EARLY MODERN CATHOLICS, ROYALISTS, AND COSMOPOLITANS

Early Modern Catholics, Royalists, and Cosmopolitans considers how the marginalized perspective of 16th-century English Catholic exiles and 17th-century English royalist exiles helped to generate a form of cosmopolitanism that was rooted in contemporary religious and national identities but also transcended those identities.

Author Brian C. Lockey argues that English discourses of nationhood were in conversation with two opposing 'cosmopolitan' perspectives, one that sought to cultivate and sustain the emerging English nationalism and imperialism and another that challenged English nationhood from the perspective of those Englishmen who viewed the kingdom as one province within the larger transnational Christian commonwealth.

Lockey illustrates how the latter cosmopolitan perspective, produced within two communities of exiled English subjects, separated in time by half a century, influenced fiction writers such as Sir Philip Sidney, Edmund Spenser, Anthony Munday, Sir John Harington, John Milton, and Aphra Behn. Ultimately, he shows that early modern cosmopolitans critiqued the emerging discourse of English nationhood from a traditional religious and political perspective, even as their writings eventually gave rise to later secular Enlightenment forms of cosmopolitanism.

Transculturalisms, 1400–1700

Series Editors:
Mihoko Suzuki, University of Miami, USA,
Ann Rosalind Jones, Smith College, USA, and
Jyotsna Singh, Michigan State University, USA

This series presents studies of the early modern contacts and exchanges among the states, polities and entrepreneurial organizations of Europe; Asia, including the Levant and East India/Indies; Africa; and the Americas. Books will investigate travelers, merchants and cultural inventors, including explorers, mapmakers, artists and writers, as they operated in political, mercantile, sexual and linguistic economies. We encourage authors to reflect on their own methodologies in relation to issues and theories relevant to the study of transculturism/translation and transnationalism. We are particularly interested in work on and from the perspective of the Asians, Africans, and Americans involved in these interactions, and on such topics as:

- Material exchanges, including textiles, paper and printing, and technologies of knowledge
- Movements of bodies: embassies, voyagers, piracy, enslavement
- Travel writing: its purposes, practices, forms and effects on writing in other genres
- Belief systems: religions, philosophies, sciences
- Translations: verbal, artistic, philosophical
- Forms of transnational violence and its representations.

Also in this series:

Philip Sidney and the Poetics of Renaissance Cosmopolitanism
Robert E. Stillman

Writing and Religion in England, 1558–1689
Studies in Community-Making and Cultural Memory
Edited by Roger D. Sell and Anthony W. Johnson

Literatures of Exile in the English Revolution and its Aftermath, 1640–1690
Edited by Philip Major

Early Modern Catholics, Royalists, and Cosmopolitans
English Transnationalism and the Christian Commonwealth

BRIAN C. LOCKEY
St. John's University, USA

LONDON AND NEW YORK

First published 2015 by Ashgate Publishing

Published 2016 by Taylor & Francis
2 Park Square, Milton Park, Abingdon, Oxon OX14 4RN
711 Third Avenue, New York, NY 10017, USA

Routledge is an imprint of the Taylor & Francis Group, an informa business

Copyright © Brian C. Lockey 2015

All rights reserved. No part of this book may be reprinted or reproduced
or utilised in any form or by any electronic, mechanical, or other means,
now known or hereafter invented, including photocopying and
recording, or in any information storage or retrieval system, without
permission in writing from the publishers.

Notice:
Product or corporate names may be trademarks or registered trademarks,
and are used only for identification and explanation without intent to
infringe.

British Library Cataloguing in Publication Data
A catalogue record for this book is available from the British Library

The Library of Congress has cataloged the printed edition as follows:
Lockey, Brian, 1968-
  Early modern Catholics, royalists, and cosmopolitans : English transnationalism and the
Christian commonwealth / by Brian C. Lockey.
    pages cm.—(Transculturalisms, 1400–1700)
  Includes bibliographical references and index.
  ISBN 978-1-4094-1871-9 (hardcover)
  1. English literature—Early modern, 1500–1700—History and criticism. 2. Christianity
and literature—England—History—16th century. 3. Royalists—Great Britain—History—
16th century. 4. Literature and transnationalism—England. I. Title.
  PR428.C48L63 2015
  820.9'3823—dc23
                                                                    2014048296
  ISBN-13: 978-1-4094-1871-9 (hbk)

Dedicated to William Varino and to my parents

Contents

List of Illustrations	*ix*
Acknowledgements	*xi*

Introduction: Catholics, Royalists, Cosmopolitans: Writing England into the Christian Commonwealth	1

PART I

1	**Papal Supremacy and the Citizen of the World**	**37**
	The Osório-Haddon Controversy	39
	Catholic Cosmopolitans and Their Interlocutors	52
	Cosmopolitan Institutions: The Society of Jesus	57
	The Pope's Scholars: The 1579 Student Revolt at the English College at Rome	64
	Catholicism and the English Nation	71
	Robert Persons's Self-Fashioning and the Papal Monarchy	76
2	**Border-Crossing and Translation: The Cosmopolitics of Edmund Campion, S.J., Anthony Munday, and Sir John Harington**	**93**
	Edmund Campion's *Ambrosia* and Spiritual Supremacy	93
	Anthony Munday and the Secular Papal Surrogate	98
	Pageants and the Cosmopolis of London	125
	Sir John Harington and the Privy Council	132
	Harington's *Orlando Furioso* and the Cosmopolitan Romance	140
3	**Cosmopolitan Romance: Philip Sidney, Edmund Spenser, and the Fiction of Imperial Justice**	**149**
	Sidney and the International Order	151
	Cosmopolitan Order in the *New Arcadia*	159
	Spenser and the Perils of Imperial Imitation	170
4	**Traitor or Cosmopolitan? Captain Thomas Stukeley in the Courts of Christendom**	**185**
	Beyond the English Nation	189
	Beyond Exile and Treason	199
	"True" Accounts of National Character	202
	Stukeley's Death and Beyond	205

viii   *Early Modern Catholics, Royalists, and Cosmopolitans*

PART II

Part II Introduction: Royalists   213

5   From Foreign War to Civil War: The Royalist Reinvention
     of the Christian Commonwealth   **225**
     The Royalist Epic   230
     Sir Richard Fanshawe's Translation of *Os Lusíadas*   240

6   The Christian Nation and Beyond: Camões's *Os Lusíadas*
     and John Milton's Cosmopolitan Republic   **263**
     Beyond the Christian Nation   264
     Puritan Antiprelatism and Milton's Transnational Elect   277

7   Royalist Turned Cosmopolitan: Aphra Behn's Portrait of the
     Prostituted Sovereign   **293**
     Anglo-Spanish Rivalry and its Dissolution   295
     Portraiture and Politics   301
     Cosmopolitanism and Commercialism from Killigrew to Behn   309

Conclusion: The Public Sphere and the Legacy of the Christian
     Commonwealth   313

Works Cited   *319*
Index   *357*

List of Illustrations

1.1 The title page of Bishop Jerónimo Osório de Fonseca's second contribution to the Osório-Haddon debate: *Amplissimi atque Doctissimi Viri D. Hieronymi Osorii, Episcopi Sylvensis ...* (Lisbon, 1567). Photo Courtesy of the Newberry Library, Chicago (Call Number: Case C 64.6469).   44

1.2 The seventh book of Nicholas Sander's *De visibili monarchia ecclesiae* (Antuerpiae, 1578), fol. 662–3. By permission of the Museum Plantin-Moretus, Antwerp.   51

1.3 From the "Martyrium describatum B. Edmundi Campiani, B. Cervini, B. Briant," fol. 39v–40 from Anglia 8, Archivum Romanum Societatis Iesu. By permission of the Society of Jesus.   84

2.1 The crime and execution of English Protestant Richard Atkins in Rome. From Anthony Munday, *The English Romayne Lyfe* (London, 1582), inset. By permission of the Folger Shakespeare Library.   101

2.2 From *The fishmongers' pageant, on Lord Mayor's Day, 1616: Chrysanaleia, the golden fishing / devised by Anthony Munday; represented in 12 plates by Henry Shaw, from contemporary drawings in the possession of the Worshipful Company of Fishmongers*, ed. John G. Nichols (London, 1844). By permission of the Folger Shakespeare Library.   128

5.1 [Europe depicted as a Queen], from Sebastian MÜNSTER, *Cosmographey oder Beschreibung all Länder Herrschaften vnd fürnemesten stetten des gantzen Erdbodens sampt ihren Gelegenheiten, Eygenschafften, Religion, Gebreuchen, Geschichten vnnd Handtheirungen ...* (Basil, 1588). By permission of the Folger Shakespeare Library.   248

5.2 The royal arms of Portugal with the encircling English Garter. Redrawn by Erin Kelly, after Roger M. Walker and W.H. Liddell, "A Commentary by Sir Richard Fanshawe on the Royal Arms of Portugal," in *Studies in Portuguese Literature and History*.   257

Acknowledgements

A year of sabbatical leave from St. John's University provided me with the opportunity to do a great deal of the research for this book at the Folger Shakespeare Library and the Newberry Library in Chicago. I am also grateful for two short-term Folger fellowships, a short-term fellowship provided by the Newberry, and a St. John's University Summer Support of Research Grant for research at the *Archivum Romanum Societatis Iesu* in Rome. Finally, I would like to thank Carolyn Williams and Jonah Siegel of the Department of English at Rutgers University, New Brunswick and the staff of the Rutgers University Library system for helping me to obtain visiting scholar status at Rutgers during the middle and final stages of this project.

I am indebted to so many friends and colleagues for assistance, editorial and otherwise, in completing this book. I would especially like to thank Elizabeth Bearden, Kathy Bond Borie, Carol Brobeck, Mauro Brunello, Edmund Campos, Elizabeth Evenden, Robert Fanuzzi, Barbara Fuchs, Tobias Gregory, Eric Griffin, Simon Healy, Rachel Hollander, Filomena Lima, Kathleen Lubey, Kathleen Lynch, Miguel Martinez, Kevin J. McGinley, Thomas McCoog, S.J., Steven Mentz, Susannah Brietz Monta, Melissa Mowry, Mark Netzloff, John W. O' Malley, S.J., Jason Pedicone, Chiara Petrolini, Goran Proot, Mark Rankin, Stephen Sicari, Scott Stevens, Stefania Tutino, Lucy Underwood, Stefano Villani, Daniel Vitkus, and Georgianna Ziegler. I would also like to thank Joanna Perez and Jessica Ayob for bibliographic assistance. I owe a special debt to Erin Kathleen Kelly for her invaluable editorial and bibliographic work and commentary in getting the final manuscript ready. Most of all, I am grateful to my wife, Chiara Cillerai, whose work on eighteenth-century American literature inspired me to think about the origins of the modern transnational sensibility. Without her advice and commentary and the countless hours she spent helping me revise the following chapters, I could never have finished this project.

Portions of chapters 1 and 2 were originally published under the title, "Catholics and Cosmopolitans Writing the Nation: The Pope's Scholars and the 1579 Student Rebellion at the English Roman College," in Barbara Fuchs and Emily Weissbourd (eds), *Representing Imperial Rivalry in the Early Modern Mediterranean* (Toronto: University of Toronto Press, 2015), 233–54. Part of Chapter 3 was published as "'Equitie to measure': The Perils of Imperial Imitation in Edmund Spenser's *The Faerie Queene*" in the *Journal for Early Modern Cultural Studies* 10.1 (Spring/Summer 2010): 52–70. A version of Chapter 4 was published under the title, "Elizabethan Cosmopolitan: Captain Thomas Stukeley in the Court of Dom Sebastian" in *English Literary Renaissance* 40.1 (Winter 2010): 1–32, and finally, a version of Chapter 7 was published as "'A Language All Nations Understand': Portraiture and the Politics of Anglo-Spanish Identity in Aphra Behn's *The Rover*" in the *Journal of Medieval and Early Modern Studies* 39.1 (Winter 2009): 161–82.

Introduction
Catholics, Royalists, Cosmopolitans: Writing England into the Christian Commonwealth

This book begins with the contested idea of the "Christian commonwealth."[1] The phrase, "Christian commonwealth," was the English translation of the Latin term, *respublica christiana*, which Catholic theologians had traditionally used both to denote the Catholic Church, as distinct from the secular realms of Europe, and the transnational ecclesiastical polity that, although mostly bureaucratically separate from the secular realms, loosely incorporated the latter entities and in certain instances had sovereignty over them and their rulers.[2] During the latter half of the sixteenth century, English Protestants increasingly used the term, "Christian commonwealth," in ways that reveal significant transformations in early modern conceptions of nationhood, temporal and spiritual governance, and the responsibilities of the Christian sovereign and subject.

In the midst of such transformations, English readers could still encounter numerous references to the traditional usage of the term, especially in works about the historical conflict with the Ottoman empire, complaints about disunity within Christendom, and in works about Catholic ecclesiastical government. Even English Protestants employed the term to denote something approximating the Catholic use of the Latin term, *respublica christiana*, especially when referencing the war with the Ottoman Turks or the Crusades, but in such instances, the term more accurately denoted the concept of "Christendom," which did not necessarily presume the existence of an ecclesiastical government. For example, Raphael Holinshed used it in precisely this way in the *Chronicles*, when he described the common perception of Henry II, who was thought "to be negligent in aiding the christian common-wealth in the holie land."[3] Elsewhere, in recounting London's response to the Christian victory over the Ottoman Turks at the Battle of Lepanto in October of 1571, Holinshed describes lavish celebrations that reflected an English consciousness of this larger transnational entity: "the banketting and great

---

[1] It was also sometimes denoted "common-wealth" or "commonweale."

[2] Stefania Tutino, *Empire of Souls: Robert Bellarmine and the Christian Commonwealth* (Oxford, 2010), 14.

[3] Raphael Holinshed, *The Third volume of Chronicles, beginning at duke William the Norman, commonlie called the Conqueror; and descending by degrees of yeeres to all the kings and queenes of England in their orderlie successions: first compiled by Raphaell Holinshed, and by him extended to the yeare 1577. Now newlie recognized, augmented, and continued (with occurrences and accidents of fresh memorie) to the yeare 1586* (London, 1586), 116.

2   *Early Modern Catholics, Royalists, and Cosmopolitans*

reioising, as good cause there was, for a victorie of so great importance vnto the whole state of the christian common-wealth."[4] The historian Richard Knolles, who published the *General History of the Turkes* in 1603, also employs the term in this manner, in order to distinguish between what he perceived as the pure motives of Christians and the impure motives of Muslims during the recent conflict with the Ottoman empire: "They fight for their Prophet, a most prophane man, author of all impietie, for spoile and prey ... for the enlarging of their dominions and territories, for worldly praise and glorie: But wee contrariwise beare armes for the sauiour of the world, for our faith and religion, for the Christian commonwealth, for our natiue countrey, for our wiues and children."[5] Here, Knolles catalogues a metonymic series of analogous entities from larger to smaller, in such a way that an encompassing "Christian commonwealth" incorporates a smaller "natiue country" which in turn incorporates an even more diminutive familial polity. Elsewhere, English readers would have encountered the traditional use of the term in English translations of continental works, such as Rene de Lucinge's *The beginning, continuance, and decay of estates wherein are handled many notable questions concerning the establishment of empires and monarchies* (1606), which condemns the disunity of the Christian commonwealth in the face of the Ottoman threat, or in works by Catholic supporters of the independence of the French Gallican Church like Edmond Richer, who sought to explain why the larger Christian commonwealth should be "gouerned by good manners, and Canons," rather than by making an example of certain temporal sovereigns through use of the papal deposing power.[6]

The second usage of the term reflects the Erastian trajectory of English Protestant politics, by denoting something equivalent to the secular *respublica* or nation or country, in which a temporal sovereign claimed supremacy over the ecclesiastical realm. In such cases, England itself or later Britain becomes a Christian commonwealth. A number of works that focus on how to eliminate sinfulness and moral turpitude from the English polity use the phrase in this manner. In 1582, the bookseller, Thomas Dawson, was selling a tract by an

---

4   Holinshed, *The Third volume of Chronicles*, 1226.

5   Richard Knolles, *The generall historie of the Turkes from the first beginning of that nation to the rising of the Othoman familie: with all the notable expeditions of the Christian princes against them. Together with the liues and conquests of the Othoman kings and emperours faithfullie collected out of the best histories, both auntient and moderne, and digested into one continuat historie vntill this present yeare 1603* (London, 1603), 272.

6   Rene de Lucinge, *The beginning, continvance, and decay of estates: VVherein are handled many notable Questions concerning the establishment of Empires and Monarchies*, trans. I.F. (London, 1606), 35. Edmond Richer, *A treatise of ecclesiasticall and politike power. Shewing, the Church is a monarchicall gouernment, ordained to a supernaturall and spirituall end, tempered with an aristocraticall order, (which is the best of all and most conformable to nature) by the great Pastor of soules Iesus Christ* (London, 1612), H4. There are also uses of other related terms such as "Christendom" or the "Christian world," but these lack any implication of an actual polity or realm as is implicit in the term, "Christian commonwealth."

Introduction 3

author identified as W. W. on the interrogation and confessions of witches taken in Essex, "Wherein all men may see what a pestilent people Witches are, and how unworthy to lyue in a Christian Common-wealth."[7] Similarly, Walter Travers wrote a response to a Papist tract defending Elizabeth's Catholic subjects from persecution, in which Travers praises Elizabeth for her ability to maintain "a Christian Commonwealth."[8] Non-conformist Protestants took a similar view. In his polemical tracts attacking episcopal governance of the English Church, the pseudonymous "Martin Marprelate" made several references to England as a Christian commonwealth, as did some Protestant ministers, such as Anthony Fletcher, Richard Leake, and Richard Rogers, in their respective attempts to purge the realm of sinfulness.[9] In contrast to traditional references to the transnational, all-encompassing Christian commonwealth, the intent in most of these instances is to promote virtue within the realm of England and thus to foster its establishment as a separate Christian nation with its own unique and consistent form of internal religious uniformity.[10]

---

[7] W. W., *A true and iust Recorde, of the Information, Examination and Confession of all the Witches, taken at S. Oses in the countie of Essex; whereof some were executed, and other some entreated according to the determination of lawe. Wherein all men may see what a pestilent people witches are, and how unworthy to lyue in a Christian Commonwealth* (London, 1582), title page.

[8] Walter Travers, *An Ansvver to a svpplicatorie epistle, of G. T. for the pretended Catholiqves: written to the right honorable Lordes of her Maiesties priuie Counsell* (London, 1583), 91. Note how this author employs the indefinite article in order to refer to England as one exemplary nation among many possible Christian commonwealths. See also Andrew Willet, *Synopsis Papismi, that is, A generall view of papistry: wherein the whole mysterie of iniquitie, and summe of Antichristian doctrine is set downe, which is maintained this day by the Synagogue of Rome, against the Church of Christ* (London, 1592), 263.

[9] Martin Marprelate, *Oh read ouer D. Iohn Bridges, for it is worthy worke: Or an epitome of the fyrste Booke, of that right worshipfull volume, written against the Puritanes, in the defense of the noble cleargie, by as worshipfull a prieste, Iohn Bridges, presbyter, priest or elder, doctor of Diuillitie, and Deane of Sarum ... Compiled for the behoofe and overthrow of the vnpreaching Parsons, Fyckers, and Currats, that haue learnt their Catechismes, and are past grace: By the reverend and worthie Martin Marprelat gentleman, and dedicated by a second epistle to the terrible priests* (London, 1588), sig. 2v. Anthonie Fletcher, *Certaine very proper, and most profitable similes, wherein sundrie, and very many, most foule vices, and dangerous sinnes, of all sorts, are so plainly laid open, and displaied in their kindes, and so pointed at with the finger of God* (London, 1595), 55. Richard Leake, *Foure sermons, preached and publikely taught by Richad Leake* (London, 1599), unpaginated epistle dedicatory. Richard Rogers, *Seauen treatises containing such direction as is gathered out of the holie Scriptures, leading and guiding to true happines, both in this life, and in the life to come: and may be called the practise of Christianitie. Profitable for all such as heartily desire the same: in the which, more particularly true Christians may learne how to leade a godly and comfortable life euery day* (London, 1603), 181.

[10] For perspective on the way in which English Protestant prelates pursued their own unique form of internal religious uniformity, without regard for continental examples, see Claire McEachern, *The Poetics of English Nationhood, 1590–1612* (New York, 1996), 61–3.

4   *Early Modern Catholics, Royalists, and Cosmopolitans*

Whether denoting a transnational body politic headed by a Papal monarch or the English polity headed by a prince with sovereignty over the temporal and ecclesiastical realm, the terminology, "Christian commonwealth," has a particular resonance in the period, implying as it does the existence of boundaries or frontiers and a governing bureaucracy headed by a monarch. The increasing use in the English language of this phrase to describe England itself is of some significance, in that it more or less confirms Richard Helgerson's main thesis in his influential work, *Forms of Nationhood: The Elizabethan Writing of England*. According to Helgerson, works as diverse as Edmund Spenser's *Faerie Queene*, Sir Edward Coke's *Institutes*, and Richard Hooker's *On the Laws of Ecclesiastical Polity* are part of a generational project of constructing a separate and distinct English polity through writing. For Helgerson, such works collectively comprise the "Elizabethan writing of England."[11]

My purpose in this book is to suggest that the scholarly focus on the literary construction of English national identity during the past 20 years has occluded the way in which other important forms of identity continued to have considerable force during the early modern period. In particular, I suggest that some older forms of identity, associated with religious orders and hierarchies, transnational humanism, travel, and commerce, may be viewed as antithetical to the prevailing trajectory of English national identity. Roman Catholicism provided the source of the most trenchant critique of the new ideology of secular and religious nationhood that culminated in Elizabethan England. The Catholic exile and recusant, not to mention the large moderate Catholic population that mostly chose to conform, were entirely excluded from Helgerson's account of English national formation. Recent works of historiography by Michael Questier and literary historical work by Allison Shell and Christopher Highley illustrate what an oversight this was in Helgerson's groundbreaking work.[12]

---

[11]   Richard Helgerson, *Forms of Nationhood: The Elizabethan Writing of England* (Chicago, 1992), 5. For subsequent discussion of the literary writing of the English nation, see Andrew Hadfield, *Literature, Politics and National Identity: Reformation to Renaissance* (New York, 1994); Claire McEachern, *The Poetics of English Nationhood, 1590–1612*; Jodi Mikalachki, *The Legacy of Boadicea: Gender and nation in Early Modern England* (New York, 1998); Willy Maley, *Nation, State and Empire in English Renaissance Literature: Shakespeare to Milton* (New York, 2003); Gillian Brennan, *Patriotism, Power and Print: National Consciousness in Tudor England* (Pittsburgh, 2003); John Kerrigan, *Archipelagic English: Literature, History, and Politics 1603–1707* (New York, 2008). Historical background on the same subject can be found in Alan G.R. Smith, *The Emergence of a Nation State: The Commonwealth of England 1529–1660* (New York, 1984).

[12]   Michael Questier, *Catholicism and Community in Early Modern England: Politics, Aristocratic Patronage and Religion, c. 1550–1640* (New York, 2006); Christopher Highley, *Catholics Writing the Nation in Early Modern England and Ireland* (New York, 2008); Alison Shell, *Oral Culture and Catholicism in Early Modern England* (Cambridge, 2007); Alison Shell, *Catholicism, Controversy and the English Literary Imagination, 1558–1660* (New York, 1999). See also John Hungerford Pollen, S.J., *The English Catholics in the Reign of Queen Elizabeth: A Study of Their Politics, Civil Life, and Government, 1558–1580, from the Fall of the Old Church to the Advent of the Counter-Reformation* (New York,

Introduction 5

The relationship between Catholicism and English national identity is far more complex than has traditionally been thought. Questier's account of the Browne-Montague family in Sussex shows how recusant Catholics, conformist Catholics, and Protestants lived amicably together in Sussex and elsewhere in the English countryside. And just as extensive Catholic communities in England were not simply related by certain tenets of faith, but rather by blood and marriage, Questier shows that Protestants and Catholics were also frequently related by blood and marriage. Moreover, the Browne-Montagues, comprising the leading Catholic noble family in Sussex, had good relations with their Protestant neighbors, with whom they even exchanged religious condolences when there occurred a death in the family.[13] At the same time, religious identity could change rather drastically from generation to generation within a particular family. During the Elizabethan period, the Earl of Montague considered himself a loyal subject of the Queen, appearing as he did alongside the Queen at Tilbury in August 1588 in the defense against the Armada. During this period, the Earl's retinue consisted solely of Marian priests, while after his death, his wife and son became more militantly Catholic, surrounding themselves with the radicalized seminarians trained at English colleges on the Continent.[14] All the while, religious discourse was steadily becoming more polarized such that, by the end of the century, certain Puritan ministers would declare that it was better for England to fight the Catholics than the Turks.[15]

Despite the comfortable situation of many rural Catholics, the question of the Queen's claim to supremacy in spiritual matters was a hard matter to ignore. For while some moderate Catholic families like the Browne-Montagues could be counted on to declare their loyalty to the Queen in the event of a Papal invasion of England, the Catholic Lawyer's argument at the beginning of the notorious Roman Catholic propaganda pamphlet known as *Leicester's Commonwealth* would have elicited the worst fears of English conformists. Responding to the Protestant Gentleman's question of whether the Jesuit priests recently executed for treason were treated justly, the Lawyer candidly admits that the religious faith of English Catholics implies (at least in theory) both a direct and an indirect threat to the English commonwealth:

> Men of a different religion from the state wherein they live may be said to deal against the state in two sorts: the one, by dealing for the increase of their said different religion, which is always either directly or indirectly against the state. Directly, when the said religion containeth any point or article directly impugning the said state (as perhaps you will say that the Roman religion doth

---

1971). For a history of the Tudor period focusing on the English reformations that occurred at the parish level, see Christopher Haigh, *English Reformations: Religion, Politics, and Society under the Tudors* (Oxford, 1993).

[13] Questier, *Catholicism and Community*, 9, 77–85.

[14] Questier, *Catholicism and Community*, 109–80.

[15] Questier, *Catholicism and Community*, 86. For an earlier account of Catholicism's decline during this period, see William Trimble, *The Catholic Laity in Elizabethan England, 1558–1603* (Cambridge, MA, 1964), 122–76.

against the present state of England in the point of supremacy), and indirectly, for that every different religion divideth in a sort and draweth from the state, in that there is no man who in his heart would not wish to have the chief governor and state to be of his religion if he could.[16]

Thus, at the outset of what eventually becomes a moderate appeal for religious toleration, the Catholic Lawyer nevertheless begins by admitting that it is inevitable that "those whom you call busy Papists in England" "may be called all traitors."[17] Moreover, when one considers the official Catholic position on what the Lawyer terms the "point of supremacy," it is clear from his argument that a completely different conception of English nationhood was at least potential in the minds of a large number of English Catholic subjects.[18]

This book begins by describing the etiology of this other conception of English nationhood, and in particular, the attempt to reintegrate England into the Christian commonwealth, according to the traditional Catholic conception of that term. The most important and singular event in this process—indeed, the event which set all subsequent events into motion from the Jesuit mission to the Armada to the Gunpowder plot— was Pope Pius V's Bull of 1570, *Regnans in Excelsis*, which excommunicated Queen Elizabeth, calling her the "pretended Queen of England and servant of crime" and seeking to deprive her "of her pretended title to the aforesaid crown and of all lordship, dignity and privilege whatsoever."[19] In the Privy Council's official response to *Regnans in Excelsis*, William Cecil, Lord Burghley, presented the pope's deposition of Elizabeth as an innovation, which would leave no temporal prince safe from papal deposition. According to Cecil, the Bull constituted a novel attempt to extend the pope's tyrannical temporal sovereignty over legitimate Christian princes.[20] But in reality, there were numerous precedents for the pope's actions, beginning as far back as 752 with Pope Zachary's deposition of Childeric, king of the Franks, and Pope Leo III's coronation of Charlemagne on Christmas day in the year 800.[21] Both acts established the authority of the ecclesiastical realm over the temporal realm, as well as laying down a precedent for subsequent popes to define the boundaries of their own realm as incorporating those of temporal sovereigns. In this respect, Pope Pius V's attempted deposition

---

[16] Anonymous, *Leicester's Commonwealth: the Copy of a Letter Written by a Master of Art of Cambridge (1584) and related documents*, ed. D.C. Peck (Athens, OH, 1985), 67.

[17] Anon., *Leicester's Commonwealth*, 67.

[18] For a broader discussion of the threat that English Catholicism presented to England, see Arthur Marotti, "The Intolerability of English Catholicism" in Roger D. Sell and Anthony W. Johnson (eds), *Writing and Religion in England, 1558–1689: Studies in Community-Making and Cultural Memory* (Burlington, VT, 2009), 47–72.

[19] "flagitiorum serva Elizabetha praetensa Angliae regina ... Quin etiam ipsam praetenso regni praedicti iure, necnon omni et quocunque dominio, dignitate, privilegioque privatam." Pope Pius V, *Regnans in Excelsis*, February 25, 1570 [http://www.papalencyclicals.net/Pius05/p5regnans.htm].

[20] William Cecil, *Execution of Justice in England* (1583), ed. Franklin L. Baumer (New York, 1938), C3–C3v.

[21] Brian Tierney, *The Crisis of Church and State 1050–1300* (Buffalo, 1988), 16–23.

Introduction 7

of Elizabeth constituted an exercise of traditional authority, going back almost a millennium. Perhaps the only real innovative aspect to the pope's actions was that, in contrast to prior papal depositions, *Regnans in Excelsis* had been printed and disseminated all over Europe.

I show that, in response to the Bull's publication, a number of English Catholic exiles, including Nicholas Sander, Robert Persons, and Edmund Campion, advanced a critique of the emerging model of English nationhood based on two related concepts that derived from Catholic religious doctrine: first, the notion of a transnational Christian commonwealth presided over by a papacy that could, in extraordinary circumstances, depose tyrannical or heretical Christian sovereigns and second, the individual cosmopolitan identity that was implicit in such a transnational claim. Although both concepts predated the early modern period, the re-emergence of the notion of a Christian commonwealth presided over by a muscular papacy and the cosmopolitan identity implicit therein constituted a fresh response to the "Statute in Restraint of Appeals of 1533," by which Henry VIII had claimed authority over both the ecclesiastical and the temporal realms. According to Sander and his colleagues, not only did there exist separate realms of the temporal and the ecclesiastical, but the authority of the sovereign was actually subordinate to ecclesiastical authority.[22] Hence, within Sander's conception of nationhood, every Christian sovereign should govern under the "specter" of chastisement by the Roman curia, which had the power to correct wayward magistrates and to remove tyrannical or heretical princes.

I show that the form of cosmopolitan identity that Campion and Persons cultivated in their public personae was predicated upon papal supremacy, according to which the pope should have the right to correct or remove bad sovereigns. In general, it is true that those involved in the planning and execution of the first Jesuit mission to England were enjoined by their superiors to demonstrate the religious nature of their cause and to emphasize that practicing Catholics could be loyal subjects of the English crown who only sought religious tolerance.[23] But as I show, from the outset, Campion's approach was actually more confrontational than scholars have traditionally thought. In Chapter 1, I show that Campion's

---

[22] Nicholas Sander, *De visibili monarchia ecclesiae, libri VIII: in quibus diligens instituitur disputatio de certa & perpetua Ecclesiae Dei tum successione tum gubernatione monarchica, ab ipso mundi initio vsque ad finem: deinde etiam ciuitas diaboli persaepè interrupta progressio proponitur, sectaeque omnes & haereses confutantur, quae vnquam contra veram fidem emerserunt: denique de Antichristo ipso & membris eius, deque vera Dei & adulterina diaboli ecclesia, copiosè tractatur ... cum indice rerum & personarum locuplete* (Antuerpiae, 1578); Richard Bristow, *A briefe Treatise of diuerse plaine and sure wayes to finde out the truthe in this doubtful and dangerous time of Heresie: conteyning sundry worthy Motiues vnto the Catholike faith, or Considerations to moue a man to beleue the Catholikes, and not the Heretikes* (Antwerp, 1574), E2, E3v. For context, see Stefania Tutino, *Law and Conscience: Catholicism in Early Modern England 1570–1625*, (Burlington, VT, 2007) 11–32.

[23] Thomas McCoog, S.J., *The Society of Jesus in Ireland, Scotland, and England 1541–1588: "Our Way of Proceeding?"* (New York, 1996), 129–41.

public self-presentation as a cosmopolitan is the reverse image of John Dee's more well-known use of this term. In different ways, both Dee and Campion exemplify competing versions of what Walter Mignolo has called the "managerial" tradition of early modern cosmopolitanism.[24] Describing himself as "a Citizen, and Member, of the whole and only one Mysticall City Vniuersall," Dee claimed to be uniquely suited to theorizing universal and transnational values that were simultaneously (and paradoxically) intended to advance English national interests.[25] It is no surprise to find that Dee's cosmopolitanism was later adopted by Richard Hakluyt, who incorporated Dee's description of himself into the first volume of the *Principal Navigations* (1599).[26] Similarly, Campion's eloquent self-presentation both in the "The Challenge" and in the *Rationes decem* and his subsequent martyrdom in 1581 were remembered by generations of Roman Catholics, eventually resulting in his canonization almost 400 years later.[27]

As I show, these two dominant traditions of cosmopolitanism were related but very different: the Catholic cosmopolitanism of Campion and Persons was rooted in the transnational *imperium* of the Roman *curia*, while Dee recounted that the source of his secular cosmopolitanism was the result of intensive study of the temporal kingdoms of the world. In the English context, the first of these two traditions generated a third form of cosmopolitanism, which until recently has received very little attention. As I show in Chapter 2, the writings of two translators of continental writings, Anthony Munday and Sir John Harington, had the effect of reconfiguring in secular terms an issue that, for the Jesuits, was a matter of church and state with political implications concerning the papal deposing power. As we shall see, Harington and Munday's fictional writings can be interpreted as championing a secular version of the Papal or Episcopal overseer, responsible for correcting an errant or tyrannical sovereign. Parallel to those Catholic exiles who sought to reintegrate the English realm into the transnational Christian commonwealth, Harington and Munday's fictional writings and translations can be read as analogously bringing the English polity closer to continental Europe.

Picking up the historical narrative after more than half a century, the second part of this book shows that this tradition of cosmopolitanism continues in the writings and translations of Sir Richard Fanshawe, whose 1655 translation of Luís de Camões's *Os Lusíadas* had an important influence on John Milton's *Paradise*

---

[24]   Walter Mignolo, "The Many Faces of Cosmopolis: Border Thinking and Critical Cosmopolitanism," in *Cosmopolitanism*, ed. Carol A. Breckenridge et al. (Durham, NC, 2002), 157–88.

[25]   John Dee, *The Perfect Arte of Navigation* [London, 1577] (reprint: New York, 1968), G3v.

[26]   Richard Hakluyt, *The Principal Navigations, Voyages, Traffiques, & Discoveries of the English Nation* [London, 1598–1600] (reprint, Glasgow, 1903), vol. 1, 16–24.

[27]   Edmund Campion, *Rationes decem quibus fretus B. Edmundus Campianus certamen adversariis obtulit in causa fidei, redditae academicis angliae [Ten Reasons proposed to his adversaries for disputation in the name of the faith and presented to the illustrious members of our universities]*, ed. and trans. John Hungerford Pollen, S.J. (London, 1914). See also Campion, "Challenge to the Privy Council," in *Ten Reasons*, 7–11.

Lost. In Chapter 6, I show that *Paradise Lost*—especially the last two books—can be viewed, if not as a repudiation of the Portuguese epic itself, then as a repudiation of the Christ-centered imperialism which Camões uses in his portrayal of the Portuguese empire and which ultimately served as the vision of English royalists such as Fanshawe. Milton intends to show that true religious devoutness transcends territorial loyalties, including by implication national loyalties. The seventh chapter considers how Aphra Behn's *The Rover* drew heavily from an earlier source, Thomas Killigrew's *Thomaso*, an autobiographical closet drama based on Killigrew's life as a royalist exile when he made a brief visit to Madrid. As I show, Behn's play endorses an alternative to the very notion of English nationhood, as it was being defined by the political theorists of the time as an entity in competition with other national entities like Spain.[28] In this respect, many of the oppositions that had developed during this period, on which national identity was based, especially those between a private and a public sphere—the domestic and the foreign, marriage and prostitution, family and state—are dissolved in the course of Behn's drama. In this respect, the play embodies a new concept of cosmopolitanism that liberates not in the name of another realm and its competing ideology but rather from the very patriarchalist ideology of nationhood, which had developed over the past century.[29]

* * *

Of the figures that I explore in the following pages, none is so central to the main thesis of this book as is Sir Philip Sidney (the subject, along with Edmund Spenser, of Chapter 3). Indeed, no English writer of fiction during the late sixteenth century had more experience and correspondence with continental Europeans than Sidney, who had travelled throughout Europe extensively from 1572 to 1575, returning to the continent in 1577 as a special ambassador to the newly elected Holy Roman Emperor Rudolph II, and finally in 1585 and 1586 accompanying Leicester's campaign to the Dutch provinces, where he was mortally wounded at the Battle of Zutphen.[30] In addition to his travels, Sidney made a large number of friends and

---

[28]   For a comprehensive study of the writings of seventeenth-century English exiles, which devotes one chapter to Thomas Hobbes and the royalist experience of exile, see Christopher D'Addario, *Exile and Journey in Seventeenth-Century Literature* (New York, 2007), 57–86.

[29]   Andrew Shifflett has made a similar argument about how both royalist poets such as Katherine Philips and republican poets such as Andrew Marvell and John Milton all subscribe to a cosmopolitan ethos, inspired by classical Stoicism. See Shifflett, *Stoicism, Politics, and Literature in the Age of Milton* (New York, 1998).

[30]   Moreover, in 1579, he and his father were deputed to meet John Casimir, younger brother of the Elector Palatine, and Sidney's friend and interlocutor, Hubert Languet, the French "Philippist" and representative of Saxony at the imperial court from 1573 to 1577. For a detailed account of Sidney's early travels, see James M. Osborn, *Young Philip Sidney 1572–1577* (New Haven, CT, 1972). For the later period, see Alan Stewart, *Philip Sidney: A Double Life* (London, 2000), 277–320. See also Michael G. Brennan and Noel J. Kinnamon, *A Sidney Chronology 1554–1654* (Basingstoke, 2003).

10   *Early Modern Catholics, Royalists, and Cosmopolitans*

acquaintances abroad, with whom he went on to maintain an ongoing correspondence throughout the remainder of his life.[31] The extensive correspondence network that Sidney maintained with continental luminaries seems to have had at least two purposes, both of which are apparent from a letter of advice which Sir Francis Walsingham is thought to have sent to his nephew when the youth commenced on his own travels to the continent. According to Walsingham, travel to foreign realms should serve both to educate the individual and to provide him with intelligence on foreign affairs, so that ultimately "you may discover much to serve yourself and commonwealth." Walsingham encourages the youth to pay particular attention to "the manners and dispositions of the people" and especially "the nobility, gentry and learned sort." The youth is encouraged to learn as much as possible about "the affairs of state and counsel of princes," for example, observing the "disposition of the French gentry" in order to determine whether they are inclined towards "the Spanish or German or English." Walsingham goes on to advise his young charge to befriend so called "men of state," by which he means the "secretaries, public notaries, and agents for princes and cities." Only by knowing their thoughts and affairs can one become cognizant of future policies.[32]

With the exception of a few instances in which Sidney seems to have frequented the house of a Venetian courtesan or involved himself with some fellow travelers of ill repute, his travels on the continent followed Walsingham's script in this letter.[33] His correspondence with his mentor Hubert Languet evinces his own and his mentor's preoccupation with his education—the books that he would be reading, practicing his Latin pronunciation, learning the German language, and encountering and conversing with other scholars—and with his intelligence gathering.[34] Sidney maintained an extensive correspondence with

---

[31]   These included Henry III, king of Navarre; Philippe du Plessis Mornay; Philip Louis I, Count of Hanau-Münzenberg; Pierre de la Ramée; Jean Lobbet; Andreas Wechel; Claude Aubéry; August I, Elector of Saxony; Théophile de Banos, the minister of the Huguenot Church in Frankfort; the historian Pietro Bizzari; John Casimir and his brother, Ludwig, the future Elector Palatine; William IV, Landgrave of Hesse-Kassel; Charles de l'Écluse; Henri Estienne; Jean de Vulcob; and William of Orange, among others. For context, see Osborn, *Young Philip Sidney*, Roger Kuin (ed.), *The Correspondence of Sir Philip Sidney* (2 vols, New York, 2012), and Jan A. Van Dorsten, *Poets, Patrons, and Professors: Sir Philip Sidney, Daniel Rogers, and the Leiden Humanists* (New York, 1962).

[32]   Cited in Conyers Read, *Mr. Secretary Walsingham and the Policy of Queen Elizabeth* (3 vols, Oxford, 1925), vol. 1, 18–20. See also, Osborn, *Young Philip Sidney*, 83–4. Languet gives Sidney similar advice on his continental education in an early letter from Sidney's first European tour. See, for example, "Hubert Languet to Sidney, Vienna, 28 January 1574," in *Correspondence of Sir Philip Sidney*, vol. 1, 99–104. See also 96–7, 123.

[33]   "Jacques Bochetel de La Forêt to Sidney, Vienna, 10 December 1573," in *Correspondence of Sir Philip Sidney*, vol. 1, 47–9; and Osborn, *Young Philip Sidney*, 74–5.

[34]   The Languet-Sidney correspondence was first published in 1633 in Frankfurt, and its purpose was clearly intended for the instruction of future diplomats and men of state. For background see Kuin, "Introduction," in *Correspondence of Sir Philip Sidney*, vol. 1, xxii–xxv. See also Steuart A. Pears (ed.), *Correspondence of Sir Philip Sidney and Hubert Languet* (London, 1845), 1–96. For further perspective on Sidney's education, see Osborn,

his continental interlocutors as a way of gathering intelligence on state affairs, relaying their knowledge of recent events and focusing especially on the state of affairs in Germany, the Low Countries, and the Mediterranean, as well as on important events involving European princes: in particular, those related to Philip II, the Duke of Anjou, the Duke of Alençon, Henry of Navarre, John Casimir, the Elector Palatine Frederick, William of Orange, and the Sultan of the Ottoman Empire.[35] These letters were written and received with the expectation of gaining information about foreign affairs, and it goes without saying that Sidney and the well-placed scholars, courtiers, and men of state throughout Europe, with whom he exchanged letters, comprised an intelligence network, the purpose of which was to exchange information on international affairs.

As represented in Sidney's correspondence, the international sphere was chaotic, lacking any order or rule of law. Venice and Vienna were threatened by Ottoman invasion. Civil wars raged in France and the Low Countries between Protestant and Catholic factions, and a state close to chaos had taken hold in both the courts of France and Poland. The Holy Roman Empire was more divided than ever along religious lines between Catholics, Lutherans, and Calvinists, a situation made even more complex by aggressive intervention by the Spanish crown and Protestant Sweden and Denmark. Closer to home, Scotland was experiencing violent turmoil, Mary Queen of Scots having been deposed and her minority young son placed under the care of regents. In Ireland, the Earl of Desmond and his supporters were in rebellion against the English crown among fears that Spain might attempt to support the Irish rebels or even invade England through Ireland. Throughout all of this turmoil, English foreign policy was primarily driven by three concerns: first, the traditional suspicion and fear of France, whose population dwarfed that of England; second, the more recent alarm at a newly aggressive Hapsburg empire that controlled Spain and spanned the entirety of Western Europe; and finally, England's newfound identity as the champion of the Protestant cause. Given these three concerns, the English crown's main foreign policy goal during this period consisted of a careful balancing act between pragmatism and idealism. During the 1570s, this entailed Queen Elizabeth exploring increasingly close ties with the French court while at the same time attempting to avoid provoking any direct antagonism from Philip II and reassuring the Spanish crown that the English crown viewed the rebellion in the Low Countries as illegal and illegitimate. At the same time, of course, the Privy Council was exploring the viability of a Protestant League that would potentially encompass England along with the Calvinist Palatinate as well as the Lutheran states within the Holy Roman Empire.[36]

Young Philip Sidney, 74–302; esp. 187–219; John Buxton, *Sir Philip Sidney and the English Renaissance* (New York, 1954), 33–94; Edward Berry, *The Making of Sir Philip Sidney* (Toronto, 1998), 28–48. For Sidney's own views on educating the reader through fiction, see Ake Bergvall, *The "Enabling of Judgement": Sir Philip Sidney and the Education of the Reader* (Stockholm, 1989).

[35]   Kuin (ed.), *Correspondence of Sir Philip Sidney*; Osborn, *Young Philip Sidney*.

[36]   See E.I. Kouri, *England and the Attempts to Form a Protestant Alliance* (Helsinki, 1981).

As a member of the Leicester circle at court, Sidney's politics were similar to his uncle's. Between the pragmatism of maintaining amicable relations with the Spanish and French crowns and the idealism of supporting the Palatinate, the beleaguered Huguenots in France or the Protestant cause in the Low Countries, Sidney assumed the latter idealistic mantle. It is this idealism that led him to pen his famous letter to Elizabeth against the planned marriage with the Duke of Alençon, to defend his uncle's reputation in the public sphere against the 1584 Roman Catholic propaganda tract, which came to be known as *Leicester's Commonwealth*, to translate DuPlessis Mornay's *De la vérité de la religion chrétienne*, and to persuade the Queen to intervene on behalf of Dutch Protestants in the Low Countries.[37] Indeed, the decisions that presaged his death on the battlefield, including his appointment as governor of Flushing in the Netherlands as well as his subsequent decision to fight alongside his uncle, the Earl of Leicester, on behalf of Dutch Protestants during the 1586 campaign, can be attributed directly to his identity as an idealistic warrior for the Protestant cause.[38]

During the 1570s, however, perhaps the most important indication of Sidney's Protestant idealism was his pursuit of the formation of a Protestant League, configured in such a way that England would occupy the league's political and financial vanguard. Sidney's involvement with a proposed Protestant League is most apparent in his 1577 embassy to the court of Rudolph II, the newly elected Holy Roman Emperor. The official purpose of Sidney's embassy was to congratulate Rudolph on his recent election and to offer condolences to him on the death of his father, as well as to offer similar condolences to Ludwig the new Elector Palatine and his brother John Casimir, whose father Frederick III had also recently passed away. Secondarily, Sidney was to attempt to reconcile Ludwig and John, whose relationship had suffered from the fact that Ludwig had recently abandoned his father's and brother's Calvinist faith and had begun to give preference to his Lutheran subjects over his Calvinist subjects.[39] A third

---

[37]   Sidney, "A Letter to Queen Elizabeth" and "Defence of Leicester," in *Miscellaneous Prose of Sir Philip Sidney*, ed. Katherine Duncan-Jones and Jan A. Van Dorsten (Oxford: 1973), 46–57 129–41; Arthur Golding and Sir Philip Sidney (trans.), *A Worke concerning the Trewnesse of the Christian Religion: A Facsimile Reproduction with an Introduction by F.J. Sypher* [London, 1587] (reprint, New York, 1976). For the debate concerning Sidney's contribution to the translation of *A Worke*, see Duncan-Jones et al. (eds), *Miscellaneous Prose*, 155–7. See also Stewart, *Sidney: A Double Life*, 218–20, 256, 260–61.

[38]   Stewart, *Sidney: A Double Life*, 274–320. According to Berry, it also influenced his presentation of himself as a poet-warrior in the *Defence of Poetry*. See Berry, *The Making of Sir Philip Sidney*, 142–63. Like other Englishmen of this period, Sidney tended to imagine English identity as based on a repudiation of what he viewed as intrinsic Spanish barbarism. See Lockey, *Law and Empire*, 47–8. See also Languet's advice to Sidney on the possible role that England could take with regard to Germany in order to counter the malign Spanish influence there. See "Languet to Sidney, Franfort, 8 January, 1578," in Roger Kuin (ed.), *The Correspondence of Sir Philip Sidney* (2 vols, New York, 2012), vol. 2, 804–8.

[39]   "Instructions for Sidney's Embassy, February 7, 1576/77" in Osborn, *Young Philip Sidney*, 525–8.

Introduction 13

unstated but presumably still official reason for the embassy involved the crown's desire to reinvigorate discussion of a Protestant League with the Palatinate and William of Orange.[40]

Sidney's pursuit of a Protestant League led by England had a number of precedents during the sixteenth century, extending back into the reign of Henry VIII. James Anthony Froude and others have explained that, from the time of Henry VIII and the proposed League of Schmalkalden, the English crown's exploration of joining the League persisted as a strategy to offset a potential alliance between the pope, the Holy Roman Emperor Charles V and Francis, King of France.[41] Rory McEntegart has neatly summarized this historical interpretation with a pithy formulation: "When Charles and Francis are together, Henry inclines towards the League; as soon as they fall out, Henry moves away from the Germans. In all this there is only political calculation; religion does not enter the frame."[42] More recently, McEntegart has challenged this view, showing that the English crown was motivated by a combination of political pragmatism and religious idealism in exploring the viability of a league of Protestant states.[43]

Among the many reasons why the English crown never joined the League of Schmalkalden, none was as important as Henry VIII's perception that such an alliance might place limitations on his own temporal and ecclesiastical authority. At the height of the negotiations in 1535, the League demanded that the king indicate his acceptance of the Confession of Augsburg. In addition, he was to cooperate with the League in opposing a papal council of the Church, and England was to provide the League with 100,000 crowns in time of war, in return for a promise that the League would provide England with 500 cavalry and 2,000 infantry against the threat of invasion. It is clear that Protestant princes in Germany were averse to angering the Holy Roman Emperor, Charles V, by involving a foreign entity in internal German affairs, but the most important obstacle to an agreement was Henry VIII's dissatisfaction with the League's desire that he accept the Confession of Augsburg, which he perceived as an implicit challenge to his position as head of the English Church. In response, Henry sought consultations with theologians including Philip Melanchthon, representative of the existing Schmalkaldic states.[44] Because events eventually derailed negotiations, this theological conference never materialized, but it does point to the most significant obstacle to England's entrance into a Protestant League during this period, namely the refusal of Henry to allow any transnational commitments, however beneficial they might be to England's foreign interests, to limit or even to define his sovereign authority.

---

[40]   Stewart, *Sidney: A Double Life*, 170; Duncan-Jones, *Sir Philip Sidney*, 120; Osborn, *Young Philip Sidney*, 450.

[41]   J.A. Froude, *History of England from the Fall of Wolsey to the Defeat of the Spanish Armada* (London, 1893), vol. 3, 269–70.

[42]   Rory McEntegart, *Henry VIII, The League of Schmalkalden, and the English Reformation* (Rochester, NY, 2002), 2.

[43]   See McEntegart, *Henry VIII*, 6–8.

[44]   McEntegart, *Henry VIII*, 51–71.

During the 1560s, proposals for a Protestant League involving England rematerialized, in part due to the English crown's increasing fear of foreign invasion and Elizabeth's need for German Reiters and Landsknechte, both for use against Catholic enemies on the continent and for England's own defense from external attack.[45] However, the more important impetus for an alliance during this period were the policies of Frederick the Elector Palatine, whose Calvinist faith excluded him from alliances with either Lutheran or Catholic princes within the Holy Roman Empire. In response to its exclusion from the Peace of Augsburg, the Calvinist Palatinate sought alliances with outside powers like England in order to counterbalance its own alienation from the surrounding princes of Germany.[46] The terms of the proposed alliance were similar to that which had been proposed during Henry's reign: England was obliged to provide money to the German Protestant states when necessary, and in return ample German Reiters and one or two regimens of Landsknechte were to be made available to Elizabeth during a limited period of time.[47] Once again, one of the most important obstacles was the failure to agree to a common religious doctrine. The German princes entered negotiations by attempting to exclude doctrinal differences, but nevertheless, religious doctrine ultimately entered into the discussions. The Lutheran princes were never sure what Elizabeth's religious views were: some were convinced she was a Calvinist, others that she was a Zwinglian, and still others that she was a Catholic. Similarly, everyone had a not inaccurate sense that English policy was driven by independent dynastic and nationalist, not religious, aims. At one point the German princes accused her of entering into the French civil war, not for religious but rather for political motives.[48] According to E.I. Kouri, this view of Elizabethan foreign policy was not inaccurate, since unlike Philip II, Elizabeth tended to judge matters from a secular, nationalist perspective and to privilege territorial and dynastic considerations before religious ones.[49] But this is only half of the story. The German Lutheran princes were also inclined to act in the name of pragmatism rather than religious idealism, and they perceived the inter-confessional alliance within the Empire based on the Peace of Augsburg to be of greater value than an alliance with a foreign prince. Most importantly, they feared any foreign alliance that might be perceived by the Hapsburgs as a violation of the terms of the peace.[50] In contrast to the Calvinist Palatinate whose confessional identity was not protected by the Peace of Augsburg, the Lutheran princes were

---

[45]   Kouri, *England and Protestant Alliance*, 196.

[46]   Kouri, *England and Protestant Alliance*, 169.

[47]   Kouri, *England and Protestant Alliance*, 157.

[48]   Kouri, *England and Protestant Alliance*, 166.

[49]   Kouri, *England and Protestant Alliance*, 195. For the alternative view that Elizabeth acted out of confessional sympathies for continental Protestants, see David J.B. Trim, "Seeking a Protestant Alliance and Liberty of Conscience on the Continent 1558–85," in Susan Doran and Glen Richardson (eds), *Tudor England and its Neighbours* (New York, 2005), 139–77.

[50]   Kouri, *England and Protestant Alliance*, 169.

content to place their trust in Emperor Maximilian, whom they perceived to be a moderate with regards to religion.

The basic structure of the tensions in English foreign policy did not change during the decade that followed. Elizabeth continued to balance national interests and religious idealism, at the same time that the focus of Elizabethan foreign policy changed. Now, events in the Low Countries and the religious civil war in France assumed center stage for the Queen and the Privy Council. Almost by default, the English crown assumed the role of protector of persecuted Continental Protestants, at one point providing a loan of 15,000 pounds to the Palatinate's mercenaries, who were sent to aid the French Huguenots.[51] In contrast, in the Low Countries, Elizabeth pursued a mediating role, attempting to send conciliatory messages to William of Orange at the same time that she publically recognized that his rebellion was an unlawful attack on Philip II's sovereignty.[52] It was within this context that Philip Sidney was sent on his embassy to visit the court of the newly elected Holy Roman Emperor, Rudolph II, among fears that Rudolph might reverse the policy of tolerance for religious difference within the German states that his father, Maximilian, had maintained. According to Fulke Greville's account of the journey, it was Sidney himself who succeeded in adding an additional ulterior purpose to his embassy, that of sounding out the Protestant princes for interest in resuscitating discussion of the Protestant alliance.[53] Whether or not we agree with Alan Stewart that Greville, who accompanied Sidney on his embassy, can be trusted on this point, it is clear that the success of Sidney's embassy depended on him acknowledging a broad range of interests other than those narrowly represented by the English crown.[54]

It is my argument that an important impetus for Sidney's pursuit of the Protestant league was his belief in the traditional conception of the Christian commonwealth. Sidney's correspondence with Languet and other continental interlocutors is especially significant for understanding why this notion of the Christian commonwealth was important for understanding Sidney's fictional writings. Sidney's correspondence with Hubert Languet was obviously intended to educate the young courtier, who was a mere 18 years of age when he first encountered Languet, and to prepare him for the life of a diplomat and statesman. That education was ultimately Languet and Sidney's purpose is illustrated by William Fitzer, who eventually published the Sidney-Languet correspondence in 1633 under the title, *The most famous Hubert Languet's political and historical epistles, formerly written to the illustrious and noble Sir Philip Sidney, English*

---

[51] Wallace T. MacCaffrey, *Queen Elizabeth and the Making of Policy, 1572–1588* (Princeton, NJ, 1981), 213.

[52] MacCaffrey, *Elizabeth and the Making of Policy*, 191–216.

[53] Fulke Greville, "A Dedication to Sir Phillip Sidney," in *The Prose Works of Fulke Greville, Lord Brook*, ed. John Gouws (New York, 1986), 25.

[54] Stewart, *Sidney: A Double Life*, 170, 179–87. Duncan-Jones and Osborne are less convinced by Greville's account. See Duncan-Jones, *Sir Philip Sidney*, 120, and Osborne, *Young Philip Sidney*, 450.

knight, son of the most illustrious Viceroy of Ireland, [and] most powerful Governor of Flushing. In which are described various accounts, stratagems, and events of things done in peace and war in his time in Germany, Italy, France, the Netherlands, Hungary, Poland, and other provinces of Christendom, to which he attached the following subtitle: "Of the greatest use and necessity to all students of matters political and historical, and also to counsellors of princes and to those at the helm of state."[55] Furthermore, Fitzer dedicated the collected letters to Sir Stephen Lesieur (Sidney's former secretary and now an aged diplomat), explaining that when Lesieur had entrusted him (Fitzer) with the letters comprising the Sidney-Languet correspondence, Lesieur had been "confident ... in the commendable expectation that they would be valuable also to other men, especially those who are noble and fit at some point to be called to the helm of the ship of state [ad Reipublicae Clauum]."[56] Fitzer's dedication implies that Languet was grooming Sidney for the position of a government official within the English court, but as we shall see, the "state [respublica]" that piqued Sidney's interest most intensely was the notional, transnational "commonwealth" that encompassed the secular realms of Europe.

The contents of these letters are also significant because so much of the Sidney correspondence concerns the chaotic and divisive state of affairs within Europe. In his letters to Sidney, Languet typically attributed the bloodshed and conflicts that were tearing apart the continent to an international Catholic conspiracy, headed by the Roman Pontiff and the king of Spain.[57] More familiar with the bloody rifts that were dividing Europe than his young protégé, Languet preferred the phrase, *orbis christianus*, which translates as the "Christian world," to the phrase, *respublica christiana*, which implies the existence of a body politic united under one governing entity. Languet's ultimate concern was that what he referred to as "these civil wars [*istis bellis civilibus*]" within Europe would enable the Ottomans to conquer first

---

[55] *Huberti Langueti viri clarissimi epistolae politicae et historicae. Scriptae quondam Ad Illustrem, & Generosum Dominum Philippum Sydnaeum, Equitem Anglum, Illustrissimi Pro-Regis Hyberniae filium. Vlissingensem Gubernatorum fortissimum. In quibus variae rerum suo aeuo in Germania, Italia, Gallia, Belgio, Vngaria, Polonia, aliisque Orbis Christiani Prouinciis Pace, Belloque gestarum, narrationes, consilia, & eventûs describuntur. Omnibus Politicarum rerum, & historiarum studiosis, Consiliariis etiam Principum, & ad ReiClauum sedentibus, maximè vtiles, ac necessariae. Nunc verò primum publicis typis divulgatae. Francofurti, In Officina Gvlielmi Fitzeri, Librarii Angli. Anno M. DC. XXXIII* (Frankfurt, 1633). English translation by Roger Kuin. See Kuin, "Introduction," in *Correspondence of Sir Philip Sidney*, vol. 1, xxiii.

[56] "fretus ... spe optima, fore, vt allis etiam, hominibus praesertim Generosis, & ad Reipubl. Clauum aliquando admouendis, vsui future forent." Original Latin from *Huberti Langueti viri clarissimi epistolae politicae et historicae* (Frankfurt, 1633), A3v–A4. English translation by Roger Kuin. See Kuin, "Introduction," in *Correspondence of Sir Philip Sidney*, vol. 1, xxii.

[57] "Hubert Languet to Sidney, Vienna, 26 March 1574," in *Correspondence of Sir Philip Sidney*, vol. 1, 144–8.

Introduction 17

Italy and then Europe itself.[58] In contrast, Sidney preferred the phrase, *respublica christiana*, and in response to Languet's conspiratorial complaints about Rome, the 19-year-old Sidney counseled his mentor to consider the problems of Christendom "one by one and separately [*singular seperatim*]" so as to avoid the conclusion that all of the problems afflicting the true "Church of God [*ecclesiae Dei*]" were attributable to one single cause. The initially flippant tone of Sidney's response to Languet's fears concerning an imminent Ottoman invasion of Italy gives way to a more serious line of thought:

> What could be more devoutly wished than that [a Turkish invasion of Italy]? In the first place it would remove that putrid limb which for so long has corrupted the whole Body of the Christian Commonwealth [*totum Corpus reipublicae Christianae*], and destroy the factory in which, as you write, the causes of so many ills are forged. Furthermore, the Christian princes [*principes christiani*] will be forced to be roused as if from a deep sleep, and your French countrymen, who are now cutting each other down, to join their forces in order to withstand a common enemy, like brawling dogs when they happen to see a wolf plundering the sheepfold.[59]

Given that, at the time that he wrote this letter, Sidney was based in Padua and was undertaking a short visit to Venice, where he had his portrait done by Veronese, it is somewhat surprising to encounter the intense anti-Italianism that was often fashionable among English gentlemen in this passage. For my purposes, the more important aspect of the passage is Sidney's desire that the Christian commonwealth unite in the face of the Turkish invasion. For his part, Languet alternatively worried about the Ottoman threat and found consolation in the fact that without the Turkish threat to Italy, the Spaniards and the Italians "would doubtless turn their forces to oppress those who profess the Reformed faith in France and the Netherlands:

---

[58] For the "civil war" reference, see *Correspondence of Sir Philip Sidney*, vol. 1, 145 [147 (Kuin's English translation. Subsequent entries follow this pattern.)]. See Sidney's references to the transnational *"respublica Christiana"* in Kuin, ed., *Correspondence*, vol. 1, 159 [162], 230 [231]; vol. 2, 736 [737]. In contrast, see Languet's and Wolfgang Zundelin's use of the phrase, "orbis Christianus" (vol. 1, 137 [139], 268 [270], 289 [291], 330 [336]; 2: 823 [826], 928 [931]). For discussion of the typical Catholic use of the phrase, "respublica Christiana," see Tutino, *Empire of Souls*, esp. 14. In a letter to Languet on March 10, 1578, Sidney refers to the French Huguenots as constituting a *"respublica Chrstiana,"* thus using it in a way that was more typical of his fellow Protestants, who often described a nation-state such as England as a Christian commonwealth (vol. 2, 820 [821]).

[59] "Qua re quid accidere potest optabilius? Primum enim tolletur illud putridum membrum quod tam diu corrupit totum Corpus reipublicae Christianae, et delebitur officina in qua vt scribis tot malorum causae cuduntur. Ad haec, cogentur principes Christiani quasi ex alto somno expergefieri, et Tui Galli iam inter se diglandiantes coniungere vires, vt communi hosti resistant, non secus ac rixantes canes, cum forte vident lupum ouile depraedantem." English translation by Roger Kuin. "Sidney to Hubert Languet, Venice, 15 April 1574," in *Correspondence of Sir Philip Sidney*, vol. 1, 158–64.

and once these are oppressed, I do not know how long you English will be able to enjoy your leisured wealth."[60] In contrast to Languet, Sidney still (perhaps naively) imagined the future possibility of a unified Christian commonwealth, comprised of the most powerful European princes, committed to resolving their religious differences and facing down the Ottoman threat.

As we shall see, it is within the context of Sidney's notion of the Christian commonwealth that we gain a better sense of his ultimate purpose in the two *Arcadias*. Sidney's pursuit of a Protestant League with German and Dutch Protestants had an obvious influence on his romance. Similar to Sidney's work on the Protestant League, the good sovereign in the *Old Arcadia*, King Euarchus of Macedonia, travels to Arcadia in search of an alliance that will serve "the universal case of Greece."[61] In Book Five, Euarchus's interest in the affairs of Arcadia proceeds from a combination of self-interest and generosity. Euarchus fears foreign invaders such as the Latins and the Asiatics, both "gaping for any occasion to devour Greece" because Basilius, Duke of Arcadia, has renounced his duties as sovereign, and as a result, "the universal case of Greece [has been] deprived by this means of a principal pillar." In response, Euarchus seeks to save "Basilius from this burying himself alive," and to convince him "to return again to employ his old years in doing good, the only happy action of man's life."[62] When he receives the report that Basilius has been murdered, he agrees provisionally to assume sovereignty over Arcadia, but it is presented narrowly as an act of charity for a valued ally, not as an act of self-interested conquest. Making sense of this narrative as an historical allegory depends on whether one identifies Queen Elizabeth's perspective as that of Euarchus or Basilius. On the one hand, some commentators on the *Old Arcadia* have speculated that the threat posed by the Latins and the Asiatics represents Sidney's perception of the contemporary threat posed to European states by Spain and the Ottoman Empire.[63] According to this interpretation, Euarchus's initial exploration of a Greek alliance involving Arcadia represents Elizabeth's attempts to forge mutually beneficial alliances with the Protestant princes of Germany.[64] On the other hand, Blair Worden has argued that Sidney sought to represent Elizabeth's reluctance to engage with potential Protestant allies such as William of Orange in his portrayal of Basilius hiding himself from effective rule and metaphorically and literally asleep to the dangers that surround him. For Worden, it makes more sense to see the Latins and the

---

[60] "hauddubie omnes suas vires converterent, ad opprimendum eos qui puriorem religionem in Gallia, & in Belgio profitentur; quibus oppressis, nescio quandiu vobis liceret isto vestro opimo ocio frui." "Hubert Languet to Sidney, Prague 13 August 1575," in *Correspondence of Sir Philip Sidney*, vol. 1, 496–510.

[61] Sir Philip Sidney, *The Old Arcadia*, ed. Katherine Duncan-Jones (New York, 1999), 309.

[62] Sidney, *Old Arcadia*, 309–10.

[63] Richard C. McCoy, *Sir Philip Sidney: Rebellion in Arcadia* (New Brunswick, 1979), 120.

[64] For my own exploration of this thesis, see Lockey, *Law and Empire*, 47–79.

Introduction 19

Asiatics encroaching against Euarchus's Macedonia as the religious threat to Sidney's Calvinist allies in the Palatinate and the Low Countries posed by the Roman Church and the Lutheran Church (identified geographically with the Germany and the Eastern portions of Europe).[65] For Worden, then, Euarchus's Macedonia represents the Palatinate and German Calvinists, while Basilius represents Elizabeth.

According to the most recent scholarship, however, Sidney would have been unlikely to endorse any such historical allegorical reading of his narrative. Robert Stillman has reminded us that Sidney tended to view the purpose of a fictional work such as the *Arcadia* not as providing the opportunity to uncover allegorical meaning but rather as a microcosm or little world that was intended to instruct the reader about moral action within the larger world.[66] From this perspective, the two versions of *Arcadia* are Sidney's way of instructing his readers through the creation of another nature, one that is "better than Nature bringeth forth."[67] Such an interpretative perspective views Euarchus not as a historical allegorical figure representing an actual European prince, but rather as an exemplary model, intended to provoke emulation and imitation. Describing the primary characteristics of the exemplary sovereign in both the *Old* and the *New Arcadia* helps us to understand the kind of action that Sidney saw as ethical in the international sphere. In his dealings abroad, Euarchus displays altruism towards the neighboring realm of Arcadia, as well as a desire to restore the rule of law in a country where chaos and disorder have taken hold. Moreover, his attempt to form an alliance with Basilius, the sovereign of Arcadia, has no religious component; rather he seeks to ally Macedonia with Arcadia based on regional solidarity, a common Greek identity, and the fact that both sovereigns find themselves in similar situations.

Sidney's own approach to political engagement overseas shows that he himself sought to emulate a similar strategy. Sidney cultivated correspondences with Catholics in Venice, Padua, and Vienna throughout the 1570s, and after 1578, Sidney was not above pursuing an alliance with Dom Antonio, the Prior of Crato, who as the pretender to the Portuguese crown shared Sidney's antipathy towards Spain and the Hapsburgs.[68] In Venice, he had befriended the English Catholic exile, Edward Windsor, Baron of Stanwell, Windsor's Italian friends, the Neopolitan nobleman Cesare Carrafa and the poet Cesare Pavese, as well as Giovanni Grimani, the Patriarch of Venice (equivalent to the Bishop of Venice), and Jean de Vulcob, the French ambassador to the Holy Roman Emperor.[69] Later, Sidney bought

---

[65] For Worden, Euarchus represents William of Orange. Blair Worden, *The Sound of Virtue: Philip Sidney's Arcadia and Elizabethan Politics* (New Haven, CT, 1996), 235–9.

[66] Stillman, *Sidney and the Poetics of Cosmopolitanism*, 86.

[67] Sir Philip Sidney, *An Apology for Poetry*, ed. Forrest G. Robinson (Indianapolis, IN, 1970), 14.

[68] Stewart, *Sidney: A Double Life*, 240–41; Osborn, *Young Philip Sidney*, 294. Similarly, the English crown and both Protestant and Catholic princes in the Holy Roman Empire were willing to enter into inter-confessional alliances out of pragmatic necessity for survival. Kouri, *England and Protestant Alliance*, 168.

[69] Osborn, *Young Philip Sidney*, 212, 507.

20   *Early Modern Catholics, Royalists, and Cosmopolitans*

3 million acres in America from Sir Humphrey Gilbert's "Commonwealth," which he went on to sell to Sir George Peckham, a prominent Catholic, so that Peckham, Sir Thomas Gerrard, and others could establish a Catholic colony.[70] Most notably, Sidney met with Campion at the court of the Holy Roman Emperor in Prague in 1577, an encounter about which Campion later confided to John Bavand that Sidney had "asked the prayers of all good men" and had given Campion alms to be distributed to the poor.[71] Although Campion later reported that Sidney seemed to be on the verge of a conversion to Catholicism, and even Robert Persons wrote that Sidney had "divers large and secret conferences with his old friend," whom he had presumably known from his time at Oxford, there is little independent evidence to suggest that Sidney's renewal of his friendship with the Jesuit amounted to anything more than the ecumenical cosmopolitanism that characterized much of his continental experience.[72]

Ultimately, Euarchus announces that his charitable intervention into the affairs of Arcadia will adhere to "the general laws of nature, especially of Greece."[73] In this respect, unlike Queen Elizabeth and her father, Euarchus is willing to submit to the dictates and demands of a regional alliance based on a higher law that will inevitably weaken his own power of prerogative in order to preserve the territorial integrity of the region. As I show, both the old and the new versions of the *Arcadia* should be read together as Sidney's progressive attempts to articulate a vision of international order, that would restrain tyrants and punish unjust aggressors.

Of course, given Sidney's background and reputation as an exemplary militant for Protestantism, one might assume that the first inspiration for Sidney's views on how to respond to tyrannical or unfit sovereigns would be such Protestant *monarchomach* tracts as the anonymous *Vindiciae, Contra Tyrannos* or George Buchanan's *De Jure Regni apud Scotos*.[74] As we see in Chapter 3, it is clear that such writings did influence Sidney's views on such matters. It is also clear, as numerous

---

[70]   Osborn, *Young Philip Sidney*, 507.

[71]   "Edmund Campion to Dr. John Bavand," cited in Richard Simpson, *Edmund Campion: A Biography* (London, 1896), 123, and Osborn, *Young Philip Sidney*, 467–8; Stewart, *Sidney: A Double Life*, 175–7; Duncan-Jones, *Sir Philip Sidney*, 124–7.

[72]   Richard Simpson's rendering of Parson's letter is cited in Simpson, *Edmund Campion*, 115. For context, see Osborne, *Young Philip Sidney*, 466–8; Stewart, *Sidney: A Double Life*, 175–7; Duncan-Jones, *Sir Philip Sidney*, 124–35. Bossy suggests that the source of a similar report on Sidney's sympathetic attitude towards Queen Mary Stuart and Catholicism by French ambassador Michel de Castelnau was Giordano Bruno, whom Sidney had entertained during the former Dominican's stay in London. See Bossy, *Giordano Bruno and the Embassy Affair* (New Haven, CT, 1991), 23.

[73]   Sidney, *Old Arcadia*, 315.

[74]   Anon., *Vindiciae, Contra Tyrannos: or concerning the legitimate power of a prince over the people, and of the people over a prince*, ed. and trans. George Garnet (New York, 1994). George Buchanan, *De jure regni apud Scotos. Or, A dialogue, concerning the due privilege of government, in the kingdom of Scotland: betwixt George Buchanan and Thomas Maitland, by the said George Buchanan. And translated out of the original Latin into English by Philalethes* (Philadelphia, 1766).

scholars have noted, that both Protestant and Catholic *monarchomachs* had *similar* (but not identical) perspectives on the right of a people to resist an illegitimate sovereign.[75] In this respect, both were responding to an almost identical problem, namely how one should lawfully respond to tyranny or illegitimacy. As is the case with the other writers of fiction considered in the pages the follow, Sidney's narrative perspective, which champions a secular imperial overseer analogous to the pope's role within the Christian commonwealth, was more complex than the perspective found in the writings of Protestant *monarchomachs*. And as we shall see in the first part of this book, Sidney's conception of the international order, like that of Munday's, Harington's, and Spenser's, is not unrelated to Persons and Sander's conception of the Christian commonwealth, governed by a papal sovereign with the power to depose unruly, evil, or heretical secular rulers. Like other writers considered in the pages that follow, Sidney's portrayal of the larger transnational commonwealths of Asia Minor and later Greece secularizes the pope-centered commonwealth of his Catholic enemies. The champions of Book Two of the *New Arcadia*, Pyrocles and Musidorus, travel throughout Asia Minor, administering an ideal of imperial justice that Persons and his Catholic compatriots would certainly have recognized as a secularized version of their own ideal of papal authority over secular sovereigns. If Greville is correct that Sidney himself was responsible for attempting to resuscitate the anti-papist alliance, his ultimate vision, as revealed by the *New Arcadia*, had an uncanny resemblance to the vision of universal papal government, promoted by his enemies.

* * *

Before examining the writings of prominent Catholic exiles and their conformist interlocutors who lived in England, we should first consider the etiology of the sixteenth-century Catholic understanding of church-state relations as well as how this understanding compared with the official outlook on matters of church and state within Queen Elizabeth's court. During the medieval period, the most significant church-state conflict concerned the basis of the Holy Roman Emperor's claim to imperial power. Did the ceremony in which the pope conferred the title of Holy Roman Emperor mean that the conferee received his imperial power from the pope? And more importantly, did this mean that the pope could depose the emperor? Finally, if so, what kinds of crimes justified taking such drastic action? During the medieval period, any response to these questions had not only to take into account the precedent of Pope Zachary's deposition of Childeric, king of the Franks, and Pope Leo III's coronation of Charlemagne during the eighth century, but it also had to conform to a systematized hierarchy, accepted widely throughout Christendom, within which the spiritual realm had certain important claims of primacy and authority over the temporal realms.

---

[75] See Quentin Skinner, *The Foundations of Modern Political Thought* (New York, 1978), vol. 1, 49–68, 139–92; vol. 2, 113–348.

22   *Early Modern Catholics, Royalists, and Cosmopolitans*

As Humbert had written in the eleventh century, "just as the soul excels the body and commands it, so too the priestly dignity excels the royal or, we may say, the heavenly dignity the earthly."[76]

Moreover, such questions took on a new urgency in the wake of the twelfth-century reintroduction of classical Roman law into the curriculum of European universities, which provided a thoroughly secular and systematized account of the origins of imperial authority, independent of ecclesiastical oversight. In response, a Bolognese monk called Gratian began systematizing the ecclesiastical law into a comparable comprehensive and organic structure and positing an administrative unity, ironically based on Roman law, centered on the pope as supreme judge in both ecclesiastical and temporal affairs. Gratian's *Decretum* and the hundreds of commentaries that it generated produced two traditions of thought with regard to papal correction of the temporal realm, both of which followed logically from Gratian's statement that Christ had conferred on Peter "the rights over a heavenly and an earthly empire [*terreni simul et celestis imperii iura comisit*]."[77] On the one hand, a moderate interpretation of Gratian's statement maintained that, while the pope wielded two swords, one spiritual and the other temporal, he was enjoined by God, who had separated the two realms, to bestow the temporal sword on the emperor.[78] According to the anonymous *Summa et est Sciendum*, this conferral of authority did not justify the papal deposing power, since emperors had existed before popes and, according to Roman law, the emperor could wield the sword by God's authority and "by virtue of his election by the people." A pope could rather only excommunicate the emperor, in the process absolving "his subjects from rendering obedience to him."[79] In this way, a pope could work together with the emperor's noble subjects towards his deposition. On the other hand, a more extreme line of interpretation, exemplified

---

[76]   Humbert, *Libri III Adversus Simoniacos*, in F. Thaner (ed.), *Monumenta Germaniae Historica Libelli de Lite Imperatorum et Pontificum* (3 vols, Hanover, 1891), vol. 1, 225: "Ex quibus sicut praeminet anima et praecipit, sic sacerdotalis dignitas regali, utputa caelestis terrestri." See the English translation in Tierney, *Crisis of Church and State*, 41–2.

[77]   Gratian, Dist. 22 c. 1, in E. Friedberg (ed.) *Corpus Iuris Canonici* (2 vols, Leipzig, 1879), vol. 1, col. 73: "Illam uero solus ipse fundauit, et super petram fidei mox nascentis erexit, qui beato eternae uitae clauigero terreni simul et celestis imperii iura commisit." See the English translation in Tierney, *Crisis of Church and State*, 119.

[78]   Alanus, Commentary on *Dist.* 96 c. 6, in A.M. Stickler, "Alanus Anglicus als Verteidiger des Monarchischen Papsttums," *Salesianum*, XXI (1959): 361–3.

[79]   *Summa et Est Sciendum* Commentary on *Dist.* 22 c. 1, in A.M. Stickler (ed.), "Imperator Vicarius Papae: Die Lehren der französisch-deutschen Dekretistenschule des 12. und beginnenden 13. Jahrhunderts über die Beziehungen zwischen Papst und Kaiser," *Mitteilungen des Instituts fur Osterreichische Geschichtsforschung*, LXII (1954): 165–212, at 203: "Item ante hodie potest imperator uti gladio quam consecretur in imperatorem, populi electione, que (per pape electionem, que: Cod Rouen) ei et in eum omne ius et omnem potestatem transfert. ... Regem autem deposuisse papa dicitur, cum eum propter aliquem contumaciam excommunicavit et ita subditos eius ab eius obedientia et servitio subtraxit." See English translation in Tierney, *Crisis of Church and State*, 120–21.

Introduction 23

by Rufinus's commentary on Gratian's *Decretum*, claimed that the pope held "a right of authority" over the earthly empire, while his steward—the emperor—held merely "a right of administration [*amministrationis*]," which the pope was called to confer conditionally on the emperor during the coronation ceremony.[80] This line of interpretation was eventually taken up by an Englishman named Alanus, giving rise to an extreme vision of papal world-monarchy: "According to the Catholic faith, [the emperor] is subject to the pope in spiritual matters and also receives his sword from him, for the right of both swords belongs to the pope. This is proved by the fact that the Lord had both swords on earth and used both as is mentioned here, and he established Peter as his vicar on earth and all Peter's successors. Therefore today Innocent has by right the material sword. If you deny this you are saying that Christ established a secular prince as his vicar in this regard."[81] This passage contains a reference to Pope Innocent III, who made his own extremist claims concerning world governance. In a letter to the patriarch of Constantinople in 1199, for example, he claims that Peter was left "not only the universal church but the whole world to govern."[82] More importantly, Innocent III was very specific about defining the papal authority as something necessary for correcting and deposing temporal rulers. He writes that temporal princes should and do acknowledge that the "right and authority [*ius et auctoritas*] to examine the person elected as king, who is to be promoted to the imperial dignity, belong to us who anoint and consecrate and crown him." He goes on to explain, "If the princes elected as king a sacrilegious man or an excommunicate [*sacrilegum quemcunque, vel excommunicatum*], a tyrant, a fool or a heretic [*tyrannum, vel fatuum, haereticum*], and that not just by divided vote but unanimously, ought we to anoint, consecrate and crown such a man?

---

[80]   Rufinus, Commentary on *Dist*. 22 c. 1, in *Summa Decretorum*, ed. H. Singer (Paderborn, 1902), 47: "Et quidem ius auctoritatis quemadmodum in episcopo, ad cuius ius omnes res ecclesiastice spectare videntur, quia eius auctoritate omni adisponuntur; ius autem amministrationis sicut in yconomo, iste enim habet ius amministrandi, sed auctoritate caret imperandi: quicquid aliis precipit, non sua, sed episcopi auctoritate indicit."

[81]   Alanus, Commentary on Dist. 96 c. 6, ed. A.M. Stickler, "Alanus Anglicus als Verteidiger des monarchischen Papsttums," *Salesianum*, XXI (1959), 361–3, at 362: "Set veritas est et fides catholica quod pape subest quoad spiritualia et etiam gladium suum habet ab eo, quia ius utrusque gladii est apud papam; quod probatur quia dominus in terris utrumque habuit et utroque usus est ut hic. Set petrum in terris vicarium constituit et omnes petri successores. Ergo et hodie innocentius habet de iure gladium materialem. Quod si negaveris dicas quod principem secularem in hoc sibi vicarium constituit et petri successores." See English translation in Tierney, *Crisis of Church and State*, 123.

[82]   "*Patriarchae Constantinopolitano. Respondet superiori epistolae*," in Jacques-Paul Migne, *Patrologia Latina* (Paris, 1855), vol. 214, col. 759D: "Jacobus enim frater Domini, qui videbatur esse columna, Jerosolymitana sola contentus, ut ibi semen fratris praemortui suscitaret ubi fuerat crucifixus, Petro non solum universam Ecclesiam sed totum reliquit saeculum gubernandum." See the English translation in Tierney, *Crisis of Church and State*, 132.

Of course not."[83] For Innocent III (and Alanus as well), the pope and his bishops preside over a court of last appeal, making the pope supreme judge over the entire Christian commonwealth. Ultimately, among canon-law jurists, both the moderate and extreme approaches to the problem of how to deal with a tyrant or heretic or incapacitated king were in agreement about the basic superiority of the spiritual to the temporal realm. The disagreement was not so much whether the pope could correct the temporal sovereign, but rather whether the pope could directly take up the temporal sword or whether the pope was constrained to employ the indirect tool of excommunication, while leaving other temporal princes or noble subjects to take up the sword in his name.

Significantly, the primary source of resistance to the entire doctrine came from temporal sovereigns, who viewed their own authority as deriving directly from God. During the thirteenth century, Emperor Frederick II endured a bitter conflict with the Papacy over his claim that his imperial title gave him sovereignty over the whole of Italy. Naturally, the Roman See opposed this claim, if only because it would have reduced the pope to a mere bishop dependent on the Emperor's good will. In 1227 and again in 1239, Pope Gregory IX deposed Frederick for the crimes of perjury, sacrilege, and heresy, pointedly omitting any mention of Frederick's ambitions in Italy.[84] Frederick responded to the pope's actions in 1246 in a letter to the kings of Christendom, in which he reminded his fellow princes that the pope now exercised a power that could conceivably threaten the sovereignty of every Christian prince: "You and all kings of particular regions [*vobis et singulis regibus singularum regionum*] have everything to fear from the effrontery of such a prince of priests [*talis principis sacerdotum*] when he sets out to depose us who have been divinely honored by the imperial diadem and solemnly elected by the princes."[85] As we shall see in Chapter 1, Frederick's denunciation of Pope Gregory IX's act of deposition bears a striking resemblance to the outrage that would be expressed by William Cecil, Lord Burghley in the *Execution of Justice* (1584),

---

[83] *Venerabilem* (*Decretales* 1.6.34), in E. Friedberg (ed.), *Corpus Iuris Canonici* (2 vols, Leipzig, 1881), vol. 2, col. 80: "Sed et principes recognoscere debent, et utique recognoscunt, sicut iidem in nostra recognovere praesentia, quod ius et auctoritas examandi personam electam in regem et promovendam ad imperium ad nos spectat, qui eum inungimus, consecramus et coronamus. ... Numquid enim, si principes non solum in discordia, sed etiam in concordia sacrilegum quemcunque, vel ecommunicatum in regem, tyrannum, vel fatuum, haereticum eligerent, aut paganum, nos inungere, consecrare ac coronare hominem huiusmodi deberemus?" See the English translation in Tierney, *Crisis of Church and State*, 133–4.

[84] Tierney, *Crisis of Church and State*, 139–49.

[85] "Frederick II's Letter to the kings of Christendom," in J. Huillard-Breholles (ed.), *Historia Diplomatica Friderici Secundi* (6 vols, Paris, 1860), vol. 6, part 1, 391: "Quid enim vobis et singulis regibus singularum regionum a facie talis principis sacerdotum timendum non superest, si nos ex principum electione solenni et adprobatione totius Ecclesie, dum cleri fide ac religione vigebant, imperali diademate divinitus insignitos, et ali regna nobilia magnifice gubernantes, deponendos agreditur." English translation in Tierney, *Crisis of Church and State*, 145–6.

Introduction 25

the crown's official response to Pope Pius V's *Regnans in Excelsis*. According to Cecil's warning for the princes of Europe, if the Papal Bull were left unchallenged, "no Empire, no kingdome, no countrey, no Citie or Towne" was secure from usurpation by the papal overseer, whose tyrannical authority would eventually undermine the integrity of every temporal realm within Christendom.[86]

During the years leading up to the papal excommunication of Queen Elizabeth (1570), English perceptions of the boundary between church and state were less settled than those of their continental counterparts. In the first decade of Elizabeth's reign, however, the debate between conformist and non-conformist controversialists was not so much about claims of papal primacy but rather the need to establish a definitive boundary between the jurisdiction of temporal authority and that of the spiritual authority.[87] As we shall see, the contours of these early debates on where precisely the temporal jurisdiction ended and the ecclesiastical jurisdiction began provide essential context to the more extreme positions later taken by Sander and Persons on papal oversight over the temporal realm. In 1565, the exiled Catholic priest who had once been a Professor of Hebrew at Oxford, Thomas Harding, attempted to refute John Jewel's *Apologia Ecclesiae Anglicanae* by charging that English prelates only knew how to seek "the favour of secular princes."[88] Jewel replied by comparing English prelates to a catalogue of biblical and historical *exempla* who were known for standing up to secular rulers: "We flatter our princes, M. Harding, as Nathan flattered King David; as John Baptist flattered Herod; as St. Ambrose flattered Theodosius."[89] The reality, of course, was that the English crown often intimidated English prelates into submission. Indeed, the Queen had begun her reign in 1559 by depriving the entire episcopal bench of its former remit. Feeble attempts by English bishops and prelates to admonish government policy illustrate how browbeaten the clergy of her realm had become. In the mid 1570s, for example, Elizabeth demanded that Archbishop Edmund Grindal suppress the practice of prophesying among country preachers, which she regarded as a threat to her own authority, going so far as to demand that he "abridge" the number of preachers in order to stop the practice. After explaining the history and benefits of such prophesying conferences and reminding her that ecclesiastical governance should be within the sole purview of the bishops, Grindal responded by invoking his conscience: "I am forced, with all humility, and yet plainly, to profess, that I cannot with safe conscience, and without the offence of the majesty of God, give my assent to the suppressing of the said exercises." In the same breath, he reminds her, in a manner that conjures up Gratian's claim for the superiority of the heavenly over the earthly kingdom, that he must choose "rather to offend our earthly majesty, than to offend the heavenly majesty of God." But rather than admonishing her, he offers to vacate his office: "If it be your Majesty's

---

[86] Cecil, *Execution of Justice in England*, C3–C3v.

[87] Tutino, *Law and Conscience*, 16.

[88] Cited in *Apologia Ecclsiae Anglicanae*, in *Works of John Jewel, Bishop of Salisbury*, ed. Rev. John Ayre (Cambridge, 1850), vol. 6, 207.

[89] *Apologia Ecclsiae Anglicanae*, in *Works of John Jewel*, vol. 6, 207.

pleasure, for this or any other cause to remove me out of this place, I will with all humility yield thereunto, and render again to your Majesty that I received of the same."[90] Ultimately, the crown did take measures to suspend Grindal from his office, though he was able to retain his spiritual authority, and he remained sequestered until his death in 1583. In other instances, whether they involved Dean of St. Paul's Alexander Nowell or Archbishop Hutton insisting that the Queen marry and produce an heir or the bishops reproving Elizabeth for keeping a little silver cross on the communion table in her chapel, the Queen was quite willing to reprove the divines "with a sharp message."[91]

For reasons that will become clear, early Catholic polemicists were fond of citing the ancient exemplum of Archbishop of Milan Ambrose standing up to Empress Justina, her son Valentinian, and most importantly to Emperor Theodosius during the so-called Battle of the Basilicas of 385–6, while Elizabethan churchmen preferred the example of Emperor Constantine.[92] It was not Constantine's donation of Rome to Pope Sylvester, already considered fraudulent by Protestants, that was important to Elizabethan prelates, however; rather it was Constantine's appointment of ecclesiastical assemblies or councils of bishops, since such appointments supported their own arguments concerning Elizabeth's claim of ecclesiastical supremacy. In the *Apologia Eccleisiae Anglorum*, for example, John Jewel, the Bishop of Salisbury wrote that "Christian Emperours in the olde time, appointed the Councelles of the Bishoppes. Constantine called the Councel at Nice: Theodosius the firste, called the Councel at Constantinople: Theodosius the seconde, the councel at Ephesus: Martian, the Councel at Chalcedon."[93] In response, Thomas Harding, the Catholic polemicist, stressed that only the pope could call a general council of bishops: "If Constantine, the two Theodosians, and Marcian called the foure firste generall Councelles by their Auctoritie onely, then were they no generall Councelles. Neither could their decrees binde the whole worlde. For although they were great Emperours, yet was not the whole Christian worlde vnder them." He goes on to add that if indeed these bodies were authentic general councils, then Constantine and his successors "called them by the assent of the Bishop of Rome." [94] In his response to Harding's tract, Jewel takes his original argument about temporal authority even further, claiming that the historical record shows precisely the opposite, namely that the pope could only call the council "by the Authoritie of the Emperoure."[95] A similar exchange,

---

[90]   *The Remains of Edmund Grindal*, ed. W. Nicholson (Cambridge, 1843), 387.

[91]   Sir John Harington, *A Briefe view of the state of the Church of England*, ed. John Chetwynd (London, 1653), 216–22 [186–9].

[92]   Patrick Collinson, "If Constantine, then also Theodosius: St. Ambrose and the Integrity of the Elizabethan *Ecclesia Anglicana*," in *Godly People: Essays on English Protestantism and Puritanism* (London, 1983), 109–33.

[93]   Cited in John Jewel, *A Defence of the Apologie of the Churche of Englande, Conteininge an Answeare to a certaine Booke lately set foorthe by M. Hardinge, and Entituled, A Confutation* (London, 1567), Iii6v.

[94]   Cited in Jewel, *Defence of the Apologie*, Iii6v.

[95]   Jewel, *Defence of the Apologie*, Kkk2.

Introduction 27

this time initiated by the English Benedictine John Feckenham, who had been the last abbot of Westminster under Queen Mary, culminated in a repetition of the same controversy.[96] In an unpublished tract, Feckenham claims that Emperor Constantine had called the council of Nice "at the request of Syluester then Bishop of Rome," and had announced to the bishops there assembled that God "had transferred to them [the bishops] the power to judge over us [temporal sovereigns] [*potestatem tradidit iudicandi de nobis*]." Additionally according to Feckenham, Emperors Constantine, Valentianus, and Theodosius were unanimous in acknowledging that authority over all ecclesiastical matters pertained exclusively to the bishops.[97] The Bishop of Winchester Robert Horne responded by noting that the evidence shows that only the Emperor had authority to call the council and furthermore that historically both the pope and the bishops had acknowledged that "the supreame power and authoritie, to sommon and call councels, whiche is a principall part of your purpose, and of the Ecclesaistical iurisdiction cohibitiue, to be in the Emperour and not in them selues." More importantly, Horne summarily rejects Feckenham's claim that it follows from Bishop Ambrose having barred Emperor's Theodosius's entrance into the Chancel, that bishops therefore exercise "the second kinde of Cohibitiue [supreme external or public] Iurisdiction over" the Emperor.[98] No such conclusion, according to Horne, should follow.

The eminent Catholic theologian Thomas Stapleton, then a professor at Louvain, responded in kind with a 500-page tome, entitled *A Counterblast to M. Horne's Vayne Blaste against M. Fekenham*, in which he recounts in some detail the historical narrative of the events pitting Bishop Ambrose against Emperor Theodosius. Stapleton begins the story at Thessalonica, whose people erupted in "sedition and an vprore," proceeding to murder some of Theodosius's magistrates.[99] In response, Theodosius commanded that the people of Thessalonica be slaughtered and the city destroyed. Later the emperor travelled to Milan, but

---

[96] For an overview of the Feckenham-Horne controversy, see A.C. Southern, *Elizabethan Recusant Prose, 1559–1582: A Historical and Critical Account of the Books of the Catholic Refugees* (London, 1950), 125–35.

[97] Cited in Robert Horne, *An Answeare Made by Rob. Bishoppe of Wynchester, to a Booke entituled, The Declaration of Suche Scruples, and staies of Conscience, touching the Othe of the Supremacy, as M. Iohn Fekenham, by wrytinge did deliuer unto the L. Bishop of Winchester, with his Resolutions made thereunto* (London, 1566), Ff4v: "Cum vos Deus sacerdotes constiturit potestatem tradidit iudicandi de nobis."

[98] Horne, *An Answeare*, Hh3. Horne draws a distinction between the "cohibitive jurisdiction" or public authority over the church, belonging to the supreme guide, i.e. the Queen in this case, and the jurisdiction "not cohibitive" or the inward court of conscience, which is directed solely by the clergy. See Tutino, *Law and Conscience*, 11–21, for a more detailed explanation of how this early controversy was actually a rather limited debate on defining the boundary between the two jurisdictions rather than on papal supremacy per se.

[99] Thomas Stapleton, *A Counterblast to M. Hornes Vayne Blaste Against M. Fekenham. Wherein is set forthe: A ful Reply to M. Hornes Answer, and to euery part thereof made, against the Declaration of my L. Abbat of Westminster, M. Fekenham, touching, The Othe of Supremacy* (Louvain, 1567), kkkkv.

28   Early Modern Catholics, Royalists, and Cosmopolitans

when he attempted to enter the Basilica to receive the sacraments, Bishop Ambrose intercepted him, barring his entrance. According to Stapleton's account,

> S. Ambrose mette hym, and forbadde him to enter: most vehementlie reprouing hym for the sayed shawghter [sic]: asking, howe he could finde in his conscience, eyher [sic] to lyfte up hiys handes to God, defiled with suche a foule murther, or with the same to receyue the holie bodie of Christe, or to receyue with hys mouthe the preciouse bloude of Christe, by whose furiouse and ragnge [sic] commaundemente so muche bloude had been shedde? Wherefore he woulde, that the Emperour shoulde turne home againe, and that he shoulde pacientlie suffer the bonde, the which God had with his heauenly sentence allowed, meaning this sentence of excommunication. The Emperour as one browght vppe in Goddes Lawes, obeyed hym, and with weapinge teares departed.[100]

As we shall see in Chapter 2, the life of Saint Ambrose, especially the story of his rebuke and excommunication of Emperor Theodosius, was important to the English Catholic perspective on papal supremacy with respect to Queen Elizabeth, because the story served as an exemplum and a precedent of the proper relationship between the ecclesiastical and the temporal realms. If Bishop Ambrose could compel the Emperor of Rome to repent and to alter and correct his governance of the temporal realm, then every subsequent pope was justified in using the same power of compulsion to correct the tyrannical or heretical rule of his temporal counterparts.

English Protestants were obviously keenly aware of what the precedent of Ambrose and Theodosius might mean for the relationship between the two realms with respect to England, especially because a bishop rather than the pope had corrected Emperor Theodosius.[101] And because it had occurred during the very early history of the Church, well before the corruption and abuse that they saw as endemic to the Roman church, it would potentially have had greater purchase than later precedents involving Pope Innocent III or Pope Boniface VIII. Given their Erastian dependence on the government of the civil ruler, however, Elizabethan Protestant martyrologists like John Foxe and conformist prelates like Richard Hooker, Bilson, and Nowell tended to neglect the entire narrative or at least to see it as an exception to the rightful supremacy of Christian princes.[102] In the *Acts and Monuments*, Foxe compares Constantine favorably with Queen Elizabeth, neglecting to mention

---

[100]   Stapleton, *A Counterblast*, kkkkv–kkkk2. A fourth and final stage in this controversy transpired with the publication of John Bridges's refutation of Stapleton's *Counterblast* and Sander's *De visibili monarchia ecclesiae, libri VIII*, entitled, *The Supremacie of Christian Princes, ouer all persons throughout their dominions, in all causes so wel Ecclesiastical as temporall, both against the Counterblast of Thomas Stapleton, replying on the Reuerend father in Christe, Robert Bishop of Winchester: and also Against Nicolas Sanders his Uisible Monarchie of the Romaine Church, touching this controuersie of the Princes Supremacie* (London, 1573), 498.

[101]   For an overview of Protestant approaches to this issue, see William A. Mueller, *Church and State in Luther and Calvin: A Comparative Study* (Nashville, 1954).

[102]   Collinson, "If Constantine, then also Theodosius," 112–14.

Introduction 29

Bishop Ambrose's confrontation with Theodosius altogether, and instead informing the reader that Ambrose, during his funeral oration for Theodosius, was responsible for the slanderous rumor of Constantine's lowly birth.[103] Bilson presents it as a unique exception to the proper relations between prince and bishop: "Saint Ambrose is the onely example in all antiquitie, which fully proueth that a Bishoppe did prohibite a Prince to enter the Church and to bee partaker of the Lordes table: which wee neither deny, nor dispraise, considering the cause and the manner of the fact."[104] He goes on to criticize his Jesuit interlocutors for finding in the story some precedent "to warrant rebellions & insurrections against Princes," when in reality it is Theodosius, who acted as an exemplum for good princes that choose to be honorable and "repent them of their sinnes."[105] Similarly, Nowell read the story of Ambrose and Theodosius as implying only that princes should be obedient to the instruction of their ministers, without suggesting that they were subject to them. Finally, Hooker discussed the Ambrose precedent at length but regarded it as an extraordinary case that had no bearing on the normal relationship between the ordinary ecclesiastical jurisdiction and the dominion of the prince.[106] Ultimately, Protestants saw the ancient story as confirming their own prejudices in favor of the sovereign's independent exercise of his own personal conscience: it was after all Emperor Theodosius who elected to reform himself in response to Ambrose's rebuke, but he was never subject to the bishop's authority. Perhaps Bilson summarized the conformist view best in a later polemical dialogue against the English Jesuits: "pastors may teach, exhort, & reprove, not force, command or reuenge: only princes be gouernors."[107]

* * *

As we shall see, *Early Modern Catholics, Royalists, and Cosmopolitans* is about those English authors that helped to secularize the religious conception of cosmopolitanism that was implicit in the Catholic notion of the transnational Christian commonwealth. In this respect, the chapters that follow comprise a pre-history of

---

[103]   John Foxe, *The Acts and Monuments of John Foxe*, with a preliminary dissertation by Rev. George Townsend, ed. Stephen Reed Cattley (8 vols, London, 1838–41), vol. 8, 657–8; vol. 1, 293.

[104]   Thomas Bilson, *The true difference betweene Christian subiection and unchristian rebellion wherein the princes lawfull power to commaund for trueth, and indepriuable right to beare the sword are defended against the Popes censures and the Iesuits sophismes vttered in their apologie and defence of English Catholikes: with a demonstration that the things refourmed in the Church of England by the lawes of this realme are truely Catholike, notwithstanding the vaine shew made to the contrary in their late Rhemish Testament* (Oxford, 1585) Cc2v.

[105]   Bilson, *The true difference*, Cc3.

[106]   Alexander Nowell, *A reproufe, written by Alexander Nowell, of a booke entituled, A proufe of certayne articles in religion denied by M. Iuell, set furth by Thomas Dorman* (London, 1565), 51; *The Works of that Learned and Judicious Divine, Mr. Richard Hooker*, ed. John Keble (3 vols, Oxford, 1836), vol. 3, 444–55. For context, see Collinson, "If Constantine, then also Theodosius," 113–14.

[107]   Bilson, *The true difference*, K8.

30   *Early Modern Catholics, Royalists, and Cosmopolitans*

more fully-realized eighteenth-century ideals of cosmopolitanism culminating with Immanuel Kant's notion of "cosmopolitan law" and Anacharsis Cloots' notion of the *république du genre humain*. In order to understand how the authors considered here fit into the larger intellectual history of cosmopolitanism, it is worth briefly considering a famous passage found in Kant's essay "Towards Perpetual Peace," which explains Kant's cosmopolitan ideal of universal community:

> The peoples of the earth have entered in varying degrees into a universal community, and it is developed to the point where a violation of laws in one part of the world is felt everywhere. The idea of a cosmopolitan law is therefore not fantastic and overstrained; it is a necessary complement to the unwritten code of political and international law, transforming it into a universal law of humanity.[108]

The ideals contained in Kant's essay are significant because they serve as the primary inspiration for the contemporary approach to cosmopolitanism. Eighteenth-century critics of Kant's notion of universal community, however, pointed out early on that such an ideal could not be realized without some overarching institution with coercive powers.[109] In the aftermath of *Regnans in Excelsis* (1570), of course, Pope Pius V and his supporters were claiming that the papacy held just such a coercive power, with the ability to punish tyrannical sovereigns and resolve conflicts between competing secular magistrates on the basis of a spiritual authority that was superior to their temporal power. During the 100 years that followed 1570, despite attempts by Robert Bellarmine, S.J. and Francisco Suárez, S.J. to sustain and bolster papal authority, it is clear that papal authority over temporal rulers was in decline. As we shall see, the second half of this book shows that, in the face of this decline, Kant's ideal of a secular non-coercive universal community, in which an enlightened state or people inspires a "federal association among other states," was already emerging within the fictional, political writings and translations of Sir Richard Fanshawe.[110] Indeed, we encounter prefigurations of Kant's vision as early as the 1590s in the plays about the adventures of Catholic exile Thomas Stukeley on the continent, which I explore in Chapter 4 of this book.

As he explains in the passage above, Kant's ideal of a "universal community" also depends for its existence on what he cites as the "idea of a cosmopolitan law," but throughout the remainder of "Perpetual Peace," Kant fails to explain in

---

[108]   Kant, *Kant: Political Writings* (New York, 1991), 107–8. For Kant's place within contemporary discussions of cosmopolitanism, see David Harvey, *Cosmopolitanism and the Geographies of Freedom* (New York, 2009), esp. 17–36; Mignolo, "Many Faces of Cosmopolis," 168–77. For an intellectual history of cosmopolitanism that presents Kant and Cloots as the gateway authors into modern cosmopolitanism, see Derek Heater, *World Citizenship and Government: Cosmopolitan Ideas in the History of Western Political Thought* (New York, 1996), 60–85.

[109]   See J.G. Fichte, "Review of Immanuel Kant, *Perpetual Peace: A Philosophical Sketch* (Königsburg: Nicolovius, 1795)," trans. Daniel Breazeale, *The Philosophical Forum* 32.4 (Winter 2001): 311–21.

[110]   Kant, *Political Writings*, 104.

Introduction 31

any detail how such a cosmopolitan law would be defined. Richard Tuck's work on the intellectual history of the ideal of international order shows that Kant's term, "cosmopolitan law," was a secularized expression of the medieval and early modern concept of natural law. According to Tuck, Kant's more immediate influences and predecessors were those political theorists such as Hugo Grotius, Thomas Hobbes, and John Locke, who had secularized traditional natural law doctrine during the seventeenth century, but the original parameters of an international order were established a century before Grotius with the *relectiones* of the Spanish Dominican, Francisco de Vitoria, and subsequent traditional neo-Scholastics who came to be known as the School of Salamanca.[111]

In most respects, Vitoria's cosmology could be described as consistent with traditional Scholasticism. For Vitoria, *ius naturalis* or natural law was the universal law, derived from the eternal law of the heavens, that applied to each and every human and every human community or people or nation. In order to be legitimate, the customary or positive law established by a particular *gens* or people had to be consistent with the universal natural law. Unlike his humanist opponents, the foundation for Vitoria's ideas was the traditional Catholic conception of the oneness of humankind—together all peoples of the earth potentially comprised one vast community before Christ.[112] Vitoria's conception of humanity's oneness stood in stark contrast to the conclusions of later humanists such as Juan Ginés de Sepúlveda, who, based on early ethnographic accounts describing the unnatural and barbaric customs and traditions of the Amerindians, had concluded that the Amerindians collectively embodied Aristotle's definition of the natural slave, thereby seeking to justify their conquest and enslavement by Spanish *encomenderos*.[113] In contrast to Sepúlveda, Vitoria allowed for only two instances in which conquest and coercive reform based on the behavior of the conquered was legitimate—cases in which innocent subjects were being victimized by unnatural sins such as cannibalism and human sacrifice, and cases in which Christians were being oppressed by non-Christian princes.[114] At the same time, Vitoria ultimately concluded his *relectio*

---

[111]   Richard Tuck, *The Rights of War and Peace: Political Thought and the International Order From Grotius to Kant* (New York, 2001). For background, see Anthony Pagden, *The Fall of Natural Man: The American Indian and the Origins of Comparative Ethnology* (New York, 1986). For discussion of how natural law discourse of the Neo-Scholastic school applies to contemporary discussion of cosmopolitanism and globalism, see Annabel S. Brett, *Changes of State: Nature and the Limits of the City in Early Modern Natural Law* (Princeton, 2011).

[112]   Pagden, *Fall of Natural Man*, 63–4.

[113]   Pagden, *Fall of Natural Man*, 109–18.

[114]   "quia habent ordinem aliquem in suis rebus, postquam habent civitates, quae ordine constant; et habent matrimonia distincta, magistratus, dominos leges, opificia, commutationes, quae omnia requirunt usum rationis." Francisco de Vitoria, *Relectio Prior de Indis Recenter Inventis*, in *Relecciones teológicas del maestro Fray Francisco de Vitoria*, ed. Luis G. Alonso Getino (3 vols, Madrid, 1933), vol. 2, 309. Francisco de Vitoria, *Relectio de Indis [On the American Indians]*, in *Political Writings*, ed. Anthony Pagden and Jeremy Lawrance (New York, 1991), 250.

32 *Early Modern Catholics, Royalists, and Cosmopolitans*

with the caveat that conquest for the education of the Amerindians should remain a temporary measure—once the Amerindians had developed into fully rational beings, their original *dominium* should be returned to them.[115]

Implicit in all of Vitoria's conclusions about the limitations on the sovereign's right of conquest was the law of nations (*ius gentium*), which held an ambiguous, intermediate position between natural and positive law, having been derived from the former and establishing a foundation for the later. In his earlier *relectio, De potestate civili [On Civil Power]*, he explained,

> The law of nations (*ius gentium*) does not have the force merely of pacts or agreements between men, but has the validity of a positive enactment. The whole world, which is in a sense a commonwealth, has the power to enact laws which are just and convenient to all men; and these make up the law of nations. From this it follows that those who break the law of nations, whether in peace or in war, are committing mortal crimes, at any rate in the case of the graver transgressions such as violating the immunity of ambassadors. No kingdom may choose to ignore this law of nations, because it has the sanction of the whole world.[116]

It is worth noting how similar this passage is to Kant's formulation of a universal community bound by a cosmopolitan law in the passage from "Perpetual Peace." The similarity between Vitoria and Kant here is the reason why Walter Mignolo has noted, in a seminal article on the history of cosmopolitanism, that "if one stripped Vitoria of his religious principles, replaced theology with philosophy, and the concern to deal with difference in humanity with a straightforward classification of people by nations, color, and continents, what one would obtain indeed would be Kant. Is that much of a difference? In my view it is not."[117] Mignolo holds up the work of both Vitoria and Kant as presenting similar ideals of cosmopolitanism, which served to critique the emerging national and imperial powers of Europe on the basis of principles derived from natural law.

But unfortunately, Mignolo misunderstands a crucial aspect of Vitoria's cosmology. The emerging nation-state, which Mignolo correctly views as the subject of Vitoria's scholastic critique, remains, for Mignolo, "coupled with the church." According to Mignolo, Vitoria's *relectiones* presented a challenge to the universal "ideology of possession enjoined by the pope and the [Holy Roman] emperor," which Vitoria sought to replace with his own "proposal in favor of

---

[115]   Vitoria, *Relectio de Indis [On the American Indians]*, 286–92.

[116]   "quod jus gentium non solum habet vim ex pacto et condicto inter homines, sed etiam habet vim legis. Habet enim totus orbis, qui aliquo modo est una respublica, potestate ferendi leges aequas et convenientes omnibus, quales sunt in jure gentium. Ex quo patet, quod mortaliter pecant violantes jura gentium, sive in pace, sive in bello, in rebus tamen, gravioribus, ut est de incolumitate legatorum. Neque licet uni regno nolle teneri jure gentium; est enim latum totius orbis authoritate." Vitoria, *De potestate civili*, in *Relectiones de Francisco de Vitoria*, vol. 2, 207. English translation from Vitoria, *Relectio de potestate civili [On Civil Power]*, in *Political Writings*, 40.

[117]   Mignolo, "Many Faces of Cosmopolis," 166.

Introduction   33

international relations based on the 'rights of the people' (community, nation)."[118] But this constitutes a serious misreading of Vitoria, who ultimately was as much a supporter of the papal deposing power as Persons, Sander, Bellarmine, or Suarez would later be. Indeed, in his most famous *relectio De indis* (the subject of Mignolo's essay), Vitoria affirms that the pope may curtail any "civil laws which promote sin," "adjudicate between princes who are threatening to come to war," and most importantly "may on occasion depose kings or institute new ones, as has sometimes happened."[119] Such passages affirm that for Vitoria, the oppressive activities of the secular authorities in the Americas had occasioned a conflict between the church and the state, and he viewed his own *relectiones* as part of a larger effort to utilize spiritual authority to correct the crimes perpetrated by oppressive temporal magistrates. In this respect, Mignolo misses a crucial difference between the early modern cosmopolitan perspective and that of the eighteenth century. For while Mignolo is correct to view Kant's cosmopolitan ideal as using philosophical principles to secularize Vitoria's theological perspective, Vitoria's notion of world governance is ultimately dependent on papal authority over temporal sovereigns, whereas Kant's conception of universal peace relies on Enlightenment principles and republican values.

In one respect, then, it seems to me that Mignolo is correct to view Kant's "Perpetual Peace" as simply a secular philosophical reformulation of Vitoria, and it is the purpose of this book to show how the traditional cosmopolitan vision of Vitoria's counterparts among the late sixteenth-century English Catholic exiles was similarly secularized in prominent works of fiction during this period. In quite another respect, this book shows that, for the writers of fiction considered in the pages that follow, the cosmopolitan ideal became even more insistent during a period in which papal authority over temporal rulers went into a period of decline from which it would never recover. Indeed, it is my view that the loss of such papal authority is what made the cosmopolitan ideal ever more pressing. As we shall see in the second half of this book, writers with as diverse political perspectives as Fanshawe, Milton, and Behn were all driven by an impetus similar to the one which drove Kant to write "Towards Perpetual Peace," namely the desire to construct an international order in the aftermath of the Thirty Years War and the irreversible decline of papal authority and the Hapsburg empire.

Finally, this book attempts to correct the dominant trend within early modern literary studies, which has focused on how fiction participates in the construction of a modern, centralized form of nationhood. As we shall see, the mainstream

---

[118]   Mignolo, "Many Faces of Cosmopolis," 166.

[119]   "Et hac ratione potest Papa infringere leges civiles, quae sunt nutritivae peccatorum … discordantibus Principibus de jure alicujus principatus et in bella ruentibus, potest esse Judex et cognoscere de jure partium et sententiam ferre … Et hac ipsa ratione potest aliquando Reges deponere et etiam novos constituere, sicut aliquando factum est." *Relectio Prior de Indis Recenter Inventis, in Relectiones de Francisco de Vitoria*, vol. 2, 328–9. English translation from Vitoria, *Relectio de Indis [On the American Indians]*, in *Political Writings*, 262.

34 *Early Modern Catholics, Royalists, and Cosmopolitans*

account of how monarchical power and national identity functioned during the Renaissance leaves out important alternative accounts of identity that do not fit into the intellectual histories of nationhood, whether it be English or British, that critics and historians locate in the period.[120] Recent contributions such as Willy Maley and David J. Baker's edited collection, *British Identities and English Renaissance Literature*, and David Armitage's collection, *British Political Thought in History, Literature, and Theory, 1500–1800*, have begun to challenge the dominant tendency by interrogating the unity of English and British identity.[121] However, like earlier criticism, such accounts still take the modern nation-state as the point of departure even if they do treat it as a multiethnic or multinational entity. In response, I argue for the importance of studying the identities of those figures who posited alternatives to the dominant narrative of nation formation. Ultimately, I show that study of the emerging ideology of English nationhood, without any consideration of the challenges posed by Catholic exiles and their eclectic imitators within England itself, presents an incomplete picture of the discourse of nationhood. The traditional conception of the Christian commonwealth was in fact far more cosmopolitan than the chaotic collection of nation-states that largely replaced it, but as the chapters that follow illustrate, remnants of the cosmopolitan perspective persisted in secularized form, enabling a powerful critique of the emerging autonomous nation-state throughout later historical periods.

---

[120] See footnote 11 for more details.

[121] The field of so-called "British Studies" has become extensive, and includes the following: J.G.A. Pocock, Gordon Schochet, and Lois G. Schwoerer, "The History of British Political Thought: a Field and its Future," in *British Political Thought in History, Literature, and Theory, 1500–1800*, ed. David Armitage (New York, 2006), 10–22; John Morrill, "Thinking about the New British History," in *British Political Thought*, ed. David Armitage, 23–46; Krishan Kumar, *The Making of English National Identity* (New York, 2003), chs 1, 2, 6; Willy Maley, *Nation, State, and Empire in English Renaissance Literature*, esp. 1–10; David J. Baker and Willy Maley, "Introduction. An Uncertain Union," *British Identities and English Renaissance Literature*, ed. David J. Baker and Willy Maley (New York, 2002), 1–10; David Armitage, *The Ideological Origins of the British Empire* (New York, 2000); Brendan Bradshaw and Peter Roberts (eds), *British Consciousness and Identity: The Making of Britain* (New York, 1998); David J. Baker, *Between Nations: Shakespeare, Spenser, Marvell, and the Question of Britain* (Stanford, 1997), esp. 1–16.

PART I

Chapter 1
Papal Supremacy and the Citizen of the World

As I show in the first two chapters of this book, the global perspective of the English Jesuits, particularly their desire to view England as part of Christendom or an encompassing Christian commonwealth, was shared to a certain extent by conformist English writers such as Sir John Harington and even one of their avowed enemies, Anthony Munday, who served the crown as a "pursuivant" of renegade Jesuit priests and Catholic recusants.[1] Moreover, this shared perspective, which I characterize as "cosmopolitan," was actually opposed to an insular belief, shared by both the old Marian Catholic establishment and some English Protestants, in the purity of Welsh or British or English identity.[2] My larger purpose here is to

---

[1] For the global character of the Jesuit order, see Luke Clossey, *Salvation and Globalization in the Early Jesuit Missions* (New York, 2008). As Markus Friedrich has shown in "Communication and Bureaucracy in the Early Modern Society of Jesus," in *Schweizerische Zeitschrift für Religions- und Kulturgeschichte* 101 (2007): 49–75, the bureaucracy of the Jesuit order was structured hierarchically like a nation, and depended on a transnational republic of letters which emanated from the office of the General for orderly function. See the *Regulae Societatis Iesu. Ad usum nostrorum tantum* (Rome, 1935), 34–5, in which the rules for the Jesuit order confirm that members should "esteem and bear a special love in our Lord for those of other nations." The rules go on to recommend that "no one at the expense of charity should make wars or dissensions between nations the subject of their conversation." Similarly, in the 1550 version of the *Formula*, members of the order are to accept that they may be sent anywhere in the world: they vow "to go to whatsoever provinces they may choose to send us, whether they decide to send us among the Turks or any other infidels, even those who live in the regions called the Indies, or among any heretics or schismatics or any of the faithful" (*The Formula of the Institute*, with *Notes for a Commentary* by Antonio M. de Aldama, S.J., trans. Ignacio Echániz, S.J. [St. Louis, 1990], 9). For background on Munday's interactions with Catholics, see Donna Hamilton, *Anthony Munday and the Catholics 1560–1633* (Burlington, VT, 2005), 7–40.

[2] For the relationship between Welsh, English, and British identities, see Schwyzer, *Literature, Nationalism and Memory*, 76–96; Kerrigan, *Archipelagic English*, 3–59, 195–219. For a recent historical account of cosmopolitanism during this period, see Margaret C. Jacob, *Strangers Nowhere in the World: The Rise of Cosmopolitanism in Early Modern Europe* (Philadelphia, 2006), ch. 3. For the intellectual traditions of cosmopolitanism during this period, see Derek Heater, *World Citizenship and Government* (London, 2002), ch. 3. For discussion of the tensions and the disagreements between the Marian Catholic exiles led by Owen Lewis and Clynnog and the Jesuits, see Bernard Basset, S.J., *The English Jesuits: From Campion to Martindale* (New York, 1967), 27–54, and for how disagreements begun at the Roman college eventually generated tensions between the secular priests and the regulars during the later Archpriest Controversy, see Basset, *English Jesuits*, 54–96; John

38   *Early Modern Catholics, Royalists, and Cosmopolitans*

use the religious context to show that perspectives on English national identity and myths of national origin often cut across confessional boundaries in ways that complicate the common view of the distinction between English Catholics and Protestants.

Before moving on to a discussion of such writers of fiction, however, I would like to explore what I call the cosmopolitan mode within the Catholic self-presentation of Jeronimo Osório de Fonseca, Edmund Campion, and Robert Persons, as well as within the institutional development of the Society of Jesus. Campion himself had a complex relationship with earlier arguments about the primacy of papal authority and the pope's right to depose sovereigns. On the one hand, as Thomas McCoog has argued, the English Jesuit mission to England before 1581 sought to minister to the religious needs of English Catholics rather than engage in more direct political involvement.[3] According to Cardinal William Allen, Campion was in support of this approach.[4] But despite Allen's testimony and the indications in Campion's writings showing that Campion saw his primary aim as promoting religious tolerance for English Catholics while outwardly maintaining a politically loyal stance towards to the crown, Campion included some subtle but clear signals that he sympathized with a more confrontational notion of how papal authority should relate to temporal magistrates.[5] These signals open a window onto the global character of the Jesuit Order as well as the writings of its most influential English member, Robert Persons.

Lastly, this chapter explores the emergence of two competing conceptions of national identity. On the one hand, with the passage of the "Statute in Restraint of Appeals of 1533," Henry VIII had claimed authority over both the ecclesiastical and the temporal realms, and Elizabeth had reaffirmed this authority. Richard Helgerson's persuasive account of Elizabethans writing the English nation describes this independent and self-determined conception of nationhood, one in which Queen Elizabeth successfully claimed sovereignty over both the temporal

---

Bossy, *The English Catholic Community 1570–1850* (New York, 1976), 35–48; Michael C. Questier, *Catholicism and Community in Early Modern England* (New York, 2006) 157–68, 288–314; and Thomas Graves Law (ed.), *The Archpriest Controversy: Documents Relating to the Dissensions of the Roman Catholic Clergy 1597–1602*, 2 vols (Westminster, 1896–98), vol. 1, ix–xxvii. See also Morys Clynnog's conception of Welsh purity in J.M. Cleary, "Dr. Morys Clynnog's Invasion Projects of 1575–76," *Recusant History* 8.5 (1966): 300–321. For an historical overview, see McCoog, *Society of Jesus 1541–1588*, 104–8.

[3]   McCoog, *Society of Jesus 1541–1588*, 138–9.

[4]   William Cardinal Allen, *A True, Sincere and Modest Defence of English Catholics That Suffer for Their Faith Both at Home and Abroad,* (2 vols, London, 1914), vol. 1, 83.

[5]   W.K. Jordan has presented early modern Catholic and Jesuit writers as insincere when they advocated for religious toleration in England. For Jordan, their real motives were restoring Catholicism. See W.K. Jordan, *The Development of Religious Toleration in England From the Beginning of the English Reformation to the Death of Queen Elizabeth* (London, 1932), 373–4. For recent interpretation of this issue, see Arthur Marotti, "The Intolerability of English Catholicism," 47–72.

and the ecclesiastical realms.[6] In contrast, the English Catholic conception of the nation was quite different: not only did there exist separate realms of the temporal and the ecclesiastical for writers like Nicholas Sander, but the authority of the sovereign was seen as subordinate to ecclesiastical authority. And most importantly, this second conception of nationhood, in which the sovereign faced the possibility of "correction" by the Roman curia, was directly opposed to Henry VIII's declaration that the "Realm of *England* is an Empire, and so hath been accepted in the World, governed by one supreme Head and King, having the Dignity and Royal Estate of the Imperial Crown of the same."[7]

The Osório-Haddon Controversy

Catholics saw Queen Elizabeth's assertion of supremacy over the spiritual realm as constituting a usurpation of the Roman curia's traditional authority. But Elizabeth's claim also constituted a challenge to the traditional relationship between the spiritual and temporal realms, whereby the former was viewed as the overseer of the latter. The crucial moment in the controversy was the papal bull issued by Pius V in 1570, *Regnans in Excelsis*, which excommunicated Queen Elizabeth, absolving her subjects of their vow of obedience to her and effectively authorizing her deposition.[8] During the years surrounding this watershed event, a number of religious controversies transpired in print between English reformers, consisting of John Jewel, William Fulke, Alexander Nowell, Walter Haddon, Thomas Bilson, George Acworth, and Bartolomew Clerke, and the English Catholic exiles and their allies, consisting of Nicholas Sander, Richard Bristowe, Thomas Stapleton, William Allen, Robert Persons, and Archdeacon and later Bishop Jerónimo Osório de Fonseca of Portugal. Much of the initial controversy that occurred in the 1560s concerned the reformers' views on purely religious issues such as transubstantiation, the devotion of saints and images, purgatory, and confession, but there were also significant debates that concerned the relationship between ecclesiastical government and civil government, especially related to questions of royal and papal supremacy.[9] One of the most famous throughout Europe and England involved the Portuguese prelate Jerónimo

---

[6]   Helgerson, *Forms of Nationhood*. Notably, Allan G.R. Smith, *The Emergence of a Nation State: The Commonwealth of England, 1529–1660* (New York, 1997), begins with the conflict with Rome resulting in the 1533 Statute.

[7]   24 Henry VIII. c. 12 (1533) in *The Statutes at large, from Magna Charta to the Thirtieth Year of King George II, inclusive, in six volumes* (6 vols, London, 1758), vol. 2, A1v.

[8]   Pope Pius V, *Regnans in Excelsis*, February 25, 1570. For context, see Thomas Clancy, S.J., "English Catholics and the Papal Deposing Power, 1570–1640 [Part I: The Elizabethan Period]," *Recusant History* 6.3 (1962): 114–41.

[9]   See Peter Milward, *Religious Controversies of the Elizabethan Age: A Survey of Printed Sources* (Lincoln, NE, 1977), 18–19.

40   *Early Modern Catholics, Royalists, and Cosmopolitans*

Osório de Fonseca and Walter Haddon, the Master of the Court of Requests at the English court.[10] The controversy began in 1563, when Osório de Fonseca published in Paris the *Epistola ad Elizabetham Angliae Reginam de Religione*, an open letter to Elizabeth adopting a respectful and deferential view of the Queen's still developing reign and offering advice to her on the relationship between the spiritual and temporal realms.[11] The controversy was joined by Haddon later that year, when he published a response in Paris called *Gualthieri Haddoni pro Reformatione Anglicana Epistola Apologetica ad Hier. Osorium. Lusitanum.*[12] Both works were subsequently translated into English: Osório's *Epistle* was translated by Richard Shacklock, an English student of the civil law at the University of Louvain, and published in 1565 in Louvain, while Haddon's response was translated by Abraham Hartwell and printed in 1565.[13] Osório's *Epistola* begins by introducing an international perspective to Queen Elizabeth's authority over the church, a perspective that assumes an important place later in Haddon's response to Osório. Osório declares that he offers his advice as a friend to Queen Elizabeth and to her realm, explaining that any good sovereign should not be concerned over whether his or her councilors are "a countrie man borne, or a straunger [*ne ciuis, an externus is*]."[14] Rather that sovereign should be concerned with the intent with which the individual offers counsel. As a friend to the Queen, Osório explains that in many cases, counsel given by foreigners is to be preferred to counsel provided

---

[10]   Matthew Racine, "A Pearle for a Prynce: Jerónimo Osório and Early Elizabethan Catholics," *The Catholic Historical Review* 87.3 (2001): 401–27; Lawrence V. Ryan, "The Haddon-Osório Controversy (1563–1583)," *Church History* 22.2 (1953): 142–54; A.C. Southern, *Elizabethan Recusant Prose*, 119–24.

[11]   Jerónimo Osório, *Epistola reuerendissimi D. Hieronymi Osorij Episcopi Syluensis, ad serenissimam Elisabetam Angliae reginam: cum facultate & approbatione reuerendissimorum patrum supremo Sanctae Inquisitionis consilio Praefectorum* (Olysippone, 1575). For the English translation, see *An Epistle of the Reuerend Father in God Hieronimvs Osorivs Bishop of Arcoburge in Portugale, to the most excellent Princesse Elizabeth by the grace of God Quene of England France, and Ireland. & c. Translated oute of Latten in to Englishe by Richard Shacklock M. of Arte and student of the Ciuill Lawes in Louaine* (Antwerp, 1565).

[12]   Walter Haddon, *Gualthieri Haddoni pro Reformatione Anglicana Epistola Apologetica ad Hier. Osorium. Lusitanum* (Paris, 1563). For the English translation, see Haddon, *A sight of the Portugall Pearle, that is, The Aunswere of D. Haddon Maister of the requests vnto our soueraigne Lady Elizabeth by the grace of God quene of England Fraunce and Irelande, defendour of the faith, & c. against the epistle of Hieronimus Osorius a Portugall, entitled a Pearle for a Prince. Translated out of lattyn into englishe by Abraham Hartwell, Student in the kynges colledge in Cambridge* (London, 1565).

[13]   In 1570, it was again translated, this time anonymously: *An Answere in action to a Portingale Pearle, called a Pearle for a Prince Geuen by a laye man in a legacie, which legacie he desireth to se executed before his death* (London, 1570).

[14]   Osório, *An Epistle*, B2v; Osório, *Epistola*, A3. Citations from Osório and Haddon are to the English translations and to the Latin in brackets for important phraseology in the original.

by the sovereign's subjects, "for many treasons [*insidiae*] are wrought against Princes of theire howseholde seruauntes [*a suis domesticis*]."[15] Most importantly, Osório has a characteristically Catholic conception of his own role as serving the welfare of the "Christian common weale [*rempublicam Christianam*]," and as a result, Osório explains that he thinks "no Christian Prince a forenner or a straunger [*nullum Christianum principem externum & alienum puto*]."[16] For Osório, there exist two separate political entities, the Christian commonwealth and the temporal realm, with the first encompassing the second, so that from the perspective of an official within the Christian commonwealth, sovereigns and magistrates within the temporal realm should submit to counsel originating from within the former entity. Osório's *Epistola* also contains a general attack on Protestantism, which he accuses of fomenting rebellion against religious authorities and eventually against temporal authorities as well. Whereas it is Christ's purpose "to gather in to one place [*in locum unum compellere*] those which stray a broade, to ioyne those which be of diuerse myndes [*animos inter se dissidentes*], in an vniforme consent, mutuall beneuolence, and charytye," Osório explains that Protestants are in league with the devil in sowing discord and division within the Christian commonwealth.[17] To the extent that Elizabeth has separated England and her subjects from Rome, she has damaged this larger commonwealth and left it "vnhealed [*rempublicam Christianam non sanauerunt*]."[18] Declaring that his own role is to "pray for the saffegard of all Christendome [*pro totius Christianae reipublicae salute*]," Osório laments the danger in which Elizabeth has placed England.[19] He explains ultimately that in order to maintain the "auncient manners and good ordres [*antiquos mores & officia rite*]" of the realm, Elizabeth must "[re]-joyne your selfe to the consent of the Catholyke churche [*ad consensum Ecclesiae totius aggregaueris*]."[20] Throughout his short book, Osório repeatedly maintains "the vnitie of Catholyke churche [*ab Eccesiae coniunctione*]," which Elizabeth's decisions have violated and endangered.[21]

Just as Osório's arguments in the *Epistola* are a reflection of his official position as Archdeacon of Evora within the Roman Church hierarchy, Haddon's response is influenced by his position within Elizabeth's government. Haddon, as one of two Masters of Requests, held an important position within the juridical court that adjudicated matters relating to the Queen's household and the hearing of poor men's causes. As a court of equity, the Court of Requests had a substantial investment in the Queen's power of prerogative, as opposed to the common law courts whose judges located the source of their jurisdictional authority in

---

[15] Osório, *An Epistle*, B2v; Osório, *Epistola*, A3–A3v.

[16] See Osório, *An Epistle*, I5v, B2v–B3; *Epistola*, C3, A3v; See also, *An Epistle*, B, I8v; *Epistola*, A3, C4, for similar language.

[17] Osório, *An Epistle*, H8v; *Epistola*, Cv.

[18] Osório, *An Epistle*, I5v; *Epistola*, C3.

[19] Osório, *An Epistle*, I8v; *Epistola*, C4.

[20] Osório, *An Epistle*, K2; *Epistola*, C4.

[21] Osório, *An Epistle*, K6; *Epistola*, C5v.

custom and tradition.[22] In his response to Osório, Haddon begins by pointing to the national differences between the Portuguese prelate and Queen Elizabeth, reminding Osório that he is indeed foreign to the English realm and that he does not understand the customs of England and its laws and government, especially regarding the role of parliament in the passage of new law.[23] Haddon goes on to admit to Osório's charge that the English sovereign has thrown off the yoke of the "imperial Bishop," explaining that the English people and their ancestors have always felt a heavy burden under the authority of the church hierarchy and that, other than Christ, there was no other authority that they needed to acknowledge.[24] He goes on to question Osório's conception of the unity of the Church under papal authority: "euen in the soundest age of the church there was one God, one fayth, and yet notwithstanding had Peter one prouince, Paul another, and Iames another, and diuers other had seuerall charge, whereas the seuering of the persons was no breach to the vnity in fayth." Claiming the current "extraordinary popish regalty" to be a recent innovation within the church, Haddon argues that at its earliest most robust stages, the church held no such monarchical authority. As far as the Queen having separated herself from the Christian unity, she only seeks her rightful authority over her own subjects in England itself, an authority which the pope had unjustly usurped. And though Elizabeth does not acknowledge the pope as "king of Bishops," she does acknowledge him as rightful Bishop of Rome.[25] Haddon thus implies that she merely asks for similar recognition of her own authority.

It is significant to note the two notions of nationhood that emerge in the first stage of this controversy. On the one hand, Osório conceives of the English realm as a rebellious province within the larger Christian entity, to which he refers as the "Christian commonwealth [*respublica Christiana*]." At the head of that Christian commonwealth, organized politically as a monarchy, is the Roman curia, and as one of this monarchy's lesser magistrates, Osório claims the prerogative to counsel temporal magistrates, which is effectively what he offers within the *Epistola*. On the other hand is Haddon's conception of a clearly demarcated English realm, whose sovereign "reygneth ouer all her subiects of Englande," and in which there exists an Erastian relationship between English political and religious culture, such that the vernacular is preferred over Latin in ecclesiastical affairs, and ecclesiastical law and policy are understood as an expression of the Queen's sovereignty over the realm.[26] Both Osório and Haddon view their own positions as traditional and conservative and the other position as an innovation. In effect, for Osório, the claims that Elizabeth has asserted over the ecclesiastical realm are a usurpation of traditional papal power, and similarly Haddon claims that the pope was traditionally simply the Bishop of Rome, without any universal or transnational oversight with regard to other bishops or temporal magistrates.

---

[22]   Theodore F.T. Plucknett, *A Concise History of the Common Law* (Indianapolis, IN, 2010), 184.

[23]   Haddon, *A sight*, A2v, C.

[24]   Haddon, *A sight*, C2v.

[25]   Haddon, *A sight*, C3, C3, C5.

[26]   Haddon, *A sight*, C4.

At the center of the debate then are two conceptions of English nationhood: one emerging from the claim of imperial sovereignty over both realms implicit in the "Statute in Restraint of Appeals of 1533," and the other emerging from a traditional understanding of the relationship between the ecclesiastical and temporal realms, re-invigorated as a counter-reformation response to the political claims made by reformers and Protestant sovereigns such as Elizabeth.[27]

While the main parameters of the debate were determined by the original *Epistola* and Haddon's initial response, the debate continued well into the 1580s. In its second stage, Osório and Haddon's positions hardened, becoming more vituperative, especially with regard to the issue of papal and regal supremacy. In 1567, Osório wrote a lengthy response to Haddon, entitled *Amplissimi atque Doctissimi Viri D. Hieronymi Osorii, Episcopi Sylvensis, in Gualterum Haddonum Magistrum Libellorum Supplicum apud clarissimam Principem Helisabetham Angliae, Franciae, & Hiberniae Reginam. libri tres*. Subsequently translated into English by John Fen, the title of the original Latin version of this book, which addressed the Queen as "*clarissimam* [most illustrious]," shows that Roman Catholics on the continent still held out hope that Elizabeth might return the English Church to the Roman Catholic fold (see Figure 1.1).[28] Shortly after the publication of Osorio's second tract, Haddon began his own response, which remained unfinished due to Haddon's untimely death in 1572. Subsequently, the Protestant martyrologist, John Foxe, finished the work, which he then published in 1577 under the title, *Contra Hieron. Osorium, eiusque odiosas insectationes pro Evangelicae veritatis necessaria Defensione, Responsio Apologetica. Per clariss. verum, Gualt. Haddonum inchoata: Deinde suscepta & continuata per Joann. Foxum*. In 1581, a translation of this work by James Bell was published.[29]

---

[27]   See 24 Henry VIII. c. 12 (1533) in *The Statutes at large*, vol. 2, A1v. For background, see Arnold Oskar Meyer, *England and the Catholic Church under Queen Elizabeth*, trans. Rev. J.R. McKee (St. Louis, 1916), 73–144.

[28]   *Amplissimi atque Doctissimi Viri D. Hieronymi Osorii, Episcopi Sylvensis, in Gualterum Haddonum Magistrum Libellorum Supplicum apud clarrisimam Principem Helisabetham Angliae, Franciae, & Hiberniae Reginam. libri tres* (Olissipone, 1567). The English translation was entitled, *A learned and very eloquent Treatie, written in Latin by the famouse man Hieronymus Osorius Bishop of Sylua in Portugal, wherein he confuteth a certayne Aunswere made by M. Walter Haddon against the Epistle of the said Bishoppe unto the Queenes Maiestie*, trans. John Fen (Louvain, 1568).

[29]   Walter Haddon and John Foxe, *Contra Hieron. Osorium, eiusque odiosas insectationes pro Evangelicae veritatis necessaria Defensione, Responsio Apologetica. Per clariss. verum, Gualt. Haddonum inchoata: Deinde suscepta & continuata per Joann. Foxum* (London, 1577). The English translation was entitled, *Against Ierome Osorius Byshopp of Siluane in Portingall and against his slaunderous Inuectiues. An Aunswere Apologeticall: For the necessary defence of the Euangelicall doctrine and veritie* (London, 1581). Finally in 1583, a related work by John Foxe was published which critiqued Osório on the subject of inherent justice entitled, *De Christo gratis iustificante. Contra Osorianam iustitiam, caeterosque eiusdem inhaerentis iustitiae patronos, Stan. Hosium. Andrad. Canisium. Vegam. Tiletanum. Lorichium, contra vniuersam denique Turbam Tridentinam & Iesuiticam. Amica & modesta defnsio. Joan. Foxij* (London, 1583).

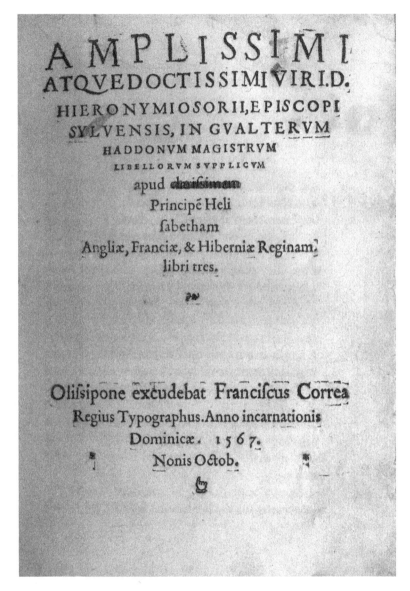

Fig. 1.1   The title page of Bishop Jerónimo Osório de Fonseca's second contribution to the Osório-Haddon debate: *Amplissimi atque Doctissimi Viri D. Hieronymi Osorii, Episcopi Sylvensis ...* (Lisbon, 1567). Note that in the Newberry Library copy above, a reader has blacked out the modifier "clarissimam [most illustrious]" presumably after the pope's excommunication of Elizabeth in 1570. Photo Courtesy of the Newberry Library, Chicago. Call Number: Case C 64.6469.

The differing conceptions of the English realm come into focus especially clearly in the response by Osório, who had recently been appointed Bishop of Silves. Towards the beginning of his response, the bishop addresses Haddon's criticism that Osório, as a foreigner, should not be meddling in the internal affairs of the English realm. Reiterating his earlier comment that the least trustworthy of the prince's counselors are often those that are closest to the prince, Osório implies that a distinct characteristic of religious discourse is that it calls on interlocutors to ignore temporal boundaries.[30] To the charge that Osório is not skilled in English affairs, he responds by saying that he speaks of "such matters as are most perfectly knowen of al men [*omnibus notissimae*]."[31] Osório goes on to refute Haddon's charge that Osório is working to malign the English polity, noting that nothing could have caused any worse a reputation for England than the actions taken by Elizabeth's father against such principled defenders of the faith as John Fisher, Bishop of Rochester and Sir Thomas More.[32]

Once again, Osório's different conception of the relationship between the temporal and the ecclesiastical emerges in his discussion of Fisher's and More's executions.[33] Osório asks Haddon what Fisher, in particular, had done to justify the charge of treason to the sovereign:

> Had [Fisher] conspired the death of the Prince? Had he entred into talke with foraine ennemies [*cum hostibus*] to betraie his owne common weale [*rep. [ublica]*]? Nothing lesse. But bicause he most constantlie refused [*recusarat*] to yeeld his consent unto a wicked statute, the holie and innocent man was so punished, as though he had ben the most detestable traitour in the worlde [*scelestorum hominum*].[34]

He goes on to describe as equally troubling the executions of More, members of the Cathusian religious order, and other bishops and priests during Henry VIII's reign.[35] Osório's implicit criticism of the English government is that such figures only exercised their conscience, according to the authority conferred on them by the church hierarchy. And given his investment in separate ecclesiastical and temporal

---

[30]   Osório, *A learned and very eloquent Treatie*, A4v–A5v; *Amplissimi atque Doctissimi Viri*, a4–a4v. Subsequent citations cite the English followed by the Latin.

[31]   Osório, *A learned and very eloquent Treatie*, A5v; *Amplissimi atque Doctissimi Viri*, a4v.

[32]   "Dicis me vniversam Britanniam inuidiosae nouitatis ream facere." Osório, *A learned and very eloquent Treatie*, A7, A8; *Amplissimi atque Doctissimi Viri*, b1v, b2.

[33]   Osório, *A learned and very eloquent Treatie*, A8; *Amplissimi atque Doctissimi Viri*, b3.

[34]   Osório, *A learned and very eloquent Treatie*, B1v–B2v; *Amplissimi atque Doctissimi Viri*, b3.

[35]   Osório, *A learned and very eloquent Treatie*, B2v; *Amplissimi atque Doctissimi Viri*, b3–b3v. For background on the persecution of priests during Henry VIII's reign, see Peter Marshall, *The Catholic Priesthood and the English Reformation* (New York, 1994), 211–32.

realms, each governed by its own sovereign, Osório views Fisher's sacrifices as an exceptional act of martyrdom in response to a government that had blurred the lines between the two realms and usurped the church's traditional authority.

In this early section of the work, Osório makes his clearest statement yet on the integrity of the Christian common weale, over which his own magistracy extends. He notes, "And whereas you charge me with curiositie for medling in a straunge common weale [aliena rep.[ublica]]: I think it is no straunge common weale, but myne owne [non alienam sed propriam estimo]. For I did not reason of the lawes of your Realme and ciuile ordinaunces [de legibus & institutis ciuilibus], but of Christian religion [Christiana religione], for the which I am not afraid to loose my life."[36] As a magistrate within the Christian commonwealth, Bishop Osório assumes the right to have used letters to "admonish [per literas admonuerim]" the Queen for putting her realm in religious peril.[37] Implicit in Osório's admonishment is that while the two realms exist separably, the ecclesiastical realm is superior to the temporal realm and assumes for itself an advisory role with regard to temporal magistrates. Thus Osório reiterates his characterization of the church as being "one and not manie [Christi ecclesiam unam esse, non plures]," and unlike his first tract, in this instance, he expands upon the nature of ecclesiastical governance. According to his formulation, just as a kingdom's unity is based on the authority of one prince, so the unity of the church is based on papal authority. Using Augustinian language, he describes a "Citie distourbed [ciuitatis ... turbari]," which can only be ameliorated under the supreme government of Peter and his heirs.[38]

Haddon and Foxe's final response to this debate, the Contra Hieron. Osorium, once again approaches the issue from the perspective of the emerging discourse of nationhood. From Haddon's nationalistic perspective, Osório's epistolae to Elizabeth are dangerous because, while they are penned by a subject of the Portuguese crown, they represent an ecclesiastical polity that encompasses that crown. In turn, Haddon will repudiate Osório's argument by ignoring that transnational ecclesiastical polity and emphasizing the network of secular Christian princes that govern Europe. He does so by addressing his response to the sovereign of Portugal, King Sebastian, under the dual assumption that Osório owes his first allegiance to his own king and that his king has a responsibility for controlling unruly subjects like Osório. He explains, "sithence Osorius through the pleasaunt blast of the Trompe of fame, hath presumed so farre upon the unspeakable clemency of our Queenes most excellent Maiestie, whom he neuer sawe: ... why should not I persaude myselfe to obteine as much, yea more rather of your [Sebastian's] Princely magnificence, and heroicall clemency?"[39] Haddon views the

---

[36] Osório, A learned and very eloquent Treatie, B4v; Amplissimi atque Doctissimi Viri, b4.

[37] Osório, A learned and very eloquent Treatie, A5; Amplissimi atque Doctissimi Viri, a4v.

[38] Osório, A learned and very eloquent Treatie, C8v, D1v; Amplissimi atque Doctissimi Viri, C3, C3v.

[39] Haddon and Foxe, Against Ierome Osorius, A1v–A2; Contra Hieron, A2v.

European political system as organized around the axis of hereditary sovereigns, whom he later says are second in authority only to God himself: "Princes [are those] whom the Lord of his infinite mearcy hath ordeyned to exercize chief rule and gouernement next vnder him upon the face of the earth [*quibus amplissimam hanc in terris dominandi potestatem divina delegauit benignitas*]."[40] In doing so, Haddon takes direct aim at Osório's conception of ecclesiastical governance, which Osório sees exercising "chief rule and government" over the spiritual realm and thus the temporal realm as well.

Ultimately Osório presents his role within the ecclesiastical hierarchy as comprising that of a potential protector or caretaker of Elizabeth's legitimacy, invoking once again the potential for Protestant sovereigns themselves to face violent revolt from rebellious religious dissidents.[41] For Osório, what is most galling about Haddon's account of the Queen's authority is the Englishman's claim that Elizabeth's sovereignty is self-enclosed, extending to almost every aspect of the subject's existence. According to Osório's summary, Haddon had claimed that "*the King's Majestie ... maistereth al persones in England* [*Regalis, inguis, maiestas omnibus dominatur Angliae personis*]." But for Osório, the notion that Haddon's prince might exercise complete mastery over her subjects made her a despot, who "would rather be accounted a tyranne, then a King [*nisi se potius tyrannum, quam regem haberi malit*]."[42]

Osório's accusation that Elizabeth risked being perceived as, or even becoming, an oppressive tyrant constitutes a crucial moment in the debate. He goes on to note the important difference between the example of the English sovereign and that of other European sovereigns, who do not claim to govern the realm in spiritual matters.[43] Once again, the matter is more complex than it might first appear to be. In one sense, of course, Osório seeks simply to preserve the separate ecclesiastical realm governed by the Roman curia. In quite another, Osório is gesturing towards the position eventually taken by Nicholas Sander and other defenders of Pope Pius V's Bull excommunicating Elizabeth, which suggested that she was a tyrant who was oppressing her Catholic subjects. Although Osório does not say so directly here, his accusation that Elizabeth's rule was sliding into tyranny contained the implicit suggestion that the Roman curia should exercise oversight over the rule of temporal magistrates for their own good. This oversight normally amounted to the very advice and counsel that Osório was offering in his *epistolae*, but in extreme circumstances, it involved correction or even deposition of a tyrannical sovereign.

It is not surprising that, in his response to Osório's charge that Queen Elizabeth risked being perceived as a tyrant, Haddon displays a more alarmed and defensive tone. "Becommeth you an old Byshop [*senem episcopum*] to utter such

---

[40]   Haddon and Foxe, *Against Ierome Osorius*, A4; *Contra Hieron*, A4.

[41]   Osório, *A learned and very eloquent Treatie*, Q7v; *Amplissimi atque Doctissimi Viri*, K4.

[42]   Osório, *A learned and very eloquent Treatie*, R6v, R7; *Amplissimi atque Doctissimi Viri*, K8, K8.

[43]   Osório, *A learned and very eloquent Treatie*, R7; *Amplissimi atque Doctissimi Viri*, K8–K8v.

mockeries?" he asks incredulously, accusing Osório of succumbing to senility and being "a laughyng stocke," and remarking finally, "I am ashamed in your behalfe." Haddon goes on to explain that, while the English sovereigns theoretically exercise authority over all matters both temporal and ecclesiastical, in practice, they "do not minister in their own persons [*ad singular manus*] in matters Ecclesiasticall [*sacris*]." And even in temporal affairs, the practice of governance is more complex, for sovereign authority is channeled through, checked by, and ministered by all manner of expert magistrates and sub-magistrates.[44] Does the intensity of Haddon's ad hominem attack on Bishop Osório betray a barely-concealed anxiety about the absence of restraints on the English sovereign's authority as a result of the emerging Tudor ideology of divine right of kings? What is clear from this final interchange is that both loyal Englishmen like Walter Haddon and critics of Queen Elizabeth like Bishop Osório were essentially in agreement that restraints on the prince's sovereignty, whether from "above" (the papal and episcopal magistrate of the Christian commonwealth) or from "below" (ecclesiastical and temporal magistrates and sub-magistrates), were necessary. Beyond this, the Osório-Haddon controversy prefigures two competing conceptions of English nationhood, one that positions England within a larger transnational polity and the other that views the realm as organically separate and self-sufficient. Bishop Osório's larger purpose is to write England and its ruler back into Christendom, in which he served as an important magistrate. In contrast, Haddon views England as a separate and self-sufficient entity, a Christian polity which was nevertheless distinct from other Christian kingdoms and the larger Christian commonwealth itself. As we shall see in the remainder of this chapter, Osório's *epistolae* to Queen Elizabeth prefigure a cosmopolitan perspective that began as a Catholic defense of the transnational Christian commonwealth but was increasingly secularized by English writers of fiction. Ultimately, this secularized cosmopolitan perspective served as a critique of the dominant ideology of English national identity that emerged during the early modern period.

In the wake of this controversy, on February 25, 1570, Pope Pius V issued his Bull *Regnans in Excelsis*, which declared Queen Elizabeth to be a heretic and that furthermore she was "to be deprived of her pretended title to the aforesaid crown and of all lordship, dignity and privilege whatsoever." *Regnans in Excelsis* was premised upon the claim, which Osório gestures at in his two *epistolae*, that the temporal magistrate was subject to the authority of the pope's ecclesiastical jurisdiction.[45] And insofar as the temporal realm was subordinate to the ecclesiastical, the pope claimed the right to depose sovereigns who had abused their secular authority. The Bull immediately produced a number of formidable defenses, most notably Nicholas Sander's *De visibili monarchia Ecclesiae* and the notorious pamphlet known in England simply as *Bristow's Motives* by fellow exile, Richard Bristow.[46] Sander's *De visibili monarchia* was a monumental

---

[44] Haddon and Foxe, *Against Ierome Osorius*, K6, K6, K6; *Contra Hieron*, R2v, R2v, R3.

[45] Pius V, *Regnans in Excelsis*, September 25, 1570.

[46] Sander, *De visibili monarchia Ecclesiae, Libri VIII*; Bristow, *A briefe treatise*.

defense of the notion that the church existed as a tangible and organized system of governance based on monarchy rather than as simply a community of like-minded souls.[47] The first six books of Sander's *De visibili monarchia* relate the reasons why the church is organized on monarchical terms rather than as a democracy or an aristocracy and then addresses questions relating to the primacy of Peter in the early church. The seventh book is more complex, presenting on each recto page a parallel chronology of both the *Civitas Dei*, consisting of the Catholic Church and the Holy Roman Empire, and the *Civitas Diaboli*, in which the writings of Protestant heretics and pseudo-churches are recounted and refuted, and on the verso, a detailed account of relevant historical events, including those in England (see Figure 1.2). It is in the second book that Sander launches into a defense of the primacy of the *potestas ecclessiastica* over the *potestas civilis*. According to Sander, while the latter was created by God "*per media iuris naturalis, gentium aut civilis*," the former derives directly from God's authority. As he goes on to explain, "Now then, as being a Christian is much more sublime than being a man, so being a minister of the Christian commonwealth is much more than being a minister of the human commonwealth."[48] In the wake of the executions of Edmund Campion and other Jesuit and secular English priests during the early 1580s, William Cecil Lord Burghley pointed out the threat that such arguments posed to every temporal sovereign of Europe: "For if these powers [of deposition] shoulde be permitted to him [the pope] to exercise, then shoulde no Empire, no kingdome, no countrey, no City or Towne, be possessed by any lawful title, longer then one such onely an earthly man, sitting (as he saith) in *S. Peters* chaire at *Rome*, should for his will and appetite (without warrant from God or man) think meete and determine."[49] Cecil was ignoring the fact that from the pope's standpoint, Elizabeth was herself a usurper who had claimed authority over the spiritual realm, but his point was still compelling. Claiming the privilege of deposing lawful sovereigns meant that the pope seemed to be overstepping the bounds of the spiritual realm and claiming authority over the temporal realm itself.[50]

Significantly, many English Catholics were also concerned about the pope having so aggressively and publicly claimed the power to depose a legitimate Christian prince.[51] For example, despite the fact that he had been secretly engaged in a number of continental plots to invade England and depose its leaders from at

---

[47]   Stefania Tutino, *Law and Conscience: Catholicism in Early Modern England, 1570–1625* (Burlington, VT, 2007), 22.

[48]   "*Nunc vero quanto sublimius est, Christianum esse, quam esse hominem, tanto etiam maius est, ministrum esse Christianae, quam humanae Reipublicae.*" Sander, *De visibili monarchia Ecclesiae Libri VIII*, E2, E3v. For context, see Tutino, *Law and Conscience*, 11–32.

[49]   Cecil, *Execution of Justice in England*, C3–C3v.

[50]   For an overview of the deposition and its aftermath in England itself, see Adrian Morey, *The Catholic Subjects of Elizabeth I* (Totowa, NJ, 1978), 54–95.

[51]   For the view that the majority of English Catholic exiles took this view until the early 1580s, see Clancy, S.J. "English Catholics and the Papal Deposing Power, 1570–1640 [Part I: The Elizabethan Period]," 114–41.

least 1575, Cardinal William Allen was candid in expressing fear that *Regnans in Excelsis* would jeopardize the situation of the Catholics in England, given that the pope had explicitly released them from their natural allegiance to their sovereign, thereby causing them to be viewed as dangerous subversives within their own country.[52] And apparently, Allen was not alone in harboring such fears. In his response to Cecil's *Execution of Justice*, Allen notes that the main defender of the Bull, Nicholas Sander, had even "suppressed to his life's end, a very learned book made in defence of Pius V. his sentence," entitled *Pro defensione excommunicationis a Pio Quinto latae in Angliae reginam*, out of concern for the plight of English Catholics. Edmund Campion had also complained to Allen that the Bull should be "mitigated, so that it should not bind the subjects, but that they might obey her, as their lawful Princess, notwithstanding any contrary sentence of the See Apostolic before given."[53] Moreover, even after the executions during the early 1580s, which considerably radicalized the views of Catholic exiles, Allen was careful to draw a distinction between what he viewed as Protestant-inspired political theories authorizing the rebellion of oppressed subjects against unjust tyrants and usurpers and Roman Catholic writers, such as himself, who argued that only the pope could authorize the deposition of an unlawful sovereign.[54] Ultimately, of course, when the opportunity presented itself, Allen argued that the Pope could authorize another sovereign, in this case, King Philip II of Spain, to invade and reform England. Thus, his *Declaration of the Sentence and deposition of Elizabeth*, published to coincide with the Spanish invasion of England in 1588, asks English subjects not to rebel against Elizabeth, but rather requests that they "vnite them selfs to the Catholike army conducted by the most noble and victorious Prince, *Alexander Farnesius, Duke of Parma and Placentia*, in the name of his Maiesty [Philip II]."[55] In the end, it is unclear whether increased persecution of English Catholics had pushed Allen from a moderate to a more extreme position or whether Allen had simply concealed his support for the Bull all along. As we shall see in the next section, Edmund Campion's views were equally complex. While early on he may have harbored doubts about the efficacy of *Regnans in Excelsis*, Campion's writings during the first Jesuit mission to England show that he was prepared to take a stance predicated on the cosmopolitan assumptions that also sustained Osório's investment in the Christian commonwealth.

---

[52] Robert M. Kingdon, "Introduction," in *The Execution of Justice in England by William Cecil and A True, Sincere, and Modest Defense of English Catholics by William Allen* (Ithaca, 1965), xxxiii–xxxvii; Albert J. Loomie, *The Spanish Elizabethans: The English Exiles at the Court of Philip II* (New York, 1963), 22–4.

[53] William Cardinal Allen, *A true sincere and modest defence of English Catholiques that suffer for their faith both at home and abrode: against a false, seditious and slaunderous libel intituled; The execution of iustice in England. VVherein is declared, hovv vniustlie the Protestants doe charge Catholiques vvith* (St. Louis, 1914), vol. 1, 83, 83.

[54] Allen, *Defence of English Catholiques*, vol. 2, 39–40.

[55] Allen [and/or Sixtus V, Pope], *A Declaration of the Sentence and deposition of Elizabeth, the vsurper and pretensed Quene of Englande* (Antwerp, 1588), fol. 1.

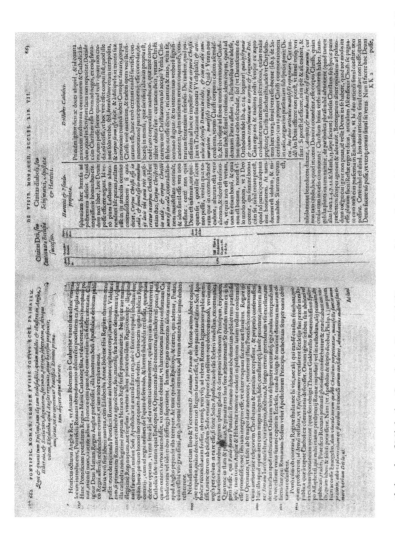

Fig. 1.2 The seventh book of Nicholas Sander's *De visibili monarchia ecclesiae* (Antuerpiae, 1578), fol. 662–663, which provides a parallel history of the *Civitas Dei* and the *Civitas Diaboli* from the beginning of time to the present (1571). See above for the beginning of the reign of Elizabeth (c. 1560). By permission of the Museum Plantin-Moretus, Antwerp.

52   *Early Modern Catholics, Royalists, and Cosmopolitans*

Catholic Cosmopolitans and Their Interlocutors

In March 1581, during the first Jesuit mission to England, Campion, while on the run from pursuivants and spies, completed his famous tract, *Rationes decem*. Published secretly by Persons at Stonor Park, Henley later that month, the *Rationes decem* contained the Jesuit's criticisms of the Anglican settlement, addressing diverse theological questions such as what authority should be given to scripture versus the church fathers, the paradoxes and sophisms of Lutheran and Calvinist doctrine, and the nature and government of the Catholic Church.[56] The climax of the tract occurs in the last few pages, where its true purpose is revealed. Here Campion addresses himself directly to Elizabeth and takes her to task for her claim of royal supremacy over the ecclesiastical realm. The passage is worth quoting in full:

> I call to witness ... Princes, Kings, Emperors, and their Commonwealths [*principes, reges, caesares, horumque respublicae*], whose own piety and the people of their realms, and their established discipline in war and peace, were altogether founded on this our Catholic doctrine. What Theodosiuses here might I summon from the East, what Charleses from the West, what Edwards from England, what Louises from France, what Hermenegilds from Spain, Henries from Saxony, Wenceslauses from Bohemia, Leopolds from Austria, Stephens from Hungary, Josaphats from India, Dukes and Counts from all the world over who by example, by arms, by laws, by loving care, by outlay of money, have nourished our Church [*nostram Ecclesiam nutrierunt*]! For so Isaias foretold: Kings shall be thy foster-fathers, and queens thy nurses (Isaias xlix, 23) [*Sic enim praecinuit Isaias (xlix. 23): "Erunt reges nutricii tui, et reginae nutrices tuae"*].
> Listen, Elizabeth, most powerful Queen [*Audi Elizabetha, Regina potentissima*], for thee this great prophet utters this prophecy, and therein teaches thee thy part [*tibi canit, te tuas edocet*]. I tell thee [*Narro tibi*]: one and the same heaven cannot hold Calvin and the Princes whom I have named. With these Princes then associate thyself [*te ... aiunge*], ... I call to witness all the coasts and regions of the world [*omne sorae plagaeque mundi*], to which the Gospel trumpet has sounded since the birth of Christ.[57]

---

[56]   Edmund Campion, *Rationes decem*. For context, see Richard Simpson, *Edmund Campion: A Biography* (London, 1896), 212–17.

[57]   Principes.—Testes item principes, reges, caesares, horumque respublicae, quorum et ipsorum pietas, et ditionum populi, et pacis bellique disciplina se penitus in hac nostra doctrina catholica fundaverunt. Hie ergo quos ab oriente Theodosios, quos ab occidente Carolos, quos Eduardos ex Anglia, Ludovicos e Gallia, Hermenegildos ex Hispania, Henricos a Saxonia, Wenceslaos e Bohemia, Leopoldos ex Austria, Stephanos ex Hungaria, Iosaphatos ex India, quos orbe toto dynastas atque toparchas possim arcessere; qui exemplo, qui armis qui legibus, qui sollicitudine, qui sumptu, nostrum Ecclesiam nutrierunt? Sic enim praecinuit Isaias (xlix. 23): *"Erunt reges nutricii tui, et reginae nutrices tuae."* Audi, Elisabetha, Regina potentissima, tibi canit, te tuas partes edocet. Narro tibi: Calvinum et hos principes unum coelum capere non potest. His ergo te principibus adiunge ... Nationes ad Christam tradvctae.—Testes iam omne sorae plagaeque mundi, quibus evangelica tuba post Christum natum insonuit. Campion, *Ten Reasons*, 84–5, 142–3.

In this passage, Campion presents himself as speaking from the perspective of a vast array of like-minded monarchs from the Continent and beyond. Campion was of course personally familiar with some of these kingdoms and their modern and ancient histories, and it is consistent with this border-crossing, cosmopolitan perspective that a few pages later, Campion ends the tract with the note, "Farewell. At Cosmopolis, City of all the World, 1581 [*Valete. Cosmopoli 1581*]."[58]

Two aspects of this passage immediately stand out with regard to the issues of cosmopolitanism and the relationship between England and the transnational Christian realm, which the Roman curia claimed as its spiritual dominion. First, Campion's self-presentation recalls the first use of the term "cosmopolitan" or "cosmopolitical" in the English language by John Dee in his *General and Rare Memorials pertayning to the Perfect Arte of Navigation* (1577), a tract whose ostensible purpose was to provide a plan for the establishment of a permanent English naval force. Like Campion, Dee also claims to have "looked into the State of Earthly Kingdoms, Generally, the whole World ouer" and now to have found "hym self, *Cosmopolites*: A Citizen, and Member, of the whole and only one Mysticall City Vniuersall: And so, consequently, to meditate of the Cosmopoliticall Gouerment therof, vnder [God] the King Almighty."[59] From the perspective of the "citizen of the world," Dee goes on to make the following judgment: "And I find … that if this Brytish Monarchy, wold heretofore, haue followed the Aduantages, which they have had, onward, They mought, very well, ere this, haue surpassed (By Iustice and Godly, sort) any particular Monarchy, else that euer was on Earth, since Mans Creation."[60] As a universal citizen, Dee views his identity as not limited to the kingdom or country of his birth—he is therefore uniquely suited to theorizing transnational values that could simultaneously (and paradoxically) defend and justify an increased centralization of English state power, and thus it is no surprise to find that Dee is also sometimes credited with being the first Englishman to refer to the construction of a "Brytish Impire."[61] Dee's ability to speak from the cosmopolis or "the city of the world" qualifies him to pronounce authoritatively on the peoples and nations of the world and especially to offer advice

---

[58] Campion, *Ten Reasons*, 87, 145.

[59] Dee, *Perfect Arte*, G3v. For context, see William H. Sherman, *John Dee: The Politics of Reading and Writing in the English Renaissance* (Amherst, 1995), 115–200; Frances A. Yates, *The Occult Philosophy in the Elizabethan Age* (Boston, 1979), 75–95; Peter J. French, *John Dee: The World of an Elizabethan Magus* (London, 1972), 182–90; and Richard Deacon, *John Dee: Scientist Geographer, Astrologer, and Secret Agent to Elizabeth I* (London, 1968).

[60] Dee, *Perfect Art*, G3v.

[61] Dee, *Perfect Art*, A2. See Sherman, *John Dee*, 148. In his *Breviary of Britaine*, Humphrey Llwyd was the first to actually use the phrase, "British Empire." See Bruce Ward Henry, "John Dee, Humphrey Llwyd, and the Name 'British Empire,'" *Huntington Library Quarterly* 35 (1971–72), 189–90.

and counsel to Christian sovereigns.[62] Campion's confessional purpose in his tract is quite different from Dee's attempts to counsel Elizabeth on defense policy in the *Memorials*, but the two stances are also similar in that each presents himself as a worldly well-travelled figure whose cosmopolitan knowledge qualifies him to advise the Queen. Moreover, Campion's claim to be a citizen of cosmopolis, the city of the world, is consistent both with Dee's claim to be a citizen of a "Cosmopolitical Gouernment" under God ("the King Almighty") and with Sander's conception of the church as comprising a *Civitas Dei* that was transnational and organized like a sovereign monarchical state. In essence, it is clear that Sander's *Civitas Dei*, Dee's "Cosmopolitical Gouvernment," and Campion's cosmopolis comprise similar transnational entities, with the caveat that Dee's Cosmopolitical Government has less of a confessional emphasis.

Second, Campion's use of the passage from Isaiah 49:23, "Kings shall be thy foster-fathers [*nutricii*], and queens thy nurses [*nutrices*]," is intended to characterize how temporal magistrates should ideally serve the Roman Catholic Church within the transnational Christian commonwealth. It is therefore central to his appeal to Elizabeth that she realign her kingdom with the Church and those sovereigns that serve it ("[*nostram Ecclesiam nutrierunt*]"). Indeed, despite Campion's assurance in the other document he published while in England, the "Challenge to the Privy Council," that he would refrain from dealing "in any respect with matter of State or Policy of this realm," Campion's more educated readers would have understood his use of the verse from Isaiah as an overt political gesture, which endorses the papal claim that the spiritual realm, presided over by the Holy See, had primacy over the temporal realm of individual Christian sovereigns.[63] In this respect, the pope was the ultimate enabler of cosmopolitanism, since his transnational subjects were capable of offering advice and correction to each of the sovereigns within his vast Christian commonwealth.

Campion's use of this verse places the entire tract within the context of contemporary writings, which utilize such claims for papal supremacy over the spiritual realm to justify the pope's right to correct or even depose a sinful, tyrannical or heretical sovereign. In 1571, for example, Sander had used the verse from Isaiah in the second book of the *De Visibili Monarchia Ecclesiae* in order to make a case for papal primacy over the temporal realm of individual sovereigns

---

[62] For discussion of the "cosmopolitics" of Dee, see Sherman, *John Dee*, 141–4. Interestingly, Dee was apparently a guest at the English hospice in Rome during the late 1560s. See Anthony Kenny, "From Hospice to College 1559–1579," in John Allen (ed.), *The English Hospice in Rome* (Exeter, 1962), 226.

[63] Campion, "Challenge to the Privy Council," in *Ten Reasons*, 7–11, esp. 8. The full title of the "Challenge" was "*Epistola ad reginae Angliae consiliarios, qua profectionis suae in Angliam institutum declarat, et Adversarios ad certamen provocat* [Letter to the counselors of the Queen of England, in which he declares the purpose of his departure into England, and calls out his adversaries to a debate]." Note that, like Osório's original *Epistola* to Elizabeth, the "Challenge" was also an *Epistola*, in this case, addressed to the Privy Council [*consiliarios reginae Angliae*].

Papal Supremacy and the Citizen of the World 55

and to justify the pope's excommunication and deposition of Elizabeth in 1570. He explains,

> Since thus it was said to the Apostles, *Go, teach all the peoples*, and when in the name of the people kings also are understood: and Bishops and priests [*Episcopi ac Presbyteri*] will have succeeded the apostles in the service of teaching [*in officio docendi successerint*]: actually in the post of teaching the Bishop is greater than his own King [*in docendi munere maior est Episcopus Rege suo*]: … Isaiah predicted *Kings will be foster fathers to the Church of Christ, and they will bow down before you with their faces to the ground; they will lick the dust at your feet. And you will know, that I am Lord?* [*Isaias praedixit*, Reges fore nutricios Ecclesiae Christi, & vultu in terram demisso adoraturos illam, & *mox subiungit*: Scies, quia ego Dominus (Isai 49)?] This [verse] is truly a sign that the Lord reigns in us [*Dominum regnare in nobis*], if we embody so much of the Church itself [*Ecclesiae ipsius*], such that it appears obvious that the ministers of Christ are greater than King and Queen are [*ministros Christi maiores quo libet Rege ac Regina esse*]."[64]

Sander's larger purpose in claiming that bishops were greater than kings and queens was to justify the Bishop of Rome's deposition of Elizabeth I, a legitimate sovereign who had nevertheless introduced dangerous heresies into her realm. Likewise, in the *Defence of English Catholics* (1584), Cardinal William Allen employs Isaiah 49:23 to justify his argument that "the spiritual hath right to correct the temporal" when the temporal realm is corrupted by heretical or tyrannical magistrates. And finally, in his *Motives*, Richard Bristow asked his readers to consider "what Church it is which conformably to these Prophecies [in Isaiah 49:23] hath brought the mighty Princes of the world, Kingdomes of the earth, and States of Commonwealthes to submit their Scepters vnto Christ our Lorde & gouernement of his Churche."[65]

Establishment Protestant apologists for the Elizabethan settlement either ignored Isaiah 49:23 or appropriated it as a justification for the Queen's claims to ecclesiastical supremacy. For example, in his own response to the Papal Bull entitled, *A View of a Seditious Bill Sent into England*, John Jewel employed

---

[64] "Cum igutur Apostolis dictum sit, *Ite, docete omnes gente (Matth. 28)*, cumque; gentium nomine reges etiam earum comprehendantur: & Episcopi ac Presbyteri Apostolis in officio docendi successerint: profecto in docendi munere maior est Episcopus Rege suo: tantum abest, vt Rex Episcopi caput in omibus rebus & causis esse queat. Qui tamen titulus non Regi modo, sed etiam Reginae ab istis hominibus, in Anglia nuper decreto publico tributus est. Isaias praedixit, *Reges fore nutricios Ecclesiae Christi, & vultu in terram demisso adoraturos illam*, & mox subiungit: *Scies, quia ego Dominus (Isaie 49)?* Hoc enim vere signum est, Dominum regnare in nobis, si tantum deferamus Ecclesiae ipsius, ut palam appareat, ministros Christi maiores quo libet Rege ac Regina esse." Nicholas Sander, *De visibili monarchia Ecclesiae*, E4v, my translation. For context, see Thomas McNevin Veech, *Dr Nicholas Sanders and the English Reformation 1530–1581* (Louvain, 1935).

[65] Cardinal William Allen, *Defence of English Catholiques*, vol. 2, 9, 13; Richard Bristow, *A Brief Treatise [Bristow's Motives]*, W3v–W4.

Isaiah 49:23 in order to defend the Queen as titular head of the church. In a muddled response to Pope Pius V's charge that Elizabeth's supremacy over the church constituted a usurpation of the Roman curia's authority over the spiritual realm, Jewel responds that Elizabeth claimed nothing that was not consistent with precedent and scripture: "To be short, queen Elizabeth doth as did Moses, Joshua, David, Salomon, Josias, Jehosaphat, as Constantine, Valentinian, Gratian, Theodosius, Arcadius, Honorius, and other godly emperors have done. God hath given charge to her of both tables. In the first she hath charge of religion, in the other of civil causes. By the prophet Esay God promiseth to his church, 'Kings shall be thy nursing-fathers and queens thy nurses.'"[66] Whether Catholic or Protestant, educated readers may have been surprised at the inclusion of Theodosius in Jewel's catalogue of emperors, given that Theodosius had been reproved, excommunicated, and finally reformed by Bishop Ambrose in an exemplary manner that Catholics thought relevant to the situation of Elizabeth herself.[67] More importantly, Jewel ignores entirely the Roman Catholic interpretation of the verse from Isaiah, according to which temporal sovereigns are enjoined to assume the role of servants (wet-nurses) with regard to the church. Instead, Jewel infers that these words should be understood as conferring on the queen authority over the spiritual realm.[68] Thus, Jewel immediately adds a second scriptural justification from the *Psalms*, "And David saith: 'Be wise therefore, ye kings, be learned, ye judges of the earth: serve the Lord in fear,'" suggesting that temporal sovereigns gain their authority over both the church and state by serving God.[69] Ultimately, Jewel's defense of Elizabeth's sovereignty over the church must acknowledge some restrictions on her ecclesiastical authority, and thus earlier in the tract, Jewel claims, reminiscent of Haddon's earlier argument, that the Queen "preacheth not, she ministereth not the sacraments, she doth neither excommunicate nor absolve from excommunication, she sitteth not to give sentence in spiritual causes, she challengeth not the dispensation of the keys of the kingdom of heaven."[70] In effect, Jewel explains—as did Haddon before him—that, in practice, Elizabeth delegates her authority over the church to her bishops.

Sir John Harington, one of the writers of fiction that I identify as a secular cosmopolitan in Chapter 2 of this book, provided a far more candid assessment of Isaiah 49:23 in his *Tract on the Succession to the Crown* (1602). Writing from the perspective of an outsider to religious controversy, Harington infuses his judgment with his signature satirical wit, confessing that he needed to consult the Queen's chaplains on the question of supremacy:

---

[66] John Jewel, *A View of a Seditious Bull Sent into England*, in *Works of John Jewel, Bishop of Salisbury*, ed. Rev. John Ayre (Cambridge, 1845–50), vol. 4, 1145.

[67] Collinson, "If Constantine, then also Theodosius," 109–33.

[68] This was also the argument that Richard Mocket made on the first pages of the crown-endorsed tract entitled, *God and the King: or, A Dialogue shewing that our Soueraigne Lord King Iames, being immediate vnder God within his DOMINIONS, Doth rightfully claime whasoeuer is required by the Oath of Allegeance* (London, 1616), A4v.

[69] Jewel, *A View of a Seditious Bull*, 1145.

[70] John Jewel, *A View of a Seditious Bull*, 1145.

If Peter being confirmed himself must confirme and conforme his fellowes, doth it followe he must place and displace kings? The prophet saith "Kings shal be thy nutricii *et reginae nutrices*," queens thy nurses: and sure when they be nurses, the milkes they give commonly is rentes and revenewes; and such milke hath that Church of Rome suckt frome their nurses of England a long tyme. But since that Churche did *luxuriari in Christo*, as St. Paul saith of the wanton widdowes, since they did like ungratefull babies suck blood for milke, and byte their nurses nipples, who can blame her if for milke she give them *Pap with a Hatchet*, as is the proverbe.[71]

Harington is presumed to have composed this manuscript for the Archbishop of York Tobias Matthew in order to champion the cause of James VI of Scotland for succession to the English throne. In this passage, Harington shows a familiarity with the reading of the verse from Isaiah that was prevalent among English Catholic exiles, but he also refutes that reading, claiming that a tyrannical church had no claim over a long-suffering and abused state. And yet, in spite of what seems to be an unequivocal view against papal supremacy, Harington does grant that some Catholic grievances concerning the Tudor crown are justified. For example, he criticizes the fact that "Henry VIII ... made Cromwell his vicegerent in Causes Ecclesiasticall, setting him, a layman, and as he writes an unlearned man, over all the bishops and clergie," and more importantly, he attacks Elizabeth herself because "contrarie to the use of all Christian countries, [during] a great part of her Majesties reigne no bishopp was of the Counsell."[72] If Catholic exiles like Sander and Allen imagined the relationship between the pope and the sovereign as one in which "the spiritual hath right to correct the temporal," then so too did Harington imagine a bishop as privy councilor playing a role analogous to the pope, correcting the sovereign from within the council when her conduct merited such correction.

Cosmopolitan Institutions: The Society of Jesus

So far we have considered how the issue of supremacy over the ecclesiastical realm was central to the Catholic cosmopolitical perspective, which posited a Christian commonwealth, over which the pope presided. We have noted how

---

[71] Harington, *A Tract on the Succession*, ed. Clements R. Markham, C.B. (London, 1880), 116. The reference to the proverb, "*Pap with a Hatchet*," meaning to punish someone by giving them a benefit, seems to be an ironical reference to John Lyly's anti-Martinist tract, *Pap with a Hatchet: Being a Reply to Martin Mar-Prelate* (1589), *Re-printed from the Original Quarto Edition with An Introduction and Notes* (London, 1844). Whereas in this passage Harington is justifying Queen Elizabeth's rejection of papal supremacy (giving them "*Pap with a Hatchet*"), Lyly's tract was written in defense of the Episcopal hierarchy within the Church of England against Martin Marprelate's attack on the English bishops and the established church's hierarchy. In this respect, Harington seems to be stressing his own conformity: he supported Elizabeth taking the "*Hatchet*" to Rome, while at the same time making reference, through his allusion to Lyly's tract, to his support for English bishops.

[72] Harington, *A Tract on the Succession*, 117.

similar this religious notion of the cosmopolitical perspective is to the secular cosmopolitan perspective of someone like John Dee. It remains to be seen how and where this ideology was institutionalized within the English exile community. In general, it is not enough simply to write from the position of an exile to embody the perspective that I have been exploring in this first chapter. It will become clear from what follows that one could be a part of the exile community, one could even support the Spanish or Catholic invasion of England, without necessarily subscribing to the broadly international Catholic perspective that Campion's and Persons's writings embody from this period. Even so, I would argue that the cosmopolitical perspective did prevail within the exile community, and it is important to understand how and why it did so.

It is my contention that the most important factor in institutionalizing this perspective within the Catholic community was the role that the Jesuits assumed within the English colleges, which allowed Robert Persons and his allies to take control of the most vital and important activity in which the exile community was engaged, namely the English mission. To assert that the Jesuits were a "cosmopolitan" or "cosmopolitical" organization is to risk reproducing a cliché about the religious order. For in the eyes of their opponents, the Jesuits did embody qualities similar to some of the negative stereotypes of the twentieth-century cosmopolitan: devotion to financial gain over national loyalty, unsavory and undue influence over legitimate political leadership, and an itinerant existence that paid little attention to national frontiers or customs.[73] At worst, it risks suggesting that the negative stereotypes which the Jesuits' opponents used to characterize them were historically accurate or even reproducing the negative associations that some modern writers came to attach to the Jesuits. As a result, it is important that we clarify what we mean when we claim that the cosmopolitical sensibility found in Dee, Campion, and others came to inhere in the institutional structure of the Society of Jesus.

Let us recall that Dee, Sander, and Campion all see themselves as citizens within the city of God, the Christian commonwealth equivalent to the cosmopolis or the city of the world in their thinking. And part of realizing that one's existence within an explicitly Christian city of the world is realizing that speaking from the cosmopolis affords one a special perspective, qualifying one to speak as an authority on the peoples and nations of the world and especially to offer advice and counsel to the sovereigns. In this respect, works such as Osório's *Epistolae*

---

[73] For an account of the early seventeenth-century forgery purporting to be secret instructions for using underhanded means to enrich and empower the Society of Jesus, see Sabina Pavone, *The Wily Jesuits and the Monita Secreta: The Forged Secret Instructions of the Jesuits, Myth and Reality* (St. Louis, 2005). See also the English translation in Appendix 1. For contemporary suspicions about Jesuit intentions in France during this period, see Thomas McCoog, *The Society of Jesus in Ireland, Scotland, and England, 1589–1597* (Burlington, VT, 2012), 205–6. For a comprehensive background on the English Jesuits to the twentieth century, see Francis Edwards, S.J., *The Jesuits in England: From 1580 to the Present Day* (Tunbridge Wells, Kent, 1985).

to Elizabeth embody an explicitly Christian version of the perspective that John Dee assumes for himself. Within the writings of Sander, Campion, and Persons, a crucial aspect of this cosmopolitical perspective is the pope's role as monarch of the Christian cosmopolis, with the bishops being his magistrates, a hierarchy that affords the Roman curia the ability to counsel and admonish sovereigns and if they become particularly wayward, to depose them.

It is clear that figures such as Campion and Persons viewed the Society of Jesus as having a special role to play within the cosmopolitical organization that they themselves were advancing. Perhaps the most notable expression of the cosmopolitan character of the Jesuits is contained in Campion's description of the English mission, which can be found at the end of his brief letter initially known as "The Challenge" and later disparagingly as "The Brag" (1580). Campion wrote the letter while hiding in a small village outside of London, with the intention of preserving a record of the true motives of the English mission, lest he and Persons be captured by English authorities and suffer his opponents' malign characterization of their aims. The letter was copied and diffused in manuscript form by Thomas Pounde and other English Catholics and later printed and widely read in refutations by William Charke and Meredith Hanmer.[74] After initially requesting separate audiences with members of the Privy Council, with the Doctors and Masters of the Universities, and with prominent temporal and spiritual lawyers of the realm in order to "discourse of religion," Campion's letter eventually challenges his Protestant counterparts to engage in a public disputation on religious doctrine before the Queen herself.[75] Finally, in the eloquent peroration to this notorious document, Campion describes the mission to which the Society will henceforth commit itself in England:

> And touching our Societie, be it known to you that we have made a league—all the Jesuits in the world, whose succession and multitude must overreach all the practices of England—cheerfully to carry the cross you shall lay on us, and never to despair your recovery, while we have a man left to enjoy your Tyburn, or to be racked with your torments, or consumed with your prisons. The expense is reckoned, the enterprise is begun; it is of God, it cannot be withstood. So the faith was planted, so it must be restored.[76]

Beyond its moving eloquence, this passage embodies a form of traditional transnationalism that is reliant on a powerful historical fiction. Much of the "Brag"

---

[74] William Chark, *An answere to a seditious pamphlet lately cast abroade by a Iesuite, with a discoverie of that blasphemous sect* (London, 1580); Meredith Hanmer, *The great bragge and challenge of M. Champion a Iesuite, commonlye called Edmunde Campion, latelye arriued in Englande, contayinge nyne articles here seuerallye laide downe, directed by him to the Lordes of the Counsail, confuted and aunswered by Meredith Hanmer, M. of Art, and student in diuinitie* (London, 1581).

[75] Campion, "To the Right Honourable, the Lords of Her Majestie's Privy Council [Campion's Challenge]," in *Rationes decem*, 7–11, esp. 8–9.

[76] Campion, "Campion's Challenge," 10.

is steeped in the expected conservative obedience to authority—indeed everything from Campion's promise not to "deal in any respect with matter of State or Policy of the Realm" to his monastic claim that he was "now as a dead man to this world and willing to put my head under every man's foot, and to kiss the ground they tread upon" can be viewed as reflecting the Society's Superior General's admonition that Persons and Campion were to proceed on the mission humbly and without any engagement with political discourse. And part of this conservative obedience is certainly found in Campion's appeal to the past Christian conversion of England, which he seeks only to "restore."[77] At the same time, Campion, Persons, and their fellow Jesuits went to England as the vanguard of a global organization, whose "succession and multitudes," Campion notes in a singular phrase, "must overreach all the practices of England." Moreover, Campion and Persons did not seek simply to restore the old faith that had once existed in England, with its special fasting days and peculiar customs that made it distinctive in Europe. Instead, their aim was that the old faith should be re-established but in a new form, cleansed of its old corruptions and superstitions, such that its antiquated customs would be brought in line with reformed continental practices.[78]

The international aspect of the Jesuits, which Campion invokes so eloquently in the passage above, was crucial to this aspect of their mission—although this was not primary in their thinking, their intervention into England would bring the country closer to the rest of Christian Europe. Significantly, the Society of Jesus was not merely a league of regulars with similar aims and goals, as Campion seeks to imply here. Rather as Markus Friedrich has shown, using documents related to Jesuit bureaucracy, the Society of Jesus comprised a vertically-organized hierarchy, and while some contemporaries may have liked to describe its structure as aristocratic, its basic structure was monarchical with the office of the Superior General in Rome at its center.[79] From the perspective of papal supremacy, the Society may even have presented itself as the ideal model on which to base a resurgent centralization of papal authority in Europe. The Jesuits had a tremendous advantage in having built their bureaucracies during the Renaissance, at a time when "the developing nation states of Early Modern Europe were more and more governed through large bureaucracies that in turn depended on new practices of information gathering and efficient administrative communication." Friedrich continues, "Large social bodies—states, trading companies, etc.—became increasingly reliant on a constant survey of their own resources, as well as on surveys of the potential competitors' status quo."[80] What distinguished the Society from earlier medieval forms of organization was the degree of centralization

---

[77] Campion, "Campion's Challenge," 8, 9, 10.

[78] McCoog, *Society of Jesus 1541–1588*, 167–8. For background on the conflicts between the Jesuits and the secular priests, see Bossy, *English Catholic Community*, 16–48.

[79] Friedrich, "Communication and Bureaucracy," 49–75, esp. 51.

[80] Friedrich, "Communication and Bureaucracy," 53. For background on the increasingly centralized nature of the Early Modern state apparatus, see Braddick, *State Formation in Early Modern England*, 11–46.

that it was able to achieve. And crucial to maintaining this centralized structure was the Jesuit system of letter writing, involving the circulation of letters and reports from the geographical peripheries to the office of the General, and an organizational structure that kept distinct various types of epistolary documents, which, according to an important manual by Francisco Sacchini and published in 1620, included "instructions; documents on visitations; rules for governing; papers pertaining to the order's relationship with the Papal Curia; several types of letters; papers on juridical affairs; and papers regarding temporal affairs."[81] While recent work stressing the importance of the Spanish, Portuguese, and French provinces in Jesuit decision-making does qualify to a certain extent the central role of Rome in the organization, the Society's *Constitutions* placed an extraordinary emphasis on correspondence with the Superior General as a means of achieving a "union of hearts."[82] As John O'Malley has noted, "rectors were to write to the provincial and the provincials were to write to the general as often as once a week; the general should respond to the provincials at least once a month, and the provincials respond just as often to the local rectors." Such rules were too demanding ever to have been observed to the letter and were only strictly adhered to during special periods such as the opening of a new school or college, but they did establish an ideal of frequent communication and an epistolary hierarchy that allowed for efficient and centralized decision-making. The most important correspondences were of course the circular letters disseminated from the office of the general two or three times a year, some of which were preserved as important documents in perpetuity.[83]

As a transnational, highly efficient and organized, monarchical organization, the Society was perfectly suited to assuming leadership over the English mission, something of which the students at the English college in Rome during the 1570s seemed to be aware. It was partly for this reason that the English scholars appealed to the Society to rescue the college from the directorship of Fr. Morys Clynnog, the Welsh secular who was then rector of the college. The conflict at the English College between the English and the Welsh scholars and the eventual Jesuit assumption of control there is important to my larger argument about early modern cosmopolitanism for three reasons. First, it illustrates many of the cosmopolitan characteristics that came to characterize the Society during this period. Second, because Persons himself gave a detailed account in his memoirs of the events at the college, it provides an important gauge of how Persons's own perspective reflected the Society's institutional characteristics.[84] Finally, the events at the English College, as complex as they were, were also recorded and

---

[81]   Cited and translated in Friedrich, "Communication and Bureaucracy," 51, 55.

[82]   *Monumenta Ignatiana Sancti Ignatii de Loyola Constitutiones Societatis Jesu* (3 vols, Rome, 1934–38), Constitution numbers 673–6, cited in John W. O'Malley, *The First Jesuits* (Cambridge, MA, 1993), 62.

[83]   O'Malley, *First Jesuits*, 62–3.

[84]   Robert Persons, "A Storie of Domesticall Difficulties in the English Catholike cause," in *Miscellanea II, Publications of the Catholic Record Society*, ed. J.H. Pollen, S.J., vol. 2 (London, 1906), 48–185.

62   *Early Modern Catholics, Royalists, and Cosmopolitans*

published by one of the Jesuits' main English enemies, Anthony Munday, whose own sojourn at the English college coincided with the famous English student rebellion against Clynnog in 1579.[85] Munday takes up an important role in Chapter 2 of this book, but in this first chapter it is important to recognize the similarities between Person's account of the rebellion and Munday's account, as we trace the evolution of cosmopolitanism and papal supremacy across the Catholic-Protestant and religious-secular fault lines that existed in England. Before turning to Person's memoirs and Munday's published account of the English student revolt, however, it is important to recount the events that occurred during the late 1570s in Rome.

In the late 1570s, Cardinal Allen successfully enlisted the Society's help in resolving an ethno-national dispute that had paralyzed the newly established English College in Rome. In 1576, Allen had helped to convert the old English hospice for pilgrims into a seminary, which came to be known as the *Collegium Anglorum*, and in late 1576, English students began to arrive from the previously-established English College at Douai.[86] Immediately, what at first might have seemed to have been an administrative dispute broke out into a "nationall quarrell ... betwene the Englishe and the Welche" students over what was perceived as both the rector's preference for the Welsh students and his plans for the future of the college.[87] During the years before the college was established, Morys Clynnog had been warden of the original English hospice, and when the hospice became a college, the post of rector fell to him by default. In 1578, Clynnog's term as warden expired, and the resident clergy elected an Englishman, Henry Henshaw, as his successor. Cardinal Giovanni Morone favored Clynnog and quickly intervened on his behalf, separating the post of warden from rector, and reappointing Clynnog to the latter position. Morone's support for the unpopular Clynnog led to a bitter struggle between the Welsh and the English residents of the college, and Allen and Morone turned to the Society for assistance in resolving the ethnic dispute.[88] By all accounts, the Society was well suited for addressing the ethnic tensions

---

[85]   Munday, *The English Roman Life*, ed. Philip J. Ayres (New York, 1980), 78–94. For discussion of Munday's strategies of self-representation in the Catholic context of the English College in Rome, see Melanie Ord, "Representing Rome and the Self in Anthony Munday's *The English Roman Life*," in *Travels and Translations in the Sixteenth Century, Selected Papers from the Second International Conference of the Tudor Symposium (2000)*, ed. Mike Pincombe (Burlington, VT, 2004), 45–64.

[86]   For background on the transition from hospice to college, see Kenny, "From Hospice to College 1559–1579," in *The English Hospice in Rome* (Exeter, 1962), 218–73.

[87]   Persons, "A Storie," 86.

[88]   Cardinal William Allen, "Dr. William Allen to Dr. Owen Lewis, archdeacon of Hainault, Paris 12 May 1579," *The Letters and Memorials of William Cardinal Allen. (1532–1594)*, ed. Fathers of the Congregation of the London Oratory, intro. Thomas F. Knox (London, 1882), 78. See also Allen's correspondence with Agazzari in "Some Correspondence of Cardinal Allen, 1579–1585," in Catholic Record Society, *Miscellanea*, vol. 7 (London, 1911), 12–105. See McCoog, *Society of Jesus 1541–1588*, 103–8; Michael E. Williams, *The Venerable English College, Rome: A History 1579–1979* (London, 1979), 1–33, and Kenny, "From Hospice to College 1559–1579," 229–63.

that were roiling the English college during this period. Unlike the older religious orders that over the centuries had developed into loose and disjointed networks of local ethno-religious communities, the Society saw itself as unified by a mission that transcended ethnic and national commitments. According to the *Regulae Societatis Iesu ad usum Nostrorum Tantum*, published in Rome in 1560, members of the society were explicitly enjoined to "be on their guard against that attitude of mind which leads some of one nationality to speak ill of those of another. Rather, they should esteem and bear a special love in our Lord for those of other nations. Hence, no one at the expense of charity should make wars or dissensions between nations the subject of their conversations."[89] As John W. O'Malley has shown, during the last year of Ignatius Loyola's life and during the First General Congregation, which followed his death, the early Jesuits suffered serious tensions between those members loyal to the Neapolitan Pope Paul IV and those members that were more comfortable with the Spanish character of the organization.[90] But to a large extent, the structure of the Society was unique among early modern religious orders in its transnational character, and this structure allowed it to resolve successfully regional and ethno-national disputes and differences that arose.[91] As Jerónimo Nadal never tired of repeating, "The world is our house."[92]

On March 19, 1579, responding to the English student's petition, Pope Gregory XIII finally ordered Cardinal Morone to accept Clynnog's resignation. Despite his continuing support for the Welshman, Morone had no choice but to accede to the wishes of the majority of students at the English College in Rome, and subsequently he commanded the fourth Superior General of the Society, Mercurian, to take charge of the situation. In turn, Mercurian quickly appointed the Italian Alfonso Agazzari as the first Jesuit rector.[93] A bull of foundation was drawn up for the new administration under which the seminarians would "be instructed in the Catholic religion in which they were born, with the aim primarily of assuring their own salvation, but also so that once instructed in the knowledge of theology they might return to England to enlighten others who had fallen away from the truth."[94] From that point on, each student who entered the college swore an oath that he would be willing to embark for England whenever his superiors at the college saw fit to send him. Thus had this transnational religious order assumed control over a college,

---

[89]   *Rules of the Society of Jesus: A New Translation from the Latin* (Woodstock, MD, 1956), 34–5.

[90]   O'Malley, *First Jesuits*, 307–9.

[91]   For discussion of the basic organization of the Society, see O'Malley, *First Jesuits*, 51–90.

[92]   Jerónimo Nadal, *Epistolae et monumenta. 5, Commentarii de instituto Societatis Jesu*, ed. Michael Nicolau (Rome, 1962), 54, 364–5, 469–70, 773–4. See O'Malley, *First Jesuits*, 67–9, and O'Malley, "To Travel to Any Part of the World: Jeronimo Nadal and the Jesuit Vocation," *Studies in the Spirituality of Jesuits* 16.2 (1984): 1–20.

[93]   McCoog, *Society of Jesus 1541–1588*, 107.

[94]   Pope Gregory XIII, "Papal Bull: Quoniam Divinae Bonitati," in Williams, *Venerable English College*, 272–80, esp. 274.

whose purpose—that of training priests and providing them with the resources to undertake missions to Protestant England—was explicitly focused on the needs of the English nation.[95] In the end, the Jesuits resolved the conflict according to what must have seemed to the English exile community to be the customary order of things, whereby a historically restive Welsh community was restored to its subordinate position, as was the case within the Atlantic context. And while the controversy between the English and the Welsh exile communities continued to malinger in subsequent years, the English Jesuits led by Robert Persons and their supporters soon became the dominant force within the exile community.[96]

The Pope's Scholars: The 1579 Student Revolt at the English College at Rome

As I show in this section, the English student revolt in Rome followed by Pope Gregory's swift deposition of its Rector Morys Clynnog was perceived as having significant geopolitical implications, especially with respect to the papal responsibility to depose tyrannical temporal magistrates. Two accounts of the 1579 student rebellion at the English College at Rome make this clear: the *English Romayne Lyfe* (1582), Anthony Munday's printed account of his travels to Rome and his sojourn at the English College, and "A Storie of Domesticall Difficulties in the English Catholike cause" (1600), Robert Persons's manuscript account

---

[95] For an exploration of the tensions between Aquaviva and Persons, who favored more direct political engagement, see John Bossy, "The Heart of Robert Persons," *The Reckoned Expense: Edmund Campion and the Early English Jesuits*, ed. Thomas McCoog (Rome, 2007), 187–208. See also McCoog, *Society of Jesus, 1541–1588*, 125–8, 221–3.

[96] In 1582, for example, an English graduate of the college named Richard Barret, having been awarded one of the college's first doctorates in theology, returned to Rheims where the fist English college at Douai had been relocated, and there he was retained by Allen as the Prefect of studies. As his letters to Agazarri show, in both Rome and Rheims, the factional disputes between the Welsh and the English students continued unabated. On sending some students to Rome to continue their studies, Barret complained to Agazzari: "Amongst those who last left for your College I have heard a certain [Richard] Edward, a Welshman, is a man of unquiet character .... While he was here, this trait was in no way discovered, either because he did not stay here long, or because he was more cautious in his behaviour. After his departure, however, some indication was given of a character too prone to anger, and too ready to defend the Welsh faction." In the middle of 1583, he sent more students to Rome and complained once again, "There is no need to add anything about the students sent to you, for I have already written two letters to your Reverence about them. Two of them are Welshmen of excellent character, but still Welshmen ... . And it will seem very remarkable to find any Welshman who, left to his own disposition and inclination, and putting aside all authority and fear of a superior—by which they can for a time be held to their duty—does not incline towards, and altogether embrace the faction followed by all of that race and nation." "Barret to Agazzari [Rheims], 16 November 1582," "Barret to Agazzari, Rheims, 14 April 1583," *Letters of William Allen and Richard Barret 1572–1598*, ed. Renold (Oxford, 1967), 39, 46.

of the rebellion.[97] As we shall see, Munday's and Persons's seemingly opposed perspectives on the revolt reveal a common view of papal intervention, which in turn yields insights into English perceptions of papal supremacy and the marginal yet significant forms of cosmopolitan English identity that I am investigating here.[98] Indeed, both Munday and Persons present papal intervention into the college revolt within the context of geopolitical concerns that suggest an analogy with the papal power to depose a tyrannical or heretical sovereign. In this respect, papal authority and prerogative within the context of the English college has the contradictory effect of simultaneously blurring the boundaries of Munday's and Persons's English identity and redrawing that identity within the broader context of the Christian commonwealth, over which the pope presided.[99]

In spite of Persons's account of events at the college having been written during the 1590s appellant crisis, long after Munday published his account in *The English Romayne Lyfe* (1582), I begin with Persons's relation. My reasons for doing so are threefold: Persons's account is more detailed than Munday's; Persons obviously knew and understood the principal figures in the dispute better than Munday and had access to the students' written appeals to Cardinal Morone and Pope Gregory XIII; and finally, his account reflects how the revolt related to other disputes within the English Catholic exile community. Persons begins his account by situating the current tensions among English Catholic exiles within the history of earlier examples of religious conflicts in England—for example, those between William the Conqueror and Stigland, the Archbishop of Canterbury, and between King Henry II and Archbishop Thomas Beckett, and between various factions during the reigns of Henry VIII, Edward VI, and Mary Tudor—in order to provide some background.[100] Significantly, these past religious controversies, which preface and contextualize Persons's relation of the recent troubles at the English College at Rome, pertain to tensions between church and state in England.

---

[97] Munday, *English Roman Life*; Robert Persons, "A Storie of Domesticall Difficulties in the English Catholike cause," 48–185.

[98] Contrast their common perspective on events at the English college to their contrasting accounts of the execution of the Protestant Englishman Richard Atkins in Rome, who had been arrested for desecration of the consecrated host during a mass at St. Peter's Church (August 1581). Persons presents Atkins as a crazed and raving zealot who finally repented while being burned at the stake, while Munday presents him as a sincere and authentic Protestant martyr. Robert Persons, *The copie of a double letter ... containing the true aduises of the cause, and maner of the death, of one Richard Atkins, executed by fire, in Rome, the seconde of August 1581* (Rheims, 1581); Munday, *English Roman Life*, 100–105.

[99] Note that this transnational perspective counters the prevailing view, which focuses on the way in which fiction and non-fictional writings channel "national and religious sentiments into the worship of the prince [i.e. Elizabeth]," "mask[ing] over and thus temporarily deflect[ing] deep social, political and theological divisions in late sixteenth-century England." *Renaissance Self-Fashioning: From More to Shakespeare* (Chicago, 1980), 168. See also Louis Adrian Montrose, "*A Midsummer Night's Dream* and the Shaping Fantasies of Elizabethan Culture: Gender, Power, Form," in *Rewriting the Renaissance*, ed. Margaret Ferguson et al. (Chicago, 1986), 65–87.

[100] Persons, "A Storie," 50–51.

66   *Early Modern Catholics, Royalists, and Cosmopolitans*

In Persons's narration, the student revolt at the college erupted immediately after its foundation at the site of the original English hospice for pilgrims, shortly after Clynnog procured a Breve from the pope that made him perpetual rector. At the time, Persons reports that there were 30 English scholars and 7 or 8 Welsh scholars living at the college. Persons, like Munday, notes that the English students complained that Clynnog's stewardship had compromised the very purpose of the college. In contrast to the majority of the English students, Clynnog's vision for the college seems to have been the more modest undertaking of preserving the organization of the English Church abroad for a future time when, it was thought, it would inevitably be restored to its rightful place in England.[101] According to the major part of English students, however, the English Catholic cause would ultimately be jeopardized if the college "should continewe in that sorte under Mr. Morrice [Clynnog] his government, whome theye avouched to have no care of making men for England, nor sending them thither, but only to entertayne them in Rome, and that such was the resolution and purpose of his Contreymen [i.e. the Welsh] in the Colledge."[102] Hence, while it is likely that the protesting English students were also biased against the Welsh, their public concern was at least for the larger goal of the mission to England and Wales, and they viewed Jesuit leadership over the college as necessary precisely because the Society was perceived to be impartial with regard to questions of national bias.[103] In a petition to Cardinal Morone, the students list three reasons for their appeal for Jesuit leadership at the college, one of which concerns the necessity of impartially adjudicating and therefore mitigating tensions between the Welsh and English within the exile community. In part, their petition reads:

> When among the two populations of England, the English and the Welsh, some natural root of discord exists, it seems necessary that such men preside over us, who are alien from affection for whichever part; in other respects now it is proved by experience, that these two peoples are unable to live together: lastly insofar as we speak with our infinite pain, we prove so at this time.[104]

Likewise, rather than overt expressions of ethnic interest, Persons's letters to his colleagues put forward the seemingly impartial argument that English dominance over the Welsh was part of the customary geopolitical order, confirmed through analogies with the current balance of power between the actual kingdoms of England and Wales. In a letter to his fellow Jesuit William Goode, Persons recounts

---

[101]   McCoog, *Society of Jesus 1541–1588*, 107.

[102]   Persons, "A Storie," 87.

[103]   See the "Memorialles given up by the Schollers against Mr Morrisse," prepared by the English students for Cardinal Morone in Persons, "A Storie," 102–17. For background, see McCoog, *Society of Jesus 1541–1588*, 105–8.

[104]   "Cum inter duos Angliae populos, Anglos et Wallos, sit aliqua naturalis radix discordiae, videtur necessarium, ut tales nobis viri praesint, qui sint alieni ab utriusque partis affectu, alioquin experientia jam probatum est, hos populos simul non posse vivere: imo quod infinito cum dolore nostro dicimus, hoc tempore probamus." "Memorialles" in Person, "A Storie," 103, my translation.

the conversation between an unnamed individual—probably a priest, perhaps even Persons himself— sympathetic to and familiar with the English students and Tolomeo Galli, the Cardinal of Como, who was initially sympathetic to Clynnog's perspective. After Como explains that he himself would have simply encouraged the English students to abandon the college if they were not prepared to submit to Clynnog, Persons goes on to explain the transformation that the anonymous interlocutor has caused in the Cardinal of Como's thinking. The Cardinal of Como confesses

> that he understood the diversity betwixt Englishmen and Welchmen was nothing more than might be betwixt two divers provinces [as] Tuscan[y] and Romagnia. Whereto replyed this man that he understood the matter farre otherwise, and thought that his Grace was not informed in the matter, for that the Welchmen and Englishmen were (putting aside Religion) as might be Mores and Spaniards. For as the Spaniards got Spayne from the Mores and after held them under, so Englishmen had done in tymes past the ould Britans, which were now called Welchmen, albeit in successe of tyme they have now imparted to them their privileges and freedoms and do account of them as of Englishmen naturall, excepting only that they use great moderation in promoting them to honours at home; and therefore naturally it is as much repugned to Englishmens harts to be subiect to the government of Welchmen as Spaniards to Mores or Frenchmen to Spaniards. These words seemed not a little to move the Cardinall whereupon after a little pause he brake out and said, I knew not of this so fully before.[105]

In the light of such geopolitical analogies, Persons himself sees the student rebellion against the colleges' magistrates under the aegis of papal authority as a model which pertains to the larger geopolitical context. In his letter to Goode, he explains in some detail how the students' audacious petition to Morone would serve them well in their confrontation with the English crown:

> This act of thers [the English seminarians] before the Cardinall [Morone] was straightway knowne and talked of all over Rome, for there were at it all the family of the Cardinall and did wonder to se such liberty of speech, before so great a personage. And albeit I think there must needs passe many excesses amongst so much as was spoken in that place, of so many Youthes; yet many men did imagine to see a certayne company of *Lawrences, Sebastians* and the like intractable fellowes, who brought Emperours and princes to desperation to deal with them, for that they could neyther with giving or taking away, neyther

---

[105]   Persons, "The copy of a larg Letter and relation wrytten by F. Persons unto F. William Goode," in Persons, "A Storie," 156–7. For an exploration of British archipelagic analogies to the relationship between the Spaniards and the Moors, see Barbara Fuchs, "Spanish Lessons: Spenser and the Irish Moriscos," *Studies in English Literature 1500–1900* 42.1 (2002): 43–62. Persons recounts the same story to Allen in a letter dated March 30, 1579, with some minor differences, including an objection by Welshmen that the analogy does not hold since Moors "are later in Spayne than the Castilians." See "Persons to Allen, Rome 30 March 1579," in Leo Hicks, S.J. (ed.), *Letters and Memorials of Father Robert Persons, S.J.*, vol. 1 (to 1588) (London, 1942), 3–4.

68   *Early Modern Catholics, Royalists, and Cosmopolitans*

with faire wordes nor with foule bring them to condesend to any one little poynt that they misliked. Many also strangers made this consequent; if these fellowes stand thus immovable before such Princes in Rome, what will they do in England before the Heretiques? And many said that they doubted before of things reported of English Priests in England, and of their bould answers, reported by Letters, but now they could beleeve anything of them.[106]

According to Persons, the courage of the English seminarians in standing up to Cardinal Morone, Archdeacon Owen Lewes, and Father Clynnog would serve them well in their confrontation with English magistrates. The seminarians are compared to the early saints, St. Lawrence and St. Sebastian, who confronted and were martyred by Pagan Roman emperors. Ultimately, of course, it is papal intervention into the affairs of the English college that authorizes and legitimizes their rebellion. In effect, the student rebellion ends with the pope's deposition of Clynnog and his ally Lewes, which by analogy justifies the papal deposing power within the geopolitical sphere of relations between Rome and the English crown. In other words, what makes their rebellion exemplary is precisely the fact that it was not a rebellion at all—rather it was a request for intervention by a supreme authority into the decisions of a lesser magistrate. By analogy, Persons and his allies sought to restore the same form of papal oversight to the English crown. Indeed, the pope's use of prerogative powers to resolve the conflict within the English college replicates the geopolitical result that Sander, Persons and other English Jesuits sought in their analogous support for Pope Pius V's public deposition of Queen Elizabeth in 1570.[107]

In publishing his own account of the English rebellion, Munday sought primarily to expose and defame the den of iniquity and treachery that, for English officials, constituted the *Collegium Anglorum*.[108] *The English Romayne Lyfe* begins with Munday and his companion Thomas Nowell traveling to France, the account of his ambush by French soldiers which he repeated in his other writings, their sojourn in Amiens with an English Catholic priest, their travels to Paris where the encountered the English ambassador and more English Catholics who persuade them finally to travel to the English college in Rome.[109] He goes on to detail the daily routine of the seminarians at the college, conversations with the English scholars, who live up to their traitorous reputation, and descriptions of the superstitions that are popular among the college's inhabitants and among the Romans in general.[110]

---

[106]   Persons, "A Storie," 146–7.

[107]   See for example, Persons, *A Conference*, D6–G6.

[108]   For independent evidence that Munday was a student at the English College, listed as a "humanista" or grammar student, see Anthony Kenny, "Anthony Munday in Rome," *Recusant History* 6 (1962): 158–62.

[109]   Munday, *English Roman Life*, 5–21. See Chapter 2 for a discussion of Munday's other works, which detail these adventures.

[110]   In her book-length study of Munday, Donna Hamilton has argued that Munday's account of his travels, like the rest of his writings, display the signs of a crypto-Catholic who was alternatively trying to conceal and remain true to his faith. Thus Hamilton focuses on how Munday's recording of the priests' voices, as they denounce Elizabeth as "that

Throughout the *English Romayne Lyfe*, Munday is clear to differentiate his own voice from those of the other English students living at the seminary, who are recorded as referring to Elizabeth as "that proud usurping Jezebel."[111] Thus, at the climax of Munday's account, when Pope Gregory XIII finally intervenes into the dispute between the English students and Father Clynnog, the pope offers the English scholars his praises for "having left your prince, which was your duty, and come so far to me, which is more than I can deserve, yet as I am your refuge when persecution dealeth straitly with you in your country by reason of the heretical religion there used, so will I be your bulwark to defend you, your guide to protect you, your Father to nourish you, and your friend with my heart-blood to do you any profit." As is typical throughout the tract, Munday separates himself here from the Catholic perspective by glossing this passage with the comment, "Behold what deceits the Devil hath to accomplish his desire."[112] At the same time, Munday's position within the college, as a new English student dependent on the goodwill of his compeers for his survival, meant that he was at least temporarily allied with the English Catholics in their conflict with the college hierarchy.

Munday notes that Clynnog, who is consistently portrayed as displaying a preference towards the Welsh students of the college, had a special antipathy towards Munday himself: "When I had been there a pretty while, I know not how Doctor Morris conceived anger against me, but he would not suffer me to tarry any longer in the College."[113] In spite of Clynnog's displeasure with Munday, the other seminarians defended Munday and protected him from Clynnog's wrath. Perceiving Clynnog's antipathy towards Munday, the other scholars

> agreed to take my part, saying that if Doctor Morris would put every Englishman he thought good on, out, in short time the College would be all Welshmen: so they bade me stick to them, and if I went away they would go away too.
>
> Besides, they moved a certain speech amongst themselves that if I were not received into the College amongst them, and used in every respect according as they were, when I returned into England, being known to come from Rome, I might be compelled to tell the names of them that were there, and what conference I had among them, so that their parents and friends should be discovered, and themselves be known against their coming in England.[114]

---

proud usurping Jezebel" and name the members of the Privy Council whom they plan to "persecute" once they return to England, has the ironic effect of recording and publishing voices that were dangerous to the Queen's rule. According to Hamilton, Munday's act of recording such seditious voices might ultimately have served as a critique of the Queen's council, and significantly, this material would be excised from the subsequent 1590 edition of the *English Romayne Lyfe*. Munday, *English Roman Life*, 25. I address Hamilton's argument in detail in Chapter 2. See also Donna Hamilton, *Anthony Munday and the Catholics*, 48. For discussion of what was cut from the 1590 edition, see Philip J. Ayres (ed.), *English Roman Life*, xxiv–xxviii.

[111] Munday, *English Roman Life*, 25.
[112] Munday, *English Roman Life*, 92.
[113] Munday, *English Roman Life*, 80.
[114] Munday, *English Roman Life*, 81.

70 Early Modern Catholics, Royalists, and Cosmopolitans

As it happens, the students' concerns about Munday returning to England were warranted: when Munday finally abandoned the college in order to return to England, he did in fact report to the authorities on the Englishmen living at the college, although it is unclear if he was compelled to do so or if he did so willingly.[115]

When he recounts the English students finally appealing to Cardinal Morone, Munday claims, in a passage redolent of self-promotion, that Clynnog's ill treatment of him was an important factor in the seminarians' decision. And in fact, Clynnog seems to single out Munday in a complaint to Morone when he notes that "the scholars used no regard to him [Clynnog], being their rector, but maintained one [Munday] lately come forth of England, both to scorn at him [Clynnog], and to offer him too much abuse."[116] In the most confrontational speech of the petition episode, Ralph Sherwin, who was later executed with Campion in London in 1581, complains to Morone that, due to favoritism shown by Clynnog, the Welsh enjoy greater provisions and luxuries at the college, in spite of the fact that all students were to be treated equally before the rector. After the appeal to Morone, Clynnog's treatment of Munday takes a turn for the worse. He informs Munday that he must immediately vacate the premises of the college, but through the intervention of the Jesuits, Munday is provided with a room near the common privy, where "all the trash of the house was put" and where Munday confesses that he "had rather have lain in the street amongst the beggars."[117] Eventually, the English students can stand Clynnog's treatment no more, and temporarily retreating to the private residence of Englishman, John Creed, they are summoned to the pope's chamber, where Gregory XIII resolves the issue by declaring, "I made the Hospital for Englishmen, and for their sake I have given so large exhibition, and not for the Welshmen. Return to your College again, you shall have what you will desire, and anything I have in the world to do you good."[118] Munday concludes by remarking, "thus was the strife ended, and myself and my fellow [Thomas Nowell] admitted by the pope's own consent to be scholars there."[119] Despite the lingering malady from which Munday claims he suffered as a result of his ill treatment at the hands of Clynnog, the pope had effectively resolved the ethnic infighting between the Welsh and English populations of the English College in a way that favorably redounded to Munday's situation within the college. More importantly, Munday's narrative of the student rebellion, like Persons's, occurs within the larger context of geopolitical tensions between Rome and England, in which English seminarians are presented as plotting to overthrow Queen Elizabeth and to "persecute" members of the Privy Council.[120] Munday presents himself as both complicit in the student rebellion at the English college and by equal measures innocent of their larger commitment to Elizabeth's overthrow, but the analogy between the two rebellions is still available to his readers.

---

[115] Hamilton, *Anthony Munday, and the Catholics*, 32–52.
[116] Munday, *English Roman Life*, 82.
[117] Munday, *English Roman Life*, 86–7.
[118] Munday, *English Roman Life*, 93.
[119] Munday, *English Roman Life*, 94.
[120] Munday, *English Roman Life*, 25.

Papal Supremacy and the Citizen of the World 71

As we will see in Chapter 2, Munday's later fictional works betray a related anxiety concerning the ability or inability to restrain or to correct a tyrannical temporal sovereign from the vantage of an imperial overseer. In this respect, Munday's "Catholic" account of these disputes at the English College ultimately seems to have had an influence on his fictional and non-fictional writings in ways that illustrate a desire for some secular equivalent to papal authority in England. Here I do not intend to argue that Munday was a secret ally of either the Catholic exiles or the conformist Catholic population in England—after all, he spent much of his adult life helping Richard Topcliffe capture and punish Catholic recusants.[121] Rather, I suggest that for Munday, the concept of papal supremacy, including the attendant deposing powers which the Roman curia claimed, held some attractions that were difficult to abandon entirely. As we shall see, much of Munday's fictional writings provide narrative spaces for imagining the benefits of independent and impartial authority figures—members of the Privy Council, nobles, bishops—that could serve as substitutes for papal authority within the new England.

Catholicism and the English Nation

Later disputes dividing the English Catholic community, such as the Archpriest controversy, bore some resemblance to the contours established during the controversy at the English college during the late 1570s.[122] They also help to contextualize broader tensions between nativist and cosmopolitan conceptions of English nationhood that were emerging during this period. In one respect, the Archpriest controversy, which began in 1597, was born of the need for a centralizing authority over the English mission. The death of Cardinal William Allen in 1594 had left the English Catholic cause without a strong unifying leader, and both the exile community and the secular priests in England desired that Catholics, both in England and on the continent, be unified under such an authority. As far back as 1579, the General of the Society of Jesus, Everard Mercurian, made fervent requests for a bishop to oversee the English mission. The secular priests favored the appointment of a bishop as well, but the Holy See had refused to appoint Catholic bishops to episcopacies held by Protestants. Resistance to appointing an English bishop to oversee the mission may well have been at the level of the pope himself, for whom the image of a beleaguered bishop traveling in disguise, fleeing from authorities, and hiding in priest holes, remained an offense to the sense of dignity inherent in the office.[123] In addition, the appointment of a bishop would have implied normalcy, and England was, in the eyes of Rome, a mission field,

---

[121] Hamilton, *Anthony Munday and the Catholics*, xxi.

[122] For a contemporary history of later controversies within the exiled Catholic community from an anti-Spanish perspective, see Sir Lewis Lewkner (?), *State of English Fugitives under the King of Spain and his ministers* (London, 1596). For background, see McCoog, *Society of Jesus 1589–1597*, 275–334.

[123] Basset, *The English Jesuits*, 90.

in which there could exist no episcopal hierarchy. The need for some form of centralizing authority over the mission eventually led to the compromise in 1598 of creating the unprecedented position of Archpriest, filled by George Blackwell. Although he was one of a number of figures responsible for this innovation, Robert Persons was accused by his enemies of personally devising the office, and Blackwell, sympathetic to the Jesuits, was accused of being Persons's man.[124] The controversy itself, which dragged on over the subsequent four years, began when a group of secular priests and Catholic laymen, henceforth known as the appellant party, sent William Bishop and Robert Charnock to Rome in October 1598 to appeal to Pope Clement VIII for redress over the appointment.[125]

According to the appellant party, the English Catholic Church had not been entirely eliminated as a functioning institution. The composition of the secular clergy, as it existed in both England and abroad, was essentially equivalent, even if existing in a diminished form, to the pre-Elizabethan Church, and the creation of the Archpriest to oversee the English mission amounted to the imposition of an unfamiliar and untraditional position of authority. In this respect, the appellant party's rejection of the Archpriest was part and parcel of a larger secular suspicion of the Jesuits, for just as the Jesuits themselves seemed to defy any traditional understanding of church hierarchy, the position of Archpriest did not fit into any existing order with which the seculars were familiar. From the perspective of the seculars, the proper place for the regulars (including the Jesuits) was the monastery, while the day-to-day affairs of the church belonged within the seculars' gamut. The Jesuits' headlong introduction of themselves into the public discussion of religion and politics by means of their printing houses in Flanders and France seemed to have obliterated this well-worn ecclesiastical division. Most alarming, the seculars saw some similarity between the Puritan critique of the traditional English Church and the Jesuit critique of the peculiar English Catholic customs of fasting and the traditional English liturgy, and in response they found in some Protestant "pseudo-bishops" such as Richard Bancroft an ally against both Puritans and Catholic "reformers."[126] The subsequent Archpriest controversy therefore may have had less to do with a dispute over bishops versus archpriests than with a larger controversy between on the one hand, those seculars who favored the traditional customs and hierarchical structure of the English Church and on the other, the cosmopolitan Jesuits and their admirers who were the main force behind the counter-reformation throughout Europe.[127]

---

[124]   Houliston, *Catholic Resistance*, 120; Basset, *The English Jesuits*, 90–91.

[125]   The appellant party consisted of priests and laymen, including Christopher Bagshaw, John Mush, Thomas Bluet, John Colleton, Anthony Copley, and William Watson, among others. See Houliston, *Catholic Resistance*, 121.

[126]   Bossy, *English Catholic Community*, 42–4.

[127]   Houliston, *Catholic Resistance*, 120. Despite the opposition which I make here between nativist traditionalists and transnational cosmopolitans, it is important to note that members of the appellant party based in England had their own transnational network that linked them to the continent. The editor of the *Wisbech Stirs*, Penelope Renold, shows

As we have seen in the previous section, during the years leading up to the English students' revolt of 1579, this fault-line was already emerging on the continent and especially within the English exile community in Rome between the Marian Catholic faction led by Clynnog and Owen Lewis and the reforming cosmopolitan faction led by Persons and Allen.[128] Earlier generations of historians generally accepted the view, expressed by W. Llewellyn Williams, that the Clynnog faction "believed only in the use of spiritual weapons," whereas the Allen-Persons faction favored confrontation and invasion.[129] In reality, however, Clynnog's faction was just as dedicated to military invasion as were their opponents. In 1575, Clynnog submitted to the pope a preliminary plan for an invasion of England, which was quickly followed by the submission of a competing invasion plan by Allen and Sir Francis Englefield. The following year, Clynnog submitted a second plan that seems to have been intended to counter various aspects of the Allen plan.[130]

The distinction between the ideological perspectives of the Persons faction and the Clynnog faction has an important bearing on each figure's conception of English nationhood, especially as the question of nationhood relates to papal supremacy. Clynnog's first plan for invasion (1575) was to have the invasion force proceed by way of entry into Wales, which Clynnog saw as a weakness in the Protestants' defense of the realm since, as he notes, the Welsh had largely preserved the ancient Roman Catholic faith.[131] This was in contrast to Allen and Englefield's subsequent invasion plan in which the invading force was to enter England by way of the borough of Liverpool.[132] Clynnog's perspective was driven by a historical narrative of immemorial Welsh Catholicism similar to the Galfridian pseudo-history that appeared in the writings of contemporary common law jurists such as Sir Edward Coke.[133] Clynnog describes Wales in the following terms:

---

that the appellant party in England was tied to a number of exiles in France and Rome, including the laymen Charles Paget and William Gifford, living in Paris and Flanders, and Hugh Griffin, who was the nephew of Morys Clynnog. The difference between the two perspectives is therefore based on political ideology rather than geography. See Penelope Renold (ed.), *The Wisbech Stirs, 1595–1598*, CRS 51 (London, 1958).

[128]   Persons, "A Storie," 64. See Bossy, *The English Catholic Community*, 25–34. For a comprehensive overview of the first faction, see Thomas H. Clancy, S.J., *Papist Pamphleteers: The Allen-Persons Party and the Political Thought of The Counter-Reformation in England, 1572–1615* (Chicago, 1964).

[129]   W. Llewellyn Williams, "Welsh Catholics on the Continent," *Transactions of the Honourable Society of Cymmrodorion* (London, 1903): 46–106, at 79.

[130]   Cleary, "Dr. Morys Clynnog's Invasion Projects," 300–322. For additional background, see Kenny, "From Hospice to College 1559–1579," 228–38.

[131]   Cleary, "Dr. Morys Clynnog's Invasion Projects," 307.

[132]   Cleary, "Dr. Morys Clynnog's Invasion Projects," 311.

[133]   This is a reference to the fact that Coke based his account of legal history in dubious sources such as Geoffrey of Monmouth's *Historia Regum Britanniae* in order to make his claim for the existence of an unbroken legacy of English legal customs going back to the ancient Britons. See Brian C. Lockey, *Law and Empire in English Renaissance Literature* (New York, 2006), 80–85.

74 *Early Modern Catholics, Royalists, and Cosmopolitans*

This region is nearly one-third of the kingdom of England: where scarcely a single man in a thousand will be found to be a heretic. The British people indeed is the original stock of that island, which to this day retains the ancient British language (which the English do not understand since they are of Saxon descent) and the ancient, the ancestral Catholic faith.[134]

Here Clynnog presents Wales's retention of its ancient Catholic identity as tied to its immemorial British character.[135] What is implicit in this passage is that subsequent conquests of the British Isles by the Saxon and Norman invaders introduced the seeds of heresy from which the English now suffer. In contrast to these outsiders, the original inhabitants of the island remain steadfast in their original pristine state.

Clynnog's position bears some resemblance to the account of Christianity's introduction into England favored by John Foxe and Richard Hooker, which Persons criticized at length in his massive *Treatise of Three Conversions of England*.[136] Similar to Clynnog's presentation of a pure British Catholicism that preceded the heretical corruptions introduced by the Saxons and Normans, for example, Foxe sees the pagan Saxon invaders as having managed almost to eradicate both native Christianity and the original Britons from the country, with the exception of those Britons that had fled to Wales.[137] But Foxe takes the argument further, suggesting that Christianity in Britain preceded any ecclesiastical allegiance to Rome. Foxe claims that, according to an ancient letter sent by Pope Eleutherius to the early British king, Lucius, Britain was already a Christian polity when Lucius asked Pope Eleutherius to assist him in setting up an ecclesiastical legal structure.[138] If this conception of Christianity's origins in ancient Britain were proved to be correct, an English sovereign, as holder of the supreme office that had originally initiated obedience to Rome, was now free to reclaim that ancient freedom from Rome. Thus according to Persons, Foxe sought to maintain that "Eleutherius conuerted not King Lucius at all: but onlie holp perhaps to conuert

---

[134] "Cambria tota (quam vulgo nunc Wallia vocant) quae regis est tertia fere pars regni Angliae: ubi vix inter mille vir unus inuenitur haereticus: Britannicus enim populus illius insulae indigena est, qui adhuc retinet, et priscam Britannorum linguam (quam Angli, ut ex Saxonia oriundi non intelligunt) et antiquam atque avitam quoque fidem catholicam." J.M. Cleary, "Dr. Morys Clynnog's Invasion Projects of 1575–76," 306; translation by J.M. Cleary.

[135] For background on the preservation of an ancient British Christianity in Wales, see Schwyzer, *Literature, Nationalism, and Memory*, 82–96.

[136] Persons, *A Treatise of Three Conuersions of England from Paganisme to Christian Religion*, 3 vols (St. Omer, 1603–4).

[137] John Foxe, *The Acts and Monuments*, vol. 1, 327–8.

[138] Persons, *A Treatise of Three Conversions*, vol. 1, F4; vol. 1, F5v. For background, see Houliston, *Catholic Resistance*, 101. For context on the early modern Protestant belief in the Christian character of ancient pre-papal Britain, see Schwyzer, *Literature, Nationalism, and Memory*, 81–5; Kerrigan, *Archipelagic English*, 121–6.

him, or to instruct him better in religion (being a Christian before)."[139] In doing so, Foxe wants to maintain that, from the very beginning, the King had prerogative over the form that the ecclesiastical polity would assume.

But Persons maintains that Foxe's account of Pope Eleutherius's missive to King Lucius is flawed because of Foxe's tendentious reading of the letter. If he had translated the original Latin version, his reader would never have doubted that even during the early period, the pope exercised supremacy over kings and temporal magistrates:

> And so he plaieth the Fox in euery thing. But, to returne againe to this latin title of the epistle, there is another cause, why Iohn Fox would not translate it into English. And this is, for that it is said therein that it was written by the Pope *ad correctionem Regis & Procerum regni, & c.* to correct the King, and nobility of the realme. Which proueth that the Pope tooke him self to be their Superiour also in those daies, and they to be subiect to his correction. For which causes Fox his schollers, *Holinshed, Hooker,* and *Harison* do leaue out this title altogeather in their chronicles.[140]

What emerges in the contrast between Persons and both his Protestant and Catholic opponents are two conceptions of the nation. Clynnog imagines a Catholic purity that has existed in Wales from the beginning of the Christian era or at least beyond any recorded memory. In the case of Foxe and his Protestant allies, a similar historical account of early Britain is used in order to make the case that claims for papal supremacy over England have no basis in ecclesiastical history.[141] In contrast, Persons champions the legacy of ancient imperial Rome, which, by conquering Britain, was understood to have introduced Christianity into the region. As a result, like Campion, Persons imagines a broadly transnational Christian commonwealth with the English realm as one province therein and the English sovereign as subordinate to papal oversight.[142] From Persons's perspective, having

---

[139]   Persons, *A Treatise of Three Conversions*, vol. 1, E8.

[140]   Persons, *A Treatise of Three Conversions*, vol. 1, F5v.

[141]   For the legal and political context here, see Glen Burgess, *The Politics of the Ancient Constitution: An Introduction to English Political Thought 1603–1642* (University Park, PA, 1992), 121–30; Brian Levack, *The Civil Lawyers in England, 1603–1641* (New York, 1973), 131–50; and Lockey, *Law and Empire*, 148–9, 163, 174–5.

[142]   Persons's notion of Britain's history is similar to that of the civil lawyers and supporters of Chancery during the early seventeenth century, who saw the English inheritance of the Roman *ius commune* as having been introduced by the Roman Empire. It is therefore no surprise to find Persons siding with the civil lawyers and attacking their bête noire, Sir Edward Coke, along similar lines in *An Answer to the Fifth Part of Reportes Lately set forth by Syr Edward Cooke*, which refuted Coke's argument that the jurisdiction of the ecclesiastical courts was subordinate to the English common law. Robert Persons, *An Answere to The Fifth Part of Reportes Lately set forth by Syr Edward Cooke, Knight, the Kinges Attorney generall* (St. Omer, 1606), B3v. See Sir Edward Coke, *The Selected Writings of Sir Edward Coke*, 3 vols, ed. Steve Sheppard (Indianapolis, IN, 2003), vol. 1, 125.

76   *Early Modern Catholics, Royalists, and Cosmopolitans*

the status of both conqueror and conquered is central to England's participation in the larger Catholic identity of the Christian commonwealth over which the pope and the Roman curia presides.

Legal historians have generally associated the notion of an unbroken legacy of British national and religious identity that we find here in Clynnog and Foxe with seventeenth-century common lawyers and Puritans, who were attempting to define the limits of the English sovereign's power on the basis of immemorial custom, which had supposedly preceded the prince's sovereignty.[143] As Clynnog's invasion plan shows, traditional Marian Catholics, who were trying to preserve their own customary outlook in the face of Jesuit reform and Protestant hegemony, believed similar myths about Britain's origins. So while the conceptions of English sovereignty and nationhood in Persons and Munday were similarly cosmopolitan, Foxe's and Clynnog's conceptions of nationhood were both based on an ideal of immemorial national purity, untrammeled by corrupting foreign invaders or institutions. Thus the widely-accepted scholarly account of the early modern ideological production of English nationhood, according to which two opposing religious conceptions of the nation existed—one Protestant and the other Catholic—is erroneous.[144] Conceptions of nationhood crossed confessional lines, and what emerges is an opposition between Catholic and Protestant cosmopolitans who saw England as an integral part of Christendom, or secular Europe, or continental affairs, and Catholic and Protestant adherents to the myth of English or British national purity.

Robert Persons's Self-Fashioning and the Papal Monarchy

I end this chapter with a discussion of how Persons fashioned English Catholic identity in relation to the larger Christian commonwealth and the papal monarchy, which oversaw that transnational polity. In one respect, Persons's strategies for

---

[143]   John Dykstra Eusden, *Puritans, Lawyers, and Politics in Early Seventeenth-Century England*, 2nd ed. (New York, 1968), 131–41. See Schwyzer, *Literature, Nationalism, and Memory*, 76–96; McEachern, *Poetics of English Nationhood*, 189–95; and Kerrigan, *Archipelagic English*, 23–4, 41, 391, 401.

[144]   See, for example, Richard Helgerson, *Forms of Nationhood*, 249–94, which uses Foxe's *Acts and Monuments* as well as Richard Hooker's *Laws of the Ecclesiastical Polity*, along with numerous secular works from the period, in order to illustrate the Elizabethan writing of the English nation. Helgerson claims that the most important event in such a writing was "the separation of the English church from the church of Rome" (251), a statement with which I would not necessarily disagree. My intention here is to show that an English conception of nationhood characterized as defined by a Protestant notion of the nation divorced from Catholicism and Catholic notions of nationhood is inaccurate. See also McEachern, *Poetics of English Nationhood*, 68, and Kerrigan, *Archipelagic English*, 121–59, for discussion of the crown's attempts to encourage religious conformity in early modern England. See Christopher Highley, *Catholics Writing the Nation in Early Modern Britain and Ireland*, for an alternative perspective.

Papal Supremacy and the Citizen of the World 77

fashioning a public Catholic identity in England resemble earlier New Historicist conceptions of early modern self-fashioning.[145] The pope governed a larger, more diffuse, less determinate realm than Queen Elizabeth, but Persons's voice is indelibly marked by a familiar attempt to imitate, ventriloquize, shape, and dialogue with the papal sovereign. In this respect, Persons's strategy for self-fashioning bears important resemblances to earlier scholarly accounts of the English subject similarly fashioning himself in relation to the English sovereign. In quite another respect, however, Persons fashions a hybrid identity that traverses the English Channel, combining continental cosmopolitanism with English-provincialism. In a comprehensive study of resistance theory in Persons's corpus, Victor Houliston notes that almost all of Persons's works were published anonymously or under pseudonyms.[146] From his first published title to his last, Persons continually published his works under an epistolary ruse in which a fictional exiled English Catholic writes a letter to his friend or acquaintance in England. His first published work, *A Brief Discours contayning certayne reasons why Catholiques refuse to goe to Church* (1580)—better known as *Reasons of Refusal*—was secretly written during Persons and Campion's mission to England and printed at the Greenstreet house of Robert Brookesby in East Ham.[147] Opening with an epistle dedicatory addressed to Queen Elizabeth, the work was signed with the pseudonym, "I. Howlet," a possible reference to fellow English Jesuit, John Howlet, as well as possibly a homonymic device intended to conjure up the phrase, "I howl it," in what Persons may have intended as a clever way to convey the author's desperate need to speak out on behalf of persecuted Catholics.[148]

Persons's presentation of the *Reasons for Refusal* relies on an elaborate fiction that would become a pattern for Persons's subsequent works. His pseudonymous identity, Howlet, explains in his dedicatory epistle that he thought it worth bringing attention to an anonymous letter written in exile "by a learned and vertuous man, to a frend of his in England."[149] In contrast to the learned and virtuous exile who composed the letter, the fictional editor, Howlet, signs the epistle as Queen Elizabeth's "most humble and obedient subiect" and seems to be intimately

---

[145]   The New Historicist account of early modern identity formation prominent in the work of Louis Montrose and Stephen Greenblatt views the English subject, especially writers of fiction and other forms of cultural production such as Sir Thomas More and Edmund Spenser, fashioning himself in relation to the sovereign's authority. See *Renaissance Self-Fashioning*, 168. See also Louis Adrian Montrose, "*A Midsummer Night's Dream* and the Shaping Fantasies of Elizabethan Culture," 65–87. For a discussion of how Persons fashioned himself as a Catholic writer, see Ronald Corthell, "Robert Persons and the Writer's Mission," in Arthur F. Marotti (ed.), *Catholicism and anti- Catholicism in Early Modern English Texts* (New York, 1999), 35–62.

[146]   Houliston, *Catholic Resistance*, 57–8. See also Peter Holmes, *Resistance and Compromise: The Political Thought of Elizabethan Catholics* (New York, 1982), 129–223.

[147]   Houliston, *Catholic Resistance*, 27–32.

[148]   Robert Persons, *A Brief Discours contayning certayne reasons why Catholiques refuse to goe to Church* (Doway [i.e. East Ham], 1580), ‡‡8v.

[149]   Persons, *A Brief Discours*, title page.

familiar with recent events in Elizabethan England, which he refers to as "this your Maiesties Realme."[150] In doing so, Persons's Howlet presents himself as the Queen's loyal subject, writing to her majesty not as an exile but from within the realm. But, in addition to presenting himself as Elizabeth's loyal subject, Howlet also invokes the transnational Christian commonwealth, of which England remains a province, arguing that "the common receaued religion of vniversal Christendome can not be soe soone abandoned by the disfauour of any one countrye, nor lacke men to speake or wryte in defence of the same, as longe as there is, ether head or hand remaining loose in the world." [151] For both Howlet, and the anonymous author of the letter itself, England's loyal Catholic subjects are inseparably linked to the continent by a common faith. The exiled anonymous author of the letter itself begins the body of the work in a manner that would become familiar to Persons's readers, by referring to a correspondence of letters between himself and a friend living in England. The author has viewed his friend's "late letters" about the pitiable state of the country, and out of solicitude for so many Catholic gentlemen who have recently been imprisoned by the crown, he is driven to write in defense of the typical Catholic recusant, whom he depicts as an obedient and loyal Englishman who chooses not to attend church for religious, not seditious, reasons.[152] He goes on to encourage other English Catholics to refuse attendance at the schismatic rite, even if the crown requires them to do so, claiming that those who have refused to fall away from the old religion (ironically) demonstrate their continuing fidelity to the crown.[153]

Persons's other early works were similarly premised upon the presentation of anonymous or pseudonymous letters. The body of Persons's *Copie of a Double Letter ... containing the true aduises of the cause, and maner of death, of one Richard Atkins, executed by Fire in Rome, the seconde of August 1581* consists of a letter "sent by an Englishe gentilman from beyond the seas, to his frende in London."[154] The first page of *The Copie of a Double Letter* displays the epistolary quality of the work: having received from his London friend an account of the

---

[150]   Persons, *A Brief Discours*, ‡3; ‡‡8v.

[151]   Persons, *A Brief Discours*, ‡2v.

[152]   Persons, *A Brief Discours*, A1.

[153]   Persons, A brief discourse, A2–A2v. Ultimately, of course, it is questionable whether Persons's efforts on behalf of English Catholics had any positive effect on the difficulties faced by actual Englishman who were determined to recuse themselves from the prescribed church attendance. And the extent to which Persons efforts may have prompted Puritan non-conformists like John Field, who famously ridiculed Persons's psuedonymic identity, I. Howlet, as a screech-owl in a widely-read refutation, to make temporary common cause with the official church indicates that Persons's efforts may have the opposite effect from which he had intended. See John Field, *A Caveat for Parsons Howlet, concerning his vntimely flighte, and schriching in the cleare daylighte of the Gospell, necessarie for him, and all the rest of that darke brood, and vncleane cage of papistes, who with their vntimely bookes, seeke the discredite of the trueth, and the disquiet of this Church of England* (London, 1581). Houliston, *Catholic Resistance*, 9.

[154]   Persons, *Copie of a Double Letter*, A2.

martyrdom of Father Everard Hanse, whom the English crown executed on July 30, 1581, the author promises to provide his own reliable account of the travails of Protestant Richard Atkins who was executed for heresy at roughly the same time in Rome.[155] Persons's *Relation of the King of Spaines Receiving in Valliodolid, and in the Inglish College of the same town, in August last past of this yere, 1592*, was "[w]ryten by an Inglish Priest of the same College, to a Gentleman and his wyf in Flaunders, latelie fled out of Ingland, for profession of the Catholique Religion."[156] Here again the author mentions a correspondence of letters, within which the current work must necessarily be contextualized.[157] Persons's *News from Spayne and Holland* (1593) is likewise "[w]ritten by a gentleman trauelour borne in the low countryes, and brought vp from a child in Ingland, vnto a gentleman his friend and ofte in London."[158] The epistolary nature of the work is crucial: in the dedication to the reader, the London friend, M.N., introduces the work by describing his happiness at having received missives from his friend concerning the affairs of Englishmen abroad in Spain and Holland.[159] The body of the work, in the form of an anonymous letter, is addressed "[t]o the right Woorshipfvl M.N. my Good Oste and Deare Frend Abiding in Graciouvs Streat in London."[160] Indeed, until the very end of his career, Persons continued to employ essentially the same epistolary structure. In 1608, he published *The Iudgment of a Catholicke English-man, living in banishment for his religion, Written to his priuate friend in England*. Once again, in the dedication to the reader, a private friend recalls his decision to publish a letter he has received "from my learned friend beyond the seas," and within the actual body of the work, the exiled author begins by thanking the private friend in England for sending him an anonymously-authored book, entitled *Triplici nodo, triplex cuneus, Or, An Apologie for the Oath of Allegiance* (authored by King James I himself), which the exiled author seeks to refute in his letter.[161] Throughout all of these tracts, Persons attempts to link English Catholics and England itself to the larger Christian commonwealth, illustrating that more complex strategies of self-fashioning persisted during this period.

In his account of the rise of the modern nation-state, Benedict Anderson points to three different forces that cohere in order to generate an "imagined community."[162] All three derive from the emergence of the vernacular print-languages that replaced

---

[155]   Persons, *Copie of a Double Letter*, A2.

[156]   Persons, *A Relation of the King of Spaines Receiving in Valliodolid, and in the Inglish College of the same towne* (Antwerp, 1592), title page.

[157]   Persons, *Relation of the King of Spaines*, A2.

[158]   Persons, *News from Spayne and Holland conteyning. An information of Inglish affayres in Spayne with a conference made thereuppon in Amsterdame of Holland* (Antwerp, 1593), title page.

[159]   Persons, *News from Spayne and Holland*, A2–A2v.

[160]   Persons, *News from Spayne and Holland*, A3.

[161]   Persons, *Iudgment of a Catholicke English-man, living in banishment for his religion, Written to his priuate friend in England* (St. Omer, 1608), 3.

[162]   Benedict Anderson, *Imagined Communities: Reflections on the Origin and Spread of Nationalism* (rev. ed; London, 1991).

the use of sacred Latin. First, the print-languages created "unified fields of exchange and communication" that existed between Latin and the spoken vernaculars, causing people to become aware of the hundreds of thousands and even millions of other users of their own particular uniform "language-field." Second, the emergence of a market for print provided a "new fixity to language," which overcame idiosyncratic and individual scribal habits. Finally, there emerged "languages-of-power" within each nation state that became associated with the bureaucratic and administrative management of the nation, pushing competing dialects and regional languages to the margins.[163] Whereas Anderson saw his "imagined communities" emerging during the eighteenth and nineteenth centuries with the advent of newsprint, Claire McEachern has drawn attention to the early modern English crown's analogous attempts at achieving religious and civic uniformity through the standard use of official religious texts such as *The Book of Common Prayer*.[164] What is remarkable about Persons's epistolary publications is the way in which his heterogeneous voice crosses the boundaries between on the one side, an emerging vernacular discourse of English nationhood, and on the other, print and manuscript ecclesiastical Latin, the emerging classical Latin of the humanists, administrative and epistolary Latin, the Italian and Spanish vernaculars of the Society of Jesus, and the competing vernacular print-languages of the continent, all of which Persons utilized at certain junctures of his career. Indeed, in one respect, Persons was adept at replicating and even positioning himself strategically within the "language-of-power" of the kingdom that had exiled him. His most influential work, *A Christian Directorie Guiding Men to their Salvation* (1585), was the most popular book of religious devotion published in English during the period—adopted, reprinted, and appreciated by Catholic and Protestant Englishmen and going through some 40 editions before 1640.[165] Ultimately the prose style of Persons's writings was appreciated by later writers, such as Jonathan Swift, who judged that "Parsons the Jesuit" was among the only writers of the period whose prose was still worth reading.[166] Thus, Persons's published works, so many of which assume the form of epistolary correspondence between English Catholics living abroad and those living in England, participate in the "print-language" that served also to establish the sense of national consciousness that McEachern and others have described in their work on the emergence of English nationhood.

---

[163] Benedict Anderson, *Imagined Communities*, 44–5.

[164] McEachern, *Poetics of English Nationhood*, 15–16. See also Kerrigan, *Archipelagic English*, 40.

[165] Persons, *The Christian Directory (1582): The First Booke of the Christian Exercise, Appertayning to Resolution*, ed. Victor Houliston (Boston, 1998), xi. Houliston organizes these editions into five stages of composition, adaptation and revision: the original 1582 Rouen edition entitled, *The first booke of the Christian exercise*; Edmund Bunny's "Protestant" version of 1584, published in London; Persons's 1585 Rouen edition and the 1598 reprint; The 1607 St. Omer edition; and finally, the 1622 edition (xxii–xxxii).

[166] Swift, *The Tatler*, no. 230: in Jonathan Swift, *Prose Works*, ed. Herbert Davis et al. (14 vols, Oxford, 1939–68), vol. 2, 177.

Papal Supremacy and the Citizen of the World 81

In quite another respect, however, other epistolary works written and published by Persons in Latin and in continental vernacular languages gesture in other directions that ultimately serve to critique that emerging national consciousness. And in contrast to Anderson's chronology whereby the sacred language of Latin is replaced by disparate vernacular print cultures, Persons's cosmopolitan critique of English nationhood does not so much constitute a last gasp of the old Medieval linguistic order as it does a modern international and polyglot field of translation and hybridity. In fact, it is worth emphasizing that whatever cognizance that Europeans obtained concerning events in England during the last decades of the sixteenth century came primarily from the published writings of figures like Persons and Allen and their fellow exiles, or alternatively figures such as Diego de Yepes whose *Historia Particular de la Persecucion de Inglaterra* (1599) shows that he was in close contact with them.[167] Persons's writings in Latin were meant to represent the English Catholic perspective to receptive continental audiences, and like his English writings during this period, they were often conveyed in epistolary form. The most widely-read of these works, *De persecvtione Anglicana*, containing accounts of English Catholic martyrdom, was presented as an extended missive from Persons himself to fellow English Jesuit John Gerard, then living in Bologna.[168] Shortly after its publication in 1581 at Persons's press in Rouen, this work was translated into French, English, Italian, and German.[169] Later Persons

---

[167] Diego de Yepes, *Historia particular de la persecucion de Inglaterra, y de los martirios mas insignes que en ella ha auido, desde el año del Señor. 1570* (Madrid, 1599). See also William Allen, *Historia del glorioso martirio di sedici sacerdoti Martirizati in Inghilterra per la confessione, & difesa della fede Catolica, l'anno 1581, 1582, & 1583: con vna prefatione, che dichiara la loro innocenza, composta da quelli, che co[n] essi praticauano mentre erano viui, & si trouorno presenti al lor giuditio, & morte. Tradotta di lingua Inglese in Italiana da vno del Collegio Inglese di Roma. S'è aggiunto il martirio di due altre Sacerdoti, & vno secolare Inglesi, martirizati l'anno 1577 & 1578* (Macerata, 1583).

[168] *De persecvtione Anglicana commentariolvs, a collegio anglicano romano, hoc anno Domini cIɔ. Iɔ xxcii. In Vrbe editus, & iam denuo Ingolstadii escusus: Additis Literis S.D.N.D. Gregoris Papae XIII. Hortatoriis ad subueniendum Anglis, & c.* (Ingolstadt, 1582), A5. It is important to note that, during the 1580s and 1590s, Persons did not himself publish accounts of persecution in English, perhaps in order to avoid inflaming the situation in England for English recusants. See McCoog, S.J., "Construing Martyrdom in the English Catholic Community 1582–1602," in Ethan H. Shagan (ed.), *Catholics and the 'Protestant Nation': Religious Politics and Identity in Early Modern England* (Manchester, 2005), 95–127.

[169] Persons, *De persecutione Anglicana, epistola. Qua explicantur afflictiones, aerumnae, & calamitates grauissimae, cruciatus etiam & tormenta, & acerbissima martyria, quae Catholici nunc Angli, ob fidem patiuntur* (Rouen, 1581) [French translation by Matthieu de Launoy; Paris: Thomas Brumen, 1582. English translation of the French translation, entitled *An epistle of the persecution of Catholickes in Englande*, trans. G.T.; Rouen: Fr. Persons Press, 1582. Italian translation, translator unidentified; Bologna: Alessandro Benacci, 1582. German translation by Johann Christof Hueber; Ingolstadt: David Sartorius, 1583.] See Houliston, *Catholic Resistance*, 195.

published the *Relacion de Algunos Martyrios, que de nueuo han hecho los hereges en Inglaterra, y de otras cosas tocantes a nuestra santa y Catolica religion* in Madrid, containing his own Spanish translation of an English letter "from a priest written in London from England, on the twenty-second of December, 1588," recounting "the martyrdoms that the heretics gave to some Catholics, after the Spanish Armada passed through those parts." In addition, the *Relacion* contained Persons's translation of a letter from Nicholas Sander's sister, Isabel, of the Bridgettine order of nuns, to an anonymous English gentleman living in Madrid (probably Sir Francis Engelfield), in which she provided an account of the order's expulsion from England in 1559.[170] Finally, his *Relation of the King of Spaines Receiving in Valliodolid* (1592), itself an epistolary work purporting to be based on a letter from an English priest living in Madrid to an Englishman in Flanders, was translated back into Spanish under Persons's supervision (1592).[171] Two other Latin titles were authored by Persons and not translated into any vernacular, the most famous of which was the *Elizabethae Angliae Reginae haeresim Calvinianum propugnantis* (1592). Published under the pseudonym Andreas Philopater, the *Elizabethae Angliae Reginae haeresim* employs an adopted identity, Philopater, as a way of allowing Persons to signal to his readers his love for God and the Holy Father, the pope, but also his continuing commitment to his ancestors and the fatherland.[172] Like his other non-English works, Persons's Philopater therefore gestures toward an awareness of national identity at the same time that it gestures in the opposite direction, toward a transnational Christian commonwealth consisting of Spanish, Italian, French, German, and Dutch interlocutors. Finally, Persons's unpublished memoirs were composed partly in English, Latin, and Italian and his vast correspondences within the network of Jesuits and his contacts among the English exiles and missionaries were written in Latin, Italian, English, and Spanish.[173]

Persons's English publications must therefore be viewed within the larger context of the administrative epistolary writings, composed in diverse ancient and vernacular languages of which Persons had mastery, as well as those non-English publications, through which Persons was able to present England and its affairs to

---

[170] "Carta de vn Sacerdote escrita en Londres de Inglaterra, a veintidos de Diziembre. 1588. de los martyrios que los hereges dieron a algunos Catolicos, despues que la armada de España passo por aquellas partes." Person, *Relacion de Algunos Martyrios, que de nueuo han hecho los hereges en Inglaterra, y de otras cosas tocantes a nuestra santa y Catolica religion. Traduzida de Ingles en Castellano, por el padre Roberto Personio, etc.* (Madrid, 1590), my translation. B, F2.

[171] Persons, *Relacion de un sacerdote ingles, escrita a Flandes, à un cauallero de su tierra desterrado por ser catolico: en el qual le da cuenta de la venida de su magestad a Valladolid y al colegio de los ingleses y lo que alli se hizo en su recebimiento/traduzida de ingles en castellano por Tomas Eclesal* (Madrid, 1592).

[172] Persons, *Elizabethae Angliae Reginae haeresim Calvinianam propvgnantis, saevissimum in Cathlicos sui regni edictum ... Cum responsione ad singula capita* (Antwerp, 1592). The other work was the *Quaestiones duae de sacris alienis non aduendis, ad vsum praximque Angliae breuiter explicatae* (St. Omer, 1607).

[173] Persons, "A Storie"; *Letters and Memorials of Father Robert Persons, S.J.*, vol. 1.

the rest of Europe. In general, his epistolary publications were intended to convey the existence of a deep level of engagement, in the form of letter-writing, between English Catholics living in England and their counterparts among the exile community on the continent. Persons's printed array of pseudo-anonymous exiled English letter-writers, providing news and information about the state of English and Continental Catholicism, would have suggested to readers the existence of a larger interested polyglot community, whose numbers were impossible to quantify. To the extent that Persons was pointing to this epistolary community, within which he himself was a central figure, consisting of members of the Society of Jesus, seminarians and missionaries, and secular Catholics both in England and abroad, he was pointing at a shifting and uncertain reality, but a reality nonetheless. The archival evidence shows that the Catholic community produced a vast quantity of correspondence about the situation in England, having produced hundreds, if not thousands, of pages of letters before the turn of the century.[174] The printed version of these letters, as a reflection of that mostly secret correspondence, suggests that the boundaries of the official vernacular print-culture were more porous and dynamic than Anderson's account suggests. And to the extent that Persons and other English Jesuits were writing, both in their printed and unprinted writings, for so many disparate and competing religious bureaucracies, national communities, and secular and religious authorities, their republic of letters becomes at once broader than the vernacular print-culture of the nation-state and simultaneously narrower in scale than the national print culture that was emerging in England. Ultimately, Jesuit memorials of martyrdom and necrologies even cross the boundaries between manuscript and print by combining the authenticity of letter writing with the permanence of the printed record (see Figure 1.3).[175]

---

[174]　The letters of early English Jesuits are a good example of this Catholic republic of letters. They can be found primarily at three archives: the Archivum Romanum Societatis Jesu (ARSI) in Rome, the Archives of the British Province of the Society of Jesus at Farm Street, London, and the Venerable English College, Rome. There are other letters archived at the Vatican. The following is an incomplete estimate of their numbers. In an unpublished survey of the letters of the British Province when they were still housed at Stonyhurst College, Thomas McCoog has numbered the contents of Anglia I, II (pre-1600), now housed at the Archives of the British Province, at 150 letters, and the contents of Anglia III, IV (pre-1641) at 241 letters. Mauro Brunello of ARSI numbers the contents of Fondo Gesuitico 651, Anglia 7, and Anglia 8 (housed at the Archivum Romanum) at 260 letters. Many of the letters have been published: Leo Hicks, S.J. (ed.), *Letters and Memorials of Father Robert Persons, S.J.*, vol. 1 (to 1588); Jessop, Augustus, *Letters of Father Henry Walpole, S.J.* (Norwich, 1873); Thomas Francis Knox, (ed.), *The Letters and Memorials of William Cardinal Allen (1532–1594)* (London, 1882); Renold (ed.), *Letters of William Allen and Richard Barret 1572–1598* (London, 1967). I would like to thank Thomas McCoog, S.J., and Mauro Brunello for their assistance.

[175]　For a comprehensive discussion of the textual and visual presentation of Catholic martyrdom during the period, see Anne Dillon, *The Construction of Martyrdom in the English Catholic Community, 1535–1603* (Burlington, VT, 2002), esp. 114–69.

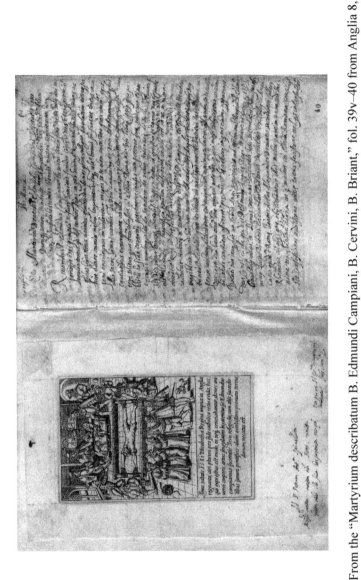

Fig. 1.3 From the "Martyrium describatum B. Edmundi Campiani, B. Cervini, B. Briant," fol. 39v–40 from Anglia 8, Archivum Romanum Societatis Iesu. Numerous epistolary and printed accounts of Campion's exemplary martyrdom circulated throughout the exiled English Catholic community. A few letters from the period included the woodcut printed image above, which resembled images from Niccolò Circignani, *Ecclesiae Anglicanae Trophaea sive Sanctor Martyrum* (Rome 1584), and [R. Verstegen], *Praesentis Ecclesiae Anglicanae Typus* (Reims, 1582), a book of woodcut images often appended to Persons's *De persecutione anglicana*. By permission of the Society of Jesus.

It is certainly tempting to consign this writing community, as Anderson does for non-print culture, to the pre-modern, to the Medieval, but as Friedrich has shown in great detail, Jesuit practices of letter writing were a particularly modern phenomenon, allowing the Society to centralize and organize monarchically in imitation of state bureaucracies. Certainly one way of understanding the printing of Persons's fictional correspondence between anonymous English priests and laymen on the continent and Englishmen living in England was as part of a conscious attempt to have this very real republic of letters, with which Persons was intimately familiar, enter into the public domain. In the end, the publication of Persons's fictional or real epistolary correspondences potentially broadens the context within which the Englishman fashioned his identity—Persons's presentation of the English Catholic subject gains legitimacy not only through his "loyal" relationship with the crown but also by means of his relationship with papal claims for supremacy over the ecclesiastical realm and the power to depose heretical, tyrannical, or sinful sovereigns.

In at least one case, the famous and widely-read *Conference about the Next Succession*, Persons's own voice is dispersed among a number of different dialogic perspectives, which constitute a community that is both transnational and transreligious.[176] Before considering relevant passages from the *Conference*, it is important to note the significance of the pseudonym, R. Doleman, which Persons used in its publication. Critics have noted that the name R. Doleman has a number of linked significances for Persons. Doleman may describe the doleful, melancholy voice of the English Catholic exile, which is invoked in the first chapter of the work. Alternatively, some secular priests in the appellant party were offended that Persons may have intended a reference to the revered Marian priest, Alban Doleman, who had remained in England after the Reformation to minister to English Catholics.[177] Of course these two possibilities do not exclude a third, namely that the combination of Persons's first name, Robert [R.], and the Marian priest's surname, Doleman, created a hybridization of the Catholic recusant in England and the exile abroad in the same way that the pseudonym *Philopater* suggested such a hybrid identity.

This influential work, in the edition printed in Antwerp, was dedicated to Robert Devereux, Earl of Essex, whom Persons seems to have thought might

---

[176]   R. Doleman [psuedo.], *A Conference about the next succession to the crowne of Ingland, diuided into two partes. Where-of the first conteyneth the discourse of a ciuill Lawyer, how and in what manner propinquity of blood is to be preferred. And the second the speech of a temporall lawyer, about the particuler titles of all such as do or may pretende within Ingland or without, to the next succession* (Antwerp, 1594 [vere 1595]). For context, see Michael L. Carrafiello, *Robert Parsons and English Catholicism, 1580–1610* (Cranbury, NJ, 1998), 33–55. For discussion of the authorship of *A Conference*, see Houliston, *Catholic Resistance*, 72–3, and Leo Hicks, "Father Robert Persons, S. J. and *The Book of Succession*," *Recusant History* 4 (1957): 104–37. I agree with Houliston that Persons was the main if not the sole author of the work.

[177]   Houliston, *Catholic Resistance*, 125.

favor the recusants if he succeeded to the throne. In Elizabeth's court, however, the dedication caused Devereux only embarrassment.[178] Persons seems to have perceived both that Essex was in the ascendant within Elizabeth's court and that he was the most outward looking of her favorites. In his rivalry with William Cecil, Lord Burghley, and Lord Burghley's son Robert, Essex was attempting to position himself as the Queen's dominant councilor on matters of foreign policy, using his expanded secretariat to set up an extensive network of intelligencers and foreign correspondences. He saw himself as bringing the English crown closer to European affairs and playing a greater role on what his close confidant, Sir Henry Unton, later called "the stage of Christendome."[179] What might have interested Persons more than anything else were signs that Essex sought to establish greater toleration for English Catholics, as long as they opposed Spain and its influence over the papacy.[180] In his dedication to Essex, in which Persons reveals "that my particuler obligation towards your honours person, riseth partly of good turnes and benefites receaued by some friendes of myne at your Lordships handes, in your last voyage and exploits in France," Persons seems to be claiming that certain individuals within the exile community were part of Essex's network of intelligencers and foreign contacts. He goes on to reveal to Essex that "the two bookes ensuing ... conteyne a conference had in Holland not long since," in which the topic of succession to the English throne was discussed at some length.[181] The Preface describes the interlocutors that took part in this conference:

> Ther chaunced not long ago (I meane in the monthes of Aprill and May of this last yeare 93.) to mete in Amsterdam in Holland, certayne Gentlemen of diuers nations, qualities and affections, as wel in religion as otherwise: (yet the most part Inglish and Irish) and they had bine in diuers countries, studied different artes, and followed vnlike professions: some of souldiars, some of lawyers both temporal and ciuil, others of meere trauelors to learn experience and pollicy: And for that the aduises which dayly came from Ingland at that tyme, (the parlament being then in hand) gaue occasion to discourse of Inglish affaires, they fell into diuers poyntes concerning the same: but yet none was treated so largly or so seriously, as was the matter of succession and competitors to the crowne, for

---

[178] Houliston, *Catholic Resistance*, 76. According to McCoog, however, Essex did in fact provide patronage to Jesuit Thomas Wright, who had argued that English Catholics should support the Queen against a Spanish invasion. See McCoog, *Society of Jesus 1589–1597*, 277–8.

[179] In a speech to parliament in 1593, Unton was describing the continent as "the stage of Christendome wherin all nacions seeke to play their tragicall partes." See Public Record Office, State Papers 12.244, fo. l65v [copy of Unton's speech March 24, 1593]; British Library, Cotton MSS, Caligula E IX(i), fo. 171 Unton to Thomas Edmondes, May 17, 1593. According to Paul Hammer, Essex himself frequently referred to Christendom in his writings. See Hammer, "Essex and Europe: Evidence from Confidential Instructions by the Earl of Essex, 1595–6," *EHR* 111 (1996): 357–81, esp. 368–9.

[180] See Hammer, *The Polarization of Elizabethan Politics: The Political Career of Robert Devereux, 2nd Earl of Essex, 1585–1597* (New York, 1999), 178.

[181] Persons, *A Conference*, 2.

that it was presumed a great while, that some thing would be determined thereof in that parlament, though one or two of the wisest of that company, held euer the contrary opinion. But when at length newes was brought, that nothing at al had bin done therin, but rather that one or two (as was reported) had bin checked or committed for speaking in the same: then came it in question among thes Gentlemen, what should be the causes of such proceding in a matter so waighty and so necessary for al Inglish men to know?[182]

In this significant passage, Persons reveals that the conference participants comprised "Gentlemen of divers nations" and of a diverse array of religious faiths and professions, whose primary focus was to "discourse of English affairs." Foremost in their collective mind was the "matter of succession and competitors to the Crown," and given news received that parliament has effectively prohibited discussion about and planning for the future sovereign, it falls to what is essentially a parliament-in-exile to broach this important discussion. One notes once again the familiar way in which Persons enjoys imagining Englishmen in dialogue with interlocutors from other European countries.

Most significantly, it is this transnational dialogue that generates Persons's famous perspective on the right of beleaguered subjects to resist the sovereign's rule. The book proceeds principally by way of a dialogue between a civil lawyer and a common lawyer, interrupted infrequently by another interlocutor from the conference. The first part of *A Conference* proves that kings do not rule by blood alone but rather that they must at least begin their rule with the consent of those they govern, while the second part reviews the legitimacy of various claimants to the English throne. A few paragraphs into the preface, the civil lawyer explains, by way of analogy with the election of the pope in Rome, that whoever succeeds to the English throne will inevitably proceed at least partially by the consent of his or her subjects: "*Your succession, said the Ciuilian, includeth also an election or approbation of the common wealth, and so doth the succession of al kings in Christendome besides, as wel appeareth by the manner of their new admission at their coronations, wher the people are demaunded agayne,* if they be content to accept such a man for their King: *thoughe his title of neernes by blood, be neuer so cleere.*"[183] What the civilian lawyer explains here and in greater detail later in the third, fourth, and fifth chapters of the first part is that consent by the subjects of the realm is actually built into the coronation ceremony itself.

But, as other commentators have noted, within Persons account of the sovereign's ascension, neither the people nor their representatives provide their direct approval to the heir who seeks to ascend to the throne. Rather, it is either the archbishop or the bishop who presides over the coronation ceremony and whose authority ultimately reflects the will of the people.[184] To be sure, within the first part of *A Conference*, the episcopate assumes a role as caretaker or custodian of the people that overshadows any assumed by the parliament. In this respect, Houliston is certainly correct to

---

[182]   Persons, *A Conference*, B–Bv.
[183]   Persons, *A Conference*, B4.
[184]   Houliston, *Catholic Resistance*, 85.

88   *Early Modern Catholics, Royalists, and Cosmopolitans*

point to Francisco Suárez as the theorist who most lucidly described the relationship between the will of the people and the will of God, even if his *De legibus ac deo legislatore* followed Persons's *Conference* by more than a decade and a half. Like most political theorists of the period, Suárez's contractual theory of the state is based on an analogy with the family. Within the context of the family, the proximate cause of the husband or father's authority is the marriage contract or the wife's consent while the ultimate cause of his authority is "the Author of nature Himself" or God.[185] Like Suárez, Persons continually draws on the marriage analogy in order to describe the contract between on the one side, the heir to the throne or the sovereign and on the other side, the commonwealth or the people.[186] For both Persons and Suárez, the sovereign is bound by a contract with the people, but the immutable substance and contours of this contract are determined by God Himself.[187]

For Persons, the will of the people and the will of God converge in the coronation ceremony and in particular in the oath that the sovereign must make before a representative of the church. Before recounting significant examples of coronation ceremonies of kings throughout history, the civil lawyer describes the general importance of the oath that the sovereign takes at the beginning of his reign:

> [I]n all good and wel ordered common wealthes, wher matters passe by reason, conscience, wisdom and consultation, and especially since christian religion hath preuailed, & giuen perfection to that natural light, which morall good men had before in matters of gouernment: since that tyme (I say) this point of mutual and reciprocal othes betweene Princes and subiects, at the day of ther coronation or admission (for al are not crowned) have bin much more established, made cleare and put in vre. And this forme of agreement and conuention, betwene the common wealth and their christian head or king, hath bin reduced to a more sacred and religious kind of vnion and concord, then before, for that the whole action hath bin donn by Bishopes and ecclesiastical Prelats, and the astipulation and promises made on both sides, haue passed and bin giuen, receaued and regestred with great reuerence in sacred places, and with great solemnity of religious ceremonies, which before were not so much vsed, though alwayes there weare some. And therefore our examples at this tyme shalbe only of christian common wealthes, for that they are more peculiarly to our purpose as you wil confesse.[188]

For Persons, the coronation ceremony is essentially a marriage between prince and subject, in which, in the midst of a religious ceremony, an archbishop, a

---

[185]   Francisco Suárez, *De legibus, ac Deo legislatore*, III iii 2, in *Selections from Three Works of Francisco Suárez*, ed. James Brown Scott, 2 vols (Oxford, 1944) vol. 1, 204, col. A and vol. 2, 378. See also Houliston, *Catholic Resistance*, 84.

[186]   Persons, *A Conference*, K7v–K8.

[187]   For a related discussion of what a Catholic subject was obligated to do when governed by an excommunicated sovereign, see *Cardinal Allen's defence of Sir William Stanley's surrender of Deventer, January 29, 1586–7*, ed. Thomas Heywood (Manchester, 1851), 22–33. Allen saw Elizabeth, after having been excommunicated, as having no right to declare war, and therefore, her Catholic soldiers, like Sir William Stanley, were obligated to disobey her.

[188]   Persons, *A Conference*, G7–G7v.

bishop or another representative of the church places the burden of conscience on the sovereign.

The subject of the papal power of deposition is not directly at issue in *A Conference*. Nevertheless, it is invoked a number of times in this complex, multifaceted work. The third chapter, entitled "Kings lawfully chastised by their common wealthes for their misgouernment," and the fourth entitled "the lawfvlness of proceeding agaynst Princes which in the former chapter is mentioned," include four historical examples in which the pope either authorized or confirmed the deposition of a lawful sovereign, one additional example in which an archbishop did so, and the example of the Holy Roman Emperor, whose election, Persons explains, is regularly presided over by the pope.[189] The first example, that of Pope Leo III's deposition of the tyrannical Empress Irene of the Eastern Roman Empire in order to crown Charlemagne as the emperor of a revived Western Empire, is the template on which all other such depositions are based. From Persons perspective, Leo deposed Empress Irene because she was a tyrant who had deposed her son, the rightful emperor, and not, as is understood by historians today, because Leo had his own enemies in Rome and saw the Eastern throne as vacant in that it lacked a male occupant.[190] The people and their direct representatives seemingly have no stake in Persons's example of Pope Leo's deposition of the Empress Irene, but in subsequent examples such as the case of Sancho II of Portugal, the deposition occurs at the people's instigation and is subsequently confirmed by the pope:

> This *Don Sancho*, after he had raigned 34. yeares, was depriued for his defects in gouernment by the vniuersal consent of al Portugal; & this his first depriuation from al kingly rule and authority (leauing him only the bare name of King) was approued by a general councel in Lions, pope Innocentius the 4. being ther present, who at the petition & instance of the whole realme, of Portugal by their Embassadors the Archbishop of *Braga*, bishop of Coimbra, and diuers of the nobility sent to Lyons for that purpose, did authorize the saide state of Portugal, to put in supreme gouernment one, *Don Alonso*, brother to the said king *Don Sancho*.[191]

According to Persons, Sancho had ruled successfully for more than 30 years, finally having been deposed by his subjects and the Thirteenth General Ecumenical Council of the Church (1245), over which Pope Innocent IV presided.[192] This is presumably the historical exemplum that Persons imagined should ideally occur

---

[189]   Persons, *A Conference*, D8–F5.

[190]   Persons, *A Conference*, E5–E5v.

[191]   Persons, *A Conference*, E8.

[192]   Perhaps because of the controversy associated with it, Persons omits to mention Pope Innocent IV's more famous and contested excommunication and deposition (1245) of the Holy Roman Emperor, Frederick II, at the same Ecumenical Council at Lyon. In fact, he would discuss Innocent IV's deposition of Frederick II in a later work, *A Discussion of the Answere of M. William Barlow, D. of Divinity, to the Booke intituled: The Judgment of a Catholicke Englishman* (St. Omer, 1612), Mmm3–Qqq4, in a section focusing not on depositions but rather on "contentions" between popes and emperors.

with regard to Elizabeth, especially with there being no prospect of an heir by blood relation.

There are at least two conclusions that can be drawn from the way in which I have attempted to situate Persons's groundbreaking work on Catholic resistance within the context of contemporary notions of cosmopolitanism and the papal deposing power. Returning to the preface of Persons's book, one should recall that Persons's conference occurs abroad in Holland and comprises Englishmen, Irishmen, and individuals from other realms.[193] In this respect, it might be compared to the General Council of Lyon, which deposed Sancho II; the main difference being that whereas the General Council was presided over by the pope, the gathering in Holland is a secular conference, presided over primarily by lawyers, who are merely exploring potential heirs to the throne and implicitly suggesting the possibility of deposing Queen Elizabeth. But despite the differences, the comparison is instructive: for the members of the conference, as for Persons himself, there is no question but that the pope has the right to depose tyrannical or abusive sovereigns. Indeed, Persons suggests that the papal right to depose a sovereign for misgovernment is supported by a broad and diverse collection of Europeans, including Elizabeth's English and Irish subjects. The civil lawyer, as the inheritor of Justinian's *Corpus Juris Civilis*, the Roman civil law, which constituted the historical basis of the systems of law practiced on the continent and in England's civilian courts, is likewise representative of the larger transnational cosmopolitanism that figures such as Persons were bringing to bear on Queen Elizabeth's rule.

What is remarkable about Persons's *Conference* is that, regardless of its investment in the papal deposing power, it was used repeatedly during the seventeenth century by parliamentarians to justify forcible removal of a legitimate sovereign. As we will see in the Introduction to Part II of this book, during the civil war, selections from Persons's *Conference* were republished as *Severall speeches delivered at a conference concerning the power of Parliament, to proceed against their King for misgovernment* (1648) in order justify parliament's deposition of Charles I, and later in 1681, Algernon Sidney even reprinted the *Conference* in order to justify excluding the Roman Catholic James II from the throne.[194] In this respect, the forces that were causing national consciousness to emerge and to invest parliament with a national identity as a representative body of the people were eventually able to occlude the *Conference*'s international appeal. But as we

---

[193] Persons, *A Conference*, B.

[194] *Severall speeches delivered at a conference concerning the power of Parliament, to proceed against their King for misgovernment* (London, 1648); R. Doleman, *A conference about the next succession to the crown of England divided into two parts* (London, 1681). See also *A Treatise concerning the broken succesion of the crown of England: inculcated, about the later end of the Reign of Queen Elisabeth. Not impertinent for the better compleating of the general information intended* (London, 1655). For perspective, see J.B. Williams [vere J.G. Muddiman], "Puritan Piracies of Father Persons' 'Conference,'" *The Month* 117 (1911): 270–78, and Houliston, *Catholic Resistance*, 85.

will see in the next chapter, this was not the case during the sixteenth century. In fact, what we find in fictional works from Anthony Munday, Sir John Harington, Sir Philip Sidney, Edmund Spenser, and George Peele is that there remained a great deal of concern around the prospect of a sovereign without the potential oversight of an imperial overseer. Ultimately, we see again and again in these writers an appeal to an imagined secular equivalent of the cosmopolitan priestly class as a guarantor of right and legitimate governance.

Chapter 2
Border-Crossing and Translation: The Cosmopolitics of Edmund Campion, S.J., Anthony Munday, and Sir John Harington

Edmund Campion's *Ambrosia* and Spiritual Supremacy

During his stay at Prague from 1574 to 1580, Edmund Campion completed three neo-Latin dramatic works, which were performed at the Clementina, the Jesuit academy where he served as a professor of rhetoric. Campion's *Ambrosia*, a play about the life of St. Ambrose first performed at the Jesuit academy in 1578, explores the issue of ecclesiastical supremacy in a way that serves as a lens through which one can better understand how Catholic exiles generally understood the relationship between temporal and spiritual magistrates.[1] It also provides some perspective on Campion's cosmopolitan perspective in the *Decem rationes*, which I have explored at the beginning of Chapter 1. Before considering how Campion's drama approaches the issue of supremacy, however, it is worth describing the contours of the events depicted within the play. The events begin in 386 CE, with tensions breaking out between Empress Justina, who ruled the Italian and African sphere of the Roman empire, and Bishop Ambrose of Milan. Empress Justina, whose court was based in Milan, was a champion of Arianism, which Bishop Ambrose and the church considered a heresy.[2]

As we shall see, the parallel between the Catholic perspective on Empress Justina and on Queen Elizabeth is clear from the outset.[3] In the opening speech of the play, Empress Justina complains that while she is "ruler over an empire [*regni potens*] that covers all Hesperia and the western region," she is still harassed by meddling church officials like Ambrose.[4] She declares that, for his part, Ambrose,

---

[1]   Allison Shell, "'We are Made a Spectacle': Campion's Dramas," in *The Reckoned Expense: Edmund Campion and the Early English Jesuits*, ed. Thomas McCoog (Rome, 2007), 119–38. For a general discussion of Jesuit dramatic works, see William H. McCabe, S.J., *An Introduction to the Jesuit Theater* (St. Louis, 1983). See also Gerard Kilroy, *Edmund Campion: Memory and Transcription* (Burlington, VT, 2005), 6–7, 46, 144.

[2]   For background on Ambrose's doctrine of church and state, see Claudio Morina, *Chiesa e Stato nella Dottrina di S. Ambrogio* (Roma, 1963).

[3]   Shell, "'We are Made a Spectacle,'" 125.

[4]   "regni potens / Hesperia quantum et occiduus axis vident." Edmund Campion, *Ambrosia: A Neo-Latin Drama*, ed. and trans. Joseph Simons (Assen, 1970), 1–2, 6–7. All citations are to the line numbers in Simons's edition of *Ambrosia*.

"sitting on his bishop's throne, … exposes himself to the threats of the sovereign by thundering his anathema against our doctrines."[5] In the scenes that follow, Justina's imperial soldiers lay siege to the Basilica in order to arrest Ambrose and his followers, who together are presented as singing joyous hymns as they prepare to die with their bishop.[6] Subsequently, Ambrose gives a sermon in which he recounts a dream in which God revealed the hidden location of the burial place of Gervasius and Protasius, two martyrs who were persecuted during the reign of Emperor Nero. Finally, the invading soldiers are persuaded of the truth of Ambrose's orthodox teachings when he performs two miracles, the "casting out" of a devil from a possessed man and the curing of a blind man.[7] The entire conflict, in which Bishop Ambrose, as an ecclesiastical authority, is presented as independent from the sources of power within the empire obviously implies a critique of contemporary Protestant realms, where religious authorities were dependent upon temporal magistrates for their authority.

The conflict between the temporal and the ecclesiastical realms comes to a head during the latter half of the play, during Ambrose's climactic dispute with the eastern Emperor Theodosius. Bishop Ambrose's triumph over the heretical Empress Justina is followed by an invasion by the usurper Clemens Maximus, causing Justina and her son Valentinian to flee the country after they have called for Emperor Theodosius's aid.[8] Theodosius's army proceeds to Italy, where he defeats Maximus, handing him over to his soldiers to be executed.[9] After the defeat of the usurper, Theodosius takes up residence in the city of Milan. Meanwhile, when his soldiers imprison a charioteer and shut down the circus back in Thessalonica, the people erupt into rebellion, killing the commander of the garrison and three senators.[10] In Italy, Theodosius is persuaded by a courtier, Ruffinus and his soldiers, that he must punish such insolence with the harshest of measures. Thus, in spite of Bishop Ambrose's admonition that Theodosius take careful account of the welfare of his soul and "Be merciful and good, as He is," the Emperor orders his soldiers to massacre 7,000 people in the town of Thessalonica.[11] When he travels to the Basilica of Milan after the massacre, however, Bishop Ambrose blocks his entrance and excommunicates him. He addresses the Emperor with the following condemnation:

> [Your] hand, which is still dripping with shed blood, could it come into contact with holy things? Shall the defiled tongue, which ordered death, venture to touch the bread of life? Leave the forecourt, shackles and bonds shall exclude you from heaven, by virtue of my power. And furthermore, you have no right to

---

[5] "Cathedraque postus regias infert minas / Anathema sectis intonans." Campion, *Ambrosia*, 35–6.

[6] Campion, *Ambrosia*, 49–141.

[7] Campion, *Ambrosia*, 141–79.

[8] Campion, *Ambrosia*, 272–306.

[9] Campion, *Ambrosia*, 567–601.

[10] Campion, *Ambrosia*, 669–744.

[11] "Secutus illum propitius esto et bonus." Campion, *Ambrosia*, 763.

enter this church [*templum*] until you have come to your senses and have washed away your guilt by penance and repentance.[12]

The other clerics express grave fears that Theodosius may retaliate, but a priest named Paulinus reminds them that they serve God not man, and that God will be able to protect those of true faith.[13] Ambrose himself holds firm, telling the clergy that Theodosius's enduring virtue and "manly disposition [*masculum pectus*]" will respond better to severe punishment than one that is mild: "We give solid food [*cibum*] to the stomach that can take it."[14] Ultimately, Theodosius attempts to repent and make amends for the violent acts that he has carried out, finally declaring on the day that he is to be readmitted into the Basilica:

> Alas, I am sullied by an immeasurable misdeed, how dare I look at this flock attached to Christ? And at myself, a criminal [*scelestum*], whose hands are shamefully red, my brothers, because they were steeped in innocent blood. By my command a city was almost completely massacred [*Exhausta paene*]. Have mercy upon me, and lament together with me, poor wretch, to see whether merciful God can perhaps bring himself, at your request, to wash my crime off. Ruler of heaven, Master of all kings, who desires not the death of anybody, who in spite of thy weariness, hast led back the lost sheep from the most distant mountains, take up the unbridled animal, reform it, bring it back to the pastures, into your fold.[15]

---

[12]　Haec quae cruorem stillat effusum manus
　　　Haec sacra contrectet? Lingua quae iussit necem
　　　Impura vitae tangere audebit cibum?
　　　Abscede vestibulo, et ligator vinculo
　　　Nexuque coelitus potestate ex mea.
　　　Nec fas deinceps ingredi templum vinculo tibi est,
　　　Donec resipiens debitam culpam abluas
　　　Poena et dolore. Campion, Ambrosia, 1020–27.

[13]　Campion, *Ambrosia*, 1048–52.

[14]　"Damus / Solidum valenti sumere stomacho cibum." Campion, *Ambrosia*, 1056–7.

[15]　Heu, sordidatus facinore immenso, quibus
　　　Oculis tuebor deditum Christo gregem?
　　　Meme scelestum, cuius imbutae manus
　　　Insonti sanguine turpiter, fratres, rubent.
　　　Exhausta paene est civitas iussu meo.
　　　Miseremini et lugete mecum perdito,
　　　Si forte crimen eluere clemens Deus
　　　Por vos rogatus sustinet. Rector poli,
　　　Regum Arbiter, qui nemini exitium cupis,
　　　Deperditam qui ex ultimis iugis ovem
　　　Lassus resumpsti, collige solutum pecus,
　　　Restitue, redde pascuis, caulis tuis.
　　　Procumbe terris, anima, et adhaereas solo,
　　　Veniam precare, et libra poenas corpori.
　　　Misere, Christe! Solvite vinclum, pater!
　　　Campion, Ambrosia, 1238–52.

96 *Early Modern Catholics, Royalists, and Cosmopolitans*

In response, Ambrose declares that Theodosius has redeemed himself, and he is finally admitted back into the good graces of the church.[16] Alison Shell has written that Ambrose's chief merit is that he corrects Theodosius's behavior without coercing him. In this regard, she contrasts Campion's example of Ambrose with Robert Persons's more extreme view of the relationship between the spiritual and the temporal realm.[17] Both see the temporal princes as subject to the spiritual power of the clergy, but Persons speaks of a "Jurisdiction of Souls," presided over by the church that is absolute in its rule.[18] According to Persons, "All Kings and Emperors that would be saved" were obligated to subject themselves to the spiritual power of the church, "as we read that our Great *Constantine* … and after him the most renouned of the rest, as *Valentinian*, the Two *Theodosius's*, *Justinian*, *Charles* the great, and others … . And yet by this did they not lose, or diminish one jot of Temporal authority, … but rather did greatly confirm and increase the same."[19] Campion's position is perhaps more moderate than that of Persons, but even Campion's more measured use of the example of St. Ambrose's correction of Theodosius would have been too much for Protestants, who seemed to consider the entire episode problematic. According to Patrick Collinson, English bishops and divines seldom employed Ambrosian exemplars when a sovereign's actions were viewed as needing correction. Richard Hooker saw Theodosius's decisions as exempt from ecclesiastical jurisdiction, while John Foxe saw Constantine, not Theodosius, as the preferred model for Protestant kings.[20] In this respect, Campion's neo-Latin play on the life of St. Ambrose should be seen as a dramatic portrayal of the kind of ecclesiastical supremacy that the Jesuits saw as integral to the Christian commonwealth and to the temporal magistrates that inhabited it. The lesson seems to be clear—those temporal magistrates such as Emperor Theodosius, who allow themselves to be corrected by the caretakers of their souls, will prosper, even if they sometimes commit outrageous moral outrages, while temporal magistrates such as Empress Justina, who attempt to defy the church or co-opt it for their own uses will ultimately be driven from their realm.

In order to emphasize his point about the spiritual correction of temporal magistrates, Campion includes a secondary plot involving Arsenius, the saintly tutor of Theodosius's son, Arcadius. By the beginning of the period depicted in Campion's play, the historical St. Arsenius had already been appointed a Deacon by Pope Damasus I. In this respect, Arsenius was a member of the church hierarchy, but Campion's portrayal of Arsenius emphasizes his role as a tutor, not as an ecclesiastical magistrate. In the *Personae Comoediae*, Arsenius is called simply "*praeceptor Arcadii* [teacher of Arcadius]."[21] The first scene in which we

---

[16] Campion, *Ambrosia*, 1253–7.

[17] Shell, "'We are made a Spectacle,'" 127–8.

[18] Persons, *The Jesuits' Memorial, for the Intended Reformation of England Under their First Popish Prince*, ed. Edward Gee (London, 1690), O3.

[19] Persons, *Jesuits' Memorial*, O4–O4v.

[20] Patrick Collinson, "If Constantine, then also Theodosius," 113–14.

[21] Campion, *Ambrosia*, 4.

Border-Crossing and Translation 97

encounter Arsenius is at the beginning of Act 3, in which Arcadius complains, "Is this to be a ruler? I seem to be a peasant or a mountain dweller born of the lowest rabble rather than a king. I, a master of the laws, am subjected to the laws of a schoolmaster [*Magistri legibus legum potens/ Subiicior*], and I, to whom my father has handed over the government because he has been called away by war, I obey my pedagogues [*paedogogis obsequor*]!"[22] The remainder of the scene presents Arsenius chastising Arcadius for his unruly and unrestrained behavior. "You are a Christian [*Es Christianus*]," Arsenius reminds him at one point, and at another he chides him, "Be ruler over yourself [*Tibi impera*]."[23] Meanwhile a lictor cautions Arsenius to remember his place, menacing him and threatening him with the executioner's axe. Arsenius's response echoes that of Bishop Ambrose—he declares that only "Future, death, judgment, heaven, hell, ... count with me, the rest is uncertain and insignificant."[24] At the end of the scene, Arcadius relents, earning Arsenius's praise.

But the next scene in which Arsenius appears opens with Arsenius praying to God and lamenting the regal and luxurious prison in which he spends all of his days. Meanwhile a hidden swordsman sent by Arcadius to assassinate the tutor secretly observes him praying and weighs the consequences of slaying him, ultimately choosing to reveal himself in order to advise Arsenius to flee. Arsenius contemplates his own duty to remain in Theodosius's court, and finally an angel appears telling him to flee the country and save himself. In response, Arsenius distributes his belongings to the poor and needy and flees the court, dedicating the rest of his life to asceticism. The portrayal of Arsenius complicates the tensions between the church and the state found throughout the rest of the play.[25] In the wake of Arsenius's flight from court, Campion's spectators would presumably have known of Arcadius's future as a disastrously weak ruler as well as Arsenius's later ascetic life culminating in him having been recognized as among the most renowned of the desert fathers of the early church, but Campion chooses to emphasize Arsenius's role as the tutor to Theodosius's children. Within the play, Arsenius is referred to as a schoolmaster [*praeceptor*], a pedagogue [*peaedogogus*], and a philosopher [*philosophus*], while his identity as a Deacon is left unmentioned.[26]

There are two ways in which to understand Arsenius's role within the tensions between the church and the state that characterize most of this play. First, the portrayal of Arsenius contains important elements of Campion's biography—his willingness to trade status and station at Oxford University, where he had been chosen to address the Queen on her visit to the University, for a life of devotion and sacrifice, for becoming "a dead man to this world and willing to put my head under

---

[22] "Hoc imperare est? Rusticulus esse videor / Potius, et ima faece monticola satus / Quam rex. Magistri legibus legum potens / Subiicior, et cui regna commisit parens, / Bello avocaltus, paedogogis obsequor." Campion, *Ambrosia*, 528–32.

[23] Campion, *Ambrosia*, 545, 550.

[24] "Futura, mortem, iudicia, coelum, Stygem, / Haec numero, reliqua incerta sunt minutaque." Campion, *Ambrosia*, 555–6.

[25] Campion, *Ambrosia*, 867–945.

[26] Campion, *Ambrosia*, 530–65.

98　　　*Early Modern Catholics, Royalists, and Cosmopolitans*

every man's foot, and to kiss the ground they tread upon."[27] Second, Arsenius's righteous role as a corrective to the unruly and rebellious Arcadius means that the role of corrector of the temporal magistrate is not limited to bishops and the papacy. In this respect, the role of spiritual corrector of the temporal magistrate is rendered more complex. Campion's portrayal of Arsenius means that the role of spiritual advisor or corrector can be assumed by a figure that is not a magistrate within the ecclesiastical hierarchy: perhaps a priest like Campion himself, a secular figure—a tutor or teacher such as Campion's portrayal of Arsenius in his neo-Latin play, or even a writer of fiction such as Sir John Harington, Anthony Munday, or Sir Philip Sidney. In this respect, Campion's portrayal of Arsenius goes some way towards secularizing the role of spiritual advisor or corrector in a direction that writers of fiction such as Munday and Harington would take further. As I will show in this chapter, two writers who came into contact with Campion were affected by his example and the issues that emerged in his trial and execution. Their response was to create fictional works in which the ecclesiastical figures of authority, championed by Persons, Sander, and Campion, were further secularized in ways that retain their transnational and cosmopolitan origins while erasing their Catholic origins.

Anthony Munday and the Secular Papal Surrogate

It has been argued that indications of Catholic sympathies can be found throughout Munday's fictional and non-fictional writing, despite the fact that he seems to have been a willing witness at the treason trials of Campion and other English seminarians during the early 1580s and that he later became a pursuivant of Catholic recusants as part of Richard Topcliffe's network.[28] His early romance, *Zelauto* (1580), includes a story in which the chivalric hero travels to Persia, where he encounters Christians being persecuted for their faith and attempting to defend them, makes a moving appeal to the ruling Soldane on behalf of a Christian lady: "This Lady for example, no straunger, but of your owne blood [i.e. country], and no enimie to your Maiestie ... If to your own blood, you will deale so tyrannically: how will you deale with me [i.e. a foreigner] poore wretch of so meane estimation?"[29]

---

[27]　Campion, "Challenge to the Privy Council," in *Ten Reasons*, 7–11, esp. 9.

[28]　The most important scholar on Munday, Donna Hamilton, argues that Munday was essentially a Catholic loyalist (see Hamilton, *Anthony Munday and the Catholics*, xvi–xvii). Hamilton's argument about Munday is that, in spite of his official capacity as a pursuivant of English Catholics, he himself was secretly a Catholic, albeit loyal to the queen. For Munday's life as a hack writer, see Celeste Turner Wright, "Mundy and Chettle in Grub Street," *Boston University Studies in English* 5 (1961): 129–38. Before Hamilton, it was argued that Munday was a committed Protestant, whose work as a pursuivant seeking to expose Catholic recusants made him an enemy of new Catholics such as Ben Jonson. According to Huntley, Jonson went on to use the character Antonio Balladino to satirize Munday in *The Case is Altered* (1609). See Frank L. Huntley, "Ben Jonson and Anthony Munday, or, *The Case is Altered* Altered Again," *Philological Quarterly* 41 (1962): 205–14, at 211.

[29]　Munday, *Zelauto, The Fountain of Fame, 1580*, ed. Jack Stillinger (Carbondale, 1963), 90.

Donna Hamilton has noted in such scenes the echoes of moderate Catholic appeals to the English crown for religious tolerance on the basis of a collective national or ethnic identity. As confirmation of her thesis, Hamilton notes that, during his apprenticeship and his early works, Munday was involved with Catholic-leaning printers such as John Allde and John Charlewood, and his first patron was Edward de Vere, Earl of Oxford, who had well-known Catholic sympathies.[30]

But although more is known about Anthony Munday's life than almost any other English writer of the period, definitively resolving the question of Munday's religious identity continues to elude scholars. What is clear is that shortly after publishing *Zelauto*, Munday publically fashioned himself as a fervent anti-Catholic, even taking up an official court position and dedicating himself to the service of ferreting out potentially treasonous Catholic recusants. By the time he had published *A banquet of daintie conceits* (1588), Munday was identifying himself as "Seruaunt to the Queenes most excellent Maiestie," while from 1588 until 1596, his name in print was followed by the title, "messenger of her Maiesties chamber."[31] More importantly, he became an intelligencer, working for Sir Richard Topcliffe in the secret effort to track down seminarians and recusants, and as late as 1612, the Catholic poet and recusant, Hugh Holland, was convicted of recusancy "ex testimonio *Anthony Munday*."[32] Despite Munday's clear attempts to represent himself as an anti-Catholic polemicist, Hamilton has argued that Munday's entire corpus illustrates a lifelong, if moderate and conformist, commitment to Catholic religious doctrine. Some fragmentary hearsay evidence exists to substantiate such a claim. During the Martin Marprelate controversy (c. 1588–89), during which Munday's talents as a spy were used to entrap Puritans, for example, a clergyman named Giles Wigginton remarked, "I was treated like a Turk or Dog ... This Mundy ... seemeth to favour the Pope and to be a great dissembler."[33] But while Hamilton's book provides a rich background to the religious controversies that were coterminous with some of Munday's works, most of her evidence is gleaned from tendentious readings of Munday's fiction. Moreover, Hamilton's portrayal of Munday fits too easily within the retrospective historiographical narrative of English Catholics as comprised, in the words of historian Michael Questier, "of

---

[30]   Hamilton, *Munday and the Catholics*, 14–18, xvii–xviii.

[31]   Munday, *A banquet of daintie conceits. Furnished with verie delicate and choyse inuentions, to delight their mindes, who take pleasure in musique, and there-withall to sing sweete ditties, either to the lute, bandora, virginalles, or anie other instrument.* (London, 1588). See, for example, *Palmerin D'Oliva.* [Part 1] *The mirrour of nobilitie, mappe of honor, anotamie of rare fortunes, heroycall president of Loue*, trans. Munday (London, 1588). For context, see Hamilton, *Munday and the Catholics*, xviii–xxiv.

[32]   Mark Eccles, "Anthony Munday," in *Studies in the English Renaissance Drama: in Memory of Karl Julius Holzknecht*, ed. Josephine W. Bennett, Oscar Cargill, and Vernon Hall, Jr. (New York, 1959), 95–105, at 103. See also *London Sessions Records, 1605–1685*, ed. Hugh Bowler, Catholic Record Society (London, 1934), vol. 34, 63–4, 71. See also I.A. Shapiro, "Shakespeare and Mundy," *Shakespeare Survey* 14 (1961): 25–33.

[33]   Cited in Celeste Turner Wright, *Anthony Mundy: An Elizabethan Man of Letters* (Berkeley, CA, 1928), 84.

right-thinking people who had a conscience in the matter of true religion." As Questier has shown, it is more accurate to view English Catholics during this period as comprising "a series of entourages and networks, often factionally aligned internally, whose ideological concerns inflected the more basic fact of their blood, kin and client relationships."[34] Hamilton's work is essential for understanding the religious context within which Munday lived and wrote, but she is unable to show that Munday was a member of any such network—in fact, the only network in which Munday did participate until at least 1612 was that of intelligencer Richard Topcliffe, who was charged by the crown with the task of hunting down Catholic recusants.[35]

After his return from Rome in 1579, Munday wrote a series of accounts of the interrogations and executions of Campion and his co-religionists, against whom Munday had testified during their trials for treason. Like his accounts of these trials, the narrative account of his travels to Italy, entitled *English Romayne Lyfe* (1582), seems to have been written with the purpose of allaying suspicions about the real reasons for his travelling to Rome.[36] And thus, it is consistent with this purpose that Munday ends the tract with a brutal account of the execution of an English Protestant, Richard Atkins, who was burned at the stake in Rome for heresy in 1579 (see Figure 2.1). I would suggest that Munday's confessional identity is ultimately impossible to define. Given Michael Questier's recent research on how closely knit were conformist Catholic and Protestant communities in the countryside—the fact for example that committed Protestants sat on recusancy commissions with figures such as Sir Thomas Leedes, George Gunter, and Edward Pelham whose families were heavily Catholicized, it is probable that religious identity was simply less determinate than once was thought.[37]

---

[34] Questier, *Catholicism and Community*, 9.

[35] For discussion of Munday's connection with the network of individuals, i.e. Robert Allot, Francis Meres, Nicholas Ling, James Robert, who edited and contributed to the John Bodenham Miscellanies, see Celeste Turner Wright, "Anthony Mundy and the Bodenham Miscellanies," *Philological Quarterly* 40 (1961): 449–61. Wright concludes that Munday edited the miscellany, *Belvedere, or, The Garden of the Muses* (1600), dedicated to Bodenham.

[36] Munday, *The araignement, and execution, of a wilfull and obstinate traitour, named Eueralde Ducket, alias House* (London, 1581); *A breefe discourse of the taking of Edmund Campion, the seditious Iesuit, and diuers other papistes, in Barkeshire: who were brought to the Towre of London, the 22. day of Iuly. 1581. Gathered by A.M.* (London, 1581); *A breefe and true reporte, of the execution of certaine traytours at Tiborne* (London, 1582); *A breefe answer made vnto two seditious pamphlets* (London 1582); *A discoverie of Edmund Campion, and his confederates* (London 1582); *The English Romayne Lyfe* (London, 1582). The last section of Munday's tract on treason argues that English papists should be pursued without mercy. See Munday, *A Watch-vvoord to Englande to beware of traytours and tretcherous practises, which haue beene the ouerthrowe of many famous kingdomes and common weales* (London, 1584), J4v–N2.

[37] Questier, *Catholicism and Community*, 49, 77–87.

Fig. 2.1 The crime and execution of English Protestant, Richard Atkins in Rome. From Anthony Munday, *The English Romayne Lyfe* (London, 1582), inset. By permission of the Folger Shakespeare Library.

What we do know is that Munday saw Campion as a traitor to the crown and was willing to testify against him in court and to write a detailed and sometimes graphic account of the proceedings of his trial and his execution. I would suggest however that, in spite of this, Munday actually adopted a cosmopolitan identity that in some respects mirrored the public persona that Campion adopted during his mission to England. From the beginning of his career, we find Munday touting his travels to the continent as a source of knowledge and wisdom. In the dedication to Edward de Vere, Earl of Oxford in his first major work, *The Mirrour of Mutabilitie*, the author trades on his travels abroad as leading to his encounter with "true noblitie."[38] Presenting his work as a continuation of the *Mirror for Magistrates* (republished in 1578), Munday recounts in great detail the reasons for his travels, his disastrous arrival in France during which French soldiers attacked him and his companion, Thomas Nowell, and robbed them of their belongings, their encounter with English Catholic exiles who afforded them with letters of introduction to the English College in Rome, their meeting with the English ambassador in Paris, and finally the list of cities that Munday visited during his subsequent travels to Italy.[39] He presents himself, at the beginning of his travels, as naive, explaining that "my wilde oates required to be furrowed in a foreiyne ground, to satisfye the trifling toyes that dayly more and more frequented my busied braine" and that he had assumed that "euery man beyond the Seas was as frank as an Emperour, and that a man might liue there a Gentlemans life, and doo nothing but walke at his pleasure." He explains how he was forced to receive garments and other favors from English Catholic exiles, who "thorowly prouided me for my iourney to Roome" and who "deliuered me diuers letters to sundry persons (whose names I remit) that there I should be placed in the office of a Preest." Immediately, Munday began to experience remorse "that we should forsake so soone the title & name of a Christian." Later, Munday is repentant when the English ambassador, described as a "second Solon" and the embodiment of "true nobilitie," warns him that allying himself with such men would be "to sell you selues willfully into such perpetuall slauery, and not only to your great ignomy, but to your freends perpetuall infamy, to your Prince and famous Contriie, if you leaue your Captaine thus cowardly." After recounting his travels into "Italy, to Roome, Naples, Venice, Padua, and diuers other excellent cities," Munday ends the dedication by returning to his native country and his patron: "And now returned, remembring my bounden duty to your Honnor, I present you with these my simple labours, desiring pardon for my bolde

---

[38] *The Mirrour of Mutabilitie*, ed. Hans Peter Heinrich (New York, 1990), 9–10. For a discussion of Munday's connections with other authors during this period, see Celeste Turner Wright, "Anthony Mundy, 'Edward' Spenser, and E.K.," *PMLA* 76 (1961): 34–9, which argues that the E.K. who prefaced Munday's *Mirrour* with verses was Edward Knight, whom Wright argues was actually Spenser's E.K., who composed the annotations to the *Shepheardes Calendar*. Wright considers the connections between Munday and Spenser, including their mutual friends and patrons: Webbe, Harvey, Lyly, Leicester, and Oxford.

[39] The complete title of the *Mirrour for Mutabilitie* was the *Mirrour of Mutabilitie, or Principall part of the Mirrour for Magistrates*.

attempt."[40] Implicit in this dedication is that the knowledge embodied within the *Mirrour* itself derives from his continental adventure. The versified stories within the Mirror, recounting the Biblical accounts of King Nebuchadnezzar, Herod, David, Ahab, and other Old Testament figures had been used since Henry VIII's break with Rome in religious controversies over papal and the temporal claims for supremacy over the church. Munday himself refrains from taking a clear position on the supremacy question in the *Mirror*; rather, his purpose seems to have been to show that he was aware of the debate.[41]

The Earl of Oxford was also the dedicatee of Munday's second major work from this period, the prose romance entitled the *Zelauto* written in imitation of Lyly's *Euphues*.[42] Once again, Munday adopts the identity of the traveller, this time in the guise of the chivalric knight, in order to introduce the work. He begins by presenting himself as similar to Don Duardos, Prince of England, and Primaleon, two characters from *Primaleon*, the Spanish chivalric romance originally published in 1512, and which Munday later translated into English in three parts.[43] He goes on to compare his book to a humble gift of flowers offered by a "poore Cittizen" to the Holy Roman Emperor, in the midst of "all the braue Gallants and woorthy Gentlemen in Roome" who in turn present him with jewels and "gifts of great value and estimation."[44] The reference to Rome in the dedication to *Zelauto* might initially seem to conform to the genre of Chivalric romance that Munday is exploring in this work, but it is actually one in a series of references to his trip to Rome in 1579, which he recounted in detail in *The English Romayne Lyfe*, printed in 1582.[45] During 1581 and 1582, Munday published a total of five pamphlets, as responses to his involvement as a testimonial witness in the interrogations and trials of Campion and other Jesuit seminarians who had travelled to England ostensibly to minister to what they considered beleaguered English Catholics. The first of these, *A breefe discourse of the taking of Edmund Campion*, was entered into the Stationer's Register on July 24, 1581, hardly a week after Campion was captured at Lyford, near Oxford. Munday seems to have been a prominent witness during the subsequent trial of Campion, Ralph Sherwin, and Alexander Briant. But what is significant and even singular about the three subsequent pamphlets on the treason trials of 1581 and 1582 is that despite his aim of laying down the boundaries of national discourse and exposing the Queen's treasonous subjects, Munday constantly invokes his continental journey to Italy and to his own vexed

---

[40]   Munday, *Mirrour*, 7, 8, 9, 10.

[41]   See Hamilton, *Munday and the Catholics*, 8–9.

[42]   For background on possible Italian sources of this work, see Geoffrey Creigh, "Zelauto and Italian Comedy: A Study in Sources," *Modern Language Quarterly* 29 (1968): 161–7.

[43]   Munday, *Zelauto*, 3.

[44]   Munday, *Zelauto*, 4.

[45]   For a discussion of *Zelauto* in relation to Munday's literary identity, see Joshua Phillips, "Chronicles of Wasted Time: Anthony Munday, Tudor Romance, and Literary Labor," *ELH* 73.4 (2006): 781–803.

104   *Early Modern Catholics, Royalists, and Cosmopolitans*

experience at the Roman seminary in particular and the knowledge with which it provided him in order to make his case.

The most important of these pamphlets is *A Discoverie of Edmund Campion, and his confederates*, printed January 29, 1582, almost exactly two months after the executions took place at Tiborne on December 1, 1581. Dedicating the tract to the members of Elizabeth's Privy Council, Munday begins by recounting "howe I haue beene in those places [i.e. Rome and elsewhere among English Catholic exiles], where I haue heard and seene more then I will heere report."[46] He goes on to repeatedly reference his travels in 1579 on the continent and to Rome, noting at one crucial moment that "it were too tedious to discourse heere" the details of his trip to Rome, concluding by announcing the subsequent publication of "a booke, which by the grace of God shall come foorth shortly, intituled, *The English Romaine lyfe*."[47] This is a pattern that occurs again in the subsequent two pamphlets: *A breefe answer made unto two seditious pamphlets*, printed March 22, 1582, and *A breefe and true reporte, of the execution of certaine traytours at Tiborne*, entered into the Stationer's Register on May 31, 1582 and printed later that year. The first of the latter two pamphlets was a response to Thomas Alfield's *A true reporte of the death & martyrdome of M. Campion Jesuite and priests, & M. Sherwin, & M. Bryan preists, at Tiborne the first of December*, printed in February 1582 and an anonymous French translation of an English account of the executions, which, at the beginning of his response, Munday describes as "The Historie of the death, which the reuerend Father *M. Edmund Campion*, Preest, of the Societie of the name of Iesus, and others haue suffered in England, for the Catholique & Roomish religion or faith, the 1. of December. 1581."[48] Both of the latter pamphlets were intended to refute the account of that execution found in Munday's *Discoverie*.

A common strategy throughout all three of Munday's pamphlets is to refer almost obsessively to his travels to the continent, as a way of granting his voice authority.[49] When Campion and his confederates deny having possessed the outlawed tract, *Bristow's Motives*, to their interrogators, Munday recounts that at the English college at Rheims, Bristow's book was "as common amongst them, as the little Catechisme heere amonge Children," while at the English College at Rome, copies of the book "were as common likewise."[50] A little later, he recounts,

---

[46]   Munday, *A Discoverie*, A4.

[47]   Munday, *A Discoverie*, C4.

[48]   Munday, *A breefe answer*, B1. For the Catholic account of Campion's execution, see Thomas Alfield, *A true reporte of the death & martyrdome of M. Campion Iesuite and prieste, & M. Sherwin, & M. Bryan preistes, at Tiborne the first of December* (London, 1582); William Cardinal Allen, *A briefe historie of the glorious martyrdom of twelve reverend Priests Father Edmund Campion & His companions* (Rheims, 1582), reprinted and edited by J.H. Pollen, S.J. (London, 1908).

[49]   For discussion of Munday's pattern of self-promotion, see Nora Johnson, *The Actor as Playwright in Early Modern Drama* (New York, 2003), 84–121.

[50]   Munday, *A Discoverie*, B5v. For a comprehensive recording and critical discussion of the events of Campion's imprisonment, including the English authorities' transcriptions of his four debates with conformist clergy, a Catholic account of the first debate, and an official

"When I came to Roome, I was allowed the Popes Scholler, and liued there in the Seminarie among them: if I should reporte all that I heard, it were more then modestie would suffer, wherefore I am constrayned to let it passe."[51] This last claim, that he was "allowed the Popes Scholler" constitutes a recapitulation of the title-page of the pamphlet where he notes that he was "sometime the Popes scholler, allowed in the seminarie at Roome amongst them" and furthermore that this book is "a discourse needefull to be read of euery man, to beware how they deale with such secret seducers."[52] The title reminds the reader of the exceptional nature of Munday's biographical narrative: the fact that, like Campion and his confederates, Munday was once a student at the English college in Rome, in danger of being on the wrong end of "how they [English authorities] deal with such secret seducers," but rather than causing him to have been executed as a traitor, his dealings with the pope are integral to his role as defender of the English crown's strategy for dealing with the Jesuit seminarians. Indeed, his knowledge of the secret and mysterious world of Catholic exiles has increased his own authority as a writer and informer.[53]

In the subsequent tract, *A breefe answer made unto two seditious pamphlets*, Munday continues to refer to the upcoming publication of the account of his travels to Rome as well as his earlier book on the *Discoverie*. In this respect, all Munday's "treason" tracts are interlinked through an incessant process of cross-referencing. Additionally, of course, this tract attempts to respond to Alfield's *A true reporte of the death & martyrdome of M. Campion*, which intended to set the record straight about Campion's execution. Alfield was responsible for penning the famous passage, in which Campion is exalted as a cosmopolitan ideal for the Christian world:

> It is not vnknowen that M. Edmund Campion Iesuite & Preist, a man reputed and taken, and by diuers his coequals plainlye confessed the flewer of Oxforde for that time he studied there, and since abrode in foreine countries one in whom our countrey hath had great honor, the frute of his learning, vertue, and rare giftes, which as they were in his childhood here among vs wonderful, so they were abrode, as in Italy, Germany, and Bohemia an honor to our country, a glasse and mirror, a light and lanterne, a paterne and example to youth, to age, to lerned, to vnlerned, to religious, and to the laytie of all sort, state, & condition, of modestie, grauitie, eloquence, knowledge, vertue, and pietie, of which iust and due commendation, some of our aduersaries can give true and certeyn testimonie, who after diligent sifting and enquiring of his life, maners, and demeinor, found nothing faulty, nothing worthy of blame.[54]

---

account of his trial, see James V. Holleran (ed.), *A Jesuit Challenge: Edmund Campion's Debates at the Tower of London in 1581* (New York, 1999). For reports of other similar trials of Catholic priests, along with records of Topcliffe's and Munday's involvement, see John Hungerford Pollen, S.J. (ed.), *Unpublished Documents Relating to the English Martyrs*, vol. 1: 1584–1603 (London, 1908), 26–8, 60–61,182–5, 200–203, 206–12.

[51]   Munday, *A Discoverie*, D1v.
[52]   Munday, *A Discoverie*, title page.
[53]   There are 19 mentions of Rome and 52 mentions of the Pope in *A Discoverie*.
[54]   Alfield, *A true reporte*, B3v–B4r.

Alfield's description of Campion in this passage is not unrelated to the ideal encountered in Dee's description of himself as the erudite individual, whose vast knowledge of the world—"the State of Earthly Kingdoms, Generally, the whole World ouer"—informs his understanding of the particular situation of the "Brytish Monarchy."[55] Like Dee's attempt to bring his knowledge of the rest of the world to bear on England's more localized situation, Alfield's description of Campion links the local—Campion was "the flower of Oxforde"—to "our countrey" and finally to the foreign and worldly—"Italy, Germany, and Bohemia." Significantly, Munday cites precisely this passage in his response to Alfield, in which he refutes the notion that Campion impressed the world with "the fruites of his learning, vertue, & rare gifts."[56] According to Munday, Campion confessed that his studies in divinity never advanced much beyond Canisius's dictates and that furthermore in Prague, he lacked the means and even books, pens, and ink with which to continue his studies, having been forced to tutor the children of gentlemen in Latin in order to support himself.[57]

For his part, Alfield characterizes Munday as Campion's unlearned opposite: an imposter and a charlatan, "neuer admitted in the seminary as he pleseth to lye in the title of his book."[58] Munday responds in kind by citing testimony by the Jesuit, Luke Kirby, who, prior to his execution on March 6, 1582, recounted the English students' meeting with the pope during their revolt against the Welsh rector of the college, Morys Clynnog. According to Munday's account of Kirby's testimony, the pope had asked for a list of the English seminary students currently living at the college. He was presented with an alphabetical list, among which appeared the names of both Thomas Nowell and Anthony Munday, thus proving Alfield to have lied about Munday not having been admitted to the seminary.[59] Munday goes on to promise to describe "the manner of [his and Nowell's] expulsion, the cause, and howe thinges happened ... in my *Englishe Romaine lyfe*."[60] It is important to note how both these pamphlets position Munday and Campion in opposition to one another using identical cosmopolitan values: knowledge of the world contributes to each man's authority, while accounts of travel abroad provide opportunities to refute opposing claims of erudition. In this respect, Munday fashions a cosmopolitan identity that is ironically modeled to some extent after Campion's own worldly erudition.

The third of the treason tracts printed in 1582, *A breefe & true reporte, of the execution of certaine traytours at Tiborne*, dedicated to Richard Martin, Sheriff and Alderman of London, included a compendium of the speeches delivered on the scaffold by two groups of Jesuits who were executed at the end of May of that year. Once again, Munday begins the work with a reference to his travels to Rome

---

[55] Dee, *Perfect Arte of Navigation*, G3v–G4.
[56] Munday, *A breefe answer*, D7v–D8.
[57] Munday, *A breefe answer*, C8–C8v.
[58] Alfield, *A true reporte*, E.
[59] Munday, *A breefe answer*, D4.
[60] Munday, *A breefe answer*, D4v.

in the dedication: "I my selfe hauing spent some time in *Roome* and other places, among them, where through I grew into such acquaintaunce with their traiterous intents and dispositions, as before some of their faces I stoode as witnesse against them, to their reproofe."[61] In this passage, Munday informs his readers of his first-hand knowledge of the exile community by virtue of his travel to the locus of iniquity itself, Rome, an experience that enabled him to assume a crucial role as witness against the traitors. Like the earlier two tracts, he concludes *A breefe and true reporte* by advertising the soon-to-be-published *English Romayne Lyfe*: "if thou desirest to be more acquainted with their Romish and Sathanicall inglinges, read my *English Romayne lyfe*, which so soone as it can be printed, shall be set foorth."[62] *A breefe and true reporte* is the shortest of the three tracts published in 1582, but it contains the most complete discussion of the issue of supremacy to be found in these early tracts. Munday once again is an eyewitness to the executions, at critical moments offering crucial testimony from the earlier arraignments of Robert Johnson and Luke Kirby.[63]

The supremacy issue is initially broached during the execution of Thomas Forde, the first priest to be executed, who declares that he acknowledged Queen Elizabeth's "supremacy in all thinges temporal, but as conserning Ecclesiastical causes I deny her, that onely belongeth to the Uicar of Christ, the Pope." Immediately after this acknowledgement, Munday declares that Forde "shewed himselfe an impious and obstinate Traytour" and after mumbling a few Latin prayers, Forde is led to his execution.[64] Similarly, on May 30, 1582, the second day of executions, Laurence Richardson declares that "the onelie Supremacie" over the ecclesiastical realm in England belonged to the pope, at which point Richardson is abruptly "committed to God."[65]

At the center of the account, however, is the execution of Luke Kirby, which occurs toward the beginning of the second day, during which Kirby is extensively interrogated on the power of the pope to depose a sinful sovereign. The crucial section begins when the Kirby is asked by a conformist clergyman "whether the Pope might lawfullie depose her Maiestie." After an initial evasion in which he declares that he must not speak of the matter since it is a matter for the "Schooles" or universities to clarify, Kirby finally confesses his belief that "if any Prince fal by infidelity, into Turscisme, Atheisme, Paganisme, or any such lyke, that the Pope hath aucthoritie to depose such a Prince," adding later that judging whether Elizabeth herself had fallen into any of these transgressions was a matter Kirby preferred to keep to himself.[66] Another member of the clergy, Robert Crowley, counters that princes derive their authority from God, and that God and only God may remove them from power. Kirby's initial refutation of Crowley's defense of the doctrine of divine right and Crowley's rejoinder are worth quoting in full.

---

[61]   Munday, *A breefe and true report*, A2.
[62]   Munday, *A breefe and true report*, C3.
[63]   Munday, *A breefe and true report*, B3v.
[64]   Munday, *A breefe and true report*, B2–B2v.
[65]   Munday, *A breefe and true report*, C3v.
[66]   Munday, *A breefe and true report*, C2v.

108   *Early Modern Catholics, Royalists, and Cosmopolitans*

> No (quoth Kirbie againe) hath it [the matter of papal supremacy] not beene
> disputed in Schooles for these fiue hundred yeeres, and will you deny it? O
> Maister Crowley, Maister Crowley, and there pawsed, as though that Maister
> Crowley had agreede with him in such a monstrous error. But Maister Crowley
> him selfe gaue me to vnderstand, that at such time as hee conferred with the
> sayde Kirbie in the Tower, about the same argument, that his aunswer was vnto
> him. If any Prince fell into any such kinde of error, that Prince were corrigible,
> but of whom? not of any earthly Prince, but of that heauenlie Prince, who gaue
> him his aucthority, and seeing him abuse it any way, correcteth him in his
> Iustice. For by his attributing to the Pope, this aucthority, he witnessed him to be
> Antichrist in that he wil depose Princes at his pleasure, & exalt him self aboue all
> that is called God, and forgiue men their sinnes at his pleasure likewise.[67]

This passage is of interest as much for what is said here as it is for what is left
unsaid. Kirby refutes the notion that only God may remove bad princes from
power by invoking the authority of the Scholastics. For Kirby and his Jesuit allies,
the pope was the ultimate arbiter of temporal magistrates. For Crowley, who in
addition to being a member of the clergy was a well-known printer and member of
the Stationer's Company, papal oversight of secular authorities was tantamount to
a usurpation of God's authority. The passage is rendered more complex by at least
two uncomfortable pauses or silences. When Kirby first confronts Crowley, the
conformist priest is silent, and Kirby pauses, assuming that Crowley has agreed
with his perspective. However, in a later private discussion, Crowley confides
to Munday that in an earlier private meeting with Kirby that covered the same
ground, Crowley had responded to him by asking, "If any Prince fell into any such
kinde of error, that Prince were corrigible, but of whom?" Crowley responds to his
own question by noting that only "that heavenlie Prince" may correct a sovereign.

Still, despite Munday's attempt to clear up the confusion, Crowley's silence at
the scaffold seems to indicate the level of tension and anxiety that surrounded the
public discussion of the papal claim to the right to depose Christian sovereigns. In
effect, Crowley seems unwilling to debate this point with Kirby in a public venue.
Moreover, what is left unsaid by this earlier private meeting is that both Kirby and
Crowley and presumably Munday all agree that bad temporal magistrates need
correction—the debate is rather over how that correction may manifest itself, with
Kirby arguing that God has entrusted the pope to depose sinful sovereigns while
Crowley and Munday see God himself as punishing such sovereigns directly. The
matter of how God carries out such correction is, however, left unaddressed. As
a result, Crowley's question concerning who ultimately corrects the error-prone
magistrate continues to haunt this passage, because the question of "who" leads to
the question of "how" and "why" and "in what circumstances" a magistrate would
need correction.

It is this anxiety over the ability or inability to correct a sinful or oppressive or
apostate prince that drives a central concern found in Munday's subsequent fictional

---

[67]   Munday, *A breefe and true report*, C3.

works, especially his dramatic works, the chivalric romances which he chose to translate, and even some of the London pageants. In many of these, one encounters figures, both secular and religious, that substitute for the pope's role as corrector of an error-prone or sinful sovereign. Before we consider some of these works, it is worth briefly remembering Munday's encounter with the pope in the work that he spent so much time advertising during these years, *The English Romayne Lyfe*, printed towards the end of 1582. In Chapter 1, I showed that Persons's and Munday's parallel accounts of what Pope Gregory XIII does with respect to the rector of the English college, intervening into the national politics of the English college in order to depose its "magistrate," is analogous to what figures such as Nicholas Sander and Richard Bristow desired him to do with respect to Queen Elizabeth I. As I noted, the pope resolves the ethnic infighting between the Welsh and English populations of the English College in a way that favorably redounds to Munday's situation within the college. What we find in this conflict, then, is that the pope utilized his prerogative powers over the ethno-national politics within the English college in a way that replicated how Catholic exiles imagined him intervening within the international sphere.

Similar to *The English Romayne Lyfe*, the extant dramatic works of Munday are pre-occupied with dramatic situations that recall, sometimes in very accessible allegories, the subject of papal supremacy. The first of these, *John a Kent and John a Cumber* (1590), is the least overtly political of Munday's plays. *John a Kent* only exists as a manuscript, which was signed "Anthony Mundy" and dated "December 1590." According to commentators, Munday probably wrote both *John a Kent* and *Sir Thomas More* for the Lord Strange's Men.[68] Typically, Hamilton reads the play as an allegorical case for religious tolerance that would benefit Catholics, arguing that its politics were quite different from the earlier magician play by Robert Greene, *Friar Bacon and Friar Bungay* (1589), which has a similar structure to *John A Kent* and probably even influenced Munday's play, but which was motivated more clearly by Protestant ideology.[69] Munday's play concerns two planned marriages: Llwellen of North Wales and Ranulphe, Earl of Chester have bid their respective daughters, Sydanen and Marian, to marry the Earl of Morton (from Scotland) and the Earl of Pembroke (an Englishman). Meanwhile, the two daughters, Sydanen and Marian, are secretly betrothed to Sir Griffin Merridock and Jeffrey Lord Powesse, both of Wales. The good magician, John a Kent, uses his magic to assist the cause of the daughters, while a second magician, John a Cumber, champions their two fathers' side in the conflict.

Powesse notes that the desire of Merridock and himself to pursue marriages with Sydanen and Marian are directly opposed to the interests of the sovereign. Moreover, should they defend their marriage plans with arms, they both

---

[68]   Scott McMillin, "*The Book of Sir Thomas More*: dates and acting companies," in *Shakespeare and "Sir Thomas More": Essays on the Play and its Shakespearean Interest*, ed. T.H. Howard-Hill (Cambridge, 1989), 62–5.

[69]   Hamilton, *Munday and the Catholics*, 114–19.

110　　　*Early Modern Catholics, Royalists, and Cosmopolitans*

"may be held as traytours to the King / that durst inuade his townes in time of Peace"(1.1.36–7).[70] Ultimately, John a Kent appears to assist the cause of the suitors, intervening in the drama with "secret arts" in order to help Griffin and Powesse pursue their aim of marrying their beloved Sydanen and Marian (1.1.107). Early in the first act of the play, Kent dons his first disguise, that of a religious hermit who has "studied hidden artes," presenting himself to Sydanem and Marian, who address him as "ffather," and bidding the young maidens to wash themselves at "Saint winifredes fayre spring," if they seek to avoid an unhappy fate (1.2.214; 1.2.237; 1.2.260). Throughout the remainder of the play, Kent uses magic in order to correct the decisions made by the two fathers, Llwellen and Ranuphe, whose authority over their own households renders them analogous to tyrannical temporal sovereigns. In this way, John a Kent's intervention into and correction of their domestic affairs allegorically recalls the pope's ability to correct tyrannical temporal magistrates. The fact that one of the maidens is named Sydanem, a name that had come to be synonymous with Elizabeth, suggests that the aims of the priest-surrogate—John a Kent—are not necessarily in conflict with the interests and desires of Queen herself.[71]

Hamilton's reading, (of this play and other plays by Munday) is that Munday seeks to allegorize the dilemma of the Catholic recusant. Should Catholic recusants disguise their identity as John a Kent does at the beginning of the play? Or should they go about their business without disguise, as the women and their lovers do at the end of the play, entering the church to be married as themselves, and thereby outwitting Kent's nemesis, John a Cumber, who expects their identity to be hidden behind an elaborate disguise? The problem with such readings is that, by the 1590s, English Catholics were not alone in debating the merits of open or clandestine recusancy. Indeed, Protestant dissenters were increasingly engaged in the same debate as well. Moreover, given Munday's edition of Jean Calvin's sermons, which appeared in 1584 (six years prior to the play), who is to say that such scenes depicting the merits of disguised or open recusancy were not rather intended to be sympathetic to the Puritan cause?[72] In Kent and Cumber's magic, Munday seems to allegorize and secularize religious authority from an ideological position that is outside of the religious controversies of the day. In this respect, a move towards secularizing religious control over the conscience of the sovereign can be found in *John a Kent and John a Cumber*. As we shall see, Munday's dramas collectively show less of an investment in the supernatural power of the priest and the fidelity of the English Catholic than a desire for any figure, secular or religious, that might replace what had been lost when the English crown rejected the church's spiritual

---

[70]　Subsequent parenthetical references to the play are from Arthur E. Pennell (ed.), *An Edition of Anthony Munday's* John a Kent *and* John a Cumber (New York, 1980). For discussion of the stages of Munday's revision of this play, see John William Ashton, "Revision in Munday's *John a Kent and John a Cumber*," *Modern Language Notes* 48 (1993), 531–7.

[71]　Pennell (ed.), *An Edition of Munday's* John a Kent, 176–7.

[72]　Jean Calvin, *Two godly and learned sermons*, trans. Robert Horne, ed. Anthony Munday (London, 1584).

Border-Crossing and Translation 111

supremacy over the conscience of the sovereign. Ultimately, Munday's portrayal of John a Kent—a magician who disguises himself as a monk in order to correct two potentially tyrannical fathers—imagines an allegorical scenario in which the sovereign's power over the domestic realm might be checked or corrected or even protected, without the authority of a religious overseer.

The Book of Sir Thomas More also only existed in manuscript form, and Munday's central role in the play's composition was established by the discovery that the manuscript was in the same hand as the manuscript *John a Kent & John a Cumber*. Sir Edward Maunde Thompson went on to date the play's composition to a few years after *John a Kent*, and most scholars now agree that Munday's part in the manuscript was finished no later than 1593, while the other hands, thought to include Henry Chettle, Thomas Dekker, Thomas Heywood, an anonymous copyist, and for three pages, the hand of William Shakespeare, date from 1593–94.[73] Munday's portions of the manuscript bear a number of marginal notes, emendations, corrections, and deletions in the hand of Edmund Tilney, the Master of the Revels at the time.[74] The play depicts the original early modern supremacy controversy, which resulted in Sir Thomas More and John Fisher Bishop of Rochester refusing to take the oath declaring King Henry VIII supreme head of the church and their subsequent execution. Significantly, despite his prominent role in the historical events dramatized, King Henry VIII never appears in the play, and there is good reason to ascribe his omission to the perception of danger inherent in the play's subject matter. Indeed, Tilney's marginal comments, in which he advises leaving out the insurrection scene at the beginning of the play and deleting the scene concerned with Fisher's impeachment and More's resignation, confirm the perilous nature of dramatizing More's life.[75]

---

[73]   Munday's hand has been confirmed by W.W. Greg, "Autograph Plays by Anthony Munday," *MLR* 8 (1913): 89–90; Sir Edward Maunde Thompson, "The Autograph Manuscripts of Anthony Mundy," 3 *Library* 14 (1915–17): 325–53; M. St Clare Byrne, "Anthony Munday and his books," 4 *Library* 1 (1920–21): 225–56; Byrne, "Anthony Munday's Spelling as a Literary Clue," 4 *Library* 4 (1923–24): 9–23. For discussion of collaborators on the play, see Vittorio Gabrieli and Giorgio Melchiori, "Introduction," in *Sir Thomas More: A Play by Anthony Munday and Others*, ed. Gabrieli and Melchiori (New York, 1990), 21–7; Scott McMillan, *The Elizabethan Theatre and the Book of Sir Thomas More* (Ithaca, NY, 1987); Stanley Wells and Gary Taylor, *William Shakespeare: A Textual Companion* (New York, 1987); Arthur Kinney, "Text Context, and Authorship of *The Booke of Sir Thomas Moore*," in Sigrid King (ed.), *Pilgrimage for Love: Essay sin Early Modern Literature in Honor of Josephine A. Roberts* (Tempe, AZ, 1999), 133–60; Jeffrey Masten, "More or Less: Editing the Collaborative," *Shakespeare Studies* 29 (2001): 109–31; John Jowett, "Henry Chettle and the Original Text of *Sir Thomas More*," in *Shakespeare and "Sir Thomas More": Essays on the Play and its Shakespearean Interest*, ed. T.H. Howard-Hill (New York, 1989), 131–50. For discussion of the dating of the revisions, see Peter Blayney, "*The Booke of Sir Thomas Moore* Re-examined," *Studies in Philology* 69 (1972): 167–91.

[74]   Gabrieli and Melchiori, "Introduction," in *Sir Thomas More*, 17–20. Parenthetical citations from the play are from this edition.

[75]   Munday et al., *Sir Thomas More*, ed. Gabrieli and Melchiori, 17–18.

But the play is also a character study of Sir Thomas More, whose innate gifts of nobility and justice enable his rise to the position of Lord Chancellor and member of the Privy Council. In this respect, More is described precisely in the cosmopolitan terms with which we are familiar. His identity is based on exchange between the city of London and the foreign, in ways that are familiar from the life trajectory of Munday himself. On the one hand, after his appointment as Lord Chancellor and member of the Privy Council, More attends a banquet with the Lord Mayor of London and his wife. Emphasizing that the city is more important to him than the state itself, he remarks, "It is not state / That can our love from London separate" (3.2.94–5). On the other hand, during his discussion with the players of a dramatic performance entitled, *The Marriage of Wit and Wisdom*, after the feast with the Lord Mayor, a player named Luggins remarks, "God bless him [More], I would there were more of his mind: 'a loves our quality, and yet he's a learned man and knows what the world is" (3.2.346–8). Similarly, the Earl of Surrey describes him to Erasmus in the following terms:

Now shall you view the honourablest scholar,
The most religious politician,
The worthiest counsellor that tends our state.
That study is the general watch of England:
In it the prince's safety and the peace
That shines upon our commonwealth are forged
By loyal industry. (3.1.139–45)

This notion that More knows the world, and brings knowledge of the world to his official capacities as advisor to the king is identical to the role that Dee sees for the cosmopolitan in the *General and Rare Memorials*, although More ultimately combines this notion of the cosmopolitan with the opposing model embodied in Edmund Campion, the seditious exile who nevertheless was also willing to utilize his knowledge of the world to offer advice to the sovereign.

The supremacy issue, of course, is central to the play, at the same time that the exact nature of what articles More is called upon to sign is left opaque during the latter half of the drama. As is the case with Oldcastle in Munday's subsequent play by that name, More repeatedly invokes his conscience as the basis for his decision not to sign the articles, something that has led readers like Hamilton and others to see the play exclusively in terms of the personal conscience of religious minorities.[76] But there is another aspect of conscience here, which has to do with More's role as a magistrate and eventually Lord Chancellor. According to the early sixteenth-century Jurist, Christopher St. German, the Court of Chancery was to be ruled according to the principles of equity and conscience, in such a way that judgment would depart from positive law and defer to natural and divine law in cases where the positive law contravened the latter two legal regimes: "for yf any lawe made by man / bynde any person by way of precept or prohibition to any thing that is against [the sayde lawes /] it is no lawe / but a corrupcyon [& a

---

[76] Hamilton, *Munday and the Catholics*, 119–26.

manyfest errour]."[77] In the *Book of Sir Thomas More*, we witness similar situations in which More departs from the law in order to arrive at a just judgment. During his intervention at the beginning of the play in response to the anti-alien riots, More promises the organizers of the rebellion that the king himself will depart from the laws regarding sedition and apply equity in his judgment of them if they will submit to their betters:

> Submit you to these noble gentlemen,
> Entreat their mediation to the king,
> Give up yourself to form, obey the magistrate,
> And there's no doubt but mercy may be found
> If you seek it. (2.3.155–9)[78]

Elsewhere during the trial of the notorious cutpurse named Lifter, More promises mercy to the thief if he "lifts" Justice Suresby's purse in order to chasten the arrogant and careless magistrate (1.3.51–200). Finally, later in the play, once he has attained the office of Lord Chancellor, he is faced with Falkner, the unkempt ruffian who "was not at barber's this three years" (3.1.107). More declares that Falkner can stay in jail for the foreseeable future, or he can "cut off this fleece, and lie there but a month" (3.1.121). In all of these cases, More utilizes the notion of equity, in which the judge departs from strict adherence to the law in order to arrive at a more universal notion of justice.

What is crucial about such scenes is that they secularize and anachronize one aspect of the religious conflict that occurred as part of Henry VIII's dispute with the Roman curia during the 1530s. An important aspect of the Statute in Restraint

---

[77] Christopher St German, *The Doctor and Student Together with Questions and Cases Concerning the Equity Thereof*, ed. T.F.T. Plucknett et al. (London, 1975), 207. For context, see John A. Guy, "Law, Equity and Conscience in Henician Juristic Thought" in *Reassessing the Henrician Age: Humanism, Politics and Reform 1500–1550*, ed. Alistair Fox and John A. Guy (New York, 1986), 179–98; Brian Levack, *The Civil Lawyers in England, 1603–1641*, 27–8; For the influence of Thomas Aquinas on St. German, see St. German, *Doctor and Student*, ed. Plucknet, 27, and Plucknet's introduction to *Doctor and Student*. See also Robert E. Rodes, Jr., *Lay Authority and Reformation in the English Church: Edward I to the Civil War* (Notre Dame, IN, 1982), 69–77; and S.B. Chrimes, *English Constitutional History in the Fifteenth Century* (Cambridge 1936), 204–14. For discussion of St. German's dispute with More over relations between the spiritual and temporal realms, see John A. Guy, "Thomas More and St. Germain: The Battle of the Books," in *Reassessing the Henrician Age*, 95–120; and John A. Guy, *The Public Career of Sir Thomas More* (New Haven, 1980). It is ironic that, despite his traditional view of the relationship between natural and common law, St. German ultimately differed with More on the church's treatment of heretics and the powers that the clergy had arrogated to themselves. Later he published *A Treatise Concerning the Power of the Clergy and the Laws of the Realm*, which argued that the only spiritual laws to bind the sovereign were pronounced by God himself.

[78] For discussion of the play's portrayal of the anti-alien riots, see Lloyd Edward Kermode, *Aliens and Englishness in Elizabethan Drama* (New York, 2009), 75–84.

114   *Early Modern Catholics, Royalists, and Cosmopolitans*

of Appeals of 1533 was the way in which it found precedence in the Statute of Provisions and *Praemunire*, a law passed during Richard II's reign, which restricted the ability of English subjects to appeal to the Roman curia.[79] During the late Elizabethan era, in which *Sir Thomas More* was written, the common law courts, comprising the King's Bench and the Court of Common Pleas, sometimes used this statute as well as related statutes to issue writs of *praemunire* in order to restrict the ability of Chancery to meddle in the affairs of competing courts. Judges on the common law courts seemed to view the Chancery, the civil law courts, and the ecclesiastical courts as foreign to the realm, and even to some extent, in league with Rome.[80] Sir Thomas More is presented in this play as the wisest member of Henry's Privy Council, one who protects the king from dangerous sedition at the beginning of the play, but who ultimately remains loyal to Rome after the Statute in Restraint of Appeals. But even more importantly, his position as Lord Chancellor would have been seen by spectators in late sixteenth-century London as a secular analogue of the Roman curia, which had been the focus of Henry's ire during the 1530s. Thus the play's portrayal of the conflict between More and the unseen Henry VIII throws what was originally a religious matter into the sphere of secular politics, such that the sympathetic portrayal of More functions as a defense of the cosmopolitan ideal as well as an analogue to the Roman curia.

Like *The Book of Sir Thomas More*, Munday's *First Part of Sir John Oldcastle* reflects issues related to contemporary controversies over papal supremacy, especially relating to papal intervention into the secular realm.[81] The dramatic action begins with a public disturbance, caused by two opposing groups of

---

[79]   The Statute of Provisions and *Praemunire* was actually based on the first *praemunire* statute of 1307, which enacted that no person shall "secretly or openly, by any Device or Mean, carry or send, or by any Means cause to be sent, any Tax imposed by the Abbots, Priors, Masters or Wardens of Religious houses their Superiors, or assessed among themselves, out of [the sovereign's] Kingdom and his Dominium, under the Name of Rent, Tallage, or any kind of Imposition." See 27 Edw. III stat. I, c. I (1353) in *The Statutes at large, from Magna Charta to the Thirtieth Year of King George II, inclusive, in six volumes* (London, 1758), vol. 1, sigs. 2N2v. See also 35 Edw. I stat. I, c. 2 [vol. 1, sig. X4v], 25 Edw III stat 6 (1350) [vol. 1, sig. 2M4–2Nv], and 16 Ric. II c. 5 (1392) [vol. 1, sigs. 3G1v–3G2v]. For context, see John A. Guy, "Henry VIII and the Praemunire Maneuvers of 1530–31," *The English Historical Review* 97.384 (July 1982): 481–503.

[80]   For context, see Lockey, *Law and Empire*, 145–86.

[81]   Philip Henslowe's diary records payment for the play going to Anthony Munday, Michael Drayton, Robert Wilson, and Richard Hathway. For a discussion of this play as the authors' response to Shakespeare's portrayal of Oldcastle in 1 and 2 *Henry IV*, see Peter Corbin and Douglas Sedge (eds), "Introduction," in *The Oldcastle Controversy: Sir John Oldcastle, Part 1 and The Famous Victories of Henry V* (New York, 1991), 9–21. See also Gary Taylor, "The Fortunes of Oldcastle," *Shakespeare Survey* 38 (1985): 85–100. For discussion of Shakespeare's "malice" against the contemporary Cobhams as a motivating factor in his own portrayal of Oldcastle [Falstaff], see Robert Boies Sharpe, *The Real Wars of the Theatres: Shakespeare's Fellows in Rivalry with the Admiral's Men, 1594–1603* (Boston, 1935), 69–70.

followers respectively of Lord Herbert and of Lord Powis, followed by a trial, over which preside two judges. According to the Sheriff, the dispute is "about religion" (1.86):

> Lord Powis detracted from the power of Rome,
> Affirming Wycliffe's doctrine to be true
> And Rome's erroneous. Hot reply was made
> By the Lord Herbert: they were traitors all
> That would maintain it. (1.87–91)[82]

In this passage, Lord Powis's affirmation of "Wycliffe's doctrine" is a reference to Wycliffe's rejection of papal authority in all its manifestations, including over temporal magistrates. According to the Sheriff's testimonial, Lord Powis had responded to Lord Herbert's accusation of treason by invoking the name of Sir John Oldcastle, Lord Cobham, who along with Powis would defend Wycliffe's doctrine, in defiance of Rome (1.94–8). One of the two judges responds that English officials must respond with caution, since "This case concerns the King's prerogative, / And 'tis dangerous to the state and commonwealth" (1.99–100). He goes on to warn of the potential for mutiny and rebellion, against the authority of King Henry V, who was busy making preparations for an invasion of France (1.105–25). In addition to illustrating the general anxiety with which the subject was associated at this time, the Judge's characterization is a puzzling response to the confrontation between Herbert and Powis: there is an implicit suggestion in his response that Powis and his supporters, who oppose "the power of Rome" in England, may be a threat to the prerogative powers of the king, when in reality, anything which limited the power of the Roman curia in England would seem to have had the effect of strengthening the king's power or prerogative.

The rest of the play clarifies early questions concerning Oldcastle's religious and political affiliations, showing that Oldcastle is both the most pious and loyal character in the play.[83] In contrast, the Catholic clergymen, the Archbishop of Rochester and Sir John the Parson of Wrothsam, are presented as pursuing their own corrupt and venal self-interest rather than the kingdom's public good. Immediately after the public disturbance between Powis and Herbert, Rochester summons Oldcastle to the ecclesiastical courts to answer charges of heresy. Taking the view that Oldcastle is a loyal subject, King Henry V asks Rochester what will occur should Oldcastle choose to appeal to the king's authority, and Rochester and the Earl of Suffolk answer in such a way that clarifies papal supremacy over temporal authorities. Henry's response is instructive of the tensions that run through the entire play:

---

[82] All parenthetical references are to the Corbin and Sedge edition of the play.

[83] See Mary Grace Muse Adkins, "Sixteenth-century Religious and Political Implications in *Sir John Oldcastle*," *University of Texas Studies in English* 22 (1942): 86–104.

116   *Early Modern Catholics, Royalists, and Cosmopolitans*

Rochester.	[Oldcastle] cannot [appeal], my Lord in such a case as this.
Suffolk.	Not where religion is the plea, my Lord.
King Henry.	I took it always that ourself stood on't As a sufficient refuge, unto whom Not any but might lawfully appeal. (2.119–22)

Henry's response in this exchange—in support of Oldcastle's right to appeal to the king—is intended both as an early challenge to the Catholic position on papal supremacy, and, as a precursor of the Church of England's position on the issue of supremacy, which would not come to fruition until the Tudor era. In effect, the early alliance between King Henry V and the Catholic clergymen masks temporarily an emerging doctrinal separation on the relationship between the Roman curia and the English crown.

This barely buried conflict between crown and church continues in a subsequent scene, in which Rochester sends a Summoner to present Oldcastle with a summons to appear in the ecclesiastical courts without the king's knowledge (4.1–90). Continuing the theme of resistance to the doctrine of Roman supremacy over the temporal realm, Oldcastle's steward, Harpoole, responds to the insolent Summoner by forcing him to swallow the writ of summons with the help of a glass of beer provided by the butler (4.55–75). Later the king himself confronts Oldcastle about his unconventional religious views, and Oldcastle responds to Henry with an anachronistic, sixteenth-century Erastian repudiation of Roman claims for supremacy over Christian kings:

My gracious Lord, unto your Majesty,
Next unto my God, I owe my life,
And what is mine either by nature's gift
Or fortune's bounty, all is at your service;
But for obedience to the Pope of Rome,
I owe him none, nor shall his shaveling priests
That are in England alter my belief.
If out of Holy Scripture they can prove
That I am in an error, I will yield,
And gladly take instruction at their hands.
But otherwise, I do beseech your Grace,
My conscience may not be encroached upon. (6.8–18)

This is without a doubt one of the most important passages in the play. There is conflict between the king and his subject here, but it does not involve a struggle for the throne. Indeed, Oldcastle's defense of his religious views reveals him to be a more robust defender and caretaker of the king's sovereignty than the king himself is. In this respect, according to the perspective of a typical, late-sixteenth-century spectator with conformist sympathies, Oldcastle is once again a forerunner of the Erastianism that would come to fruition during the reign of Queen Elizabeth. Oldcastle's statement of where he owes his allegiance, to God and the king under Him, recapitulates the Protestant rejection of the papal supremacy as well as the

Protestant view of the "authentic" spiritual hierarchy, which placed no entity but God over the sovereign. In the next sentence, Oldcastle rejects any loyalty to Rome or to any of its English representatives on the basis of Holy Scripture and personal conscience. Indeed, like Sir Thomas More, Oldcastle bases his beliefs and decisions on a code of personal conscience.

Subsequently, tensions between the king and Rochester continue to worsen, the king at one point complaining that Rochester is "intending to forestall / Our regal power" by summoning Oldcastle to an ecclesiastical court (6.78–9). At this point, the dramatic action turns away from the conflict between church and state in order to explore two different rebellions, the first led by Sir Roger Acton and motivated by Wycliffe-associated religious devotion and the second, Lord Scroop's rebellion, motivated by dynastic considerations. Because of Oldcastle's reputation for integrity, both groups of rebels invoke his name as either an ally or a potential ally. Scroop and his allies, the Earl of Cambridge, Sir Thomas Gray, and Chartres, the French factor, approach Oldcastle to enlist him to their cause, an offer in which he originally feigns interest in order to reveal the plot to King Henry (7.80–161). Rochester takes advantage of the first rebellion, led by Acton and comprised of commoners, in order to implicate Oldcastle in the treasonous plot, and the king is in momentary agreement with him that Oldcastle must be arrested and executed for treason (12.52–81).

At this point in the drama, an implicit comparison is drawn between Oldcastle and Rochester in terms of each figure's role as caretaker of King Henry V's sovereignty. Oldcastle refutes Rochester's charges of complicity in the commoner's Wycliffian rebellion, and then he quickly provides evidence that the Earl of Cambridge, Scroop, and Gray are planning a rebellion against the king (12.82–146). In protecting the king from the conspirators involved in Scroop's rebellion, Oldcastle takes on a role analogous to the role that Rochester has claimed for himself from the beginning of the play, namely that of protecting the king from internal and external conspirators and traitors. But there is also a crucial difference. Whereas Oldcastle has the welfare of the king as his primary objective, Rochester continually disguises his own corrupt and private interests in the guise of concern for the public welfare. Indeed, the notion that Rochester pursues Oldcastle in the interests of the commonwealth disguises Rochester's personal interest in eliminating Oldcastle in order to maintain the corrupt ecclesiastical hierarchy that has served his personal interests. By the end of the first part of the play (the second part has presumably been lost), Oldcastle manages to avoid capture by the ecclesiastical authorities. Indeed at a critical moment towards the end of the play, he is forced to disguise himself by putting on the Bishop of Rochester's ecclesiastical robes in order to conceal himself from his tormenters. In doing so, he symbolically reveals the way in which his relationship with the king is analogous to the ideal relationship between the bishop and the king, namely that of protector and advisor and sometimes corrector of the king's conscience (14.49–59). Once again, then, we see that Munday was deeply ambivalent about the supremacy issue, wanting to maintain the king's independence from church interference, but

118   *Early Modern Catholics, Royalists, and Cosmopolitans*

also seeking to maintain the historical role of the church as teacher and guide of the king's rule. Indeed, the arrest of Scroop, Gray, and Cambridge provides a context within which to introduce innovative ways of understanding the king's relationship with the Privy Council. On arresting the conspirators, Henry declares that the plan was "To have the King at Council, and there murder him, / As Caesar was amongst his dearest friends" (16.43–4). Here, the council should ideally have the role of protecting the king's authority and person. In this case, however, it is precisely Oldcastle whom Henry thanks next to God: "God have the praise for our deliverance; / And next our thanks, Lord Cobham, is to thee, / True perfect mirror of nobility"(16.55–7). The parallel with the pope is clear: just as the pope was directly under God as corrector and protector of the sovereign's authority so too is Oldcastle the protector of King Henry's authority under God. The king's declaration in this scene embodies Munday's use of the dramatic genre in order to reorient the issue of papal supremacy in secular terms.

Perhaps, the most intriguing of Munday's dramatic works concerning the issue of papal supremacy are his two Robin Hood plays: *The Downfall of Robert, Earl of Huntington* and *The Death of Robert, Earl of Huntington*, both of which were staged in the late 1590s and printed in 1601.[84] The *Downfall* begins with an induction in which the poet John Skelton and a fictional John Eltam are preparing a play for the king, who is absent and unnamed, but whom we can assume, given the time period in which the historical Skelton lived, is Henry VIII. This is significant of course because Henry VIII presided over the greatest crisis of ecclesiastical supremacy during the history of England. The play that follows the induction combines the legend of Robin Hood with historical events that occurred during the reign of King John I, who presided over the most serious medieval crisis involving issues of supremacy and the power of papal deposition prior to the reign of Henry VIII.[85] Before Munday's Huntington plays, King John had been commemorated from a Protestant perspective by playwright John Bale in the early Tudor play *King Johan* (1538) and by martyrologist John Foxe in the *Acts and Monuments* as a medieval exemplum for later Protestant rulers.[86] The reign of King John was also commemorated from a more secular nationalist perspective in an anonymous two-part play called *The Troublesome Raigne of Iohn King of England* (1591) and by Shakespeare in his early play, *The Life and Death of King John* (1594).[87]

---

[84]   See Hamilton, *Munday and the Catholics*, 132–7. For background on the legend of Robin Hood during the period, see Jeffrey L. Singman, *Robin Hood: The Shaping of the Legend* (Westport, CT, 1998).

[85]   For a discussion of Munday's self-conscious approach to the relationship between history and the Robin Hood legend, see Liz Oakley-Brown, "Framing Robin Hood: Temporality and Textuality in Anthony Munday's Huntington Plays," in *Robin Hood: Medieval and Post Medieval*, ed. Helen Philips (Portland, OR, 2005), 113–29.

[86]   John Bale, *King Johan*, ed. Barry B. Adams (San Marino, CA, 1969); John Foxe, *The Acts and Monuments of John Foxe*, vol. 2, 319–42.

[87]   Anon., *The troublesome raigne of Iohn King of England* [electronic edition] (Cambridge, 1994).

At the beginning of the induction to Munday's first Huntington play, Skelton recounts how King Richard I has gone abroad to join the crusades on behalf of Christendom, leaving the Bishop of Ely, Lord Chancellor in charge in his absence:

> Richard calde Cor de Lyon takes his leave,
> Like the Lords Champion, gainst the Pagan foes
> That spoyle Judea and rich Palestine.
> The rule of England and his princely seate
> He leaves with Ely, then Lord Chancellor,
> To whom the mother Queene, her sonne, Prince John,
> Chester, and all the Peeres are sworne. (1.63–9)[88]

The dramatic action begins soon thereafter, with Robert Hood, the Earl of Huntington, having invited Prince John, the king's younger brother, the Queen Mother Eleanor, and other members of the court to celebrate his betrothal with Matilda.[89] Meanwhile, we learn that Justice Warman, the steward serving the Huntington's household, has betrayed his master into the hands of Huntington's evil uncle, Gilbert de Hood, the Prior of York, who subsequently banishes his nephew from his property and declares him an outlaw (2.140–64). Making matters more complex, Prince John is in love with Matilda, Huntington's betrothed, while the Queen Mother Eleanor is secretly in love with Huntington himself, all of which make it necessary for Huntington and Matilda to escape to the green world (5.560–658). After the escape of Robin (Huntington) and Matilda, Prince John uses the opportunity of Hugh Lacy's murder to usurp the throne from the regent, the Bishop of Ely (5.659–790). The Bishop of Ely attempts to arrest Prince John for the brutal murder of Hugh Lacy, and in response, the Prince presents fraudulent letters along with his brother's forged signature, authorizing him to assume the crown:

> But here are letters from his Majesty,
> Sent out of Joppa, in the holy land,
> To you, to these, to mee, to all the State,

---

[88] Anthony Munday, *The Downfall of Robert, Earle of Huntington*, in *Robin Hood and Other Outlaw Tales*, ed. Stephen Knight and Thomas Ohlgren (Kalamazoo, MI, 2000), 303–401. All parenthetical citations to the play are to this edition.

[89] Until line 781, "Matilda" is named "Marian." For the significance of Munday presenting Robin Hood as a nobleman, and specifically as the Earl of Huntington (a first in the history of the Robin Hood legend), see Malcolm Nelson, *Robin Hood Tradition in the English Renaissance*, (Elizabethan and Renaissance Studies, Salzburg Studies in English Literature, Salzburg, 1974), 119–31, and Meredith Skura, "Anthony Munday's 'Gentrification' of Robin Hood," *English Literary Renaissance* 33.2 (2003): 155–80; Stephen Knight, *Robin Hood, A Complete Study of the English Outlaw* (Cambridge, MA, 1994), 123; and David Bevington, *Tudor Drama and Politics. A Critical Approach to Topical Meaning* (Cambridge, MA, 1968), 295–8. Unlike Hamilton, Bevington sees the name of Huntington as motivated by the Admiral's Men's efforts "to give sympathetic expression to [their] Puritan viewpoint" (295), while Knight argues that Munday's noble portrayal of Robin Hood amounts to a process of both "gentrification and emasculation" (117).

120 *Early Modern Catholics, Royalists, and Cosmopolitans*

> Containing a repeale of that large graunt,
> And free authoritie to take the seale,
> Into the hands of three Lords temporall. (5.744–9)

The three lords temporal are Prince John, and his close allies, the Earl of Leicester and Hugh Lacy's corrupt brother, the Lord Lacy. As commentators have noted, it is hard to know where legitimate rule is centered in these two plays, given that, with the exception of the absent Richard, magistrates over both the temporal [Prince John] and the ecclesiastical realms [the Prior of York and at the beginning of play, the Bishop of Ely] are corrupt.[90] The Bishop of Ely eventually redeems himself, joining the band of Robin Hood's outlaws, along with numerous former allies of Prince John. In the end, Prince John disguises himself as one of Robin's outlaws in order to escape the consequences of the collapse of his own legitimacy. Robin captures Prince John, and on Richard's triumphant return to England, Robin presents Prince John to the crown, newly repentant and reformed:

> Here is Prince John, your brother, whose revolt
> And folly in your absence, let me crave,
> With his submission may be buried.
> For he is now no more the man he was,
> But duetifull in all respects to you. (15.2757–61)

Whereas the ecclesiastical magistrate, the Bishop of Ely, had been powerless before Prince John, Huntington declares here that John's former sinful behavior has been corrected and reformed. Representing the pastoral purity of the green world, Munday's Robin Hood acts as a substitute for papal or episcopal authority, correcting the conscience of a sinful secular magistrate when he goes astray.[91] In this respect, Robin finds himself allied with both temporal and ecclesiastical authorities in redeeming Prince's John's corrupt and tyrannical rule. Richard's legendary role within the Crusades, fighting "gainst Pagan foes," orients all of these dramatic events within the larger transnational Christian realm.

The sequel, *The Death of Robert, Earl of Huntington*, portrays tensions between the temporal and ecclesiastical realms more directly. Indeed, even if Munday's earlier dramatic works betray barely allegorized alarm at the prospects of an English sovereign governing without spiritual supervision, *The Death of Robert* shows that Munday wanted to be seen as a conformist, ready to endorse an ecclesiastical hierarchy that was answerable only to the English sovereign. Indeed from the outset, this play seems ruthlessly clear about where Munday's political loyalties lay, when ecclesiastical matters arose. By the end of the first third of the play, the evil Prior of York has poisoned Robin Hood with a deadly concoction,

---

[90] Hamilton, *Munday and the Catholics*, 129–30.

[91] For a discussion of the moral purity and universalism that was often associated with the pastoral during this period, see Lockey, *Law and Empire*, 36–41.

Border-Crossing and Translation 121

which he had prepared for Huntington and the king (508–824).[92] As Huntington lays dying, King Richard asks the Bishop of Ely if there are any laws that allow the state to convict "This Prior, that confesseth murders thus," to which the Bishop responds, "He is a hallowed man, and must be tried, / And punisht by the censure of the Church" (713–15). The now repentant Prior corrects them, confessing

> Richard, King Richard, in thy Grandsires daies,
> A law was made, the Cleargie sworne thereto,
> That whatsoever Church-man did commit
> Treason, or murder, or false felonie,
> Should like a seculer be punished. (718–22)

At the end of Robin Hood's life, then, King Richard is finally able to claim sovereignty over a corrupt ecclesiastical realm. The rest of this play takes an abrupt turn that provides some context to how some of Munday's pageants would treat this issue. *The Death of Robert* is actually two plays interlinked by a common theme, the English nobles' correction of the king's tyranny, and an induction scene in which, in the wake of Robin Hood's premature demise, the actor playing the Earl of Chester declare that they plan to end the play with "*Matildaes* Tragedie," which recounts the tumultuous reign of King John in the wake of the death of King Richard (871). Munday drew the story of John and Matilda from a number of recent English retellings: most notably, John Stow's translation of Nicholas de Bromfield's "Dunmow Chronicle" and Michael Drayton's narrative poem simply entitled, "Matilda."[93] In Munday's version, following his brother's death, Prince John has ascended the throne, but he is surrounded by competing claimants and threats to the crown. Meanwhile, he has also rekindled his passion for Matilda, who refuses his advances. Throughout the remainder of the play, King John's intemperate pursuit of Matilda and his cruel murder of Lady Bruse and her son— he orders that they be imprisoned in a dungeon without food, leading to their starvation—embody the characteristics of untrammeled tyranny that came to be associated with the historical King John's reign. Meanwhile, the noblemen, consisting of Fitzwater, the Bruses, the Earl of Leicester, and the Earl of Richmond, persist in rebellion against the king.

Ultimately, Matilda finds false refuge in the convent of Dunmow, whose corrupt Abbess attempts to sell her to the king for the price of 100 marks. Trapped between surrendering her chastity to the king and certain death, she chooses to drink a cup of poison provided to her by the king's servant. By the end of the play, King John, defeated by the rebelling nobles, has turned penitent for murdering Matilda, Lady Bruse, and her son. The Earl of Leicester suggests that the nobles

---

[92]   Subsequent citations are to line numbers from Munday, *The Death of Robert, Earl of Huntington*, in *The Huntingdon Plays: A Critical Edition*, ed. John Carney Meagher (New York, 1980), 284–461.

[93]   John Stowe, *The Annales of England* (London, 1592); Michael Drayton, "Matilda," in *The Works of Michael Drayton*, ed. William J. Hebel (Oxford, 1961), vols 1 and 5. See Hamilton, *Munday and the Catholics*, 132–3 for context.

122   *Early Modern Catholics, Royalists, and Cosmopolitans*

swear allegiance to Lewis the Dolphin of France, who has been sent with an army to help the beleaguered English subjects, but Oxford suggests that it is not "for loue of England [that] Lewis comes" (2994). In the end, the nobles choose to resubmit to King John, with the Earl of Leicester admonishing him:

> My Lord, once more your subiects do submit,
> Beseeching you to thinke how things haue past,
> And let some comfort shine on vs your friends,
> Through the bright splendour of your [future] vertuous life. (3028–31)

To which the king vows to "be better than I yet haue beene" (3033). As in Campion's *Ambrosia*, the sovereign repents his tyrannical behavior, ultimately redeeming himself and re-legitimizing his own rule. But the situation is more complex than this, illustrating as it does the important strains of convergence that can be found in Catholic resistance theory and sixteenth-century Protestant monarchomach tracts. On the one hand, in *A Conference*, Persons makes an important example of the tyranny of King John, who "by his euel gouernment ... made himselfe both so odious at home & contemptible abroade ... as first of al he was both excommunicated and deposed by sentence of the pope at the sute of his owne people." Persons explains that, promising to make war against the Turks, King John was temporarily able to ally himself with the pope, but the "Barons" were not mollified and proceeded "to his depriuation which they did effectuate, first at Canterbury and after at London, in the eighteenth & last yeare of his reigne."[94] According to Persons, a successful rebellion against the tyrant was only averted by the death of the king in 1216.[95] On the other hand, the situation in Munday's play also conforms to the contours of legitimate rebellion set out in the anonymous Huguenot tract, *Vindiciae, Contra Tyrannos* (1579). Munday's King John violates the second part of the two-fold covenant that, according to the *Vindiciae*'s author, binds the sovereign's temporal realm to the will of the people.[96] As a result, the kingdom's magistrates, that is, the English nobles in this case, who function "like patrons who should protect the public welfare, and the safety and liberty of the people," are obliged to admonish the king when he seeks to infringe on the rights of the people.[97]

---

[94]   Persons, *A Conference*, F1v–F2.

[95]   Allen uses the papal excommunication of King John and the rebellion against his rule as a way to justify acts of disobedience by English Catholics such as Sir William Stanley's surrender of Deventer to the Spanish crown on January 29, 1586/7. See *Cardinal Allen's defence of Sir William Stanley's surrender*, 26.

[96]   The first part of the *Vindiciae* author's two-fold covenant is the spiritual one between God, the people, and the sovereign. Anon., *Vindiciae, Contra Tyrannos: Or Concerning the Legitimate Power of a Prince over the People, and of the People over a Prince*, ed. and trans. George Garnet (New York, 1994). The original Latin edition was titled Stephano Ivnio Bruto Celta, *Vindiciae, contra tyrannos: sive, De Principis in Populum, Populique in Principem, legitima potestate* (Edimbvrgi, 1579). Citations are to the modern English translation followed by the Latin original in brackets.

[97]   "tanquam Patroni, qui vtilitati publicae, Populique saluti & libertati patrocinentur." Anon, *Vindiciae*, H4v.

Whether the model of restricting and resisting temporal rule in this second Huntington play was exclusively Catholic—or Protestant—inspired or some combination of the two is impossible to say, but within the context of Munday's entire dramatic corpus, the issue may not matter. The ending of the second Huntington play, in which the English nobles collectively correct John's tyranny and prompt the king to redeem himself, certainly complicates the earlier model whereby Munday explored how a uniquely-wise and cosmopolitan figure with origins in the secular world—More, Oldcastle, Robin Hood—could take on a role analogous to the pope or the bishop with regard to correcting the king's conscience, but it does not reject it altogether. After all, at the end of the second Huntington play, King John undergoes a familiar process of reformation that is similar to the first Huntington play, asking Bruse to forgive him and vowing to undergo "penance for this wrong" (3044).

In the end, comparing both of Munday's Huntington plays to Shakespeare's *The Life and Death of King John* clarifies important insights about the unique nature of Munday's approach to issues surrounding the education and correction of the sovereign. Unlike Munday's second Huntington play, Shakespeare's *King John* provides rich historical detail concerning the actual conflict between King John and the pope, which transpired during the first two decades of the thirteenth century. In 1207, Pope Innocent III appointed Stephen Langton as Archbishop of Canterbury. When John rejected Langton's appointment, the pope issued an interdict against the English crown, followed in 1212 by a papal bull deposing the king. In Shakespeare's *King John*, all of this is staged at the beginning of the third act, when Cardinal Pandulph, the papal legate, enters on stage and interrupts the terms of peace to which King John and King Philip of France have agreed before the walls of the besieged town of Angers. Announcing himself to the two kings, Pandulph directly addresses John, demanding of him, in the name of the pope, "why thou against the Church, our holy mother, / So willfully dost spurn" (3.1.141–2).[98] John responds by claiming supremacy over all ecclesiastical matters within his realm:

> Thou canst not, Cardinal, devise a name
> So slight, unworthy, and ridiculous,
> To charge me to an answer, as the Pope.
> Tell him this tale, and from the mouth of England
> Add thus much more, that no Italian priest
> Shall tithe or toll in our dominions;
> But as we, under God, are supreme head,
> So under Him that great supremacy,
> Where we do reign, we will alone uphold
> Without th' assistance of a mortal hand.
> So tell the Pope, all reverence set apart
> To him and his usurp'd authority. (3.1.149–60)

---

[98] Subsequent parenthetical citations are from William Shakespeare, *King John*, in *The Riverside Shakespeare*, ed. G. Blakemore Evans (2nd ed., New York, 1997).

In response to John's claim of supremacy, Pandulph announces the king's excommunication and enlists King Philip to "raise the power of France upon his head / Unless he do submit himself to Rome" (3.1.193–4). This scene presents the supremacy controversy threatening John's authority as one specifically concerned with the right to appoint bishops, therefore leaving out the more serious imputation of the king's tyranny. In comparison, the focus of Munday's Huntington plays is more directly on King John's tyranny, treating the conflict between Rome and the English crown obliquely and indirectly in terms of an ongoing contest between the English Church and state: in the general corruption of the English clergymen represented in the play, in the Prior of York's attempt on King Richard's life and his response (520–80), and finally in the Monk and Abbess's underhanded dealings with Matilda at the end of the play (2489–603).

It was of course the conflict with the pope that made King John an exemplary ruler in Bale's earlier dramatic account of his reign.[99] Unlike previous Protestant-inspired incarnations of King John, Shakespeare does not take the side of the English king here. Like every other major character in the play—King Philip, Lewis the Dolphin, Pandulph, and even the Bastard Philip of Faulconbridge, John is presented as motivated primarily by Machiavellian self-interest. For example, John will stand on principle in this scene, but when later in the play he perceives his rule to be threatened, he will quickly cut a deal with the papal legate to save himself (5.1.1–29). Pandulph is similarly full of machinations, first convincing Lewis, the despairing French prince, that John's capture of Arthur, the young French-sponsored claimant to the English throne, would ultimately strengthen Lewis's own claim to the English crown, while soon after making a deal with King John, which allows the king to preserve his title (3.4.107–83). Unlike Munday's tyrannical portrayal of John, the legitimacy of Shakepeare's King John is threatened not so much by the king's bad behavior but by the suspect nature of his claim to the throne and the existence of so many better competing claimants. In the end, Shakespeare's play does include a figure, the Bastard Falconbridge, who has certain characteristics in common with Munday's portrayals of Robin Hood and Oldcastle. At various points, Falconbridge seems to function as the king's caretaker (2.1.350–407). But whereas Robin Hood directly corrects the moral failings of King John and whereas Oldcastle assumes the role of the Henry V's caretaker, Falconbridge's role is ultimately more the Tamburlaine-like Machiavel than the protector of the king. At crucial moments, he advises the king to imitate his own grandiosity: "Be great in act, as you have been in thought. / Let not the world see fear and sad distrust / Govern the motion of a kingly eye" (5.1.45–7). But he is incapable of correcting the king's moral failings or preventing the collapse of his authority and final demise. Remarking in his final speech, "This England never did, nor never shall, / Lie at the proud foot of a conqueror, / But when it first did help to wound itself" (5.7.112–14), Falconbridge is better at assuming the role of brutal truth-teller, driving home a lesson about loyalty to the nation above all else. Indeed, whereas Munday's Huntington plays are about correcting

---

[99] Bale, *King Johan.*

Border-Crossing and Translation

the king's personal moral failings and his tyrannical rule, Shakespeare's play is more about the need to maintain a united England in the face of manipulative and self-interested foreign predators.[100]

Pageants and the Cosmopolis of London

Perhaps the most cosmopolitan series of dramatic works that Munday composed are the pageants that he created for the annual Lord Mayor's Show. These works have received little attention from scholars, but in their day, the Lord Mayor's pageants were probably the most widely-viewed dramatic productions of the period, because they occurred in the squares and streets of London and on the banks of the Thames River where the inhabitants of the city could hardly have avoided them.[101] As David Bergeron has noted, Munday's relationship to the Lord Mayor's Shows was essentially identical to the relationship of Ben Jonson to the court masque: "Munday dominates the scene," having "had a hand in at least fifteen Lord Mayor's Shows during the period 1602–1623."[102] Bergeron has noted that one remarkable aspect of these works is the way in which they combine adoration of the city with celebration of King James's court.[103] But within the context of the cosmopolitan mode that we are exploring here, the most salient aspect of these works is the way in which they contextualize the city within the international sphere.

One characteristic of the Lord Mayor's Shows, in particular, was common to the masque tradition, namely the use of the exotic and unfamiliar in order to portray the

---

[100] For an extended discussion of Munday's influence on Shakespeare, including *King John*, see David Womersley, "Shakespeare and Anthony Munday," in *Literary Milieux: Essays in Text and Context Presented to Howard Erskine-Hill*, ed. David Womersley and Richard McCabe (Newark, 2008), 72–91.

[101] For Munday's place within the civic culture of the city of London, see Tracy Hill, *Anthony Munday and Civic Culture: Theatre, History and Power in Early Modern London, 1580–1633* (New York, 2004).

[102] Anthony Munday, *Pageants and Entertainments of Anthony Munday: A Critical Edition*, ed. David M. Bergeron (New York, 1985), xi. See also Bergeron, "Anthony Munday: Pageant Poet to the City of London," *Huntington Library Quarterly* 30 (1967): 345–68, and Bergeron, *Practicing Renaissance Scholarship: Plays and Pageants, Patrons and Politics* (Pittsburgh, 2000). For the importance of the Pageants and the Lord Mayor's shows to London's civic culture, see M.C. Bradbook, "The Politics of Pageantry: Social Implications in Jacobean London," in *Poetry and Drama 1570–1700: Essays in Honour of Harold F. Brooks*, ed. Antony Coleman and Antony Hammond (London, 1981), 60–75; Theodore B. Leinwand, "London Triumphing: The Jacobean Lord Mayor's Show," *Clio* 11.2 (1982): 137–53; Gail Kern Paster, "The Idea of London in Masque and Pageant," in *Pageantry in the Shakespeare Theater*, ed. Bergeron (Athens, 1985), 48–64; and Sergei Lobanov-Rostovsky, "The Triumphes of Gold: Economic Authority in the Jacobean Lord Mayor's Show," *ELH* 60.4 (1993): 879–98; James Knowles, "The Spectacle of the Realm: Civic Consciousness, Rhetoric and Ritual in Earl Modern London," in *Theatre and Government Under the Early Stuarts*, ed. J.R. Mulryne and Margaret Shewring (New York, 1993), 157–89.

[103] Munday, *Pageants*, xii.

city or the court as wealthy and cultured. Munday's pageants tend to link London to the international sphere by means of commerce and religion. The position of Lord Mayor was inevitably inflected with commercial concerns since the Lord Major was a member of one of the Twelve Great Livery Companies, and he was elected by members of all the Livery Companies of London. Munday's pageants were written and performed in order to celebrate the guild from which the Lord Mayor originated. Thus, Munday's first extant pageant, *The Triumph of revnited Britania* (1605), which celebrated the Merchant Taylors and inaugurated Sir Leonard Holliday as Lord Mayor, begins with a dialogue between the Master and Mate of a Ship called the "*Royall Exchange*," which according to the Master, has recently "made a rich returne, / Laden with *Spices, Silkes,* and *Indico*" (112–13).[104] In fact, Holliday was a founder of the East India Company and the owner of a real merchant ship called the "Royal Exchange," a vessel whose name commemorates the mercantile forces linking the actual Royal Exchange in London to the rest of the world. In addition to the celebration of commerce and travel, Munday's commitment to London's Livery Companies often invokes transnational and ecumenical Christianity. For example, in the dedicatory epistle of his contemporary *Briefe Chronicle of the Successe of times, from the Creation of the World, to this instant* (1611), Munday links the current success of the Merchant Taylors, originally known as the Guild and Fraternity of St. John the Baptist, to its supposed origins in the transnational religious order of the Knights Hospitaller, which in 1240 had "within Christendome nineteene thousand Lordships or Mannors" and was anciently responsible for serving Christian pilgrims in Jerusalem.[105] Munday goes on to present the growth of the Merchants Taylors as coterminous both with the development of the city of London itself and with the history of the English crown, noting that from the time of Edward III, the kings of England "thought it no indignity to themselues, to be stiled in the Brother-hood of S. Iohn Baptist," wearing the livery on their shoulders and attending religious services at the Merchant Taylor's Hall.[106] Thus, in addition to their importance for maintaining commercial ties to Europe and the rest of the world, the Merchant Taylors and the city of London form a nexus linking the English crown to the transnational Christian realm.

Elsewhere, at the beginning of the Lord Mayor's pageant of 1614, entitled *Himatia-Poleos, The Triumphs of olde Draperie, or the rich Cloathing of England,*

---

[104] Munday, *The Triumphes of Re-United Britannia* (1605), in *Pageants and Entertainments*, 1–24. Citations are by line number. For Munday's relationship with the Merchant Taylors, see Charles R. Forker, "Two Notes on John Webster and Anthony Munday," *English Language Notes* 6 (1968): 26–34.

[105] Munday, *A Briefe Chronicle, of the Successe of times, from the Creation of the World to this instant. Containing, the Originall & liues of our ancient Fore-fathers, before and after the Floude, As also, of all the Monarchs, Emperours, Kinges, Popes, Kingdomes, Common-weales, Estates, and Gouernments, in most Nations of this Worlde: And how in alteration, or succession, they have continued to this day* (London, 1611), A4v. Note that in his typically cosmopolitan approach, Munday purports to have written a brief but comprehensive history of the world to the very instant that he was writing.

[106] Munday, *A Briefe Chronicle, of the Successe of times*, A5–A6.

which celebrated the Company of Drapers, Munday writes that the city had become the conduit through which just rule had anciently been established over the entire nation (1–10).[107] In Munday's formulation, just as Sparta or Lacedemon was responsible for introducing just rule into Rome, so did Rome introduce "our form of rule" into London and later England itself (5). Furthermore, the Great Twelve Livery companies were an integral part of this *translatio imperii*, which links England and "all other [modern] Nations" to the example of ancient Rome, which, like London, distinguished certain trade associations over others that were deemed of less importance (5). According to Munday's formulations in this pageant, commerce, related to the drapers' trade of making garments, increases the security of the city and therefore the country as well:

> The walles of any Citty, were termed by the *Grecians*, according as we title our instant discourse, *Himatia Poleos*, the Cloathing or garments of the Cittie. Intimating thereby, that as garments and cloathing doe ingirt the body, defending it continually from the extremities of colde and heat: so walles, being the best garments of any Citie, do preserve it from all dangerous annoyances. Hereon we lay the foundation of our devise, in the honour of *Draperie* the rich Clothing of *England*, which … clothed both Prince and people all alike, to the no mean renowne of the Kingdome, and admiration of forraigne nations, to whom our Draperie … by meanes of navigation and commerce, affoorded the rich Liverie of this land; better imbraced by them and much more highly esteemed, then all other trafficque whatsoever. (87–100)

In this passage, the commercial cloth trade is presented as erecting a wall of metaphorical drapery around the city that protects and defends its inhabitants, ultimately providing the same protection for the entire nation. At the same time, the Drapers' participation in a network of international trade is something that ties London and by extension England to the rest of the world "by meanes of navigation and commerce."

Something similar can be found in references to London and England's place within the transnational context of Christendom as well. The first lines of the 1616 Lord Mayor's pageant, *Chrysanaleia: The Golden Fishing: or, Honour of Fishmongers*, which celebrated John Lemon of the company of Fishmongers, make reference to the London merchants who helped European knights during the first Crusade, led by Godfrey, the Duke of Bouillon.[108] Like the subjects of "every Christian Kingdome [who] did ayde him [Godfrey] with their best assistance,"

---

[107]   Munday, *Himatia-Poleos, The Triumphs of olde Draperie, or the rich Cloathing of England* in *Pageants and Entertainments*, 71–84. Citations are by line number.

[108]   Munday, *Chrysanaleia* (1616) in *Pageants and Entertainments*, 101–22. Citations are by line number. For discussion of how pageants merge the languages of religion and commerce, see Daryl W. Palmer, "Metropolitan Resurrection in Anthony Munday's Lord Mayor's Shows," *Studies in English Literature 1500–1900* 46.2 (2006): 371–87. See also David Cressy, "The Protestant Calendar and the Vocabulary of Celebration in Early Modern England," *The Journal of British Studies* 29.1 (1990): 31–52.

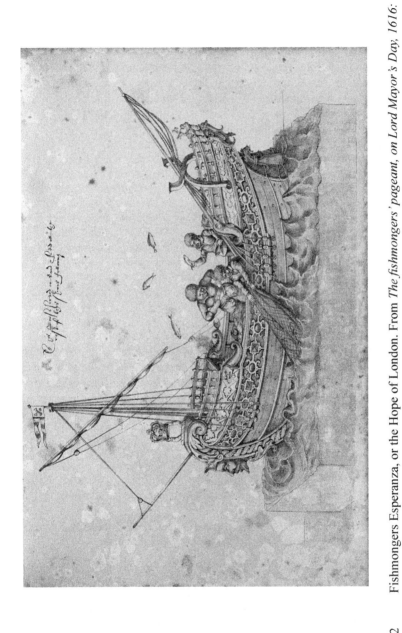

Fig. 2.2 Fishmongers Esperanza, or the Hope of London. From *The fishmongers' pageant, on Lord Mayor's Day, 1616: Chrysanaleia, the golden fishing* / devised by Anthony Munday; represented in 12 plates by Henry Shaw, from contemporary drawings in the possession of the Worshipful Company of Fishmongers, ed. John G. Nichols (London, 1844). By permission of the Folger Shakespeare Library.

English merchants, especially the Fishmongers and the Goldsmithes, did their part to contribute to the cause, eventually joining together to rebuild the ruined walls and gates of Jerusalem (17–18). Interestingly, when they return home, they joined together in order to rebuild England's own Jerusalem, "our famous Metropolis *London*" (38). All of this is placed in the context of transnational religious doctrine and international commerce that links London with other cities of the world. Thus, it is no surprise that the first device in the pageant was a fishing "busse" called the Fishmongers Esperanza, or the Hope of London, which is meant either to symbolize St. Peter's fishing boat, from which Peter was called by Christ to be a fisher of men, or to symbolize an English fishing vessel "which not only enricheth our kingdome with all variety of fish the Sea can yeelde: but helpeth also (in that kind) all other lands" (79–81; see Figure 2.2). Thus, in this pageant, London becomes a city of God and of the world, linked by international religious and commercial ties to other significant cities such as Jerusalem.[109]

The issues of papal or sovereign primacy are less obviously present in Munday's pageants. One reason for their absence may be the genre itself, which was focused on the city of London rather than the crown. Another reason may be simply that King James I's preference for ecumenism over confrontation with England's Catholic enemies meant that it was easier for writers like Munday to emphasize England's relationship with the Christian world while ignoring the underlying political and religious tensions over issues of allegiance and supremacy. Of course, controversies surrounding the papal claim for a right to depose heretical sovereigns continued into the beginning of James's reign, albeit at a less frenzied pace, eventually emerging in full force in the aftermath of the Oath of Allegiance (1606), and especially with the publication of James I's *Triplici nodo, triplex cuneus* (1608), Robert Bellarmine's *Responsio ad librum: Triplici nodo, triplex cuneus* (1608), his subsequent *Tractatus de potestate summi pontificis in rebus temporalibus* (1610), and Francisco Suarez's *Defensio catholicae fidei contra anglicanae sectae errores* (1613).[110] But in comparison to the Elizabethan years,

---

[109]   Note that in the 1611 pageant, entitled *Chruso-Thriambos. The Triumph of Gold* (in *Pageants and Entertainments*, 49–70), which inaugurated Sir James Pemberton, a similar theme opens the masque, likening Richard the Lionheart's establishment of the position of Lord Mayor with his role in the Crusades (187–99).

[110]   Anon., *Triplici nodo, triplex cuneus: Apologia pro iuramento fidelitatis, aduersus duo breuia P. Pauli Quinti, & epistolam Cardinalis Bellarmini, ad G. Blackvellum, Archipresbyterum nuper seriptam. Authoritate Regia* (Londini, 1608) [see *Triplici nodo, trplex cuneus* in *King James VI and I: Political Writings*, ed. J.P. Sommerville (New York, 2006), 85–131]; Robert Bellarmine, *Responsio Matthaei Torti Presbyteri, et theologi papiensis, ad librvm inscriptvm, Triplici nodo triplex cvnevs* (Coloniae Agrippinae, 1608) in *Ven. Cardinalis Roberti Bellarmini Politiani SJ Opera Omnia*, ed. J. Fevre (12 vols, Paris, 1870–74), vol. 12, 209–56; *Tractatus de potestate svmmi pontificis in rebvs temporalibvs: aduersus Gvlielmvm Barclaivm* (Coloniae Agrippinae, 1611); and Francisco Suarez, *Defensio Fidei Catholicae et Apostolicae Adversvs Anglicanae Sectae Errores cum responsione ad Apologiam pro Juramento Fidelitatis, & Praefationem monitoriam Serenissimi Jacobi Magnae Britanniae Regis* (Cologne, 1614) [*A Defense of the Catholic*

130   *Early Modern Catholics, Royalists, and Cosmopolitans*

concerns about ecclesiastical supremacy had to a large extent been mitigated by James's official efforts at achieving religious reconciliation among Christians of many persuasions as well as his pursuit of peace with the Spanish crown.[111]

In any event, the only royal pageant Munday was responsible for creating, the 1610 pageant celebrating Prince Henry's investiture entitled *Londons Love, to the Royal Prince Henrie*, does provide evidence of Munday's continued investment in such issues. *Londons Love* was a major undertaking, commissioned by all the companies of London and the Lord Mayor in order to receive the Prince, who arrived by barge on May 31, 1610, into the city proper. Once again, the pageant places the city at the center of national affairs, but more importantly, Munday's introduction of the pageant itself celebrates the fact that Henry would be invested in the court of parliament. Munday lists 10 previous princes who were invested successfully in parliament, and then he goes on to give a cautionary note concerning subsequent sovereigns—"Richard the second, Edward the fift, and Edward the Sonne of Richard the third"—who were not invested there: "And those that were created out of Parliament, were Princes of hard and disaster fortune. For Richard the second was deposed: Edward the fifte murdered, and Richard the third, his Sonne dyed within three moneths after, as a just judgement of god for his Father's wickedness" (65–71).[112] The desire to have the future king invested in Parliament resembles the notion found in the *Vindiciae, Contra Tyrannos* that the sovereign should be answerable to the people's representatives. However, it also reminds us of the importance that Robert Persons placed on the coronation ceremony presided over by a bishop in his *Conference*.[113] In Munday's royal pageant, the prince's investiture by parliament serves to secularize Persons's perception of correct relations between church and state, as reflected in his view of the bishop's essential role in the coronation ceremony. Both bishop and parliament play the same role with regard to the temporal sovereign, serving to correct and modify his rule on behalf of God and the people.

Faith and Apostolic Faith— In refutation of the Errors of the Anglican Sect with a Reply to the Apologie for the Oath of Allegiance and to the Admonitory Preface of His Most Serene Majesty James, King of England], collected in *Selections from Three Works of Francisco Suarez*, ed. James Brown Scott, 2 vols (Oxford, 1944). For discussion of how English Catholics viewed the papal deposing power during the reign of James I, see Thomas Clancy, S.J., "English Catholics and the Papal Deposing Power, 1570–1640 [Part II: The Jacobean Period]," *Recusant History* 6/5 (1962): 205–28. For a notable Protestant response to Bellarmine, see chapter 9 of John Donne, *Pseudo-Martyr: Wherein out of Certaine Propositions and Gradations, This Conclusion is evicted. That those which are of the Romane Religion in this Kingdome, may and ought to take the Oath of Allegeance*, ed. Anthony Raspa (Buffalo, NY, 1993), 179–89.

[111]   W.B. Pattinson, *King James and the Reunion of Christendom* (New York, 1997), esp. 36–57.

[112]   Munday, *Londons Love, to the Royal Prince Henrie* (1610), in *Pageants and Entertainments*, 35–48. Citations are to line numbers.

[113]   Persons, *A Conference*, B4.

Finally, *Chrysanaleia*, the 1616 celebration of the inauguration of John Leman to the position of Lord Mayor, also briefly touches on such concerns. In this pageant, Munday chooses to celebrate the mayoralty of another fishmonger, William Walworth, who served as Lord Mayor in 1374 and 1381. Munday recalls that, during the second term of 1381, Walworth defended Richard II during Wat Tyler's Rebellion in a way that is reminiscent of John Oldcastle's role with respect to Henry V in Munday's earlier play. One of the devices of the pageant presented Walworth being resurrected at his tomb, giving his blessing to Lemon (177–82).[114] A subsequent device represents in allegorical terms the divinely sanctioned protection, which Walworth provided to Richard II, in the form of a Pageant Chariot drawn by Mermen and Mermaids:

> Our Pageant Chariot, is drawn by two Mare-men and two Mare-mayds, as being the supporters to the Companies coate of Armes. In the highest seat of eminence, sits the triumphing Angell, who that day smote the enemy by *Walworth's* hand, and laid all his proud presuming in the dust. With one hand (King *Richard* sitting a degree beneath her) [the angel] holds his Crowne on fast, that neither forrein Hostilitie, nor home-bred Trecherie should ever more shake it. In the other hand shee holds his striking Rodde, inferring thus much thereby: *By mee King's reigne, and their enemies are scattered.* (183–92)[115]

Note that Walworth's suppression of Tyler's revolt was guided by the hand of an angel, who is the true protector of the king. Ultimately, this is the answer to the discussion between Crowley and the Jesuit Luke Kirby, which Munday had recorded in his account of Kirby's execution. For conformists, God and his angels guide and protect his sovereigns by means of councilors, nobles, and magistrates such as Lord Mayor Walworth. The papal overseer of temporal sovereigns—found in the work of Sanders and Persons—becomes secularized in Munday's fictional portrayal of wise and worldly figures such as Walworth, Oldcastle, Huntington, and More, who function in a manner that is analogous to the Roman curia. As we shall see in the next section in which we consider a number of works by Sir John Harington, Munday was not alone in secularizing papal oversight of the temporal realm.

---

[114] For a contemporary drawing of this device, see Munday, *The Fishmongers' Pageant on Lord Mayor's Day, 1616, Chrysanaleia: The Golden Fishing, Devised by Anthony Munday, Citizen and Draper. Represented in Twelve Plates by Henry Shaw, F.S.A. from Contemporary Drawings in the Possession of the Worshipful Company of Fishmongers, Accompanied with Various Illustrative Documents and an Historical Introduction*, ed. John Gough Nichols (London, 1844), folio 21. For a discussion of the theme of resurrection in Munday's pageants, see Palmer, "Metropolitan Resurrection in Anthony Munday's Lord Mayor's Shows," 371–87.

[115] For a contemporary drawing of this device, see Munday, *The Fishmongers' Pageant*, ed. John Gough Nichols, folios 22–3.

Sir John Harington and the Privy Council

While presenting himself as an adherent to the established church, the first English translator of Ariosto's *Orlando Furioso*, Sir John Harington (1561–1612), nevertheless frequently conveyed empathy for the plight of English Catholics throughout his writings.[116] Recently, Gerard Kilroy has put forth the related claim that both John Harington of Stepney (1517–82) and his son, Sir John, had an abiding interest in the writings of Edmund Campion, the former reportedly having read on his deathbed Henry Walpole's poem commemorating Campion's death on December 1, 1581 and the latter having transcribed the only two extant copies of Campion's Virgilian poem, *Sancti salutiferi nascentia semina verbi*.[117] It is no surprise then to find that one of Harington's principal interlocutors throughout his writing career was Campion's partner during the first Jesuit mission, Robert Persons. Harington's first engagement with Persons's writings can be found in the English translation of *Orlando Furioso* (1591), the early work for which he is primarily known to subsequent generations. In the coda to the translation, Harington begins the penultimate commentary entitled, "A Briefe and Summarie Allegorie of Orlando Furioso," with a defense of his translation against the charge, found in the 1585 edition of Persons's *Christian directorie*, that "dissolute poets and other loose writers" are ultimately held responsible in the afterlife for the souls of future readers corrupted by their writings.[118] Later, in *A New Discourse of a Stale Subject, Called the Metamorphosis of Ajax* (1596), Harington makes reference to the libelous tract known as *Leycesters Commonwealth* or *Father Parson's Greencoat*, assumed at the time to have been authored by the Jesuit.[119] Harington's most important response to Persons, however, can be found in a manuscript, which its nineteenth-century editor Clements R. Markham entitled *A Tract on the Succession to the Crown* (1602), the principal purpose of which seems to have been to defend James VI's future claim to the English throne against Persons's influential *Conference on the Next Succession* (1594), which favored the Spanish claimant, Isabella Clara Eugenia.[120]

---

[116] Kilroy, *Edmund Campion*, 89–120.

[117] Kilroy, *Edmund Campion*, 68–70, 149–93.

[118] Sir John Harington (trans.), *Ludovico Ariosto's Orlando Furioso*, ed. Robert McNulty (Oxford, 1972), 558.

[119] Sir John Harington, *A New Discourse of a Stale Subject, Called the Metamorphosis of Ajax*, ed. Elizabeth Story Donno (New York, 1962), 225. For the attribution of *Leicester's Commonwealth* to Persons, see Anon., *Leicester's Commonwealth: The Copy of a Letter Written by a Master of Art of Cambridge (1584) and Related Documents*, ed. D.C. Peck (London, OH, 1985), 3.

[120] Jason Scot-Warren makes a persuasive—albeit mostly conjectural—case that Harington intended the manuscript for the private perusal of Tobie Matthew, Bishop of Durham and later Archbishop of York, whose copious annotations can be found throughout the margins of the only surviving scribal copy found in the Chapter Library at York. *Sir John Harington and the Book as Gift* (New York, 2001), 154–61.

Harington declares at the beginning of the tract that his purpose is to defend the claim of James VI to the three religious communities governed by the English crown, "Papists, Protestants, and Purytans," but in so doing, he is determined to persuade his diverse readers "more with other men's wordes then myne owne."[121] In the first chapter, Harington makes his case for James VI to the conformists by reviewing a Latin tract by Edward Seymour, Duke of Somerset, published in 1548, which sought to persuade the Scots of the wisdom of a marriage arrangement between King Edward VI and Mary Stuart.[122] In the second and third chapters, he makes his case to the Puritans by quoting from an earlier response to Persons's *Conference* by radical parliamentarian Peter Wentworth, entitled *A discourse containing the authors opinion of the true and lawfull successor to her Maiestie*, which also supported the claim of James VI.[123] Most of the rest of the tract addresses the Catholics, first by using *Leycesters Commonwealth*, to show that neither foreign birth nor religious identity should impede succession, and then by addressing several other works by Catholics including *Delle relationi universali* by philosopher Giovanni Botero, *Examen pacifique de la doctrine des Huguenots* by the English convert, Henry Constable, and finally and most importantly, Robert Persons's *A Conference About the Next Succession*.[124]

Although Harington presents his own tract as an ecumenical attempt to address the concerns of all the religious identities governed by the English crown, his main interlocutor is clearly Persons, who serves as a second interlocutor in the two chapters on Wentworth's response to the *Conference*, chapter 4 on *Leycesters Commonwealth* (attributed to Persons), and Harington's own response to the *Conference* in chapter 6.[125] Moreover, unlike the previous chapters, Harington's response to the *Conference* is framed as a refutation, in which Harington confesses that, from his first reading of the tract, he had been predisposed to view Persons's tract "with professed hate and malice" because its author was "notod [sic] as a speciall oppugner of the Scottishe tytle," which Harington favored.[126] He goes on to note, however, that in spite of the tract's seeming support for the Spanish claimant, the *Conference* ultimately contradicts itself, since of all the claimants

---

[121] Sir John Harington, *Tract on the Succession*, B3, B2.

[122] Edward Seymour, *Epistola exhortatoria ad pacem, missa ab illustrissimo Principe, Domino Protectore Angliae, ac caeteris Regiae Maiestatis consiliarijs, ad nobilitatem ac plebem, uniuersumq[ue] populum Regni Scotiae* (Londini, 1548).

[123] *A discourse* is appended to *A pithie exhortation to her Maiestie for establishing her successor to the crowne* of 1587 under the title, *A Treatise Containing M. Wentworths Iudgement Concerning the Person of the Trve and lawfull successor to these Realmes of England and Ireland* (Edinburgh, 1598).

[124] Giovanni Botero, *Delle relationi vniversali* (Roma, 1591); Henry Constable, *Examen pacifique de la doctrine des Huguenots* (Paris, 1589); Harington, *Tract on the Succession*, G3.

[125] Moreover, more of the tract (chapters 4, 5, 6 and much of 8) is dedicated towards the concerns of the English Catholics than the other two confessions.

[126] Harington, *Tract on the Succession*, L.

reviewed in Persons's tract, James is shown to be the "next in bloode, against whome [Persons] make[s] so poore and weeke objections." Moreover, Harington conveys basic agreement with the argument encountered in first part of Persons's *Conference* about deposing tyrannical, unfit or heretical sovereigns, in which Persons "enforced much the lawfulness of putting back unworthy successors and deposing present possessioners."[127] Harington goes on to address the supremacy issue directly in the eighth and final chapter of the *Tract on Succession*, not by engaging Persons's earlier tract, but rather by invoking the famous Rainolds brother, John and William, the former of which was reputed to have begun his university career at Christ Church, Oxford as a Catholic and to have later become a Puritan, while the latter began at New College as a Protestant and converted to Catholicism. In the eighth chapter, it quickly becomes clear that Harington's perspective on papal supremacy is more nuanced than one might expect from an outspoken adherent to the national church.

Harington's ostensible purpose in drawing attention to the Rainolds brothers is to illustrate the need for religious tolerance. Harington sees religious controversy as "growen to that height as to divide brothers and brothers, fathers and sonnes, husbandes and wyves one frome another in opinions and belief," and thus he expresses a perhaps unrealistic desire that a complete separation emerge between state and religious matters, such that divergent devotional practices—like those exercised by the Rainolds brothers—would be subject only to personal conscience.[128] Reviewing John and William Rainolds' opinions on ecclesiastical governance, he finds that he agrees with aspects of both perspectives. On the one hand, Harington concurs with Sir John Rainolds' (Protestant) opinion that the pope's supremacy claim had effectively usurped Christian sovereigns of their rightful governance of the spiritual realm: "For this poynte of *Supremacie* I was throughly resolved not long since by a great doctor, and one of hir Majesties chaplaines, that it is a mere temporall and politique constitution, and may accordingly be reteined or transferred or assigned by a Christian prince, and being so done byndes the subject in conscience till by lawful authoritye it be revoked or altered."[129] In other words, Christian kings, who are also after all ordained by God, could delegate rule over the spiritual realm to the pope, but, given that such kings also represented "lawful authoritye," they could also seize back rule over the spiritual realm.

On the other hand, Harington agrees with William Rainolds's (Roman Catholic) criticisms of the Henrician reformation and the Elizabethan settlement. "In some thinges," Harington explains, William Rainolds' "reprehensions be just and his complaintes so trewe against some open scandall of our Churche and

---

[127] Harington, *Tract on the Succession*, L2v. Harington nevertheless objects to Persons's dedication of the *Conference* to the disgraced Earl of Essex. As Scott-Warren notes, Harington's comments about Essex are ironic, given his own earlier loyalty to Essex, as found in his prior work, *A New Discourse* (see below for more details). Scott-Warren, *Sir John Harington and the* Book, 157.

[128] Harington, *Tract on the Succession*, Q1v.

[129] Harington, *Tract on the Succession*, Q2v.

our neighbours of Scotland for contempt of our ministerie here, spoiling of the Churche, and making zeale the cloak of oppression there, even in the heart of their reformacion, as I am sorye to fynde it, and unable to defend it." He goes on to enumerate three of Rainolds's criticisms of the English Church, two of which concern the issues of supremacy and governance of the spiritual realm. According to Harington, Rainolds complained

> 1. Namely, how in King Henry the 8th his tyme, he made Cromwell his vicegerent in Causes Ecclesaisticall, setting him, a layman, and as he writes an unlearned man, over all bishops and clergie.
> 2. How contrarie to the use of all Christian countries, a great part of her Majesties reigne no bishopp was of the Counsell.[130]

Rainolds's first point, that Henry had appointed a layman to oversee the English bishops, strikes at the heart of controversies over ecclesiastical self-governance. Harington agrees that, by appointing Cromwell as viceregent of ecclesiastical affairs, Henry had assumed a role that reproduced within the temporal realm what Pope Pius V had assumed for himself with regard to Elizabeth within the spiritual realm. In other words, just as the pope held that he had a right to depose a temporal magistrate like Elizabeth, thus making himself a supreme sovereign over temporal sovereigns, so Henry had appointed a temporal magistrate as head of the English Church, thus making him a supreme secular overseer of prelates. From Harington's moderate perspective, Henry's act was unjust not only because it constituted a usurpation of the ecclesiastical realm similar to what the pope had tried unsuccessfully against Elizabeth's temporal realm; it also constituted a dangerous blurring of the temporal and spiritual realms.

The second point—William Rainolds's complaint that, during a substantial portion of her reign, Elizabeth had refused to appoint a bishop to the Privy Council—is even more crucial to an understand of Harington's ambivalence about the supremacy issue. As we shall see from his other work, Harington seems to have viewed members of the Privy Council as a secular force that could function in a manner analogous to the pope's corrective function with regard to sovereigns.[131] One finds the most detailed expression of this aspect of Harington's perspective in his earlier parodical, Rabelaisian tract, *A New Discourse of a State Subject, Called the Metamorphosis of Ajax*, published anonymously in 1596.[132] The *New*

---

[130] Harington, *Tract on the Succession*, Q3. For a deeper discussion of the views of William Rainolds and other English Catholics on the papal deposing power, see Thomas Clancy, S.J., "English Catholics and the Papal Deposing Power, 1570–1640 [Part I: The Elizabethan Period]," *Recusant History* 6/3 (1962): 114–41, esp. 124–5.

[131] For background on Harington, see Steven W. May, *The Elizabethan Courtier Poets: Their Poems and their Contexts* (Columbia, MO, 1991), 140–65; D.H. Craig, *Sir John Harington* (Boston, 1985), and Jason Scott-Warren, *Sir John Harington and the Book*.

[132] Sir John Harington's *A New Discourse of a Stale Subject, Called the Metamorphosis of Ajax*, ed. Elizabeth Story Donno (New York, 1962). Unless otherwise noted, all parenthetical references are to this volume.

136   *Early Modern Catholics, Royalists, and Cosmopolitans*

Discourse is putatively about Harington's servant Thomas Combe's invention of the first primitive flushable privy, or the "device" as it is referred to throughout the tract, which is described in some detail in the middle section entitled, "An Anatomie of the Metamorpho-sed Ajax."[133] It has long been noted that the *New Discourse* is substantially more complex than simply constituting a space within which to introduce the invention of the "device."[134] For example, it is clear from certain passages in the tract that Harington's purpose was to convey his solidarity with the English Catholic community, especially their suit for religious tolerance. What attracted Harington to that community as well as to Wardour Castle, the seat of the recusant Arundells and the place where the first such flushable device was installed, is the perceived cosmopolitan character of some members of that community.[135]

Recently, Gerard Kilroy has made a persuasive case that Harington's real purpose in writing the tract was to sue for religious tolerance for Catholics and to attack through satire the network of official spies and "promoters," of which Anthony Munday was an upstanding member, that were informing on English Catholic recusants.[136] One of the crucial pieces of evidence that Kilroy points to in order to illustrate the Catholic politics of this work can be found in Lord Lumley's copy of the work, which can now be found at the Folger Shakespeare Library.[137] Harington gifted this copy of the *New Discourse* to Lord Lumley after having

---

[133] As a number of commentators have pointed out, the second section of the *New Discourse* that describes the invention was probably written by Combe, not Harington. See Scott-Warren, *Sir John Harington and the Book*, 57. See also Henry Sigerist, "An Elizabethan Poet's Contribution to Public Health: Sir John Harington and the Water Closet," *Bulletin of the History of Medicine* 13 (1943): 229–43.

[134] Indeed, it should be noted in passing that Harington's *New Discourse* is one of the most self-consciously literary texts that, for whatever reason, is not regularly read by literary scholars. It is dense, difficult, opaque, and most importantly for my purposes, it is a quintessentially cosmopolitan work, including as it does numerous untranslated or tendentiously translated Latin, Greek, and Italian phrases and epigrams by Martial, Sir Thomas More, John Heywood, and numerous references to continental writers such as Rabelais. For a broad discussion of how Harington relates to Rabelais, see William E. Engel, "Was Sir John Harington the English Rabelais?," in *Rabelais in Context: Proceedings of the 1991 Vanderbilt Conference*, ed. Barbara C. Bowen (Birmingham, AL, 1993), 147–56. For a discussion of the interplay between the scatological and the religious, see T.G.A. Nelson, "Death, Dung, the Devil, and Worldly Delights: A Metaphysical Conceit in Harington, Donne, and Herbert," *Studies in Philology* 76 (1979): 272–87.

[135] See Donno's commentary in Harington, *A New Discourse*, 232 n.149; Kilroy, *Edmund Campion*, 90–96; and Scott-Warren, *Sir John Harington and the Book*, 86–98.

[136] Gerard Kilroy, *Edmund Campion, Memory and Transcription* (Burlington, VT, 2005), 90–96. For Harington's Epigrams, in which he condemns "Base spies disturbers of the publicque rest" (Epigram 76), see Harington, *The Epigrams of Sir John Harington*, ed. Gerard Kilroy (Burlington, VT, 2009), 121. For context, see Kilroy, "Part 1: The Pleasant Learned Poet," in *Epigrams*, 61–2.

[137] Lumley-Folger copy, STC 12779.2.

added clarifying marginal annotations.[138] The most significant of these annotations can be found in the margin of the passage which describes the moment the "devise" was first conceived and discussed:

> For I assure you the devise was first both thought of and discoursed of, with as brode termes as any belongs to it, in presence of six persons, who were (all save one) enterlocutors in the dialogue, of which I was so much the meanest, that the other five, for beuty, for birth, for vallew, for witt, and for wealth, are not in manie places of the realme to be matched. Neither was the place inferior to the parsons, being a castle, that I call, the wonder of the West, so seated without, as England in few places affoords more plasures, so furnished within, as China nor the West Indies scant allowes more plenty. Briefly, at the very coming in, you wold think you were come to the *Eldorado* in *Guiana* (174–5).[139]

To the right of this passage, Harington writes in precise letters the five persons that were present: "Erl of Southhamp/ Sr Mat. Arundel/ Count Arundel/ La Mary Arundel/ Sir Hary Davers," And after a space, he identifies the location, "Warder Castle," the historic seat of the Arundells near Tisbury, Wiltshire. As Kilroy notes, members of the Arundell family and the Southamptons were leading Catholic recusants, and thus, the annotations give "the whole inspiration of the 'device' a strongly recusant ring."[140] In his *Tract on the Succession*, Harington declares that he is "neither Papist, Protestant, nor Puritan, or [but] a protesting Catholique Puritan," a clever phrase which seems to indicate that he was committed to the Elizabethan settlement, but it is clear that Harington also sympathized with the plight of the Catholic community, which the above passage shows had a definite cosmopolitan character.[141] Just as Munday's pageants linked the metropolis of London to the international sphere, so this passage links Wardour Castle with China, the West Indies, and finally Eldorado in Guiana, which Harington had doubtless read about in Sir Walter Raleigh's *Discovery of Guiana*. England is presented negatively in the passage, as a realm that "in few places affoords more plasures" than those that can be found at Wardour. In effect, the singularity of Wardour is that it provides a link to the outside world, to the non-English, to travel and to the exotic.

Furthermore, one of the most memorable parts of the *New Discourse* has a bearing on matters concerning the pope's correction of temporal magistrates. Harington begins by recounting an ancient letter from the Roman magistrate, Plinius Secundus (Pliny the Younger) from the city of Amestris in Asia Minor,

---

[138] For a brilliant discussion of how the marginal is often central to Harington's books and manuscript copies, see Gerard Kilroy, "Advertising the Reader: Sir John Harington's 'Directions in the Margent' [with Illustrations]," *English Literary Renaissance* 41.1 (2011): 64–110.

[139] See Lumley-Folger copy of *A new discourse of a stale subiect, called The metamorphosis of Aiax* (London, 1596), K1.

[140] Kilroy, "Part 1: The Pleasant Learned Poet," in *Epigrams*, 8.

[141] Harington, *Tract on the Succession*, 108. For additional perspective on Harington's tolerant perspective on English Catholics in his *Epigrams*, see May, *Elizabethan Courtier Poets*, 150–51.

138   *Early Modern Catholics, Royalists, and Cosmopolitans*

to the Roman Emperor Traianus during the beginning of the second century CE. Plinius sends a missive in which he complains to the emperor about the open sewer running through the city of Amestris, a sewer "which as it is foule & most uncleanly to behold, so is it infectious with the horrible vile savour." He goes on to request Traianus's permission to have the sewer vaulted, to which Traianus's immediately replies that it is indeed proper "that the water be covered that runs by the city of Amestrians," and that "money for the work" is no object. Harington's commentary on this exchange is first of all to commend Emperor Traianus for even answering Plinius's suit. Indeed, Harington expresses astonishment that Plinius did not instead receive an insolently-worded missive from one of the Emperor's secretaries, declaring that "the Emperor, not vouchsafing to answer your letter him selfe, hath commanded me to write thus much to you, that he marvels you will presume to trouble his divine Majestie with matters of so base regard" (133).

    He goes on to imagine a similar contemporary scenario involving his hometown of Bath. Imagining himself as the magistrate of the town, he composes his own letter to Emperor Traianus, in which he asks the Emperor to "authorise me, or some wiser then me" to install covered sewers in Bath that will improve the promising but decaying infrastructure of his own town (143).[142] A number of aspects of Harington's Bath analogy are significant in terms of the supremacy issue. First, note that Harington does not draw a direct analogy between Emperor Traianus and Queen Elizabeth, as one would expect. Rather than writing to Elizabeth, he writes to the Roman Emperor himself (136).[143] Second, he suggests that the contemporary equivalent of Traianus was none other than Robert Devereux, Earl of Essex, member of the Privy Council and, at the time, Elizabeth's court favorite. The passage in question reads as follows:

> And I have thought sometime with my selfe, that if I were but halfe so great an officer under our most gracious Emperesse, who is indeed worthy, and onely worthie to be Trajans Mistresse, as Plinius secundus was under that Trajan; I would write for the mending of such a lothsome fault in my neighbour town of Bath (where many noble persons are oft annoyed with it) as Plinie did for Amestris. Yet whie may I not by *Poetica licentia*, and by an honest & necessarie figure (in this age) called *Reprehensio*, imagine my selfe for halfe an houre to be

---

    [142] In 1611, Harington was still petitioning the crown for improvements in Bath, suggesting in a humorous note to a Lord of the Privy Council that King James I refute Nicholas Sander's remark that Henry VIII's more savvy courtiers had to wait until the king was content after having relieved himself in order to press suits for the granting of bells and roofing lead from dissolved monasteries. According to Harington, James should assist in repairing the Bath Abbey Church by granting timber to the cause after one of his own evacuations (Hugh Craig, "Sir John Harington: Six Letters," in *English Manuscript Studies 1100–1700*, ed. Peter Beal and Jeremey Griffiths [London, 1995], 43–63, at 55–7).

    [143] Earlier he groups Traianus with Nero, Domitianus, Antonius, and the popes as rulers of Rome who anciently persecuted Christians and Romans: *"Nero, Domitianus, Traianus, Antonius, Pontifices Romanos laniarunt* [Nero, Domitian, Trajan, Antony, Pontiffs persecuted Romans]."* See Donno (ed.), *A New Discourse*, 136 n.157.

Secundus, and suppose some other, that perhaps at this houre is not farre from Trajans countrey, to be that worthiest Trajan? (141)

The last sentence in which he imagines "some other" being "at this hour ... not farre from Trajans countrey" as Traianus is a notable reference to the Earl of Essex being one of the commanders of the expedition to Cádiz, which set sail on June 1, 1596 and returned during the first week of August. (*A New Discourse* appeared in print later that year.)[144]

The response to Harington's tract was, to say the least, not positive. Almost immediately after its publication, Harington was threatened with a suit in the Star Chamber, ostensibly due to very direct criticisms of the Earl of Leicester found in the tract.[145] However, Jason Scott-Warren has suggested that passages such as the one above, which figures Essex as Emperor Traianus and seems to discuss the prohibited subject of the Queen's marriage (Harington calls her "our most gracious Emperesse, who is indeed worthy, and onely worthie to be Trajans Mistresse" [141]), were the real cause of Harington's troubles.[146] I would suggest further that the entire episode can be understood as a secular reconfiguration of the supremacy issue. The actual letter to Traianus which follows this passage is conflicted about the relationship between the Emperor and the Queen—Harington addresses Traianus as "your Lordship" suggesting that the letter is meant throughout to be understood as referencing Essex, the Queen's favorite courtier. And yet, within the imaginary, anachronistic universe of the Roman empire, Harington's analogy with Plinius's original letter suggests that England is one province within the Roman empire and that, by writing this letter to Emperor Traianus rather than Queen Elizabeth, Harington is appealing to a "higher" imperial authority that supervises the Queen's power.[147] It is also not hard to imagine that the entire episode is intended to be

---

[144]   For context, see Scott-Warren, *Sir John Harington and the Book*, 75–80.

[145]   Harington writes, "so we may one day be put into the Chronicles, as good members of our countrey, more worthily then the great Beare that caried eighte dogges on him when Monsieur was here" (*A New Discourse*, 171). The "great Beare" is taken as a reference to Leicester. See Dorothy Auchter, *Dictionary of Literary and Dramatic Censorship in Tudor and Stuart England* (Westport, CT, 2001), 237. Harington's cousin, Robert Markham, was apparently informed that the Queen understood the work to have "aimed a shafte at Leicester." See Henry Harington (ed.), *Nugae Antiquae* (3 vols, London, 1792), vol. 2, 288.

[146]   Referencing Elizabeth with the title, "Mistresse," has a double-edged meaning in the late sixteenth century. On the one hand, this title references Queen Elizabeth's sovereignty over her subjects, including Essex. On the other hand, "Mistresse" could also have a more suggestive meaning: "a woman loved and courted by a man; a female sweetheart" (*OED*). Scott-Warren, *Sir John Harington and the Book*, 79–80.

[147]   Harington, *A New Discourse*, 142–3. Note that Harington ascribes his nomination to the position of Steward of Bath to the members of the Privy Council, rather than the Queen: "This I do the rather write, because your Lordship, and the rest of her Majesties most honorable counsel, thought me once worthie to be Steward of that towne ..." (143). In so doing, his letter reflects, by way of analogy with imperial Rome, the notion that the Privy Council had a quasi-imperial supervisory role with regard to Elizabeth's sovereignty.

critical of Elizabeth's authority—Harington's expression of astonishment that the original Emperor Traianus was sufficiently conscientious to respond to Plinius's request suggests perhaps that Harington's contemporary local magistrates could expect much less attention from their queen. In this respect, the passage seems motivated by the same reasons that later motivated Harington to complain that Elizabeth had declined to appoint a bishop to the Privy Council for so long a period of time during her reign. In effect, Harington conjures up an ancient Roman emperor who would play a moderating role analogous to the role of Sander's pope, a figure who could oversee the English sovereign, and who could be appealed to, when she herself proved to be delinquent in her duties.

In addition, of course, the passage seems to suggest Essex as a potential husband and overseer of Elizabeth, something Harington had obliquely suggested earlier in his lengthy commentary on the fifth book of his translation of *Orlando Furioso* (1591), in which he had written about Genevra's marriage to a social inferior: "it is no disparagement for the greatest Emperesse in the world to marrie one that is a gentleman by birth."[148] Indeed, like his fictional letter to Traianus in the *New Discourse*, Harington's commentaries on his translation of *Orlando Furioso* reveal anxious ruminations about the exercise of temporal sovereignty without some form of papal or imperial oversight. Thus, Harington's opening commentary on the first canto recounts the story of Pope Leo III's deposition of the tyrannical Empress Irene, and Pope Leo's subsequent coronation of Charlemagne as Holy Roman Emperor, which Persons included as an example in his argument in favor of the papal deposition of tyrannical monarchs in the *Conference on the Next Succession* (1594). But unlike Persons who upholds the primacy of the spiritual realm over the temporal, the events of Ariosto's poem occur under the auspices of a code of transnational justice that is more chivalric than Christian (28).[149]

Harington's *Orlando Furioso* and the Cosmopolitan Romance

I would like to conclude this chapter by noting the way in which important translations of prominent continental works of fiction present a cosmopolitan model of national identity that is opposed to the model of national identity that has prevailed among literary scholars since Richard Helgerson's groundbreaking work on this subject.[150] Translations by both Munday and Harington offer more clarity

---

[148] Sir John Harington (trans.), *Ludovico Ariosto's Orlando Furioso*, 68. All subsequent quotations from the critical apparatus to this work are cited as page numbers in parenthetical references. Quotations from the poem itself refer to canto.stanza. For a discussion of the gender politics of Harington's translation, see May, *Elizabethan Courtier Poets*, 159–65.

[149] See Persons, *A Conference*, E5–E5v.

[150] For his analysis of how Protestantism contributed to the writing of Elizabethan England, see Helgerson, *Forms of Nationhood*, 249–94, which uses Foxe's *Acts and Monuments* as well as Richard Hooker's *Laws of the Ecclesiastical Polity*, along with numerous secular works from the period, in order to illustrate the Elizabethan writing of the

Border-Crossing and Translation 141

on this point, portraying as they do protagonists who are constantly traveling across boundaries and frontiers. Munday's translation of *Palmerin of England, part 1*, printed in 1596, recounts a crisis in "Great Britain" which involves the loss of an heir to the throne. But in the kingdom's hour of need, knights from all over Christendom, led by the Emperor Palmerin d'Oliva of Constantinople, come to lend assistance.[151] Similarly, in Harington's 1591 translation of *Orlando Furioso*, one of the most important translations of the period, an alliance of knights from all over Europe, including the English knight Astolfo submit to and serve Charlemagne in the defense of Christendom.

Similar to the *New Discourse*, Harington's commentary on his 1591 Englishing of Ariosto's *Orlando Furioso* translates a secularized form of papal supremacy into the English public sphere.[152] The translation begins with "A Preface or Rather, A Brief Apologie of Poetrie and of the Author and Translator of this Poem," in which Harington defends poetry in terms that would have been recognizable to contemporary readers of George Puttenham and Sidney, both of whose works he mentions at the beginning of the preface (1–15).[153] Throughout the translation,

---

English nation. Helgerson claims that the most important event in this collective process of "writing" the nation was "the separation of the English church from the church of Rome" (251). In this respect, Helgerson's model of nationhood was based on the Statute in Restraint of Appeals of 1533 in which Henry VIII had claimed authority over both the ecclesiastical and the temporal realms. My intention here is to show that an English conception of nationhood characterized as defined by a Protestant notion of the nation divorced from Catholicism and Catholic notions of nationhood is inaccurate. See Christopher Highley, *Catholics Writing the Nation*, for some perspective.

[151] *The [first] seconde [sic] part, of the no lesse rare, historie of Palmerin of England*, trans. Anthony Munday (London, 1596). For context, see Hamilton, *Munday and the Catholics*, 80–86. Munday's other translations of *Amadis de Gaule*, *Palmerin d'Oliva*, and *Primaleon of Greece* were all romances of chivalry, in which knights enforce a universal chivalric code that functions as a transnational order. *The first book of Amadis of Gaule*, trans. Anthony Munday (London, 1590); *Palmerin d'Oliva [Part 1] The mirrour of nobilitie*, trans. Anthony Munday (London, 1588); *The first booke of Primaleon of Greece*, trans. Anthony Munday (London, 1595). For context, see Lockey, *Law and Empire*, 17–46; Phillips, "Chronicles of Wasted Time," 781–804; John J. O'Connor, *Amadis de Gaule and its influence on Elizabethan literature* (New Brunswick, NJ, 1970), 25–42, 61–84.

[152] For discussion of Harington's translation of the *Orlando* as a key to understanding poetic translation during the period, see Massimiliano Morini, "Sir John Harington and the Poetics of Tudor Translation," in *Travels and Translations in the Sixteenth Century*, (Burlington, VT), 120–36. Daniel Javitch, in *Proclaiming a Classic: The Canonization of* "Orlando Furioso" (Princeton, NJ, 1991), 134–57, argues that Harington translation transformed the work into something entirely more didactic than the original. See also Rich Townsend, *Harington and Ariosto: A Study in Elizabethan Verse Translation* (New Haven, 1940).

[153] See T.G.A. Nelson, "Sir John Harington as a Critic of Sir Philip Sidney," *Studies in Philology* 67 (1970): 41–56. Rich, *Harington and Ariosto*, 36–50, 151–4, suggests that Harington's textual apparatus is meant to be parody, while Nelson elsewhere suggests that Harington was simply skeptical of allegorical interpretation. See Nelson, "Sir John

142   *Early Modern Catholics, Royalists, and Cosmopolitans*

Harington ends each canto with a detailed analysis of the moral of the canto, its historical content, its allegorical character, and its literary allusions. Finally, the translation ends with two separate essays, "A Brief and Summarie Allegorie of Orlando Furioso," in which he examines the larger allegorical significance, and "The Life of Ariosto, briefly and compendiously gathered out of sundrie Italian writers by John Harington," the facts of which he reports to have gathered from Ariosto's Italian commentators, Gierolamo Porro, Gierolamo Garofalo, and Simon Fornari (558–78).

The first thing to note about Ariosto's *Orlando* is how well the original work lends itself to the secular cosmopolitan outlook, especially with regard to what I have characterized as Harington's secularization of the power of papal supremacy. At the center of the poem, of course, is a titanic religious war between the Christian forces, led by Emperor Charlemagne, and the Muslim forces, led by King Agramante, but Ariosto makes clear that, at the same time, Christian and Muslim knights share common chivalric values such as honor and good faith that are based on ancient Roman military codes that influenced both Christian and Islamic civilizations. As I have noted elsewhere, chivalric romances are narratives in which the universalizing martial ethos of chivalry, which emerged coterminously with the medieval and early modern traditions of *ius gentium* and just-war doctrine, transcends national and religious boundaries.[154] Ariosto provides a good example of this early in the first canto, during the encounter between the Christian knight, Rinaldo, and the Spanish Saracen, Ferrau, both of whom are infatuated with Angelica. After the two knights engage each other in personal combat, Ferrau agrees to make an alliance with Rinaldo based on the universal code of chivalry, as Ariosto's description of the terms, in Harington's translation, makes clear:[155]

> Feraw (that felt small pleasure in the fight)
> Agreed a sound and frendly league to make.
> They lay aside all wrath and malice quight,
> And at the parting from the running lake
> The Pagan would not let the Christen knight
> To follow him on foot for manners sake
> But prays him mount behind his horses backe,
> And so they seeke the damsell by the tracke.

Harington and the Renaissance Debate over Allegory," *Studies in Philology* 82 (1985): 359–79; Sidney, *A Defense of Poetry*, ed. Jan van Dorsten (New York, 1966); George Puttenham, *The Art of English Poesy: A Critical Edition*, ed. Frank Whigham and Wayne A. Rebhorn (Ithaca, NY, 2007).

[154] See Lockey, *Law and Empire*, 19–36.

[155] Rinaldo is chasing Angelica, when she passes Ferrau, who immediately falls in love with her. Ferrau attempts to protect Angelica from Rinaldo, and the two knights enter into vicious battle with one another. When it becomes clear that neither of the knights are able to dominate the other one, Rinaldo proposes that they "make a truce," and join forces in order to find her (1.18).

O auncient knights of true and noble hart:
They rivals were, one faith they liv'd not under;
Beside they felt their bodies shrewdly smart
Of blowes late given, and yet (behold a wonder)
Through thicke and thin suspicion set apart,
Like frends they ride and parted not a sunder
Untill the horse with double spurring drived
Unto a way parted in two arrived, (1.21–2)[156]

It is worth noting that Ariosto's original Italian, in which the word, "cavallieri" (knight), is used, reveals a common etymological origin with the word, "cavaleria" (chivalry), thus stressing the chivalric code more than does Harington's translation, which simply uses the word, "knight." Most significantly, Ariosto remarks that the two knights "eran di fé diversi" ["one faith they liv'd not under"], and yet, the code of chivalry provides a common universal ethical regime that regulates their behavior, allowing each knight to escape the religious dictates which would make them enemies.

The non-sectarian regime of chivalric values that imbues Ariosto's poem might be termed cosmopolitan quite apart from Harington's intervention; as we shall see, however, Harington's reading of *Orlando Furioso* in his critical apparatus illustrates a number of concerns having to do with the secularization of papal supremacy that we have become familiar with from Harington's *New Discourse*. As we have noted in the previous chapter, Persons's account of Leo III's deposition of Empress Irene in favor of Charlemagne (encountered in the *Conference on the Succession*) formed the basis of his argument in favor of the

---

[156] Al pagan la proposta non dispiacque:
così fu differita la tenzone;
e tal tregua tra lor subito nacque,
sì l'odio e l'ira va in oblivione,
che 'l pagano al partir de le fresche acque
non lasciò a piedi il buon figliol d'Amone:
con preghi invita, et al fin toglie in groppa,
e per l'orme d'Angelica galoppa.

Oh gran bontà de' cavallieri antiqui!
Eran rivali, eran di fé diversi,
e si sentian degli aspri colpi iniqui
per tutta la persona anco dolersi;
e pur per selve oscure e calli obliqui
insieme van senza sospetto aversi.
Da quattro sproni il destrier punto arriva
ove una strada in due si dipartiva. (21–2)
Citations are from Ludovico Ariosto, Orlando Furioso, ed. Gioarcchino Paparelli, 2 vols (Milano, 1991).

144   *Early Modern Catholics, Royalists, and Cosmopolitans*

overthrow of tyrannical monarchs.[157] As the good and just sovereign at the center of Ariosto's poem, Charlemagne figures as the foil of the unwise and sometimes tyrannical King Agramant of Africa, who leads the Muslim army. What Ariosto leaves mostly unremarked throughout the poem is that Charlemagne attained his position as leader of the Christian world through papal intervention in his favor. In contrast, Harington is careful to point this out in the critical apparatus appended to the first canto in which he attributes to the Venetian historian Marcus Antonius Coccius Sabellicus the historical basis for much of Ariosto's narrative: "Further the said author [Sabellicus] affirmeth that the same *Charlemaine*, for his great favor showed to the Church of Rome was by *Leo* the third named Emperour of Rome and that he was a just, a fortunate, and a merciful Prince, and one that within Europe as well as without did attain great conquests, suppressing the violent government of the Lumbards and taming the rebellious Saxons, Hunnes, and Bavarians, and conquering a great part of Spain" (28). Harington provides this background on the papal coronation of Charlamaigne as a way of contextualizing some of the examples of good monarchy and tyranny that are contained in the poem.

Elsewhere, at the end of the twenty-sixth book, Harington goes on to refute anti-papal readings of the poem which assume that the monster who has terrorized Europe during the age in which Ariosto lived and whom King Charles V, King Henry VIII, and King Francis of France eventually subdue was the pope: "Some verie fondly have surmised and published the same in print that this [monster] was alluded to the Bishop of Rome, but how absurd that imagination is, the praise of the pope then living, following in 32 staffe [stanza], doth plainely show" (298). Indeed, in the thirty-second stanza, Pope Leo X is recounted capturing the monster, albeit after the latter has been wounded by the temporal sovereigns mentioned above: "*Leo* the tenth the Lion fierce is called / Who chast him [the monster] and fast caught him by the eare / And in the chase the beast so tyred and galled / As others took him while he held him theare" (26.32, 26.36).[158] Once again, given that Harington seems to agree with Simone Fornari in seeing the monster as a temporal prince, this episode embodies the logic used by Catholics to justify the pope's right to depose a tyrannical prince or authorize legitimate temporal princes to do so. In this case, the pope captures the monster by the ear until the temporal princes are able to catch up with him and detain him.

Harington reads at least one other episode in canto 9 involving the deposition of a tyrannical sovereign as reflecting a logic similar to that involving the traditional papal deposing power. But whereas Empress Irene and the monster of canto 26 are deposed by means of papal authority, the tyrannical king, Cymoscos, is deposed by the actions of Orlando, the chivalrous knight. In the middle of canto 9, Orlando encounters Olimpia, a distressed maiden, who relates the following story: King Cymoscos attempted to force the beautiful Olimpia to marry his son, Arbantes. When Olimpia, having already been betrothed to Byreno, refused, Cymoscos

---

[157]   Persons, *A Conference*, E5–E5v.

[158]   "Decimo ha quel Leon scritto sul dosso, / ch'al brutto mostro i denti ha ne l'orecchi; / e tanto l'ha già travagliato e scosso, / che vi sono arrivati altri parecchi" (26.36).

invaded the kingdom of Holland where Olimpia's father was king. Cymoscos ended up taking Olimpia hostage, and his son, Prince Arbantes, forced her to marry him, but before the marriage could be consummated, her servant killed Arbantes allowing Olimpia to make her escape. Meanwhile, King Cymoscos assembled his navy and encountered Byreno by sea, taking him prisoner. When Cymoscos found his son dead, he decreed that he would spare Byreno's life if Olimpia yielded herself as his prisoner. Olimpia tells Orlando that she would deliver herself to King Cymoscos if she could be assured that he would be true to his word and spare Byreno's life. Orlando and Olimpia travel to Cymoscos's kingdom of Friseland, where Orlando challenges the king to a duel before defeating him, his 30 knights, and Cymoscos's secret weapon, the cannon. Ultimately, Orlando kills King Cymoscos and frees Byrenos, who goes on to conquer Friseland, marrying King Cymoscos's daughter to his own younger brother, who ends up inheriting the kingdom (9.18–87). Orlando's deposition of the evil King of Friseland bears important similarities to how English Catholics envisioned the pope's role in authorizing the rise of good and just sovereigns such as Charlemagne and the deposition of evil tyrants such as Empress Irene and the monster of the twenty-sixth canto. More to the point, Harington's commentary on the episode would have reminded readers of the pope's recent use of his spiritual authority to authorize Catholic sovereigns, especially Philip II, to invade Elizabeth's kingdom: "In his comming to succour the distressed Olympia we may note how God sends unexpected reliefe to the afflicted. In Olympia we may see a rare mirror of constancie which I doubt too few of her sex will imitate. By Cymoscos tyrannie and death all Princes may take a warning that no engins nor strategems can keep a tyrant safe in his estate but only clemancy and bountie that to lawfull Princes breedes evermore love and loyaltie in this subject" (110). In Harington's gloss on the episode, Orlando's deposition of King Cymoscos reflects the divine order, by which the Christian God governs the universe. At the same time, the agent of deposition, Orlando, does not explicitly represent a Christian order of justice, but rather, he represents the order of chivalry, which, although imbued with Christian values, is not their equivalent. From the vantage point of 1591, three years after Spain's unsuccessful invasion of England, this passage must have conjured up uncomfortable parallels with the Duke of Parma's recent attempt to restore God's divine order to England.

At the same time, it seems to me that it would be pushing the point too hard for one to claim that Harington was using Ariosto's *Orlando Furioso* to make the pro-Catholic case in favor of the papal right to depose temporal sovereigns. We should recall that Harington makes clear in the *Tract on Succession* that he was a supporter of the Church of England; rather, his main criticism of the Elizabethan settlement was that it left the Church of England unable to influence crown policy. Indeed, one of Harington's main points of agreement with William Rainolds was that, during most of Elizabeth's reign, there had been no bishop that had served on the Privy Council. In this respect, I would argue that Harington's point in his commentary on his translation was closer to Edmund Campion's purpose in his neo-Latin play,

Ambrosia, in which Bishop Ambrose chastises Emperor Theodosius and ultimately helps him seek redemption after the Emperor has massacred 7,000 Thessalonicans for rioting and killing the Roman governor of Thessalonica. Indeed, in the preface to *Orlando Furioso* in which Harington defends poetry, he enlists the example of Bishop John Fisher's confrontation with King Henry VIII as indicative of the worth of poetic allegory. Given the theme of deposition of or chastisement of wayward sovereigns found in both Harington's translation and the *New Discourse*, we can assume that Harington views Fisher as exemplary for a number of reasons. In describing the value of allegory, Harington recounts a confrontation between the bishop and the king during Henry's suppression of the monasteries in which Bishop Fisher used a parable as a way of resisting the king's plans:

> Bishop Fisher, a stout Prelate (though I do not praise his Religion) when he was assaid by king Henrie the eight for his good will and assent for the suppression of Abbeys, the king alledging that he would but take away their superfluities and let the substance stand still or at least see it converted to better and more godly uses: the grave Bishop answered it in this kind of Poeticall parable: He said there was an axe that wanting a helve came to a thicke and huge overgrowne wood and besought some of the great okes in that wood to spare him so much timber as to make him a handle or helve, promising that if he might finde that favour he would in recompence thereof have great regard in preserving that wood, in pruning the braunches, in cutting away the unprofitable and superfluous boughes, in paring away the bryers and thornes that were combersome to the fayre trees and making it in fine a grove of great delight and pleasure, but when this same axe had obtained his suit, he so laid about him and so pared away both timber and top and lop that in short space of a woodland he made it a champion and made her liberalitie the instrument of her overthrow.
>
> Now though this Bishop had no very good successe with his parable, yet was so farre from being counted a lye that it was plainly seen sooner after that the same axe did both hew down those woods by the roots and pared him off by the head and was a peece of Prophecie as well as a peece of Poetrie, and indeed Prophets and Poets have been thought to have a great affinitie as the name Vates in latin doth testifie. (6–7)

Ultimately, as Harington explains, the king would not submit himself to the corrective wisdom of his bishop, and Harington's description of the scene implies, along with his admiration of Fisher, some corresponding criticism of the king for the way in which he ultimately treated Fisher. Harington is obviously forced to walk a fine line here, carefully making clear that while he does not approve of Fisher's religion, he still admires the bishop's attempt to use a parable in order to correct the king's abuse of power. Indeed, both in this instance as well as in the *New Discourse* and in the *Tract on Succession*, he seems to suggest that sovereigns such as King Henry VIII should subject themselves to the wisdom and learning of a surrogate papal figure: in the *New Discourse*, Traianus or the Earl of Essex assumes this role with regard to Elizabeth while in the *Tract on the Succession*, it is the bishop that Queen Elizabeth never appointed to the privy council.

Elsewhere, in the final "Briefe and Summarie Allegorie of Orlando Furioso," Harington explains that Ariosto conceived his poem in such a way that "all the parts thereof" are to be referred "to two principall heads and common places, namely, Arms and Love" (559). After exploring the theme of love in the work, Harington takes on the more serious "common place," namely Arms. He describes Ariosto's poem as constructed around a comparison between the "two mightie Emperors," Charlemagne and Agramant, the first of which "directeth all his counsells by wisedome, learning, and Religion," while the second "being rash and unexperienced ruined himselfe and his countrie" (559). Significantly, the place of good and bad counselors is central to Harington's explanation of how the latter occurred, and in Harington's reading, the figure of Sobrino, the wise and good councilor whose advice King Agramant continually ignores throughout the narrative, is especially noteworthy. He explains, "Yet we see Agramant hath his grave Sobryno that adviseth him at the first not to invade other mens countryes but to keep his owne, that adviseth him to prevent mischiefe in time and to sue for peace, that adviseth him to put the matter to a combat of one man and the partie overcome to pay yearely tribute, and finally that not onely with faithful counsell but with valiant service sticketh to him to the last, but Agramants owne rashnesse and follie overthrowes all the good that could be done him" (366). For Harington, Sobrino is the secularized equivalent of the wise Bishop Fisher in King Henry VIII's court—he is the equivalent of Traianus or Essex in the *New Discourse*. He is the equivalent of Campion's Bishop Ambrose and Munday's Earl of Huntington, Sir Thomas More, and Sir John Oldcastle: the cosmopolitan noble with the wisdom to chastise and correct erring sovereigns. In turn, it seems apparent that, for Harington, the central purpose of Ariosto's poem is to show what occurs to those sovereigns who ignore or disobey such figures.

Ultimately, it is clear that Harington saw himself as potentially embodying the figure of the wise noble who could educate contemporary sovereigns and magistrates, and he imagined his books as one means of doing so.[159] This was certainly one purpose behind the *Epigrams*, which Harington presented to King James VI of Scotland in 1603 and to Henry Prince of Wales two years later. As Gerard Kilroy has noted, the *Epigrams* "constitute a moral, political, and theological critique of the state of the nation," in which Harington seems to be advertising himself as a potential educator of the heir apparent.[160] Indeed, Harington seemed to adopt this role of gift-giving educator of princes and magistrates in the most unlikely of places. In 1599, Harington had been an officer in Essex's failed

---

[159] As Scott-Warren has shown, the book as gift is a constant theme in Harington's authorial self-fashioning: Harington compulsively presented both his published and manuscript works as gifts to his patrons. Scott-Warren, *Sir John Harington and the Book*, 1–24.

[160] Kilroy, Preface in *The Epigrams*, vii. His translation of the *regimen sanitatis salernitanum*, published later as *The Englishmans Docter. Or, the Schoole of Salerne* (London, 1607), also seems to have been intended to educate the young prince. See "Part 1: The Pleasant Learned Poet," in *The Epigrams*, 20.

148   *Early Modern Catholics, Royalists, and Cosmopolitans*

campaign to put an end to the Earl of Tyrone's rebellion in Ireland (it was during this campaign that the Earl conferred a knighthood on Harington along with some 60 other English officers).[161] Following preliminary discussions between Essex and Tyrone, which eventually led to Essex's premature retreat to England at the end of September 1599, Harington presented a gift of his translation of Ariosto to the Earl of Tyrone's two sons. In a subsequent letter to George Carew, Earl of Totnes, Harington explains the context in which he presented his copy of the translation to the two boys:

> [Harington] took occasion the while to entertain [Tyrone's] two sons, by posing them in their learning, and their tutors, which were one Fryar Nangle, a Franciscan; and a younger scholer, whose name I know not; and finding the two children of good towardly spirit, their age between thirteen and fifteen, in English cloths like a nobleman's sons; with velvet gerkins and gold lace; of a good chearful aspect, freckle-faced, not tall of stature, but strong, and well set; both of them [learning] the English tongue; I gave them (not without the advice of Sir William Warren) my English translation of 'Ariosto,' which I got at Dublin; which their teachers took very thankfully and soon after shewed it the earl, who call'd to see it openly, and would needs hear some part of it read. I turn'd (as it had been by chance) to the beginning of the 45th canto, and some other passages of the book, which he seemed to like so well, that he solemnly swore his boys should read all the book over to him.[162]

At the time of this exchange, the Earl of Tyrone and Sir William Warren were engaged in heated negotiations over a temporary truce, which concluded with the signing of formal documents halting hostilities. The beginning of the forty-fifth canto of the *Orlando Furioso* concerns the forces of ephemeral Fortune, which alternatively subverts the well-being of kings and princes and restores them to "the happy hour" (45.2). Harington's message to Tyrone and his sons seems to have been that only through education and preparation can one guard against the ebbs and flows of fortune, which are inevitable with the passing of time.[163]

---

[161] For context, see Adam N. McKeown, *English Mercuries: Soldier Poets in the Age of Shakespeare* (Nashville, TN, 2009), 125–43.

[162] Harington, "To Justice Carey [Ireland, October 1599]," in *The Letters and Epigrams of Sir John Harington together with The Prayse of Private Life*, ed. Norman Egbert McClure (New York, 1977), 77.

[163] Rick Bowers speculates that Harington was sent to Ireland explicitly in order to spy on Essex and report back to the privy council. See Bowers, "Sir John Harington and the Earl of Essex: The Joker as Spy," *Cahiers Élizabéthains* 69 (2006): 13–20.

Chapter 3
Cosmopolitan Romance:
Philip Sidney, Edmund Spenser, and the
Fiction of Imperial Justice

The previous chapter suggests that the works of fiction and translation by Anthony Munday and Sir John Harington were shaped by the cosmopolitan perspective of Edmund Campion and other Catholic exiles, even as these two writers viewed themselves as opposed to the politics of Catholic exiles in other respects. In particular, I suggest that their fictional works and some of their other writings translate into secularized form the concept of papal supremacy, imagined by Catholic exiles such as Sander and Allen as laying the foundation for papal claims for the right to depose heretical or tyrannical leaders. In the fictional works by Harington and Munday, we encounter again and again characters such as Emperor Traianus in Harington's *A New Discourse* and Robin Hood in Munday's *Earl of Huntington* plays, who serve to correct the conscience of the crown in ways that are reminiscent of Campion's Bishop Ambrose in his Latin play, *Ambrosia*. This chapter considers similar forms of cosmopolitan identity within the context of two canonical fictional works, Philip Sidney's *The New Arcadia* and Edmund Spenser's *Faerie Queene*, both of which provide insight into the ways that writers imagined order and justice within the international sphere.

Before considering Sidney and Spenser in more detail, it is worth pausing to evaluate what I present in the previous chapter as the secularized translation of papal supremacy into the fictional works of Munday and Harington. According to my account of Munday and Harington, the impetus behind the fictional portrayal of figures who rein in untrammeled sovereign power was driven by some of the same anxieties that caused Catholic exile Robert Persons to write *A Conference on the Next Succession*, namely the necessity of councilors, advisors—or for Persons, bishops and popes—that could bind the sovereign's conscience or correct the sovereign's behavior when he or she fell into sin. My argument does not depend for its viability on the claim, made respectively by Donna Hamilton and Gerard Kilroy, that Munday and Harington harbored clandestine Catholic sympathies. At the same time, the fact that both Munday and Harington were known to have consorted with the English Catholic community, both at home and abroad, and that their non-fictional writings illustrate an abiding interest in the issue of papal supremacy at the very least makes my argument about the nature of the cosmopolitan identity that their writings explore more persuasive.

Unlike Munday and Harington, Sidney and Spenser were identified with the circle of writers and scholars surrounding Robert Dudley, Earl of Leicester, who

150 *Early Modern Catholics, Royalists, and Cosmopolitans*

was at the center of the militant Protestant faction at Elizabeth's court.[1] A number of scholars have moreover presented both writers as having Calvinist sympathies and have argued that, along with Leicester and Sir Francis Walsingham, Sidney and Spenser mostly identified with the persecuted Huguenots across the channel, while other scholars have presented Sidney and Spenser as loyal and even enthusiastic supporters of the Elizabethan settlement or of having been influenced by the moderate reformer, Philipp Melanchthon.[2] Whatever their true religious affiliations, I show in this chapter that Sidney and Spenser came to similar conclusions to those that Munday and Harington arrived at, namely that the international sphere was prone to chaos without some external force that was capable of correcting the sinful or tyrannical sovereign.[3]

---

[1]   Jan Karel Kouwenhoven, "Sidney, Leicester, and *The Faerie Queene*," in *Sir Philip Sidney 1586 and the Creation of a Legend*, ed. Jan Van Dorsten et al. (Leiden, Netherlands, 1986), 149–70; Alan Stewart, *Philip Sidney: A Double Life*, 9–35, 51, 57–78, 162, 165, 183, 185–6, 248, 250–1; Duncan-Jones, *Sir Philip Sidney*, 5, 15, 70, 150–51, 156–7, 220, 267–9, 281; Osborn, *Young Philip Sidney*, 179–80. Spenser's link to the Leicester circle was more tenuous and ambivalent. See Andrew Hadfield, *Edmund Spenser: A Life* (New York, 2012), 101, 107–10, 146–7, 151, 275–8.

[2]   For the Sidney-as-Calvinist argument see, Andrew D. Weiner, *Sir Philip Sidney and the Poetics of Protestantism* (Minneapolis, 1978); Alan Sinfield, "Protestantism: Questions of Subjectivity and Control," in *Faultlines: Cultural Materialism and the Poetics of Dissident Reading* (Berkeley, CA, 1992), 143–80; Nadra Perry, "Imitatio and Identity: Thomas Rogers, Philip Sidney, and the Protestant Self," *English Literary Renaissance* 35.3 (2005): 365–406. For the latter argument that Sidney was a conformist, see Eileen Z. Cohen, "Gentle Knight and Pious Servant: A Study of Sidney's Protestantism," Dissertation, University of Maryland, College Park, MD, 1965; Roger Kuin, "Querre-Muhau: Sir Philip Sidney and the New World," *Renaissance Quarterly* 51.2 (Summer 1998): 549–85; Kuin, "Sir Philip Sidney's Model of the Statesman," *Reformation* 4 (1999): 93–117. For the Sidney-as-Philippist argument, see Robert E. Stillman, *Philip Sidney and the Poetics of Renaissance Cosmopolitanism* (Burlington, VT, 2008). For the Arcadia as a "Protestant" narrative, see Tiffany Werth, "The Reformation of Romance in Sir Philip Sidney's *The New Arcadia*," *English Literary Renaissance* 40.1 (Winter 2010): 33–55. Spenser's religious influences were equally complex and heterogeneous. Hadfield notes especially the influence of Jan van der Noot, often seen as a Calvinist author, who later converted to Catholicism. Hadfield presents him, I think correctly, as a conformist, using the 1559 *Book of Common Prayer*, but having an "eclectic faith" that perhaps changed over time. Notably his sons Sylvanus and Peregrine became Catholic. See Hadfield, *Edmund Spenser*, 39–54, 116–18, 222–6.

[3]   For Harington's relationship with Sidney's oeuvre, see Nelson, "Sir John Harington as a Critic of Sir Philip Sidney," 41–56, and P.J. Croft, "Sir John Harington's Manuscript of Sir Philip Sidney's *Arcadia*," in *Literary Autographs*, ed. Stephen Parks et al. (Los Angeles, 1983), 39–75. Kilroy notes that with the help of two scribes, Harington was transcribing and elaborating on the *Arcadia* at the same time that he was translating *Orlando Furioso*. See Kilroy, "Advertising the Reader," 65–6. See also H.R. Woudhuysen, *Sir Philip Sidney and the Circulation of Manuscripts, 1558–1640* (New York, 1996), 346, for the dates of Harington's transcription of this and other works by Sidney. For Ariosto's influence on Sidney, see Freda L. Townsend, "*Sidney* and *Ariosto*," *PMLA* 61 (1946): 97–108. For Munday's relationship

Sidney and the International Order

The messy ending of the *Old Arcadia* reveals the impossibility of establishing a regime of justice within the transnational sphere.[4] With Basilius presumed dead, Euarchus assumes the position of protector of Arcadia in an attempt to restore the rule of law in the troubled dukedom and obtain justice for Basilius's killers. But Euarchus's ability to establish justice in Arcadia is hampered by his own anxieties over public perception of his own dynastic ambitions (312).[5] His first order is therefore that "no man, under pain of grievous punishment name me by any other name but protector of Arcadia; for I will not leave any possible colour to any of my natural successors to make claim to this, which my free election you have bestowed upon me" (316; see also 307). As the exemplum of the good sovereign, Euarchus's motivations are presented as mostly charitable, Philanax remarking at one point, "Thou wilt lend thine arms unto her, and as a man take compassion of mankind" (311). Indeed, Euarchus's only selfish motive is the protection of the "universal case of Greece," which he views as threatened by Basilius's abdication of his responsibilities. For the narrator, Euarchus is the exception to the bad behavior of "most princes," who would have thought Basilius's retreat into the pastoral "a sufficient cause ... to have sought the enlarging of their dominions, wherein they falsely put the more or less felicity of an estate" (309).

In spite of the attempt to differentiate Euarchus from "most princes," however, the anxiety about the motivation behind his actions persists to the very end of the trial of the accused regicides, at which point the morality of the king's motivations is sorely tested. He is faced with an impossible dilemma: once he knows that the two youths accused of killing Basilius and kidnapping the princesses are his son Pyrocles and his nephew Musidorus, he must choose between preserving his family and his dynastic legacy and fulfilling his responsibility to uphold unbiased justice in the troubled realm of Arcadia. As it happens, Euarchus is committed to impartial justice over the pursuit of personal or familial interests, even if the pursuit of justice might jeopardize his basic dynastic interests in Macedonia. Indeed, it is tempting to view Basilius's resurrection from his deathly sleep allegorically as Euarchus's

---

with Spenser, see Turner Wright, "Anthony Mundy, 'Edward' Spenser, and E.K.," 34–9. For a discussion of how Spenser's *Faerie Queene* relates to the *Arcadia*, see T.P. Harrison, Jr, "The Relations of Spenser and Sidney," *PMLA* 45.3 (1930): 712–31.

[4] Lockey, *Law and Empire*, 47–79. For an overview of both the *Old* and the *New Arcadia* and its continental and classical sources, see A.C. Hamilton, *Sir Philip Sidney: A Study of His Life and Works* (New York, 1977). On the question of sources, see also Thelma Greenfield, *The Eye of Judgment: Reading the New Arcadia* (Toronto, 1982), 123–42; Clark L. Chalifour, "Sir Philip Sidney's *Old Arcadia* as Terentian Comedy," *Studies in English Literature* 16.1 (1976): 51–63; V.L. Forsyth, "Polybius's Histories: An Overlooked Source for Sidney's *Arcadia*," *Sidney Journal* 21.2 (2003): 59–65; and David Kalstone, "The Transformation of Arcadia: Sannazaro and Sir Philip Sidney," *Comparative Literature* 15.3 (1963): 234–49.

[5] All parenthetical citations from the *Old Arcadia* are from Sidney, *The Old Arcadia*, ed. Katherine Duncan-Jones (New York, 1999).

152   *Early Modern Catholics, Royalists, and Cosmopolitans*

reward for staying true to the ideal of impartial justice.[6] But Sidney ultimately shows that whatever choice Euarchus makes in the trial, he is bound to be accused of privileging his own dynastic interests above the ideal of impartial justice.[7]

In spite of such a cautionary note, Euarchus's intervention within Arcadia conforms to the prescriptions of the most important Protestant *monarchomach* treatise, the *Vindiciae, Contra Tyrannos*, in its recommendations concerning what a good sovereign should do when he encounters tyranny within a neighboring kingdom.[8] Like the narrator in the *Arcadia*, the anonymous author of the *Vindiciae* warns against a good king using injustice to advance his own interests: "I too definitely do not consider that under this pretext [that of charitable intervention] you may invade foreign borders, or seize the jurisdiction of another for yourself, or remove the harvest of a neighbor to your area as many do under this pretense."[9] Making reference to Cicero's *De republica*, the *Vindiciae* explains in great detail

---

[6] For a consideration of Baslius's revival, see Charles Ross, *Elizabethan Literature and the Law of Fraudulent Conveyance: Sidney, Spenser, and Shakespeare* (Burlington, VT, 2003), 60–62.

[7] Lockey, *Law and Empire*, 70–79. Despite the two youths accused of regicide having been revealed as his son, Pyrocles, and his nephew, Musidorus, Euarchus decides that their execution must go forward. But as soon as he decides on this course, Euarchus is immediately accused of executing his nephew, the heir to the Thessalian throne, in the name of his dynastic interests in the realm of Thessalia. Musidorus remarks, "Enjoy thy bloody conquest, tyrannical Euarchus ... Let thy flattering orators dedicate crowns of laurel unto thee, that the first of thy race thou hast overthrown a prince of Thessalia," and later Eurarchus's own son, Pyrocles, chastises him "lest seeking too precise a course of justice, you be not thought most unjust in weakening your neighbors mighty estate by taking away their only pilar" (356, 358). For related readings of Euarchus's imperfect judgment, see Robert Stillman, *Sidney's Poetic Justice: The Old Arcadia, Its Eclogues, and Renaissance Pastoral Traditions* (Cranbury, NJ, 1986), 214–28; Elizabeth Dipple, "'Unjust Justice' in the *Old Arcadia*," *Studies in English Literature 1500–1900* 10.1 (1970): 83–101, esp. 93–4; Clifford Davidson, "Nature and Judgement in the *Old Arcadia*," *Papers on Language and Literature* 6 (1970): 348–65; Joan Rees, "Justice, Mercy, and a Shipwreck in *Arcadia*," *Studies in Philology* 87.1 (1990): 75–82; Rees, *Sir Philip Sidney and Arcadia* (Cranbury, NJ, 1991), 127–41; and Ann W. Astell, "Sidney's Didactic Method in the *Old Arcadia*," in *Studies in English Literature 1500–1900* 24.1 (Winter 1984): 39–51. For discussion of the complex sense of closure in the fifth book of the *Old Arcadia*, see Stephen Greenblatt, "Sidney's *Arcadia* and the Mixed Mode," *Studies in Philology* 70.3 (1973): 269–78.

[8] For context, see William Dinsmore Briggs, "Political Ideas in Sidney's *Arcadia*," *Studies in Philology* 28.2 (1931): 137–61; Worden, *Sound of Virtue*, 282–92; Robert E. Stillman, "The Truths of a Slippery World: Poetry and Tyranny in Sidney's *Defence*," *Renaissance Quarterly* 55.4 (2002): 1287–319. For refutation of Briggs's argument that Sidney was influenced by the *Vindiciae*, see Irving Ribner, "Sir Philip Sidney on Civil Insurrection," *Journal of the History of Ideas* 13.2 (April 1952): 257–65; Ribner, "Machiavelli and Sidney: The *Arcadia* of 1590," *Studies in Philology* 47.2 (1950): 152–72.

[9] "nec ego sane consulo, vt eo pretextu fines alienos invadas, iurisdictionem alterius ad te rapias, messem vicini in aream tuam traducas, quad pleriq; eo pretextu faciunt." Anon., *Vindiciae, Contra Tyrannos*, 183 [Q4v].

Cosmopolitan Romance   153

what a "neighboring prince" is obligated to do when confronted by tyranny on his borders:

> Briefly, if a [tyrannical] prince rides roughshod over the fixed limits [*limites*] of piety and justice, then a neighbour will be able to rush forth from his borders [*limites*] piously and justly, not in order to invade another's, but to command him to be content with his own. Indeed, he would himself be impious and unjust if he were to neglect to do so. If a prince practices tyranny against a people, a neighboring prince should be no less zealous in rendering assistance to it, than he would be to the prince of the people engaged in sedition. Indeed, he ought to be more ready to do so in so far as it is more wretched for many to suffer than one.[10]

The culmination of a number of such tracts published during the 1570s in response to the Saint Bartholomew's Day massacre of 1572, the anonymous *Vindiciae* justified the people's fundamental right to rebellion, especially when they faced the threat of religious persecution.[11] In this respect, its purpose was not unlike that of Pope Pius V, who, in issuing his famous Bull, *Regnans in Excelsis* (1570), excommunicating Queen Elizabeth, sought to succor persecuted English Catholics and to absolve them from their obligation to the English crown. Despite their political and theological differences, neither Catholic supporters of *Regnans in Excelsis* nor the author of the *Vindiciae* wanted to authorize all forms of popular rebellion against an unjust or tyrannical or heretical sovereign. Thus, in 1580, Pope Gregory XIII issued a clarification of *Regnans in Excelsis*, in which he observed that English Catholics should remain loyal subjects of Queen Elizabeth until an opportunity for liberating themselves from Elizabeth presented itself, by which was presumably meant a Catholic invasion of the kingdom by a legitimate sovereign.[12] Similarly, while the *Vindiciae* sought to justify resistance to tyranny, such resistance could only occur according to two narrowly-defined covenants that bound the sovereign, the magistrates, and the people of a particular kingdom. According to both covenants, local magistrates and neighboring princes were entitled or even obligated to resist or intercede into the affairs of the tyrant who persecuted his people either for religious or secular reasons. In contrast, private

---

[10]   "Breuiter, si princeps fixos peitatis & iustitiae limites violenter transilit, poterit vicinus pie iusteque extra limites suos prosilire, non vt invadat aliena, sed vt suis illum contentum esse iubeat: quin impius & iniustus erit, si negligat. Si princeps in populum tyrannidem exerceat, non minus aut segnius illi opem feret, quam illi, si populus seditionem moueat: imo eo promptius debebit, quo plures quam vnum pati miserabilius est." Anon., *Vindiciae, Contra Tyrannos*, 184 [Q4v].

[11]   See Skinner, *The Foundations of Modern Political Thought*, vol. 2, 306–48.

[12]   This clarification can be found as Item 11 in the "Facultates concessae Patribus Roberto Personio et Emundo [sic] Campiano pro Anglia die 14 Aprilis 1580," printed as an appendix in Meyer, *England and the Catholic Church Under Queen Elizabeth*, 486–8, at 487. There are other copies of Gregory's clarification (Public Record Office, State Papers Domestic, Elizabeth November 1580 and April–May 1582). For the larger context, see McCoog, *The Society of Jesus 1541–1588*, 139–41.

subjects of the king must learn to endure the rule of an oppressive tyrant and hope for liberation through the actions of a magistrate or an extraordinary liberator.[13]

Similar to Persons's *Conference*, the prescriptions found in the *Vindiciae* were premised on an international order based on the notion of the Christian commonwealth.[14] But whereas Persons and Sander could claim that the superior authority of the spiritual realm allowed the pope to depose a tyrannical sovereign for either religious or secular reasons, the author of the *Vindiciae* and his Huguenot co-religionists were looking forward to a world without popes in which sovereigns had been delegated power over both the spiritual and temporal realms. As a result, the *Vindiciae* establishes a complex network of princes and magistrates that together are responsible for resisting and eliminating tyrants or heretical princes who persecute the faithful. Within this network, the good princes within Christendom are given the role of correcting and deposing evil or heretical sovereigns, a role that Persons and Campion saw as the exclusive right of the pope or bishop. Like Persons, the author of the *Vindiciae* can find numerous historical precedents for this position. Moreover, like Sander, Bristow, Allen, and Campion, his argument draws on Isaiah 49:23, with which we are now familiar from our discussion in Chapter 1:

> Without any doubt, where the glory of God and the kingdom of Christ is concerned, no limits [*limites*], no frontiers [*fines*], no barriers [*cancelli*], ought to restrict the zeal of pious princes ... Many Christian princes have followed these examples of pious ones, as a result of which the church—which was at first confined to Palestine—has spread throughout the whole world. There were the two emperors Constantine and Licinius, the former in the east and the latter in the west. They were colleagues possessed of equal power. The common proverb should be noted: an equal has no command over an equal. Yet nevertheless Constantine waged war against Licinius, who banished, ravaged, and butchered Christians—amongst whom were many nobles—on account, or on the pretext, of their religion. So Constantine secured by force the free practice of the Christian religion. And finally, when Licinius broke faith and reverted to his original

---

[13] According to the first sacred covenant, God is the lord, while according to the second secular covenant, the people are lord. According to the first covenant, the sovereign and his magistrates, who are representative of the people, were co-tutors bound to protect the true worship of God. According to the second secular covenant, the king and his magistrates, once again representing his people, were bound to protect the laws of the kingdom, provinces, and the cities. There are some differences between the two covenants—local magistrates are locally bound according to the second secular covenant, while they are universally bound according to the first sacred covenant, which means that they should resist a tyrant who violates the first covenant regardless of boundaries or frontiers (Anon., *Vindiciae, Contra Tyrannos*, 41, 46–60, 59, 66, 155, 158–60, 165–7, 170–71).

[14] Interestingly while the author expressed contempt for papal monarchical claims, he drew heavily from canon law as precedent in his analysis of both parts of the covenant. See Anon., *Vindiciae, Contra Tyrannos*, 126, 147, 163–5. For context, see also Garnett, "Editor's Introduction," xliv.

Cosmopolitan Romance   155

savagery, he [Constantine] ordered him to be put to death in Thessalonica. This was, I say, that same Constantine the Great whose piety was celebrated by all the theologians of that era to such an extent that some would wish to say of him what is said by Isaiah the prophet: "Kings shall be the foster-parents and pastors of the church [*Reges Ecclesiae nutricios & pastores futuros*]."[15]

In this crucial passage, the author of the *Vindiciae* uses the war between the Eastern Roman Empire and the Western Roman Empire to make his point that temporal rulers like Constantine, rather than popes or bishops such as Bishop Ambrose of Milan, have the right to depose a tyrannical or heretical sovereign such as Licinius. Moreover, Christian sovereigns, rather than evangelizing clerics, were responsible for the spread of the Christian Church outside of Palestine, and indeed, such sovereigns can and should continue to serve the church by acting as Constantine did in protecting and defending those Christians whom the tyrant, Licinius, persecuted. In contrast to Catholic commentators, the *Vindiciae*'s citation of Isaiah 49:23 avoids using the Latin Vulgate Bible, in which kings are referred to as "*nutricii* [foster-fathers]" and queens "*nutrices* [wet-nurses]." Rather, its citation of the verse adds the Latin word, "*pastores* [pastors]," which subtly blurs the distinction between princes and clergy, temporal and spiritual rulers. For the author of the *Vindiciae*, secular princes are the equivalent of spiritual princes, and they have the same authority over the church. In the *Vindiciae*'s deployment of this Biblical verse, then, secular princes no longer function as servants to an authoritative church—rather, they are its governors. Ultimately, whereas Nicholas Sander saw this verse as justifying the exaltation of the spiritual realm above the temporal, popes and bishops over kings and temporal magistrates, the author of the *Vindiciae* interprets it as justification for temporal rulers to become direct caretakers of the church and to exercise a borderless sovereignty over evil rulers within Christendom.

Not unlike the *Vindiciae*, one purpose of Sidney in the *Old Arcadia* seems to have been to theorize the establishment of an international order. And similar to the examples found in the *Vindiciae*, the order that emerges in the *Old Arcadia* is maintained at the behest of the secular ruler. Thus, no figures of transnational

---

[15] "Nimirum vbi Dei gloria, vbi Christi regnum agitur, nulli limites, nulli fines, nulli cancelli, piorum principum zelum arcere debent. Sin vis forte maior immineat recordentur horum exemplo, qui vere Dominum timent, neminem metuere posse. Haec piorum principum exempla, ex quo ecclesia, quae prius Palestina circuscribebatur, per vniuersum orbem diffusa fuit, Christiani principes multi insequuti sunt. Erant Constantinus & Licinius imperatores ambo: ille Orientis, hic Occidentis. Erant & collegae pari potestate praediti. Notum vero est, quod vulgo dicitur: Parem in parem non habere imperium. Nihilo minus tamen Constantinus Licinium Christianos, in iisque nobiles plaerosque, religionis sive causa, sive praetextu, relegantem, divexantem, contrucidantem, bello petit, religionis liberum cultum Christianis vi impetrat: fidem denique frangentem, & ad pristinam saeuitiam revertentem Thessalonicae morte mulctari iubet. Constantinus, inquam, ille Magnus, cuius vsque adeo pietas ab omnibus illius saeculi Theologis celebratur, vt de eo quidam dictum velint, quod est apud Esaiam Prophetam: Reges Ecclesiae nutricios & pastores futuros." Anon., *Vindiciae, Contra Tyrannos*, 176–7 [P6v].

156 *Early Modern Catholics, Royalists, and Cosmopolitans*

authority emerge in the *Old Arcadia* that might be construed as analogous to the pope in sixteenth-century Europe. Nor are there any overarching imperial figures analogous to the Roman emperor from the ancient world or the Holy Roman Emperor from the contemporary world. Euarchus is described by way of comparison with Basilius as the "mightiest prince of Greece," and early on in the narrative when we first encounter him, Euarchus is presented as defending himself against the neighboring kings of Thrace, Pannonia, and Epirus, evil sovereigns whom Euarchus eventually conquers (309; 9). In this respect, he is a natural inheritor of the ancient conquerors of Greece, Philip of Macedon and his son Alexander. But his imperial inheritance is mostly irrelevant insofar as Euarchus rejects or only reluctantly assumes the traditional role of imperial conqueror. When Euarchus intervenes in the affairs of Arcadia, he is acting only as the King of Macedonia and his purpose is self-serving insofar as restoring Arcadia to right rule will assist him in protecting Macedonia from foreign invasion. In other words, Euarchus's actions in Arcadia seem to embody one of the situations that the author of the *Vindiciae* imagined, that of a neighboring prince "extend[ing] a helping hand to a stricken people and a prostrate commonwealth."[16]

But in terms of political theory, the Protestant *monarchomach* tradition was not the only influence on Sidney's romance. Sidney's conception of failed rule embodied in the weak and ineffectual Basilius is very different from the tyranny imagined by the author of the *Vindiciae*, when he prescribes that good princes should intervene into the affairs of their oppressive neighboring princes. By way of analogy, the author of the *Vindiciae* maintains that it is "all the more lawful for a good prince, who is rendering assistance to and protecting not some slave against a ferocious owner, or sons against a raging father, but the kingdom against a tyrant, the commonwealth against the private desire of one man, the people—the owner [*domino*], I say—against a public slave and agent."[17] Sidney's portrayal of Basilius is not the type of ruler that is analogous to a "ferocious owner" or a "raging father." Rather, his faulty rule consists in him neglecting his sovereign duties, which leads to a collapse of the "natural" order in the court and finally chaos and insurrection in the country itself.

As my earlier work on the *Old Arcadia* has shown, another probable influence on Sidney, given his use of the legal concepts of equity, natural law and the law of nations, comprised the early and mid-sixteenth-century writings of the Spanish Neo-Scholastics, especially Francisco de Vitoria and Bartolomé de las Casas.[18]

---

[16] "populo afflicto, reipublicae prostratae, manum auxiliarem porrigas." Anon., *Vindiciae, Contra Tyrannos*, 183 [Q2v].

[17] "an non multo magis licebit bono principi, non seruis quidem adversus saeuientem dominum, aut filiis adversus furentem patrem: sed regno adversus tyrannum, republicae adversus priuatam vnius libidinem, populo, domino inquam, adversus seruum & actorem publicum, opem ferre & patrocinari." Anon., *Vindiciae, Contra Tyrannos*, 182–3 [Q3v].

[18] See Lockey, *Law and Empire*, 64–70. See Francisco de Vitoria, *De Indis [On the American Indians]*, 231–92; See Bartolomé de las Casas, *Una brevísima relación de la destruyción de las Indias* (Sevilla, 1552), and its French and English translations: *Tyrannies et cruautés des Espagnols perpétrées ès Indes occidentales* (Antwerp, 1579), and *The*

Cosmopolitan Romance 157

Taking into account Sidney's Protestant humanist predilections, it might strike one as improbable that Sidney's *Arcadia* could have been influenced by a writer as central to the orthodoxy of the Roman Catholic Church in Spain as Vitoria had been. But given his hostility to the Spanish crown, Sidney would undoubtedly have found common cause in Vitoria's and Las Casas's respective critiques of the oppressive policies in the Americas pursued by the Spanish conquistadores.[19] Moreover, Arcadia's descent into unnatural vice, incest, and ultimately barbarism as well as Euarchus's subsequent charitable intervention into the neighboring kingdom, the purpose of which is to re-establish natural law, accurately embody a narrow set of justifications for conquest that Vitoria favored. For Vitoria, if the mental state of a people is so impaired that "they are unsuited even to governing their own households," then "for their own benefit," a prince "might take over their administration ... so long as this could be proved to be in their interest."[20]

Perhaps the biggest difference between the Huguenot *monarchomach* and the neo-Scholastic theorists on just war and conquest was their differing views on natural law, with Vitoria viewing natural law from the traditional Thomist

---

Spanish Colonie, or Briefe chronicle of the acts and gestes of the Spaniardes in the West Indies (London, 1583). See also *A Short Account of the Destruction of the Indies*, ed. and trans. Nigel Griffin, intro. Anthony Pagden (London, 1992). My argument for Vitoria and Las Casas's influence on Sidney notes the possibility that Sidney might have encountered them through his acquaintance with Alberico Gentili, whom Fr. Luis G. Alonso Getino has shown to have been heavily influenced by Vitoria, his studies at Padua, or even his brief stint at Oxford. See Getino, "Introducción," *Relecciones teológicas del maestro Fray Francisco de Vitoria* (Madrid, 1933), Tomo 3, xxxvi–xliiii. For the other Spanish influences on Sidney that have been documented, see Gustav Ungerer, *Anglo-Spanish Relations in Tudor Literature* (Bern, Switzerland, 1956), 67–9; Elizabeth Bearden, "Sidney's 'mongrell tragicomedy' and Anglo-Spanish Exchange in the *New Arcadia*," *Journal for Early Modern Cultural Studies* 10.1 (2010): 29–51; Paul J. Cooke, *The Spanish Romances in Sir Philip Sidney's* Arcadia, Dissertation, University of Illinois, Urbana-Champaign, 1939; and Judith M. Kennedy, "Introduction," *A Critical Edition of Yong's Translation of George of Montemayor's* Diana *and Gil Polo's* Enamoured Diana (Oxford, 1968), xxxiii–xxxiv.

[19] Echoing Bartolomé Las Casas's account of Spanish atrocities committed in the Americas, Sir Fulke Greville wrote that Sidney felt that the "inhuman cruelties [of the Spanish] had so dispeopled and displeased those countries [of the New World]" that Sidney hoped that the "relics of those oppressed Cimaroons would joyfully take arms with any foreigner, to redeem their liberty, and revenge their parents blood." Sir Fulke Greville, "A Dedication to Sir Philip Sidney," in *The Prose Works of Fulke Greville, Lord Brooke*, ed. John Gouws (New York, 1986), 65, lines 21–66, line 2. For Vitoria's and Las Casas's critique of Spanish imperialism, see Pagden, *The Fall of Natural Man.* For an analysis that opposes the humanism of just-war theorists such as Alberico Gentili and Hugo Grotius to the scholasticism of Vitoria, see Richard Tuck, *Rights of War and Peace*, 16–50.

[20] "Nec sunt satis idonei ad gubernandam rem familiarem ... pro utilitate eorum possent Principes Hispani accipere adminstrationem illorum ... dummodo constaret hoc illis expedire." *Relectio Prior de Indis Recenter Inventis*, in *Relectiones de Francisco de Vitoria*, vol. 2, 378; Vitoria, *Relectio de Indis [On the American Indians]*, in *Political Writings*, 290.

158   *Early Modern Catholics, Royalists, and Cosmopolitans*

perspective as one rung in a hierarchy that also comprised the eternal law, the divine law, and the human law. Because natural law was derived from the eternal law and coterminous with the divine law (according to scripture, the gentiles have the law written in or carved into their heart), the natural law ultimately formed the foundation of human law and custom.[21] This in turn justified a good sovereign taking measures to bring unnatural human laws or customs into conformity with natural law through war or conquest.[22] In contrast, the author of the *Vindiciae* perceives natural law as emerging from a state of natural liberty. Natural law is that which emerges from nature itself, which teaches us "to preserve and protect our life and liberty—without which life is scarcely life at all—against all force and injustice."[23] Robert Stillman's recent work on Sidney's poetic theory has presented Philip Melanchthon's theological writings as responsible for Sidney's references to nature (*natura naturans*) and natural law in the *Defence of Poetry*, and he is doubtless correct in ascribing the general Protestant revitalization of interest in natural law doctrine that emerged in the work of John Ponet, George Buchanan and Languet to a republic of letters that was Philippist in spirit.[24] But Sidney's perspective on natural law in both the *Old* and the *New Arcadia* also has important similarities to the traditional Scholastic perspective.[25] The good King Euarchus implies that Greek and Arcadian law is derivative from and consistent with the laws of nature: when he arrives in Arcadia and assumes the position of protector, he promises that "to the uttermost of my skill, both in the general laws of nature, especially of Greece, and particularly of Arcadia (wherein I must confess I am not unacquainted), I will not only see the past evils duly punished, and your weal hereafter established, but for your defence in it, if need shall require, I will employ the forces and treasures of mine own country" (315–16). Implicit in this passage

---

[21]   Letter to the Romans 2:14–15. Thomas Aquinas, *Summa Theologiae*, ed. and trans. Thomas Gilby, O.P. (New York, 1966), vol. 28, 1a2ae 91–6.

[22]   Vitoria, *De lege [On Law]*, in *Political Writings*, 153–204. For the laws regulating conquest, see Vitoria, *Relectio de Indis [On the American Indians]*, 231–92 and *De Indis Relectio Posterior, sive de iure belli [On the Law of War]*, 293–328. For the English context, see Lockey, *Law and Empire*, 150–59.

[23]   "vitam & libertatem nostram, qua sine vita vix vitalis est, adversus omnem vim & iniuriam conseruare & tueri." Anon., *Vindiciae, Contra Tyrannos*, 149 [N3].

[24]   Stillman, *Sidney and the Poetics*, 103–22, 192–204. Stillman also argues that Sidney inherited much of his thought on how natural law applies to tyranny and the state from the *Vindiciae* and other monarchomarch tracts during this period. For a related discussion of Sidney's interest in the divine poetry of French Huguenot Du Bartas, see Alan Sinfield, "Sidney and Du Bartas," *Comparative Literature* 27.1 (1975): 8–20.

[25]   Long ago, Lois Whitney showed that Sidney's understanding of natural law was ultimately Aristotelian and Thomist, even if it was often presented in contradictory terms. See Whitney, "Concerning Nature in *The Countesse of Pembroke's Arcadia*," *Studies in Philology* 23 (1927): 207–22. Similarly, Constance Miriam Syford recognized Sidney's interest in the "unifying Force and Wisdom of an Universal, Eternal Nature." See Syford, "The Direct Source of the Pamela-Cecropia Episode in the *Arcadia*," *PMLA* 49.2 (1934): 472–89, at 479.

Cosmopolitan Romance   159

is the Thomist notion of a hierarchy of law ("general laws of nature, especially of Greece, and particularly of Arcadia"), which allowed the Neo-Scholastics to argue that all human law had to be consistent with natural law to be legitimate.

Ultimately, despite their differences on religious doctrine, Vitoria and the author of the *Vindiciae* were addressing the identical problem of how to foster an international order that would authorize just acts of foreign intervention and prohibit unjust ones. Indeed, it is clear that Catholics such as Vitoria and Persons as well as Protestants such as the author of the *Vindiciae* were all endeavoring to answer crucial questions about the legitimacy of sovereignty from a perspective external to the nation-state. And while their religious and methodological perspectives were vastly different, they shared a common debt to the *Corpus Iuris Civilis* and the *Corpus Iuris Canonici* as well as to medieval jurists such as Bartolus of Sassoferato.[26] For Vitoria, who was addressing a slightly different set of questions, such legitimacy could be found in a Thomist conception of natural law, while for Persons it could be found in the spiritual realm, presided over by the Roman curia. For the author of the *Vindiciae* it came directly from God and then from the people and their representatives, the good princes and magistrates who ruled according to natural law. Sidney's *Old Arcadia* is concerned with the same basic question of what form the international order should take in order to legitimize and protect good sovereigns, reform or punish tyrants, and restore states where the rule of law has collapsed. Euarchus's motivations in assuming the temporary protectorship of Arcadia and sitting in judgment of the accused regicides are laudable. And yet, in spite of the fact that Euarchus's intervention into Arcadia proceeds according to an ideal of justice inspired by traditional conceptions of natural law, the suspicion that he is acting in order to advance his own self-interests casts doubt on his motives until the very end of the narrative.

Cosmopolitan Order in the *New Arcadia*

The ending of Sidney's first version of his romance suggests that a transnational realm governed by so-called good sovereigns like Euarchus will forever be open to the accusation that such state actors conceal their real motivations beneath a veneer of morality.[27] The *New Arcadia* takes up the same problem but resolves it by locating the source of moral action outside of the realms of secular rulers.[28] Let us recall that, throughout the *Old Arcadia*, Greece lacks an imperial overseer that is capable in an impartial manner of restoring natural law in Arcadia.[29] As a

---

[26]   Anon., *Vindiciae, Contra Tyrannos*, 188–90; See "Index," in Vitoria, *Political Writings*, 392–3.

[27]   See Lockey, *Law and Empire*, 76–9.

[28]   For a related reading of justice in the *New Arcadia*, see William Craft, *Labyrinth of Desire: Invention and Culture in the Work of Sir Philip Sidney* (Newark, DE, 1994), 25–52.

[29]   For a comprehensive discussion of the relationship between the *Old* and the *New Arcadia*, see A.G.D. Wiles, "Parallel Analyses of the Two Versions of Sidney's *Arcadia*, including the Major Variations of the Folio of 1593," *Studies in Philology* 39.2 (1942):

160 *Early Modern Catholics, Royalists, and Cosmopolitans*

result, Arcadia must ultimately turn to the neighboring sovereign, Euarchus, who strives to administer right rule and justice but cannot escape the accusation that his intervention into Arcadia will be self-serving. In contrast, in the *New Arcadia*, Pyrocles and Musidorus establish a regime of transnational justice throughout the kingdoms of Asia Minor that is utterly divorced from the interests of any kingdom or sovereign claim.[30] In this respect, Pyrocles and Musidorus together assume the role of "secular pope" or "secular bishop" that we encountered in the works of Munday and Harington. Together they embody a power that is able to correct or depose tyrannical princes as well as protect and restore vulnerable kingdoms, all the while abjuring any territorial interest.[31]

The New Arcadia begins with a civil insurrection in Laconia, where the helots are engaged in a rebellion against the gentlemen of Lacedaemon.[32] After the shipwreck that occurs at the beginning of the narrative, Palladius (Musidorus in disguise) finds himself in the house of the Arcadian nobleman, Kalendar, whose son, Clitophon, had previously travelled to Laconia to help his friend, Argulus, recently taken prisoner by the helots. When Clitophon is also taken prisoner, Palladius (Musidorus) and Kalendar lead a force of Arcadians against the helot rebels. When Palladius (Musidorus) encounters the helot captain in battle, Palladius's helmet is knocked off, revealing to the helot captain the prince's identity. The helot captain, none other than Palladius's best friend, Daiphantus (Pyrocles in disguise), spares Palladius, after which Daiphantus (Pyrocles) persuades the helot rebels to allow all the Arcadians to return to their country. Afterwards, Daiphantus (Pyrocles) achieves a just peace with the Lacedaemonians on behalf of the helots (26–48).[33]

Aspects of the Lacedaemonian-helot civil war in Laconia conjure up the kind of conflict which the author of the *Vindiciae* imagined in the third and most

---

167–206. For more insight into how Sidney revised the *Arcadia*, particularly with regard to the transition from dialogue in the original to exemplum or incompletion in the revision, see Jon Sherman Lawry, *Sidney's Two Arcadias: Pattern and Proceeding* (Ithaca, NY, 1972), 154–289, and Gavin Alexander, *Writing After Sidney: The Literary Response to Sir Philip Sidney, 1586–1640* (New York, 2006), 1–56. See also Margaret M. Sullivan, "Amazons and Aristocrats: The Function of Pyrocles' Amazon Role in Sidney's Revised *Arcadia*," in *Playing with Gender: A Renaissance Pursuit*, ed. Jean R. Brink et al. (Urbana, IL, 1991), 62–81; Victor Skretkowicz, "Categorising Redirection in Sidney's *New Arcadia*," in *Narrative Strategies in Early in Early English Fiction*, ed. Wolfgang Görtschacher and Holger Klein (Lewiston, NY, 1995), 133–46.

[30] The two princes' correction of tyrannical and unjust governments was recognized early on by Edwin A. Greenlaw, who drew parallels with Xenophon's *Cyropaedia*. "Sidney's *Arcadia* as an Example of Elizabethan Allegory," *Anniversary Papers by Colleagues and Pupils of George Lyman Kittredge* (Boston, 1913), 327–37, at 331–3.

[31] For a discussion of how Pyrocles and Musidorus conform to the heroic types of *sapienta et fortitudo*, see Alan Isler, "The Allegory of the Hero and Sidney's Two *Arcadias*," *Studies in Philology* 65.2 (1968): 171–91.

[32] For context, see Irving Ribner, "Machiavelli and Sidney: The *Arcadia* of 1590," *Studies in Philology* 47.2 (1950): 152–72.

[33] All citations from *The New Arcadia* are from Sir Philip Sidney, *The Countess of Pembroke's Arcadia (The New Arcadia)*, ed. Victor Skretkowicz (New York, 1987).

important question of the four which the *Vindiciae* treats, namely, "whether, and to what extent, it be lawful to resist a prince who is oppressing or ruining the commonwealth: also by whom, how, and by what right it may be allowed."[34] In the case of the helot rebellion at the beginning of the *New Arcadia*, a subjugated people rise up to resist their oppressive rulers, and they are led successfully by an extraordinary deliverer, Daiphantus (Pyrocles), who ultimately negotiates a just result in response to their grievances (41). For the author of the *Vindiciae*, a tyrant could only be overthrown by a magistrate, or a legitimate representative of the people, a role that Daiphantus (Pyrocles) assumes when he leads them into battle and later secures a just resolution of their plight. But the result from the Lacedaemonian-helot civil war also combines aspects of the fourth question in the *Vindiciae*, "whether neighbouring princes may by right, or ought, to render assistance to subjects of other princes who are being persecuted on account of pure religion, or oppressed by manifest tyranny?"[35] Daiphantus (Pyrocles) has apparently been adopted by the helots as one of their own, but in reality, Daiphantus is Pyrocles in disguise—and Pyrocles is of course a neighboring prince and heir to the throne of Macedonia.

Pyrocles does not reveal his true identity as a prince to the helots, instead disguising himself as Daiphantus, a fake identity inspired by an earlier disguise assumed by the original Zelmane, daughter of the evil King Plexirtus, when she pursues Pyrocles's love, eventually becoming his page (260–61). Moreover, even if Pyrocles is a prince in reality, there is no sign that he holds sovereignty over any land or kingdom. In this respect, the first political conflict in the *New Arcadia* seems purposely to exist outside of any of the categories or prescriptions in the *monarchomach* tract that Sidney was almost certainly reading during this period. Daiphantus both is and is not a foreign prince interceding in the helot rebellion; he is and he is not a noble representative of the helots; he is and he is not allied with the Arcadian forces that are at loggerheads with the helots, who have kidnapped an Arcadian nobleman.

Most importantly, Pyrocles's intervention into Laconia stands in stark contrast to his father's just but still self-interested intervention into Arcadia in Sidney's prior work, the *Old Arcadia*. Whereas Euarchus's intervened into Arcadia as a neighboring prince, interested in protecting the borders of his kingdom, Pyrocles has no such self-interest at stake. As I show in this section, Sidney's new international order in the *New Arcadia* is both an extension of Euarchus's successful intervention into Arcadia as well as a rejection of that state-based order. Like Euarchus, Musidorus and Pyrocles establish an international order that punishes and overthrows evil tyrants while coming to the aid of sovereigns that

---

[34] "An, et quatenus principi rempublicam aut opprimenti, aut perdenti, resistere liceat. Item, quibus id, & quo modo, & quo iure permissum sit." Anon., *Vindiciae, Contra Tyrannos*, 67 [F5].

[35] "An ivre possint, avt debeant vicini Principes auxilium ferre aliorum Principum subditis, religionis purae causa afflictis, aut manifesta tyrannide oppressis?" Anon., *Vindiciae, Contra Tyrannos*, 173 [P3v].

162   *Early Modern Catholics, Royalists, and Cosmopolitans*

are in peril from such evil forces. But unlike Euarchus, Musidorus and Pyrocles do not have states of their own—nor do they represent state actors or state interests.

One contemporary analogy might be the Holy Roman Emperor, even if the analogy ends when one considers both the confessional identity of the Emperor and the fact that the Emperor was not just an elected position; rather he was also sovereign of his own territory within the Empire. More to the point, the ability of Pyrocles and Musidorus to punish tyrants and protect legitimate sovereigns from the position of those who have abjured any self-interest in the temporal realm recalls an idealized version of the papal power of deposition and correction that we have explored in the first two chapters. In the *New Arcadia*, the two princes perfect this transnational aspect of the pope's power, perhaps responding to the Protestant criticism that the pope's authority was vitiated by his own territorial interests. After all, the pope had always exercised both a direct temporal authority and a spiritual authority over various territories in Italy.[36]

Although one of Sidney's biographers has suggested that we take seriously Campion's report that Sidney had seriously considered converting to Roman Catholic, his correspondence with Languet and other continental Protestants illustrates the disdain for the pope and for the Roman Church felt by the circle of Protestant humanists of which he was a member.[37] In a letter to Sidney in March 1574 during Sidney's sojourn in Venice, for example, Languet describes the Roman Pontiff as the source of all of the turmoil that had been tearing apart Christendom. He laments "these civil wars [*bellis civilibus*] in which the Christian princes [*Principum Christianorum*] are undermining their strength" such that "the way is being prepared for the Turks to conquer Italy." He explains that the source of the current turmoil in Europe is clear: "the Roman Pontiff is twisting himself into every shape to prop up his crumbling tyranny [*tyrannidem*]."[38] In his response, Sidney gently reproves his mentor for his overly pessimistic outlook on recent events, counseling Languet to consider such events "one by one and separately, so that you do not pile up griefs all at the same time and give the impression of being crushed under too great a weight of Fortune." The exchange reveals that the 19-year-old Sidney was skeptical of a historical account that ascribed all the bloodshed in Europe to the Pontiff, thus displaying a more lucid and impartial understanding of

---

[36]   In places like Ireland he took up the sword, and he had his own temporal holdings throughout Italy. See Cecil, *Execution of Justice*, C3–D4v, for a summation of Protestant criticisms of papal authority over the temporal realm. For a defense of the pope's claim to execute some temporal powers, see Allen, *True, Sincere and Modest Defence of English Catholics*, vol. 2, 62–7.

[37]   See, for example, "Hubert Languet to Sidney, Vienna, 1 April, 1574," in Kuin (ed.), *Correspondence of Sir Philip Sidney*, vol. 1, 149–52. See also "Sidney to Wilhelm, Landgrave of Hess, Frankfurt 13 May 1577," vol. 2, 735–41. For context, see Osborn, *Young Philip Sidney*, 477.

[38]   "Istis bellis civilibus, quibus atteruntur vires Principum Christianorum, sternitur via Turcis ad occpandam Italiam"; "Vertit se Pontifex Rom. in omnes formas, ut ruentem suam tyrannidem fulciat." "Hubert Languet to Sidney, Vienna, 26 March 1574," in Kuin (ed.), *Correspondence of Sir Philip Sidney*, 144–8.

recent European events than his mentor. In the same letter, Sidney shows the first inkling that he might be prompted to use historical or allegorical fiction in order to comprehend and put in perspective recent events in Europe: "Should I console you with Letters, and bring up faraway examples of other kingdoms [*longe petita exempla aliorum regnorum*] which were in far more hopeless state, yet afterwards not only revived but tamed the whole world?"[39] In the *New Arcadia*, the role that Pyrocles and Musidorus assume in Asia Minor is that of idealized figures of transnational authority, unencumbered by the corruption and mundane interests that a fervid Protestant such as Languet would associate with Rome. In effect, Sidney's portrayal of Pyrocles and Musidorus embody the idealized power of the pope or the Holy Roman Emperor—the imperial might, the singular focus on justice, the ability to punish tyrants and usurpers and uphold rightful sovereigns—while eschewing all those elements that made these figures so unappealing to Protestants—their confessional bias and error-prone theologies, their temporal interests, and the threat they posed to the Protestant states, including England itself.

In this respect, the *New Arcadia* seems to reject the international order, promoted by the author of the *Vindiciae*, in which the bad behavior of princes is corrected by magistrates and the ethical interventions of good princes. In the third and final book of the *New Arcadia*, Amphialus and his mother Cecropia might superficially seem well-suited for the role of the *Vindiciae*'s magistrates (*universi*), who lead the subjects in revolt against a bad sovereign.[40] And yet, they rebel against Basilius, not to correct a bad king who has led Arcadia to the brink of ruin, but rather to sate Amphialus's lust for Basilius's daughter Philoclea (316–22).[41] In contrast, the role that Musidorus and Pyrocles play in Asia Minor is more analogous to the Catholic ideal of papal deposition with respect to Christian sovereigns except for two significant differences. The international order that Musidorus and Pyrocles establish is purely secular, and the two princes simultaneously assume and reject an imperial role. Indeed, their authority does not come from any claim of conscience or spiritual equity. Secondly, there is no Christian commonwealth at stake here—the imperial force that Musidorus and Pyrocles alternatively adopt and reject is transnational, but its limits are not defined by anything more definite than the boundaries of Asia Minor.

Sidney's revisions of the *Arcadia* render his new work less focused on the foreign policy of kingdoms and nation-states. Rather, Sidney's heroes, Pyrocles and Musidorus, pursue an ideal of transnational justice that is only remotely

---

[39] "singula seperatim consideres, ne dum simul dolores accumules, nimium fortunae succumbere videaris." "consoler ne te per literas, adducamque longe petita exempla aliorum regnorum, quae multo magis desperata tamen postea non tantum respirarunt, sed et fraenum orbi terrarum iniecerunt?" "Sidney to Hubert Languet, 15 April 1574," in Kuin (ed.), *Correspondence of Sir Philip Sidney*, 158–64.

[40] See Martin N. Raitiere, *Faire Bitts: Sir Philip Sidney and Renaissance Political Theory* (Pittsburgh, 1984), 19–38.

[41] For a different reading connecting the captivity episode of Book 3 to the heroic travels of Book 2, see Elizabeth Dipple, "The Captivity Episode and the *New Arcadia*," *Journal of English and Germanic Philology* 70.3 (1971): 418–31.

164   *Early Modern Catholics, Royalists, and Cosmopolitans*

linked to the interests of any one kingdom or nation-state. The difference here, it must be noted, is one of degree. Like Pyrocles's father, Euarchus, the two princes Musidorus and Pyrocles pursue justice in the international context, but whereas Euarchus's "charitable intervention" in the *Old Arcadia* is explicitly linked to Macedonian interests, Musidorus and Pyrocles enforce a regime of transnational justice that is itinerant and radically dislodged from loyalty to any one people or state. The transnational justice that is the subject of romances such as the *New Arcadia* owes a large debt to the medieval tradition of chivalry, and to the degree that Musidorus and Pyrocles are presented as embracing the chivalric ideal in the *New Arcadia*, the itinerant regime of justice that they attempt to enforce should be seen as embodying a sensibility that precedes, in historiographical terms, the early modern rise of the nation-state.[42] Additionally, the pastoral element embodied in Musidorus's costume as the shepherd Dorus, the ecloguic intermissions between books of the romance, and the pastoral retreat taken by the Arcadian royal family are significant, since traditionally, the pastoral mode has been used to critique the metropolis, the imperial capital, and the court, from the perspective of the primitive, natural, universalist shepherd.[43] In this respect, the pastoral is, like the chivalric element, a convention within the genre of romance that critiques the early modern rise of the nation state from the perspective of an earlier period that was both more localized and also more cosmopolitan.[44]

One element that is truly new about the revised *Arcadia* then is the introduction of the transnational sensibility of Musidorus and Pyrocles that is opposed to the national concerns that are still identified with Euarchus's rule over Macedonia.

---

[42]   For context, see Lockey, *Law and Empire*, 29–36; Maurice H. Keen, *Chivalry* (New Haven, CT, 1984), 1–17; Maurice H. Keen, *The Laws of War in the Late Middle Ages* (Toronto, 1965), 239–47; Aldo Scaglione, *Knights at Court: Courtliness, Chivalry, and Courtesy from Ottonian Germany to the Italian Renaissance* (Berkeley, 1991), 81–3; Richard McCoy, *The Rites of Knighthood: The Literature and Politics of Elizabethan Chivalry* (Berkeley, CA: 1989), 9–27, 55–78; and Alex Davis, *Chivalry and Romance in the English Renaissance* (Rochester, NY, 2003), 1–39. For a very different reading of Sidney's ideals of courtesy and chivalry in the *Old Arcadia*, see May, *Elizabethan Courtier Poets*, 69–102.

[43]   For a discussion of how romantic love poses a threat to the family's unity in Sidney's romance, see Lisa Hopkins, "Passion and Reason in Sir Philip Sidney's *Arcadia*," in *Prose Fiction and Early Modern Sexualities in England, 1570–1640*, ed. Constance C. Relihan and Goran V. Stanivukovic (New York, 2003), 61–76.

[44]   Lockey, *Law and Empire*, 36–41. See also Paul Alpers, *What is Pastoral?* (Chicago, 1996), 191, and Michael McKeon, "The Pastoral Revolution," in *Refiguring Revolutions: Aesthetics and Politics from the English Revolution to the Romantic Revolution*, ed. Kevin Sharpe and Steven N. Zwicker (Berkeley, 1998), 267–90, at 284–9. For background on Sidney's use of pastoral, see Elizabeth Dipple, "Harmony and Pastoral in the *Old Arcadia*," *ELH* 35.3 (1968): 309–28; V.L. Forsyth, "The Two Arcadias of Sidney's Two *Arcadias*," *Studies in English Literature 1500–1900* 49.1 (2009): 1–15; Judith Haber, *Pastoral and the Poetics of Self-Contradiction: Theocritus to Marvell* (New York, 1994), 53–97; Peter Lindenbaum, *Changing Landscapes: Anti-Pastoral Sentiment in the English Renaissance* (Athens, GA, 1986), 22–90; and Stillman, *Sidney's Poetic Justice: The* Old Arcadia, *Its Eclogues, and Renaissance Pastoral Traditions* (Lewisburg, PA, 1986).

This new sensibility is introduced chronologically as superseding Euarchus's early devotion to the welfare of Macedonia. The *New Arcadia* begins *in medias res*: whereas the work itself begins with the aftermath of a dramatic shipwreck from which Musidorus washes up on the shores of Arcadia and Pyrocles washes ashore in Laconia, the earliest actual events, relating to Euarchus's rise to power, are recounted by Musidorus at the beginning of Book 2. In this framed narrative, Musidorus, disguised as the shepherd Dorus, recounts to Pamela the establishment of Euarchus's rule over the kingdom of Macedonia, which prior to his inheritance of the kingdom, had descended into lawless anarchy (158–63). Musidorus recounts that, when Euarchus grew old enough to assume sovereignty over Macedonia, the kingdom had descended into bitter infighting between various "great lords and little kings" (159). By offering himself as an exemplum of the just sovereign to his subjects, Euarchus achieved an internal pacification of Macedonia, and then very quickly, Euarchus found himself dealing with the most pressing issue: the foreign threats that surrounded his nascent kingdom.

According to Musidorus's historical account, Euarchus chose to make an important alliance by marrying off his sister to Dorilaus, King of Thessalia, later consolidating this alliance with Thessalia by taking Dorilaus's sister as his own wife (162). Dorilaus's wife gave birth to a son, Musidorus, whose identity came to the attention of the King of Phrygia (162). Bothered by certain prophesies about the infant, the King of Phrygia invaded Thessalia, with the help of the kings of Lydia and Crete (162). King Euarchus assisted King Dorilaus in defending his kingdom, but soon after he had left Macedonia, the kings of Thrace and Pannonia invaded Macedonia (162). Ultimately, Euarchus is able to turn these invasions back on the invaders, achieving "the conquest of all Pannonia and almost Thrace," and finally, bringing "the conclusion of all to the siege of Byzantium" (164). It is in fact this counter-invasion that sets the narrative of the *New Arcadia* in motion, for during the period that Euarchus fights to defend his country by conquering the invading countries, the two princes, Euarchus's son Pyrocles and Dorilaus's son Musidorus are coming of age in the kingdom of Thessalia. Their initial voyage from Thessalia is launched with the purpose of travelling to Byzantium and assisting Euarchus in his siege of that city (165).

In other words, the impetus for the romance narrative that eventually occurs is a voyage to assist Euarchus in making the kingdom of Macedonia safe from external invasion. Of course, because of a shipwreck, chronologically the first in a series of three shipwrecks in the *New Arcadia*, Musidorus and Pyrocles never arrive at the gates of Byzantium. Pyrocles ends up being taken prisoner by the old enemy of Musidorus's father, the King of Phrygia, while Musidorus drifts to the shores of Pontus where he ends up at the house of a noble (169–71).[45] The King of Phrygia is typical of the tyrants that populate Sidney's revised romance—he is a stereotypical evil sovereign, "wickedly sad (ever musing of horrible matters), suspecting (or rather, condemning) all men of evil because his mind had no eye to espy goodness" (169). Added to his malevolence, however, is a special fear of Musidorus, about

---

[45] See Steven R. Mentz, "Reason, Faith, and Shipwreck in Sidney's *New Arcadia*," *Studies in English Literature 1500–1900* 44.1 (2004): 1–18.

which the tyrant is haunted by "numbers of soothsayers who affirmed strange and incredible things should be performed by that child" (162). There is an element of King Herod's fear of the prophecies of Christ's birth in this tyrant's obsession with Musidorus. Ultimately, by means of a series of substitutions and machinations, Musidorus and Pyrocles defeat the King of Phrygia and kill him and his son (174).

At this point, the politics of transnational justice, which the two princes represent, begin to replace Euarchus's politics of national self-interest. The princes' victory over the King of Phrygia does not directly serve the same sort of national cause that Euarchus's prior victories over his enemies served. With the tyrant of Phrygia defeated, the country's inhabitants unanimously offer the Phrygian crown to Musidorus, but he declines the offer. Musidorus's alter ego, the shepherd Dorus, recounts his decision in the third person:

> But [Musidorus], thinking it a greater greatness to give a kingdom than get a kingdom, understanding that there was left of the blood royal, and next to the succession, an aged gentleman of approved goodness ... did, after having received the full power to his own hands, resign all to the nobleman, but with such conditions, and cautions of the conditions, as might assure the people with as much assurance as worldly matters bear, that not only that governor, of whom indeed they looked for all good, but the nature of the government, should be no way apt to decline to tyranny. (175)

In this passage, Musidorus explicitly renounces any interest in sovereignty over Phrygia, even if such sovereignty might emerge as the clear unintended consequence of bringing a tyrant to justice.

From this point until the princes eventually arrive at Arcadia, by the means of yet another shipwreck, their journey involves defending justice throughout Asia Minor. Beginning with the King of Pontus episode (which frames the interrelated King of Galatia episode, the narrative basis for the Gloucester subplot in Shakespeare's *King Lear*), the two princes encounter a series of good and evil sovereigns, into whose kingdoms the princes intervene in order to restore justice. Again and again, the princes punish malefactors, usurpers, and invaders and restore beleaguered and oppressed sovereigns to their rightful thrones with no regard for their own benefit (176–271). Ultimately, their only benefit is an ill-defined form of imperial fame or recognition without the sovereign powers that normally accompany empire. Towards the end of Book 2, after Musidorus has once again rescued the King of Pontus, this time from the evil King Otanes and two giants, we are told that princes from around the world have assembled in Pontus to acknowledge their debt to the princes. Pyrocles, partially disguised as Zelmane, recounts a union of princes that convenes in order to honor the valiant deeds of the two heroes:

> Thither (understanding of our being there) flocked great multitudes of many great persons, and even of princes—especially those whom we had made beholding unto us, as the kings of Phrygia; Bithynia; ... of Pontus and Galatia; and Otanes, the prisoner by Musidorus set free; and thither came Plexirtus of Trebizond, and Antiphilus (then king of Lycia), with as many mo great princes, drawn either by our reputation, or by willingness to acknowledge themselves obliged unto us for

what we had done for the others, so as, in those parts of the world, I think, in many hundreds of years, there was not seen so royal an assembly, where nothing was let pass to do us the high honours which such persons ... could perform—all, from all sides, bringing unto us right royal presents (which we to avoid both unkindness and importunity liberally received); and not content therewith would needs accept, as from us, their crowns, and acknowledge to hold them of us—with many other excessive honours which would not suffer the measure of this short leisure to describe unto you. (271)

This passage, especially the last few phrases, describes the princes' collective attempt to grant Musidorus and Pyrocles formal imperial oversight over the kingdoms of Asia Minor. It is clear, however, that the princes seek no such role, and instead of accepting such vows of loyalty, the princes become "aweary" of the ceremony (271). Longing for Greece, they remain indifferent to the appeals and quickly begin their travels back home. Still, throughout Book 2, the princes have already assumed a quasi-imperial role throughout Asia Minor, and yet unlike the traditional imperial role, their rule throughout Asia Minor is not attached to any kingdom or state. One should recall the more traditional imperial role assumed by Euarchus, in order to gain some perspective on their role. Recounting the reconstitution of Macedonia, Musidorus describes Euarchus's kingdom as one "which in elder time had such a sovereignty over all the provinces of Greece that even the particular kings therein did acknowledge, with more or less degrees of homage, some kind of fealty thereunto" (158). More importantly, Euarchus's conquest of Pannonia and Thrace and his ongoing siege of Byzantium embody precisely the imperial identity that Pyrocles and Musidorus forego in the passage above. Thus, whereas Euarchus's conquests are intended to strengthen his own rule over Macedonia and neighboring territories, Musidorus and Pyrocles's regime of justice throughout Asia Minor is attached neither to sovereignty nor to the interests of a particular kingdom.

In this respect, this romance offers its readers an important alternative to the prevailing national and imperial order that served as the political locus of so many fictional works of this period. The traditional New Historicist account of individual identity, of course, has theorized identity as constituting itself through the individual's relationship with the sovereign. According to Stephen Greenblatt, for example, Renaissance fictions normally channel "national and religious sentiments into the worship of the prince [i.e. Elizabeth]," "mask[ing] over and thus temporarily deflected deep social, political and theological divisions in late sixteenth-century England."[46] In later New Historicist accounts, the sovereign's identity was also shown to be constituted by means of a complex negotiation of language and representation generated by both sovereign and subject. What is different about the narratives recounted by Musidorus and Pyrocles is that they define identity as radically itinerant and transnational. In one respect, of course,

---

[46] Stephen Greenblatt, *Renaissance Self-Fashioning*, 168. See also Louis Adrian Montrose, "*A Midsummer Night's Dream* and the Shaping Fantasies of Elizabethan Culture: Gender, Power, Form," in *Rewriting the Renaissance*, ed. Margaret Ferguson et al. (Chicago, 1986), 65–87.

168   *Early Modern Catholics, Royalists, and Cosmopolitans*

Greenblatt's notion of identity applies to the two princes. Throughout their narratives, they are fashioned and fashion themselves in a series of encounters with royal figures and subjected peoples. But in quite another respect, the princes fashion their identities, not in the static relationship with one sovereign or with one kingdom or people, but in the movement between competing authority figures and kingdoms, a result of the princes traveling from court to court and verifying again and again their own independent self-worth. Each separate situation reaffirms a form of sovereignty over the self that gives each prince an independence and self-determination that seems to exist outside of one binding relationship to a centralizing authority or state apparatus.

It was perhaps a form of sovereignty, to which Sidney himself had aspired and towards which his mentors had encouraged him to strive. In an early letter written to Sidney during his continental travels, for example, Languet counsels Sidney on the role of learning in Sidney's process of self-fashioning. He notes that, given his station in life, Sidney will probably be unable to afford the luxury of growing old "reading books [*in literarum studiis*]." Rather Sidney's travel and education should prepare him for guiding the nations of the world:

> So learn as much as possible of the essentials and of those things the knowledge of which is useful for properly planning and carrying out your career; and remember that that word of the Poet, "you ... have to guide the nations by your authority [*Tu regere imperio populos*]" [Virgil, *Aeneid* 6.851–3], etc., applies to you, and that the greatest contribution to that is (as that other one [Homer, *Odyssey* 1.3.] says) to have contemplated the customs and cities of many men [*homimum multorum, ut ait ille, mores & urbes considerasse*], for which you will have even less opportunity when you are back home than for reading.[47]

Apart from John Dee's description of the *cosmopolite* in the *Memorials*, there are few more succinct and effective expressions of the secular cosmopolitan ideal than Languet's advice to Sidney in this letter. Languet's reference to Virgil's *Aeneid* is especially significant. The speaker of this verse is the shade of Aeneas's father, Anchises, whom Aeneas encounters in the underworld. He reminds Aeneas that, as the eventual founder of Rome, he will have a special purpose in the world: "You, Roman, must remember that you have to guide the nations by your authority, for this is to be your skill, to graft tradition onto peace, to show mercy to the conquered, and to wage war until the haughty are brought low."[48] In citing this

---

[47]   "Disce igitur maxime necessaria, & quorum cognitio ad vitam recte instituendam & transigendam est utilis, & memineris ad te pretinere illud Poëtae, Tu regere imperio populos &c. & ad eam rem plurimum conferre, hominum multorum, ut ait ille, mores & urbes considerasse: quod tibi minus licebit, ubi patriam redieris, quam literis incumbere." "Hubert Languet to Sidney, Vienna 28 January 1574," in Kuin (ed.), *Correspondence of Sir Philip Sidney*, vol. 1, 99–104.

[48]   "tu regere imperio populos, Romane, memento / (hae tibi erunt artes), pacisque imponere morem / parcere subiectis et debellare superbos." Virgil, *Aeneid*, trans. W.F. Jackson Knight (New York, 1956).

Cosmopolitan Romance 169

verse, Languet was encouraging Sidney to fashion himself as a humanist, a man of state, a counselor of princes, but he was also encouraging him to model his own identity after Aeneas, founder of imperial Rome. The *New Arcadia* shows that Sidney had taken Languet's advice to heart, although perhaps not exactly as Languet had intended. Languet was preparing Sidney for life as a cosmopolitan counselor, but Sidney had his own ideas about poetry, which led him to explore, along with Sir John Harington, the writing of fiction as a more subtle way of guiding the nations. Looking back to the *New Arcadia*, it is clear that Anchises's advice to his son, the future founder of Rome, could be used to describe the imperial role that Pyrocles and Musidorus assume throughout Asia Minor—like the Roman emperor, they guide the nations, they show mercy to the conquered and wage war against the haughty. As for Sidney himself, it is likely that in his singular way, he aspired to a similar role as a writer of fiction, his creation of the Arcadian world constituting his own way of asserting his authority and becoming a guide to nations.

Finally, the cosmopolitan and transnational definitions of identity found in romances such as the *New Arcadia* serves as an important corrective to the ongoing theoretical paradigms that has viewed Early Modern political identity as principally nationally bound. The revisions that emerged in the 1593 version of Book 5 are also significant in this respect. It is unclear whether these revisions were carried out by Sidney himself, the Countess of Pembroke, or Fulke Greville in accordance with Sidney's wishes, but whatever the case, the revised version of Book 5 depicts the cosmopolitan sensibility, which I have been describing, as having finally contaminated Euarchus's narrative.[49] What is interesting is how Euarchus's motivations for traveling to Arcadia are transformed in the new version. In the *Old Arcadia*, as I noted, Euarchus's visit to Arcadia is specifically motivated by the threat of the invading Latins and Asiatics. He seeks to prop up the rule of a valuable neighbor and ally in order to protect Macedonia and Greece from foreign invaders. In the revised version, Euarchus makes specific preparations, putting "his people in a readiness for war," that effectively frustrate the Latins' plans for invading Macedonia before he begins his travels (788).[50] Additionally, the events of his travels are different from the original. In the revised version, Euarchus's sojourn in Arcadia begins with his voyage by ship to his newly-conquered territory of Byzantium in order to assemble the force necessary to bring Plexirtus and Artaxia to justice. On the way, his ship encounters a violent tempest and is stranded in Laconia, which places him in precisely the situation that his son,

---

[49]   For discussion of the post-1590 revisions of the *New Arcadia*, see William Leigh Godshalk, "Sidney's Revision of the *Arcadia*, Books III–V," *Philological Quarterly* 43.2 (April 1964): 171–84; Victor Skretkowicz, "Building Sidney's Reputation: Texts and Editons of the *Arcadia*," in *Sir Philip Sidney 1586 and the Creation of a Legend*, 111–24. See also Skretkowicz, "Textual Introduction," in Sidney, *The New Arcadia*, ed. Victor Skretkowicz, liii–lxxxi.

[50]   Parenthetical citations from Book 5 of the 1593 printed version of the *New Arcadia* refer to Sir Philip Sidney, *The Countess of Pembroke's Arcadia*, ed. Maurice Evans (New York, 1987).

Pyrocles found himself in at the beginning of Book 1 (790–91). Because hostilities between the helots and the Lacedomonians have broken out again, Euarchus flees to Arcadia, where he selflessly assumes the reins of power in order to prevent the kingdom from descending into anarchy (790–97). In contrast to the original version of the romance, Euarchus's intervention into Arcadia is not motivated by a desire to bolster the security of his own kingdom by strengthening a valued ally. Instead, it is the purely altruistic gesture of a stranded sovereign who has followed his son into the transnational role of the knight errant, restoring justice to embattled regimes, without regard to any self-interest. In other words, in the final episode of *New Arcadia*, King Euarchus of Macedonia has taken up the role of itinerant romance hero, which his son Pyrocles's devotion to Philoclea has caused Pyrocles himself to abandon.

Ultimately, in Sidney's revisions of Book 5, Euarchus seems unwittingly to have been influenced by his son's itinerant acts of heroism, which comprise a will to do justice without regard to national self-interest. Sidney's revision therefore renders the work less amenable to the emerging ideologies of nationhood that Helgerson and others have theorized concerning early modern England. Given that the *New Arcadia* was one of the most widely read fictional works during this period, going through 13 editions in the century after its publication in 1593, it seems significant that the *New Arcadia* cuts against the grain of English national formation. Against the standard account of the writing of Renaissance England, the case of the *New Arcadia* illustrates that a more nuanced and complex political imagination survived.

Spenser and the Perils of Imperial Imitation

In the second half of this chapter, I make a related argument concerning Book 5 of Spenser's *The Faerie Queene*, by way of a brief detour concerning the role of equity in the poem. Although the term, "equity" was employed in a variety of different ways during the Renaissance, it was most importantly the legal principle that was applied in the court of Chancery and the Star Chamber.[51] In cases that were tried in such venues, justice proceeded according to a conception of equity or conscience that superseded the rigidity of the law itself.[52] According to the early sixteenth-century jurist, Christopher St. German, equity amounted to the chancellor's understanding of natural law according to his conscience, and thus equity functioned to correct an injustice that would have resulted by following the common law too closely.[53] Where the law gave no remedy, Chancery had the

---

[51]   See Mark Fortier, *The Culture of Equity in Early Modern England* (Burlington, VT, 2005), 4–23, for a discussion of the wide array of definitions of equity that were employed during this period.

[52]   See Fortier, *Culture of Equity*, 29–58.

[53]   Christopher St. German, *The Doctor and Student*, ed. T.F.T. Plucknett and J.L. Barton (London, 1975), 111–13.

power to bind a party by that individual's own conscience and order him to do something on pain of committal for contempt.[54] While St. German might have seen his position as rooted in a conservative common-law juridical perspective, there were at least some common lawyers who viewed St. German's defense of equity as a direct threat to the integrity and self-sufficiency of the common law courts. One such response to St. German's writings claimed that the common law was simply infallible and should therefore not be deviated from: "Wherefore if you observe and keep the law ... in doing all things that is for the common weal, and eschew all things that is evil, and against the common weal, you shall not need to study so much upon conscience, for the law of the realm is a sufficient rule to order you and your conscience."[55] Finally, the application of equity was traditionally identified with the sovereign's extraordinary powers, in that the prince's use of the prerogative also constituted a deviation from the strict adherence to the common law.[56]

Spenser may have had a professional stake in such controversies. In the late 1570s, Spenser's position as secretary to John Young, Bishop of Rochester would have insured that the young poet had extensive dealings with the ecclesiastical courts, and later in 1581, not long after his arrival in Ireland, he was appointed clerk for faculties in the Irish court of Chancery, an office that he subsequently held for seven years.[57] I would like to suggest that, in Book 5 ("The Book of Justice") of Spenser's poem, equity functions as a critique of the overly rigorous

---

[54] See Louis Knafla, *Law and Politics in Jacobean England, The Tracts of Lord Chancellor Ellesmere* (New York, 1977), 159–70.

[55] Anon., *A Replication of a Serjeant at the Laws of England, Appended to Christopher St. German, The Doctor and Student*, ed. William Muchall (Cincinnati, 1874), 349. For context, see Plucknett, "Introduction," *Doctor and Student*; Robert E. Rodes, Jr., *Lay Authority and Reformation in the English Church: Edward I to the Civil War* (Notre Dame, IN, 1982), 69–77; S.B. Chrimes, *English Constitutional History in the Fifteenth Century* (Cambridge, 1936), 204–14, Burgess, *Politics of the Ancient Constitution*, 122–3; John A. Guy, "Law, Equity, and Conscience in Henrician Juristic Thought," in *Reassessing the Henrician Age: Humanism, Politics and Reform 1500–1550*, ed. Alistair Fox and John A. Guy (New York, 1986) 190–98. For discussion of the authorship of the *Replication*, see John A. Guy (ed.), *Christopher St German on Chancery and Statute* (London, 1985), 56–63.

[56] For context, see JohnH. Baker, *Introduction to English Legal History* (London, 1971), 50, and Fortier, *Culture of Equity*, 87, 92–101.

[57] See Willy Maley, A *Spenser Chronology* (Lanham, MD, 1994), 18–19, 37–8, 46. For a more comprehensive account of Spenser's dealings with the court of Chancery and the civil law, including his early stint as the Bishop of Rochester's secretary, see Hadfield, *Edmund Spenser*, 110–19; 174–5; 202–6. For some critical context on Spenser's writings on Ireland, see Nicholas Canny, *Making Ireland British: 1580–1650* (New York, 2003), 1–58; Patricia Coughlan, "'Some secret scourge which shall by her come unto England': Ireland and Incivility in Spenser," in *Spenser and Ireland: An Interdisciplinary Perspective*, ed. Patricia Coughlan (Cork, 1989), 46–74; Patricia Palmer, *Language and Conquest in Early Modern Ireland: English Renaissance Literature and Elizabethan Imperial Expansion* (New York, 2001), 8–39, Richard McCabe, *Spenser's Monstrous Regiment: Elizabethan Ireland and the Poetics of Difference* (New York, 2002), and Andrew Hadfield, *Edmund Spenser's Irish Experience, Wild Fruit and Salvage Soyl* (New York, 1997).

172   *Early Modern Catholics, Royalists, and Cosmopolitans*

regime of justice that the hero of Book 5, Sir Artegall, champions in his travels throughout Faerie Land. Moreover, despite the anti-Spanish thrust of Book 5, the manner in which the principle of equity is applied in the book resembles the Spanish Dominican use of natural law to weigh the ethics of Spanish intervention in polities that either persecuted the innocents, oppressed Christians or had established and practiced unnatural customs.[58]

In Book 5 of *The Faerie Queene*, the champions Artegall and Britomart face an analogous situation when they confront the Amazon, Radigund, who rules over an oppressive polity that the narrator characterizes as unnatural. Artegall fails to exercise equity correctly and the result of his failure is his capture and imprisonment by Radigund as well as his eventual liberation by the female knight, Britomart. Britomart's intervention into the narrative identifies equity as a feminine principle, presumably in order to identify the exercise of equity with Britomart's real-life counterpart, Queen Elizabeth. However, Britomart's application of equity in Book 5 leads to some unsettling conclusions about English or British imperial identity in general. Most significantly, her intervention into and reform of Radigund's unnatural polity closely adheres to Neo-scholastic constructions of papal supremacy, especially those having to do with the papal power to depose unlawful temporal sovereigns. In the Radigund episode at the center of Book 5, Spenser's poem is caught in a contradiction between Spenser adherence to the principle of "feminized" equity in foreign contexts and his insistence on basic principles of natural law, which were responsible for naturalizing patriarchal gender relations. As a result, one important and available (mis)reading of the book is that the narrative ironically justifies the (Papal or Spanish) conquest of England itself and its own "Amazon" queen, Elizabeth, in the interest of restoring a regime based on traditional conceptions of natural law.[59]

One characteristic of Faerie Land is that there are no boundaries that might distinguish a domestic realm from the international sphere. Without encountering any frontiers, heroes and heroines such as Red Crosse, Guyon, Britomart, and Artegall travel across Faerie Land and confront figures that are alternatively familiar and foreign. Book 5 is no exception to this in that there is no point in Artegall's journey, when the knight of Justice comes upon a frontier that definitively separates a domestic realm from a foreign context. Nevertheless, it is also fair to say that the first five actions on behalf of justice that Artegall takes have a more

---

[58]   Anthony Pagden, "Dispossessing the Barbarian: The Language of Spanish Thomism and the Debate over the Property Rights of the American Indians" in *The Languages of Political Theory in Early-Modern Europe*, ed. Anthony Pagden (New York, 1987), 79–98, and Pagden et al., "Introduction" in Francisco de Vitoria, *Political Writings*, xxv. See also Pagden, *The Fall of Natural Man*, 27–56, 109–11.

[59]   For analysis of the paradoxical combination of admiration and fear Spain inspired in Spenser and others, see Barbara Fuchs, "Spanish Lessons: Spenser and the Irish Moriscos," *Studies in English Literature 1500–1900* 42.1 (2002): 43–62. For comparative analysis of the emergence of the Spanish and English empires, see Pagden, *Lords of All the World: Ideologies of Empire in Spain, Britain and France 1500–1800* (New Haven, CT, 1995), 1–102.

Cosmopolitan Romance 173

domestic character—most of them involve disputes over property or rights of way, while the encounter that begins in canto 4 with Queen Radigund and her nation of Amazons introduces a foreign, even exotic, element into Artegall's adventures.[60] Significantly, Artegall's travels subsequent to the Amazon encounter continue to invoke this foreign element. Artegall and Arthur go on to encounter figures who are clearly identified as sovereigns such as Queen Mercilla and tyrants such as Geryoneo and Grantorto, who oppress legitimate sovereigns. In this respect, the trajectory of Artegall's adventures in Book 5 is from domestic legal disputes to disputes between competing regimes.

Toward the beginning of Book 5, the narrator recounts that the goddess Astrea has instructed Artegall "to weigh both right and wrong / In equall ballance with due recompence, / And equitie to measure out along" (1.7).[61] Moreover, similar to the manner in which St. German formulates the relationship between equity and the law, Astrea has taught Artegall to "dispence" with "rigour" in instances where adhering to the letter of the law would result in injustice (1.7).[62] Despite his upbringing, most critics agree that Artegall, who tends to enforce a harsh and unyielding form of justice, is "not an apt student of equity."[63] And yet Artegall does manage in certain instances to defend an egalitarian definition of equity by which nature is perceived as distributing resources in a just and equitable manner. For example, whereas the Egalitarian Giant seeks to return the earth to its primordial

---

[60]   See Clare Carroll, "The Construction of Gender and the Cultural and Political Other in *The Faerie Queene* 5 and *A View of the Present State of Ireland*: The Critics, the Context, and the Case of Radigund," *Criticism* 32.2 (1990): 163–92.

[61]   Citations (canto.stanza) are from *The Faerie Queene*, ed. A.C. Hamilton (New York, 1977).

[62]   St. German, *Doctor and Student*, 111–13, 207.

[63]   Andrew Majeske, *Equity in English Renaissance Literature: Thomas More and Edmund Spenser* (New York, 2006), 97. According to Majeske, Artegall's initial "exploits in Book 5 ... are illustrations of rigorous ('harsh') justice rather than equity" (97). Thus, Artegall has his mechanical squire, Talus, ruthlessly slaughter the guilty parties, Pollente, Munera, and the Egalitarian Giant, along with their followers in the first two cantos of the book. See Annabel Patterson, *Reading Between the Lines* (Madison, WI, 1993), 96–9. Moreover, as Katherine Eggert has noted, even Artegall's disastrous defeat by Radigund does not mitigate Artegall's passion for rigorous, unyielding justice in the later cantos. See Katherine Eggert, *Showing Like a Queen: Female Authority and Literary Experiment in Spenser, Shakespeare, and Milton* (Philadelphia, 2000), 45. For further discussion of Artegall's harsh version of justice, see Alastair D.S. Fowler, *Spenser and the Numbers of Time* (London, 1964), 44; James E. Phillips, "Renaissance Concepts of Justice and the Structure of *The Faerie Queene*, Book V," *Huntington Library Quarterly* 33 (1970): 103–20, esp. 106; Judith H. Anderson, "'Nor Man It Is': The Knight of Justice in Book V of Spenser's *Faerie Queene*," *PMLA* 85 (1970): 65–77, esp. 65; and Elizabeth Fowler, "The Failure of Moral Philosophy in the Work of Edmund Spenser," *Representations* 51 (Summer 1995): 47–76. For a general discussion of the legal matters explored in Book 5, see T.K. Dunseath, *Spenser's Allegory of Justice in Book Five of the* Faerie Queene (Princeton, 1968). For a discussion of the legal concept of equity, see Fortier, *Culture of Equity*, 146–50.

174 *Early Modern Catholics, Royalists, and Cosmopolitans*

state of equal distribution, Artegall defends the existing order of celestial justice that "doth among [all earthly things] raine, / That every one doe know their certain bound" (2.36). Similarly, in the property dispute between the brothers Amidas and Bracidas, Artegall defends the "equitable" natural forces that have redistributed much of Bracidas's land and deposited it on Amidas's island and washed Amidas's treasure away and deposited it on Bracidas's island (4.1–20).[64]

In contrast to his application of this egalitarian form of equity, Artegall has trouble applying the Greek form of equity, or *epieikeia*, responsible for correcting the severity of the law.[65] The best, early example of this difficulty is at the end of the third canto, in which Sir Guyon comes forward to claim back his stolen horse from the scoundrel, Braggadochio. Guyon describes an identifying mark in the horse's mouth, which the horse only allows Guyon to reveal, and subsequently Artegall judges the horse to be Guyon's property (3.32–5). In the immediate aftermath of Artegall's judgment, Artegall's first impulse is to strike the thief and imposter, Braggadochio, with his sword. The narrator, however, explains that

> *Guyon* did [Artegall's] choler pacify,
> Saying, Sir knight, it would dishonour bee
> To you, that are our iudge of equity,
> To wreake your wrath on such a carle as hee:
> It's punishment enough, that all his shame doe see. (3.36)

In this episode, Artegall reveals himself to be incapable of restraining himself from violently lashing out at Braggadochio, hardly the respectable or proper role for the judge to play in the affair. Only though the intervention of Guyon, who refers to him deferentially as "our iudge of equity," is Artegall restrained. Of course, it is hard not to perceive a hint of irony when considering this episode in the context of the entire poem. Throughout Book 2, Guyon, the Knight of Temperance, is unable to control his own intemperate and violent outbursts, constantly needing the tutelage of the Palmer in order to moderate his propensity for violence.[66] In this instance, Artegall is reminded of his role as "iudge of equity" by the only other knight hero in *The Faerie Queene* who has a tendency toward intemperate violence. In this way, Spenser seems to be showing how Artegall's own propensity toward rigor and immoderate violence even exceeds that of Guyon, whose quest some commentators view as ending in failure.[67]

Britomart embodies the form of equity, the corrective of an overly rigorous interpretation of the law, which is largely missing in Artegall's severe applications of justice. Britomart, however, does not make an appearance until Artegall has

---

[64] See Herbert B. Nelson, "Amidas v. Bracidas," *Modern Language Quarterly* 1.3 (1940), 393–9.

[65] See Knafla, *Law and Politics*, 159–70; Fortier, *Culture of Equity*, 3–7.

[66] See Greenblatt, *Renaissance Self-Fashioning*, 177.

[67] See, for example, Louis Adrian Montrose, "The Elizabethan Subject and the Spenserian Text," *Literary Theory / Renaissance Texts*, ed. Patricia Parker and David Quint (Baltimore, 1986), 303–40, esp. 329.

failed to extend his regime of justice to the Amazons of Radegone, where Queen Radigund reigns supreme. After resolving the conflict over property between Bracidas and Amidas, Artegall continues on his travels and has Talus disperse the troop of Radigund's women warriors who are about to execute the good knight, Sir Terpine. Later Artegall himself intercedes on Terpine's behalf and defeats Radigund in battle (4.22–43). Feeling humiliated, Radigund subsequently proposes to him that they fight a duel, declaring the following as the conditions of the fight: "That if I vanquishe [Artegall], he shall obay / My law, and euer to my lore be bound, / And so will I, if me he vanquish may" (4.49). The next morning, they fight a long battle, in which, at a certain point, Artegall removes the Amazon's helmet in order to behead her. But when he discovers the beauty of her face, his heart is instead filled with pity. He throws away his sword, is promptly overcome (5.6–17), and is made "a womans slaue," forced by her followers to "spin both flax and tow" and to live in penury (5.23).

Two aspects of Artegall's initial confrontation with Radigund are significant in terms of the Renaissance understanding of equity and law. First, Radigund's proposal for the conditions of her duel with Artegall orients her struggle with him as one between two competing regimes of law, a gynocentric legal regime and a patriarchal one.[68] In contrast, Artegall seems to misunderstand his role as the more limited one of taking revenge for the personal affront made to fellow knights. In this respect, he declares that he will "not rest, till I her might doe trie, / And venge the shame, that she to Knights doth show" (4.34). Artegall thus articulates a code of chivalry in defense of personal honor that ignores the fact that his conflict with the polity of Radegone occurs within an "international" sphere of action, where conflicts cease to be over personal honor and revenge and are rather about competing systems of law.[69]

Second, Artegall's response to seeing Radigund's beautiful face reads like yet another misapplication of the legal principle of equity (in the sense of equity as defined as leniency or mercy).[70] The narrator tells us,

> At sight thereof [of her face] his cruell minded hart
> Empierced was with pittifull regard,
> That his sharpe sword he threw from him apart,
> Cursing his hand that had that visage mard. (5.13)

In this passage, Artegall finally tempers his rigorous form of justice with mercy, but no sooner has he done so than Radigund overcomes him and enslaves him.

---

[68] For contemporary context, see Henry Spelman, who writes that conquest of a foreign kingdom was normally accompanied by the imposition of the conqueror's laws on the people conquered ("Of the Union," in *The Jacobean Union, Six Tracts of 1604*, ed. Bruce Galloway et al. [Edinburgh, 1985], 181).

[69] For the relationship between chivalry and the legal tradition of *ius gentium*, that formed the basis of international law, see Maurice H. Keen, *The Laws of War*, 239–47, esp. 241.

[70] For the sense of equity as mercy or leniency, see Fortier, *Culture of Equity*, 7, 29–58, and 117–20.

The scene indicates Artegall's inability to apply equity in a way that would not involve his own personal desires.[71] In this respect, his application of equity echoes the contemporary criticisms of its use in the courts of law. For example, John Selden poked fun at the lack of consistency in the chancellor's use of conscience, by comparing the application of equity to the size of the chancellor's feet: "One Chancellor has a long Foot, another a short Foot, a Third an indifferent Foot: 'Tis the same thing in the Chancellor's Conscience."[72]

Ultimately, it is Britomart who embodies the correct application of equity by grounding the concept in the universal doctrine of natural law that St. German had explored in his writings. After Talus finds Britomart, she begins her long trek to Radegone, and along the way, she sojourns at the Temple of Isis, where the Temple priests reveal the statue of the goddess Isis, presented as partially standing on the statue of a crocodile (later identified as Osyris). At the beginning of the Temple of Isis episode, we learn that Osyris is the god of justice, and Isis the goddess of equity. The narrator explains:

> [Osyris's] wife was *Isis*, whom they likewise made
> A Goddesse of great power and souerainty,
> And in her person cunningly did shade
> That part of Justice, which is Equity
> Whereof I have to treat here presently. (7.3)

According to the priest's later interpretation of Britomart's violent dream in which the crocodile attacks her, prompting Isis's intercession on her behalf, the statue of the crocodile represents both Osyris and Artegall, and the fact that the crocodile is under Isis's foot shows that justice's "stern behests" and "cruel dooms" are to be restrained by equity (7.22). The Temple of Isis episode ultimately has the effect of linking Britomart with Isis, the goddess of equity, and once again identifying Artegall, through his link with Osyris in the dream, as the champion of a rigorous, inflexible definition of justice (7.22).

Britomart ventures on to Radigund's castle and defeats the Amazon queen in an epic battle (7.33–4), and then she enters the castle itself, encountering the imprisoned male knights attired in womanish clothes. She assumes sovereignty over Radegone in order to reform its laws so that they conform with patriarchal rule:

> During which space she there as Princess rained,
> And changing all that forme of common weale,
> The liberty of women did repeale,
> Which they had long vsurpt; and them restoring
> To mens subiection, did true Iustice deale. (7.42)

In the next stanza, she transforms the captive male knights into magistrates of the city and finally makes everyone swear allegiance to Artegall. A number of critics have pondered the paradox at the center of Britomart's renunciation of her own

---

[71] See Fortier, *Culture of Equity*, 75.
[72] John Selden, *Table-Talk* (Westminster, 1895), 46.

rule: throughout *The Faerie Queene*, Britomart is identified as the perfect knight and ruler, but in this instance, she nevertheless instructs the female inhabitants of Radegone that women have no right to inhabit positions of authority and to rule. In this respect, Katherine Eggert sees the episode as indicative of a shift from more digressive feminine modes of narrative found in earlier books to a masculine narrative, comprised of historical allegory, while Andrew Majeske sees Britomart's decision as allegorically prefiguring Elizabeth's own preference for James Stuart over his cousin Arabella.[73] But such readings fail to take into account the full significance of equity and its relationship with natural law discourse in Book 5. The use of equity, according to St. German, involved a correction of the existing human law, in cases where following the law itself would result in injustice.[74] Since the application of equity to correct the law was seen as originating in the sovereign's power of administering justice outside of the ordinary channels, it was often associated with the sovereign's power of prerogative.[75] It is at this juncture in St. German's writings that his ideas overlap with writers such as John Major and Juan Ginés de Sepúlveda, both of whom made the case for conquering peoples and nations whose customary laws violated the principles of natural law. Major and Sepúlveda focused on reports of unnatural vices such as cannibalism, sodomy, and idolatry among the Amerindians, the presence of which Major and Sepúlveda claimed provided justification for the Spanish crown's project of reforming such polities and bringing their human laws in conformity with universal natural law.[76] Note that the role they saw the Spanish sovereign playing with regard to Amerindian customs was similar to the role St. German staked out with regard to the injustices that sometimes occurred by following the common law, which comprised the English customary law.[77] It is also analogous to the role that Britomart assumes with regard to the reform of Radegone.

In this respect, Britomart's intervention into Radegone, rather than an application of equity in the sense of leniency, functions as a corrective to a legal regime that fails to reflect the laws of nature.[78] The "true justice" that Britomart restores to

---

[73] Eggert, *Showing Like A Queen*, 27; Majeske, *Equity in English Renaissance Literature*, 108.

[74] See St. German, *Doctor and Student*, 111–13. For context, see Fortier, *Culture of Equity*, 59–86, and Guy, *St. German*, 67–75.

[75] See Baker, *Introduction to English Legal History*, 50.

[76] See John Major, *In secundum librum setentiarum* (Paris, 1519) and Juan Ginés de Sepúlveda, *Demócrates Segundo, o, de las justas causas de la guerra contra los indios*, ed. Ángel Losada, (Madrid, 1984). For critical discussion, see Pagden, *The Fall of Natural Man*, 38–41, 109–11, and Pagden, "Dispossessing the Barbarian," 91.

[77] For a general discussion of this analogy, see Lockey, *Law and Empire*, 145–59.

[78] See Fortier, *Culture of Equity*, 65–74. For a discussion of equity as leniency in Spenser, see 117–20. For a contextualization of Book 5 of Spenser's *Faerie Queene* within broader English attempts to reform "barbaric" (Irish) custom, see Bradin Cormack, *A Power to Do Justice: Jurisdiction, English Literature, and the Rise of the Common Law, 1509–1625* (Chicago, 2008), 133–76. Where I differ with Cormack is the greater importance that I attribute to the doctrine of natural law within Spenser's writings.

178 *Early Modern Catholics, Royalists, and Cosmopolitans*

Radegone is a traditional conception of justice comprised of a patriarchal regime that subordinates women based on the doctrine of natural law.[79] From here we are inevitably led to two contradictory conclusions. On the one hand, the rigorous (common-law inspired) form of justice, which Artegall deploys effectively in the domestic contexts, is shown to be incompatible with the universal regime of natural law that was thought to govern the international sphere.[80] Subsequent encounters bear this out. Both Artegall and Arthur go on to confront a number of other figures such as the Souldan, Geryoneo, and Grantorto, whose injustices have to do with oppressing legitimate sovereigns such as Belge and Irena, representing the Low Countries and Ireland. But Artegall's final battle with Grantorto, while initially successful, ends in failure. After he defeats Grantorto, Artegall's tendency toward justice without equity undermines his attempts to reform the land of Irena, in precisely the same way that the Spenser of *A View* presents the English common law as failing to reform Ireland.[81] In the last canto, the narrator implies that Gloriana, the Faerie Queene, has reservations about Artegall's strategy for reform:

> But ere he could reforme it thoroughly,
> He through occasion called was away,
> To Faerie Court, that of necessity
> His course of Iustice he was forst to stay,
> And *Talus* to reuoke from the right way,
> In which he was that Realme for to redresse.
> But envies cloud still dimmeth vertues ray. (12.27)

This passage constitutes an allegorical commentary on Spenser's patron, Lord Arthur Grey of Wilton, who served as lord deputy of Ireland, and whose scorched-earth campaign in Ireland was considered disastrous by the English crown.[82]

On the other hand, the use of equity based on natural law in order to enforce a patriarchal regime of justice in Radegone inevitably brings into question the exalted position that Britomart has throughout *The Faerie Queene*, both as the ancestor of the future line of English sovereigns and as an ancient, mythological type for Elizabeth herself. In this respect, Britomart's enforcement of patriarchal rule in Radegone holds out a tantalizing misreading concerning Elizabeth's rule in England. If equity was to be used to reform unnatural polities in the same way that Spanish jurists justified the conquest of the Americas, should not such rationales also be used to reform Elizabeth's rule of England itself? This question is even more significant when we consider that, among members of the English Catholic community in exile, the justification of a Spanish invasion of England was based on the notions of equity

---

[79] See, for example, John Knox, *The First Blast of the Trumpet Against the Monstrous Regiment of Women* (1558), in *Political Writings* (Washington, 1985), 42, 70.

[80] For context, see Lockey, *Law and Empire*, 145–59.

[81] For a related discussion of *A View*, see Lockey, *Law and Empire*, 113–42.

[82] For context, see "Grey, Arthur, Fourteenth Baron of Wilton," in *The Spenser Encyclopedia*, ed. A.C. Hamilton et al. (Buffalo, NY, 1990), 341–2, and Hadfield, *Edmund Spenser*, 153–95.

Cosmopolitan Romance 179

and natural law.[83] On the eve of the Spanish invasion of England, for example, Cardinal Allen sought to reassure his fellow English Catholics "that the controuersyes which may arise by the depriuation of this woman [Elizabeth] ... shalbe decyded and determined wholy accordinge to iustice and Christian equity without iniury or preiudice to any person."[84] Similarly, Persons held that the sovereign was bound by a contract with the commonwealth, such that her rule should conform to "al law, both of nature and nations, and so conform to al reason and equity, that it is put among the very rules of both the Ciuil and cannon law."[85] Accordingly, the queen's subjects were fully justified by virtue of natural law in rebelling against her, because she had abused her authority and persecuted her subjects unjustly.

As we have noted, English Catholic writers generally disavowed an absolute right to resist an unjust sovereign. Like Persons, Allen preferred that temporal sovereigns be corrected by the pope, who would intervene and correct their behavior from above. Thus, four years before the Spanish Armada, Allen began the fifth chapter of his *Defence of English Catholics*, in an obvious reference to Elizabeth's rule, by complaining that "Princes being not subject to superiors temporal, nor patient of correction or controlment by their inferiors, may easily fall to grevious disorders, which must tend to the danger and ruin of whole countries." He goes on to describe the world's first kings, whom God corrected through the agency of his "prophets or priests in manner as overseers." Ideally, he goes on to say, there is such a "concurrence and subalternation" between the civil and ecclesiastical authorities "that the inferior of the two (which is the civil state) must needs (in matters pertaining any way either directly or indirectly to the honour of God and benefit of the soul) be subject to the spiritual, and take direction from the same." In special cases, Allen notes, where the temporal power "resisteth God, or hindereth the proceeding of the people to salvation; there the spiritual hath the right to correct temporal." Thus, Allen adheres to Francisco de Vitoria's defense of acts of war and intervention for delivering the oppressed from tyranny.[86] The *Relectiones* of Vitoria describe a limited gamut in which such acts were justified, but two very clear cases were instances in which innocent subjects are being victimized by unnatural sins such as cannibalism and human sacrifice, and cases in which Christians are being oppressed by non-Christian sovereigns.[87] Allen seems to have the second case in mind in terms of his justification of the Spanish invasion.

Moreover, in contrast to Persons's contractual theory of sovereignty, Allen draws a distinction between Protestant political theorists who authorized the

---

[83]   For perspective, see Stefania Tutino, *Law and Conscience: Catholicism in Early Modern England 1570–1625* (Burlington, VT, 2007), esp. 11–80; McCoog, *The Society of Jesus 1541–1588*, 1–177; Bernard Basset, S.J., *The English Jesuits: From Campion to Martindale* (New York, 1968), 1–224.

[84]   Cardinal William Allen [and/or Sixtus V, Pope], *A Declaration of the Sentence and deposition of Elizabeth, the usurper and pretensed Queene of England* (Antwerp, 1588), fol. 1.

[85]   Persons, *A Conference*, G2.

[86]   Allen, *Defense of English Catholics*, vol. 2, 1, 12, 13, 12.

[87]   See Vitoria, *De usu ciborum, sive temperantia [On Dietary Laws, or Self-Restraint]*, in *Political Writings*, 225–6 and *De indis [On the American Indians]*, 286–8.

180   *Early Modern Catholics, Royalists, and Cosmopolitans*

rebellion of oppressed subjects against unjust tyrants and usurpers and Catholic writers, like himself, who argued that only the pope could authorize the deposition of a sovereign.[88] Ultimately, of course, Allen argued that the pope had an absolute right to authorize the Spanish sovereign to invade and reform England. Thus, his *Declaration of the Sentence and deposition of Elizabeth*, published to coincide with the Spanish invasion of England, asks English subjects not to rebel against Elizabeth, but rather requests that they "vnite themselfs to the Catholike army conducted by the most noble and victorious Prince, Alexander Farnesius, Duke of Parma and Placentia, in the name of his Maiesty [Philip II]."[89] It should be obvious that the model that Spenser uses with regard to Radigund bears a striking resemblance to Allen's model of the pope authorizing the overturning of tyrannical or heretical regimes. Recall that Britomart, before arriving at the city of Radegone, travels to the Temple of Isis, whose priests of equity provide a kind of imprimatur on their champion's subsequent actions.

Use of the doctrines of equity and natural law were not confined to the writings of English Catholic exiles such as Persons and Allen. In the *Defensio Fidei Catholicae, et Apostolicae Adversus Anglicanae Sectae Errores* (1613), for example, the Spanish Jesuit Francisco Suárez employed the natural-law reasoning that Vitoria had applied to Amerindian polities in order to reformulate Allen's argument in strict scholastic terms. In terms of equity, Suárez wrote that the pope's application of "prudence and equitable justice [*prudentiam, & iustitiae equitatem*]" extends to an ability to authorize temporal means to correct princes who fall into sin.[90] Suárez goes on to enumerate a list of instances in which the pope used such power to correct temporal princes, and he concludes by noting that the pope's corrective function serves to defend and deliver beleaguered subjects: "it is a function of the papal office to defend the subjects of an heretical or perverse prince, and to free them from the evident peril … Consequently, [the pope] can, through this power, deprive a prince of his dominion; he can prevent the latter from injuring the subjects; and he can release those subjects from their oath of allegiance, or declare them to be released, since such an oath is always understood to carry with it the condition that it may be thus dissolved."[91] Thus, in Suárez's account, the pope's power to authorize intervention derives from his ability to apply "equitable justice."

For their part, common law jurists such as Sir Edward Coke had substantial concerns about the doctrine of equity, which they identified with Roman civil

---

[88]   Allen, *Defense of English Catholics*, vol. 2, 39–40.

[89]   Allen [and/or Sixtus], *Declaration*, fol. 1.

[90]   Francisco Suárez, *A Defense of the Catholic and Apostolic Faith* in *Selections from Three Works*, vol. 1, 336; vol. 2, 692.

[91]   "Ergo ad Pontificis munus spectat, subditos heretici, vel peruersi Principis defendere, & ab illo euidenti periculo liberare, … Ergo per illam potest, & talem Principem dominio suo priuare, & arcere, ne noceat subditis, & hos à iuramento fidelitatis soluere, vel solutos declarare, quia illa conditio in tali iuramento semper intelligitur inclusa." Suarez, *A Defense of the Catholic and Apostolic Faith*, in *Selections from Three Works*, vol. 1, 340; vol. 2, 700–701.

law and thus saw as foreign to the realm.[92] For Coke and other adherents to the common-law ideology, there was a clear parallel between Chancery's intervention into the jurisdictions of the common law courts and pre-Reformation attempts by the pope to interfere in English domestic affairs. The writ of *praemunire* had historically been employed to restrict the power of the Catholic Church in England, especially the papal ability to collect tithes and transport them outside the realm.[93] Throughout the Elizabethan and Jacobean periods, the writ was also used, or misused, by English jurists in order to restrict the authority of the court of Chancery and the ecclesiastical courts, where the principle of equity was frequently employed.[94] The best indication of how Coke's domestic concerns about the doctrine of equity also had ramifications for the foreign context can be found in Persons's response to Coke in *An Answer to the Fifth Part of Reportes Lately set forth by Syr Edward Cooke, Knight, the Kinge's Attorney General, written as a refutation of Coke's Fifth Report* (1605). In the latter work, Coke famously cites cases showing that the jurisdiction of the ecclesiastical courts was subordinate to common-law courts, given that the English sovereign was also head of the church.[95] In his response to Coke's preface, Persons defends the church and the ecclesiastical hierarchy from what he considers to be a usurpation of its ancient privileges, but he begins his response by defending the right of the "iust Prince" to "administer iustice, by law of nature [i.e. equity] and nations, if he will."[96] Significantly, Persons seems as worried by Coke's assault on the doctrine of equity and the limiting effect his formulation would have on the sovereign's power of prerogative as he is by the implications of Coke's formulations for the ecclesiastical courts. In terms of Spenser's poem, it is noteworthy that Persons shared Spenser's notion of the sovereign as a dispenser of equity, or justice outside of the strict bounds of law, because it bolstered his idea that the pope was justified in using the same doctrine to amend the consciences of heretical sovereigns such as Elizabeth or James.[97] Like Spenser who imagined a victorious Britomart utilizing

---

[92]   For context, see William Lambarde, *Archeion or, a Discourse upon the High Courts of Justice in England*, ed. Charles H. McIlwain et al. (Cambridge, MA, 1957), 45 and W.J. Jones, *The Elizabethan Court of Chancery* (Oxford, 1967), 464.

[93]   See 35 Edw. I stat. 1, c. 2, in *The Statutes*, X4v. See also 25 Edw. III stat. 6 (1350) [Mm4], 27 Edw. III stat. 1, c. 1 (1353) [Nn2–Nn2v], and 16 Ric. II c. 5 (1392) [Gggv–Ggg2v].

[94]   See Knafla, *Law and Politics*, 140–44, 158–69; Brian Levack, *The Civil Lawyers in England 1603–1641* (New York, 1973), 76–9.

[95]   Sir Edward Coke, *The Selected Writings of Sir Edward Coke*, ed. Steve Sheppard (3 vols, Indianapolis, IN, 2003), vol. 1, 125.

[96]   Robert Persons, *An Answere to The Fifth Part of Reportes Lately set forth by Syr Edward Cooke, Knight, the Kinges Attorney generall* (Antwerp, 1606), B3v.

[97]   For similar, less religiously motivated responses to Coke's Reports, see Thomas Egerton Ellesmere, Lord Chancellor. "The Lord Chancellor Egertons Observacions vpon ye Lord Cookes Reportes," in *Law and Politics*, ed. Louis Knafla, 297–318, and "Some Notes, and Remembrances, Concerning Prohibitions, for Staying of Suites in the Ecclesiasticall Courts, and in the Courts of the Admiralty," in *Law and Politics*, 282–96.

182   *Early Modern Catholics, Royalists, and Cosmopolitans*

the principle of equity in order to justify toppling illegitimate regimes such as that of Radigund, Persons imagines the pope's use of equity justifying essentially the same actions being taken against heretical English sovereigns.

So what is the natural law that Spenser sees Radigund as violating? In canto 5, Spenser specifies that it is a violation of patriarchal rule:

> Such is the crueltie of womenkynd,
> When they have shaken off the shamefast band,
> With which wise Nature did them strongly bynd,
> T'obay the heasts of mans well ruling hand,
> That then all rule and reason they withstand,
> To purchase a licentious libertie. (5.25)

This passage embodies the contradiction at the heart of Book 5 of *The Faerie Queene*, and to some extent exposes an unbridgeable rift within the entire poem. Spenser attempts to lay the groundwork for an imperial English polity, one that would be based on the doctrine of equity. The problem of course is that the doctrine of natural law, the very basis of equity, was generally understood to be inconsistent with the notion of women rulers. Thus the Scottish Protestant reformer, John Knox, condemned the rule of Mary Stuart and Elizabeth explicitly on the basis of equity: "to promote a woman to bear rule, superiority, dominion, or empire above any realm, nation or city is repugnant to nature, contumely to God, a thing most contrarious to his revealed will and approved ordinance, and finally, it is the subversion of good order, of all equity and justice."[98] Probably because of Queen Mary Tudor's restoration of the Catholic faith, writers such as Allen and Persons took a more nuanced view of female rulers. Both granted the legitimacy of Queen Elizabeth's temporal rule, but objected, on the grounds of natural and divine law, to the notion that she could claim any authority over Christ's church. After invoking Adam's authority over Eve in the garden, and Paul's admonition to women to cover their heads while praying, Persons concludes that "deductions from the law of Nature" argue conclusively for the "subjection, and subordination of women."[99] For both Allen and Persons, women are naturally inferior to men in spiritual matters.[100]

Therefore, in order to carve out this imperial identity for England, Spenser must make an exception for Elizabeth. He finishes the stanza, cited above, by reminding us of the singular nature of Elizabeth:

> But vertuous women wisely vnderstand,
> That they were borne to base humilities,
> Vnlesse the heauens them lift to lawfull souereintie. (5.25)

Here, the heavens have singled out Elizabeth as one uniquely lifted up "to lawfull sovereigntie." The singular nature of Elizabeth of course invokes the singular nature

---

[98]   Knox, *First Blast*, 42.
[99]   Persons, *An Answere*, K3v.
[100]   Allen, *Defence of English Catholics*, vol. 2, 128.

of her valiant forbearer, Britomart, who is ultimately responsible for reforming Radigund's unnatural polity. The exceptional nature of Britomart is embodied in her visit to the Temple of Isis, where the priests that reside there confer a kind of legitimacy on her that parallels the scene from Book 4 in which Britomart, in a battle that foreshadows Radigund's defeat of Artegall, vanquishes the Knight of Justice, causing him to fall "humbly downe vpon his knee [before Britomart], / And of his wonder [make] religion, / Weening some heauenly goddess he did see" (4.6.22). As I have noted, the priests confer on Britomart the status of equitable rule that transcends the law. But as in the scene from Book 4, in which Artegall falls to his knees and worships Britomart as a goddess, an additional, obvious interpretation would view the priests conferring on Britomart (and Elizabeth) a legitimate religious authority that figures such as Allen, Persons, and Suarez saw as a violation of natural law for her to claim. Once again, however, the scene cuts both ways, since the priests that confer a form of religious legitimacy on Britomart might easily be compared to the pope himself. At the center of the analogy that links Britomart's conquest of Radegone to the rise of an English imperial stance is the slippery doctrine of equity that also served as the pope's justification for Spanish invasion of England. Throughout the Radegone episode, one sees Spenser caught in a kind of labyrinth, trying to divert his reader away from an obvious analogy that links the doctrine of equity to the principles that justified a Catholic conquest of England itself at the same time that he seeks to provide an imperial stance for Elizabeth based on natural law. The dissonance surrounding the way in which Spenser's female champions must mimic and replicate the very doctrines that were being employed to justify their own deposition is thus manifold.

It would of course be ridiculous to suggest that an ostensibly nationalistic writer such as Spenser would be giving aid and comfort to the English and Spanish enemies of the English queen. What we see in Book 5 of *The Faerie Queene*, however, is how difficult it was for English Protestant writers, during this period, to imagine an imperial identity based on the prior traditions of equity and natural law, because such traditions directly conflicted with the religious and legal traditions of England as well as with the gender identity of its sovereign. Spenser himself obviously understood how potentially dangerous the putting to paper such imaginings could be. Toward the end of Book 5, Spenser imagines a supposedly good poet named BonFont turned bad and renamed MalFont. The tongue of this formerly "good poet" has been nailed to a post because "he falsely did reuyle, / And foul blaspheme that Queene for forged guyle" (9.25). What I have illustrated with regard to the Radigund episode in Book 5 suggests that Spenser himself understood that a poem that imagined and celebrated an emerging imperial English identity contained the potential for generating certain misreadings that suggested the justice of subverting Queen Elizabeth herself. His portrayal of Malfont, the good poet gone bad, is therefore perhaps the articulation of a legitimate fear that the use of a traditional legal concept such as equity, ironically connected to the sovereign's extraordinary powers, could be used to justify the usurpation of Elizabeth herself whom Spenser ostensibly had intended to celebrate throughout the poem. As Spenser conceives of the principle of equity here, the very doctrine that embodied the queen's power to correct and restrain the English common law was ultimately a double-edged sword that threatened the basis of her own legitimacy.

In the end, cosmopolitan identity and the Christian commonwealth are, it seems to me, central to Spenser's imperial imagination in Book 5. It is noteworthy that in *A View of the Present State of Ireland*, in the midst of a discussion of the hybrid identity of the Spanish, Ireneus offers the following remark about Christendom: "I [thincke] theare is no nacion now in Christendome nor muche farther but is mingled and Compounded with others, for it was a singuler providence of god and a moste admirable purpose of his wisdome to drawe those Northerne heathen nacions down into these Cristian partes wheare they mighte receaue Christianitye and to mingle nacions so remote so miraculouslye to make as it weare one kindred and bloud of all people and each to have knowledge of him."[101] In this passage, Spenser describes how the mixed heritage of Christendom, based on frequent migrations of populations from the North to the South, has fostered a providential and miraculous unity among the kingdoms of Europe. What I have shown in my reading of Book 5 is that Spenser perceived a similar unity within the scholastic foundations of imperialism, a unity that could equally provide a basis in natural law both for Dee's "Brytish Impire" and for Sander's imperial *monarchia Ecclesiae*.[102]

---

[101] Edmund Spenser, *A View of the Present State of Ireland*, in *The Works of Edmund Spenser: A Variorum Edition*, ed. Rudolf Gottfried (Baltimore, 1949), lines 1374–80.

[102] For a related discussion of Spenser's ambivalence towards Rome, found in particular in *The Ruines of Time*, see Hadfield, *Edmund Spenser*, 274–8.

Chapter 4
Traitor or Cosmopolitan?
Captain Thomas Stukeley in the Courts of Christendom

During the second half of the sixteenth century, English sailors such as Sir Francis Drake were touted as national heroes, and numerous pamphlets were published commemorating their seafaring exploits. Tracts such as Henry Roberts's *Most Friendly Farewell to Sir Francis Drake* (1585) framed Drake's exploits as the natural product of English nationalism. Roberts compares Drake to the ancient heroes of epic and repeatedly mentions his sacrifices for his "countries welth," portraying him as acting solely in his country's interest.[1] If in one sense such encomium reflects an undeniable aspect of Drake's enterprises, in another it obfuscates the manner in which the activities of privateers such as Drake were related to those of the pirate, who had no loyalty to the state. Privateers, like pirates, acted primarily out of their own self-interest, and privateers could act as pirates on one mission and as licensed privateers on another.[2] In this respect, what is really novel about Drake is the way in which an existing tradition going back to medieval times of warfare by non-state actors, of which Drake was a recent participant, was translated by writers such as Roberts into an ideology of incipient nationhood. This incorporation was largely produced by means of writings after the fact that attempted to situate the voyages of privateers within the larger national narrative.[3] According to political scientists, the ability either to eliminate non-state actors or alternatively to incorporate them into a coherent

---

[1] Henry Roberts, *A Most Friendly Farewell to Sir Francis Drake* ([1585 reprint] Boston, 1924), B3. For the context of Drake's 1585 voyage to the West Indies, see Simon Adams, "The Outbreak of the Elizabethan Naval War against the Spanish Empire: The Embargo of May 1585 and Sir Francis Drake's West Indies Voyage," in *England, Spain and the Gran Armada 1585–1604: essays from the Anglo-Spanish conferences, London and Madrid, 1988*, ed. M.J. Rodriguez-Salgado and Simon Adams (Edinburgh: John Donald, 1991), 45–69.

[2] Hans Turley, *Rum, Sodomy and the Lash: Piracy, Sexuality, and Masculine Identity* (New York, 1999), 30–31. See also Barbara Fuchs, *Mimesis and Empire: The New World, Islam, and European Identities* (New York, 2001), 118, and Daniel Vitkus, "Introduction," *Three Turk Plays from Early Modern England* (New York, 2000), 29–30.

[3] See John Cummins, *Francis Drake: The Lives of a Hero* (New York, 1995), 44–5, for instances during Drake's career when his privateering interests did not coincide with the English government interests.

186   *Early Modern Catholics, Royalists, and Cosmopolitans*

national framework is one of the processes that heralds a more centralized sense of nationhood.[4]

And yet, the artificiality of such narratives is clear when we consider the story of a privateer/pirate born almost a generation before Drake named Thomas Stukeley, who died in the famous Battle of Alcazar in 1578, precisely at the time that Drake was commencing his most ambitious and lucrative high seas ventures.[5] Early in his career, Stukeley's life was also subsumed into the national narrative. In 1563, Robert Seall composed a tribute to Stukeley entitled *A Comendation of the adve[n]terus viage of the worthy Captain M. Thomas Stutely Esquyer and others, towards the land called Terra Florida*, in which he praised the seafarer in terms that remind us of the nationalistic rhetoric that Roberts used to write about Drake's heroism.[6] It is clear, however, that there were already grave doubts about the accuracy of Seall's biographical narrative of Stukeley as the loyal subject of Elizabeth—in particular, references to "vain talk" about Stukeley's loyalties.[7] Posthumous evaluations of Stukeley's contribution to the English national project are far less sanguine than Seall's. William Camden called Stukeley "a Ruffian, and a ryetous spender, and a notable boaster of himselfe," and Richard Johnson portrayed Stukeley as a traitor who finally repented his immoral life: "thus haue I left my contry deere, / To be so vildly murthered heere: / euen in this place wheras I am not known."[8] Such posthumous accounts effectively portray Stukeley as having betrayed his native allegiance to the English crown.

What occurred after Stukeley's voyage to Terra Florida—in short, his defection to Spain and his aborted mission to "liberate" Ireland from English rule—obviously ruled out the more typical Drakean narrative of service for the national cause.[9] And yet, what is surprising about the two Elizabethan plays that portray Stukeley, George Peele's *The Battle of Alcazar* (1589; printed 1594) and the anonymously-authored *The Famous History of the Life and Death of Captain Thomas Stukeley* (1596; printed 1605), is that they take a relatively nuanced view of his life. Both

---

[4]   Janice E. Thomson, *Mercenaries, Pirates, and Sovereigns: State-Building and Extraterritorial Violence in Early Modern Europe* (Princeton, 1994). For a historical account of the English crown's attempts to suppress piracy, see David Delison Hebb, *Piracy and the English Government, 1616–1642* (Brookfield, VT, 1994), esp. 7–20. For background on piracy in English literature during the period, see Claire Jowitt, *The Culture of Piracy, 1580–1630: English Literature and Seaborne Crime* (Burlington, VT, 2010).

[5]   A contemporary account of the battle can be found in John Polemon, *The Second Part of the Booke of Battailes, fought in our age* (London, 1587), R3Y3.

[6]   Robert Seall, *A comendation of the adue[n]terus viage of the wurthy Captain. M. Thomas Stutely Esquyer and others, towards the land called Terra florida* (London, 1563).

[7]   Thus, later on in his tribute to Stukeley, Seall tells the sea captain to "hoice thy sail, / Thy wished land to find: / And neuer doo regard vain talke, / For wurds they are but wind."

[8]   William Camden, *The Historie of the Life and Reigne of the Most Renowned and Victorious Princesse Elizabeth, late Queene of England* (London, 1630), Bk 1, 6–12. Richard Johnson, *The Crown Garland of Golden Roses: Consisting of Ballads and Songs*, ed. W. Chappell (London, 1842), 38.

[9]   For a recent account of the biographical Stukeley, see Juan E. Tazon, *The Life and Times of Thomas Stukeley (c. 1525–78)* (Burlington, VT, 2003).

portrayals refuse Stukeley a settled role within the narrative of emerging English identity, neither presenting him as exclusively English nor as the typical traitor to the English crown who might easily be excluded from any relationship to his native country. Rather, by presenting Stukeley as involved in a network of religious and secular authorities that defied the official narrative of English nationhood, in which the sovereign was the sole authority, they offer an alternative to the emerging narrative of nationhood in which figures such as Drake both intentionally and unintentionally participated. This alternative and more diffuse political structure often was not necessarily in opposition to the incipient notion of a unique English character. In fact, Stukeley's Englishness is central to these plays, for the more Stukeley distances himself from his native loyalty to the English sovereign, the more his English identity is stressed. The portrayal of Stukeley is therefore the product of a dialectical relationship existing between his English identity and the transnational or "cosmopolitan" identity that his Englishness enables. In contrast to the secular papal substitutes championed by Munday, Harington, Sidney, and Spenser, the two fictional portrayals of the life of Captain Thomas Stukeley constitute a departure from the centralized vision of Christendom or Europe that we have encountered in other cosmopolitan works of the period. Whereas these other writers of fiction found ways to maintain the Christian commonwealth of Persons and Allen while transforming it into a secular transnational entity, the Stukeley plays ultimately present Stukeley's Englishness as a window onto an imagined network of Christian sovereigns that should ideally act as caretakers for one another. While defense of "Christendom" is referenced throughout the two Stukeley plays, these dramatic works should nevertheless not be understood as attempting to define a common and transnational Christian identity but rather as presaging the system of mutually supportive sovereigns later imagined by royalists such as Sir Richard Fanshawe, as we will eventually find in Chapter 5.

In recent years, there has been a flurry of interest in the life and the dramatic portrayals of Stukeley, including a full length biographical study of Stukeley's life, a new collected edition of the two plays that include his name in their title, and a number of literary critical articles on the subsequent dramatic portrayals of his life.[10] The literary criticism has sought to situate the two dramatic portrayals

---

[10]   Tazon, *Life and Times of Stukeley (c. 1525–78)*; Charles Edelman (ed.), *The Stukeley Plays: The Battlle of Alcazar by George Peele, The Famous History of the Life and Death of Captain Thomas Stukeley* (New York, 2005); Daniel Vitkus, "Adventuring Heroes in the Mediterranean: Mapping the Boundaries of Anglo-Islamic Exchange on the Early Modern Stage," *Journal of Medieval and Early Modern Studies* 37.1 (2007): 75–95; Jean E. Howard, "Gender on the Periphery," in *Shakespeare and the Mediterranean*, ed. Tom Clayton et al. (Newark, 2004), 344–62; Emily C. Bartels, "The Battle of Alcazar, the Mediterranean, and the Moor," in *Remapping the Mediterranean World in Early Modern English Writings*, ed. Goran V. Stanivukovic (New York, 2007), 97–116; Leeds Barroll, "Mythologizing the Ottoman: The Jew of Malta and the Battle of Alcazar," in *Remapping the Mediterranean World in Early Modern English Writings*, 117–30. Of these essays, only Bartel's captures the cosmopolitan nature of Stukeley, whose career, she says, "cannot be contained or explained by any set terms of Englishness, nation, or religion" (106).

of Stukeley's adventures within the context of England's complex relationship with the Ottoman Empire by setting them beside other dramatic depictions of English travelers in the Mediterranean world. Jean Howard has labeled this genre the "adventure play," at the center of which is "the conversion paradigm, the actual or threatened transformation of the English hero into something alien: into a Turk, a Muslim, a traitor, a renegado." According to Howard, "such plays almost always end with a recuperative gesture through which renegade masculinity looks homeward, renounces the seduction of the periphery, and is reconciled to a larger English or Christian community."[11] In effect, the threat of conversion to Islam functions as part of what Daniel Vitkus calls "English identity formation" and what Howard refers to as the production of "Early Modern religious, cultural, and racial categories of difference."[12]

As groundbreaking as Vitkus's and Howard's work is, it remains indebted to Helgerson's *Forms of Nationhood* which argues, in similar fashion, that such challenges to English national ideology as Spenser's privileging of an atomistic and aristocratic Gothic sensibility over royal authority are ultimately recuperated into the national project through their contribution to the formation of a unique English character.[13] A number of historians and literary critics have begun to interrogate such Anglo-centric accounts of national identity, by taking up J.G.A. Pocock's call more than 30 years ago for a "British history" that would challenge the traditional paradigms of English history.[14] According to Pocock, such a historiographical approach would ultimately be an antinationalist endeavor that would strive to be a "pluralist and multicultural" account of the competing identities that inhabited the Atlantic Archipelago.[15] One of Pocock's standard-bearing literary critics, David J. Baker has since remarked that a "thoroughgoing British literary criticism" may

---

[11]   Howard, "Gender on the Periphery," 349, 358.

[12]   Vitkus, "Adventuring Heroes in the Mediterranean," 79; Howard, "Gender on the Periphery," 348.

[13]   Helgerson, *Forms of Nationhood*, 19-59. For notable developments of Helgerson's thesis that English literary texts had an important ideological role in producing a common national identity, see Clare McEachern, *The Poetics of English Nationhood*, 134, and Philip Schwyzer, *Literature, Nationalism, and Memory in Early Modern England and Wales*, 112. Spenser figures prominently in both McEachern and Schwyzer. See also Jodi Mikalachki, *The Legacy of Boadicea: Gender and Nation in Early Modern England*, and John Kerrigan, *Archipelagic English: Literature, History, and Politics 1603–1707*.

[14]   This field has become extensive, and includes the following published in recent years: J.G.A. Pocock, Gordon Schochet, and Lois G. Schwoerer, "The History of British Political Thought: A Field and its Future," 10–22; John Morrill, "Thinking about the New British History," 23–46; Krishan Kumar, *The Making of English National Identity*, chs 1, 2, 6; Wiley Maley, *Nation, State, and Empire in English Renaissance Literature*, esp. 1–10; David J. Baker and Willy Maley, "Introduction. An Uncertain Union," 110; David Armitage, *The Ideological Origins of the British Empire*; Brendan Bradshaw and Peter Roberts, (eds) *British Consciousness and Identity*; David J. Baker, *Between Nations*, esp. 116.

[15]   J.G.A. Pocock, "British History: A Plea for a New Subject," *Journal of Modern History* 47 (1975): 601–28, 616.

be impossible, given England's political and literary dominance in Britain.[16] And yet, a "British" approach to historiography has the benefit of considering the hegemony of England from a multi-centered perspective, sustained and cultivated in hybrid identities, exile communities, and the interactions between and among British ethnicities. It is clear from Baker's work, for example, that English identity emerges in relation with and in response to the other national, ethnic, and tribal identities within Britain.[17]

This chapter pushes the envelope of such an approach still further. Helgerson and later work on English nationhood was groundbreaking because it challenged and "unmask[ed] the nation's claim to a 'natural' or 'immemorial' origin," but Helgerson's approach remained limited by the presuppositions of an Anglo-centric tradition of historiography.[18] Baker, Willy Maley, and other literary critics inspired by Pocock's call for a British historiography went a long way towards overcoming such limitations by locating their readings in the spaces between England and the surrounding polities that comprised the Atlantic Archipelago. But textual phenomena that can be attributed to Britain and British identity are in some sense overdetermined. In such work, Englishness continues to be a function of contrast with what is non-English, even if interesting and fertile interpenetrations between competing British identities are sometimes uncovered. As my reading of the dramatic works based on the life of Thomas Stukeley shows, Pocock's transcultural approach to British history can be extended still further in order to consider the way in which English identity exists in relation to an older but still persistent transnational or "cosmopolitan" identity inherent in the familiar notion of Christendom. In such works, cosmopolitanism emerges dialectically with national identity: Stukeley's Englishness is the window onto a broader transnational identity that ultimately works to dislodge and destabilize national identity itself.

Beyond the English Nation

In order to comprehend the form of cosmopolitanism that appears in the dramatic works portraying the life of Thomas Stukeley, let us recall that when John Dee invoked a secular cosmopolitan perspective in his *General and Rare Memorials pertayning to the Perfect Arte of Navigation* (1577), his ostensible purpose was to provide a plan for the establishment of a permanent English naval force that would afford "PERPETVALL POLITIK SECVRITY and better preseuation of this famous Kingdom, from all Forrein danger, or Homish disorder."[19] At this point

---

[16]   Baker, *Between Nations*, 16.
[17]   Baker, *Between Nations*, 1–16.
[18]   Helgerson, *Forms of Nationhood*, 301.
[19]   Dee, *The Perfect Arte of Navigation*, A4v, e3v. For analysis of the place of this tract within Dee's entire corpus, see Sherman, *John Dee: The Politics of Reading and Writing in the English Renaissance*, 115–200; Yates, *The Occult Philosophy in the Elizabethan Age*, 75–95; French, *John Dee: The World of an Elizabethan Magus*, 182–90; and Deacon, *John Dee: Scientist Geographer, Astrologer, and Secret Agent to Elizabeth I*.

190   *Early Modern Catholics, Royalists, and Cosmopolitans*

in English history, of course, there was no English navy to speak of, but rather a motley collection of mariners that could act as free agents or even agents of foreign powers if they so desired. To address the problem, Dee presents himself in the figure of the classical Stoic cosmopolitan,[20] the individual who has both an allegiance to humanity as a whole (Dee's "one Mysticall City Vniversall") and to the country in which he was born (his "Brytish Monarchy"), in order to claim a privileged perspective on England and to advance a corresponding argument about its need for a centralized, standing navy. As a universal citizen, Dee sees himself as uniquely suited to theorizing transnational values that could simultaneously (and paradoxically) defend and justify an increased centralization of English state power.[21] Although Dee's text is more complex than I am giving it credit for at the moment, his early invocation of a "Brytish Impire" confirms Walter Mignolo's argument that the dominant forms of cosmopolitanism throughout history have been "managerial" in nature.[22] As I noted in the Introduction, it is not surprising that Richard Hakluyt eventually incorporated Dee's account of the patriotic cosmopolitan into the opening pages of the first volume of the *Principal Navigations*.[23] For Hakluyt and others who were even more engaged in such matters, just such a perspective enabled the emergence of future national and imperial maritime policies. I would suggest that the portrayal of Stukeley in these two plays embodies Mignolo's notion of "critical cosmopolitanism," which tends to resist imperial and state power from the perspective of the marginalized,

---

[20]   For background on the cosmopolitanism of the Stoics, see A.A. Long and D.N. Sedley, *The Hellenistic Philosophers* (New York, 1987), vol. 1, 364. For a contemporary take on Dee's cosmopolitan identity, see Kwame Anthony Appiah's notion of the "rooted cosmopolitan" in "Cosmopolitan Patriots," in *Cosmopolitics: Thinking and Feeling beyond the Nation*, ed. Pheng Cheah and Bruce Robbins (Minneapolis, 1998), 91–116. For a general history of cosmopolitan thought, see Derek Heater, *World Citizenship and Government*.

[21]   Dee, *The Perfect Arte*, A4v. See Sherman, *John Dee*, 148. Interestingly Schwyzer views Dee's vision of an Imperial British monarchy as succinctly embodying "both the aims and spirit of sixteenth-century British nationalism" (Schwyzer, *Literature, Nationalism, and Memory*, 11).

[22]   Mignolo's main examples of this critical stance are the *relectiones* by Francisco de Vitoria, which challenged the legal and theological foundations of the Spanish conquests of the New World. See Walter Mignolo, "The Many Faces of Cosmopolis: Border Thinking and Critical Cosmopolitanism," 157–88. In the past decade a number of scholars have discussed the notion of cosmopolitanism by tracing its history and evaluating its roles in modern western cultural and political history. See for example Cheah and Robbins (eds), *Cosmopolitics: Thinking and Feeling beyond the Nation*; Vinay Dahrwadker (ed.), *Cosmopolitan Geographies: New Locations in Literary Culture* (New York, 2001); Joshua Cohen (ed.), *For Love of Country: Debating the Limits of Patriotism* (Boston, 1996); Carol A. Breckenridge and Sheldon Pollock (eds), *Cosmopolitanism* (Durham, NC, 2002). On the notion of a cosmopolitanism that transgresses national boundaries by rooting itself in places and cultures, see Kwame Anthony Appiah, *Cosmopolitanism: Ethics in a World of Strangers*, (New York, 2007).

[23]   Richard Hakluyt, *Principal Navigations*, vol. 1, 16–24.

exiled, or banished subjects of the imperium.[24] Whereas a figure such as Dee in the *Perfect Arte of Navigation* employs the cosmopolitan perspective in order to prescribe a strengthening of the state apparatus, the dramatic portrayals of Stukeley's cosmopolitan perspective tend in the opposite direction, constituting a critique of early modern ideologies that saw individual identity as connected to the emerging sense of English nationhood.[25]

The first Stukeley play, whose complete title is *The Battel of Alcazar, Fought in Barbarie, betweene Sebastian king of Portugall, and Abdelmelec king of Marocco, With the death of Captaine Stukeley*, focuses on King Sebastian's defeat on the famous battlefield of that name in 1578. The play begins in Morocco with political intrigue over the Moroccan crown between the rival pretenders, Abdelmelec and Muly Mahamet, with Sebastian supporting Mahamet in his attempt to overthrow Abdelmelec and reclaim the throne. Stukeley appears in the second act, after the alliance between Sebastian and Mahamet has been established. Along with his lieutenants Jonas and Hercules, an unnamed Irish Bishop, and his small army, Stukeley stops in Lisbon on his way from Rome to Ireland. After being welcomed by Diego Lopes, the Governor of Lisbon, the Irish Bishop announces that they are on a mission to reconquer Ireland in the name of Pope Gregory, who has financed the mission, and to restore Roman Catholicism to the island. Diego Lopes is surprised to find that an honorable Englishmen, as Stukeley is reputed to be, would attack territory belonging to the English crown.

As with Dee's writings, Stukeley's response to Diego Lopes gestures toward a cosmopolitan outlook on the world. But unlike Dee's "managerial cosmopolitanism," which uses the cosmopolitan perspective to endorse strengthening the power of the English crown, Peele's play works in the opposite direction, showing how national identity might serve as a window onto broader, transnational forms of identity rooted in European Christendom. On one level, of course, Peele's Stukeley loosely represents the biographical Stukeley, the English traitor who eventually sided with the Spanish enemy and planned to overthrow English rule in Ireland in the name of Roman Catholicism. But on a deeper level, Peele's portrayal embodies the cosmopolitan ideal in such a way that Stukeley balances his original English character with the cosmopolitan perspective. Thus Stukeley responds,

> Lord Governor of Lisbon, understand
> As we are Englishmen, so are we men,
> And I am Stukeley so resolved in all
> To follow rule, honour and empery,
> Not to be bent so strictly to the place

---

[24]   Mignolo, "Many Faces of Cosmopolis," 159.

[25]   Joseph Candido first used the phrase, "citizen of the world," to describe the dramatic portrayals of Stukeley (55). See "Captain Thomas Stukeley: The Man, the Theatrical Record, and the Origins of Tudor 'Biographical Drama,'" *Angia-Zeitchrift fur Englische Philologie* 105 (1987): 50–68.

192   *Early Modern Catholics, Royalists, and Cosmopolitans*

> Wherein at first I blew the fire of life,
> But that I may at liberty make choice
> Of all the continents that bounds the world.
> For why, I make it not so great dessert
> To be begot or born in any place,
> Sith that's a thing of pleasure and ease,
> That might have been performed elsewhere as well. (2.2.26–36)[26]

In this passage, Stukeley's English identity bleeds into his general human identity. His subsequent declaration that he is "resolved in all / To follow rule, honour, and empery" reflects the fact that Stukeley sees himself as following an ethical code comprised of rule, honor, and allegiance to a ruler's absolute dominion. But note that his allegiance to "empery" is not attached to England or to any other particular kingdom. The lack of specificity indicates that Stukeley's allegiances are not limited to his country of birth or any other country. He makes this clear in the next line, declaring that he is "Not to be bent so strictly to the place / Wherein at first I blew the fire of life / But that I may at liberty make choice / Of all the continents that bounds the world." In essence, Peele renders Stukeley as an individual who claims to be faithful, rule-bound, and honorable at the same time that Stukeley's loyalties obviously go beyond the limits of national origin.

Ironically, in the dialogue that follows, it is the Irish Bishop who tries to correct Stukeley by invoking the traditional patriarchalist analogy between the family and the state, on which English monarchical ideology was based. Implicitly reproaching Stukeley for his bawdy reference to his own conception ("a thing of pleasure and ease, / That might have been performed elsewhere as well"), the Bishop remarks, "We must affect our country as our parents" (2.2.42). In the Bishop's terms, loyalty to the country of one's birth is implicitly enjoined by the Decalogue's admonition to honor thy parents. This analogous or, more accurately, metonymic relationship between the state and family serves to naturalize monarchical political ideology by presenting the state as a larger organic version of the family.[27] Both Stukeley and his lieutenant, Hercules, express skepticism towards the Bishop's defense of this tradition, however, complaining that the Bishop is speaking in insincere platitudes. Stukeley responds to the Bishop sarcastically: "Well said, Bishop, spoken like yourself / The reverent lordly Bishop of Saint Asses" (2.2.48–9). And Hercules explains that the Bishop has been speaking "according to his coat / And takes not measure of it by his mind" (2.2.50–51). In this exchange, an important opposition emerges between the Bishop's defense of traditional patriarchalism and Stukeley's and Hercules's ridicule of that ideology. As Michael McKeon has recently shown, one mark of the modern is the critique of and eventual breakdown of the traditional

---

[26]   All parenthetical citations are from George Peele, *The Battle of Alcazar* in Edelman (ed.), *The Stukeley Plays*.

[27]   The relationship in the play between Stukeley's family and his country is based on metonymy rather than analogy, since Stukeley and his family comprise a part of the country. For an in-depth discussion of the relationship of the family to the state, see Michael McKeon, *The Secret History of Domesticity: Public, Private, and the Division of Knowledge* (Baltimore, 2005), 115, 110–61.

early modern political analogy, which figures the family as a smaller version of the state or the state as a larger version of the family.[28] What we see in Stukeley's ridicule of the Bishop is a very early challenge to this traditional political analogy, on which the entire edifice of the early modern state was based.

The displacement of the linkage between the state and family allows a relationship to develop between the state and the subject in cosmopolitan terms. Such a relationship, implied in Stukeley's ironic response to the Bishop's word, takes visible shape in the second play. *The Famous History of the Life and Death of Thomas Stukeley* dramatizes Stukeley's biography by following the trajectory of a picaresque narrative, and partly as a result, it initially presents a more negative assessment of his character.[29] In the first half of the play, Stukeley assumes the identity of the stereotypical lovable rogue, an identity based on self-exile when he sequentially abandons the analogous familial body and the body politic. The first six scenes depict Stukeley abandoning his family for the life of a soldier. Initially, he persuades Curtis, a rich alderman, to grant his daughter Nell's hand in marriage to him (1.70–120). Nell marries Stukeley ahead of Vernon, Stukeley's rival, and Stukeley fulfills everyone's suspicions about his true intentions by using her family's money to pay off his debts (5.15–22). Afterwards, he defies Nell's father as well as his own by abandoning his family and traveling to Ireland to serve in the wars. He declares his voluntary exile from the familial body by claiming the need to honor a prior vow to the state: "I vowed in heart / To be a soldier, and the time now serves / And now my vow shall be accomplish'd" (6.106–8). Stukeley's claim to be acting honorably and in England's interest, however, is insincere. As soon as he arrives in Ireland, he brags about having "made away [his wife's] portion and her plate, / Her borders, bracelets, chains and all her rings / And all the clothes belonging to her back" (9.59–62).[30] Still, the fact that he has traveled to Ireland in order to defend English rule against the Irish revolt renders his betrayal of his family and his subsequent abandonment of England more complex. Indeed, one might view his decision to fight in Ireland as a dramatization of the renewed struggle to extend English rule into Ireland that would serve England's interest but would also eventually pose a challenge to English identity by incorporating both England and Ireland into a broader British identity.[31] As in the first play, *Thomas Stukeley* seems to invoke the traditional analogy between the family and state in order to illustrate its limitations.

---

[28] McKeon, *Secret History*, 11–15.

[29] For a discussion of the picaresque genre as a critique of national identity, see Barbara Fuchs, "An English Picaro in New Spain: Miles Philips and the Framing of National Identity," *The New Centennial Review* 2.1 (Spring 2002): 55–68.

[30] All parenthetical citations are from Anonymous, *The Famous History of the Life and Death of Captain Thomas Stukeley* in Edelman (ed.), *The Stukeley Plays*. Parenthetical citations appear as scene and line number.

[31] For Ireland's place within the early modern notion of Britain, see Nicholas Canny, *Making Ireland British, 1580–1650* (New York, 2003). For a succinct discussion of the relationship between English nationalism and the Welsh origins of Britain, see Schwyzer, *Literature, Nationalism, and Memory*, 69, 76–96.

194   *Early Modern Catholics, Royalists, and Cosmopolitans*

In Ireland, Stukeley encounters his old enemy Captain Jack Harbert, who is now the English governor of Dundalk, and hostilities resume between the two figures (10.6–51). Before they can duel, however, the Irish attack and the English army finds itself defending the town against an onslaught by Shane O'Neill's band of rebels. Not content to stay behind the walls of the fortress, Stukeley ignores Harbert's orders and attacks the Irish invaders outside the gates, and subsequently he is symbolically ejected from the body politic when Harbert refuses to let him re-enter the town (11.20–25). Once again, it is possible to see the dispute between Stukeley and Harbert as one between the future "British" perspective (Stukeley), which actively seeks to pacify and incorporate Ireland into a new polity, and the defensive English perspective (Harbert), which seeks to maintain the status quo by remaining behind the town walls and maintaining discipline over rebellious Englishmen such as Stukeley. When Harbert succeeds in keeping Stukeley out of the walled English settlement, however, Stukeley's response is to extend the gamut of his shifting identity to the continent. In the scenes that follow, he flees to Spain, eventually making contact with Philip II.

A constant theme running throughout this entire sequence is the extent of Stukeley's loyalty to his country, but as the play complicates the nature of that polity, the question of his loyalty or disloyalty is also rendered more complex. In contrast to his devilish roguery in England, his subsequent actions in Ireland, Spain, and alongside the Portuguese sovereign reveal that Stukeley retains a recognizable code of honor that seems to immunize him from the charge of treason. When Stukeley arrives in Cales, Spain, the Governor assumes that he is a pirate and immediately has him imprisoned on that basis (13.44). Subsequently, Stukeley encounters the Governor of Cales's wife, who quickly becomes enamored of the Englishman, swearing secret loyalty to him. Stukeley responds to her advances with the following vow:

> Madam,
> How much your noble Spanish courtesy hath power in me
> A faithful English heart shall manifest,
> And I will be the champion of your honour
> Wherever I become in Christendom. (13.116–20)

As in the *Battle of Alcazar*, Stukeley embraces his English identity here, claiming it as faithful and honorable. Once again, however, Stukeley's national identity enables him to claim a more universal identity, based on the chivalric notion of honor within the "realm" of Christendom. In the process, Stukeley retains his Englishness, along with qualities such as ingenuousness, faithfulness, and honesty that contemporary English playwrights associated with portrayals of Englishmen abroad.[32] The Stukeley that later fights beside King Sebastian in Barbary embodies all of these traits. In the *Battle of Alcazar*, at the start of the crucial battle, Stukeley

---

[32]   See, for example, the figure of Posthumus in Shakespeare's *Cymbeline*.

declares himself ready to die for the cause of the Portuguese sovereign.[33] Similarly, in the second play, Stukeley declares himself ready to ignore his own tactical knowledge out of loyalty to the authority of King Sebastian.[34] These moments are meant to suggest that Stukeley lives and dies by a code of chivalry that was at once a system of values belonging to an earlier era and one that was experiencing a resurgence during the Elizabethan period.[35] Indeed, such chivalric codes are bound up with English identity while also extending beyond such an identity.[36]

Ultimately, both plays deflect the accusation of treason onto more diabolical figures. For example, Stukeley's last words in Ireland are a condemnation of the traitorous acts of the Irish rebel, Shane O'Neill: "Farewell O'Neill, if Stukeley here had stayed, / Thy head for treason, soon thou shouldst have paid" (*Thomas Stukeley*, 11.96–7). The scene in which Stukeley makes this remark is directly followed by a scene in which O'Neill enters with "a halter about his neck," at the end of which he and his secretary Neil Mackener are killed by two Scottish soldiers as traitors to the crown (12.69–75). Likewise, the author of *Thomas Stukeley* simply omits the longstanding friendship that the historical Stukeley maintained with O'Neill, from the early 1560s when O'Neill made a trip to Elizabeth's court.[37] In the *Battle of Alcazar*, the role of true exiled traitor is similarly deflected onto the figure of Muly Mahamet, who according to the Presenter has assassinated his uncle and his two brothers in order to consolidate his rule of Morocco. In contrast, both works partially elide the real-life Stukeley's role as traitor to the crown, and in doing so, they forestall the corresponding uncomplicated recuperation into English national discourse that would occur as a result of drawing a more definitive demarcation between Stukeley and England.[38] This process of elision is especially apparent in an early fractured scene in *The Battle of Alcazar* in which Stukeley encounters

---

[33]   "For my part, lords, I cannot sell my blood / Dearer than in the company of kings" (4.2.68–9).

[34]   In spite of the fact that "Our men are weak, the enemy is strong, / Our men are feeble, they in perfect health" and that it would be "better discipline, ... / To let them seek us here, than we them there," he vows to be the first across the river that separates Sebastian's army from the enemy (23.11–21). Later, at the start of the crucial battle and in the face of insurmountable odds, Stukeley swears loyalty to Sebastian, assuring him: "Rise when you will, his foot that is foremost, / His sword that's soonest drawn, my foot and sword / Shall be as forward and as quickly drawn" (23.40–43).

[35]   For discussion of chivalry in England during the late sixteenth century, see Richard McCoy, *The Rites of Knighthood: The Literature and Politics of Elizabethan Chivalry* (Berkeley, 1989).

[36]   See Lockey, *Law and Empire*, 17–46.

[37]   This friendship led O'Neill to intercede on Stukeley's behalf, when he was arrested for acts of piracy against Spanish ships, and also prompted Stukeley to attempt to purchase the estate adjoining O'Neill's land from Nicholas Baganel (Edelman, Introduction in *The Stukeley Plays*, 6).

[38]   For the place of treason within early modern discourses of the state, see Lisa Steffen, *Defining a British State: Treason and National Identity, 1608–1820* (New York, 2001), 1–47.

King Sebastian. Throughout this scene, the dialogue falters under the weight of two conflicting imperatives: to promote English nationalism and to rehabilitate Stukeley as an honorable gentleman. When Stukeley appears before the Portuguese sovereign with his lieutenants, Hercules and Jonas, Sebastian assumes that he officially represents the English crown. Sebastian, holding court, requests that the Duke of Avero "call in those Englishmen, / Don Stukeley and those captains of the fleet / That lately landed in our bay of Lisbon" (2.4.54–6). Sebastian then invites Stukeley and his men to join him in his planned invasion of North Africa "in honour of thy country's [England's] fame" (2.4.85). In the next part of this scene, Stukeley reveals that he no longer serves the English sovereign and that his intention is to invade Ireland. In response, Sebastian's delivers a long speech in which the Portuguese king explains why Ireland is impervious to invasion.

In one respect, this is the most clichéd speech of the play, since it is meant to satisfy its English audience that, according to another European sovereign, Queen Elizabeth's realm is secure from external invasion. In another respect, however, these verses are the most important of the play since they obscure the historical record in order to rehabilitate Stukeley as a heroic Englishman. Stukeley tells Sebastian that his mission is to invade and overthrow the current regime in Ireland, to which Sebastian replies,

> For Ireland, Stukeley? Thou mistak'st wondrous much,
> With seven ships, two pinnaces, and six thousand men?
> I tell thee, Stukeley, they are far too weak
> To violate the Queen of Ireland's right,
> For Ireland's queen commandeth England's force.
> Were every ship ten thousand on the seas,
> Manned with the strength of all the eastern kings,
> Conveying all the monarchs of the world
> To invade the island where her highness reigns,
> Twere all in vain, for heavens and destinies
> Attend and wait upon her majesty. (2.4.98–108)

Sebastian has just heard word that Stukeley means to invade territory that belongs to the sovereign, Queen Elizabeth, to which the captain owes his allegiance. Instead of acknowledging this fact, however, Sebastian speaks of the "Queen of Ireland's right," as if such a queen were distinct from Elizabeth, the sanctioned object of Stukeley's loyalties. Only secondarily does Sebastian identify this queen as a figure who "commandeth England's force," thus obscuring her primary identity as the sovereign of England. In Sebastian's formulation, Stukeley is invading Ireland, not England, and by speaking of a Queen of Ireland in this way, the play momentarily occludes Stukeley's relationship with Elizabeth.[39]

---

[39] One editor, John Yoklavich, has noted that this speech "is probably the most corrupt in the play, [and] it is impossible to know just where there have been imperfect revisions and deletions" (*The Battle of Alcazar*, in *The Life and Works of George Peele*, ed. Yoklavich (New Haven, CT, 1961), 359).

At the end of the passage, the king invites Stukeley to join his crusade against the King of Morocco: "If honour be the mark whereat you aim'st, / Then follow me in holy Christian wars, / And leave to seek thy country's overthrow" (2.4.134–6). Here, at the end of 38 lines of verse, Sebastian finally acknowledges Stukeley's treasonous mission ("to seek thy country's overthrow"), but at the same moment, Sebastian invites Stukeley to consider remedying his defection by joining Sebastian's campaign to extend the boundaries of "Christendom." Sebastian's invitation substitutes a commitment to the broader transnational Christian identity for the mission to invade Ireland on the basis of narrower partisan interests. Thus, Sebastian's Christian transnationalism both replaces Stukeley's treasonous mission and reinvigorates his English identity.[40]

Given that Sebastian's invitation approximates the transnational character of Stukeley as he originally formulated his identity earlier in Act 2 ("As we are Englishmen, so we are men"), it is no surprise that Stukeley immediately commits to Sebastian's cause. But he tells Sebastian that while he himself "will be the first / To die with honour for Sebastian" (2.4.142–3), he must consult with his co-leaders of the expedition. At this point, another rupture is revealed in the scene. Sebastian asks the Bishop and Stukeley's two English lieutenants, Hercules and Jonas, if they are also willing to join his invading force: "Tell me Lord Bishop, captains, tell me all, / Are you content to leave this enterprise / Against your country and your countrymen?" (2.4.145–7). The following is their response:

Bishop.	To aid Mahamet, King of Barbary,
	Tis against our vows, great King of Portugal.
Sebastian.	Then captains, what say you?
Jonas.	I say, my lord, as the Bishop said,
	We may not turn from conquering Ireland.
Hercules.	Our country and our countrymen will condemn
	Us worthy of death, if we neglect our vows. (2.4.148–54)

The Bishop's response seems initially to refer to a religious obligation. But Hercules's reference to their "country" and "countrymen" orients the entire matter along a national trajectory. In response to King Sebastian's request, Hercules replies that joining Sebastian's African campaign would mean betraying his own "country." But to what "country" and "countrymen" is Hercules referring in his response? This is an important question since his response both echoes and contradicts the spirit of Sebastian's initial demand to Stukeley's men, that they "leave this enterprise / Against your country and your countrymen [their fellow Englishmen]." Hercules's response, that joining Sebastian's campaign

---

[40] Both Peele's *Battle of Alcazar* and the anonymous *Thomas Stukeley* contain multiple references to Christendom and the mission to advance transnational Christian unity, which Sebastian presents himself as championing. See, for example, *The Battle of Alcazar* (2.4.66; 2.4.135; 2.4.165; 3.1.31; 3.4.16; 3.4.76; 5.1.59; 5.1.225), and *Thomas Stukeley* (13.120; 14.47–8; 14.124–7; 17.25; 19.194–6; 20.54; 22.98–104).

would constitute a betrayal of "our country and countrymen," uses Sebastian's own language to suggest that breaking their vow to invade Ireland would in itself constitute a betrayal.

In arguing that his "countrymen" are counting on their invasion of Ireland, is Hercules suggesting that England is not what it seems to be, that Englishmen themselves seek to be liberated by Stukeley the English Catholic? Is he referring to the oppressed Irish and English Catholics, or perhaps the larger Catholic community, as his "country"? Or is he calling his Italian sailors his "countrymen," and their fleet of sailing vessels his "country"? Ultimately, it is impossible to identify with any specificity the "country" to which Hercules is referring because the language of nationalism that is being employed here expresses loyalties and vows that extend beyond the national entity. Indeed, the language of nationalism that one finds in Hercules's response reveals how nationalism itself can exceed its own definitions and incorporate its opposite, the transnational, into itself. It also reveals how any expression of collective loyalty was already bound up with the language of nationhood at this time.

This problem becomes even more complex when we consider the late scene in which Stukeley is murdered by Hercules and Jonas, now belatedly identified as Italian soldiers. Towards the beginning of Act 5, there appears the following stage direction: "*Alarums. Enter* Stukeley *with two* Italians" (5.1.109). This is followed by a scene in which Hercules and Jonas, now apparently Italian, accuse Stukeley of being a traitor to the cause of retaking Ireland for Catholicism and mortally wound him. "Stand, traitor, stand ambitious Englishman, / Proud Stukeley stand, and stir not ere thou die," says Hercules before stabbing Stukeley (5.1.109–10). The most recent editor of *The Battle of Alcazar*, Charles Edelman, makes an interesting point when he writes that the contradiction between the national identities of Hercules and Jonas in the second and the fifth acts "is a problem only for readers: an audience in the theatre does not hear speech headings."[41] Edelman assumes that the same actors who played Hercules and Jonas at the beginning of the play might have also played Stukeley's assassins at the end in a way that would be unproblematic for the spectator. But from the perspective of national loyalty, the problem is only slightly mitigated through performance. When Diego Lopes and Sebastian encounter Hercules and Jonas in the second act, they explicitly identify and address them as Englishmen. In contrast, before Hercules and Jonas kill Stukeley at the end of the play, Stukeley identifies them as "proud malicious dogs of Italy" (5.1.126). Thus, the larger question which fractures both the written and the performed text is the nature of the entity to which Hercules and Jonas seek or sought to remain loyal.

Hercules and Jonas seek to be loyal to some originary conception of the nation in both the meeting with Sebastian and in the assassination scene, but the true identity of the entity or entities, to which they refer, is occluded by Hercules's ambiguous response in Act 2 and later textual problems. The only printed Quarto edition of *The Battle of Alcazar* (1594) is a corrupted text, and it is likely that

---

[41] Edelman, *Stukeley Plays*, 231.

a number of passages are missing from the play or that the printed text is the result of a conflation of two or more versions of the play.[42] Whatever its cause, the indeterminacy of their national and religious identity has the effect of rendering Stukeley's contrasting cosmopolitan identity that much more substantial. Stukeley exists along an axis of transnational principles, which both encompass the sense of English national identity that is developing during this period and move beyond that identity and subvert it. Initially, of course, Stukeley and Hercules are almost reflections of each other. Stukeley introduces himself as an Englishman whose very Englishness leads to the transnational, while Hercules declares himself loyal to an undefined and thus potentially transnational "country." But Hercules's desire to remain loyal to his "country" represents a vague and perhaps even disguised loyalty that contrasts with Stukeley's more defined, expansive view of the world. Ultimately, Stukeley's transnational identity ties into his Englishness in such a way that it both clarifies and synthesizes Hercules's contradictory and ill-defined sense of identity.

Beyond Exile and Treason

As we have seen, it is impossible to discuss the cosmopolitan perspective in this play without invoking the question of the individual's loyalty or disloyalty to the state. To illustrate the uniqueness of such themes in these two portrayals of Thomas Stukeley, it is helpful to consider other contemporary plays that thematize treason and religious betrayal. A number of plays have been used as points of comparison with the Stukeley plays, including Thomas Heywood's *The Fair Maid of the West, Part 1* (1604), John Day, William Rowley, and George Wilkins's *The Travels of the Three English Brothers* (1607), Robert Daborne's *A Christian Turned Turk* (1612), and Philip Massinger's *The Renegado* (1623). Of these, Daborne's *Christian Turned Turk* is especially helpful for illustrating what normally occurs to figures who betray their native religious or national identity.[43] The protagonist, John Ward, an Englishman-turned-corsair, betrays England and

---

[42]   Edelman, Introduction to *The Stukeley Plays*, 19. One intriguing possibility is that Hercules and Jonas have been masquerading as Englishman in the early scenes in the court of Sebastian and then later reveal their true Italian identity in a missing scene. If this were the case, then Hercules and Jonas present a more sinister form of cosmopolitanism than the "rooted cosmopolitanism" that Stukeley represents. For discussion of the term "rooted cosmopolitanism," see Appiah, "Cosmopolitan Patriots," 91.

[43]   Thomas Heywood, *The Fair Maid of the West, Parts I and II*, ed. Robert K. Turner, Jr. (Lincoln, 1967), John Day, William Rowley, and George Wilkins, *The Travels of the Three English Brothers* in *Three Renaissance Travel Plays*, ed. Anthony Parr (New York, 1995), 55–134, Robert Daborne, *A Christian Turned Turk*, in *Three Turk Plays from Early Modern England*, ed. Daniel Vitkus, 149–240; Philip Massinger, *The Renegado* in *Three Turk Plays from Early Modern England*, 241–344. See Daniel Vitkus, "Adventuring Heroes in the Mediterranean," and Howard, "Gender on the Periphery," for discussion of these other plays.

the Christian polity by converting to Islam and undergoing circumcision in order to marry the beautiful Voada (8.10–11).[44] Ward's conversion leads to poverty, rejection, and episodes of agonizing soul-searching during the last quarter of the play, in which the pirate laments, "Should I confess my sin, / There's not an ear that can with pity hear / A man so wicked" (13.108–10). Finally, his despair drives him to commit suicide, at which point he belatedly longs for home and attempts to reconcile himself with the Christian realm and the English nation, which he feels he abandoned and betrayed:

> Or may, O may, the force of Christendom
> Be reunited and all at once requite
> The lives of all that you [Muslims] have murdered,
> Beating a path out to Jerusalem
> Over the bleeding breasts of you and yours.
> . . .
> Let dying Ward tell you that heaven is just,
> And that despair attends on blood and lust. (16.309–13, 320–21)

In the ultimate lines of the play, the Governor of Tunis recounts Ward's betrayal and his resulting punishment: "His monument in brass we'll this engrave: / 'Ward sold his country, turned Turk, and died a slave'" (16.325–6).

The lesson of *A Christian Turned Turk* is clear, as Daniel Vitkus points out: "when brought into contact with Islamic power and wealth, remain steadfast in your Christian faith and you will return home a hero; forsake your country's religion and you will be punished (as Stukeley and Ward were)."[45] In *A Christian Turned Turk*, the series of narrative events, in which Ward betrays his country and religion, later repents his actions, and then takes his own life, functions to reify English national identity and to draw a figurative boundary that excludes traitors such as Ward. But Stukeley should not be compared to Ward here, since he presents an obvious problem for such a conclusion. While it is clear that Ward is punished for forsaking "his country's religion," it is by no means true in Stukeley's case since Stukeley never even considers converting to Islam and he never completely abandons his English identity. At the end of *Thomas Stukeley*, far from confessing and lamenting any acts of treason on his own part, Stukeley's last words are instead to curse the "treasonous" Italian soldiers that mortally wound him: "What fortune never yet / Did cross Tom Stukeley in, to show her frown, / By treason suffers him to be overthrown" (28.60–63). In contrast to Ward, Stukeley's last words cast him as a victim of betrayal.

Needless to say, there are important similarities between *A Christian Turned Turk* and the Stukeley plays, the most important being the prevalence of speeches inspired by Christopher Marlowe's *Tamburlaine*, in which the protagonist declares his refusal to be subject to a king and his ambition to be his own sovereign.

---

[44]   Parenthetical citations (scene and line number) are from the Vitkus edition the play.
[45]   Vitkus, "Adventuring Heroes in the Mediterranean," 90.

Like *Tamburlaine*, Ward and both portrayals of Stukeley express this iconoclastic ambition. But in contrast to the specifically religious iconoclasm of Tamburlaine and Ward, there is no analogous moment of religious heresy or defection in the Stukeley plays.[46] Despite his identity as a Catholic exile, the fictional Stukeley expresses very little opinion on religion in both plays. Instead, the iconoclasm expressed in his Tamburlaine speech in Peele's version is an expression of a purely secular aspiration. "King of a mole-hill had I rather be / Than the richest subject of a monarchy" (2.2.69–84), declares Peele's Stukeley, while the second portrayal of Stukeley similarly remarks, "[I] scorn to be controlled, / Of any man that's meaner than a king" (11.93–6).

Ultimately, both the Stukeley of *Thomas Stukeley* and Peele's Stukeley do undergo a kind of defection, but it is in exactly the opposite direction from the Christian who turns Turk. Peele's version of events includes the scene in which Stukeley defects from his original purpose (the invasion of Ireland), but in doing so, he ends up unintentionally allying himself with England's anti-Spanish ally, Portugal. On a superficial level, the fact that Stukeley aligns himself with a Catholic sovereign such as Sebastian would by itself make him a traitor to Protestant England. But in this case, the situation is more complex. Portugal was historically an important ally of England's that originally helped England to check the Spanish threat. In this respect, the aftermath of Sebastian's disastrous campaign in North Africa posed significant challenges for the English government. In 1580 Philip II took possession of the Portuguese crown, and the popular Portuguese pretender, Dom Antonio, Prior of Crato, went into exile first to the Azores, then to France and finally to England, where a number of Queen Elizabeth's courtiers, including Sir Philip Sidney, initially took up his cause. Later, in 1589, at precisely the time that it is presumed that George Peele was writing *The Battle of Alcazar*, Sir Francis Drake and Sir John Norris were commanding an expedition to the coast of Portugal on Dom Antonio's behalf to persuade the Portuguese to rise up against Spanish occupation. In 1589, the most probable date for the composition of *The Battle of Alcazar*, Peele himself composed a poem entitled, *A Farewell Entitled to the famous and fortunate generalls of our English forces: Sir Iohn Norris & Syr Frauncis Drake Knights, and all theyr braue and resolute followers*, a work which once again attempted misleadingly to situate

---

[46] For example, early in *Tamburlaine Part 1*, Tamburlaine heretically aspires to divinity and expresses disdain for orthodox accounts of divinity: "Jove sometimes masked in a shepherd's weed, / And by those steps that he hath scaled the heavens / May we become immortal like the gods" (1.2.199–201). This theme continues throughout Part 1 and Part 2, the end of which has Tambulaine burning the "Alcoran" as he claims, "There is a God full of revenging wrath, / ... / Whose scourge I am" (5.1.180–82). Likewise, Ward expresses his iconoclasm at the moment when he decides to turn Turk and undergo circumcision: "I'll rather lead on slaves / Than be commanded by the power of kings" (7.191–2). In the process, Ward completes his defection from the religious and temporal authorities to which he once owed allegiance.

within the English national narrative a voyage that served a variety of different private and dynastic interests.[47]

Given this history (which follows directly the fictional history recounted in the play), Stukeley's decision to join King Sebastian's campaign in Northern Africa might be seen as inadvertently advancing a stronger position for England by strengthening an ally with respect to a mutual enemy, Spain. That the anonymous author of *Thomas Stukeley* also supported Elizabeth in her support of Portuguese independence from Spain is illustrated at the end of *Thomas Stukeley*, when Dom Antonio makes an appearance at the side of King Sebastian, who declares Antonio to be the rightful heir to the Portuguese throne (19.69–70). In the process, the fictional King Sebastian renders Elizabeth, who became Dom Antonio's most important royal sponsor, an executor of his royal will. In the *Battle of Alcazar*, Stukeley recognizes the perfidy of the Spanish sovereign from the beginning, a recognition that makes him an unconscious link between Portugal and England in each kingdom's confrontation with Spanish aggression and occupation (3.2.61–2). Stukeley has one foot in Portugal, a realm of his own choice, but he maintains a tip of his toe in the English polity as well, in such a way that his identity includes but also exceeds the boundaries of his native English identity.

"True" Accounts of National Character

What I have been arguing is that Stukeley's cosmopolitan identity is enabled by his retention of an English character. As we shall see, a figure whose national character was truly indeterminate could pose a more serious threat to sovereignty. The threat emerges because such a figure could claim to be anything, even a competing claimant to a throne. Contrast, for instance, the fictional recognitions of Stukeley's innate nobility in these plays with a related account of a true story, which was roughly contemporaneous with these two plays and which was translated into English by Anthony Munday in 1601. In this case, our context is once again the Portuguese defeat at Alcácer Quibir. Two years after the disastrous defeat of the issueless King Sebastian of Portugal, Philip II of Spain took control of the Portuguese crown, but rumors persisted that Sebastian had survived the battle and that he would someday return to Portugal and free his countrymen from Spanish control. Throughout the 1580s and 90s, various claimants to the throne appeared in Portugal, were proved fraudulent, and were summarily executed.[48] But in 1598, a most intriguing claimant emerged. In June of that year, an individual

---

[47] He also made reference to his Stukeley play in this poem. Addressing Drake and Norris's men, he writes, "Bid Theaters and proude Tragedians, / Bid *Mahomets Poo*, and mightie *Tamburlaine*, / King *Charlemaine, Tom Stukeley* and the rest / Adiewe: to Armes, to Armes, to glorious Armes." (George Peele, *A Farewell Entituled to the famous and fortunate generalls of our English forces: Sir Iohn Norris & Syr Frauncis Drake Knights, and all theyr braue and resolute follower* [London, 1589]).

[48] Tazon, *Life and Times of Stukeley*, 13.

arrived in Venice and declared himself to be the long-lost King Sebastian. Various Portuguese merchants who inhabited Venice at the time made contact with him and became convinced that he was their lost king.

The Venetian Sebastian recounted that 20 years earlier, he had been badly wounded in the battle in which the Portuguese invaders were defeated, but that he had ultimately succeeded, along with several Portuguese noblemen, in escaping to the Portuguese coast by ship. When he arrived to the Algarve, however, he decided not to reveal himself because of his shame in having led his army into such a disastrous defeat. Instead, he resolved to travel throughout Europe and Asia, where he fought in various wars as a mercenary. Finally, he decided to do penance by spending the remainder of his days as a recluse. On hearing his story of royal origins, however, a hermit advised him to do penance by returning to Portugal and reclaiming his throne. Sebastian thus shipped off to Sicily and resolved to travel to Rome in order to reveal himself to the pope. On the way, however, he was assaulted and robbed, which left him unable to complete his trip to Rome. Instead, he traveled to Verona and then to Venice where he announced himself to the Venetian authorities. For a while his presence was tolerated, but when the Spanish crown found out about the man's claims, the Spanish ambassador to Venice complained that he was an imposter from Calabria and requested successfully that the Venetian authorities throw him in prison. Soon after, a Portuguese priest, named José Teixeira, acting as his sponsor, published a series of letters to a French bishop, in which the priest gave "proof" that the figure in Venice truly was the long-lost Sebastian.[49]

Anthony Munday translated this tract into English in 1601, under the title, *The Strangest Adventvre That Ever Happened: Either in the ages passed or present. Containing a discourse concerning the successe of the King of Portugall Dom Sebastian.*[50] Information that Sebastian might be alive would have been of keen interest to an older generation of Englishmen who had assisted Dom Antonio, the Prior of Crato, in his claim to the contested Portuguese throne, now firmly held by Philip III. From my perspective, the more interesting aspect of this tract is how it fits into the questions of recognition that are significant in the Stukeley plays. The testimony of José Teixeira and others concerning the Venice claimant to the Portuguese throne combines fantastical elements with other elements that have a realistic and even legalistic quality to them. The claimant's story reads like a contemporary romance narrative. The tract even includes that signature romance trope—the identifying birth mark—in this case, in the form of testimony by a Friar

---

[49]   José Teixeira, *The Strangest Adventvre That Ever Happened: Either in the ages passed or present. Containing a discourse concerning the successe of the King of Portugall Dom Sebastian,* trans. Anthony Munday (London, 1601).

[50]   Two additional tracts recounting subsequent events surrounding Dom Sebastian were later translated and published in England: José Teixeira, *A Continvation of the Lamentable and Admirable Adventvres of Dom Sebastian, King of Portugall,* trans. Anthony Munday (London, 1602); José Teixeira, *The Trve Historie of the late and lamentable aduentures of Don Sebastian, King of Portugall,* trans. Anthony Munday (London 1603).

Stephen de Sampayo that the claimant "hath all the markes on his body, without failing in any one of them, as he had in his infancy, onely the wounds excepted which he received in the bloudy day at Affricke."[51] But throughout the tract there is a competing element of legalistic realism. In a letter included by Teixeira in the tract as official testimony, a Father Juan De Castro assures us that the claimant bears marks on his body that conform to official testimony about King Sebastian's body, verified by public Notaries. José Teixeira himself lists these marks at the end of the letter, and they comprise such un-romance–like characteristics as, "He hath little pimples on his face and hands, and very apparent: but such as knows it not cannot discerne them," and "He hath the fluxe of seed, or Gonorrhaea."[52]

In light of the Stukeley plays, what is important about the Venetian Sebastian's *Strange Adventure* is that, in spite of unmistakable attempts to situate the experiences of the claimant within romance-derived tropes, neither his royal nor his national identity is readily apparent to those who encounter him. Indeed, unlike the fictional Stukeley whose Englishness is instantly recognized as a form of nobility, even the nationality of the claimant is contested—he is accused of not speaking Portuguese and of being from Calabria. In this respect, the encounter with the Sebastian of Venice is a very different kind of cosmopolitan phenomenon. The Sebastian of Venice is not identified primarily because his provenance cannot be determined. His supporters swear that he is the king, based on physiological traits. However, one cannot rule out self-interest on their part since they are all Portuguese subjects suffering under Castilian rule. His doubters claim that he cannot be the Portuguese king because he does not have the proper characteristics that signify his claimed national origins.

The fictional Stukeley, in contrast, is instantly recognizable as an Englishman. Hence, what is ironic about the Stukeley plays is that Stukeley inadvertently draws attention to the existence of an English character at the very moment that he is ostensibly denying his loyalty to the English nation and the monarch with which it was identified. Having a cosmopolitan identity is thus paradoxically enabled by the English identity, curiously re-emphasizing the nation from which it represents an escape. This may be the reason that the Stukeley plays, which seem to valorize a Catholic traitor to the crown, were allowed to be staged and ultimately printed. But the comparison between Stukeley's fictional experience of being instantly recognized as both English and noble and the very different experience of the Venetian Sebastian has other ramifications. Like Sebastian in Venice, the real Stukeley faced intense suspicion from foreign sovereigns when he appealed for support in his proposed venture to invade Ireland. In reality, Philip II made a show of empowering Stukeley, by bestowing various titles on him, but he never

---

[51] Teixeira, *The Strangest Adventvre*, F4. For discussion of the romance genre, see Steve Mentz, *Romance for Sale in Early Modern England: The Rise of Prose Fiction* (Burlington, VT, 2006); Lockey, *Law and Empire*, 15–142; Lori Humphrey Newcomb, *Reading Popular Romance in Early Modern England* (New York, 2002); and Barbara Fuchs, *Romance* (New York, 2004).

[52] Teixeira, *The Strangest Adventvre*, K4.

trusted Stukeley's loyalties enough to finance his plans to invade Ireland. Pope Gregory was more generous, giving him 600 soldiers and some munitions, but the ships with which he provided Stukeley were unseaworthy, which was probably the most significant reason why Stukeley never got farther than Lisbon.[53] In fact, with the exception of the Portuguese king, most foreign magistrates seemed to harbor suspicions about who Stukeley was and to whom he owed his true loyalties. Even Persons reports that Stukeley had encountered "great variance and open hostility" during his sojourn in Spain. However, the attitude of suspicion toward Stukeley seems to have been less pervasive within the English exile community. In his memoirs, Persons lists Stukeley's name along with Sir Francis Englefield, Sir Richard Shelley, Saunders, Allen, Lewis, and Clynnog as among those who "wished well the conversion of there countrey, but agreed not well in the means or maner of consultation." He reports that in Rome Stukeley had allied himself with the Welsh faction headed by Lewis and Clynnog, and against the faction of Saunder and Allen and implicitly Persons himself.[54] In 1575, when Stukeley arrived in Rome, of course, Lewis and Clynnog held the reins at the English hospice in Rome and constituted the established, longstanding power center within the exile community. Given Stukeley's unsavory reputation as a privateer and a pirate and the fact that most patronage in Rome seemed to follow strict ecclesiastical hierarchies, Stukeley probably sided against the upstart party of Allen and Persons out of an acute awareness of the tenuousness of his own situation in Rome.

The contrast between the fictional Stukeley and the real Stukeley reveals that identities that were not moored stably to some nation posed a serious challenge to sovereigns of the period. The fictional Stukeley can navigate the transnational realm precisely because his national identity is never in question. Thus his cosmopolitan identity is intimately tied to his national identity. Indeed, George Peele and the anonymous author of *Thomas Stukeley* want to imagine that national identity is easily and instantly recognizable, but the experience of the biographical Stukeley demonstrates that those figures whose national or ecclesiastical identity or purpose could not be easily identified were often shunted to the margins.

Stukeley's Death and Beyond

At the end of *The Battle of Alcazar*, Stukeley's identity is structured around a tension between his noble English character and his transnational existence. In the last act, a mortally wounded Stukeley delivers a long final speech in which he recounts the life he has lived, focusing on his travels throughout continental Europe. The account is marked most prominently by his encounters with the sovereigns of those Mediterranean countries that he has visited. He first details his visit to the court of King Philip in Spain where "Tom Stukeley [did] glitter all in gold, / Mounted upon his jennet white as snow, / Shining as Phoebus in

---

[53] See Tazon, *Life and Times of Stukeley*, 144–68, 232–3.
[54] Persons, "A Storie," 64.

King Philip's court" (5.1.146–8). He then recalls his travels to Rome where he was "Received with royal welcomes of the Pope" (5.1.155). He recounts, "There was I graced by Gregory the Great, / That then created me Marquess of Ireland" (5.1.156–7). Finally, he recounts his relationship with "sweet Sebastian," mourning that he did not provide better advice to the Portuguese king (5.1.169). Throughout this speech, Stukeley imagines his life as a series of relationships with sovereigns, in which his desire to be his own sovereign is partially achieved. In Philip's court he shines like a "Phoebus" that seems to outshine Philip himself, and in the pope's presence, he is created "Marquess of Ireland."

As was the case in my analysis of Sidney in the prior chapter, it is important to contrast this with an older account of identity formation prominent in the work of Louis Montrose and Stephen Greenblat, which would see in this speech an English subject fashioning himself in relation to such authority figures.[55] In one respect, Stukeley's last speech is related to the New Historicist notion of the subject gaining a sense of self through his relationship to authority. The foreign courts that Stukeley describes in his final speech are perhaps just one court, with a different sovereign, Philip, Gregory, or Sebastian at its head, and Stukeley is "fashioned" and "fashions" himself in a series of encounters with such royal figures. But in quite another respect, something very different is happening here. First of all, these three sovereigns have different interests that at least in the case of Philip and Sebastian are diametrically opposed to each other. The subject thus gains his identity, not in the static relationship with one sovereign, but in the movement between competing authority figures, a result of Stukeley traveling from court to court and verifying again and again his own independent self-worth. Each separate sovereign recognizes in Stukeley a sovereignty over the self that gives Stukeley an independence and self-determination that seems to exist outside of one binding relationship to a centralizing authority. Indeed their recognition of his innate nobility has the effect of transforming Stukeley into something like an independent sovereign, who reigns over his own person.[56]

But does not Stukeley's death signal the containment of whatever cosmopolitan perspective that he initially might have symbolized in the same way that Ward's death functions in *A Christian Turned Turk*? Does it not constitute a reaffirmation of the English nation that Stukeley left behind? Of course, in one respect, these two plays are obligated to present Stukeley's death by virtue of their claim to be reproducing a true history of his life. Nevertheless, it is hard not to entertain

---

[55] According to Greenblatt, Renaissance fiction channeled "national and religious sentiment into the worship of the prince [i.e. Elizabeth]," "mask[ing] over and thus temporarily deflected deep social, political and theological divisions in late sixteenth-century England." *Renaissance Self-Fashioning*, 168. See also Louis Adrian Montrose, "*A Midsummer Night's Dream* and the Shaping Fantasies of Elizabethan Culture: Gender, Power, Form," 65–87.

[56] This anticipates the absolutism that Catherine Gallagher has claimed seventeenth-century women writers used to carve out a sphere of personal dominion over their body and mind. See Gallagher, "Embracing the Absolute: the Politics of the Female Subject in Seventeenth-Century England," *Genders* 1 (1988): 24–39.

the conclusion that Stukeley's death is, in some sense, a punishment for his transgression of the national sphere. In both plays, for example, Stukeley renders a final salute to England at the moment when he dies (5.1.175–6; 28.60–62). But Stukeley's death raises as many questions as it answers. For one thing, the issue is not dissimilar to the equally irresolvable question that has often been asked about cross-dressing during the Renaissance: whether such dramatic portrayals of cross-dressing as occur in plays such as *As You Like It* constitute attempts to subvert patriarchy or are ultimately contained within patriarchal ideology when the cross-dressing female is inevitably married off at the end of the play.[57] Even here though, the comparison is ultimately not an exact one. Stukeley's cosmopolitanism is distinct, since his perspective is not subversive in the same way as cross-dressing. Most literary historians see dramatic portrayals of cross-dressing as signaling a traditional "gender system under pressure" from those who were oppressed by the patriarchal order.[58] Cosmopolitanism may to some extent have been the perspective of the recusant or exiled English Catholic, but it is not "subversive" in quite the same way since it predates the rise of the modern nation-state by several hundred years.[59] Nor is the national perspective conservative in the same way that patriarchy is with respect to women who subversively cross-dressed, for the modern nation emerged as an entity out of a period that was essentially more cosmopolitan, not less. In this respect, Stukeley's cosmopolitan perspective is possibly more conservative than the national perspective that we are used to seeing celebrated in contemporary history plays.

But if the English nation prevails to some extent at the end, it is certainly a more complex conception of the nation than we might at first expect to encounter in such plays. As I have noted, the end of *Thomas Stukeley* includes a scene in which Stukeley gestures toward a reconciliation with England. This reconciliation occurs by way of a final dialogue with the Englishman, Vernon, who was Stukeley's old rival for his wife, Nell. During the first half of the play, Vernon plays the "good" Englishman—honorable, humble, and genuine—to the ambitious, manipulative, and proud Thomas Stukeley. But Vernon is ultimately Stukeley's double as well, for like Stukeley, Vernon abandons England for self-exile. In Vernon's case, exile occurs as a response to Stukeley winning the heart of his beloved Nell. Claiming that his relationship with his native country has been spoiled by Stukeley's success, Vernon expresses a desire for travel: "I am fired with a desire to travel / And see the fashions, state and qualities / Of other countries" (4.53–5). At the end of the play, Stukeley contemplates the prospect of

---

[57] See for example the disagreement on this issue between on the one hand, Valerie Traub and Jean Howard, and Dympna Callaghan, on the other. See Traub, *Desire and Anxiety: Circulation of Sexuality in Shakespearean Drama* (New York, 1992), 14–56; Jean Howard, *The Stage and Social Struggle in Early Modern England* (New York, 1994), 93–128; and Dympna Callaghan "'And all is semblative a woman's part': Body Politics and Twelfth Night," *Textual Practice* 7.3 (1993): 428–52.

[58] Howard, *The Stage*, 94.

[59] Heater, *World Citizenship*, 1–59.

208   *Early Modern Catholics, Royalists, and Cosmopolitans*

his own death by embracing Vernon, and then he makes reference to their shared "English blood," which will be "commixed" with "the blood of kings" (28.31–3). Thus, in a contradictory moment, Stukeley invokes England while simultaneously embracing his cosmopolitan double: a representative of positive English traits who for his own reason has exiled himself from his native land. In this respect, the ending both gestures towards England and gestures away from it at the same moment.

Peele's play is even more fascinating in dealing with the question of Stukeley's death. As I have mentioned above, in his last speech, Stukeley begins by recounting his travels through the courts of Mediterranean Europe, where he has been treated by each potentate as if he were himself a king. He ends with the following invocation of his native land:

> Stukeley, the story of thy life is told,
> Here breathe thy last and bid thy friends farewell.
> And if thy country's kindness be so much,
> Then let thy country kindly ring thy knell.
> Now go, and in that bed of honour die
> Where brave Sebastian's breathless corse doth lie. (5.1.173–8)

This is Stukeley's farewell gesture to England, whose spectators are enjoying the very dramatic spectacle that contains these verses. Several aspects of this passage render this speech more complex than it might first appear. First, note that Stukeley refers to England as his "country," that indeterminate term that Hercules has by now corrupted to such an extent that it has become difficult to identify its proper referent. Second, note that Stukeley asks for his dead corpse to be buried in Sebastian's grave. This is significant because Stukeley's dying speech directly precedes Sebastian's own death, but curiously, Peele does not give Sebastian his own farewell speech.

At the end of the play, Zareo reports to Muly Mahamet Seth, the new King of Barbary, that the Portuguese have been searching for the king's corpse, and the last time we see the Portuguese king is 35 lines after Stukeley finishes his speech, when "*two* PORTUGALS [enter] *with the body of the king.*" The Portuguese corpse-bearers identify the corpse as Sebastian's, and Seth is satisfied, but the fact is that we never see the Portuguese king die. In fact, past critics have suggested that Stukeley's speech may function dramatically as the death speech of the absent King Sebastian.[60] With the substitution of Stukeley's farewell speech for that of Sebastian and the suggestion that Stukeley is buried in Sebastian's grave, Peele seems to be gesturing towards the Portuguese tradition of "Sebastianismo," the millennial belief that the Portuguese king miraculously survived the famous battle. If Peele knew about the legends of Sebastian's survival of the Battle of Alcácer Quibir, which is probable, then the final cosmopolitan gesture of this play is the

---

[60]   David Bradley, *From Text to Performance in the Elizabethan Theatre: Preparing the Play for the Stage* (New York, 1992), 170.

suggestion that Stukeley becomes Sebastian's double in death, a substitute corpse for a miracle king that would supposedly go on to experience his own exiled, itinerant, and decentered adventure.

Ultimately, it is worth reflecting on such figures as Stukeley as a way of revising the account of the nation and its formation now standard in Renaissance studies. Consider for example that my introductory account of how Drake's voyages were ultimately and somewhat misleadingly commemorated as expressions of English national unity is largely consistent with Helgerson's account of how Luís de Camões's *Os Lusíadas* and Richard Hakluyt's publication of the *Principal Navigation* functioned within their respective national discourses. Indeed, Helgerson shows that Hakluyt's entire project entailed re-inscribing epic nationalism into voyages that were taken primarily for mercantile profit.[61] But such an account of the writing of English nationhood overlooks the way in which such narratives might have simultaneously challenged emerging national ideologies. Works of fiction, such as the Stukeley plays, cut against the grain of English national formation. Against the standard account of the writing of Renaissance England, the case of Thomas Stukeley illustrates that more complex, transnational identities survived in dramatic fictions.

---

[61] Helgerson, *Forms of Nationhood*, 149–92.

PART II

Part II Introduction
Royalists

Historical continuity can be found between the Catholic exiles of the late sixteenth century and the royalists of the mid-seventeenth century, but it is complicated by the enormous transformations that occurred within English politics during the intervening period.[1] To be sure, those points of continuity that exist, as circumstantial as they often are, are compelling. In 1640, for example, during the early conflict with the Scottish Covenanters, among the first to rise up on behalf of Charles I's efforts against the rebelling Scots was the Earl of Strafford's Irish army, composed primarily of Irish Catholics. Later in October 1641, when a number of Ulster Catholic gentry, led by Sir Phelim O'Neill, rose up and took control of English forts and castles, they claimed their actions were taken "by authority from His Majesty out of England, and by consent of the prime nobility and gentry of Ireland" and were intended "for the preservation of His Majesty's prerogative" and "their own religion and liberties against the Puritan faction in England, Scotland, and Ireland."[2] And during the later period in exile, some of the most committed adherents to the royalist cause, especially those that surrounded Queen Henrietta Maria's court in France, were Catholics, and even conformist royalist adherents to the Queen such as Sir William Davenant were reputed to have taken the opportunity of being in exile to convert to Catholicism.[3] Obviously,

---

[1]   There are a wide array of theories concerning the origins of the English civil war in general and the royalist party in particular. Lawrence Stone famously locates the origins of the conflict between royalists and parliamentarians in the early sixteenth century, while on the other extreme Ronald Hutton claims that all-out war only became possible in March 1642 and that a royalist identity formed soon after. See Stone, *The Causes of the English Revolution 1529–1642* (New York, 1972), 47–147; Hutton, *The Royalist War Effort 1642–1646* (New York, 1982), 3–32. See also Conrad Russell, *The Fall of the British Monarchies 1637–1642* (New York, 1991), 1–146; Russell, *The Causes of the English Civil War: The Ford Lectures Delivered in the University of Oxford, 1987–1988* (New York, 1990). For the influential debate about the decline of the gentry, see R.H. Tawney, "The Rise of the Gentry, 1558," *Economic History Review* 11.1 (1941): 1–38 and H.R. Trevor-Roper, "The Elizabethan Aristocracy: An Anatomy Anatomized," *Economic History Review* 3.3 (1951): 279–98. For a more recent discussion of the formation of a royalist identity, see Gerome de Groot, *Royalist Identities* (New York, 2004).

[2]   Cited in Nicholas Canny, *Making Ireland British*, 471.

[3]   Alfred Harbage, *Sir William Davenant, Poet Venturer, 1606–1668* (Philadelphia, 1935), 104–5. For a discussion of Queen Henrietta Maria's court as it relates to her Catholic courtiers, see Quentin Bone, *Henrietta Maria: Queen of the Cavaliers* (Chicago, 1972), esp. 94–141, 190–202. For a highly readable discussion of Davenant's place among the cavaliers and their poets, see John Stubbs, *Reprobates: The Cavaliers of the English Civil War* (New York, 2011), 112–20. For discussion of how the experience of exile influenced the writings of Englishmen, see D'Addario, *Exile and Journey*, esp. 57–86.

English Catholic perceptions of the crown had undergone a drastic transformation during the period between the end of the sixteenth century and the civil war period. Whereas the early Jesuits saw Elizabeth as a heretic queen who had not only usurped the pope's rightful claim to the ecclesiastical realm but was introducing heresy into her realm, English Catholics during Charles I's reign had become accustomed to relying on Charles I's absolutist claims to sovereignty, especially his exercise of the sovereign's extraordinary powers, to insure whatever limited *de facto* tolerance that they enjoyed. A wide array of Catholic perspectives existed during the seventeenth century: between the idiosyncratic position taken by later English Catholics such as Kenelm Digby and Thomas White who supported a Roman Church divested of the Court of Rome's authority and the more orthodox position of Robert Persons and Fr. Robert Bellarmine, S.J., most English Catholics were doubtless somewhere in the confused middle. But because Charles I's policies were perceived as more generous to the old faith than his Puritan opponents, most Catholic supporters of the crown seemed all too eager to ignore the fact that from the Church's perspective, like Elizabeth and James I, Charles had also effectively usurped the ecclesiastical realm and was responsible for presiding over the introduction of dangerous heresies into the body politic.[4]

The enormous transformation in English Catholic perspectives on the English crown were matched by equally impressive changes occurring within English Protestantism during this period. The perceived threat of subversion by Jesuit infiltrators and Catholic recusants in the immediate wake of the Gunpowder Plot (1605) led to a renewed upswing in anti-papist zealotry among Puritan divines. Ecclesiastical authorities within the established church and the crown tolerated and even had a certain regard for such expressions of anti-popery. Among many conformist and non-conformist Protestants in late sixteenth-century England, expression of hatred for the pope and his supporters was how one manifested adherence to the true religion.[5] A heightened sense of the threat posed by the Antichrist pope was a certain sign of election for Puritan divines, but it also served as a political strategy used to endear the Puritans to the establishment.[6] By the early 1620s, however, a number of conformist voices had begun questioning whether

---

[4]   Moreover, while Charles told the Venetian envoy that he did not "approve of so much rigour ... against the papists," his efforts to curb the practice of Catholicism among his subjects were often aggressive. See *Calendar of State Papers Venetian, 1628–1629*, 167. For context on his efforts to enforce conformity, see Kevin Sharpe, *The Personal Rule of Charles I* (New Haven, CT, 1992), 301–8.

[5]   For a discussion of anti-popery as a religious tenet within English Protestantism, see Arthur Marotti, "The Intolerability of English Catholicism," 52–4. For a review of attempts at fostering religious unity and uniformity in England, see Conrad Russell, "Arguments for Religious Unity in England, 1530–1650," in *Unrevolutionary England, 1603–1642* (Ronceverte, WV, 1990), 179–204. See also Kevin Sharpe, *The Personal Rule of Charles I*, 275–402, and Julian Davies, *Caroline Captivity of the Church: Charles I and the Remoulding of Anglicanism, 1625–1641* (New York, 1992).

[6]   Anthony Milton, *Catholic and Reformed: The Roman and Protestant churches in English Protestant Thought 1600–1640* (New York, 1995), 37–45.

Part II Introduction 215

works of anti-papist controversy had a potentially dangerous seditious purpose rather than being simply a tenet of the faith. With alarming frequency, the accusations of anti-popery were now directed at conformists and representatives of the established church rather than being limited to those that actually held communion with the Roman Church. According to Anthony Milton, this was especially the case during the height of the unrest over the Spanish match in 1622.[7] At the same time, there was increasingly some substance to the accusations of crypto-popery directed toward the established church, if only because the "Arminians" were slowly disengaging from the anti-papal system of values that had formed the basis of the earlier alliance between the Puritans and the established church. More alarming, from the anti-papist perspective, the boundaries between the Church of England and the Roman Church seemed to be blurring.[8] In their appeal to Catholic recusants, the Laudians had attempted to crack down on anti-papist expression typical of earlier generations. Likewise, like Roman Catholics, the Laudians increasingly approved traditional doctrines, to which Catholics subscribed, such as the notion that good works were a legitimate pathway towards salvation.[9] Finally, during Charles I's reign, purveyors of traditional anti-papist discourse found their work challenged and even censored for being divisive or even politically seditious.[10]

Meanwhile, there no longer existed a clear distinction between the so-called "Church papists" and the recusants, because the latter group increasingly did not perceive the ceremony of the established church to be foreign to their own

---

[7] Milton, *Catholic and Reformed*, 50–52.

[8] As Russell and others have noted, it is simplistic and inaccurate to reduce the early seventeenth-century world to one in which the conformists and the Puritans comprised a two-party system. The situation was more complex. See Conrad Russell, *Unrevolutionary England 1603–1642*, xxiii; Russell, *The Fall of the British Monarchies*, 15–26; Peter Lake, "Calvinism and the English Church 1570–1635," *Past and Present* 114 (1987): 32–76; Sharpe, *Personal Rule of Charles*, 275–402; Julian Davies, *Caroline Captivity of the Church* (New York, 1992); James Loxley, *Royalism and Poetry in the English Civil Wars: The Drawn Sword* (New York, 1997), 13–15. See also Nicholas Tyacke, *Anti-Calvinists: The Rise of English Arminianism c. 1590–1640* (New York, 1987); Tyacke, "Puritanism, Arminianism, and Counter Revolution," in *The Origins of the English Civil War*, ed. Russell (New York, 1973), 119–43.

[9] Laud himself, however, had written an important and influential rebuttal of the claims of the papacy. See William Laud, *A relation of the conference between William Laud, late Lord Arch-Bishop of Canterbury, and Mr Fisher the Jesuite* (London, 1673). For context, see Kevin Sharpe, *Personal Rule of Charles I*, 284–301; Peter Lake, "The Laudian Style: Order, Uniformity, and the Pursuit of Beauty of Holiness in the 1630's" in *The Early Stuart Church, 1603–1642*, ed. Kenneth Fincham (Stanford, 1993), 161–85.

[10] Milton, *Catholic and Reformed*, 71. For background on the relationship between Puritans and the established church, see Peter Lake, *The Boxmaker's Revenge: "Orthodoxy," "Heterodoxy" and the Politics of the Parish in Early Stuart London* (Stanford, 2001), and Kenneth C. Fincham and Peter Lake, "The Ecclesiastical Policy of King James I," *Journal of British Studies* 24.2 (1985): 169–207. As for the Elizabeth period, see Peter Lake, *Anglicans and Puritans? Presbyterianism and English Conformist Thought from Whitgift to Hooker* (London, 1988) and Peter Lake, *Moderate Puritans and the Elizabethan Church* (Cambridge, 1982).

traditions and were therefore conforming in increasing numbers.[11] In fact, this seems to have been part of the Laudian plan for attracting more Roman Catholic recusants to the established church. But far from unifying the church on the basis of established doctrine, both newcomers and existing conformists were increasingly confused by an intentional blurring between the national and the Roman Catholic rite.[12] At the same time that such transformations in attitudes towards recusants and the Roman Church were occurring within conformist circles, other important shifts were occurring among Roman Catholic attitudes toward Rome. Without a unifying figure such as Cardinal William Allen, tensions within the Catholic community both at home and abroad emerged between the supporters of the Archpriest, George Blackwell, and the appellant supporters of the papal appointment of an English bishop. The appellant controversy revealed the existence of longstanding tensions between the Jesuit regulars and the secular parish priests, who increasingly viewed the Jesuits as rebellious interlopers, ignoring their monastic vows in order to meddle in affairs that had traditionally belonged within the gamut of the seculars' authority. For their part, the Jesuits viewed their secular counterparts as provincial and superstitious traditionalists, who were either unwilling or incapable of adapting to the new reality of the counter-reformation. At one time, the appellant controversy was viewed as a victory for those elements within the English Catholic community that chose loyalty to the queen over loyalty to the pope; however, given that the appeal was directed to the pope and therefore implicitly acknowledged his authority, the appellant perspective was never one that placed loyalty to the English crown over religious authorities.[13]

Still, the appellant controversy presaged the emergence of an important distinction between English Catholic expressions of loyalty to the Court of Rome and loyalty to the Church of Rome.[14] Subsequent controversies surrounding the Oath of Allegiance of 1606 did not follow precisely the lines of division established by the prior conflict, but the result was similarly disruptive to the Catholic cause, causing a rift between those Catholics who believed they could take the oath without abandoning their fundamental spiritual allegiance to Rome and those that did not. The Catholic response to both the Gunpowder Plot and the Oath was complex and heterogeneous. In his first breve to King James, Pope Paul V condemned the plot and called for English Catholics to maintain their obedience to the crown in its aftermath, while also unequivocally proscribing the Oath itself. Perhaps misunderstanding the papal call for civil obedience, Blackwell advised English Catholics that they could submit to the Oath in good conscience. After he was captured and examined in June 1607, Blackwell went on to take the Oath himself. Even after the publication of a second papal breve and a letter by Fr. Robert Bellarmine, S.J. reiterating the curia's official condemnation of the Oath, Blackwell continued to maintain his position by drawing a distinction between

---

[11]   Milton, *Catholic and Reformed*, 52–4.
[12]   Milton, *Catholic and Reformed*, 83.
[13]   Basset, *The English Jesuits*, 90–91, Houliston, *Catholic Resistance*, 120.
[14]   Milton, *Catholic and Reformed*, 340–45.

Part II Introduction   217

the pope's obvious right to excommunicate the king and the more extreme claim that papal excommunication of a temporal ruler was the equivalent of deposition.[15]

In the aftermath of Blackwell's capture and imprisonment, King James I published an anonymous defense of the Oath of Allegiance, the *Triplici nodo, triplex cuneus*, and Persons promptly responded in a series of refutations of the official English position.[16] In his *Judge-ment of a Catholicke Englishman* and his subsequent *Discussion of the Answer of M. William Barlow*, Persons focused less on the papal deposing power itself and more on the impossible demands that the King was making of his Catholic subjects, who after all had only sought "liberty of Conscience, and equality with other Subiects."[17] While Persons drew attention to the difficult situation in which English Catholics found themselves, it fell to Bellarmine and Francisco Suárez, S.J. to clarify the doctrine of papal authority over temporal rulers. Bellarmine's characterization of the papal deposing power as derived from a *potesta indirecta* was very different from the account offered by Sander and Persons, who had never drawn any such distinction between direct and indirect authority. In this respect, his notion of the pope's *potesta indirecta* was an innovative clarification of earlier ideas on the subject. According to Bellarmine, the pope was not, as Cecil had averred in the *Execution of Justice*, simply a temporal prince bent on usurping legitimate sovereigns when it suited his interests.[18] Outside of his traditional sovereignty over the papal states, the pope had no temporal power, only spiritual power. In his response to the Erastianism of William Barclay, who had put forth an absolutist argument establishing that the French king enjoyed supreme authority over the Gallican Church, Bellarmine explained,

> In regard of all other Christian provinces and Christian princes, (theologians) accord to the Pope only a spiritual power [*potestam solum spiritualem*], which of itself properly regards only the spiritual, and regards the temporal only as it is

---

[15] *A Large Examination taken at Lambeth, according to his Maiesties direction, point by point, of M. George Blackwell* (London, 1607), C4v–F4v. See also *Mr. George Blackwel, (Made by Pope Clement 8. Arch-priest of England) his Answeres vpon sundry his Examinations: Together with his Approbation and taking of the Oath of Allegeance: And his Letter written to his Assistants, and brethren, moouing them not onely to take the said Oath, but to aduise all Romish Catholikes so to doe* (London, 1607). For context, see Houliston, *Catholic Resistance*, 139–43; Bossy, *The English Catholic Community*, 41–8; Questier, *Catholicism and Community*, 344.

[16] Anon. [King James I], *Triplici nodo, triplex cuneus: or, an Apologie for the Oath of Allegiance, Against the two Breues of Pope Pavlvs Qvintus, and the late Letter of Cardinal Bellarmine to G. Blackwel the Arch-priest* (London, 1607 [vere 1608]).

[17] Persons, *The Ivdgment of a Catholicke English-man, living in banishment for his Religion ... Concerninge A late Booke set forth, and entituled: Triplici nodo, triplex cuneus, Or An Apologie for the Oath of Allegiance* (St. Omer, 1608), E4v; Persons, *A Discussion of the Answere of M. William Barlow, D. of Diuinity, to the Book intituled: The Iudgment of a Catholicke Englishman* (St. Omer, 1612).

[18] Cecil, *Execution of Justice*, C3–D4v. For a defense of the pope's claim to execute some temporal powers, see Allen, *A True, Sincere and Modest Defence of English Catholics*, vol. 2, 62–7.

subordinate to the spiritual [*subordinantur spiritualibus*]. And therefore, when we speak properly, we say that the Pope has a power in the temporal [*Potestate in temporalibus*], but as Pope he has no temporal power [*potestam temporale*]. From which it follows that the difference conveyed by the terms 'direct' and 'indirect' does not refer to the manner of acquiring the power, as Barclay falsely asserts; the words are used to set forth the secondary, and consequent [*secundarium, & consectaneum*], object of the supreme spiritual power, which primarily and directly regards the spiritual, and regards the temporal secondarily and indirectly, that is, in its relation to the spiritual [*secundario & indirecte, id est, in ordine ad spiritualia, respicit temporalia*].[19]

In contrast to Sander and Persons for whom it was enough to assert the superiority of the spiritual realm over the temporal realm to justify the papal power to depose a temporal sovereign, Bellarmine clarified that whatever supremacy the pope wielded over the temporal realm was "indirect." Indeed, the pope enjoyed no true temporal authority over a particular kingdom; rather any temporal authority he did enjoy proceeded only from the fact that he held supreme authority over the spiritual realm, which was superior to the temporal. Later, Bellarmine explained that the pope does not hold the ordinary jurisdiction over temporal sovereigns that he holds, for example, over his bishops, which he could depose as their ordinary judge. Rather, it was only in extraordinary circumstances that, "as the supreme spiritual ruler, he can change the royal power, taking it away from one and conferring it on another, if this be necessary for the salvation of souls."[20]

Despite these nuances, from the perspective of Bellarmine and Suárez, Blackwell's advice to English Catholics that they could take the Oath in good conscience without contradicting the pope's spiritual authority was the equivalent

---

[19] "In reliquas Prouincias Christianas, & Principes Christianos, tribuunt Pontifici potestatem solum spiritualem, quae per se, & proprie respicit spiritualia; temporalia vero respicit, vt subordinantur spiritualibus. Et ideo quando proprie loquimur, dicimus Pontificiem habere potestatem in temporalibus, non autem habere potestatem temporalem, qua Pontifex est. Ex quo sequitur vt discrimen vocum, directe & indirecte, non referatur proprie loquendo, ad modum acquirendi potestatem, vt Barclaius falso dicit; sed ad explicandum obiectum secundarium, & consectaneum supremae spiritualis potestatis, quae vt supra diximus, primario, & directe respicit spiritualia, secundario & indirecte, id est, in ordine ad spiritualia, respicit temporalia." Roberto Bellarmino, *Tractatus de potestate. Summi Pontificis in rebvs temporalibvs aduersus Gvlielmvm Barclaivm* (Coloniae Agrippinae, 1611), 15. English translation found in John Courtney Murray, "St. Robert Bellarmine on the Indirect Power," *Theological Studies* 9 (1948): 491–535, 497. For a notable Protestant response to Bellarmine, see chapter 9 of Donne, *Pseudo-Martyr*, 179–89.

[20] "Tamen potest mutare regna, & vni auferre, atq; alteri conferre, tanquam summus Princeps spiritualis, si id necessarium sit ad animarum salutem, vt probabimus." Roberto Bellarmino, *Tertia Controversia Generalis, De Svmmo Pontifice*, ed. Jacques Amyot and Simon Goulart (Ingolstadii, 1587), lib. V, cap. VI, 611. See also *Opera Omnia*, ed. Sisto Riario Sforza (Neapoli, 1856), I, 532; translation found in Murray, "St. Robert Bellarmine," 498. For context, see Tutino, *Empire of Souls*, 9–48; Houliston, *Catholic Resistance*, 142–6.

Part II Introduction 219

of encouraging them to deny their religious faith.[21] But in Blackwell's initial response to Bellarmine, which quoted extensively from prior works by both Bellarmine and Suárez, it is clear that the purpose behind Blackwell's distinction between the pope's power to excommunicate and the power to depose was to reconcile his own position with that of his Catholic critics. And despite what might seem to be Bellarmine and Suárez's definitive intervention into the debate, the entire controversy simply exacerbated the unbridgeable rift for English Catholics that was emerging between loyalty to the Roman Church and loyalty to the Roman curia.[22]

Eventually, subsequent English Catholics such as Thomas White (alias Blackloe) and Sir Kenelm Digby would be unapologetic in their choice of the former loyalty over the latter. To see how different their perspective was from the perspective of Bellarmine and Persons, one need look no further than the speech that Digby gave at a parliamentary commission to defend himself from the charge that he had tried to convert the young Thomas Pope, second Earl of Downe, to the Roman faith. Digby professed his faith to be a moderate one and went on to declare that nothing could shake his loyalty to the king: "I conceive my bond of allegeance to the King my Master and my duty of obedience to the lawe of this kingdome, to be so firme and strong as no other on earth can absolve me from it. But whenever any attempt should be made against it upon pretence of any authority whatsoever I would readily draw my sword, and expose my life and spend my fortunes in opposition of it."[23] As Stefania Tutino has noted, Digby seems to have seen no conflict between his political and religious allegiances and furthermore to have believed that the English Catholic cause was equivalent to the king's political cause.[24]

White's position on political obedience, while bearing certain similarities to Digby's, had been further radicalized by the execution of King Charles I and the rise of the Commonwealth government. His seminal political work, *The Grounds of Obedience and Government* (1655), melded consent theory with Catholic theology and the doctrine of natural law. According to White, the state had as its *telos* an Aristotelian notion of the common good, which it was the purpose of the government to foster and pursue. If the supreme magistrate failed to pursue

---

[21]   In this respect, both Bellarmine and Suárez considered the Oath of Allegiance to be the latest in a series of usurpations of papal sovereignty over the spiritual realm that had been initiated by James and Elizabeth before him. In the *Defensio Fidei Catholicae et Apostolicae* (1613), Suárez responded to the Oath by reaffirming the pope's right to depose a usurper or a heretical or tyrannical king. Suárez argued that the Oath of Allegiance, ironically intended by James to forestall potential usurpation of the English crown, itself constituted a usurpation of the pope's ecclesiastical authority. Suárez, *A Defense of the Catholic and Apostolic Faith*, in *Selections from Three Works*, vol. 2, 724.

[22]   Milton, *Catholic and Reformed*, 263–9.

[23]   British Library, Additional Mss. 41846, ff. 113r–117v, at f.115v. Cited in Stefania Tutino, *Thomas White and the Blackloists: Between Politics and Theology during the English Civil War* (Burlington, VT, 2008), 11.

[24]   Tutino, *Thomas White and the Blackloists*, 10–11.

220   *Early Modern Catholics, Royalists, and Cosmopolitans*

the common good or was perceived to be striving against the common good, then according to White, it was natural for men to resist him. Resistance came about because the magistrate had violated his "contract" with the people, whose own contractual obligations stipulated that they would obey him insofar as their own obedience would result in the commonwealth's common good. White's controversial endorsement of Cromwell's regime followed from his contract theory, for at a certain point in the *Grounds*, White concludes that pursuing the common good justifies maintaining Cromwell's government even if King Charles II is the lawful possessor of the throne, since it is clearly in the best interests of the people "to stay as they are, then to venture the restoring of him [Charles II], because of the publicke hazard."[25] White's position on the people's right to resist an unjust magistrate has led many commentators to draw parallels with the views on resistance of Sander, Persons, and Suárez.[26] But in reality, White's position on the common good is very different from the Jesuits. As Victor Houliston has shown, for Persons and the tradition of resistance that he represents, the custodians of the people's will are not the elected members of parliament but rather the archbishop or bishop who presides over the sovereign's coronation oath. As we have seen, Persons thought that only religious authorities could authorize a rebellion against and the deposition of a heretical or tyrannical sovereign.[27]

In contrast, White's plan for the English Catholic Church was essentially based on an Erastian model that was closer to Thomas Hobbes's position that the subject could cede practically everything to the state—even his religious instruction—than to Persons's position that the governors of the temporal state must be supervised by the caretakers of the spiritual realm.[28] Indeed, the 1647 proposal for Catholic toleration that the Blackloists drew up introduced a radical reform into the relationship between the pope and English Catholics. According to Henry Holden and White's formulation in the 1647 declaration, in return for parliament recognizing the natural rights of English Catholics, the Catholics should be prepared to undergo a radical transformation of the traditional episcopal governance structure. According to the document, Catholics should be governed by six or eight bishops that would be chosen and ordained by parliament, and the pope should "have no Power over them to the preiudice of the state."[29] John Bossy has correctly pointed to Holden and White's plan as severing "the connection between the envisaged Catholic Church

---

[25]   Thomas White, *The Grounds of Obedience and Government* (London, 1655), G9. For background, see Tutino, *Thomas White*, 71–3, and Wolfram Schmidgen, *Exquisite Mixture: The Virtues of Impurity in Early Modern England* (Philadelphia, 2013), pp. 59–101.

[26]   See, for example, Tutino, *Thomas White*, 71, and Schmidgen, *Exquisite Mixture*, pp. 77–8.

[27]   Houliston, *Catholic Resistance*, 83–5.

[28]   Tutino, *Thomas White*, 78.

[29]   R. Pugh, *Blacklo's Cabal Discovered in severall of their Letters Clearly expressing Designs Inhvmane against Regulars, Vnivst against the Laity, Scismatical against the Pope, Crvel against Orthodox Clergy men And owning the Nvllity of the chapter, their opposition of Episcopall Authority* (s.l, 1680), 36–40, at 37. For background, see Tutino, *Thomas White*, 44–5.

Part II Introduction

and the Pope," and thus, it is no surprise that the Blackloists were overwhelmingly condemned as heretic separatists by the Roman curia and the Jesuits.[30] The 1647 proposal for toleration demonstrates that White, despite his support for the doctrine of popular resistance, was distinct from the Jesuit tradition of Catholic resistance both in terms of his conception of the common good and in terms of his notion of the relationship between church and state.[31]

And yet, it is also clear that contemporaries tended to blur the distinction between White's position and what they perceived as Persons's position. Thus in 1648, for example, attempting to provide a rationale to justify the deposition of King Charles I, parliamentarians appropriated excerpts of Persons's *Conference* under the title, *Severall Speeches Delivered At a Conference concerning the Power of Parliament, to proceed against their King for Misgovernment.*[32] As we have seen in Chapter 1, Persons's *Conference* is organized as a dialogue between a civil lawyer, who declares in Part 1 that he is an expert in the canon and civil law, and a "Temporall Lawyer," who in Part 2 recounts the "particular titles" that potential claimants might make to the English throne.[33] Throughout Part 1 of the *Conference*, the civil lawyer instructs the temporal lawyer on the nature of monarchical government and the limits that the ecclesiastical authorities and parliamentary bodies place on sovereigns, thereby replicating the traditional English Jesuit conception of the relationship between the spiritual and the temporal realms that we have become familiar with from Chapter 1. In contrast, the *Severall Speeches* reduces Persons's *Conference* to a series of anonymous speeches, without identifying the civil lawyer as their origin or the temporal lawyer as his interlocutor. Indeed, the very title of the pamphlet announcing that the "Severall Speeches" contained therein were delivered "at a Conference concerning the Power of Parliament" suggests that the speeches were nine separate arguments made by supporters of the English parliament in favor of the deposition of King Charles, rather than one continuous argument delivered by a representative of the ecclesiastical realm meant to educate a representative of the temporal realm. The *Severall Speeches* is ambiguous on the source of the parliament's power to depose the king. On the one hand, some of the speeches transcribed in the pamphlet do reproduce Persons's original invocation of the "canon law" (that is, appeals to "our law both Civill & Canon" are used to

---

For context on the parliamentary and Puritan view that the parliament should oversee the church and church doctrine, see Russell, *The Fall of the British Monarchies*, 231–6.

[30] Bossy, *English Catholic Community*, 66.

[31] Thus, White's perspective provides an excellent example of Thomas Morton's description of those English Catholics who privileged the Roman Church over the Court of Rome. Thomas Morton, *A Discharge of Five Imputations of Mis-Allegations, Falsly Charged upon the (now) Bishop of Duresme, by an English Baron* (London, 1633), T3v–T4.

[32] Anon. [Robert Persons], *Severall Speeches Delivered At a Conference concerning the Power of Parliament, to proceed against their King for Misgovernment* (London, 1648). For context, see J.B. Williams [J.G. Muddiman], "Puritan Piracies of Father Persons' 'Conference,'" *The Month* 117 (1911): 270–78.

[33] Persons, *A Conference*, title page, F6.

justify limitations on the power of the monarchy).[34] On the other hand, the tract omits, in the fifth speech, entitled, "The Coronation of Princes, and manner of their admitting to their authority," the civil lawyer's original parenthetical declaration that the canon law "is part also of my profession."[35] Hence, the "Severall Speeches" seeks to eliminate the original tension between the ecclesiastical and the temporal realm that characterizes Persons's *Conference*, even while retaining the authority of the civil and canon law in order to advance a universal argument in favor of the English parliament's right to depose King Charles.

Once the English civil war had commenced, Catholics within the three kingdoms were pre-disposed to side with Charles I simply to maintain the sovereign who had used his royal power to provide some security to their own tenuous existence. And it is here that one finds the most important common element between English Catholics at the turn of the seventeenth century and both Catholic and conformist royalists at the beginning of the civil war. It is worth recalling in Chapter 3 that Persons's refutation of Coke's *Reports* primarily focused on Coke's claim that the ecclesiastical courts should be subordinate to the common law courts. But he began his defense of equity and the ecclesiastical courts by defending the right of the "iust Prince" to "administer iustice, by law of nature [i.e. equity] and nations, if he will."[36] Behind Persons's defense of the extraordinary power of the prince to exercise the prerogative, of course, was an implicit defense of the pope's analogous right to exercise his extraordinary powers to depose a heretical or tyrannical sovereign. For Persons, Coke's attempt at limiting and restricting the so-called prerogative courts was an attempt to limit both the sovereign's extraordinary power to administer justice and the pope's analogous power to exercise his own prerogative. Similarly, the tensions that led up to the civil war consisted of a conflict over the king's power to use his prerogative to raise revenue for the crown without having to consult with parliament, which in turn sought to curb the royal prerogative. In this respect, the late sixteenth-century attempt by Jesuits to defend the pope's extraordinary powers against the encroachment of temporal rulers was almost indistinguishable from both the Catholic and the *conformist* royalist position on the legitimacy of Charles I's right to exercise his royal prerogative.

As we shall see in the next chapter, the cosmopolitan investment in the traditional conception of the transnational Christian commonwealth, which persisted within royalist political theory, remained as an essential legacy of the late sixteenth-century English Catholic exiles. Once King Charles had been deposed and executed in 1649, the Erastianism that the English sovereigns had formerly promoted might have seemed an impediment to the restoration of the monarchy since no supporter of the king's claim to the throne could now make a retroactive case for its restoration based on papal oversight.[37] Given the English sovereign's

---

[34]   Anon. [Robert Persons], *Severall Speeches*, D2, D2v, D3.

[35]   Anon. [Rober Persons], *Severall Speeches*, D2; Persons, *A Conference*, F6.

[36]   Persons, *An Answere*, B3v.

[37]   For a discussion of the royalist conception of the relationship between monarch and nation, see de Groot, *Royalist Identities*, 20–54.

position as head of the ecclesiastical realm, the English king's legitimacy could not be supported by reference either to the pope's transnational authority over the Christian commonwealth or to the Catholic cosmopolitanism that we explored respectively in the works of Sander and Persons. The obvious question then is who inherited the tradition of transnationalism that is celebrated in the works of these late sixteenth century writers? How was one to justify the restoration of the English monarchy without reference to transnational values that encompassed the three kingdoms? It is my argument in the following chapter that an innovative conception of the Christian commonwealth emerged in the royalist use of the epic genre in order to address this complex question.

Chapter 5
From Foreign War to Civil War: The Royalist Reinvention of the Christian Commonwealth

During the civil war and its aftermath, two competing foundational claims for the sovereignty of princes coexisted. On the one hand, supporters of the monarchy sought to justify the king's legitimacy on the basis of divine right, the legacy of James I's famous tract, *The True Law of Free Monarchies*, which maintained both that the king owed his authority to his role as God's representative and that, on that basis, there could be no basis for the resistance against a legitimate sovereign.[1] On the other hand, a competing claim, first put forward in the sixteenth-century anonymous Huguenot tract, *Vindiciae, contra Tyrannos,* that legitimate authority could only be justified on the basis of a social contract between the people and their sovereign, became the preferred theory of the supporters of the parliament, since it justified the deposition of Charles on the basis of the claim that such an implied contract had been violated.[2] The civil war and the execution of King Charles I had done great damage to the first rationale for legitimate sovereignty, but as I show in this chapter, Sir Richard Fanshawe sought to use the epic to reinvent the tradition of divine right by linking it to ancient protective and mutually beneficial alliances between threatened Christian sovereigns. As I show, this is one legacy of the earlier religious-inspired form of cosmopolitanism that sought to protect and correct legitimate sovereignty and correct and depose illegitimate sovereigns.

Nigel Smith and David Norbrook have written eloquently on the way in which the epic genre was used during the English civil war to provide commentary on current events.[3] During the Elizabethan and Jacobean periods, Virgil's *Aeneid* enjoyed the most prominence among the ancient epics, in terms of English

---

[1] James VI and I, *The Trew law of Free Monarchies*, in *The Political Works of James I*, ed. Charles Howard McIlwain (New York, 1965), 53–70, esp. 58–9.

[2] Anon., *Vindiciae contra Tyrannos*, 138. For context, see Quentin Skinner, *The Foundations of Modern Political Thought*, vol. 2, 318–38. For the most famous seventeenth-century adherents to the notion of a social contact, see Hugo Grotius, *De iure praedae commentarius*, vol. 1, trans. G. L. Williams (New York, 1950), 91–2, and Thomas Hobbes, *Leviathan*, ed. with intro. Richard Tuck (New York, 1991), 94–100; For a broader understanding of Grotius's and Hobbes's views on sovereignty in the context of their discussion of the international sphere, see Tuck, *Rights of War and Peace*, 1–16, 78–139.

[3] David Norbrook, *Writing the English Republic: Poetry, Rhetoric, and Politics, 1627–1660* (New York, 1999); Nigel Smith, *Literature and Revolution in England, 1640–1660* (New Haven, CT, 1994).

226   *Early Modern Catholics, Royalists, and Cosmopolitans*

translations and imitation, but during the civil war, while imitation and translation of Virgil continued among royalist writers, the epic that occupied the most prominent role was undoubtedly Lucan's *Pharsalia*, also known as *De Bello Civili*, the unfinished account of the events of the civil war between Julius Caesar and the Roman Senate.[4] Lucan originally wrote his epic as a pro-republican account of the rise of Julius Caesar and the end of the Roman republic—ultimately, the work that he produced constituted a refutation and parody of the Virgilian epic, meant to show that the epic could never accurately represent the chaotic forces at work in a civil war. Lucan's epic was also a political intervention into contemporary Roman politics during the reign of Emperor Nero, whom he later conspired to overthrow in a plot that eventually led to the young poet committing suicide while reciting his own pro-republican poetry. In terms of seventeenth century English politics, Norbrook has written eloquently about how "Lucan was the central poet of the [English] republican imagination, and his traces can be found again and again amongst leading Parliamentarians."[5] But as Nigel Smith has noted, royalists were also willing to appropriate Lucan's *Pharsalia* for their own purposes, in spite of the bizarre set of analogies that such appropriations often caused.[6]

The most important translation of Lucan's *Pharsalia* during this period was that of Thomas May, who would later become a supporter of parliament and would eventually be commissioned to write the *History of Parliament*, which appeared in 1647.[7] The first three books of May's translation of Lucan's *Pharsalia* first appeared in 1626, followed in 1627 by the complete translation, and his own English Continuation of the *Pharsalia* in 1630.[8] In 1640, May's *Supplementum Lucani*—the Latin translation of his English continuation of the *Pharsalia*—appeared in print in Leiden, prefaced by a collection of commendatory verses by friends.[9] Among those who contributed was Richard Fanshawe, who would later become Secretary of War to Charles II during the civil war. As Syrithe Pugh has noted recently, Fanshawe is often characterized, based on a superficial reading of the "Ode on the Proclamation" as an inveterate and unyielding absolutist, a view which does not do justice to the complexity of his views on governance.[10] Pugh's

---

[4]   Smith, *Literature and Revolution*, 203–4.

[5]   Norbrook, *Writing the English Republic*, 24.

[6]   Smith, *Literature and Revolution*, 207–17.

[7]   Smith, *Literature and Revolution*, 205.

[8]   Thomas May, *Lvcan's Pharsalia: or the Civill Warres of Rome, betweene Pompey the great and Ivlivs Cæsar. The three first Bookes* (London, 1626). May, *Lucan's Pharsalia: or The Civill Warres of Rome, betweene Pompey the great, and Ivlivs Cæsar: The whole ten Bookes*. Englished by Thomas May (London, 1627). May, *A Continvation of Lucans Historicall Poem till the death of Ivlivs Cæsar* (London, 1630).

[9]   Thomas May, *Supplementum Lvcani librii VII* (Lugduni Batavorum, 1640).

[10]   See, for example, Loxley's reading of this poem in *Royalism and Poetry in the English Civil Wars*, 46–8. For discussion of the city-versus-country opposition in this poem as it relates to how Fanshawe saw England within an international context, see Hammond, *Fleeting Things: English Poets and Poems 1616–1660* (Cambridge, MA, 1990), 26–8.

work on Fanshawe relies on analysis of the diplomat's early poetry and translations in order to suggest that in fact Fanshawe was committed to limited monarchy. Fanshawe's early English translation and dedication to Prince Charles II of the *Genethliacon*—George Buchanan's poem originally composed to commemorate the birth of James VI—in 1645 is perhaps the best example of Fanshawe's use of poetic translation in order to make the case for limited monarchy.[11]

Pugh's argument that Fanshawe intended his translation of Buchanan's *Genethliacon* to be read as a remonstrance of King Charles I for his dereliction of proper governance seems clear enough, but her additional claim, that Fanshawe was a champion of limited monarchy and rejected the absolutist claims of the king and his father, James I, is less convincing. Certainly, one possible interpretation of certain lines in Fanshawe's translation such as, "They [the people] serve, because they need not serve [*Et domino servit, quia non servire necesse est*]" and "And of their own accords [they] invite that yoke, / Which if inforc't on them, they would have broke [*Deposcitque jugum quod vi cogente metuque / Rejecturus erat*]," is that the English people have the power of consent over the laws that govern them (53, 55–6).[12] Similarly, Fanshawe's inclusion, during his translation of Buchanan's condemnation of typical tyrants, of Buchanan's negative reference to Catiline, who led the failed conspiracy against the Roman senate during the first century BCE, is an indication that Pugh is not wrong to ascribe some belief in limited monarchy to Fanshawe (102).[13] At the same time, other verses suggest a more complex picture:

> And *Hee* [the king] again, with this more tender grown
> More *Father of his People*, on his *owne*
> *Shoulders* assumes *their burthens*, beats the way
> Which they must tread, and is the first t'*obey*
> What he *commands*; to pardon others prone,
> Inexorable to *himself* alone.

> [*contra indulgentior ille*
> *Rexque paterque suis adimit, subit ipse labores,*
> *Quaeque jubet primus praeit, et legum aspera jussa*
> *Mollia parendo facit, erratisque suorum*
> *Parcere non durus, sibi inexorabilis uni.*] (57–62)

---

[11] Syrithe Pugh, *Herrick, Fanshawe and the Politics of Intertextuality: Classical Literature and Seventeenth-Century Royalism* (Burlington, VT, 2010), 4, 99–119. See also Gareth Alban Davies, "Sir Richard Fanshawe, Hispanic Cavalier," *University of Leeds Review* 20 (1977): 87–119. For the text of Buchanan's *Genethliacon*, see *George Buchanan: A Memorial*, ed. David Alexander Millar (St. Andrews, 1907), 324–31; See also George Buchanan, *George Buchanan: The Political Poetry*, ed. and trans. Paul J. McGinnis and Arthur H. Williamson, Scottish Historical Society, 5th series, no. 8 (Edinburgh, 1995).

[12] English citations in parenthesis are from Sir Richard Fanshawe, "Presented to His Highnesse, in the West, Ann. Dom. 1646," in *The Poems and Translations of Sir Richard Fanshawe*, ed. Peter Davidson (2 vols, New York, 1999), vol. 1, 143–6. The Latin is from Buchanan, *George Buchanan: A Memorial*, ed. Millar, 325.

[13] Pugh, *Herrick, Fanshawe*, 97–105.

228   *Early Modern Catholics, Royalists, and Cosmopolitans*

This passage suggests that the king's subjects exist in a kind of symbiosis with him, such that the king's self-restraint and good behavior provides an example, which his subjects willingly follow. Indeed, Buchanan's original poem was intended as an extended commentary on the future education of the infant prince, James VI. Accordingly, the most important manner in which the king's powers are "limited" are through his personal education, by which the monarch would ideally learn to "curb his pleasures, and suppresse / Those weeds which make a *Man* a *Wildernesse* [*Ipse voluptatum cum Princeps frena coercet, / Et nimium laetam vitiorum comprimit herbam*]" (75).

Pugh would no doubt mostly agree with my assessment of this poem and Fanshawe's other early writings. Fanshawe's Latin poem, *Maius Lucanizans*, intended to celebrate May's *Supplementum*, the Latin version of his *Continuation of Lucan's historicall poem*, is according to Pugh yet another indication of Fanshawe's investment in limited monarchy. But in fact, as she notes, Fanshawe's celebration of May's *Supplementum* has very little to do with restrictions placed on monarchy by the representatives of the people.[14] Rather, Fanshawe once again emphasizes sovereignty that is judicious and honorable, owing to the instruction and counsel provided by poets such as May and Fanshawe. *Maius Lucanizans* begins not with a celebration of republican virtue, but rather with a celebration and exaltation of the virtuous ruler over the evil emperor. Comparing Nero to Julius Caesar, Fanshawe addresses Lucan in the person of May (Lucan's ghostly incarnation) not as a defender of the republic, but rather, as Fanshawe himself aspired to be, as the caretaker of virtuous leadership:

> Vivis (Io!) Lucane sacra revocantur ab urna
> Purpurei manes, et *noto major Imago.*
> Caesareo turgent exhaustae crimine venae,
> Dum melior *Caesar* Capitolia, vindice versu,
> Conspergit moriens, ipsumque cruore *Tonantem.*

> [Lo, Lucan, you live! Your purple ghost is recalled from the sacred urn, and this apparition is greater than your well known form. Your veins, emptied by the crime of a Caesar [Nero], swell, while a better Caesar [Julius], with your verse playing the avenger, dies, and spatters with blood the Capitol and Jove himself] (1–5).[15]

Even more significantly, Fanshawe uses his poem to urge May to transform the *Pharsalia*, through his *Supplementum*, into a traditional Virgilian epic, ending with the triumphant imperial rule of Augustus Caesar, the quintessentially virtuous leader. Providing May with advice about how to end the epic, Fanshawe counsels,

> Prima *Cleopatra* Camena
> Dicta tibi, summo poscit jam carmine dici,
> Nondum tota micat, media plus parte laborat

---

[14]   Pugh, *Herrick, Fanshawe*, 151–4; 175–6.

[15]   Fanshawe, *Poems and Translations*, 77–9. Translation by Syrithe Pugh in *Herrick, Fanshawe*, 175–6.

Luminis, et privata mori, *Regina* veretur,
Altisono properes nisi tu succurrere versu
Exaequesque animos dictis, anguesque ministres.
Formam pinge *Ducum* victricem; Haud tempore victam:
Pinge *Ducem* molli vinctum fera colla cathena:
Actiacasque acies; Tyroni ubi gloria cana
Cessit. Saepe *Virum* retrahebat conscia virtus
Factorum veterum, *Martis*que innata Cupido,
Navali sed enim pugna plus posse probavit,
Aequoream *Venerem*. Fugiens quem vincere posset,
Victricem sequitur Fugientem: Et parte recedens
Imperii, laxas *Augusto* tradit habenas.
Hic suspende Tubas. Hic cum *Nasone Maronem*,
Et Flaccum, dulcesque choros agnosse *Tuorum*.
Egregius *Victor* pacato carmine Mundo
Auscultat, totamque *Hederis* indulgent *Olivam*.
Emeritus vates agat otia grata sub illo.

[Cleopatra, recounted to you by your first Muse, now demands to be told in a final song; the whole of her does not yet shine forth; it is more in the mid-part of her life's light that she toils: the Queen is afraid, unless you hurry to help with your lofty verse, to calm her spirits with your words and to provide her with serpents. Paint her beauty, a conqueress of Generals: in no way has she been conquered by time. Paint the General bound, with his fierce neck in a tender chain. Paint the battle array of Actium, where his grey eminence yielded to a beginner. Often his courage conscious of former deeds, with an innate cupidity for Mars, used to drag this man back again into the fray; but in the naval battle he proved that seaborn Venus has more power. Fleeing a man he could conquer, he follows the conqueress as she flees; and retiring from his part in empire, he hands over the slack reins to Augustus.

Here hang up your trumpet. Here recognize, along with Ovid, Virgil, and Horace too, the sweet choruses of your work! The outstanding victor [Augustus], with the world pacified by song, pays heed, and adorns the whole olive branch of peace with poetry's ivy leaves. Under him, the deserving bard may follow his favoured pursuits]. (31–50)

May's *Supplementum* to Lucan's original poem brought the history of Rome up to the assassination of Julius Caesar, presenting the assassination as retribution for Caesar's betrayal of the republic. But Fanshawe encourages May to finish the epic, by bringing the historical narrative up to the establishment of the empire under Augustus. Similarly, Fanshawe's catalogue of those Roman poets—Ovid, Virgil, and Horace—whom the poet should emulate includes only those who lived during Augustus Caesar's reign and who mostly aspired to imperial laurels rather than republican virtue. With the rise of Augustus, who takes up the slack reins from the fallen and less virtuous Antony and who "Auscultat [pays heed]" to poets like May and implicitly Fanshawe himself, we once again have a model of the sovereign led by virtuous poetry. Hence, the good sovereign is only bound—limited—by those intellectuals and poets, like Fanshawe, that are capable of inculcating good moral doctrine through their writings.

230 *Early Modern Catholics, Royalists, and Cosmopolitans*

With the exception of Fanshawe's translation of the Buchanan poem, the vast majority of Pugh's examples of limitations placed on monarchy are what she refers to as "humanist counsel," the instruction and counsel that the sovereign should expect from learned intellectuals and poets such as Fanshawe himself.[16] Pugh sees this aspect of Fanshawe's early poetry as reflective of a nostalgia, among both future royalists and republicans, for a definition of monarchy that was willingly limited by wise counsel.[17] And indeed, Fanshawe was not alone among royalists in seeing the poet or the intellectual as educating and correcting magistrates through the written word. In the preface to his epic poem, *Gondibert*, for example, William Davenant provides perhaps the best description of this aspect of the poet's function with regard to powerful rulers:

> The common Crowd (of whom wee are hopelesse) wee [poets] desert; being rather to be corrected by lawes (where precept is accompany'd with punishment) then to be taught by Poesy; for few have arriv'd at the skill of *Orpheus*, or at his good fortune, whom wee may suppose to have met with extraordinary Grecian Beasts, when so successfully he reclaim'd them with his Harpe. Nor is it needfull that Heroique Poesy should be levell'd to the reach of Common men; for if the examples it presents prevaile upon their Chiefs, the delight of Imitation (which wee hope wee have prov'd to be as effectuall to good as to evill) will rectify by the rules which those Chiefs establish of their own lives, the lives of all that behold them; for the example of life, doth as much surpasse the force of precept, as Life doth exceed Death. (13)[18]

As it is described in this passage, Davenant's notion of the poet's role is roughly equivalent to that of Fanshawe—laws are for the "common Crowd" while the poet, like the bishop or pope before him, is responsible for correcting and shaping the moral character of the magistrate.[19]

The Royalist Epic

At the center of Fanshawe's conception of sovereignty then is the traditional conception of what I call the cosmopolitan who shapes and corrects the sovereign through wise counsel. But this is only one aspect of the particular mode of cosmopolitanism that can be found in Fanshawe's corpus. The other important aspect of Fanshawe can be found in his account of the rise of the nation-state. Critics sometimes present Fanshawe as viewing the world through the lens of

---

[16]   Pugh, *Herrick, Fanshawe*, 121.

[17]   Pugh, *Herrick, Fanshawe*, 11.

[18]   All parenthetical citations to Davenant's preface are to page numbers from Gladish's edition of the poem: Sir William Davenant, *Sir William Davenant's* Gondibert, ed. David F. Gladish (New York, 1971).

[19]   For a reading of Gondibert within the context of Davenant's plays, see Kevin Sharpe, *Criticism and Compliment: The Politics of Literature in the English of Charles I* (New York, 1987), 54–108.

Virgilian epic; this is because he translated parts of the *Aeneid* as well as the most significant modern Virgilian epic of the period, Luís de Camões's *Os Lusíadas*, into English.[20] But it is clear that Fanshawe was as shaped by various accounts of the Roman civil war, to be found in Lucan and other classical writings, as he had been shaped by the *Aeneid*. Indeed, at the inception of Portugal's history as it is recounted in the first cantos of *Os Lusíadas* is the story of a civil war between Castile and the first kings of Portugal. But unlike the outcome of the English civil war, the civil war at Portugal's inception ended with an independent Portuguese sovereign who enjoys a special relationship with Christ.

Of course, Fanshawe was not the only royalist poet whose work was shaped by the interplay between Virgilian epic and Lucanian anti-epic. Indeed, to understand how Fanshawe viewed the Portuguese epic and the narrative account of the rise of the Portuguese nation found therein, it is important first to consider prior royalist attempts to apply the genre of epic to recent events within the English civil war. As Smith has noted, royalist pamphlets exploited "epic language right up to the execution of Charles," often preferring to view events through the lens of the Troy legend, "with royalist commanders appearing as Agamemnons, Parliamentarians as traitorous Thersites, and the New Model Army as destructive 'bloody Myrmidons.'"[21] This was the familiar imperial epic, the preferred language of royalism, but in at least one case, that of Abraham Cowley's *The Civil War*, the lens of Lucanian anti-epic was also incorporated into the epic form to frame the royalist perspective. Cowley wrote the existing three books of his epic during summer or autumn of 1643, at the height of the fighting between the royalists and the parliamentary forces, and he ultimately gave up work on the poem after the royalist cause suffered its decisive defeat at the first Battle of Newbury.[22] In a subsequent preface to his collected poems after parliament's victory and the execution of King Charles I, he claims to have destroyed the poem, although a truncated version of Book I was published in 1679 twelve years after his death.[23] The rest of the poem was assumed to have been lost until the discovery of two manuscript copies of the three books among the Cowper family papers in the Panshanger MSS at the Hertford County Record Office in 1967 by Allan Pritchard. As Pritchard has noted, stylistically Cowley's *Civil War* owes much to Virgil's *Aeneid*: Cowley employs the Virgilian half-line or hemistich, the classical supernatural machinery, and echoes and even translates Virgil in some of his elegies for dead royalists and

---

[20]   Norbrook, *Writing the English Republic*, 65–6, 159–60. For context, see Geoffrey Bullough, "Introduction," in *Luís de Camões The Lusiads in Sir Richard Fanshawe's Translation* (Carbondale, IL, 1963), 9–28.

[21]   Smith, *Literature and Revolution*, 212.

[22]   Allan Pritchard (ed.), *The Civil War by Abraham Cowley* (Buffalo, NY, 1973), 15. The relationship between the *Aeneid* and the *Pharsalia* is explored in depth in David Quint, *Epic and Empire: Politics and Form from Virgil to Milton* (Princeton, 1993), chs 1, 2, 4. For a discussion of how the epic form finally engulfs and disables the work's poetic form, see Loxley, *Royalism and Poetry in the English Civil Wars*, 86–8.

[23]   Abraham Cowley, *A Poem on the Late Civil War* (London, 1679).

232 *Early Modern Catholics, Royalists, and Cosmopolitans*

in his description of the battles as well.[24] However, the primary classical model in terms of content and purpose for Cowley's poem was Lucan's *Pharsalia*, with Charles's royalist forces ironically taking the place of the (eventually defeated) republican army led by Pompey. At the same time, Cowley's poem was clearly influenced by the divine right theorists that were publishing in Oxford during the first half of the English civil war.[25] The events of the civil war are framed by an elaborate theological cosmic conflict between the royalist army of the king, implicitly the earthly representative of God who supported the royalist cause, and the parliamentary forces, aided and abetted by Lucifer and the rebel angels who participated in an original rebellion in heaven. In a scene that uncannily predicts Milton's portrayal of Satan's parliament in Book II of *Paradise Lost*, the end of Book II in Cowley's poem includes an elaborate description of a parliament in hell: "Here Rebell Minds in envious torments ly; / Must here forever Live, forever Dy" (2.385–6).[26] The inhabitants of hell, rebels against God's sovereignty, forge countless acts of rebellion throughout history, and in particular, they inspire the current rebellion against the English king:

> The Sinne they Love in man, and punish most,
> Is proud Rebellion, their great Sonne, and Sire;
> Which kindled first, now blowes the'æternall fire.
> A tall and dreadfull Feind! with double Face,
> One virgin like, and full of painted Grace.
> Faire seem'd her hew, and modest seemd her guise;
> Her Eyne cast up towards Heaven in holy wise.
> From her false mouth kind words did alwayes fly,
> Religion, Reformation, Liberty! (2.400–408)

In these verses, Cowley presents the androgynous allegorical figure of Rebellion voicing parliamentary slogans, while later, Satan inveighs against "Charles his dull and godly raigne" and calls on his minions "the Bishops pride [to] behold, / Which sixteene hundred yeares hath us controul'd" (2.531–3), before commanding his followers to possess the souls of the commanders of the parliamentary forces, "Saint-Johns, the Vanes, Kimbolton, Pym, and Say," as they proceed into battle (2.545).

The cosmological context which drives the terrestrial events in this play renders Cowley's poem markedly different from Lucan's original, where the only supernatural elements are portents, the traditional consultation of oracles, and Pompey's son Sextus's meeting with the gruesome witch of Thessaly, Erictho, who

---

[24] Pritchard (ed.), *Civil War*, 40. Robert Wilcher argues that Cowley intended the verses that comprises Book 1 of the *Civil War* to be a self-contained poem, and that his plan for a larger epic, comprised of further books, came later. See Wilcher, *The Writing of Royalism 1628–1660* (New York, 2001), 183–92.

[25] Smith, *Literature and Revolution*, 105.

[26] All parenthetical citations are from Cowley, *The Civil War*, ed. Allan Prichard, referring to book and line numbers.

reveals the future by reanimating the corpses of dead soldiers.[27] For Cowley, the English civil war was part of a larger cosmological war between Heaven and Hell. God was committed to the side of Charles and his royalist supporters, and Satan was similarly committed to the parliamentary forces. The cosmological context of the poem, however, was soon overtaken by the events of history, when it was clear, after the Battle of Newbury, that the royalist cause was doomed. Cowley's response was to abandon his work and later to commit himself to religious history as the basis of epic. In an extraordinary passage from the preface to his *Poems* (1656), he explains his abandonment of the project:

> I have cast away all such pieces as I wrote during the time of the late troubles, with any relation to the differences that caused them; as among others, *three Books of the Civil War it self*, reaching as far as the first *Battel of Newbury*, where the succeeding *misfortunes* of the *party* stopt the *work*; for it is so uncustomary, as to become almost *ridiculous* to make *Lawrels* for the *Conquered* ... When the event of battel, and the unaccountable *Will* of *God* has determined the controversie, and that we have submitted to the conditions of the *Conqueror*, we must lay down our *Pens* as well as *Arms*, we must march out of our *Cause* itself, and *dismantle* that, as wel as our *Towns* and *Castles*, of all the *Works* and *Fortifications* of *Wit* and *Reason* by which we defended it. (a4)[28]

In this passage, Cowley explains that "the event of battel, and the unaccountable *Wil* of *God* has determined the controversie," therefore providing a divine judgment against the king and the royalist forces. He goes on to recommend "the *Art* of *Oblivion*" of the Athenian general, Themistocles, who according to Cicero, sought an art of forgetting rather than an art of memory (a4–a4v).[29] To forget the past and "to burn the very copies" of his first attempt at epic: this is Cowley's response to God's judgment with respect to his epic account of the English civil war (a4v).

But Cowley's response went beyond the abandonment of his first attempt at epic, causing him also to abandon completely the traditional Virgilian epic framework linking the supernatural world and the secular historical world within which European kingdoms such as England had emerged. God's judgment against the English royalist cause, of which Cowley was a representative, is incontrovertible, and to continue to celebrate a cause, which God has obviously abandoned, would be akin to blasphemy. Cowley might have given up on the entire ideology of the divine right of kings, but as we shall see, his transformation was more limited, amounting to a more modest recognition that Charles was simply not God's representative on earth. In response, he turned to writing epics about religious history, wherein one could legitimately draw a linkage between the divine and

---

[27] See *Lucan*, trans. J.D. Duff (Cambridge, MA, 1928).

[28] Parenthetical citations are to the signatures from Abraham Cowley, *Poems: Viz. I. Miscellanies II. The Mistress, or, Love Verses. III. Pindarique Odes. And IV. Davideis, or, A Sacred Poem of the Troubles of David* (London, 1656).

[29] Cicero, *De Oratore*, trans. E.W. Sutton, ed. H. Rackham (Cambridge, MA, 1967), II.lxxiv. 298–300.

the terrestrial. In his second attempt at epic, Cowley wrote the *Davideis*, a heroic poem based on the life of King David and the divinely sanctioned nation of which he was the chief representative. Putting a definitive date of composition on the *Davideis* is nearly impossible, with some commentators even arguing that Cowley started writing the poem at Oxford before the civil war broke out, but whatever the date of its original inception, it is clear that the final version, eventually included in the *Poems* (1656), contained passages that Cowley had adapted from his earlier *Civil War*.[30] And indeed, in his preface to the *Poems*, Cowley describes a progressive transition away from the classical and historical epic towards an epic based on religious history.[31] Whereas before it was the republican cause that had been corrupted by Satan's influence, now it is secular poetry itself that shows Satanic influences, and Cowley explains that the *Davideis* is an attempt to recover poetry from such devilish corruption:

> Amongst all holy and consecrated things which the *Devil* ever stole and alienated from the service of the *Diety*; as *Altars, Temples Sacrifices, Prayers*, and the like; there is none that he so universally, and so long usurpt, as *Poetry*. It is time to recover it out of the *Tyrants* hands, and to restore it to the *Kingdom* of *God*, who is the *Father* of it. It is time to *Baptize* it in *Jordan*, for it will never become clean by bathing in the *Waters* of *Damascus* ... . Besides, though those mad stories of the *Gods* and *Heroes* [from the Classical world], seem in themselves so ridiculous; yet they were then the *whole Body* (or rather *Chaos*) of the *Theologie* of those times. They were believed by all but a few *Philosophers*, and perhaps some *Atheists*, and served to good purpose among the *vulgar* (as pitiful things as they are) in strengthening the authority of *Law* with the terrors of *Conscience*, and Expectation of certain rewards, and unavoidable punishments. There was no other *Religion*, and therefore *that* was better then *none at all*. But to us who have no need of them, to us who deride their *folly*, and are wearied with their *impertinencies*, they ought to appear no better arguments for *Verse*, then those of their worthy *Successors*, the *Knights Errant*. (b2–b3)

In this passage, Cowley criticizes the pagan epic—"those mad stories of the *Gods* and *Heroes*"—as based on untruths, their only real purpose being a form of Machiavellian education of the "vulgar" by means of "strengthening the authority of *Law* with the terrors of *Conscience*." In contrast, Cowley goes on to explain his own epic as participating in the most virtuous tradition of poetry, namely "the

---

[30] See Cowley, *Poems*, Aaaa1–Tttt5v. For the dating of the *Davideis*, see Thomas Sprat, "An Account of the Life and Writings of Mr Abraham Cowley," preface to the *Works of Mr. Abraham Cowley* (London, 1668), c1; Arthur H. Nethercot, *Abraham Cowley: The Muse's Hannibal* (Oxford, 1931), 153–5; Frank Kermode, "The Date of Cowley's *Davideis*," *RES* 25 (1949): 154–8. For parallels between Cowley's *Civil War* and his *Davideis*, see Jean Loiseau, *Abraham Cowley, sa vie, son oeuvre* (Paris, 1931), 81, 403, and Prichard, "Introduction," *The Civil War*, 52–5.

[31] For a broader discussion of the relationship between the royalist politics of *Davideis* and the *Civil War*, see Raymond A. Anselment, *Loyalist Resolve: Patient Fortitude in the English* (Newark, DE, 1988), 155–84.

Books of the *Bible*," which "are either already most admirable and exalted pieces of *Poesie*, or are the best *Materials* in the world for it" (b3). Ultimately, Cowley's poem will serve as a kind of mirror for princes: "For what worthier *subject* could have been chosen among all the *Treasuries* of past times, then the *Life* of this young *Prince* [David]; who from so small beginnings, through such infinite troubles and oppositions, by such miraculous virtues and excellencies, and with such incomparable variety of wonderful actions and accidents, became the greatest *Monarch* that ever sat upon the most *famous* Throne of the whole Earth? whom should a *Poet* more justly seek to *honor*, then the highest person who ever *honored* his Profession?" (b2). Cowley's epic effectively removes the heroic struggle from the purview of pagan or secular history or the rise of the nation-state and empire, where God's cause is difficult if not impossible to perceive. Thus at the beginning of the poem itself, King David's rule is immediately and unproblematically identified as synonymous with God's rule, and thus, he is opposed by the hellish regime of Satan: "*Angels* and *Men* did *Peace* and *David* love, / But *Hell* did neither *Him*, nor *That* approve" (Aaaa3). As in the earlier *Civil War*, hell is once again the realm of those who "Lov'ed to *Rebel*," but in contrast to recent English history where the rebel cause eventually did prove victorious, in the religious context of *Davideis*, even Satan can be certain that his rebellion will ultimately be "*in vain*" (Aaaa2v). Moreover, all of the familiar certainties about the divine right of kings, the Christian cosmological war, and Christ's divinity, which Cowley had abandoned by giving up his first historical epic, are retrieved. For Cowley, the only legitimate subject of a heroic poem is the original nation of Israel, out of which all other nations—indeed the very notion of nationhood itself—emerged in imitation.

Other royalists employed related strategies in order to shape the genre of epic to the new reality. As we have seen, Cowley removed the epic narrative from temporal history in order to refashion the genre as one based on Biblical events, thereby recovering the genre from his earlier failed attempt to link English history to the divine. In contrast, Davenant chose to remove the epic narrative from both the Biblical contest and the secular historical context. Davenant's *Gondibert: An Heroic Poem* (1651) is set in Lombardy and involves an extended but incomplete chivalric narrative, which begins with a civil conflict between two factions of the fictional King Aribert's court, comprising the rival armies of Gondibert and Oswald.[32] Prior to the publication of Gondibert, Davenant published a preface (1650) to the poem in the form of a letter to "His Much Honor'd Friend, M. Hobbes," to which Thomas Hobbes composed a rejoinder.[33] Davenant begins the preface by addressing what he perceives as Lucan's failures within the *Pharsalia*.

---

[32] For a discussion of *Gondibert* in relation to Davenant's biography and the general history of the cavalier poets, see Stubbs, *Reprobates*, 415–38. For a discussion of Davenant's preface that relates it to the royalist politics of the day, particularly its veiled attacks on Puritan divines and parliament, see Wilcher, *Writing of Royalism*, 317–23.

[33] For a related reading of the preface to *Gondibert*, see Sharpe, *Criticism and Compliment*, 101–8.

236   *Early Modern Catholics, Royalists, and Cosmopolitans*

According to Davenant, "Lucan who chose to write the greatest actions that ever were allow'd to be true … did not observe that such an enterprize rather beseem'd an Historian, then a Poet" (4–5). This is the beginning of a constant refrain that runs through Davenant's preface, namely that good poets realize "the truth in the passions" or the "truth operative," as he later calls it, while historians prefer to record "the truth of actions" or the "Truth narrative" as he calls it later (5, 10). His own heroes, he goes on to say, are Christians, not because of Cowley's claim about the truth of Biblical scripture but rather because "the Principles of our Religion conduce more to explicable vertue" (9). Indeed, the Christian context is not valuable in and of itself; rather it allows Davenant to develop an important aspect of his poem: "My Argument I resolv'd should consist of Christian persons; for since Religion doth generally beget, and governe manners, I thought the example of their actions would prevaile most upon our owne, by being derived from the same doctrine and authority" (9). Religion has a civilizing effect on humankind, and the fact that Christianity is the religion of his audience means his own poem will also participate in the civilizing function of religious doctrine. More importantly, unlike Judaism, which forces the Jews into a "sullen separation of them selves from the rest of the humane flesh," and Islam, which "consisted in the vain pride of Empire," Christianity

> did anciently in its politicks rather promote the interest of Mankinde then of States; and rather of all States then of one; for particular endeavors only in behalfe of our owne homes, are signes of a narrow morall education, not of the vast kindnesse of Christian Religion which likewise ordain'd as well an universall communion of bosoms, as a community of Wealth. Such is Christian Religion in the precepts, and was once so in the practise. (10)

The appeal of Christianity, according to Davenant, is that it is transnational—it is coterminous with the interests of humanity rather than one state or one political entity. Moreover, it combines the interests of "all states," rather than of one state. Presumably, Davenant's ideal of the heroic poem will attempt to make the same kind of universal appeal.[34]

It is therefore no surprise to find him subsequently identifying "Heroique Poesy" as functioning analogously to the way in which the spiritual realm traditionally functions with regard to temporal magistrates. Whereas the "common Crowd" are "rather to be corrected by lawes," heroic poetry, like Persons's and Campion's bishops, directs the morality of Davenant's magistrates, the "Chiefs" of the common men:

> Nor is it needfull that Heroique Poesy should be levell'd to the reach of Common men; for if the examples it presents prevaile upon their Chiefs, the delight of Imitation (which wee hope wee have prov'd to be as effectuall to good as to

---

[34]   Contrast this post-civil-war sensibility with Davenant's earlier Caroline masques, which, according to Reid Barbour, celebrate the religious heroism of the established church. See Reid Barbour, *Literature and Religious Culture in Seventeenth-Century England* (New York, 2002), 24–34.

evill) will rectify by the rules, which those Chiefs establish of their owne lives, the lives of all that behold them; for the example of life, doth as much surpasse the force of precept, as Life doth exceed Death. (13)

And given that laws are eventually modeled after the good behavior of the "Chiefs," the "example" of those good magistrates corrects the behavior of the common men as well. In this respect, heroic poetry functions like religious doctrine, instructing magistrates and the courts in good morality, which is then applied to the body politic. Davenant expounds upon this later when he says that while poetry may be subordinate to religion in regulating the morality of the state, it effectively regulates morality by doing the same thing as religion. Moreover, in the best circumstances, it also assists in reinforcing the beneficial effects of religious doctrine:

> Poesy, which (like contracted *Essences* seems the utmost strength and activity of Nature) is as all good Arts, subservient to Religion; all marching under the same Banner, though of lesse discipline and esteeme. And as Poesy is the best Expositor of Nature (Nature being mysterious to such as use not to consider) so Nature is the best Interpreter of God; and more cannot be said of Religion. And when the Judges of Religion (which are the Chiefs of the Church) neglect the help of Moralists in reforming the People (and Poets are of all Moralists the most usefull) they give a sentence against the Law of Nature: For Nature performes all things by correspondent aids and harmony. And tis injurious not to think Poets the most usefull Moralists; for as Poesy is adornd and sublim'd by Musick, which makes it more pleasant and acceptable; so morality is sweetned and made more amiable by Poesy. (40–41)

In effect, divines should accept the assistance of poets in directing morality, which is "sweetned and made more amiable by Poesy," especially because the severity and austerity with which some divines approach their craft makes instruction in moral doctrine unpalatable. Finally, Davenant goes on to note that, throughout history, like divines, both the leaders of armies and statesmen have all been dependent on poetry in order to perfect their craft. Ultimately, it is clear that Davenant views the role that poetry plays as similar to that played by religious doctrine, that of a transnational set of values that ideally regulates the morality of sovereigns and magistrates, eventually filtering down into the common people by writ of law and the people's natural desire to imitate their superiors.

Hobbes's response to Davenant's preface reiterates Davenant's central thesis (of his preface) about the moral value of poetry, at the same time that Hobbes steers the discussion away from Davenant's comparison between the divine and the poet, substituting instead a comparison of the poet and the philosopher. Only among the ancients were divines and poets comparable, since "their Poets were their Divines; had the name of Prophets; Excercised among the People a kind of spirituall Authority" (48). Like Davenant, Hobbes thinks the purpose of the poet is to teach good morality, and that Davenant himself has "no other motive of [his] labour, but to adorne vertue, and procure her Lovers; then which there cannot be a worthier designe, and more beccoming noble Poesy" (48). But in

238 *Early Modern Catholics, Royalists, and Cosmopolitans*

contrast to Davenant's comparison between poetry and religion, Hobbes thinks that poetry is more comparable to philosophy, even assuming pre-eminence over philosophy when philosophical precepts fail, "as they have hetherto fayled in the doctrine of Morall vertue" (49–50). Hobbes goes on to explain, "He therefore that undertakes an Heroique Poeme (which is to exhibite a venerable and amiable Image of Heroique vertue) must not onely be the Poet, to place and connect, but also the Philosopher, to furnish and square his matter, that is, to make both body and soule, coulor and shaddow of his Poem out of his owne store" (50). In essence, Hobbes's effectively secularizes Davenant's original comparison between divines and poets by figuring the poet as a moral philosopher.

The poem itself continues the process of secularization, which Davenant and Hobbes began in Davenant's preface and Hobbes's *Answer*. Unlike both Cowley's *Civil War* and the *Davideis*, Davenant's *Gondibert* does not link terrestrial events to a supernatural realm. Whereas Cowley saw victory in war as tied to God's judgment, Davenant begins *Gondibert* with a meditation on war, in which God's judgment is strangely missing. Indeed, Davenant's conception of war as the necessary precondition for establishing a state based on the rule of law invokes Hobbes's idea that the international sphere, in which nation-states exist in an eternal state of war, replicates the original state of nature.[35] According to Davenant, King Aribert had perfected the study of war, which "to the good [ruler]" is "more needful ... then [study of] Law" (I.I.3).[36] War is the only force that allows sovereigns to control the chaotic forces of nature, as well as to protect and maintain the state:

4. To conquer Tumult, Nature's sodain force,
War, Arts delib'rate strength, was first devis'd;
Cruel to those whose rage has no remorse,
Least civil pow'r should be by Throngs surpris'd.

5. The feeble Law rescues but doubtfully
From the Oppressor's single Arme our right;
Till to its pow'r the wise war's help apply;
Which soberly does Man's loose rage unite.

6. Yet since on all War never needful was,
Wise *Aribert* did keep the People sure
By Laws from little dangers; for the Laws
Them from themselves, and not from pow'r secure.

---

[35] For Hobbes, who had witnessed both the Thirty Years War and the English civil war, the international scene effectively replicated the chaotic state of nature before the emergence of the state. He explained that war between nations was perpetual and that a system of natural law that would regulate such international conflict simply did not and could not exist: "The notions of Right and Wrong, Justice and Injustice have there no place. Where there is no common Power, there is no Law: where no Law, no Injustice. Force, and Fraud, are in warre the two Cardinall vertues." See Hobbes, *Leviathan*, 90.

[36] All parenthetical citations to *Gondibert* are to the book, canto, and line numbers of the Gladish edition.

7. Else Conquerors, by making Laws, o'recome
Their own gain'd pow'r, and leave mens fury free;
Who growing deaf to pow'r, the Laws grow dumb;
Since none can plead where all may Judges bee. (I.I.4–7)

This is a complex passage that requires close attention. In stanza 4, the state of nature is one of "tumult," which a "civil power" must master through the art of war, and in turn, that civil power must maintain a monopoly on violence to keep the chaotic throngs at bay. Law becomes important as a secondary measure to protect the people from "little Dangers," but law is feeble and powerless before a hostile foreign power ("the Oppressor's single arm"), against which, once again, war is necessary to protect the rule of law ("to its pow'r the wise war's help apply"). Most importantly, however, the laws should only protect the people "from themselves" without rendering them "from pow'r secure." In other words, the sovereign himself should be exempt from the law, "else conquerors … o'recome / Their own gain'd power," thereby leaving subjects free to exercise their own individual interpretation of justice (a situation in which "all may Judges bee"). The background to this passage of course is the English civil war, which Davenant seems to view as a period in which the "Laws grow dumb" and "mens fury [was] free." The Hobbesian absolutism that is implicit in these verses makes clear that the chaotic state of nature must be overcome by war, and stability must be maintained by the threat of force. Without God as the final arbiter of war and national conflict, humanity is effectively cut off from direct access to the divine powers in *Gondibert*—in addition, the priesthood is corrupt, abusing its power through oppressive taxation and depending on the warrior class for its power (II.I.50–75). Only in the court of Astragon does the Baconian study of nature reveals the new way to the divine truth, which the "schools," that is, scholastic learning, have corrupted: "Here Art by such a diligence is serv'd / As does th'unwearied Planets imitate; / Whose motion (life of Nature) has preserv'd / The world, which God vounchsaf'd but to create" (II.V.7). The philosopher, Astragon, is reminiscent of Davenant's poet from the preface, who interprets the "law of nature" (41). For Davenant and Hobbes, the poet and the philosopher replace the priest as the caretakers of the divine, which they access through the study of nature. Direct access to the divine is not possible in *Gondibert*, and the borderless, divided polity over which King Aribert presides is governed only by the sovereign threat of force.

While Cowley's revision of the epic located the plot within the context of Biblical scripture, where one could be certain of understanding God's will, Davenant utterly replaced an authoritative supernatural realm with the authority of nature, as it was interpreted by poets and natural philosophers. Ultimately, both Cowley and Davenant came up with a coherent cosmology in the wake of the collapse of the traditional belief in the divine right of kings, but at the same time, it is hard to argue that their newly-incarnated epics were not denatured and even politically irrelevant within the context of the aftermath of the English civil war.

240   *Early Modern Catholics, Royalists, and Cosmopolitans*

In contrast to Davenant and Cowley, Fanshawe was able to engage with the epic in ways that renewed its traditional transnational appeal as well as its viability as a form linking temporal history with the traditional epic architecture of the supernatural. As we shall see in the next section, Fanshawe's translation of the great Portuguese epic was central to his grand vision of a transnational ecumenical order of Christian monarchs, an order sustained by the loyal industry of diplomats and ambassadors such as Fanshawe himself.

Sir Richard Fanshawe's Translation of *Os Lusíadas*

Luís de Camões's *Os Lusíadas* is generally viewed as a traditional Virgilian epic, written in celebration of the relationship between on the one hand, the divine realm and on the other, the Portuguese people and their sovereign, who in turn are the primary agents within a narrative of national foundation and imperial expansion.[37] Fanshawe's translation of Camões's national epic, entitled *The Lusiad, or Portugals Historicall Poem*, might therefore seem to be precisely the kind of work that would support the royalist doctrine of the divine right of kings. Within the context of the genre of epic that we have been exploring here, Fanshawe's translation would seem to reclaim the traditional focus of the modern epics by Camões, Tasso, and Spenser on the relationship between the divine realm and temporal history, which Cowley and Davenant had abandoned. And given the two primary accounts of national sovereignty of the day, namely contract theory and the divine right of kings, we might assume that Fanshawe's publication of his translation would have been understood as siding with the latter.[38]

In reality, Fanshawe seems to have viewed his translation of *Os Lusíadas* through the lens of Lucan's *Pharsalia* as much as the lens of traditional Virgilian epic. Indeed, the evidence points to two divergent conclusions. On the one hand, by the time he had begun translating Camões, Fanshawe seems to have been predisposed towards Virgilian epic, having translated Book IV of the *Aeneid*, which he had published with his translation of Guarini's *Il Pastor Fido* in 1648.[39] The *Aeneid* IV contains the ill-fated love-story of Aeneas and Dido, which would

---

[37] Helgerson's argument about Camões's *Os Lusíadas* is that the poem is about the formation of "the aristocratic and the nationalist ideology already strongly associated with the classical epic." At the same time, he sees it masking certain commercial interests that were seen as in competition with traditional values. See Helgerson, *Forms of Nationhood*, 155. For Quint, *Os Lusíadas* celebrates the traditional victory of imperial forces over figures of resistance like Adamastor and the digressive romance of canto 6. See Quint, *Epic and Empire*, 113–25.

[38] For an exploration of the politics of subsequent Spanish and English translations of this poem, see Miguel Martinez, "A Poet of Our Own: The Struggle for *Os Lusíadas* in the Afterlife of Camões," *Journal for Early Modern Cultural Studies* 10.1 (2010): 71–94.

[39] Fanshawe, "The Fourth Booke of Virgills *Aeneis*," in *Poems and Translations*, vol. 1, 104–29. For background on Fanshawe's translation of *Il Pastor Fido*, see J.H. Whitfield, "Sir Richard Fanshawe and *The Faithful Shepherd*," *Italian Studies* 19 (1964): 64–82.

From Foreign War to Civil War 241

become a favorite narrative for royalists during this period, reminding them of a possible parallel with Prince Charles's itinerant and romantic exile before a hoped-for assumption of the duties of governance.[40] On the other hand, Fanshawe's translation of *Os Lusíadas* is prefaced by the translation of a poetic excerpt from Petronius's *Satiricon*, known since antiquity as the *Bellum Civile* or *De Bello Civili*, which relates in elegant poetic form the causes of and the beginning stages of the Roman civil war.[41] As we shall see, Fanshawe obviously intended his translation of the *Bellum Civile* to serve as an aesthetic guide for his reader's understanding of Camões's larger purpose in *Os Lusíadas*.

The history of how this poetic excerpt from the *Satiricon* has been used since antiquity provides some insight into the reasons why Fanshawe may have included it in the prefatory material to his publication of *The Lusiad*. From an early period, at least going back to the Carolingian period in Europe, abstracted portions of Petronius's *Satiricon* like the *Cena Trimalchionis*, the story of the Widow of Ephesus, and the brief poetic fragment called the *Bellum Civile* were circulated independently.[42] Harry Thurston Peck notes that from a very early date, this poetic fragment, explained and recited by an itinerant and impoverished poet named Eumolpus while he and his companions are travelling to the city of Crotona, was well-known, having been used for reading and instruction in the schools.[43] In the pages of *florilegia* that flourished from the eleventh century until the fourteenth century, there appear frequent abstracts from eight different passages from the *Bellum Civile*, captioned with titles. From the same period, there are four manuscript versions of the poem, with captions that had been drawn from the titled abstracts that were excerpted in the *florilegia*. These captions—*De luxuria* [On extravagance] (introducing lines 32–8, 24–6, 87–9 from Petronius's *Bellum Civile*), *De avaritia* [On greed] (for lines 40–44); *De egestate* [On want] (for lines 56–7); *De gloria* [On ambition] (for lines 61–6); and *De fortuna* [On fortune] (for lines 79–81)—show that from an early period, the exegetical focus on the poem was on the depravity of Rome that led to the civil war.[44] This interpretation is affirmed in two other manuscripts from the fifteenth century, which include more extensive interpretive apparatuses. The first bears an inscription, "*Satira Petronii*

---

[40] Pugh, *Herrick, Fanshawe*, 165–9, 172; Lois Potter, *Secret Rites and Secret Writing: Royalist Literature, 1641–1660* (New York, 1989), 77–8; Norbrook, *Writing the English Republic*, 74.

[41] Fanshawe, "Out of the Satyr of Petronius Arbiter, pag 48," in *The Lusiad, or, Portugals Historicall Poem*, in *Poems and Translations*, ed. Davidson, vol. 2, 9–26.

[42] A. Fred Sochatoff, "The Purpose of Petronius' *Bellum civile*: A Re-examination," *Transactions and Proceedings of the American Philological Association* 93 (1962): 449–58, at 452.

[43] Harry Thurston Peck, *A History of Classical Philology from the Seventh Century, B.C. to the Twentieth Century A.D.* (New York, 1911), 246.

[44] Paris. 17903, Escorial Q.i.14, Paris. 7647, and Atreb. 64. Cited in Sochatoff, "Purpose of Petronius' *Bellum civile*," 454. See also B.L. Ullman, "Petronius in the Medieval Florilegia," *Classical Philology* 25 (1930): 11–21.

242   *Early Modern Catholics, Royalists, and Cosmopolitans*

poetae sathirici contra uicia Romanorum [Satire of Petronius the satirical poet against the vices of Romans]," while the *titulus* of the second reads, "*Petronii Arbitri Satyrarum quae ex suis extat sola integra incipit. Fuit hic poeta Claudii Neronis temporibus coetaneus Parsio qui miro artifico in Romanorum auaritiam et luxuriam suis satiris inuectus est* [Here begins the only complete example of Petronius Arbiter's Satires which exists among his writings. In the time of Claudius Nero and contemporaneous with Perseus, this poet with admirable skill inveighed against the avarice and decadence of the Romans in his satires]."[45] In addition, the *argumentum* attributed to the author in both manuscripts affirms an interpretation of the poem in which the author "*Reprehendit ... uitia Romanorum* [attacked the vices of the Romans]."[46] Throughout the first century of printing, the *Bellum Civile* was alternatively published as an independent excerpt and with the rest of the *Satiricon*. As in the manuscript versions, the first edition printed in 1500 introduced the poem in familiar terms: "*Petronii Arbitri Satura, in qua vitia Romanorum reprehenduntur* [the Satire of Petronius Arbiter, in which the vices of the Romans are attacked]."[47]

Modern critical perspectives on the poem are also applicable to Fanshawe's inclusion of the poem in the front matter of his translation. There is a debate within modern criticism about whether Petronius's *Bellum Civile* is simply an imitation of Lucan's *Pharsalia*, an attempt to parody Lucan or whether it is a conservative attack on both the moral degeneracy as well as the analogous literary style that the *Pharsalia* had come to represent in Nero's Rome.[48] The latter perspective on the poem sees Petronius as displaying conservatism in both literary and moral terms, despite his well-known reputation for moral laxity and riotous living.[49] Fanshawe's use of the poem to preface his translation seems to gesture in a number of different directions. His own commentary on his translation makes clear that he saw it, in stylistic terms, as a response to and even perhaps a refutation of Lucan's *Pharsalia*. He notes that the rules that Petronius followed in his epic fragment are those that Camões would eventually follow in *Os Lusíadas*. Accordingly he writes that he included the *Bellum Civile* in order to offer a poetic map for understanding Camões's epic. His intention was

---

[45]   Codex Dresdensis Dc 141; Codex Monacensis 23713. Cited in Sochatoff, "Purpose of Petronius' *Bellum civile*," 454–5. For an examination of these manuscripts, see Sochatoff's unpublished dissertation, "The Commentaries in the Manuscripts d, k, m of Petronius"; see *Abstracts of Theses, University of Pittsburgh Bulletin* 31.1 (1934): 294–301.

[46]   According to Sochatoff, phrasing in Desdensis Dc 141 varies slightly from that of Monacensis 23713, cited here.

[47]   Petronius Arbiter, *Petronius Arbiter poeta Satyricus* (Leipzig, 1500). See Sochatoff, "Purpose of Petronius' *Bellum civile*," 455.

[48]   William Arrowsmith (trans. and ed.), *The Satyricon* (Ann Arbor, 1959), 184; Florence Theodora Baldwin, "Introduction," in *The Bellum Civile of Petronius* (New York, 1911), 12; Evan T. Sage, "Atticism in Petronius," *Transactions and Proceedings of the American Philological Association* 46 (1915): 55–7; Evan T. Sage, *Petronius: Satyricon* (New York, 1929), 208.

[49]   Sochotoff, "Purpose of Petronius' *Bellum civile*," 456–8.

From Foreign War to Civil War 243

to shew the *Rule* and *Model*, which (*indubitably*) guided our CAMOENS in the raising his GREAT BUILDING, and which (except *himself*) that I know of, no POET ever followed that *wrought in great*, whether *ancient*, or *modern*. For (to name no more) the Greek HOMER, the Latin VIRGIL, our SPENCER, and even the Italian TASSO (who had a *true*, a *great*, and *no obsolete story*, to work upon) are in effect wholly fabulous: and LUCAN (though *worthily* admired) is as much censured by *some* on the other side for sticking too close to *truth*. As FABIUS for one;— LUCAN full of flame and vigour, and most perspicuous in his Sentences: yet (that I may speak what I think) rather to be reckoned amongst orators then the poets. And SERVIUS for another, with less manners in his expression; *That which I said, that the Art of Poetry is forbidden to set down a naked story, is certain: for* LUCAN *deserved not to be in the number of* POETS, *because he seems to have compiled a* HISTORY, *rather than a* POEM. Amounting to the same which is *objected* above in the *Introduction* to this *Essay* (which glanceth *particularly* at LUCAN) and *mended* (as the *Author* thereof conceived) by the *Essay* itself, which is of a mixt nature between *Fable* and *History*.[50]

There are a number of important points that emerge in Fanshawe's commentary here. First, it is clear that Fanshawe sympathized with the view put forward in Petronius's *Bellum Civile* that the Roman civil war was the direct result of Rome having descended into depravity. At the end of his English translation of Guarini's *Il Pastor Fido*, Fanshawe included a prose and verse account of the Roman civil war, entitled, "A Summary Discourse of the Civil Warres of Rome, extracted out of the best Latine writers in Prose and Verse," which he addressed to Prince Charles.[51] As in Petronius, the incipit of the "Summary" puts forward the thesis that Rome had fallen into luxury and moral degeneracy, leading directly to the civil discord which followed.[52] Hence, both Fanshawe's translation of the *Bellum Civile*, which dwells on the topic of Roman depravity for approximately a fifth of the entire poem, and his earlier prose summary stress the theme of Rome's luxury and moral degeneracy. For its part, Lucan's *Pharsalia*, which devotes only a brief section in Book 1 to Rome's moral degeneracy, has generally been seen as de-emphasizing the Sallustian view that Rome was undermined by moral degeneration in private and public life.[53] It is possible that Fanshawe's interest in both the "Summary" and the *Bellum Civile* was to draw a parallel to the (supposed) moral degeneration that had blighted

---

[50]   Fanshawe, *The Lusiad*, in *Poems and Translations*, ed. Davidson, vol. 2, 26.

[51]   Fanshawe, Poems from *Il Pastor Fido*, in *Poems and Translations*, ed. Davidson, vol. 1, 135–42. Subsequent references appear in parenthesis.

[52]   "Most Excellent Prince, When, by the subversion of Carthage, Rome had lost her two spurres, Emulation and Feare, she sunke presently in her vertue, I mean all her vertues, except her Fortitude; there was but too much of that left still to doe her selfe mischiefe withall" (Fanshawe, "A Summary," 135).

[53]   K.F.C. Rose, *The Date and Author of the Satyricon*, with an introduction by J.P. Sullivan (Leiden, 1971), 63.

244 *Early Modern Catholics, Royalists, and Cosmopolitans*

the reign of Charles I.[54] But more likely, Fanshawe intended the *Bellum Civile* to be read as a commentary on a more recent descent into moral depravity, which fellow royalists had perceived to have occurred in the newly-founded English republic. Indeed, royalist writers had recently composed a number of dramatic works and play pamphlets, such as *The Famous Tragedy of King Charles I*, *The Levellers Levelled, Craftie Cromwell*, and *The Tragedy of that Famous Roman Oratour Marcus Tullius Cicero* (1651), in which Oliver Cromwell and his fellow republicans were represented as Machiavellian, apostate, or lascivious.[55]

Second, Fanshawe's last sentence in the passage, in which he mentions an "Introduction to this [Poetic] Essay (which glanceth particularly at Lucan)," refers directly to the original explanation of the *Bellum Civile*, in which the itinerant poet, Eumolpus, declares his intention to distinguish his own poetic attempt to convey the events of the Roman civil war from Lucan's earlier version.[56] The following is Fanshawe's translation of Eumolpus's introductory discourse to his poetic fragment: "*Behold a great Task*, THE CIVIL WAR? *Whoever will touch that burthen (unless abounding with* letters) *shall sink under it. For not* things done *should be comprehended in verse (which is much better performed by* Historians) *but the free spirit must throw it self headlong in digressions, and in personatings of Gods, and in fabulous ornaments upon the rack of invention: that it may seem rather an ebullition of some prophetik truths, amidst a world of pleasant extravagancies, from a breast inflamed with fury; than a deposition, as of sworn witnesses to* tell the truth, all the truth, and nothing but the truth."[57] In this passage, Eumolpus suggests that Lucan's epic on the civil war failed because it was too devoted to the truth of history rather than the "free spirit" of letters. In his own commentary on the *Bellum Civile* in the passage cited previously, note that Fanshawe's commentary

---

[54]   As I have noted, Pugh has shown throughout Fanshawe's corpus that contrary to the prevailing view of Fanshawe as a fervid supporter of the king, he often offers criticisms of Charles I's reign in his lyrical poetry. Even in very early poems such as his "on the Proclamation of 1630," which has traditionally been read as an example of Caroline pastoral idealism, Pugh offers an alternative reading of the poem as presenting the excluded view of the gentry who had been ordered to renounce their traditional duties and rights, and abandon the *res publica* to absolute rule, and to retire into a life of *otium*. Pugh, *Herrick, Fanshawe*, 114.

[55]   Smith, *Literature and Revolution*, 80.

[56]   For the entire *Satiricon*, see Petronius, *Satyricon*, Seneca, *Apocolocyntosis*, ed. E.H. Warmington, trans. W.H.D. Rouse and Michael Heseltine, no. 15 (Cambridge, MA, 1975), esp. 250–75.

[57]   "*Caeteri enim aut non viderunt viam qua iretur ad carmen, aut versum timuerunt calcare. Ecce* belli civilis *ingens opus! Quisquis attigerit, nisi plenus literis, sub onere labetur. Non enim res gestae versibus comprehendendae sunt (quod longe melius historici faciunt) sed per ambages Deorumque ministeria, et fabulosum sententiarum tormentum praecipitandus est liber spiritus: ut potius furentis animi vaticinatio appareat, quam religiosae orationis sub testibus fides: Tanquam si placet hic impetus etsi nondum recepit ultimam manum*" (Petronius, *Satyricon*, ed. E.H. Warmington, 250–52; Fanshawe [trans.], *The Lusiad*, in *Poems and Translations*, 8–9).

reiterates Eumolpus's criticism here that Lucan was not a poet. For both Fanshawe and Eumolpus, Lucan was rather a historian who had transcribed a "naked story" or provided a deposition. In contrast, the type of poet to which Camões aspired—according to Fanshawe—combined the fabulous with the historical in order to improve upon Lucan's imperfect historical poem.

Petronius's *Bellum Civile* attempts a similar mixture of history with fable. The middle portion of the poetic fragment contains a conversation between Pluto and Fortuna, in which Pluto complains vociferously about the corruption and iniquity that has developed within Rome and especially about the Romans having invaded Pluto's subterranean domain in order to pursue the mining of precious stones. In response, he demands that Fortuna commence a war, which will "possess with rage the Roman breasts, and throng / Our Realms with funerals" (107–8).[58] After Fortuna expresses her own hatred for Rome, predicting the events of the civil war at Phillipi, Thessaly, Spain, Libya, Egypt, and Actian, Jove sends a bolt of lightning to earth, avalanches commence, civil war erupts, and the dead are raised from their tombs. It is at this point in the poem that Caesar is presented as abandoning the Gallic wars and taking up arms against Rome, complaining of the wrongs, including that of having been expelled and placed into exile, that Rome has committed against him. The parallel with Charles II's exile is clear—one that Fanshawe had explored earlier in a poem "presented TO HIS HIGHNESSE THE PRINCE OF WALES, At his going into the West, *Anno* M.DC.XLV. *Together with* CESAR'S COMMENTARIES," in which the prince is encouraged to "set Cesar's glorious Acts before your sight" and emulate them.[59] It is here that the differences with Lucan's approach to the civil war come into focus, for whereas Lucan's perspective is that of the Pompeians and the republicans, the perspective of Petronius (and Fanshawe) is that of Julius Caesar, who is presented as returning to Rome from exile in order to cleanse Rome of its iniquity. Still, Fanshawe's imperial take on the Roman civil war should not distract us from comprehending his ultimate purpose in including Petronius's *Bellum Civile* in the prefatory material of his translation of Camões's national epic. Fanshawe sought to invoke Lucan's *Pharsalia* and the Roman civil war as a typological framework from which to comprehend recent historical events, at the same time that he favored Petronius's imperial perspective to Lucan's republican perspective. Moreover, he preferred Petronius's superior stylistic approach combining the fabulous and the historical to Lucan's strictly historical approach.

For Fanshawe, Camões's *Os Lusíadas* combined many of the elements of the traditional Virgilian epic involving the birth of a nation and subsequent imperial conquest, but the history of the birth of Portugal is first and foremost a history of

---

[58]   Subsequent parenthetical references are to line numbers from Fanshawe's translation of Petronius's *Bellum Civile* found in Fanshawe (trans.), *The Lusiad*, in *Poems and Translations*, ed. Davidson, 9–25.

[59]   Fanshawe, "Presented to His HIGHNESSE THE PRINCE OF WALES, At his going into the West, *Anno* M.DC.XLV. *Together with* Cesar's Commentaries," in *Poems and Translations*, ed. Davidson, vol. 1, 143, l.3.

246 Early Modern Catholics, Royalists, and Cosmopolitans

civil war between two provinces of the Christian or European commonwealth: Portugal and Castile. To be sure, Camões's poem actually focuses on the integrity of two overlapping bodies politic: Portugal and Christendom. The narrator's first address to King Sebastian at the beginning of the first canto addresses the tension between these two entities:

> E, vós [Sebastião], ó bem nascida segurança
> Da lusitana antiga liberdade,
> E não menos certíssima esperança
> De aumento da pequena Christandade;
> Vós, ó novo temor da maura lança,
> Maravilha fatal da nossa idade,
> Dada ao mundo por Deus, que todo o mande,
> Pera do mundo a Deus dar parte grande. (1.6)

> And *you* [King Sebastian], a present *Pawn* to PORTUGALE
> Of the old *Lusitanian-Libertie*;
> Nor the less certain *Hope* t'extend the Pale
> One day, of *narrow* CHRISTIANITIE:
> New *Terrour* of the *moorish Arsenale*:
> The foretold *Wonder* of our *Centurie*:
> Giv'n to the World *by* GOD, the World to win,
> To give *to* GOD much of the World again. (1.6)[60]

In this passage, Camões and Fanshawe, in his translation, figure Portugal's sovereign within the larger Christian commonwealth, at the same time that they invoke the dream of using Portugal's resources to extend ("esperança de aumento") the narrow bounds of Christendom. Later at the beginning of canto 3, which contains the history of Portugal's origins, Camões continues this transnational theme by describing the geographical region in which "Prowd EUROPE lyes [jaz a soberba Europa]" (3.6). After describing Northern, Eastern, and Southern Europe, he describes France and finally Spain,

> Eis aqui se descobre a nobre Espanha,
> Como cabeça ali de Europa toda,
> Em cujo senhorio e glória estranha
> Muitas voltas tem dado a fatal roda. (3.17)

> Lo! Here displays it self illustrious SPAIN,
> As *Head* there of all EUROPE: In whose strange
> Successes of their *Wars*, and ways of *raign*,
> Fate's wheel gave many a *turn*, wrought many a *change*. (3.17)

---

[60] Parenthetical citations to the Portuguese original are to the canto and stanza from Luís de Camões, *Os Lusíadas*, ed. Frank Pierce (New York, 1973). Parenthetical citations to Fanshawe's translation are to the Davidson edition, vol. 2, 1–330.

A description of Portugal follows in the next stanza:

Eis aqui, quasi cume da cabeça
De Europa toda, o Reino Lusitano,
Onde a terra se acaba e o mar começa
E onde Febo repousa no Oceano.
Este quis o Céu justo que floreça
Nas armas contra o torpe Mauritano,
Deitando-o de si fora; e lá na ardente
África estar quieto o não consente. (3.20)

The LUSITANIAN KINGDOM here survay,
Plac't as the *Crown* upon fair EUROPE's Head:
Where (the *Land* finishing) begins the *Sea*,
And whence the *Sun* steps to his watry Bed.
This, first in *Arms* (by gracious HEAV'N's decree)
Against the filthy MAURITANIAN sped:
Throwing him out of *Her* to his old Nest
In burning AFFRICK; nor *there* let him rest. (3.20)

Within Camões's geographical account, Europe is conceived of as a female body in which Spain forms the head and Portugal the crown. (A woodcut image of a map resembling this description of an anthropomorphized Europe had appeared in print throughout Europe from at least 1537 [see Figure 5.1]).[61] Hence, once again there are two bodies politic that are at the center of this poem—the first being the kingdom of Portugal and the second being that of Christian Europe, in which the Portuguese comprise the vanguard against the Muslim infidels.

Later in the same canto, Camões describes the history of the establishment of the Portuguese crown. King Afonso VI of Castile and León awards Henry of Burgundy the Condado of Portugal for the assistance Henry had provided during the Castilian reconquista against the Moors. Henry subsequently marries Afonso's (illegitimate) daughter, Teresa, and is given the territory of Galicia as a dowry. After the death of Henry, Teresa attempts to disinherit her first son, Afonso Henriques, who eventually rebels against her, resulting in an intra-familial conflict:

De Guimarães o campo se tingia
Co sangue próprio da intestina guerra,
Onde a mãe, que tão pouco o parecia,
A seu filho negava o amor e a terra. (3.31)

The blushing Plains of ARADUCA groan,
With *one-same* blood of *War intestine* dide;
In which the *Mother* (whose *deeds* spake her *none*)
The *Son* her *love*, and his own LAND deny'de. (3.31)

---

[61]   Peter Meurer, "Europa Regina. 16th century maps of Europe in the form of a queen," *Belgeo* 3–4 (2008): 355–70.

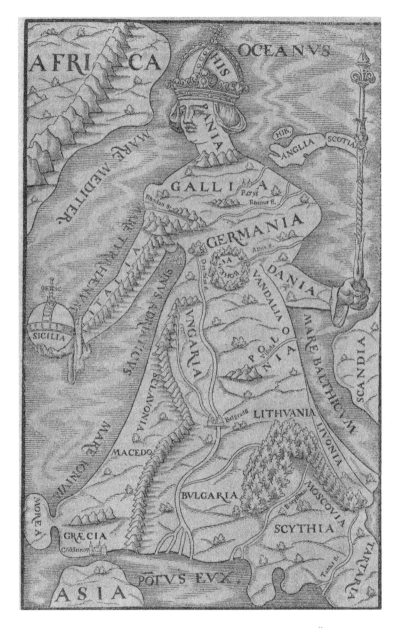

Fig. 5.1 [Europe depicted as a Queen], from Sebastian MÜNSTER, *Cosmographey oder Beschreibung all Länder Herrschaften vnd fürnemesten stetten des gantzen Erdbodens sampt ihren Gelegenheiten, Eygenschafften, Religion, Gebreuchen, Geschichten vnnd Handtheirungen* ... (Basil, 1588).
By permission of the Folger Shakespeare Library.

From Foreign War to Civil War 249

This passage invokes the familiar analogy between the family and the state. Teresa's criminal "*Incontinence* [Incontinencia]" leads to a conflict within the family, a struggle which both serves as an analogy to and causes an internecine conflict between the Castilian monarch, who supports Teresa, and Afonso Henriques, who subsequently seeks independence from Castile (3.32). Afonso Henriques easily defeats his mother and her new husband, at which point Castile unites all of its forces against the nascent kingdom of Portugal.

Subsequently, the epic alternates between a narrative of Virgilian nation-building and Christian conquest of the Saracens and one relating the internecine civil quarrel between the Portuguese and the monarchs of Castile and León, in which the Roman civil war is repeatedly invoked as a historical type. King Afonso Henriques defeats a variety of different Muslim kings, beginning with the famous Battle of Ourique, where according to legend his historical counterpart vanquished five Muslim kings immediately after Christ appeared to him on the cross before the famous battle commenced. A series of conquests of cities and towns in central Portugal follow, culminating in the conquest of Lisbon, surrounded by its "ULYSSEAN WALLS [muros ulisseus]" (3.58). Finally, Afonso Henriques's conquest of the city of Badajoz marks the return of the Lucanian civil war with Castile (3.66–74). With the city weakly defended by his men, the Portuguese king is surrounded by "LEON-MEN [Leoneses]" and is promptly defeated (3.70). It is at this point that Camões compares King Afonso Henriques's curtailed conquest of the region to the unfinished accomplishments of Pompey:

> O famoso Pompeio, não te pene,
> De teus feitos ilustres a ruína,
> Nem ver que a justa Némesis ordene
> Ter teu sogro de ti vitória dina.

> O famous POMPEY! Be not *Thou* in pain
> To see thy *Glories*'s sad *Catastrophie*;
> Or that just NEMESIS should pre-ordain
> Thy *Father-in-Law* to triumph over *Thee*. (3.71)

Camões goes on to catalogue a long list of Pompey's famous conquests, over the fierce Eniochians and Arabs and finally over the "SCYTHIAN-TAURUS with erected Crown [o scítico Tauro, monte erguido]" (3.73), as well as Pompey's infamous defeat by Caesar at Pharsalus. He then compares Pompey's defeat to Afonso Henrique's defeat by the Spanish at Badajoz:

> Porque Afonso verás, soberbo e ovante,
> Tudo render, e ser depois rendido.
> Assi o quis o Conselho alto celeste,
> Que vença o sogro a ti, e o genro a este. (3.73)

> For *high* and *great* ALPHONSO thou shalt see
> Bear *All* before him, and at last bourn down.

250   *Early Modern Catholics, Royalists, and Cosmopolitans*

By a *Cross-match* of FATE were *Both* undon,
Thou [i.e. Pompey] by a FATHER-IN-LAW [i.e. Caesar], *He* [Afonso Henriques] by
a SON [i.e. Ferdinand II of León, his son-in-law]. (3.73)

According to this passage, Afonso is Pompey returned, having confronted a similar fate—and here the analogous civil strife within the family and the state continues—of having been defeated in a civil war by his own family member. Eventually, Afonso is restored as sovereign of Portugal, soon to be followed by his son, Sancho, who continues the war of conquest against the Moorish kings, signaling a return to Virgilian epic. And within this trajectory, alliances are even temporarily made with the "CASTILIAN KING [o rei sublime castelhano]," who entreats "Help from the valiant PORTINGALL [ajuda ao forte lusitano]" in his own war against the Moors, while at other moments of weakness, the "CASTILIAN [Castelhano]" conquers Portugal "uncomptrold / … wasting so the weake disnerved *State* [devastando/ As terras sem defesa]" (3.101, 3.138).

In the first half of canto 4, the theme of civil war returns with a vengeance, when Camões recounts the Portuguese interregnum crisis of 1383–85 that followed the death of King Ferdinand I, during which King John I, the Castilian pretender, and John of Avis, the Portuguese pretender, vied for the Portuguese throne. The Pharsalian analogy emerges during the famous description of the crucial Battle of Aljubarrota (4.28–45), in which around 600 English soldiers and longbow men supported the outnumbered Portuguese army. The battle itself is described in the familial terms, which characterize most of Camões's civil-war scenes:

Eis ali seus irmãos contra ele [Joao de Aviz] vão,
(Caso feio e cruel!) mas não se espanta,
Que menos é querer matar o irmão,
Quem contra o Rei e a Pátria se alevanta:
Destes arrenegados muitos são
No primeiro esquadrão, que se adianta
Contra irmãos e parentes (caso estranho!),
Quais nas guerras civis de Júlio e Magno. (4.32)

Loe now his [John of Avis'] *Brother's* swords against him bent
(Cruel, and ougly)! But *Hee* [John of Avis] wonders not.
For they, who 'gainst their *King*, and *Countrey* went,
Would never stick to cut a *Brother's* Throat.
Of these *Revolters* many did present
Themselves in the first Ranks: And *who* so hot
To kill their *Friends*, as *They*? So kindred Hoasts
Of yore incountred in *Pharsalian* Coasts. (4.32)

Note that the reference to Lucan is more direct in Fanshawe's version than in Camões's version, in which the poet makes only a general reference to the civil war between Caesar and Pompey [Magno]. Ultimately, the Portuguese pretender, John of Avis, prevails, and peace is concluded by means of a marriage alliance with "two illustrious English ladies [duas ilustríssimas inglesas]":

From Foreign War to Civil War

Despois que quis o Padre omnipotente
Dar os Reis inimigos por maridos
Às duas ilustríssimas inglesas,
Gentis, fermosas, ínclitas princesas.

After the KING OF HEAV'N, for ever blest,
To the *Foe-Kings* in holy marriage gave
Of ENGLISH SISTERS an unequall'd pair,
Illustrious, lovely, beautiful, and Fair. (4.47.5-8)

The respective marriage of Philippa of Lancaster to João I of Portugal, and of her sister Catherine of Lancaster to Henrique III of Castile would mark the conclusion of the crisis and establish peace in the Iberian Peninsula. And from this point on, the epic returns to the Virgilian model of conquest and imperial expansion against the Moors.

Of course, it is ultimately unclear, when considering Fanshawe's English translation of *Os Lusíadas*, how much emphasis the translator himself might have placed on the relatively small portions of the larger poem that we have considered here. Fortunately, we possess a later manuscript that provides us with a more lucid perception of Fanshawe's own preoccupations as he himself read the poem.[62] In preparation for one of his two embassies to Portugal from September to December 1661 or from September 1662 to August 1663, Fanshawe translated into Latin a collection of prefatory poems and prose passages from the famous 1639 Spanish edition of *Os Lusíadas* edited and annotated by the Spaniard Manuel de Faria e Sousa.[63] Fanshawe also composed an elegant Latin description of the relationship between the English Order of the Garter and the Portuguese Coat of Arms, and most importantly, he completed a Latin translation of canto 1 and half of canto 4 from *Os Lusíadas*.

Significantly, Fanshawe's Latin translation of canto 4 breaks off after stanza 47, which describes the uniting of Portugal and Castile through the pair of English marriages discussed above:

His, alijsque, diu cedebat *Iberia* retro
Casibus adversis: *Tunc, Pacis* amabile munus
Dat *Victor*, Victis; cum, par Regale sororum
Nupserat, Anglarum, Commissis *Regibus*: Ambae
Oribus, et virtute, pares; *Lancastrides*, Ambae. (362; The original Portuguese and Fanshawe's English translation of canto 4, stanza 47 are provided above and in the footnote below.)[64]

---

[62] *Specimen Rerum a Lusitanis*, MS BDM2˚LXXXIX(C.). Fundação da Casa de Bragança, Vila Viçosa, Portugal.

[63] Manuel de Faria e Sousa (ed. and trans.), *Lusíadas de Luís de Camoens, principe de los poetas de España* (Madrid, 1639).

[64] Parenthetical references to page numbers are from Fanshawe, *Specimen Rerum a Lusitanis*, in *Poems and Translations*, ed. Davidson, vol. 2, 331–62. For reference, the first

252 *Early Modern Catholics, Royalists, and Cosmopolitans*

This is followed by a short commentary, also in Latin:

> Quondam Hymen erit alter, et altera Regia Virgo
> Quae, vice tunc versa, Diademate laeta Britanno
> Lusa nurus fulgebit; erint etiam altera Bella
> Hesperidum: Haec eadem semper Fortuna Sequetur;
> Haec itidem Regi Rex Anglus amicus utrique
> Inter Ulysseum componet et inter Iberum. (362)

> [One day there will be another marriage, another Royal virgin; who, with roles reversed, a happy daughter of Lusus, will shine in the British diadem; and there [will] also be another war of the Hesperians; this same Fortune will always follow in the same way. The English king will be friend to this same King, and will compact peace between Spain and Portugal. (660; trans. by Davidson)]

These haunting and complex verses, added at the end of the Latin translation in the hand of Richard Fanshawe's brother Lyonel, reveal a central preoccupation that runs throughout Fanshawe's entire corpus of poetry.[65] Indeed, they provide crucial insight into Fanshawe's work as a translator of works by Guarini, Horace, Virgil, Camões, and Antonio de Mendoza into English, as well as of works by John Fletcher and Camões into Latin.[66] Finally, they provide insight into Fanshawe's life as a diplomat, who worked tirelessly for the cause of the triple alliance in Lisbon and Madrid, as well as an understanding of Fanshawe's conception of a network of Christian sovereigns dedicated to protecting and correcting legitimate sovereignty within the frontiers of Christendom or Europe.

---

four lines of this stanza in the original and in Fanshawe's English translation are provided here: "Destas e outras vitórias longamente / Eram os Castelhanos oprimidos, / Quando a paz, desejada já da gente, / Deram os vencedores aos vencidos, [With these and other Victories opprest / A tedious while were the CASTILIANS brave, / When *Peace,* and *now* by both desired *Rest,* / The *vanquisht* People from the *Victors* have:]" (4.47.1–4).

[65]   Even if these lines comprise Lyonel Fanshawe's own commentary on Fanshawe's Latin translation of *Os Lusíadas*, they can still be understood as also reflecting Fanshawe's views on the pair of marriage. See Davidson's commentary in *Poems and Translations*, 660–61.

[66]   Sir Richard Fanshawe, *Il Pastor Fido: The faithfull Shepheard. With an Addition of divers other Poems, Concluding with a short Discourse of the Long Civil Warres of Rome* (London, 1648); *Selected Parts of Horace, Prince of Lyricks; And Of all the Latin Poets the fullest fraught with Excellent Morality. Concluding With a Piece out of Ausonius and another out of Virgil. Now newly put into English* (London, 1652); *La Fida Pastora, Comoedia Pastoralis* [Latin trans. of John Fletcher's *The Faithful Shepherd*] (Londini, 1658); *The Lusiad, or Portugals Historical Poem: Written In the Portingall Language by Luis de Camoens; And Now newly put into English by Richard Fanshaw, Esq* (London, 1655); *Querer Por Solo Querer: To Love only for Love Sake: A Dramatick Romance. Represented at Aranjuez Before the King and Queen of Spain, To Celebrate The Birth-Day of that King by the Meninas ... Written in Spanish by Don Antonio de Mendoza, 1623. Paraphrased in English, Anno 1654* (London, 1670).

From Foreign War to Civil War   253

An attempt to understand them fully, however, first has to acknowledge how they seem to refer simultaneously to a number of different contexts, past, present, and future. The first most obvious context, of course, is the first half of canto 4 of *Os Lusíadas*, which recounts the Battle of Aljubarrota, that famous 1385 conflict between Portugal and Castile that ended with the enduring alliance between Portugal and England, the oldest of its kind in European history, based on the marriage alliances described in stanza 47 between the House of Lancaster and the crowns of Portugal and Spain. The second context is the War of Portuguese Restoration, which began in 1640 as a Portuguese rebellion against Castilian rule and ended in 1668 with full Portuguese independence from Spain. This war was no doubt Fanshawe's most immediate concern—in August 1662, he was appointed to serve as ambassador to Portugal, where he would direct English military and financial support to the Portuguese crown, and later sent to Spain in 1664 to negotiate a complex peace treaty between, on the one hand, the Spanish and English crowns, and on the other hand, between Portugal and Spain. Like the ongoing aggression between Castile and Portugal recounted in cantos 3 and 4 of *Os Lusíadas*, there was a similar lack of clarity concerning the nature of the War of Portuguese Restoration. Was it a foreign war between two separate crowns, or was it a civil war between two geographical regions or dynasties within the same polity? Clearly, the English crown saw it as the former, but there were prominent voices during this period that perceived the war as civil in nature. The French ambassador to Portugal during the 1660s, Frémont d'Ablancourt, described the prevailing view of the conflict as inaccurate in a letter to the Prince of Turenne: "It may seem strange to you to hear me talk after such a fashion, but I beg you to consider that there is no question here of an enemy foreign in religion, manners or language, or who has done such injury to this nation as to make reconciliation impossible. When they meet they dispute the ground foot by foot and fight obstinately about the streams and passages of the smallest importance. But it is simply one part of a country rising up against the other, and is rather a civil than a foreign war."[67] Similar to d'Ablancourt, Fanshawe seems to have been disposed to viewing Portugal, England, and Spain as part of the same transnational political entity. In this respect, any war within Christendom had a civil as well as a foreign element.

The third context is the English one, and here there are two different but related issues. The first is the marriage contract between King Charles II and Catherine of Braganza, for whose retinue Fanshawe provided essential assistance in arranging travel to England in 1661. The appended commentary on canto 4, stanza 47 from Fanshawe's Latin translation of *Os Lusíadas* describes a reversal of roles: this time, instead of an English princess marrying a Portuguese prince, a Portuguese infanta will marry an English king. The reference is obviously to Catherine and Charles, but depending on when this commentary was written, it either predicts

---

[67] "M. De Fremont a S[on] A[ltesse] M[onsieur] L[e] P[rince] D[e] T[urenne], July [13–]23, 1663," in Sophia Crawford Lomas (ed.), *The Manuscripts of J.M. Heathcote, Esq., Conington Castle* (Norwich, 1899), 124–6. Original letter has been translated and/or summarized by Lomas.

254   *Early Modern Catholics, Royalists, and Cosmopolitans*

the marriage that occurred in 1662, or it constitutes a reference to that marriage, and predicts an eternal return of yet another marriage alliance between England and Portugal. Interestingly, the eternal return of important historical events and conflicts assumes a significant role throughout Fanshawe's corpus. Like many Englishmen of this period, Fanshawe saw the English civil war as a conflict that reprised the Roman civil war in ancient times. But he also saw recurring patterns in recent relations between Portugal and England that hearkened back to more recent European history. In a letter to Lord Clarendon in October of 1662, for example, he warned that the failure of the English crown to act decisively and to support the Portuguese side in the present conflict against Castile would reprise Queen Elizabeth's loss of Portugal during the 1580 Portuguese succession crisis, which resulted in King Philip II's ascension to the Portuguese throne. For Fanshawe, the commander of the Spanish forces, the Duke of Albuquerque, was the contemporary incarnation of the Duke of Alva during the earlier crisis, in which the Portuguese pretender, Antonio, Prior of Crato, was finally driven into exile to the English court.[68] During that earlier crisis, Fanshawe complains that Elizabeth I had failed to act quickly enough in support of Portugal, and the Duke of Alva's invasion force overran the kingdom while she dawdled. Similar to his exploration of the parallels between historical periods, Fanshawe also tended to find parallels between contemporary European kingdoms. His pair of Escurial poems is a good example. The first is a 1637 poem entitled, "On the Escurial, built by King Philippe the Second of Spaine and dedicated to St. Laurence," written as a celebration of the monumental royal palaces outside of Madrid, while the second parallel poem, entitled "On His Majesties Great Shippe lying almost finisht in *Woolwich* Docke *Anno Dom*. 1637. and afterwards called *The Soveraigne of the Seas*," was written to commemorate Charles I's construction of the famous 90-gun warship, the biggest of her class.[69] Both poems appeared sequentially in parallel texts in Latin and English at the end of Fanshawe's translation of Guarini's *Pastor Fido*, and both commemorate the building of giant enduring edifices that represent the strength of the polity itself. Fanshawe's purpose in pairing the two poems together is revealed at the beginning of the second poems, where he addresses the great ship as the "*Escuriall of the Sea*," but the parallel extends into other aspects of the two poems (1).[70] Like the real Escurial, whose builders comprised a cosmopolitan collection of artisans from India, Germany, Flanders, Greece,

---

[68] "Sir Richard Fanshawe to Lord Chancellor Clarendon," in *The Manuscripts of J.M. Heathcote, Esq.*, 37–40; at 38–9. Parts of original letter have been summarized by Lomas.

[69] The Latin title of the first is, "In Aedes magnificas quas *Philippus* Secundus *Hispaniarum* Rex Escuriis aedificavit, et Sancto *Laurentio* dedicavit," and of the second is, "*Ad eximiae magnitidinis Navem sub auspiciis Caroli Magnae Britanniae Regis constructam.* Anno Dom. *1637. Cui postea nomen* REGINA MARIUM." Both are found in the *Poems and Translations*, ed. Davidson, vol. 1, 60–77. Subsequent references to these poems are to the line numbers from the English versions.

[70] For an analysis of the politics of landscape in Fanshawe's lyrical poetry, especially those poems appended to Fanshawe's translation of *Il Pastor Fido*, see James Turner, *The*

Denmark, France, Italy, and England, combining harmoniously with the Spanish to construct this edifice (33–48), the "sacred Oakes" that supplied the wood for the masts of the "*Escuriall of the Sea*" might come from Britain or Denmark or Norway (20–21). Together the two poems draw an obvious parallel between Spain and England, the Spanish crown and the English crown.[71]

The second related issue concerns how Fanshawe might have viewed the recent troubles in England within the context of the international sphere. To be sure, if the Portuguese war of rebellion against Castile had both a foreign and a civil dimension, what were the implications for a royalist understanding of the English civil war? And if England, Portugal, and Castile being part of the same broader Christian polity seemed to justify English intervention into the conflict, other European sovereigns should have had a similar obligation towards England during its moment of crisis. As we shall see, during his subsequent embassy to the Spanish court, Fanshawe was instructed to respond to any complaints concerning English interference in Spanish and Portuguese affairs by rebuking the Spanish crown for not having provided more assistance to Charles II during his long period of exile on the continent. In this respect, the most significant document of Fanshawe's *Specimen a Lusitanus*, his Latin description of the historical relationship between the English Order of the Garter and the royal arms of Portugal, as they were revised during the reign of King John II (1481–95), contains further clues about the international order that Fanshawe seems to be promoting. According to this document by a professional amanuensis, later emended in Fanshawe's own hand, King John II "finally fixed and established" the form that the Portuguese arms would take until Fanshawe's own day, including the arms' encirclement by the English Garter on which appeared the famous motto in middle French, "Honi soit qui mal y pense" (see Figure 5.2).[72] During the second part of this two-page description of the Portuguese arms, presumably intended to be presented to the Portuguese crown, Fanshawe describes the Order itself as an international network of heroic and like-minded European sovereigns, which King Edward III had established in order to unify the military leaders of Europe. "How, you Portuguese ask, did this thing [membership in the Order] become his [King John II's]?" Fanshawe asks, before responding with the following passage detailing the origin and history of the Order:

Politics of Landscape: Rural Scenery and Society in English Poetry 1630–1660 (Cambridge, MA, 1979), 49–56, 94–9.

[71]   Gerard Hammond suggests that Fanshawe addressing the vessel as the "Escurial of the Sea" was especially unfortunate, given the suspicions of the crown's collusion with Spain. See *Fleeting Things: English Poets and Poems*, 157–60.

[72]   Original Latin is from the *Specimen Rerum a Lusitanis* in *Poems and Translations*, ed. Davidson, vol. 2, 335–6, at 335. English translation is found in Roger M. Walker and W.H. Liddell, "A Commentary by Sir Richard Fanshawe on the Royal Arms of Portugal," in *Studies in Portuguese Literature and History in Honour of Luís de Sousa Rebelo*, ed. Helder Macedo (London, 1992), 155–70, at 159. For background on the order, see Sir Colin Cole, "The Most Noble Order of the Garter," *The Coat of Arms, n. s. 6* (1984–85): 89–95.

256   *Early Modern Catholics, Royalists, and Cosmopolitans*

For it seemed good to the Kings of England, from the very inception of this most august Order [of the Garter], that it should become a decoration not only for their own deserving subjects, but that it should also be an incentive and a reward for the foreign valor of Christian princes [*externae virtuti Christianorum Principum*], however distantly related by blood, with the result that men of the highest rank in Europe [*primae magnitudinis in Europa*] did not think they had proved their renown until they became known to this royal Fellowship and had been nominated [*fuissent electi*] to this most noble Order. And no affinity or kinship, no treaty was a more sacred bond, a closer tie than the ribbon binding together the members of the Knightly Order of Saint George. And nine emperors, fifty-five crowned kings, four hundred illustrious nobles and magnates (although, however, the Knights could not exceed twenty-six in number at any one time) had already some years previously made their names and heroic deeds immortal in the records of this most glittering Order. There you will find this shield [*hoc scutum*] (of John II of Portugal) painted in bright colors in the book of the Knights of the Garter of the most illustrious Edward IV, King of the English.[73]

In reward for his unwavering loyalty to the crown, King Charles II had awarded Sir Richard Fanshawe, among other honors, the Chancellorship *pro tem* of the Order of the Garter (during the absence of the Chancellor Sir Henry de Vic), and before he left on his first royal embassy for Lisbon in September 1661, Fanshawe seems to have taken a genuine interest in reviving the Order and reorganizing its affairs, after it had fallen into disarray during the preceding decade. According to his description above, membership in the order, rather than being heritable or determined by familial or dynastic ties, was purely based on personal merit, and King John II had been awarded membership because of the priority he had given to exploring the coast of Africa and the East.[74] Thus, Fanshawe's celebration of the Portuguese members of the Order was yet another iteration of Fanshawe's faith in a voluntary international order involving a network of like-minded sovereigns, linked to the English crown by virtue of their personal and political values. In this respect, Fanshawe's diplomatic involvement in the attempts to establish a peace

---

[73]   Regibus enim Angliae, ab initio hujus augustissimi Ordinis, visum est, ut non solum suis subditis benemerentibus in ornamentum cederet, sed etiam externae virtuti Christianorum Principum (quantumvis remoti sanguinis) irritamento, et applausui, foret: ita ut, primae magnitudinis in Europa, non videbantur sibi satisfecisse famae suae, donec huic regali societati innotuissent, et in hunc celeberrimum ordinem fuissent electi: neque ulla necessitudo, aut consanguinitas, ullum faedus, sanctius vinculum, strictior copula quam, inter socios Equestris Sancti Georgiani ordinis, subligaculum: Et, novem Imperatores, quinquaginta quinque Coronati Reges, quatercentum inclyti proceres et magnates (cum interim commilitones numerum viginti sex, uno eodemque tempore, excedere non possint) jam, ante aliquot annos, consecraverint nomina sua, et Heröica Gesta, in Archivis hujusce fugentissimi Ordinis, Aeternitati. Ubi et hoc scutum (Iohannis secundi Portugalliae) vivis coloribus depictum, libro, Equitum Garterij, inclytissimi Anglorum Regis Eduardi quarti. From *Specimen Rerum a Lusitanis,,*in *Poems and Translations*, ed. Davidson, trans. Roger M. Walker and W.H. Liddell, vol. 2, 336; Walker and Liddell, "A Commentary," 159–60.

[74]   For background, see Walker and Liddell, "A Commentary," 155–7, 166.

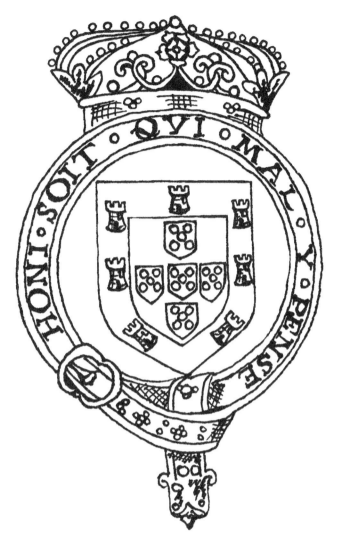

Fig. 5.2 The royal arms of Portugal with the encircling English Garter. In the middle of Fanshawe's description of the Order, there was a space where the royal arms were to appear, according to the following instructions, surrounded by a circle: "Place for the shield / of Portugal / With a garter round it / John II, King of Portugal." I would like to express my gratitude to Erin Kathleen Kelly for assistance in reproducing this image.[75]

---

[75] This is a copy of an image found in Walker and Liddell, "A Commentary by Sir Richard Fanshawe on the Royal Arms of Portugal," in *Studies in Portuguese Literature and History*, 155–70, at 165.

258   *Early Modern Catholics, Royalists, and Cosmopolitans*

treaty that would bind England, Portugal, and Spain is relevant as well. Rather than an order based on papal authority that corrects the temporal sovereigns of Europe, Fanshawe perceived one in which European sovereigns took responsibility for correcting and protecting their peers.

In practice, much of this work would be done by ambassadors like Fanshawe himself. In Charles II's instructions to Fanshawe in 1664 on his embassy to the Spanish court, Charles makes clear the same kind of reciprocation that has existed between Portugal and England must continue in the future. And just as the Portuguese court had assisted the English crown in the immediate aftermath of the English civil war, so must the English crown assist the Portuguese crown during its current travails. Charles II instructed Fanshawe to inform Ramiro Núñez de Guzmán, the Duke of Medina de las Torres and Sumiller de Corps of Philip IV's court, that, despite the English king's enduring regard for the Spanish crown, he had firmly resolved to continue his assistance to the Portuguese:

> You shall tell him, that you were made choice of by us, for our Ambassador to that Court, out of the knowledge we had of your affection to that Crown [Castile], having spent many years in that Court [Madrid], and that it would be an unspeakable misfortune, if you should be put to return to us without effecting that good understanding between us you desired, but that rather than you would seem to admit any debate upon a particular so contrary to our Honour, you would take your leave to Morrow of that Court, and return to us. That you must again put him in mind that we sent our Ambassadors to *Madrid*, to renew that Alliance in the strictest terms they could propose, and to excuse what had been formerly done with reference to *Portugal*, as done (as in truth it was) after the beginning of that Parliament which raised the Rebellion against our Father; That all our Overtures [to the Spanish Court] were then rejected, and our Ambassadors required to depart from that court, and at the same time, and after our Cousin Prince *Rupert*, Admiral of our Fleet, was inhibited to come into the Ports of *Spain*, and such of our said Fleet were by Storm driven into *Cartagena*, and there Stranded, the Ships Pillaged, and the Tackle and Ordnance of our Ships most injuriously detained from us, and denied to be restored to us tho' often demanded. That at this time, and after all this, our Fleet was Received and Protected in *Lisbon* against all the Threats of *Cromwell*, and tho' it was evident at the same time, that *Portugal* it self would by that Act of Generosity, become engaged in a war against *England*, as it quickly fell out to be, which brought infinite loss and damage upon them; and now after all these Offices performed to us in our lowest distress; And after we have taken to Wife the Daughter of that Crown, to Renounce that Alliance, and to look on whilst that Kingdom is destroyed, would be a thing so Dishonourable, that if we should be guilty of it, it would so lessen us in the Reputation of the World, that our Friendship would not be thought valuable to any of our Neighbours.[76]

---

[76]   King Charles II, "Instructions for Sir *Richard Fanshawe*, Going Ambassador to the Catholick King, January the 14th. 1663/4." in *Original Letters of his Excellency Sir Richard Fanshaw, During his Embassies in Spain and Portugal* (London, 1701), B–C3, at B4–B4v.

As we see in this passage, Charles's instructions are based on a historical account that assumes that European crowns are linked by a common royalist ideology. Charles begins by requesting that Fanshawe ask the Spanish crown's pardon for English support provided to Portugal at the outset of the Portuguese rebellion, blaming such support on the English parliament. Implicit in Charles II's apology is a retrospective awareness that England had been in breach of the 1630 peace treaty with Spain, which forbid either crown from lending support to rebellious parties in the other's kingdom.[77] Nevertheless, he rebukes the Spanish crown for denying him assistance during the decade of exile, reminding the Duke, that, unlike the Spanish crown, the Portuguese crown gave ample assistance to the English king in exile as well as to the royal fleet of Prince Rupert, while in the process placing its own future relations with Commonwealth-led England in jeopardy.

Fanshawe's further negotiations with the Spanish crown make clear that English negotiations towards a common alliance with the Spanish and the Portuguese crowns were being pursued not simply to satisfy the self-interest of the English crown. They were also intended to assist the Spanish crown and to correct its excesses. In a subsequent letter to Fanshawe, the Secretary of State and the king's most influential minister, Henry Bennet, explains that the English crown was concerned that the Spanish crown should understand that it has over-extended itself and may destabilize its own legitimacy as a result. Fanshawe's diplomatic initiative on behalf of the English crown is therefore also intended to serve the interests of the Spanish crown as well:

> Do they not see and feel their own Weakness? Have they not had Peace with all Christendom besides, for five years past, only to intend with more vigor the Conquest of *Portugal*? What progress have they made in it? Do they not see and feel the dying Condition of their King, and the young, tender, and uncertain Health of their Prince? Do not they see *France* with their Swords Drawn, ready to Invade them on all sides? What Friends have they to stand by them, if the Emperor hath made Peace with the Turk (as this weeks Letters say he hath) is [sic] there not a Fire already Kindled in *Germany*, in their Disputes between the Elector of *Mentz* and the City of *Erford*, which with the other Factions and Partialities reigning in the Empire, is likely to throw it into a worse state than even the War with the Turk, against which all hands went unitedly? If, I say, to sum up all these Reflections do not awaken them, and oblige them to turn themselves otherwise than they do, to cultivate the King our Master's Friendship, it must be concluded, some irresistible Fate or Judgment from Heaven attends that Monarchy, which their own skill cannot divert; therefore it would become your Excellency to awake them the best you can ... .[78]

---

[77] Indeed, reference to the terms of the 1630 treaty between Spain and England are ubiquitous in Fanshawe's epistolary account of negotiations between the crowns of Spain and England. See the *Original Letters*.

[78] "Henry Bennet to Fanshawe, August 25, 1664," *Original Letters*, T6–U1, at T8–T8v.

260   *Early Modern Catholics, Royalists, and Cosmopolitans*

In the middle of this passage, Bennet predicts that the recent Peace Treaty of Vasvár signed between the Leopold I, the Holy Roman Emperor, and the Ottoman Empire would further isolate the Spanish crown from its allies in Northern Europe, since the specter of the Ottoman Turk would no longer have the effect of uniting Christian Europe against a common foe. Bennet suggests that the Spanish crown should recognize the threat that was emerging from France and immediately commence negotiations on an alliance with England and Portugal in order to ward off the threat of a French invasion. In order to conclude such a triple alliance, Fanshawe had received authority from the Portuguese crown to negotiate directly with Spain on behalf of Portugal. During 1665, Fanshawe successfully negotiated a treaty with the Duke of Medina, which was signed on December 17 of that year without being ratified by the English crown. It was eventually held in the English court that Fanshawe had exceeded his instructions, and he was subsequently recalled, a development which Lady Ann Fanshawe blamed on the Earl of Clarendon "and his party" who, according to Fanshawe's wife, had conspired against Fanshawe's embassy.[79] Edward Montagu, the Earl of Sandwich, was chosen to replace Fanshawe in Madrid and quickly concluded a peace treaty, the groundwork of which Fanshawe had been preparing meticulously for five years. The reasons for the crown's recall of Fanshawe are still unclear to historians. Most likely, while members of the Privy Council were more or less satisfied with the Anglo-Spanish treaty that Fanshawe had signed on December 17, they balked at his failure to resolve the differences between Spain and Portugal.[80]

Though Fanshawe's embassy to the Iberian peninsula ended in failure, his vision of a transnational and ecumenical commonwealth sustained by a network of temporal sovereigns persisted. In this respect, it is worth returning to *Os Lusíadas* in order to comprehend the full significance of Fanshawe's efforts in Portugal and Spain. The example of Egas Moniz, the tutor to King Afonso Henriques of Portugal, who served as the Portuguese ambassador to the king of Castile during the twelfth century, may have served as a narrative exemplum for Fanshawe's own ambassadorship to the Spanish crown. The beginning of canto 3 recounts the civil war between Castile and the nascent kingdom of Portugal during the twelfth century. When the first King of Portugal, Afonso Henriques, is surrounded by the armies of Castile in Araduca, his tutor, Egas Moniz, offers himself to the Castilian king as Afonso Henriques's surety, with the promise that the Portuguese sovereign would later submit to Castile. Ultimately, Afonso Henriques refuses to submit to the Castilian crown, but Egas Moniz remains true to his promise to Castile, submitting his own life, along with those of his wife and children, to the Castilian sovereign, King Fernando, in lieu of the defiant Portuguese king. For Camões (and doubtless for Fanshawe as well), Egas's sacrifice is a sign of ultimate obedience

---

[79]   Lady Ann Fanshawe, *The Memoirs of Ann Lady Fanshawe*, ed. Herbert Charles Fanshawe (London, 1907), 181.

[80]   For a detailed discussion of the negotiations that led up to the Anglo-Spanish Peace Treaty of 1667, see Herbert Charles Fanshawe, "Appendix IV: The Spanish Treaty, Proposed by Sir Richard Fanshawe, December 1665," in *The Memoirs of Ann Lady Fanshawe*, 234–51.

to the Portuguese crown: "O grao fidelidade portuguesa / De vassal que a tanto se obrigava! [O great, and Portingal-Fidelitie / Payd by a Subject to his Prince]" (3.41). But it is also a sign of Egas Moniz's submission to the transnational Christian commonwealth that bound the crowns of Portugal and Castile together that Moniz was unwilling to break his promise to King Fernando of Castile.

Like Egas, Fanshawe ultimately saw his role as that of serving his own king, but through Charles II, Fanshawe viewed himself as serving the larger European commonwealth as well. In this respect, Fanshawe's vision differed crucially from that of Camões in that Fanshawe's ideal of such a commonwealth, rather than depending on a unified religious identity, was secular or at least ecumenical in character. Ironically, like William Davenant, Fanshawe might have seemed to be the perfect candidate for conversion to the Roman faith during the civil war. He had always been a passionate Hispanophile who had first visited Spain as a student in 1633, and from 1635–38, he had served as secretary to England's ambassador to Spain, Baron Walter Aston, who had himself converted to the Roman faith in 1623. Recognized (along with John Milton) as one of the most accomplished Latinists of his day, Fanshawe ultimately replaced Milton as *Secretarius Pro Lingua Latina* after the restoration, during a period when use of Latin as the lingua franca of Europe was experiencing a dramatic revival.[81] He obviously loved the Spanish and Portuguese languages like no other Englishman of the period, and thus one might have expected someone like Fanshawe to have been warmly disposed towards Catholicism, perhaps even a secret convert. And this expectation was doubtless the reason why his widow Lady Ann chose to begin her memoirs about her life with him by describing her husband's lifelong commitment to the national church: "He loved and used clearness in all his actions, and professed his religion in his life and conversation. He was a true Protestant of the Church of England, so born, so brought up, and so died."[82] Fanshawe remained a committed conformist until his death, but his poetry and translations betray a cosmopolitan commitment to the European polity, bound by a common thread of secularized cultural, literary, and linguistic traditions.

---

[81] For more on Richard Fanshawe's biography, see Roger M. Walker, "A Rediscovered Seventeenth Century Literary Friendship: Sir Richard Fanshawe and Dom Francisco Manuel de Melo," *Seventeenth Century* 7.1 (1992): 15–24; Walker, "Sir Richard Fanshawe's 'Lusiad' and Manuel de Faria e Sousa's *Lusiadas Comentadas*: New Documentary Evidence," *Portuguese Studies* 10 (1994): 44–64.

[82] Lady Ann Fanshawe, *Memoirs*, 4. As she recounts, Fanshawe was so committed to the English Church that he found a way to bury his daughter, Elizabeth, in Madrid in 1650 and his son, Richard, in Lisbon in 1663 according to the rites of the Church of England, at a time when there was no Protestant burial ground in those two cities and the practice of Protestantism was forbidden. Lady Ann Fanshawe, *Memoirs*, 67, 112. See also Fanshawe's Latin epitaphs for these two children in *Poems and Translations*, ed. Davidson, vol. 2, 365.

Chapter 6

The Christian Nation and Beyond: Camões's *Os Lusíadas* and John Milton's Cosmopolitan Republic

Although the extent of Milton's knowledge of the Portuguese poet, Luís de Camões, is unknown, critics ranging from E.M.W. Tillyard to Louis Martz have made persuasive cases for the influence of Camões's epic, *Os Lusíadas*, on *Paradise Lost*.[1] The majority of these cases are based on the discovery of echoes and parallels between the two poems. Given the nature of the similarities, it is likely that Milton knew Fanshawe's 1655 translation of the epic, although considering Milton's remarkable command of modern languages, it is not altogether impossible that he also knew the Portuguese original or that he used Faria e Sousa's annotated 1639 prose translation into Spanish.[2] The abundance of internal evidence certainly shows that one of the epics Milton had in mind while writing *Paradise Lost* was *Os Lusíadas*. But it is clear that, rather than adopting Camões's perspective, Milton intended *Paradise Lost* as a repudiation of the Christian nationalism which seems to play such a large role in certain episodes of the Portuguese epic.[3] Camões's vision of the Portuguese king and nation had obvious resonances with the aims of the disenfranchised royalists during the Interregnum in England. In this respect, Fanshawe's own royalist affiliations are not insignificant. As I have noted in Chapter

---

[1]   See E.M.W. Tillyard, *The English Epic and its Background* (New York, 1954), 238–50, and Louis L. Martz, *Milton: Poet of Exile* (New Haven, 1986), 155–68. Also see C.M. Bowra, *From Virgil to Milton* (London, 1948), 194–5 and Robert Ralston Cawley, *Milton and the Literature of Travel* (New York, 1970), 140. The most complete study of Camões's influence on Milton is James H. Sims, "Christened Classicism in *Paradise Lost* and *The Lusiads*," *Comparative Literature* 24.2 (1972): 338–56. See footnote 1 in Sims for a more exhaustive list. See also James Sims, "The Epic Narrator's Mortal Voice in Camões and Milton," *Revue de Littérature Comparée* 51 (1977): 374–84. In *Epic and Empire, Politics and Generic Form from Virgil to Milton*, 253–6, David Quint has uncovered a further series of echoes of *Os Lusíadas* in *Paradise Lost*.

[2]   In 1649, the Council of State of the Commonwealth of England appointed Milton to the post of Secretary for Foreign Languages, which he held until the Restoration, when King Charles II appointed Sir Richard Fanshawe to the position. See Robert Thomas Fallon, *Milton in Government* (University Park, PA, 1993), 1–22.

[3]   Tillyard, Bowra, and Sims are the best examples of critical accounts that have held that in echoing him, Milton was essentially adopting Camões's perspective (Tillyard, *The English Epic*; Bowra, *From Virgil to Milton*; Sims, "Christened Classicism"). Martz's *Milton: Poet of Exile* is more complicated. After initially placing the perspectives of the two poets at odds, Martz finally goes on to find that their two epics share the same pessimistic view of the universe (165–8).

264 *Early Modern Catholics, Royalists, and Cosmopolitans*

5, his 1655 translation of *Os Lusíadas* might be seen as a timely attempt to reassert the divine connection between the nation and the monarch: significant episodes in Camões's *Os Lusíadas* like Vasco da Gama's account of the Battle of Ourique portray the Portuguese king as directly inspired by Christ and his obedient soldier-subjects as responsible for carrying out Christ's continued works in the world. In this respect, English readers would have read the Portuguese epic as an indictment of the Commonwealth government and the polity that it was trying to conceive.

In the first section of this chapter, I show that *Paradise Lost*—especially the last two books—can be viewed as a repudiation of the conception of the Christian kingdom that Camões used in his portrayal of Portugal and which ultimately would have been viewed as congenial to the vision of English royalists. In Book XI of *Paradise Lost*, in which Michael's prophecies to Adam begin, Milton points to Adam and Eve's excessive religious attachment to the territory and history of Eden as a sign of their fallen state. Milton means to show that true religious devoutness transcends all such territorial loyalties, including by implication national and dynastic loyalties. As for the nation itself, the twelfth book presents the institution of nationhood—in the form of the Hebrew nation—as an interim measure, which finally produces its own dissolution with the coming of Christ. Henceforth, according to Milton, all Christian faith should be understood as transcending temporal boundaries in the manner that Paul sets out in the Epistles.

In the second part of this chapter, I show that, while Milton's perspective on the character of the English nation changed after the Restoration, his notion of a transnational elite that would replace the Episcopal hierarchy of the Roman and English Churches remained a consistent theme within his prose works. As I show, this transnational elect, of which Milton saw himself as a member, was essential to Milton's republican approach to secular cosmopolitanism.[4] In the end, Milton's perspective on England and its place in the world both harkens back to earlier sixteenth-century forms of cosmopolitanism and has important elements in common with the cosmopolitanism of his royalist opponents such as Sir Richard Fanshawe.

Beyond the Christian Nation

However much Fanshawe may have sought to present *Os Lusíadas* as principally about a civil war within Christendom, it is clear that a substantial portion of the poem comprises a traditional epic account of one nation's conquests—more than two-thirds of Camões's epic can be viewed as relating the history of Portuguese expansion. The epic's main narrative, the story of Vasco da Gama's 1498 voyage to India, is not only a major chapter in this history but also functions as a narrative

---

[4] For discussion of Milton's republicanism, see Martin Dzelzainis, "Milton's Classical Republicanism," in *Milton and Republicanism*, ed. David Armitage et al. (New York, 1995), 3–24; Thomas N. Corns, "Milton and the Characteristics of a Free Commonwealth," in *Milton and Republicanism*, 25–42. For a discussion of Milton's *Paradise Regained* that relates Milton's cosmopolitanism to the classical Stoic tradition, see Shifflett, *Stoicism, Politics and Literature in the Age of Milton*, 129–54.

frame for the rest of the historical events of Portuguese expansion. However, Camões's poem is not simply an account of imperialist expansion. Indeed, in the tradition of *The Aeneid*, *Os Lusíadas* can equally be seen as a history of divinely-sanctioned royal dominion over territory as well as of the achievement of sovereignty over a Christian polity (of which da Gama and his crew are members) by a legacy of rightful sovereigns. In this vein, much of the recounted history of Portuguese expansion can be re-characterized as the story of the foundation of a Christ-inspired and Christ-sanctioned kingdom, which ends with the establishment of the boundaries that existed when Camões was writing.[5]

The history of Portugal, largely told by Vasco da Gama in the third and fourth cantos of *Os Lusíadas*, begins with an account of the events leading up to the gift of a portion of land by King Alfonso of Spain to Count Anrique, the father of the first Portuguese king, Afonso Henriques. The land, from which the nation of Portugal will eventually stem, is given in recompense for Count Anrique's assistance in the Christian struggle against the Moors. According to da Gama's narrative, Count Anrique had spent his life fighting for the territorial expansion of Christianity, both within the Iberian peninsula and during the Crusades to the Holy Lands (3.26–7). In return for Anrique's fidelity, King Alfonso marries his daughter Teresa to the French count and presents him with a large portion of land as a dowry (3.25).[6] The establishment of Anrique's dominion is the first step in the ultimate foundation of Portugal as a Christian kingdom. Given that a noble's property rights and a sovereign's right to govern were all discussed under the broad legal term, *dominium rerum*, a lord's right to his territory was viewed in religious and legal terms as analogous to a king's right to govern his realm.[7]

---

[5] My use of the word "nation" here and elsewhere assumes that the modern conception of nationhood replaced an older conception of the dynastic realm during the sixteenth century. In *Imagined Communities*, 9–48, Anderson locates the foundations of our modern conception of nationhood in early modern print culture, which caused separate European vernaculars to replace Latin as the language of government. In *Nationalism: Five Roads to Modernity* (Cambridge, MA, 1992), 31–5, Liah Greenfeld notes that the sixteenth century brought crucial changes in vocabulary reflecting the development of national consciousness. In *Forms of Nationhood*, Richard Helgerson finds that sixteenth-century English writers were active not so much in reflecting national consciousness as in forming it. For Helgerson, Camões played a major role in producing his own nation's national consciousness—he writes, "there can be few examples in history of a poet or of a poem more intimately linked with the identity of a nation than Camões and *The Lusiads* have been with that of Portugal" (163). In Helgerson's discussion, the aristocratic concerns of Camões figure as a point of comparison with the economic concerns of Richard Hakluyt and the English explorers (151–63).

[6] Citations from the poem are to canto and stanza from Camões, *Os Lusíadas*, ed. Frank Pierce. English translations are my own.

[7] In Camões's version, Da Gama explains that Anrique "das terras tomou posse [took possession of those lands]," while Fanshawe's Da Gama explains that Henry gained "The *Livery and Seisin* of that Land" (3.25). Anthony Pagden, "Dispossessing the Barbarian," 79–98, for a discussion of juridical debates concerning claims of *dominium* in the New World.

Such analogies are important in terms of da Gama's narration of the establishment of the nation of Portugal since the account of Count Anrique gaining *dominium* will ultimately develop into an account of the achievement of royal sovereignty by his son, Afonso Henriques. More importantly, whether he is recounting the process of achieving *dominium* or national sovereignty, da Gama sets up an equation between fidelity to Christ and the acquisition of land. From the beginning, the acquisition of the territory that will become Portugal is explicitly linked to the divine.

It comes as no surprise then that the context for the actual foundation of Portuguese sovereignty is the battle of Ourique which figures as the miraculous origin of the nation's symbols and religious purpose and links religious fervor to the development of national consciousness. In the conflict, both Anrique's son, Prince Afonso, and, through him, the Portuguese are marked by God as the collective agents of Christian expansionism as they defeat the overwhelming forces of five Moorish kings. With the miraculous victory over the combined Moorish forces, Portugal is founded as a quintessentially Christian kingdom. The battle of Ourique functions typologically as a victorious re-enactment of the events surrounding Christ's crucifixion. The vision which Afonso has before the battle is the first step in this re-enactment, conferring the very identity of king on the prince. Hence, immediately after the stanza which describes the miracle, Camões refers to Afonso as "seu Rei natural [their natural king]" for the first time and subsequently portrays the army lifting up the new king and, in a moment of divine recognition, crying out, "Real, real, / Por Afonso, alto Rei de Portugal [Royal, royal / For Afonso, high King of Portugal]" (3.46.3, 7–8). In doing so, Camões involves the entirety of the Portuguese people in his account of the miraculous founding of Portugal.

In the vision itself, Camões presents Afonso's response to Christ's appearance as informed by a number of canonical and Biblical precedents. Here is his account of the vision:

> A matutina luz, serena e fria
> As estrelas do Pólo já apartava,
> Quando na cruz o Filho de Maria,
> Amostrando-se a Afonso, o animava.
> Ele, adorando quem lhe aparecia,
> Na Fé todo inflamado, assi gritava:
> —"Aos infiéis, Senhor, aos infiéis,
> E não a mi, que creio o que podeis!" (3.45)

> [The light of dawn, cold and serene, chased the stars from the sky, when on the cross the Son of Mary, revealing himself to Afonso, inspired him. He [Afonso], adoring Him that appeared, all inflamed in his faith, shouted, "Unto the faithless! Unto the faithless, show Thyself, Lord, and not to me, for I believe in Thy power!"]

The most obvious parallel here is the legendary appearance of Saint James the Greater (called the Matamoros or Moor-slayer) to King Ramiro I of Asturias, during his legendary defeat of the Moors at the Battle of Clavijo during the twelfth century. There are Biblical references as well. Obviously, the appearance of Christ bathed in light references the various appearances of the resurrected Christ to the Apostles in the Gospels and the Book of the Acts of the Apostles, including of course His appearance to Saint Paul on the road to Damascus. By attempting to persuade Christ to appear to the Moors rather than to Afonso himself, the king momentarily refuses his role as an agent of Christ's presence in the world, thus obliquely alluding to Saint Peter's denial of Christ on the eve of the crucifixion as well as to those Apostles who doubted the earliest accounts of Christ's resurrection. Later, after the battle is won, Camões acknowledges Afonso spending three days at Ourique in order to satisfy the requirements of the *sessio triduana*, or "three-day sit-down," which conferred *dominium* on the victor of a battle.[8] Given the religious context here, however, there may be a further reference either to the three-day sequence comprising Christ's crucifixion and resurrection or to Saint Paul's three days of blindness in Damascus before the scales fell from his eyes (3.53).[9]

Ultimately, the battle is also memorialized by symbolism that presents Afonso's defeat of the five Moorish kings as mystically connected to Christ's five wounds during the crucifixion. At the end of the battle of Ourique, King Afonso devises the escutcheon of Portugal as a way of commemorating his glorious defeat of the Moorish kings:

> Aqui pinta no branco escudo ufano,
> Que agora esta vitória certifica,
> Cinco escudos azuis esclarecidos,
> Em sinal destes cinco reis vencidos. (3.53)

> [Here [the king] paints on the proud white shield, that has sustained this victory, five clear blue shields, which signal the five defeated [Moorish] kings.]

---

[8] See James Q. Whitman, *The Verdict of Battle: The Law of Victory and the Making of Modern War* (Cambridge, MA, 2012), 183–8.

[9] The oldest extant work which mentions the miracle is Fernão Lopes's *Chronicle of the First Seven Kings of Portugal of 1419*—an account which was responsible ultimately for a number of attempts to have Afonso canonized as a saint. Indeed, the myth remained powerful for centuries after Camões's own death, and later versions made more explicit what Camões had rendered symbolically. For example, in an account written in 1632 by chronicler Antonio Brandão, Christ speaks to Afonso, telling him, "Eu sou o fundador, & Destruidor dos Reynos, & Impérios, & quero em ti, & teus descendentes fundar para mim hum Império, por cujo meio seja meu nome publicado entre as Nações mais estranhas … [I am the founder and destroyer of kingdoms and empires and I want in you and your descendants to found for myself an empire, by whose means my name will be published throughout the most foreign nations]" *Monarchia Lusitana*, III parte, Livro X, cap. v, quoted in Ana Isabel Buescu, "Um mito das origens da nacionalidade: o milagre de Ourique," *A memoria da Nação, Colóquio do Gabinete de Estudos de Simbologia, realizada na Fundação Calouste Gulbenkian, 7–9 outubro, 1987*, ed. Francisco Bethencourt and Diogo Ramada Curto (Lisboa, 1991), 49–69, at 57.

268   *Early Modern Catholics, Royalists, and Cosmopolitans*

This stanza inevitably invokes Camões's earlier description of the symbolism of the Portuguese arms in the first canto of the epic:

> Vede-o no nosso escudo, que presente
> Vos amostra a vitória já passada,
> Na qual vos deu por armas e deixou
> As que Ele pera si na Cruz tomou; (1.7)

> [Behold it on our escutcheon, that now displays the past victory [at Ourique], that He [Christ] gave to you through arms and left to you through the wounds which He suffered on the cross.]

There is an obvious if implicit connection between the two stanzas which figures the victory at Ourique as retribution for Christ's crucifixion—in effect, five infidel kings are defeated for the five wounds which Christ suffered on the cross. The newly-formed kingdom of Portugal is responsible for carrying out such retribution. Ultimately, Camões portrays the kingdom of Portugal as an agent of divine justice—as such, it is responsible for the expansion of territory in the name of Christ and the sovereign who is His contemporary incarnation.

Milton's earlier prose writings, unlike *Paradise Lost*, show conflicted sympathy for the idea of a modern English nation ordained by Christ.[10] In *A Second Defense of the English People*, while for the most part Milton stresses the folly of those who would view kings as "the viceroys, indeed, and vicars of Christ," the echoes of an English nation through which Christ performs his works are notable.[11] In *A Second Defense*, Milton claims that as an Englishman, he holds a special office, not as the disseminator of the Word of Christ as was the case with Portugal, but as the disseminator of liberty to other nations: "I seem to be leading home again everywhere in the world, after a vast space of time, Liberty herself, so long expelled and exiled. And like Triptolemus of old, I seem to introduce to the nations of the earth a product from my own country, but one far more excellent than that of Ceres. In short, it is the renewed cultivation of freedom

---

[10] For Paul Stevens's analysis of what he calls Milton's Janus-faced nationalism, see Stevens, "'Leviticus Thinking' and the Rhetoric of Early Modern Colonialism," *Criticism* 35.3 (1993): 441–61; "Milton's Janus-faced Nationalism: Soliloquy, Subject, and the Modern Nation State," *Journal of English and Germanic Philology* 100.2 (2001): 247–68; and "Milton's Nationalism and the Rights of Memory," in *Imagining Death in Spenser and Milton*, ed. E.J. Bellamy et al. (New York, 2003), 171–84.

[11] Milton, *A Second Defence of the English People*, in *Complete Prose Works of John Milton: 1650–1655*, ed. Don M. Wolfe (New Haven, CT, 1966), vol. 4, part 1, 551. All subsequent citations from Milton's prose works are from the *Complete Prose Works* (*CPW*) and are cited by volume and page number. "Nondum enim Tyrannis res sacra erat; nondum tyranni, Christi scilicet proreges atque vicarii repente facti." Latin quotations are from John Milton, Joannis Miltoni Opera Omnia Latina [*A complete collection of the historical, political and miscellaneous works of John Milton*] (3 vols, Amstelodami, 1698), vol. 3, K4v.

The Christian Nation and Beyond   269

and civic life that I disseminate throughout cities, kingdoms, and nations."[12] But underneath the secular facade here, Milton's dissemination of liberty has an explicitly religious purpose. As the champions of liberty, the English will help to cleanse from the mind "the superstitions that are sprung from ignorance of real and genuine religion"; hence, England's role as the transporter of freedom is shown to be almost equivalent to that of a transporter of uncorrupted religious faith.[13] In carrying out this function, England presumably serves in the spread of Christ's reformed and "true" message. In general, then, while Milton perhaps does not want England to adopt the Christian ideology with which we saw Portugal identified in Camões's epic, England is still figured here as a Christian realm, responsible albeit indirectly for the dissemination of the word of Christ. Milton's view of England as a disseminator of liberty was of course fueled by his anti-Catholic views. In the *Areopagitica*, for example, Milton had railed against the 1643 parliamentary ordinance for licensing the press, claiming that such book-licensing had come not "from any ancient State, or politie, or Church, nor any Statute left us by our Ancestors elder or later; nor from the moderne custom of any reformed Citty or Church abroad; but from the most Antichristian Councel and the most tyrannous Inquisition that ever inquir'd."[14] Milton was referring to the Council of Trent and the Spanish Inquisition of the mid-sixteenth century and their efforts to expunge dangerous Protestant publications. Against what he perceived as the forces of tyranny and repression, Milton conceived of England and the idealized forces of English liberty as tied to the Protestant cause on the continent and elsewhere.

By the time he had completed *Paradise Lost*, however, Milton seems to have re-evaluated his earlier sympathy for the ideal of the Christian polity with the responsibility of disseminating liberty and the uncorrupted faith to the rest of the world. The re-emergence of the royalist ideology of absolutism in the late 1650s as well as Milton's own disillusionment with the Commonwealth ideals seems to have radically altered Milton's position with regard to the relationship between Protestantism and an elect English nation.[15] During the Interregnum,

---

[12]   *Second Defense*, in *CPW*, vol. 4, part 1, 555–6. "Videor jam mihi, tantis circumseptus copiis, ab Herculeis usque columnis ad extremos Liberi Patris terminos, libertatem diu pulsam atque exulem, longo intervallo domum ubique gentium reducere: Et quod Triptolemus olim fertur, sed longe nobiliorem Cereali illa frugem, ex civitate mea gentibus importare; restitutum nempe civilem liberumque vitae cultum, per urbes, per regna, perque nationes disseminare." Milton, *A complete collection*, vol. 3, L.

[13]   *Second Defense*, in *CPW*, vol. 4, part 1, 680. "superstitiones animis, religionis verae ac solidae ignoratione ortas, abegetitis … ." Milton, *A complete collection*, vol. 3, O4.

[14]   *Areopagitica*, in *CPW*, vol. 2, 505.

[15]   See Christopher Hill, *Milton and the English Revolution* (New York, 1979), for a discussion of how *Paradise Lost* can be seen as reflecting Milton's disillusionment with the Commonwealth in the late 1650s as well as his reaction to the Restoration in 1660. For further context, see Andrew Milner, *John Milton and the English Revolution: A Study in the Sociology of Literature* (Totowa, NJ, 1981), 195–209. J.G.A. Pocock has identified a general decrease "in the vocabulary of Godly Rule and the Elect Nation" after 1660. See Pocock, *The Machiavellian Moment: Florentine Political Though and the Atlantic Republican Tradition* (Princeton, 1975), 403.

270 *Early Modern Catholics, Royalists, and Cosmopolitans*

supporters of the exiled king translated classical and continental works with a view toward promoting the ideal of divine right favored by the Caroline court. Like Sir John Denham's "free" translation of the second book of *The Aeneid* published in 1656, Fanshawe's translation of *Os Lusíadas* was meant to serve a counter-revolutionary cultural and political ideology that would restore the lost hegemony of the Caroline crown and aristocracy.[16] Fanshawe's ultimate purpose was both to restore the discourse of the divine right of the English sovereign and to reintroduce the notion of England as one province within a transnational Christian or European commonwealth. In the face of this reinvigorated royalist form of Christian nationalism, Milton sought to illustrate the dangers inherent in the conception of England, or any nation, as divine. David Quint's work has been sensitive to the purpose of Milton's allusions to Fanshawe's translation of *Os Lusíadas*. Quint's work suggests that the parallels which Milton establishes between the Portuguese voyage to India and Satan's journey to Eden were meant to show that the imperialistic expansionism of Portugal or any other European nation was the work of the devil. Quint goes on to argue that *Paradise Lost* is largely a repudiation of the Roman Catholic ideals of empire.[17]

I would argue, however, that, while repudiating the prospect of a Roman Catholic empire was certainly one of Milton's purposes in *Paradise Lost*, more important still was his interrogation of the political and social entity that Camões identifies as responsible for such expansionism, namely, the divinely-sanctioned Christian realm.[18] Milton does so especially in the last two books of *Paradise Lost* by offering an account of Biblical history that addresses the proper place of the nation within

---

[16]   See Lawrence Venuti, "The Destruction of Troy: Translation and Royalist Cultural Politics in the Interregnum," *Journal of Medieval and Renaissance Studies* 23.2 (1993): 197–219, for an account of the politics of translation by royalists during the Interregnum. Venuti pays particular attention to Denham's 1656 translation of the second book of *The Aeneid* entitled, *The Destruction of Troy, An Essay upon the Second Book of Virgils Aeneis*. Venuti shows how seventeenth-century translation theory advocating translation of the spirit rather than the grammar of the text allowed Denham and others to adapt their translations to the political events of contemporary England. In commendatory verses extolling Sir Richard's Fanshawe's translation of Guarini's *Il Pastor Fido* (1647), Denham calls this "free" form of translation "a new and nobler way."

[17]   In *Epic and Empire*, David Quint uncovers a series of Miltonic allusions to Fanshawe's translation, all of which suggest the notion that Milton based his account of Satan's journey on da Gama's voyage to India (253–5). However, Quint is somewhat reductive in setting up this parallel: "as da Gama opened up a route to the Indies for the trade and imperialism of Europe—particularly Catholic Europe—so Satan blazes a trail for Sin and Death to build their bridge by 'art/ Pontifical' from Hell to earth" (255). His emphasis on Milton's repudiation of the Catholic empire occludes the more important sense in which Milton was also repudiating the prospect of any Christianized empire, even an English one. See also David Armitage, "John Milton: Poet against Empire," in *Milton and Republicanism*, 206–26.

[18]   For a consideration of this aspect of Milton in relation to Puritan notions of the apocalypse, see Michael Fixler, *Milton and the Kingdoms of God* (London, 1964).

The Christian religion. While a great deal of this history closely follows the biblical account of the primary figures in the Old Testament, Milton gives special attention throughout both books to the issues of property, territory, and nationhood which we have encountered in *Os Lusíadas*. In doing so, Milton's purpose is to demonstrate that a national identity purportedly based on Christ contravenes a correct reading of biblical history; indeed, he portrays the entire institution of nationhood as an interim measure whose importance ends with the coming of Christ.[19]

Just as we saw in the case of Camões, Milton begins his treatment of the *topos* of nationhood by invoking the notion of property. At the beginning of Book XI, Adam and Eve are banished from the Garden, and the necessity of leaving what they now consider to be their own land causes them at least as much pain as the initial decree of death caused them. Their attachment to the land of Eden is one of the first signs of their fallenness. They display a new penchant for localizing the presence of God in the world and regard their banishment as causing their separation from what is divine. After they have heard the new decree, Adam explains,

> Departure from this happy place, our sweet
> Recess, and only consolation left
> Familiar to our eyes, all places else
> Inhospitable appear and desolate,
> Nor knowing us nor known: …
> … This most afflicts me, that departing hence,
> As from his face I shall be hid, depriv'd
> His blessed count'nance; here I could frequent,
> With worship, place by place where he voutsaf'd
> Presence Divine … . (XI.303–7, 315–19)[20]

A number of important facets of fallenness are shown in this long passage. Among the most important is the connection that is implicitly drawn between Adam's attachment to locations and the potential for such attachment to become idolatry. Indeed, in the lines which follow, "here I could frequent / … and to my Sons relate; / On this Mount he appear'd, under this Tree / Stood visible, among these Pines his voice / I heard, here with him at this Fountain talk'd" (XI.317–22), Adam imagines himself relating the history of God's presence in Eden to his offspring and unwittingly begins to localize God. In doing so, he threatens to privilege the place or icon above the God which it supposedly represents: "So many grateful Altars I would rear / Of grassy Turf, and pile up every Stone / Of lustre from the brook, in memory / Or monument to Ages …" (XI.319–26). Thus Michael's rejoinder stresses the ubiquity of God's presence within the world:

---

[19] For a related reading focusing on typology in the last two books of *Paradise Lost*, see Philip J. Donnelly, *Milton's Scriptural Reasoning: Narrative and Protestant Toleration* (New York, 2009), 172–87.

[20] All citations from *Paradise Lost* are from John Milton, *The Complete Poems and Major Prose*, ed. Merritt Y. Hughes (New York, 1957).

> Adam, thou know'st Heav'n his, and all the Earth,
> Not this Rock only; his Omnipresence fills
> Land, Sea, and Air, and every kind that lives,
> Fomented by his virtual power and warm'd: ...
> ... surmise not then
> His presence to these narrow bounds confin'd
> Of Paradise or Eden: (XI.335–8, 340–42)

In general, then, Milton uses these passages to show that limiting God to certain locations carries a potential for limiting God's power in the world, for confining what should be a frontierless presence to a set of boundaries, and for transforming reverence of God into something equivalent to a pagan ritual.

Book XI ends with a lesson about the sinfulness of the reverential form of territorialization which Adam and Eve favor at the beginning of their fall from grace. The context is Michael's prognostications concerning the story of Noah and the flood. Michael predicts that when the deluge falls from the heavens, no location will claim sacredness apart from the living men who inhabit it:

> ... then shall this Mount
> Of Paradise by might of Waves be mov'd
> Out of his place, push'd by the horned flood,
> With all his verdure spoil'd, and Trees adrift
> Down the great River to the op'ning Gulf,
> And there take root an Island salt and bare,
> The haunt of Seals and Orcs, and Sea-mews' clang.
> To teach thee that God attributes to place
> No sanctity, if none be thither brought
> By Men who there frequent, or therein dwell. (XI.829–38)

Again, the subject of territory and nationhood are implicitly invoked in this passage. By relocating Paradise and transforming it into an unremarkable island inhabited by seals and whales, Milton makes clear that in the fallen world, the land that once comprised Paradise is no more blessed—and perhaps even less so—than any other land. In the process, he inevitably alludes to newly-discovered pastoral-island paradises where such sea animals were also found and which were described in the contemporary accounts of explorers in the Eastern seas. Such islands as well as their primitive inhabitants were often idealized for not having suffered what were seen as the corrupting influences of civilization, but according to this passage, such idealizations would seem to be an error as well.[21] As this passage shows, Milton wanted to separate any notion of territory from religion and instead, claim that all religiosity originated in the hearts of Christians.

The last book of Milton's epic introduces a slight change of focus to these issues. As we saw, the eleventh book is almost solely concerned with questions of property and territory, and the theme of nationhood is only implicitly related. In the twelfth book, Milton takes up the question of nationhood more directly—

---

[21] See Pagden, *The Fall of Natural Man.*

indeed, he uses the word "nation" at least 17 times in what constitutes the epic's second shortest book comprised of slightly more than 600 lines. Like many of the words of Latin origin that Milton uses in *Paradise Lost*, the use of the word "nation" is highly ambiguous throughout Book XII. The word registers two levels of significance. Within the context of the Old Testament history that Milton is recounting, the word "nation" is equivalent to the Latin *natio*, meaning "a race or a stock of people." Within Milton's more immediate context, the word carries the more modern meaning of "a country or native soil."[22] Drawn together in one word, the two meanings play an important role in Milton's purpose for the book: he will remain true to the letter of biblical verse, but he will also produce a critical commentary on the contemporary notion of the divinely-sanctioned nation.

Although at times it is somewhat associational and difficult to trace, the logic of this commentary describes the advent and the final dissolution of the nation connected to God. According to Michael, the cleansing effects, which the flood afforded, are only temporary. The inhabitants of the second stock are said to "dwell / Long time in peace by Families and Tribes / Under paternal rule" (XII.22–4). But before long, a more ambitious and oppressive polity comes about. Nimrod becomes the first tyrant, "who not content / With fair equality, fraternal state, / Will arrogate Dominion undeserv'd / Over his brethren, and quite dispossess / Concord and law of Nature from the Earth" (XII.25–9). Tyranny is thus introduced into the world. In his next paragraph, Michael explains that the creation of tyranny is a necessary evil which supplements the inner usurpation which Nimrod's rebellion represents and which Adam's transgression made inevitable.[23] The argument seems to be a combination of familiar interpretations of Genesis and Aristotle's argument on the "natural slave" in the *Politics*: because man is unable to utilize his reason to govern his passions from within, in short, because he is enslaved by his passions, it is necessary that he suffer enslavement from without.[24] Enslavement from without

---

[22]   In fact, most sixteenth- and seventeenth-century writers of Latin dictionaries failed to give the classical definition of natio ("a race or stock"). According to Liah Greenfeld's *Nationalism: Five Roads*, Thomas Cooper's *Theasaurus Linguae Romanae et Britannicae* (1565) translates *natio* as "a nation" and then goes on to explain "a people having their beginnyng in the countrey wheare they dwell." In Thomas Elyot's *Latin English Dictionary* (1538), *natio* is simply rendered by "a nation"; Elyot does not feel compelled to give further explanation. John Rider's *Bibliotheca Scholastica* (1589) translates the English "a countrey" as *regio, natio, orbis* and the entry "nation" starts with "A Nation, or countrey"—"Nation" and "countrey" were apparently interchangeable for Rider (32). For an explanation of how the creation of the first nation of Israel is actually implicit in the creation myth itself, as recounted in *Genesis*, see Regina M. Schwartz, *Remembering and Repeating: Biblical Creation in* Paradise Lost (New York, 1988), 2.

[23]   This episode in Book XII has also been read as reflecting Milton's hostility to patriarchalism and, in Nimrod's rejection of "fair equality, fraternal state," continued investment in republicanism. See Su Fang Ng, *Literature and the Politics of Family in Seventeenth-Century England* (New York, 2007), 145–7.

[24]   Aristotle, *Politics*, ed. and trans. H. Rackham (Cambridge, MA, 1990), 1253 a1–40, 1254 b1–40.

274   *Early Modern Catholics, Royalists, and Cosmopolitans*

insures that his enslavement from within will not completely take over. Tyranny is thus a necessary supplement to man's incomplete and incompetent inner system of government:

> Therefore since hee permits
> Within himself unworthy Powers to reign
> Over free Reason, God in Judgment just
> Subjects him from without to violent Lords;
> Who oft as undeservedly enthral
> His outward freedom: Tyranny must be,
> Though to the Tyrant thereby no excuse. (XII.90–96)

Of course, the question of multiple, oppressive tyrants, or as Milton says above, multiple "violent Lords," immediately brings to the fore the question of the multiple territories which they govern. It is therefore no surprise that the next sentence introduces the subject of the nation. For just as tyranny becomes necessary to the restraint of the inner passions and their imminent usurpation, the institution of the nation becomes a necessary, temporary measure which will finally lead to the dissolution of outward usurpation or tyranny and, in the process, will itself become deconstituted.

Indeed, God chooses to favor one nation in order to cause the dissolution of all other temporal rulers and nations. He leaves all other peoples to their iniquities and makes a covenant with Abraham and his descendants. According to Michael, God will lead Abraham's people

> into a Land
> Which he will show him, and from him will raise
> A mighty Nation, and upon him show'r
> His benediction so, that in his Seed
> All Nations shall be blest. (XII.122–6)

The nation of Israel which Abraham fathers is necessary because the benediction which God has afforded its people is capable finally of overcoming all national boundaries.[25] Hence, for Milton, Israel takes up a position as God's chosen nation and in the process, contributes ultimately to a negation of its own status as nation. Indeed, nationhood, like tyranny, is another necessary evil that finally helps to unite all nations under Christ. Thus, in a later section, Michael predicts the coming of Christ and His apostles who are ultimately responsible for spreading

---

[25]   The importance of the notion that "All Nations shall be blest" through Abraham's descendants is highlighted by the fact that Milton repeats the last verse of this passage almost word for word at lines 146 and 147. These lines read, "This ponder, that all Nations of the Earth / Shall in his Seed be blest." Incidentally, both passages allude to Genesis 18:17–18 of the King James translation of *The Bible*: "And the Lord said, Shall I hide from Abraham the thing which I do; Seeing that Abraham shall surely become a great and mighty nation, and all the nations of the earth shall be blessed in him?"

His word: "Thus they win / Great numbers of each Nation to receive / With joy the tidings brought from Heav'n" (XII.502–4). This short passage stresses the traditional belief that only the faithful will be saved by Christ; but it also predicts that Christ's coming will fissure the loyalty that is inherent in a united sense of nationhood. Christ is not so much the ruler of all nations here as He is the savior of the believers of each nation.[26]

Finally, let us look at what Milton has to say concerning the role that Christ plays with regard to the land that was promised to Abraham as the territory of the nation of Israel. During the Old Testament period in which God solely favored the one nation of Israel, He promises to the Israelites the land of Canaan as a national territory. Such a territory had a direct relation with God in the manner with which we are already familiar; in fact, in a typological sense, the Portugal of *Os Lusíadas*, and every other modern nation which has claimed such a relation, is based on similar claims. In Milton's account of biblical history, Christ's coming transforms Canaan into a despatialized, spiritual locale of well-being. In effect, the Canaan that earlier was the mundane seat of Israel now transforms to become an "eternal Paradise of rest." And thus, although Moses is "Conducted by his Angel to the Land / Promised to Abraham and his Seed" (XII.259–60), it is not Moses who finally leads his people to the true promised land. This task will instead be performed by Christ:

> And therefore shall not Moses, though of God
> Highly belov'd, being but the Minister
> Of Law, his people into Canaan lead;
> But Joshua whom the Gentiles Jesus call,
> His Name and Office bearing, who shall quell

---

[26]   In an earlier section, Michael predicts the advent of Christ Himself:
> That of Royal Stock
> Of David (so I name the King) shall rise
> A Son, the Woman's Seed to thee foretold,
> Foretold to Abraham, as in whom shall trust
> All Nations, and to Kings foretold, of Kings
> The last, for of his Reign shall be no end. (XII.325–30)

In this passage, Christ's reign is portrayed as an empire over which Christ is the ultimate and final king. That Milton portrays Christ in this way might suggest that the poet is far less serious than I have been claiming about telling a story of the triumph over the institution of the nation—after all, the development of empire is deeply invested in nationhood as an extension of the conquering nation. But although Milton does use the terms "king" and "reign" to characterize Christ's triumph, Christ is not portrayed here as the ruler of all nations but rather as one "in whom shall trust/ All Nations." Moreover, his reign-without-end implies a reign without the spatial or temporal restrictions which bind a truly temporal ruler. In many ways, then, this characterization of Christ as ruler of the world is similar enough to traditional notions of rulers to convey the power involved but different enough to stress that the traditional notion of a ruler is being overcome. Thus, Milton uses the traditional portrayal of a king but stretches it enough so that it becomes deconstituted in the process.

The adversary Serpent, and bring back
Through the world's wilderness long wander'd man
Safe to eternal Paradise of rest. (XII.307–14)

The Israelites might be "in thir earthly Canaan plac't" by Moses, but it takes Christ to lead "long wander'd man" to his true "Canaan," now a metaphor for the Heavenly kingdom. In this deeply orthodox account of the Savior's entrance into the world, Christ represents the triumph over a relation between the divine and one single territory. The idea that one nation is favored by God above all others is cast as an Old Testament paradigm which is revised with the coming of Christ. In effect, the privileged nation is portrayed as an interim measure, and the coming of Christ insures that no nation will ever again attain the same privileged status. With regard to what we have said about Portugal and its place within *Os Lusíadas*, it is clear that Milton's religious history is a repudiation of Camões's portrayal of a Portuguese territory or nation ordained by Christ.[27]

In the years after the first edition of *Paradise Lost* was published, Milton's distrust for the institution of nationhood and national loyalties only grew in intensity. Both *Samson Agonistes* and *Paradise Regained* raise the concerns that the final books of *Paradise Lost* voice surrounding the nation and its relation to God and Christ. However, these later works are so absolute in their condemnation of the institution of nationhood and national loyalties that the complexity of the issues is greatly reduced. Indeed, in the third and fourth books of *Paradise Regained*, the debate between Satan and Christ over the nature of Christ's kingdom has little room for gray areas. Satan is relentless in his attempts to worry the question of how Christ's kingdom relates to secular nations and empires. And Milton's Christ is just as relentless in rejecting any association between them. In the end, *Paradise Regained* seems to repeat in more overt terms the lessons of the final books of *Paradise Lost*. In *Paradise Regained*, we are made to understand that, throughout history, the nations and empires of the world have been aligned with Satan, used and manipulated by him, just as they are being used to tempt Christ into betrayal. Not only is the institution of nationhood not to be trusted, it is figured as wholly evil. In turn, Christ's justice will be all the more absolute in its destruction: his season shall be "as a stone that shall to pieces dash / All Monarchies besides throughout the world."[28] Here Christ's coming is not simply the dissolution of all nations, but the complete destruction of their monarchical governments.[29] In this

---

[27] For discussion of how this relates to the Puritan notion of history ending with the "Kingdom of Christ," see Fixler, *Milton and the Kingdoms of God*, 13–46, 226–34.

[28] *Paradise Regained*, IV.148–9, in John Milton, *The Complete Poems and Major Prose*, ed. Merritt Y. Hughes.

[29] For context, see Bryan Adams Hampton, *Fleshly Tabernacles: Milton and the Incarnational Poetics of Revolutionary England* (Notre Dame, IN, 2012), 167–226. For the relationship between *Samson Agonistes* and *Paradise Regained*, see David Loewenstein, *Representing Revolution in Milton and his Contemporaries* (New York, 2001) 276–81, Joseph Wittreich, *Interpreting Samson Agonistes* (Princeton, NJ, 1986), 80, and Walter S.H.

respect, Christ's entrance into the world signals the collapse of an entire ideology by which monarchical rule is justified by its connection to the divine.

Puritan Antiprelatism and Milton's Transnational Elect

As I have shown, the last two books of *Paradise Lost* constitute a critique of the popular contemporary notion that England (or Portugal for that matter) could have an important place within God's divine plan, similar to that of the nation of Israel within the Old Testament. Consistent with this conclusion, Victoria Kahn has shown in a recent essay on *Samson Agonistes* that, like his portrayal of Samson, Milton's Delila is able to articulate a rational account of the self-interest of her own Philistine nation, thus effectively extending Milton's Christ-centered critique of divinely-sanctioned nationhood into ancient biblical history as well. According to Kahn, the inevitable conclusion one takes from such a poem is that, based on natural law or reason, no nation can be committed to God any more than any opposing nation.[30] Thus, it seems that, by the time of the Restoration, Milton had given up on an earlier optimistic conception of the English nation as the new Israel or Jerusalem, which would bring religious liberty to the rest of the nations of the world.[31] Milton's disillusionment with nationhood and nationalism at the end of his life obviously does not in itself constitute a form of cosmopolitanism. But an epistolary exchange that Milton had later in his life does at the very least suggest that Milton subscribed to a cosmopolitan perspective that was not so foreign to the perspective of his royalist opponents such as Fanshawe.

In this case, the interlocutor was Peter Heimbach, whose father was chancellor in Heimbach's native duchy of Cleves. Having been informed that Milton had been taken by the plague in the winter of 1665–66, Heimbach wrote from the duchy in broken Latin, expressing his surprise that Milton was still living: "But it was reported that you had been restored to your heavenly *patria*, and that, freed from our earthly follies, from on high you now looked down upon them.

Lim, *John Milton, Radical Politics, and Biblical Republicans* (Newark, 2006), 126–69. For discussion of the apocalypse in Milton, see Ken Simpson, "The apocalypse in *Paradise Regained*," in *Milton and the Ends of Time*, ed. Juliet Cummins (New York, 2003), 202–23, and for a general discussion of how the Restoration transformed perceptions of an approaching apocalypse, see Jonathan Rogers, "'We Saw a New Created Day': Restoration Revisions of Civil War Apocalypse" in *The English Civil War in the Literary Imagination*, ed. Claude J. Summers and Ted-Larry Pebworth (Columbia, MO, 1999), 186–201. For *Paradise Regained* as an account of the birth of liberty, see Joan S. Bennett, *Reviving Liberty: Radical Christian Humanism in Milton's Great Poems* (Cambridge, MA, 1989), 161–204.

[30] Victoria Kahn, "Disappointed Nationalism: Milton in the Context of Seventeenth-Century Debates about the Nation-State," in *Early Modern Nationalism and Milton's England*, ed. David Loewenstein and Paul Stevens (Toronto, 2008), 249–72.

[31] For an in-depth discussion of Milton's "ongoing commitment to religious radicalism" during the Restoration, see Sharon Achinstein, *Literature and Dissent in Milton's England* (New York, 2003), 115–53.

278 *Early Modern Catholics, Royalists, and Cosmopolitans*

And since no correspondence is allowed into that kingdom, I have hitherto had to restrain and repress my pen so eager to write to men such as you."[32] Milton responds by describing himself as having suffered from a kind of internal exile—he writes that the virtue which "you call *Policy* (and which I would prefer you call *Patriotism*) after having allured me by her lovely name, has almost *expatriated* me, as it were." And then he concludes by writing somewhat obliquely, "One's *Patria* is wherever it is well with him [*Patria est, ubicunque est bene*]."[33] The phrase lacks the bombast of John Dee's claim to have been a "Citizen, and member, of the whole and only one Mysticall City Vniuersall," but it is not far off in terms of sentiment.[34]

Milton's exchange with Heimbach provokes a question which we will attempt to address in the remainder of this chapter: how did someone who had so self-consciously identified himself with his country during his authorship of the *First* and the *Second Defense of the People of England*, both of which he signed as "Joannis Miltoni Angli" come to see himself as having been so radically dislodged from his place of birth by the end of his life?[35] There are two possible responses to this question. One is that, after the Restoration, Milton became disillusioned with the notion that England was a nation chosen by God to spread the reformed religion to the rest of the world, or in his words, to "set up a Standard for the recovery of *lost Truth*, and blow the first *Evengelick Trumpet* to the *Nations*, holding up, as from a Hill, the New Lampe of *saving light* to all Christendome."[36] The second response to this question, which I find more persuasive, is that Milton felt ambivalent about the narrative of the English as the new divine elect from a relatively early stage of his career and that this ambivalence developed into resolute pessimism over time. We can perceive this ambivalence not directly in his

---

[32] Peter Heimbach, "Letter XXXIII, Peter Heimbach to Milton, May 27, June 6, 1666," in *CPW*, vol. 8, 2. "Ferebant enim te nostris nugis exemptum, patrio coelo redonatum esse, terrisque sublimiorem quavis nostra dispicere. Ad hoc regnum, ut non datur aditus, sic calamum meum satis ad tui símiles scripturientem hactenus cohibere, ac reprimere debui." Latin comes from *The Works of John Milton* (8 vols, London, 1851), vol. 1, cxcvi.

[33] Milton, "Letter 41, To Peter Heimbach August 15, 1666," in *CPW*, vol. 8, 4. "quam enim Politicam tu vocas, ego Pietatem in Patriam dictam abs te mallem, ea me pulchro nomine delinitum prope, ut ita dicam, expatriavit." Joannis Miltonii Angli, *Epistolarum Familiarium Liber Unus* (Londini, 1674), E, or *The Works of John Milton*, vol. 7, 410. For a reading of how the state of internal exile influenced Milton's late works, see D'Addario, *Exile and Journey*, 87–123.

[34] Dee, *Perfect Arte*, G3v. For a related reading of Milton's exchange with Heimbach, see Shifflett, *Stoicism, Politics, and Literature in the Age of Milton*, 151–4.

[35] Milton, *Joannis MiltonI Angli Pro Popvlo Anglicano Defensio contra Clavdii Anonymi, alias Salmasii, Defensionem Regiam*, (Londini, 1651), title page; *Joannis MiltonI Angli Pro Populo Anglicano Defensio Secunda*. (Londini, 1654), title page.

[36] Milton, *Of Reformation*, in *CPW*, vol. 1, 525. See Victoria Kahn, "Disappointed Nationalism," 249–72. For discussion of the development and transformations in Milton's political thought, see John T. Shawcross, *The Development of Milton's Thought: Law, Government, and Religion* (Pittsburgh, PA, 2008), 1–24.

writings about the English nation but rather in his antiprelatical tracts stretching back to the beginning of the civil war.[37]

Given Milton's identity as a Puritan, my literary history of cosmopolitanism might have begun with the Protestant response to Catholic claims for a transnational Christian commonwealth in order to better incorporate Milton's sensibility.[38] As I showed in the Introduction and in Chapter 3, the ideal of a unified transnational Protestant Christendom, with the purpose of countering the Catholic league, was partially realized in the Schmalkaldic league, and Sir Philip Sidney's diplomatic embassy in 1577 shows that the English government seriously entertained joining such an alliance.[39] But because of confessional differences among Protestant sovereigns, these attempts at grand Protestant alliances seemed to have been inherently unstable in comparison to the centralized, bureaucratic structure of the Roman Catholic Church, a structure that was replicated in the religious orders as well. As we shall see, Milton seems to have been acutely aware of the instability and disunity at the heart of any collective transnational Protestant endeavor, and thus his own cosmopolitan perspective emerges, not as a natural outgrowth of earlier attempts to organize European Protestants, but rather as a critical response to the hierarchical unity of both the Roman Church and its schismatic counterpart in England. Milton could rail against papistry as well as any of his Puritan counterparts, but what captured Milton's early political imagination more strongly was his rejection of the episcopal hierarchy which had remained largely intact after the English crown's break with Rome.[40] Milton's antiprelatical writings were inspired first and foremost by the desire to abolish the church hierarchy and bring England closer to the congregationalism that characterized the Calvinist movement on

---

[37] For analysis of how the focus of Milton's antiprelatical tracts is on discipline not doctrine, see Thomas N. Corns, "Milton's Antiprelatical Tracts and the Marginality of Doctrine," in *Milton and Heresy*, ed. Stephen B. Dobranski and John P. Rumrich (New York, 1998), 39–48.

[38] Milton had a complex relationship with Puritanism. Stephen M. Fallon argues that Milton's writings were not "representative of Puritan practice and perspective," but he nevertheless argues that, based on his religious beliefs, Milton was still a Puritan (21). See Stephen M. Fallon, *Milton's Peculiar Grace: Self-Representation and Authority* (Ithaca, NY, 2007), chs 1–3. See also A.L. Rowse, *Milton the Puritan: Portrait of a Mind* (London, 1977). For the opposing view, see Catherine Gimelli Martin, *Milton among the Puritans: The Case for Historical Revisionism* (Burlington, VT, 2010), 1–30.

[39] See McEntegart, *Henry VIII, The League*; and Kouri, *England and Protestant Alliance*.

[40] For the religious context in which Milton was writing, see Nigel Smith, *Perfection Proclaimed: Language and Literature in English Radical Religion 1640–1660* (New York, 1989), 1–104. Kevin Sharpe and Anthony Milton have shown how Puritans tended deliberately to confuse the "Arminianism" and high-church characteristics of the Church of England with Catholicism. See Kevin Sharpe, *Personal Rule of Charles I*, 301–8, and Milton, *Catholic and Reformed*, 71.

280 *Early Modern Catholics, Royalists, and Cosmopolitans*

the continent.[41] In this respect, Milton's cosmopolitan sensibility is not so very different from the royalist cosmopolitanism found in Fanshawe's writings, which also incidentally emerged as a response to the Roman Catholic cosmopolitanism that preceded it. In contrast to Fanshawe, for Milton, it is what comes to substitute for the bishops' authority that constitutes the basis of his cosmopolitan critique of both temporal and ecclesiastical authorities. Indeed the decentering of the monarchical realm that we see in the last two books of *Paradise Lost* is actually implicit very early on in Milton's critique of the Episcopal structure of both the Roman and the English Churches.

As is clear from Michael's account of religious history at the end of Book XII of *Paradise Lost*, Milton's antiprelatical polemic goes hand in hand with his critique of the divinely-sanctioned nation.[42] At the end of Michael's account of religious history, the episcopal hierarchy is identified as the primary source of corruption in the Church. Soon after the original Apostles have ministered "Great numbers of each Nation" with "the tidings brought from Heav'n," corruption begins to manifest itself among their heirs:

> at length
> Thir [the Apostles'] Ministry perform'd, and race well run,
> Thir doctrine and thir story written left,
> They die; but in thir room, as they forewarn,
> Wolves shall succeed for teachers, grievous Wolves,
> Who all the sacred mysteries of Heav'n
> To thir own vile advantages shall turn
> Of lucre and ambition, and the truth
> With superstitions and traditions taint,
> Left only in those written Records pure,
> Though not but by the Spirit understood.
> Then shall they seek to avail themselves of names,
> Places and titles, and with these to join
> Secular power, though feigning still to act
> By spiritual, to themselves appropriating
> The Spirit of God, promis'd alike and giv'n
> To all Believers. (XII.503–20)

As in other important places in Milton's oeuvre, the "Wolves" that succeed the first apostles refer to the members of the ecclesiastical hierarchy that turn the Christian faith to their own personal advantage, resulting in their own enrichment and entitlement. In particular, there seems to be a reference to the bishops who enrich themselves with "names, / Places and titles, and with these ... join / Secular power,

---

[41]   Milton, *Of Reformation*, in *CPW*, vol. 1, 526–7. For the historical context of Milton antiprelatism during the 1640s, see Thomas N. Corns, *Uncloistered Virtue: English Political Literature, 1640–1660* (New York, 1992), 11–37.

[42]   In contrast to my analysis of Milton's prose and poetry, Robert Thomas Fallon argues against attempts to reconcile Milton's poetry and prose. See Robert Thomas Fallon, *Divided Empire: Milton's Political Imagery* (University Park, PA, 1995).

The Christian Nation and Beyond   281

though feigning still to act / By spiritual." Furthermore, these prelates claim the
right to restrain the individual's conscience, but they are only able to do so through
the corrupt temporal power that they have accrued to themselves.[43]

Milton made a similar point about the topic of Church discipline in a number
of his prose works. In the *Treatise of Civil Power in Ecclesiastical Causes* (1659),
Milton explains that the Roman Church's appropriation of temporal powers
through "corporal inforcement" and "the forfeture of monie" comprise the "two
arms of Antichrist."[44] The church might employ these "corporal punishments"
to compel the conscience of an individual, but because of the inherent liberty
of the conscience, they will ultimately be unable to enfetter the soul itself.[45] As
he explains elsewhere in the same tract, "Christ hath a government of his own,
sufficient of it self to all his ends and purposes in governing his church; but much
different from that of the civil magistrate; and the difference in this verie thing
principally consists, that [Christ's government] governs not by outward force, and
that for two reasons. First, because it deals only with the inward man and his
actions, which are all spiritual and to outward force not lyable."[46] Here, Milton
explains the essential freedom of the individual's conscience, which Christ's true
church acknowledges. An individual's conscience is subject to the invisible church
of Christ and is therefore ultimately insulated from physical compulsion, for no
matter how such compulsion may disguise itself as occurring under the regime
of a spiritual realm, it occurs at the behest of a secular power.[47] For Milton, the
papacy's claim to authority over the spiritual realm was fraudulent, since it was
enforced through temporal means.

In turn, Roman Catholicism can never be tolerated in Milton's England because
it is the equivalent of loyalty to a foreign prince:

> But as for poperie and idolatrie, why they also may not hence plead to be
> tolerated, I have much less to say. Their religion the more considerd, the less
> can be acknowledgd a religion; but a Roman principalitie rather, endeavouring
> to keep up her old universal dominion under a new name and meer shaddow of
> a catholic religion; being indeed more rightly nam'd a catholic heresie against
> the scripture; supported mainly by a civil and, except in *Rome*, by a forein
> power: justly therfore to be suspected, not tolerated by the magistrate of another
> countrey.[48]

For Milton, English Roman Catholics, rather than professing another religion,
were actually professing loyalty to another temporal sovereign. In this respect,

---

[43]   For a related reading of Milton's views on ecclesiastical coercion, see Donnelly,
Milton's Scriptural Reasoning, 49–72; 175–7.

[44]   Milton, *A Treatise of Civil Power in Ecclesiastical Causes*, in *CPW*, vol. 7, 245.

[45]   Milton, *Treatise of Civil Power*, in *CPW*, vol. 7, 260–62.

[46]   Milton, *Treatise of Civil Power*, in *CPW*, vol. 7, 255.

[47]   Thus in Milton's early poem "Lycidas," the "two-handed engine at the door," can
only "smite once, and smite no more" (130–31). See "Lycidas" in Merritt Y. Hughes's
edition of *Complete Poems and Major Prose*.

[48]   Milton, *Treatise of Civil Power*, in *CPW*, vol. 7, 254.

Milton's position was not that different from the position of the English crown during the sixteenth and early seventeenth centuries, which had tried Jesuits as traitors to the crown rather than as heretics to the English Church. But there is another more important aspect of this passage—what distinguishes the Roman Church is that, in reality, it is ancient imperial Rome reincarnated in such a way that it can "keep up her old universal dominion under a new name." In essence, Milton readily acknowledges that the purpose of the church hierarchy is to enforce Christian discipline, but since no temporal power, neither Roman nor English, can compel what is inward, invisible, and inviolable, the regime of discipline enforced by the Roman Church is both illegitimate and ineffective.

In fact, Milton's conception of church discipline, central to his entire antiprelatical polemic, never underwent the radical transformation that occurred within his conception of English nationhood.[49] Thus, in an early work of antiprelatism such as *The Reason of Church Government* (1642), Milton inveighs against the divisions within ecclesiastical edifices that separate the clean from the unclean, the consecrated from the unconsecrated, the hallowed from the unhallowed. Just as there should be no essential difference between bishop and priest, so should there be no essential difference between priest and parishioner. For Milton at the beginning of the civil war, the congregation comprises a collective and fraternal priesthood that should ideally discipline individual members that go astray. After the elimination of priests and bishops, "the congregation of the Lord [would] soone recover the true likenesse and visage of what she is indeed, a holy generation, a royall Priesthood, a Saintly communion, the houshold and City of God."[50] Rather than descending from within a vertical church hierarchy, discipline should proceed horizontally from councils and community. The individual should be disciplined not by a priest but rather "in the presence of two or three his faithfull brethren appointed thereto."[51] And the ultimate act of discipline, excommunication, should proceed through a communal process, at the end of which, "if, neither the regard of himselfe, nor the reverence of his Elders and friends prevaile with [the individual], to leave his vitious appetite, then as the time urges, such engines of terror God hath given into the hands of his minister as to search the tenderest angles of the heart." What follows is a collective act in which the congregation together will "dissolve their fellowship with him, and holding forth the dreadfull sponge of excommunion, pronounce him wip't out of the list of God's inheritance, and in the custody of Satan till he repent."[52]

Milton's ideas on congregationalism lead to the inevitable question of how to unify the church. Early on in *The Reason of Church Government*, for example,

---

[49] For analysis of how the focus of Milton's antiprelatical tracts is on discipline not doctrine, see Thomas N. Corns, "Milton's Antiprelatical Tracts and the Marginality of Doctrine," in *Milton and Heresy*, ed. Stephen B. Dobranski and John P. Rumrich (New York, 1998), 39–48.

[50] Milton, *Reason of Church Government*, in *CPW*, vol. 1, 844.

[51] Milton, *Reason of Church Government*, in *CPW*, vol. 1, 846.

[52] Milton, *Reason of Church Government*, in *CPW*, vol. 1, 847.

The Christian Nation and Beyond   283

Milton struggles with the unwelcome reality of sectarianism that inevitably creates divisions between different groups of the faithful. He admits that a church hierarchy of prelates culminating in an archbishop has the advantage of serving as a unifying force. But he surmises that establishing an office of archbishop as head of the national church in order to resolve schisms must logically lead to the institution of a Protestant pope, with a transnational jurisdiction:

> so I observe here, that if to quiet schisme there must be one head of Prelaty in a land or Monarchy rising from a Provinciall to a nationall Primacy, there may upon better grounds of repressing schisme be set up one catholick head over the catholick Church. For the peace and good of the Church is not terminated in the schismelesse estate of one or two kingdomes, but should be provided for by the joynt consultation of all reformed Christendome: that all controversie may end in the finall pronounce or canon of one Arch-primat, or Protestant Pope. Although by this meanes for ought I see, all the diameters of schisme may as well meet and be knit up in the center of one grand falshood.[53]

Indeed, because Christianity is an inherently universalist and transnational religion, not tied to the well-being or divinity of one nation over others, the institution of an archbishop over the kingdom will inevitably imply the need for a pope to preside over "all reformed Christendome." And thus the institution of bishops and archbishops over the national Church will inevitably be the "very wombe for a new subantichrist to breed in."[54] Indeed the problem of how to reconcile the desire for unity with the inviolable freedom of conscience is something that haunts all of Milton's antiprelatical tracts.

Later in the same tract, he responds to these concerns by arguing that prelatry, far from preventing schisms, actually causes them since prelates separate themselves from and privilege themselves before other Christians. Thus, once again, he argues first that "the chiefest remedy we have to keep Christendom at one ... is by councels" and second that the purveyance of good education on the basis of scripture is crucial for unity.[55] Beyond councils and sound education, Milton views the search for the truth as inevitably causing divisions to occur, making schism the natural result of reforming and redeeming the church. According to the section on sects and schisms (chapter 7 of Book I), the reforming of a church is "never brought to effect without the fierce encounter of truth and falshood together."[56] This notion, which Eve articulates in the crucial passage presaging Satan's temptation in Book IX of *Paradise Lost*, that virtue or truth must encounter and overcome vice or falsehood, is central to Milton's entire corpus (IX.322–41). Truth is not truth and virtue is not virtue without "the fierce encounter" with vice in the public realm, the "exterior help" which Eve says "sustains" virtue (IX.336). In this respect, Milton seems to be acknowledging that, no matter how injurious they are to the fabric of

---

[53] Milton, *Reason of Church Government*, in *CPW*, vol. 1, 783.
[54] Milton, *Reason of Church Government*, in *CPW*, vol. 1, 783.
[55] Milton, *Reason of Church Government*, in *CPW*, vol. 1, 791.
[56] Milton, *Reason of Church Government*, in *CPW*, vol. 1, 796.

284 *Early Modern Catholics, Royalists, and Cosmopolitans*

reformed Christendom, schism and differences among the various sects are at least beneficial for the search for the truth.

Later in *Areopagitica* (1644), Milton would argue that there could be a kind of unity among the separatism and sectarianism that characterized Protestant England. In *Areopagitica*, Milton's purpose is to reinvigorate the godly nation of England "as a knowing people, a Nation of Prophets, of Sages, and of Worthies," and paradoxically schism and separatism is an integral part of the process.[57] He imagines rebuilding the godly nation of England based on the analogy of building the Jewish Temple in Jerusalem:

> there must be many schisms and many dissections made in the quarry and in the timber, ere the house of God can be built. And when every stone is laid artfully together, it cannot be united into a continuity, it can but be contiguous in this world; neither can every peece of the building be of one form; nay rather the perfection consists in this, that out of many moderat varieties and brotherly dissimilitudes that are not vastly disproportionall arises the goodly and gracefull symmetry that commends the whole pile and structure. Let us therefore be more considerat builders, more wise in spirituall architecture, when great reformation is expected.[58]

In *Areopagitica* at least, these "moderat varieties and brotherly dissimilitudes" are able to cohere into a unitary and godly "house of God" in such a way that, in this process of separatism and sectarianism, there remains a kind of unity to the body politic, from which a unitary truth emerges. England is like the Temple because, like the Jews, the English comprise the divine elect, a "Nation chos'n before any other" to spread liberty and the reformed religion.[59] This is the England that Milton, later in the same work, compares to Samson, "a noble and puissant Nation rousing herself like a strong man after sleep, and shaking her invincible locks."[60]

On the one hand, then, in the *Areopagitica* and certain other early writings by Milton, the English people have a special mission to spread the light of liberty to the world. On the other hand, Milton could elsewhere display profound pessimism about dangerous division and disunity being introduced into the English body politic through sectarianism. Whereas in *Areopagitica* and the *Second Defense*, Milton sees unity arising out of sectarianism, elsewhere, in the *Tenure of Kings and Magistrates* (1649), Milton was not so sanguine. In this tract, Milton observes that the rampant sectarianism that resulted in the civil war means that certain

---

[57] Milton, *Areopagitica*, in *CPW*, vol. 2, 554.

[58] Milton, *Areopagitica*, in *CPW*, vol. 2, 555. For context, see David Loewenstein, "Milton's Nationalism and the English Revolution: Strains and Contradictions," in *Early Modern Nationalism*, 25–50, at 31.

[59] Milton, *Areopagitica*, in *CPW*, vol. 2, 552.

[60] Milton, *Areopagitica*, in *CPW*, vol. 2, 558. See also the *Second Defense*, in which Milton describes the English comprised of "citizens, with pre-eminent virtue and a nobility and steadfastness surpassing all the glory of their ancestors." Milton, *Second Defense*, in *CPW*, vol. 4, part 1, 548–9.

elements of the English populace will never develop the enlightened view that Milton and his congregationalist allies have championed.[61] He singles out the king and his supporters for special derision, comparing their attempt at subjugating the English people to a foreign conquest by England's arch-enemy, the King of Spain: "For look, how much right the King of *Spaine* hath to govern us at all, so much right hath the king of *England* to govern us tyrannically."[62] He goes on to redefine the bonds of liberty and enlightenment as not confined to England's frontiers in ways that remind us of the cosmopolitan perspective of his political and religious enemies. Indeed, it is here that we see that Milton's cosmopolitan perspective mirrors that of his royalist opponents such as Fanshawe:

> Who knows not that there is a mutual bond of amity and brother-hood between man and man over all the world, neither is it the English sea that can sever us from that duty and relation: a straiter bond yet there is between fellow-subjects, neighbours, and friends; But when any of these doe one to another so as hostility could do no worse, what doth the Law decree less against them, then op'n enemies and invaders? or if the Law be not present, or too weake, what doth it warrant us to less than single defense, or civil warr? and from that time forward the Law of civil defensive warr differs nothing from the Law of forren hostility. Nor is it distance of place that makes enmitie, but enmity that makes distance. He, therefore, that keeps peace with me, neer or remote, of whatsoever Nation, is to mee, as farr as all civil and human offices an Englishman and neighbour: but if an Englishman forgetting all Laws, human, civil and religious, offend against life and liberty, to him offended and to the Law in his behalf, though born in the same womb, he is no better then a Turk, a Sarasin, a Heathen.[63]

Although it may not be immediately apparent, there is an important religious subtext to this passage. In the sentences that precede these important words, Milton emphasizes those "many thousand [devout] Christians destroy'd" by the royalist army of King Charles I during the civil war.[64] In the passage itself, Milton explains that he has more in common with similarly enlightened Christians overseas than he does with King Charles and his militants. It may be that the law, "a straiter bond," binds him to the king's English and Scottish supporters, but the open hostilities that occurred during the civil war have transformed Charles's royal army into invaders no different from an invading foreign army. In this respect, Milton claims that there is no difference between a civil war and a foreign war—the aggression of the king's party transforms them into foreigners. Milton concludes by saying that any Englishman that offends "against life and liberty ... though born in the same womb, ... is no better then a Turk, a Sarasin, a Heathen." Once again, those Englishmen that lack the enlightened religion and persecute true Christians are the

---

[61] For discussion of the immediate political context of this work, especially Milton's attempt to address his Presbyterian opponents, see Corns, *Uncloistered Virtue*, 194–220.

[62] Milton, *The Tenure of Kings and Magistrates*, in *CPW*, vol. 3, 214.

[63] Milton, *The Tenure of Kings and Magistrates*, in *CPW*, vol. 3, 214–15.

[64] Milton, *The Tenure of Kings and Magistrates*, in *CPW*, vol. 3, 214.

286   *Early Modern Catholics, Royalists, and Cosmopolitans*

equivalent of the non-Christian heathen—they are radically other in both religious and political terms.

Similar to the manner in which Fanshawe perceived the Portuguese rebellion against the Castilian crown as a civil war analogous to the English civil war, Milton presents the English civil war as a war of foreign aggression initiated by King Charles, whom he compares to the king of Spain. It is here that Milton's cosmopolitan perspective seems to mirror Fanshawe's perspective in that from opposite sides of the religious and political spectrum, Milton and Fanshawe both perceive themselves to be participating in a transnational polity that exceeds the boundaries of their nation. To be sure, it is this same instinct to look past the nation that ultimately causes Milton to reject majority rule in *The Readie and Easie Way*, in which Milton shows a reluctance to submit to what fellow republican Sir Henry Vane complained was the "depraved, corrupted, and self-interested will" of the English populace, if left to "its own free motion."[65] If, for example, a majority of the English people chose a return to monarchy, Milton's enlightened minority should compel them to reverse their decision:

> is it just or reasonable, that most voices against the main end of government should enslave the less number that would be free? More just it is doubtless, if it com to force, that a less number compell a greater to retain, which can be no wrong to them, thir libertie, then that a greater number for the pleasure of thir baseness, compell a less most injuriously to be thir fellow slaves. They who seek nothing but their own just libertie, have alwaies right to winn it and to keep it, when ever they have power, be the voices never so numerous that opposed it.[66]

Thus, the enlightened minority ultimately has the prerogative to overrule the populace when they choose a path towards tyranny.[67] Notice once again the parallel with the position of Persons and Sander who similarly saw the pope and his bishops as comprising an enlightened minority with the prerogative authority to correct or depose a sovereign that implemented tyrannical or heretical policies.[68]

It is tempting to see Milton as simply inconsistent on this point, but there remains an important continuity that runs through all of Milton's prose work, namely, that what qualifies an enlightened minority to wield such power is Milton's notion that they comprise an elect community of "prophets" or "Sages" or "worthies."[69]

---

[65] Sir Henry Vane, *A Needful Corrective or Ballance in Popular Government* (London, 1659), A3v.

[66] Milton, *Readie and Easie Way to Establish a Free Commonwealth*, in *CPW*, vol. 7, 455. For some perspective on this passage, see Warren Chernaik, "Milton, the English Nation, and Cromwell," in *Early Modern Nationalism*, 73–114, at 101–2, and 111 n.91.

[67] For a discussion of this aspect of Milton within the context of his later pessimistic prose tracts, see D'Addario, *Exile and Journey*, 98–102.

[68] See Chapter 1. For a discussion of Milton's views on civil idolaters who would make a god out of their king, see Richard F. Hardin, *Civil Idolatry: Desacralizing and Monarchy in Spenser, Shakespeare, and Milton* (Newark, DE, 1992), 164–201.

[69] Milton, *Areopagitica*, in *CPW*, vol. 2, 554.

In other words, for Milton, the elect should take up the role of the church hierarchy within the republic. As Milton says in *The Tenure of Kings and Magistrates*, the power of the sovereign derives from the people and it is people "in whom the power yet remains fundamentally."[70] Similarly, he sees the republic as energized when it becomes, according to Paul Stevens, "a priesthood of all believers, a nation of prophets or individuals thinking dialogically within the framework of reason."[71] In effect, Milton has only eliminated the office of bishop in order to replace it with congregations comprised of individual enlightened members, each of which becomes his own priest and bishop, with the analogous ability to correct the sovereign through his representatives in parliament.

Thus, if on the one hand Milton had an agonistic relationship with English nationalism throughout his career, one can find, on the other hand, a consistency within his antiprelatical tracts, for it is in these works that Milton identifies the individual enlightened Christian as subsuming the office of the prelate, and this in turn forms the basis of his cosmopolitan perspective. Indeed, in his last prose tract, *Of True Religion, Heresy, Schism, and Toleration*, he shows that his views on the pope and the bishops had not altered since his earliest prose pamphlets, written during the Bishops' Wars of the early 1640s. Indeed, Milton's *Of True Religion* contains his clearest articulation of the political danger of the papacy and the church hierarchy to the sovereignty of temporal powers:

> Popery is a double thing to deal with, and claims a twofold Power, Ecclesiastical, and Political, both usurpt, and the one supporting the other.
>
> But Ecclesiastical is ever pretended to Political. The Pope by this mixt faculty, pretends right to Kingdoms and States, and especially to this of *England*, Thrones and Unthrones Kings, and absolves the people from obedience to them; sometimes interdicts to whole Nations the Publick worship of God, shutting up their Churches; and was wont to dreign away greatest part of the wealth of this then miserable Land, as part of his Patrimony, to maintain the Pride and Luxury of his Courts and Prelates.[72]

Here, Milton harshly ridicules the papal power of prerogative over temporal sovereigns, but it is worth noting that traditional Catholic writers from Sander to Persons and on to Bellarmine would have had no trouble recognizing their own claims for the papal power of deposition in this caricature. Whereas Milton's perspective on English nationalism and the English people might have undergone a radical transformation during these years, Milton's condemnation of the papal deposing power found in this passage is indistinguishable from his position almost 30 years earlier in *Areopagitica*, where he had written that "Popery ..., which as it extirpats all religions and civill supremacies, so it self should be extirpat."[73]

---

[70] Milton, *The Tenure of Kings and Magistrates*, in *CPW*, vol. 3, 202.

[71] Paul Stevens, "How Milton's Nationalism Works," in *Early Modern Nationalism*, 273–304, at 291.

[72] Milton, *Of True Religion, Heresy, Schism, and Toleration*, in *CPW*, vol. 8, 429.

[73] Milton, *Areopagitica*, in *CPW*, vol. 2, 565.

288   *Early Modern Catholics, Royalists, and Cosmopolitans*

For Milton, the problem with popes and bishops had always been that they claimed the power to intervene in the affairs of the temporal realm, and from a very early point in his career, Milton was unequivocal in claiming that rather than strengthening kings, bishops and the pope actually weakened monarchs. By claiming, as he does here, that "Popery" poses the ultimate threat to "civill supremacies," Milton was in part responding to James I, who had once explained that if bishops were eliminated from the church, "I know what would become of my supremacy." The king had famously continued: "No bishop, no King. When I mean to live under a presbytery I will go to Scotland again."[74] In response to such arguments, Milton repeatedly argues throughout his early tract, *Of Reformation*, that prelates actually weaken legitimate sovereignty, including that claimed by kings. According to Milton, history is replete with examples of popes and bishops interfering in temporal affairs, fomenting rebellions, deposing rightful sovereigns, and extracting "heaps of *gold*, and *silver*" from the country through the ecclesiastical courts.[75] Later in *The Reason of Church Government*, Milton compares the church hierarchy to Delila, clipping the hair of Samson, who represents the sovereign, "laying down his head among the strumpet flatteries of Prelats."[76] Milton goes on to call England's bishops "clippers of regal power and shavers of the Laws" and to warn of their attempts to restrict the power of parliament itself: "how they stand affected to the law giving Parliament, your selves, worthy Peeres and Commons, can best testifie; the current of whose glorious and immortal actions hath bin only oppos'd by the obscure and pernicious designes of the Prelats: until their insolence broke out to such a bold affront, as hath justly immur'd their haughty looks within strong wals."[77] Milton's reference to the prelates' "bold affront" refers to the "Petition and Protestation of all the Bishops" of December 10, 1641 in which Bishop Joseph Hall and 11 other bishops declared recent proceedings, which excluded the bishops from parliament, to be "null and of no effect." On December 30, 1641, in response to the bishops' "Humble Petition," the Court of Parliament ordered 10 bishops committed to the Tower of London and 2 to be turned over to the Black Rod.[78] For Milton, the pope and the church hierarchy had, throughout history, sought to usurp legitimate temporal sovereignty, and the English bishops' attempt to disregard and declare illegal the law which had recently excluded them from parliament, was a further indication of Milton's claim that throughout history, whether Roman or English, the episcopal hierarchy had sought to undermine legitimate temporal authority.[79]

---

[74]   Cited in David Harris Willson, *King James VI & I* (London, 1963), 207.

[75]   Milton, *Of Reformation*, in *CPW*, vol. 1, 592.

[76]   Milton, *The Reason of Church-Government*, in *CPW*, vol. 1, 859.

[77]   Milton, *The Reason of Church-Government*, in *CPW*, vol. 1, 860.

[78]   John Rushworth, *Historical Collections: Abridg'd and Improv'd* (8 vols, London, 1706), vol. 4, Q4–Q4v.

[79]   For an exploration of the larger historical context of these early tracts and Milton's attempts to position himself within the mainstream politics, see Sharon Achinstein, "John Milton and the Communities of Resistance, 1641–2" in *Writing and Religion in England, 1558–1689: Studies in Community-Making and Cultural Memory*, ed. Roger D. Sell and Anthony W. Johnson, (Burlington, VT, 2009), 289–304.

The Christian Nation and Beyond   289

Finally, it is worth noting that Milton also comments extensively on the role of Pope Eleutherius in Britain's ecclesiastical history, which is significant given the importance that Persons attributes to Eleutherius's letter to King Lucius in his refutation of John Foxe, which we explored at the end of Chapter 1. Predictably, in contrast to the role that Pope Eleutherius plays in Persons's *Treatise of the Three Conversions*, Milton's portrayal of Eleutherius confirms his antiprelatism. In his early tract, *Of Reformation*, Milton refutes the English bishops' claim that "no forme of Church government is agreeable to monarchy, but that of Bishops" by calling on them to follow the advice put down by Pope Eleutherius in his response to King Lucius's request that the Bishop of Rome help him introduce into Britain a Christian ecclesiastical regime.[80] According to Milton, Eleutherius wrote that King Lucius should simply organize religious and civil law by following scripture. According to Milton's account, Pope Eleutherius bid King Lucius "to betake himselfe to the old, and new Testament, and receive direction from them how to administer both Church, and Common-wealth."[81] On the basis of Eleutherius's letter, Milton concludes that church governance by bishops was not part of the earliest Christian government.

Later, however, Milton reveals himself to have been doubtful concerning the entire exchange between Pope Eleutherius and King Lucius. In *The History of Britain, That part especially now called England*, which he seems to have begun in 1648, then abandoned and then finally published in 1670, Milton recounts Bede's account of King Lucius requesting Eleutherius's help in establishing a Christian commonwealth, only to dismiss Lucius's missive itself as "an improbable Letter" and speculating that Bede may have erred in his account, having lived "neer 500 years after."[82] In general, Milton's *History of Britain* is both a skeptical and pessimistic history of the island, which repeatedly calls into question the truth of the events recounted therein.[83] At the same time, as Thomas N. Corns notes, the *History* is brimming with "a playful anticlericalism and an abrasive puritanical Protestantism."[84] Indeed, even Milton's skeptical perspective on British history tends to confirm his antiprelatical stance. Thus, the History reveals that the clergy, as represented by figures like the monk, Elmer, who claimed the power of prophecy but "could not forsee, when time was, the breaking of his own Legs" during an experiment in manned flight, consist primarily of charlatans and

---

[80]   Milton, *Of Reformation*, in *CPW*, vol. 1, 573.

[81]   Milton, *Of Reformation*, in *CPW*, vol. 1, 574.

[82]   Milton, *The History of Britain, That part especially now called England*, in *CPW*, vol. 5, part 1, 97.

[83]   Gary D. Hamilton, "The History of Britain and its Restoration audience," in *Politics Poetics, and Hermeneutics in Milton's Prose*, ed. David Loewenstein et al. (New York, 1990), 241–55, at 246.

[84]   Thomas N. Corns, "Milton and the Limitations of Englishness," in *Early Modern Nationalism*, 205–17, at 212. In his 1698 biography of Milton, John Toland noted that a number of the most anti-clerical passages in Milton's *History* were expunged. See Helen Darbishire (ed.), *The Early Lives of Milton* (London, 1965), 237–8.

mountebanks.[85] In other instances, Milton questions the very monastic sources that he later acknowledges "must be follow'd," calling the monks "dubious Relaters," who wrote history "to the best advantage of what they term holy Church, meaning indeed themselves."[86] Forced to use sources that were implicated in the very church hierarchy Milton had spent his life critiquing, Milton finally eschews a progressive or providential conception of national history, which might have provided insight on contemporary England.[87]

More revealing contradictions in his antiprelatical stance can be found in *Eikonoklastes*, Milton's response to *Eikon Basilike*, Charles I's posthumous memoir on the civil war, which was probably written in part or at least compiled by Charles's supporters after his execution. At a critical moment in *Eikon Basilike*, Charles declares that the crown of England was never "bound by any coronation oath" or obliged "to consent to whatever its subjects in Parliament shall require." Furthermore, he has always refused to submit to those that seek to deprive him "of the liberty of using my reason with a good conscience," the capacity of which, he claims, every individual enjoys.[88] In his response, Milton condemns the king for admitting openly the desire to subject his people to tyranny: "What Tyrant could presume to say more, when he meant to kick down all Law, Government, and bond of Oath?" According to Milton, the coronation oath was an ancient guarantor that the king did not "make himself Superiour to his whole Kingdom" and insures that the king understands that he himself is subject to two superiors, "the Law and his Court of Parliament." What is notable about Milton's stance on the coronation oath, however, is that although Milton could even recite the portion of the Latin and Old English versions of the oath that were relevant to his argument, he would not allow himself to mention that the oath itself was administered by the Archbishop of Canterbury or that the first of the king's three pledges was to defend the church.[89] It is worth recalling that, for Persons, the coronation oath was crucial to the Catholic defense of the papal right to depose or correct a wayward sovereign. In contrast, for Milton, the coronation oath is crucially important because it verifies the king's obligation to obey the English law and consult with the parliament. In order to champion the coronation oath, Milton must omit the role of the archbishop and the portion of the oath itself that pertains to the church in order to focus on the second and third portions of the oath in which the king agreed to uphold the law and submit himself to parliament.[90] Similarly, towards the

---

[85]   Milton, *History of Britain*, in *CPW*, vol. 5, part 1, 394.

[86]   Milton, *History of Britain*, in *CPW*, vol. 5, part 1, 128, 127.

[87]   Far from glorifying the English as a chosen people, the unfinished *History* ends with William the Conqueror's conquest of the island. See Corns, "Milton and the Limitations of Englishness," 211. For the opposing view that Milton's *History of Britain* shows an investment in historical progress, see Andrew Escobedo, *Nationalism and Historical Loss in Renaissance England: Foxe, Dee, Spenser, Milton* (Ithaca, NY, 2004), 185–245.

[88]   *Eikon Basilike; The portraiture of His Sacred Majesty in his solitudes and sufferings*, ed. Philip A. Knachel (Ithaca, NY, 1966), 26.

[89]   Milton, *Eikonoklastes*, in *CPW*, vol. 3, 414–15.

[90]   Milton, *Eikonoklastes*, in *CPW*, vol. 3, 414, n.20; 415.

The Christian Nation and Beyond   291

end of *Eikonoklastes*, Milton finds support for his republican views by referencing Ambrose's excommunication of Emperor Theodosius for ordering the massacre of Thessalonica in 390 CE, without mentioning Ambrose's status as Bishop of Milan. Instead, Milton claims that simply by virtue of being Theodosius's "subject," Ambrose had a right to correct his emperor's bloody behavior.[91]

Such omissions and contradictions reveal important insights into Milton's conception of the political relationship between sovereign and subject. It is worth recalling that, for Milton, the conscience of any individual, whether king or subject, is ultimately not subject to any external ecclesiastical authority. In this respect, Charles I's refusal to submit to an external coronation oath administered by the archbishop ironically confirms Milton's own argument, advanced consistently throughout his antiprelatical writings, that each individual's conscience is subject, not to ecclesiastical authority, but rather to his own reason and reading of the Scripture. In the end, Milton would perceive the conscience of Charles to be no different from the conscience of any other individual, declaring in the second edition of *Eikonoklastes* that just as the king considered his coronation oath to be simply a "brutish formality," the English people shall henceforth view the Oaths of Allegiance and Supremacy as merely "brutish and as formal," since by the king's "own sentence" they are "no more binding to us then his Oath to him."[92] During the same year that Milton published *Eikonoklastes*, he published the *Tenure of Kings and Magistrates*, in which he follows a collection of Protestant divines including Martin Luther, Zwinglius, Jean Calvin, Martin Bucer, Peter Martyr, John Knox, Thomas Cartwright, Dudley Fenner, Anthony Gilby, and Christopher Goodman in claiming that the people may violate their oath and depose a tyrannical sovereign.[93] And yet, at the end of this tract, Milton attributes to these divines a less radical position than might be expected, namely, that "to doe justice on a lawless King, is to a privat man unlawful, to an inferior Magistrate lawfull."[94] For Milton, the only party that could legitimately correct a king was an "inferior Magistrate," presumably a noble who would assume the role of Campion's and Persons's bishop: caretaker of the realm and of the king's conscience.

Whether in the form of an "inferior Magistrate" or his borderless nation of saints or prophets, Milton was ultimately counting on the power and authority of kings to be limited by elect individuals that eschewed the formal ecclesiastical authority and ceremony of bishops. As I have noted, Milton's elect polity, to which he presumably belonged, was not coterminous with England or Britain. Milton's perception of his own future prospects during the Restoration, evinced in the bleak outlook of his *Treatise of Civil Power* and the *Readie and Easie Way*, may have led to his pessimism over the future of the English people, which can be found in

---

[91]   Milton, *Eikonoklastes*, in *CPW*, vol. 3, 587.

[92]   Milton, *Eikonoklastes*, in *CPW*, vol. 3, 415.

[93]   Milton, *Tenure of Kings and Magistrates*, vol. 3, 242–50. For discussion of these works within their immediate political context, see Corns, *Uncloistered Virtue: English Political Literature, 1640–1660*, 194–220.

[94]   Milton, *Tenure of Kings and Magistrates*, vol. 3, 257.

those tracts. But as I have shown, one can find the roots of this pessimism towards the English nation in his earliest antiprelatical tracts such as *Of Reformation*, in which he declares in the first few pages that he seeks to bring the English churches in conformity with "the rest of the [Protestant] *Churches* abroad."[95] Milton's perspective on such matters was not limited to the frontiers of England; rather, it was based on a transnational community of educated elites, who would assume the role that the transnational church hierarchy had once assumed both within the spiritual and the temporal realms. Thus, Milton's nation could ultimately be said to be a borderless, egalitarian, and elite collective of substitute "bishops," willing to self-discipline on the religious front and to serve as a check on the worst instincts of their own magistrates. Not unlike sixteenth-century English writers considered in Part 1 of this book, Milton managed to transform and appropriate that aspect of the ecclesiastical order, whose responsibility it was to correct the excesses of the temporal order, while rejecting the ecclesiastical hierarchy itself.

---

[95] Milton, *Of Reformation*, in *CPW*, vol. 1, 527.

Chapter 7

Royalist Turned Cosmopolitan:
Aphra Behn's Portrait of the
Prostituted Sovereign

Up to this point in my account of literary manifestations of cosmopolitanism, I have focused on political and religious ideologies and have ignored the role of commerce. But as historians of early modern political thought have shown, commercial interests constituted an important factor in the rise of the Enlightenment ideal of the world citizen.[1] Furthermore, commerce was often viewed optimistically as countervailing what were perceived as the violent and backward-looking forces of tribe and nation. For example, in 1711, Joseph Addison and Richard Steel, describing the dizzying mixture of peoples, faiths, and languages on the floor of the Royal Exchange in London, arrived at an optimistic philosophical ideal of classical cosmopolitanism: "I am infinitely delighted in the mixing with these several Ministers of Commerce, as they are distinguished by their different Walks and different Languages: Sometimes I am jostled among a body of *Armenians*: Sometimes I am lost in a Crowd of *Jews*, and sometimes make one in a Groupe of *Dutch-men*. I am a *Dane, Swede, or French-Man* at different times, or rather fancy myself like the old Philosopher, who upon being asked what Countryman he was, replied, That he was a Citizen of the World."[2] It should be clear that one of my aims in this book has been to correct the widely accepted historical narrative of cosmopolitanism as having its origins in the Enlightenment values of free commercial exchange and secular philosophical reason, embodied in this passage. As we have seen, the history of early modern cosmopolitanism is far more nuanced, having its roots in a complex secular engagement with the Roman Catholic conception of the Christian commonwealth. In this chapter, I show that in the wake of the Restoration, Aphra Behn's perspective on commercial cosmopolitanism was as conservative as it was groundbreaking, revealing a complex combination of nostalgia for and derision towards the national rivalries and international conflicts of an earlier age.

Behn's famous two-part play, *The Rover* (1677, 1681) drew heavily from an earlier source, Thomas Killigrew's *Thomaso*, a closet drama supposedly based on Killigrew's life as a royalist exile when he made a brief visit to Madrid.[3] Both

---

[1]   Jacob, *Strangers Nowhere in the World*, 1–13, 66–94.

[2]   *The Spectator*, Sunday 19 May 1711, reprinted in *The Royal Exchange*, ed. Ann Saunders(London, 1997), 206–7.

[3]   See Nancy Copeland, "'Once a Whore and Ever'? Whore and Virgin in *The Rover* and its Antecedents," *Restoration: Studies in English Literary Culture 1660–1700* 16.1

294   *Early Modern Catholics, Royalists, and Cosmopolitans*

Killigrew's and Behn's plays harken back to an earlier period of intense Anglo-Spanish rivalry. In both versions, cunning Spaniards make reference to stealing from "Old Queen *Besse*" or Queen Elizabeth and, in Behn's version, further reference is made to Spain having had "a quarrel to her [i.e. with Elizabeth] ever since *Eighty-Eight*," a reference to the defeat of the Armada.[4] But, in contrast to Killigrew, Behn's play references a more specific facet of the rivalry with Spain whereby Englishmen were presented as potential liberators of peoples victimized by the Spanish imperium. Behn sets her play in Spanish-occupied Naples, where a group of English royalists arrive and "liberate" the oppressed women, or subjects, that inhabit the city. What is singular about the play is that, since the protagonists, Belvile and Willmore, are exiled royalists, they are liberators according to a monarchical ideology that was anachronistic within Commonwealth England. Of course, Behn's play was first performed in 1677 after the Restoration, and thus, one might expect it to show support for the restored monarchical ideology. But as Helen M. Burke has argued, Behn's English "liberators" are ridiculed throughout the play.[5] In particular, they fail to live up to the sixteenth- and early seventeenth-century ideal of the English privateer, whom Sir Philip Sidney, Sir Walter Ralegh, and others presented as gallantly rescuing the oppressed from the clutches of Spanish tyranny.[6]

In this final chapter, I suggest that Aphra Behn's play both conveys nostalgia for an idealized Elizabethan past and presents an alternative to the traditional adoration of the sovereign, which had formed the basis of late sixteenth-century English national identity.[7] I consider the play as part of a trajectory of dramatic

---

(Spring 1992): 20–27; Elaine Hobby, "No Stolen Object, but Her Own: Aphra Behn's *Rover* and Thomas Killigrew's *Thomaso*," *Women's Writing* 6.1 (1999): 113–27; DeRitter Jones, "The Gypsy, *The Rover*, and The Wanderer: Aphra Behn's Revision of Thomas Killigrew," *Restoration: Studies in English Literary Culture 1660–1700* 10.2 (1986): 82–92. On the question of whether *Thomaso* really is a closet drama, see Marcus Nevitt, "Thomas Killigrew's *Thomaso* as Two-Part Comedy," in *Thomas Killigrew and the Seventeenth-Century English Stage: New Perspectives*, ed. Philip Major (Burlington, VT, 2013), 113–32.

[4] Aphra Behn, *The Rover*, part 1, 3.2.69–70, in *The Works of Aphra Behn*, ed. Janet Todd (7 vols, Columbus, 1996), vol. 5, 445–521; part 2 of *The Rover* is in vol. 6, 225–98. All citations are of part 1 of the play, except for one instance where part 2 is indicated in the text. Thomas Killigrew, *Thomaso*, in *Comedies and Tragedies* (London, 1967), 313–464, part 1, 375. Further citations of *The Rover* are parenthetically in the text by act, scene, and line number, while citations from *Thomaso*, indicating part 1 or part 2 of the play, are given by page numbers.

[5] Helen M. Burke, "The Cavalier Myth in *The Rover*," in *The Cambridge Companion to Aphra Behn*, ed. Derek Hughes and Janet Todd (New York, 2004), 118–34.

[6] For this view of Ralegh, see John Holmes, "The Guiana Projects: Imperial and Colonial Ideologies in Ralegh and Purchas," *Literature and History* 14.2 (2005): 1–13. For a related view of Sidney, see Brian C. Lockey, *Law and Empire*, 47–79.

[7] On similar nostalgia within Killigrew's dramatic works, see Karen Raber, "Warrior Women in the Plays of Cavendish and Killigrew," *Studies in English Literature* 40.3 (Summer 2000): 422–4.

works that formed an incremental critique of Elizabeth's defining place within the late sixteenth- and seventeenth-century English imagination. Behn was herself a Tory and her critique of English monarchy was not from the perspective of the Whig opposition. Neither was it exclusively from the position of sexual politics or proto-feminism, although it is clear that sexual politics play an important role in this critique.[8] Rather it was in the service of a cosmopolitan perspective, through which distinctions between various national identities are viewed as under pressure from new transnational commercial forces that cause such identities to collapse into one another.[9] Behn's cosmopolitan perspective substitutes commercial values for the religious and political cosmopolitanism that we have encountered in earlier chapters. As Willmore says in the second part of *The Rover*, "money speaks sense in a Language all Nations understand, 'tis Beauty, wit, Courage, Honour, and undisputable Reason— … *Socrates*, without ready money to lay down, must yield" (3.1.343–7). Ultimately, the play moves past nostalgia for the less complex definition of English national identity to a post-imperial perspective that substitutes the vitiated courtesan for the virgin queen.

Anglo-Spanish Rivalry and its Dissolution

When *The Rover* was staged in 1677, England confronted the most complex and chaotic international situation that it had faced since the beginning of the Thirty Years War. Spain's decline and the second and third Anglo-Dutch wars had irrevocably damaged England's traditional anti-Spanish alliance with the Dutch.[10] Viewing *The Rover* as a product of the transformations that had occurred since the Elizabethan period is instructive in this respect. During the late sixteenth century, English writers viewed Spain with an uneasy combination of admiration, fear, and contempt because of what they perceived as the cruel and oppressive policies initiated by the Spanish crown in the Americas and Continental Europe. Thus, in the opening pages of his 1595 tract entitled the *Discovery of Guiana*, Sir Walter Ralegh recounts his arrival at the island of Trinidad, where he encounters the leaders of various native communities, who complain of being persecuted by the Spanish governor Antonio de Berrío. Before leaving for the mainland of South America, Ralegh provides an account of a meeting with the inhabitants in which he presents Elizabeth as a protector against Spanish oppression:

---

[8] For a discussion of Behn's Tory politics and feminism, see Susan Owen, "Sexual Politics and Party Politics in Behn's Drama, 1678–83," in *Aphra Behn Studies*, ed. Janet Todd (New York, 1996), 15–29.

[9] For a recent historical account of cosmopolitanism during this period, see Jacob, *Strangers Nowhere in the World*, 66–94. For the intellectual traditions of cosmopolitanism during this period, see Heater, *World Citizenship and Government*, 60–88.

[10] See Charles Wilson, *Profit and Power: A Study of England and the Dutch Wars* (Boston, 1978).

> I called all the captains of the island together that were enemies to the Spaniards ... And by my Indian interpreter which I carried out of England, I made them understand that I was the servant of a Queen, who was the great cacique of the north, and a virgin, and had more caciqui under her than there were trees in that island; that she was an enemy to the Castellani in respect of their tyranny and oppression, and that she delivered all such nations about her, as were by them oppressed; and having freed all the coast of the northern world from their servitude, had sent me to free them also, and withal to defend the country of Guiana from their invasion and conquest. I showed them Her Majesty's picture which they so admired and honoured, as it had been easy to have brought them idolatrous thereof.[11]

Here, Ralegh presents the English sovereign as "delivering" nations that the Spanish had conquered and had oppressed.[12] This passage owes an obvious debt to the legends of Spanish brutality, made popular throughout Europe by Bartolomé de las Casas's account of Spanish atrocities in the New World.[13] In response to Las Casas, the idea that Englishmen should "deliver" or liberate those peoples oppressed by the bloodthirsty Spanish took on a life of its own. Late sixteenth- and early seventeenth-century Englishmen repeatedly saw their nation in competition with Spain, and much of this competition involved the idea that England had a more ethical strategy of foreign engagement than Spain had.[14]

As we shall see, nostalgia for a time of more intense anti-Spanish sentiment concerning English colonial competition with Spain is central to Behn's *The Rover*.

---

[11] Sir Walter Ralegh, *The Discovery of Guiana*, NetLibrary eBook (Hoboken, NJ, 1990s), 8. It is worth recalling that, when he arrived to the West Coast of North American during his circumnavigation, Sir Francis Drake erected a post which bore a brass plate, stating Queen Elizabeth's sovereignty over the area, in which a hole had been cut revealing a silver sixpence stamped with an image of the queen's head. See John Cummins, *Francis Drake: The Lives of Heroes* (New York, 1995), 118.

[12] For a discussion of the role of Elizabeth's portraits in representation of the crown, see Kevin Sharpe, *Selling the Tudor Monarchy: Authority and Image in Sixteenth-Century England* (New Haven, CT, 2009), 358–416.

[13] Bartolomé de las Casas, *Una brevíssima relación de la destruyción de las indias*, (Seville, 1552), was translated into French (*Tyrannies et cruautes des Espagnols* [Antwerp, 1579]), and from French into English in 1583 (*The Spanish Colonie, or Briefe Chronicle of the Acts and gestes of the Spaniardes in the West Indies, called the newe World, for the space of XL. yeeres* [London, 1583 (reprint, Ann Arbor, MI, 1966)]). For consideration of the so-called "black legend" of Spain throughout history, see *Rereading the Black Legend: The Discourses of Racism in the Renaissance Empires*, ed. Walter Mignolo, Margaret Greer, and Maureen Quilligan (Chicago, 2007); Maria DeGuzman, *Spain's Long Shadow: The Black Legend, Off-Whiteness, and Anglo-American Empire* (Minneapolis, 2005); and Charles Gibson, *The Black Legend: Anti-Spanish Attitudes in the Old World and the New* (New York, 1971).

[14] See William S. Maltby, *The Black Legend in England, the Development of Anti-Spanish Sentiment, 1558–1660* (Durham, NC, 1971); Richard McCabe, *Spenser's Monstrous Regiment: Elizabethan Ireland and the Poetics of Difference* (New York, 2002), 226–7; and Lockey, *Law and Empire*, 65–9.

The Madrid setting of Killigrew's original work lends itself more immediately to the politics of the itinerant exiled royalists.[15] For Killigrew, Madrid is an exotic and unfamiliar setting in which there certainly remains the sense of the historic competition between England and Spain, but Killigrew's setting of the play in Madrid also removes the center of such competition from the colonial context. In contrast, Behn's *Rover* is set in Spanish-occupied Naples and thus places the imperial context at the center of the play's themes. Las Casas's *Brevíssima relación* is important in this respect, since inhabitants of European countries such as the Netherlands that were governed by the Spanish crown during the late sixteenth century often perceived themselves as sharing with the Amerindians a common experience of being oppressed by a ruthless tyrannical power.[16] English readers, for example, could not help but see Las Casas's account of Spanish brutality as a warning to Europeans who faced Spanish aggression, since the first translation of Las Casas's book into English included the preface of the French translator, the Flemming Jacques de Miggrode or, as he is known in the English translation, James Alligrodo, who presented the *Brevíssima relación* as a warning to the Dutch on the importance of uniting the provinces against Spanish rule.[17] Spanish-governed Naples found itself in a similar situation during the seventeenth century, since it was ruled by a series of Spanish viceroys who often placed the interests of Spain ahead of those of Naples. During the seventeenth century, the joint kingdom of Naples and Sicily sustained a series of violent rebellions against perceived Spanish tyranny, the first occurring in 1647 in the cities of Naples and Palermo and the last occurring in Messina in 1674, in response to increased taxes on food, which the bankrupt Spanish government had been forced to impose.[18]

One inconsistency in the analogy that I am drawing here between Ralegh and Behn is that Behn's play contains no figures that are clearly identified as native Neapolitans besides possibly the fleeting entrance of the anonymous men and women dressed in "*Masquing Habits*," celebrating the carnival at the beginning of the play.[19] However, like many other dramatic and fictional works by Behn, this play seems to structure imperial and colonial politics around the issue of gender. In this respect, the female characters stand in for the oppressed subjects of Spanish imperial rule. Most significant of these are Pedro's sisters, Florinda and Hellena,

---

[15] For a comprehensive discussion of the politics of exile in Killigrew's play, see J. P. Vander Motten, "Recycling the Exile: *Thomaso, The Rover*, and the Critics," in *Thomas Killigrew and the Seventeenth-Century English Stage*, 133–50.

[16] Benjamin Schmidt, *Innocence Abroad: The Dutch Imagination and the New World, 1570–1670* (New York, 2001), 68–122.

[17] James Aliggrodo, preface to Bartolomé de las Casas, *The Spanish Colonie*, ¶2. For a modern edition of the original French translation, see *La destruction des Indes*, trans. Jacques de Miggrode, with preface by Alain Milhou (Paris, 1995).

[18] For context, see Anthony Pagden, *Spanish Imperialism and the Political Imagination* (New Haven, CT, 1990), 65–90.

[19] *The Rover*, 1.2.74–5, s.d. For a discussion of the carnivalesque in the play, see Linda R. Payne, "The Carnivalesque Regeneration of Corrupt Economics in *The Rover*," *Restoration: Studies in English Literary Culture: 1660–1700* 22.1 (1998): 40–49.

and Angellica Bianca, a native Italian courtesan from Padua, whose services had been purchased by Pedro's uncle, the now deceased Spanish General.

The gender-based colonial context of this play surfaces in the first scene, in which Don Pedro tells his sister, Florinda, that she is to marry Don Vincentio, identified as an ancient suitor who has made a great fortune in the Indies. Florinda and her sister Hellena are of course horrified, especially since Florinda is in love with the dashing young English cavalier Belvile. In a revealing exclamation, Hellena remarks, "*Don Vincentio! Don Indian!* he thinks he's trading to *Gambo* still, and wou'd Barter himself (that Bell and Bawble) for your Youth and Fortune" (1.1.125–6). Important aspects of the colonial context surface in Hellena's witty and sexually charged comment about Vincentio's "Bell and Bawble," a reference to his genitalia. The mention of Vincentio bartering "that Bell and Bawble" alludes to the European practice of trading worthless objects in order to exploit the resources of the indigenous populations in Africa and the New World, and "*Gambo*" functions as a reference to the slave trade in Gambia, West Africa. In Hellena's witty analogy, Vincentio is trading for the "Youth and Fortune" of Florinda, placing Florinda and her sister in the position of the exploited African slaves. Don Vincentio is the marriage choice of the siblings' absent father, whereas later in the scene, Pedro reveals his own desire that Florinda marry his friend, Antonio, the son of the Spanish viceroy of Naples. Even so, a marriage to Antonio amounts to essentially the same thing in the eyes of Florinda, who resists the patriarchal figures of control around her. Like Vincentio, Antonio's family has also obviously benefited from Spanish imperialism (in Italy).

In contrast to the Spanish suitors stands the valiant but destitute English suitor Belvile, who has played precisely the role that English explorers and privateers had played during an earlier period in relation to the oppressed New World subjects of the Spanish empire.[20] Before the events recounted in the play, Belvile seems to have been a mercenary, employed by the French during their invasion of the northern Spanish city of Pamplona, where Florinida happened to be residing. Florinda explains, "when I was expos'd to such dangers as the Licens'd Lust of common Souldiers threatned, when Rage and Conquest flew through the City— then *Belvile*, this Criminal for my sake, threw himself into all dangers to save my Honour" (1.1.66–70). In effect, Belvile turned against the French invaders, who employed him, in order to save Florinda's honour. Likewise, in the first act, Belvile promises once again to rescue her, going so far as to ask his former lieutenants to assist him in the rescue (1.2.237–55; 309–11), when a masked Florinda "invites [him] to deliver her from the threatned violence of her Brother" (1.2.237–8).[21] Thus while the Spanish (and French) men at the beginning of the play fit the stereotype of Spain as the oppressor of conquered peoples, Belvile fits the stereotype of the valiant Englishman prepared to risk his life to rescue the oppressed.

---

[20] Adam R. Beach, "Carnival Politics, General Satire, and Nationalist Spectacle in Behn's *The Rover*," *Eighteenth-Century Life* 28.3 (2004): 12.

[21] For a discussion of rape in the play, see Anita Pacheco, "Rape and the Female Subject in Aphra Behn's *The Rover*," *ELH* 65.2 (1998): 323–45.

Royalist Turned Cosmopolitan   299

As we shall see, however, this simplistic structure, Spanish oppressors versus English liberators, quickly collapses in a manner that blurs such identities and begins to challenge English national identity.[22] This collapse occurs around the figure of Angellica Bianca, the Italian courtesan, who advertises her services for the royal sum of 1,000 crowns a month by putting out portraits of her image in the street for passers-by. Angellica is trying to attract one of the rich Spaniards of the city, and she specifically mentions as possible suitors Florinda's brother, Pedro, and Florinda's official betrothed, Antonio. A violent confrontation occurs when a smitten Willmore pulls down the smallest of Angellica's portraits for a keepsake. Antonio takes offense and orders Willmore to "Restore the Picture, Sir" (2.1.208). When Willmore refuses to do so, the traditional Anglo-Spanish rivalry asserts itself. The Spaniards join Antonio's side, while the Englishmen Belvile, Frederick, and Blunt join Willmore's side. The Englishmen prevail, and in a telling comment, which situates the quarrel in historic Anglo-Spanish rivalry over the Low Countries, Willmore tells the retreating Spaniards: "A plague on your *Dons*; if they fight no better they'l ne're recover *Flanders*" (2.1.243–4).

In the events that occur next, things become more complex. Angellica falls in love with Willmore and invites him into her house, where he ends up enjoying her services without paying for them (2.1.274–431). On the most superficial level, Willmore is once again assuming the traditional position of the English soldier who offers to liberate Angellica from the oppressive Spaniards to which she is subjected. But in contrast to Florinda and Hellena and Ralegh's Elizabeth, Angellica is no virgin.[23] Rather she is an experienced courtesan who seeks to exploit those putative Spanish oppressors for the outrageous price of 1,000 crowns per month. Moreover, Willmore is certainly not in any position of power with regard to Angellica. The fact is that Willmore is in no position to save anyone—he is utterly destitute, and confesses that he is living from meal to meal (2.1.329).

The traditional narrative in which the English liberator fights to protect the virgin territory of the New World from the rapacious Spanish oppressor clearly do not apply to Angellica, but in spite of this, Willmore initially pushes matters in that direction by attempting to transform her into a "virgin" by reforming her.[24] At the same time, he also confesses that, like the wealthy Spanish youths, if he had sufficient money, he would gladly pay her for her services. Thus, Willmore embodies contradictory desires, telling her,

> Yes, I am poor—but I'm a Gentleman,
> And one that Scornes this baseness which you practice;

---

[22] For a recent article that treats the subject of national identity in the play, but comes to different conclusions from mine, see Beach, "Carnival Politics," 1–19.

[23] See Heidi Hutner, "Revisioning the Female Body: Aphra Behn's *The Rover*, Parts I and II," in *Rereading Aphra Behn: History, Theory, and Criticism*, ed. Heidi Hutner (Charlottesville, 1993), 102–220, and Copeland, "'Once a Whore and Ever'?".

[24] For context, see Louis Montrose, "The Work of Gender in the Discourse of Discovery," in *New World Encounters*, ed. Stephen Greenblatt (Berkeley, 1993), 177–217.

> ... Tho' I admire you strangely for your Beauty,
> Yet I contemn your mind.
> —And yet I wou'd at any rate enjoy you,
> At your own rate—but cannot—see here
> The only Sum I can command on Earth;
> I know not where to eat when this is gon. (2.1.320–29)

Here, Willmore both chastises Angellica for her moral turpitude and confesses that he would gladly pay the sum—it would be a "mean trifling sum if I cou'd pay it down"—if he had the money (2.1.334). In the latter declaration, Willmore blurs the heretofore clear distinction between the identity of the "ethical" English liberator and the exploitative identity of Pedro and Antonio, who have both the desire and the means to take up Angellica's offer. To Willmore's surprise, of course, Angellica has already fallen in love with him, and she offers her services free of charge. In so doing, she tries to divest her own identity of its commercial reality and invest it with innocent romance. Attempting to transform herself into the innocent virgin that Willmore clearly desires her to be, she asks him if he can "forget those mean effects of vanity / Which set me out to sale, and, as a Lover, prize my yielding joy" (2.1.367–8). And for the moment, they enjoy a sexual interlude that falls outside the commercial relations that govern all such relations involving spouses and courtesans in the play.

But love is a romantic illusion in this scene, and Willmore is motivated solely by a desire to satisfy sexual urges. In this respect, Willmore has cozened Angellica into providing her services for nothing—he has no intention of this relationship being more permanent. I remarked earlier how, in his courtship of Angellica, Willmore's speeches are split between the desire to pay for Angellica's services and the desire to chastise her for her immoral life. In fact, by the end of his encounter with Angellica, he begins to take on the stereotypical characteristics of the Spaniard. When he leaves Angellica's house, Willmore is clearly taken with the sensual aspects of his experience. On meeting Belvile, his speech is peppered with Latinate phrases: "Oh such a Bona Roba! to sleep in her Arms is lying in Fresco, all perfum'd Air about me" (3.1.92–3). And when Frederick suggests they have some French wine to celebrate his victory, he insists on Canary wine or Sack (3.1.94–107).

The rest of the play is full of a series of situations in which identity is blurred in precisely this way. Shortly after his encounter with Angellica, a drunken Willmore encounters Florinda, Belvile's love, in the garden where she is waiting for Belvile (3.2.110–75). Unfortunately, Willmore expects all such encounters to replicate his seduction of Angellica and, when Florinda resists him, he ends up almost raping her. In the process, he sets himself against his friend Belvile, becoming indistinguishable from the foreign troops who tried to rape her in Pamplona. Other confusions follow in which Belvile stands in for Antonio during the duel with Pedro (4.1.105–46), the Englishmen and Spaniards together chase Florinda attempting to rape her (5.1.1–114), and Blunt gets cozened by Lucetta and ends up dressed in the clothes of a Spaniard (5.1.513–15). In this way, the Anglo-Spanish rivalry breaks down such that English stereotypes about Spanish and English identity become confused and blurred.

Portraiture and Politics

In contrast to Elizabeth's portrait, which constituted an iconic symbol of the kingdom that Elizabeth ruled, Angellica's portrait represents the new more intense commercial forces, which drove the Anglo-Dutch wars of the latter part of the century.[25] Ralegh's original use of Elizabeth's portrait was in the service of a monarchical ideology that figured the sovereign as the pure, virginal center of the nation.[26] When he had shown the Trinidadians the portrait of Elizabeth, their potential deliverer, Ralegh remarked that the natives began immediately to revere her image: "I showed them Her Majesty's picture which they so admired and honoured, as it had been easy to have brought them idolatrous thereof." In contrast, the purpose of Angellica's portrait is commercial in a way that is potentially disruptive to Neapolitan authority.

As a force that threatens the traditional state authority, Angellica represents the new power of international commerce that does not distinguish between buyers of different nations. Commercial interests break down boundaries that separate different states and nationalities, different categories of knowledge and aesthetic principles, as well as the distinction between virtue and vice itself.[27] For Behn, Angellica's portrait is also central to the new commercial and cosmopolitan sensibility that enabled her own writing career. In the postscript of the printed version of the play (1677), Behn defends herself against charges that she plagiarized the play from Killigrew's original source by comparing herself to Angellica. Admitting some borrowings from Killigrew, she notes, "I, vainly proud of my Judgment, hang out the Sign of Angellica, (the only stoln Object) to give Notice where a great part of the Wit dwelt" (postscript, 8–10). She goes on to announce that her play is simply one iteration in a series of such literary appropriations—she notes that Killigrew's *Thomaso* itself was drawn from an earlier work by Richard Brome (10–12). I would like to suggest further that there is a trajectory of dramatic and literary works, in which portraits are used to inspire devotion, adoration, idolatry, that occur from the late sixteenth century throughout the seventeenth century linking Ralegh to Behn. As we shall see, a number of such plays happen to concern relations between Spain and England. By tracing this trajectory, we find that Angellica's portrait, which Behn declares as the

---

[25]   See Wilson, *Profit and Power*.

[26]   For background, see Kim F. Hall, *Things of Darkness: Economies of Race and Gender in Early Modern England* (Ithaca, NY, 1995), 1–24. For a related reading of Shakespeare from such a perspective, see Linda Woodbridge, "Palisading the Elizabethan Body Politic," *Texas Studies in Literature and Language* 33.3 (1991): 327–54.

[27]   As Jacobs writes, "if the cosmopolitan emerged in these settings [the exchanges] it did so after a national or perhaps just a local identity had been firmly fixed" (*Strangers Nowhere in the World*, 69). She goes on to note how national identities competed with professional and religious identities once the exchanges were well established (70). In terms of the dissolution of the distinction between virtue and vice, recall Bernard Mandeville's maxim: "Private Vices, Public Benefits."

302   *Early Modern Catholics, Royalists, and Cosmopolitans*

most important symbol of *The Rover*, signals a fundamental transformation and displacement in the relationship between the sovereign and the realm.

The process by which Ralegh's portrait of the virginal Elizabeth becomes the portrait of Angellica, the courtesan, begins during the late sixteenth century. In Ralegh's description above, the natives idolize Elizabeth's image, not her just rule or her wisdom in matters of statecraft. In this respect, Ralegh is making a point about Elizabeth's beauty and appearance and the effect that that appearance might have on the onlooker. Certainly, contemporary readers of this passage would have noted that the Trinidadian response to the image of the queen was little different from the frequent expressions of adoration for the queen afforded by English courtiers of the period. Ralegh was not the only writer of this period to translate this tradition of courtly adoration of the queen into the colonial context. In William Warner's prose romance, *Syrinx, Or A Sevenfold History* (1583), Queen Dircilla is exiled on an island full of savages. The Queen civilizes the natives and is henceforth described in terms of the role that Ralegh wanted Elizabeth to play in the New World: "By this means, therefore, it came to pass that those islanders had already in devotion deified their governess *Dircilla*, for such as was *Pallas* to the *Grecians*, and *Isis* to the *Egyptians*, so and such was she to this people."[28] Elsewhere, Warner focuses on the Queen's appearance, "her beauty" and "the majesty of her looks," as the tool with which Dircilla pacifies the savages.[29]

Both Ralegh's passage describing the reception of Elizabeth's portrait and Warner's account of Queen Dircilla pacifying the islanders through her beauty participate in the Erastian ideology that figures the queen as the gendered center of the church and state. An important essay by Ann Rosalind Jones and Peter Stallybrass shows that this Erastian ideology owes a debt to the sonneteers' tradition of love poetry, exemplified by Sidney's *Astrophil and Stella*, in which the male lover worships the virginal beauty of the beloved lady. Jones and Stallybrass claim that, throughout *Astrophil and Stella*, Stella's image repeatedly strikes Astrophil with admiration and adoration, which serves as an analogy for the relationship between the courtier and Queen Elizabeth.[30] Ralegh himself drew on this analogy between the personal and public adoration of the queen in the poetic fragment, *The 21st and Last Book of the Ocean to Cynthia*. At the beginning of the poem, the speaker describes Cynthia, or Queen Elizabeth, in the following terms:

> Such force her angelic appearance had
> To master distance, time, or cruelty,
> Such art to grieve, and after to make glad,
> Such fear in love, such love in majesty.[31]

---

[28]   William Warner, *Syrinx, Or A Sevenfold History*, ed. Wallace A. Bacon (Evanston, IL, 1950), 164.

[29]   Another analogous example may be found at the beginning of the *Faerie Queene* when the salvage nation begins to worship the pious Una (Book 1.6).

[30]   Ann Rosalind Jones and Peter Stallybrass, "The Politics of *Astrophil and Stella*," *Studies in English Literature* 24 (1984): 53–68.

[31]   Sir Walter Ralegh, *The 21st (and Last) Book of the Ocean to Cynthia*, in *Selected Writings*, ed. Gerald Hammond (Manchester, 1984), 37–49, 112–15.

Royalist Turned Cosmopolitan 303

In this passage, written a number of years before Ralegh's *Discovery of Guiana* was published, Ralegh presents the "art" of Cynthia's "angelic appearance" as something that could cause complete devotion in the onlooker, thus predicting Ralegh's description of the effect Elizabeth's portrait would have on the inhabitants of the New World. Ralegh's desire that the inhabitants of the New World would grow to idolize Elizabeth participates in a political and a personal history that involves the romance tradition as well. Popular romances such as Henry Roberts's *Pheander, the Maiden Knight* and Margaret Tyler's translation of Diego Ortuñez de Callahora's *Espejo de Principes y Caballeros* begin with episodes in which a knight falls in love with a princess on the basis of her "report."[32] Of the romances published during this period, however, Sidney's *New Arcadia* is certainly the most significant, and it contains an early scene in which the portrait of a beautiful woman inspires devotion. The first time we encounter Basilius's daughter, Princess Philoclea, is by way of her portrait in the house of Kalander, an Arcadian nobleman. Musidorus, disguised as Palladius, is touring the house and encounters a portrait of the royal family. Kalander explains that the young woman in the portrait is the "younger daughter" of the Arcadian sovereign, who along with the rest of the royal family, has gone into hiding in order to avoid the fulfillment of a prophesy.[33] Significantly, the young prince's initial fascination with the beauty of Philoclea leads to Kalander's discussion of the current state of "this country of Arcadia." In other words, Kalander's description of Arcadia is invoked at the moment that Palladius/Musidorus views Philoclea, the virginal symbol of that country.[34] Later Musidorus's cousin, Pyrocles, falls in love with Philoclea's image, a process which Pyrocles describes in sonnet form: "For from without came to mine eyes the blow, / Whereto mine inward thoughts did faintly yield / ... Thus are my eyes still captive to one sight; / Thus all my thoughts are slaves to one thought still."[35] Pyrocles's description of being "taken" by the image of Philoclea is once again precisely what Ralegh hoped would occur to the Trinidadians with regard to Elizabeth.

From early New Historicist work by such critics as Louis Montrose on the iconography surrounding Elizabeth, it has become clear that the adoration of

---

[32] *The Mirror of Princely Deeds* begins with the siege of Belgrade, in which the good emperor Trebatio hears talk of Briana, the King of Hungary's beautiful daughter, immediately falls in love with her, and ends up marrying her and impregnating her while disguised as her fiancé, Prince Edward. *Pheander* begins with an account of how Dionisius, a Prince of Numedia, has fallen in love with the Princess Nutania of Thrace after hearing report of her "exceeding beauty." Margaret Tyler [reprint of Diego Ortúñez's *The Mirror of Princely Deeds and Knighthood*, trans. M.T. (London: 1580)], ed. Kathryn Coad (Brookfield, VT, 1996), B1v–C3; Henry Roberts, *The Historie of Pheander, The Mayden Knight* (London: 1617), B.

[33] Sidney, *The Countess of Pembroke's Arcadia [The New Arcadia]*, 15.

[34] Sidney, *The New Arcadia*, 16.

[35] Sidney, *The New Arcadia*, 69.

304   *Early Modern Catholics, Royalists, and Cosmopolitans*

Elizabeth and her image served to shore up her monarchical power.[36] I would suggest that the analogy that tied late sixteenth-century love poetry to Elizabethan court politics was related to, and was even perhaps one version of, the more important analogy that existed between the family and the state. Like the analogy between the family and the state, the analogy between courtly love and Elizabethan court politics had the effect of naturalizing the monarchical structure of England's government. To trace out the trajectory which links Ralegh's portrait of Elizabeth to Behn's portrait of Angellica is to recount the dismantling of this important nexus of political analogies, through which the political structure of the state was sustained through frequent comparison to the personal and the familial.[37]

The kind of iconic role that Elizabeth inhabited within the poetic and narrative traditions of this period was, to some extent, already being manipulated by poets and playwrights in new and unorthodox ways during the first intense period of Anglo-Spanish rivalry. Perhaps the most famous example of such unorthodox use of this trope occurs in the third book of Spenser's *Faerie Queene*. Despite Spenser's traditional description of the poem as a "pourtraict" and "mirrour" of Queen Elizabeth, the heroine of the third book, Britomart, reverses the gender roles typically found in the trope of portraiture (3.proem.1, 5). Early in Book 3, Britomart finds her father's magic "looking glasse," sees her future husband, Artegall, and falls madly in love with his image (2.18, 22–6). The transgressive potential of this unorthodox use of the trope is quickly contained through the fulfillment of Britomart's role as the champion of chastity, but similar dramatic use of a portrait could simultaneously signal the danger of bold expressions of female desire and delineate national difference. The case of Robert Greene's *Friar Bacon and Friar Bungay* (1589) is instructive in this respect. Along with late 1580 and early 1590 dramas such as Thomas Kyd's *The Spanish Tragedy* (1587–89), George Peele's *Edward I* (1590), Peele's *The Battle of Alcazar* (1589), the anonymous *The Life and Death of Captain Thomas Stukeley* (1594), and tracts such as Edward Daunce's *A Brief Discourse of the Spanish State* (1590), Greene's *Friar Bacon* registers the threat posed by Spain in the aftermath of the Spanish Armada by

---

[36] See most recently, Louis Montrose, "Spenser and the Elizabethan Political Imaginary," *ELH* 69.4 (2002): 907–46. See also Louis Montrose, "The Elizabethan Subject and the Spenserian Text," in *Literary Theory / Renaissance Texts*, ed. Patricia Parker and David Quint (Baltimore, 1986), 303–40, and "Spenser's Domestic Domain: Poetry, Property, and the Early Modern Subject," in *Subject and Object in Renaissance Culture*, ed. Margreta de Grazia, Maureen Quilligan, and Peter Stallybrass (Cambridge, 1996), 83–130. See also, the essays contained in *The Reign of Elizabeth I: Court and Culture in the Last Decade*, ed. John Guy (Cambridge, 1995).

[37] For the most recent discussion of the break-down of this analogy, or rather metonymy as Michael McKeon notes, between the family and the state, see McKeon, *The Secret History of Domesticity: Public, Private, and the Division of Knowledge* (Baltimore, 2005), 11–16, 110–61. See also Constance Jordan, "The Household and the State: Transformations in the Representation of an Analogy," *Modern Language Quarterly* 54.3 (1993): 308–26.

considering England's historical relationship with the Spanish crown.[38] At the center of the play is Greene's portrayal of the medieval philosopher Roger Bacon, whom many writers during the sixteenth century considered to be a demonologist and a sorcerer.

Friar Bacon is set at the time of King Henry III, and it concerns the marriage opportunities of his son, Edward I, who was destined to marry Princess Eleanor of Castile. At the beginning of the play, Edward is enamored of the humble and virginal daughter of the Keeper of Fressingfield, Margaret. Edward's original description of Margaret, the English country girl, owes an obvious debt to the tradition of courtly love in which the young female serves as the pure, virginal center of the nation (i.50–61, i.73–86). Set against the nationalistic symbolism of Margaret is Eleanor, Princess of Castile, who takes on a special significance after the failed Armada. It turns out that Eleanor has traveled to England, daring "to brook Neptunus' haughty pride," and has decided to woo the prince in person (iv.18). Eleanor's attraction to the prince reverses the stereotypical romance plot whereby the prince falls in love with the princess on the basis of her picture or her report. She recounts her reasons for traveling to England "After that English Henry, by his lords, / Had sent Prince Edward's lovely counterfeit, / A present to the Castile Eleanor," which, she explains, "Led both mine eye and thoughts in equal link / To like so of the English monarch's son / That I attempted perils for his sake" (iv.21–30). Here Eleanor assumes the stereotypical role of the male hero of the romance genre. For an English audience, this gender reversal may well have raised doubt about the value of the dynastic union with the crown of Castile.[39]

Significantly, visual representations, whether painted or "speaking," figure national identity in this play.[40] The events of *Friar Bacon* set up a comparison between the representative art embodied in painting, symbolized by the portrait of Edward, which has enflamed Eleanor's passion and has motivated her to travel to England to woo him, and Friar Bacon's "glass prospective [sic]," which is able to generate an image of the beautiful English commoner, Margaret of Fressingfield (v.105). The play also pits the future bloody history of England, presumably caused by Edward's marriage to Eleanor, against the history that might have occurred, had Bacon's demonic invention of a magical "brazen head," intended to protect England from the external world, been successful. Thus, in response to Henry's query, "[W]hat shall grow from Edward and his queen?" Friar Bacon predicts that England will undergo endless wars before arriving at the peaceful present of

---

[38] Parenthetical citations are from Robert Greene, *Friar Bacon and Friar Bungay*, ed. Daniel Seltzer (London: Edward Arnold, 1964).

[39] See Eric Griffin, *Ethno-poetics and Empire: English Renaissance Drama and the Specter of Spain* (Philadelphia, 2009), 50–56, for a related discussion of George Peele's damning portrayal of "Elinor" in *Edward I*.

[40] Hall, *Things of Darkness*, 1–24. For related discussions of how the female body symbolizes national or racial identity during the Renaissance, see Kim F. Hall, *Things of Darkness: Economies of Race and Gender in Early Modern England* (Ithaca, NY: Cornell University Press, 1995), esp. pp. 1–24.

Elizabeth (xvi.41, 49–50). Ultimately, the historical reality of Edward's union with Eleanor is triumphant in spite of the fact that it will bring about future wars for the English people.

Robert Greene was not the only playwright of this early period to reverse the gender roles of the traditional narrative episode in which a male viewer falls in love with a princess or noblewoman through the medium of her picture. John Webster and Thomas Dekker include a similar scene in their 1607 play, *The Famous History of Sir Thomas Wyat*, which dramatizes the events surrounding the younger Wyatt's rebellion against Queen Mary I at the time that she was planning her marriage to Philip II of Spain.[41] In this play, Mary takes the role of Eleanor and falls in love with the portrait of Philip. Like Eleanor's love for Edward, Mary's love for Philip comes "at the first sight of his delightfull picture." She continues, "That picture should haue power to tingle / Loue in Royall brests: the Dartes of loue are wordes, pictures, conceite."[42] Similar to the earlier play, Mary is depicted as the suitor in this future marriage, to which the patriotic Wyatt naturally objects. The stakes are obviously higher in *The Famous History* than in *Friar Bacon*, but the idea is the same: both plays reverse the gender roles of a stock narrative episode in order to show the extent to which amorous relations with Spain have the potential for endangering the English royal family and thus the state as well.

Both Greene's play and Webster and Dekker's play show that the iconic system, which positions the queen's virginal identity at the center of the nation, was already being manipulated at the same moment that it was certainly the most powerful ideological framework for defining the kingdom's identity. The next time that Spain captured England's dramatic imagination in a way that was similar to the years following 1588 was during the year 1623, when the Duke of Buckingham was negotiating with the Spanish crown over the Spanish match between Charles I and the Infanta Maria Anna, Philip III's daughter. A number of plays were written and staged during this period that either directly or indirectly commented on the Spanish match, of which Philip Massinger's *The Renegado* (1624) deploys the familiar trope of the portrait.[43] *The Renegado* begins with the story of a Venetian gentleman disguised as a merchant named Vitelli visiting the city of Tunis in secret search of his sister Paulina.[44] In the opening scene, his servant, Gazet, has set up shop in the city market and sells trinkets to the Tunisians. Among these trinkets are a collection of "choice pictures," and for each painting, Gazet has rehearsed a sales pitch in order to entice naive buyers (1.1.4). In reality, Gazet is hocking portraits of courtesans and telling unsuspecting buyers that they represent the royalty of Europe (1.1.6–13). On the surface, Gazet's use of the pictures resembles Ralegh's

---

[41] John Webster and Thomas Dekker, *The Famous History of Sir Thomas Wyat* [London, 1607] (reprint: New York, 1970).

[42] Webster and Dekker, *The Famous History*, C4v.

[43] Jerzy Limon, *Dangerous Matter: English Drama and Politics in 1623–24* (Cambridge, 1986), 1–39, 98–129.

[44] Philip Massinger, *Renegado*, in *Three Turk Plays From Early Modern England*, ed. Daniel Vitkus (New York, 2000), 241–339. Further citations are given in the text by act, scene, and line number.

original use of Elizabeth's portrait in order to spread the fame of his sovereign. To the unsuspecting buyer, Gazet seeks to spread the fame and reputation of the royal women of Christian Europe, who represent the virginal center of that entity and its countries.[45] Both Gazet and Ralegh presume to extend the imperial ambit of those whom they represent. But Gazet's pictures fraudulently present courtesans and prostitutes as royalty, thereby undermining the authenticity of the feminine purity at the center of the Christian or European commonwealth. In reality these women are imposters—prostitutes—whose bodies are bought and sold in an economy that challenges the boundaries of the prevailing conception of the early modern nation. Not surprisingly, Gazet believes himself to be radically cosmopolitan. He brags that "he would not be confined / In my belief," explaining that "in the mean time, / Live I in England, Spain, France, Rome, Geneva: / I'm of that country's faith" (1.1.32–3, 35–7). To put it bluntly, Gazet confesses that he would willingly "prostitute" himself out to whatever country in which he resides.

Recent work by Michael McKeon on the early modern history of the domestic realm traces some important transformations in the way that prostitutes were being viewed during the seventeenth century. According to McKeon, the signs that might have differentiated the streetwalker from a "lady of quality" were breaking down during this period. London courtesans dressed in a way that was indistinguishable from fashionable women, and in turn, some writers complained that fashionable women enjoyed emulating the clothing and makeup of the streetwalker. The hypocrisy was such that the crown itself was not exempt from criticism by the more astute observers. Samuel Pepys noted that while rioting crowds during Easter week of 1668 pulled down a number of brothels, they would not "go and pull down the great bawdy house at Whitehall," which the court of Charles II had supposedly become. Similarly, the publication of a 1683 tract called *The Whore's Rhetoric* was in part an attempt to compare the public whore to the prince, offering itself as a book of statecraft for the prostitute and repeatedly comparing her to a public magistrate.[46] Ultimately, the line that separated legitimate households from illegitimate ones (brothels) began to blur so that even the royal household was not exempt from critique. Massinger's *The Renegado* can be seen as a first step in this process, a process that ends with the elevation of Angellica to the position of a kind of anti-sovereign in *The Rover*. The second scene of *The Renegado* depicts a conversation between Donusa, niece to the Ottoman emperor, and her eunuch, the English-born Carazie, discussing the relative freedom of English ladies. In a dialogue that alludes directly to the fraudulent identity of Gazet's "queens," Carazie declares that "Women in England, / For the most part, live like queens," while at the same time, confessing that English law allows a woman to have "a private friend" in order to relieve the husband of his strenuous sexual obligations

---

[45]   Hall, *Things of Darkness*, 9.

[46]   Michael McKeon, *The Secret History of Domesticity: Public, Private, and the Division of Knowledge*, 205; see also 194–211. See also James Grantham Turner, *Liberties and Radicals in Early Modern London: Sexuality, Politics, and Literary Culture, 1630–1685* (New York, 2002), 1–46.

towards her (1.2.28–9, 46). In other words, English women inhabit precisely the place that the courtesans portrayed in Gazet's pictures inhabit: they are both queens and whores at the same time. The virginal representative of the English nation has transformed into its polar opposite.

All of this takes an interesting turn when Donusa, the Turkish princess and symbolic feminine symbol of the Ottoman Empire, goes to the market in order to survey the wares sold there. Donusa encounters Vitelli and Gazet at their vending stall, and Vitelli explains to the princess that they are selling portraits of beautiful European women by great painters such as Michelangelo: "They are indeed / The rarest beauties of the Christian world / And nowhere to be equaled" (1.3.134–6). Donusa takes offense at this boast, unveils herself, and offers up her own competing image by holding a mirror to her face. When Vitelli expresses wonderment, Donusa becomes enraged and breaks some of Gazet's wares, implicitly resisting the commercial forces that surround her. But she has already fallen in love with Vitelli, and she tells Gazet that his master can expect to receive payment for the broken wares by paying a visit to her in her private chambers. In subsequent scenes, she seduces him and then has sexual relations with him. Throughout her interactions with Vitelli, Donusa is both queen and courtesan, alternatively overpowering him with her position in the court and using her body to reimburse him for his broken wares in a commercial transaction.

As in Behn's *The Rover*, it is tempting to see Donusa's simultaneous position of power and the commercialization of her body as combining in a way that allows her to transcend traditional national and religious politics. As the plot progresses, however, it becomes clear that *The Renegado* is as invested in the same traditional national and religious politics as its predecessors, since in the end, Vitelli converts Donusa to Christianity and takes her away to Italy with the other Christians (and lapsed Christians such as Grimaldi), and Vitelli's sister Paulina refuses the viceroy of Tunis's advances towards her.[47] Applying precisely such an Erastian logic, Claire Jowitt has argued convincingly that the play should be read as an attempt to imagine a successful Spanish match that would redound favorably to the religious and political interests of the English crown, with the Venetian Christians taking the place of the Protestant English and the Turkish rulers of Tunis taking the place of the Roman Catholic Spanish. But in contrast to the demands made on Charles that he renounce his religious authority and convert to Catholicism, Vitelli is able to conquer Donusa sexually and convert her to Christianity (that is, Protestantism in Jowitt's analogy). Even here, then, in the main plot having to do with the relationship between Vitelli and Donusa, Erastian politics prevail over transnational commercialism.[48] Hence, *The Renegado* occupies at best an interim stage within the trajectory, which links

---

[47] For accounts of how literary representations shaped nationalistic attitudes towards Muslims, see Nabil Matar, *Turks Moors, and Englishmen in the Age of Discovery* (New York, 1999), 3–18, 43–82; Vitkus, "Adventuring Heroes in the Mediterranean: Mapping the Boundaries of Anglo-Islamic Exchange on the Early Modern Stage," 75–95; and Barbara Fuchs, *Mimesis and Empire: The New World, Islam, and European Identities*, 118–38.

[48] Claire Jowitt, "Massinger's *The Renegado* (1624) and the Spanish Marriage," *Cahiers Elizabethains* 65 (2004): 45–54.

the traditional oppositional national ideology of Ralegh's portrait to Aphra Behn's more complex use of Angellica's portrait.

Cosmopolitanism and Commercialism from Killigrew to Behn

Because Behn's portrait scene in *The Rover* appropriates so much from Thomas Killigrew's original, it is worth considering *Thomaso* in some detail before considering Behn's version. Although an exiled Catholic cavalier, it is clear that Killigrew was heavily invested in the kind of secular cosmopolitanism that we encountered in Fanshawe's writings in Chapter 5. Having been appointed as the exiled crown's representative to the Doge of Venice in 1650, Killigrew appealed to a natural alliance among Christian sovereigns—reminiscent of Fanshawe—that demanded a European response to the English parliament's execution of King Charles I: "If all Christian princes do not make opportune provision for this there is no doubt that the poisonous breath of [the English parliament's] rebellion will corrupt all peoples, far and near, wherever malcontents are found. But with God's help and the magnanimous assistance of Christian princes we hope that serene skies will return to England and that you will see our triumphal fires lighted with those very sticks with which we are now beaten, and that the hateful carcases of these parricides will have become food for the flames, as they deserve."[49] In contrast to this appeal, Killigrew's 1654 play, purportedly based on his own experience of travelling to Madrid, seems to be less about transnational politics and more about the emergence of anarchic forces of commerce that threatened to destabilize the Erastian political ideologies to which both Fanshawe and Killigrew had more or less dedicated themselves during the Interregnum. Act 2 opens with Angellica appearing at the balcony with her bawd, Anna. Below is the pillar, "upon which hangs her Picture, and by it stand two Bravoes to protect it from affronts" (1 *Thomaso*, 326). Meanwhile, the men who gaze longingly at the picture repeatedly compare Angellica to a prince, based on the sum that she demands. Seeing the price that Angellica is demanding, for example, Thomaso makes the following exclamation, which Behn would later appropriate for Willmore: "A Thousand Crowns? By this Day, a thousand Kingdoms were not dear" (334; cf. *The Rover*, 2.1.98–100). Likewise, on seeing Angellica's advertisement of herself, one of three "Monsieurs without cloaks" exclaims that the thousand crowns that Angellica demands is "a portion for the *Infanta*, and a good one too, if we keep *Catalonia* and *Massaniello Naples*," a line that Behn gives to Frederick (327; cf. *The Rover*, 2.1.105). Even the service of Angellica's Bravoes is in lieu of service to the crown. If he were not guarding her picture, the second Bravo would be "a frozen naked Sentinel in *Flanders*" (329). In this respect, Angellica replaces the central authority of the prince with an authority based on commerce that demands similar payments of tribute.

---

[49]   "Venice: February 1650," in *Calendar of State Papers Relating to English Affairs in the Archives of Venice, 1647–1652*, ed. Allen B. Hinds (London, 1927), vol. 28, 135–41.

310 *Early Modern Catholics, Royalists, and Cosmopolitans*

Within this commercial "realm," men of diverse national origins all acknowledge Angellica's authoritative beauty, marveling at the price she is demanding and expressing the wish that they had enough money to afford her services.[50] In this respect, the original scene from *Thomaso* is even more cosmopolitan than Behn's version. Whereas in Behn's version only the English and the Spaniards are tempted by Angellica's portraits, in *Thomaso*, first an Italian from Milan admires the portrait and expresses interest in Angellica's company. He is followed by the three destitute "Monsieurs," presumably Frenchmen, who are in turn followed by a "Polish *Prince*," and a Flaunders Merchant, who offer to pay her Bravoes with credit. All of them are summarily refused (327–8). Only then do the Spaniards and the English appear and enter into an altercation over Thomaso's affront to Angellica. The case of the "*three* Monsieurs" is particularly noteworthy within the parade of nationalities that stops to admire Angellica's picture, since the lines that are attributed to the third Monsieur suggests a blurring of national identities. Angellica obviously sees them as French, exclaiming "Monsieur! Monster," and Anna, Angellica, and one of the Bravoes makes subsequent reference to France after they have left the stage (327–8). However, when the third Monsieur exclaims that Angellica's price is "a portion for the *Infanta*, and a good one too, if we keep *Catalonia*, and *Massaniello Naples*," his use of the pronoun "we" shows that he identifies himself with the Spanish crown's attempt to put down the rebellions that began in Catalonia in 1640 and in Naples in 1647 (327). Anna and Angellica take this blurring of national identity even further by suddenly referring to the "Monsieurs" as if they were English cavaliers. Anna mentions their poverty and licentiousness ("[their whores] are seldom paid, but always robb'd when they come among'st them") and their depraved exiled prince ("Their Prince will beat his Whore") and their "dead King" (328). Angellica then describes as equivalent the identities of the Frenchmen, Englishmen, and Spaniards. Recounting how the subjects of all three crowns show no respect to their sovereigns, she asks, "The three Christian Kings are so us'd by their vassals; *Frondeur*, Round-head, and a Massaniellian; which is the worst devil of the three?" (328). *Frondeur* was a contemporary French term for someone who believed the king's power should be limited, while a *Masaniellian* was a Neapolitan supporter of the Naples revolt against the Spanish Hapsburgs. Anna answers that the Roundheads were the worst, but the parallel that Angellica has made gives the further impression that all European men are equivalent before her.

In fact, Killigrew's play reflects a more radical leveling of national identity than Behn's later play, and in this respect, it is not surprisingly a product of its context. The repeated talk of the Spanish general's death seems to reference the recent execution of Charles I, which ushered in a period in which the royalist cause of restoring Charles Stuart to the throne seemed hopeless. Cromwell had been proclaimed Lord Protector while Killigrew was writing the play, and like many exiled cavaliers, Killigrew had little prospect of ever returning to his native

---

[50] See Beach, "Carnival Politics," 12.

Royalist Turned Cosmopolitan   311

country.[51] It is therefore not surprising that, at the end of Killigrew's original work, Thomaso resolves to remain in Madrid with "this Star, bright *Serulina*, whose Friendship thus has fixt the Wanderer" (2 *Thomaso*, 464).

Like Killigrew's original, Angellica's pictures in *The Rover* are not in the service of a centralized monarchical state as are the portraits of Elizabeth. They appeal to individuals regardless of national origin. Moreover, Angellica's small portraits exist in relation to a series of similar "trifles," as she calls the money she gives to Willmore, or the "Bell[s] and Bawble[s]," as Hellena jokingly calls the objects with which Don Vincentio will use to barter for Florinda's hand in marriage (4.1.229; 1.1.126). Recall that Florinda gives a small portrait to Belvile (3.1.255), and Lucetta, the jilting wench, and Blunt exchange a worthless bracelet and a "Toy of a diamond" (2.1.50). All of these trifles are intended to cause the men who receive them to worship the female giver in a way that reminds us obliquely of the portrait of Ralegh's Queen. Thus, the commercial world of Angellica is no longer the centralized monarchical state in which, according to Stephen Greenblatt, Renaissance fiction channeled "national and religious sentiment into the worship of the prince [i.e. Elizabeth], … mask[ing] over and thus temporarily deflect[ing] deep social, political and theological divisions in late sixteenth-century England."[52] Rather signs and symbols and even plays are quickly used and discarded in order to elevate an individual's commercial value. The commercial motives at the center of Behn's play are thus a deeply decentering force which ultimately posed a challenge to the traditional way in which concepts such as nation, empire, and religious identity were configured during this period.

At the same time, it is important to acknowledge that Behn diminishes the cosmopolitan character of Killigrew's original portrait scene somewhat, by reducing it to an almost exclusive contest between the English and the Spanish. Behn's play also returns us nostalgically to the Petrarchan adoration of the sovereign, which was more thoroughly critiqued in Killigrew's original play.[53] This nostalgia expresses itself as a yearning both for earlier, less jaded expressions of affection and for loyalty to the uncontested monarchical power for which such expressions were often analogies. Indeed, Thomaso's expressions of courtly adoration of Angellica are tepid in comparison with those expressed by Behn's Willmore. Thomaso tells Angellica that he will wear her picture as "a Buckler against all that dare be angry, what ere they be" (1 *Thomaso*, 336), a line which Willmore restates in a way that conveys the full extent of his affection with a Petrarchan conceit: "I saw your Charming Picture and was wounded; quite through my Soul each pointed Beauty ran; and wanting a Thousand Crowns to procure my remedy—I laid this little Picture to my Bosom—which if you cannot allow me, I'll resign" (2.1.225–8). Similarly, Angellica's song in *The Rover*, which mentions how "Caelia in her charming Eyes/ Wore all Love's sweets, and all [Damon's] cruelties" (2.1.161–2), renders Petrarchan an original song in *Thomaso* that

---

[51]   Hobby, "No Stolen Object, but Her Own," 116.

[52]   Greenblatt, *Renaissance Self-Fashioning*, 168.

[53]   Pacheco, "Rape and the Female Subject," 336–7.

312   *Early Modern Catholics, Royalists, and Cosmopolitans*

promises a leveling satisfaction for all ("Youths," "Old men," "Fools," and "mad men") that approach Angellica and ask for her services (334–5).[54]

Perhaps most significant is Angellica's attitude to her potential buyers in each play. In *Thomaso*, Angellica advertises herself not primarily in the interest of monetary profit but rather for her pleasure. She complains that, while the General made her wealthy, "his jealousy made me lye hid in the world, neither seen nor enjoy'd" (326–7). In contrast, Behn's Angellica declares that "nothing but gold shall charm my heart" (2.1.129–30). Thus, when Killigrew's Angellica and Behn's Angellica surrender to their respective English cavaliers, the monetary economy is displaced in favor of an economy based on love and deception, but the degree to which this occurs is different in each version. In both plays, of course, Angellica's falling in love with an Englishman goes some way towards disrupting the commercial cosmopolitanism that I have been describing here. And yet, English national sentiment resurfaces more strongly in Behn's 1677 version. Whereas Killigrew's Angellica is seeking enjoyment when she encounters Thomaso, Willmore's attraction to Behn's Angellica is such that, in spite of her desire to keep her relations with prospective buyers strictly commercial, she still falls for him. In doing so, Willmore stands out among the Spanish and English nationals such that an English audience is rewarded with the idea that Englishmen prevail over other nations in matters of the heart. Additionally, Killigrew's Angellica falls in love with Thomaso, but she does not become possessive in her affection for him—she even assists him in his endeavors to bed other courtesans (2 *Thomaso*, 393–6). Behn's Angellica, in contrast, turns so violently possessive of Willmore's affections that she ultimately draws a gun on him (5.1.299).

Nevertheless, the more pronounced stress on English national identity must be measured against the dissolution of the boundaries between Spanish and English identity explored in the first section of this chapter. In the postscript, Behn herself seems to see her own authorial position as radically and commercially cosmopolitan. Her play is one in a series of stolen objects: plays, portraits, bodies, affections, dowries. In her declaration that she "hang[s] out the Sign of Angellica (the only stoln Object)," Behn identifies herself with Angellica, the "royal" courtesan whose authority both challenges and reifies the distinction between competing national identities (postscript 9).[55] Moreover, through her plagiarism of Killigrew's original, Behn also identifies herself with Willmore, the figure who steals both Angellica's portrait and her affections, and whom, in a crucial reversal, Angellica pays for doing so (4.1.225–9). Thus, Behn also challenges the distinction between male and female, benefactor and courtesan, buyer and seller, along with the distinction between English and non-English in such a way that all forms of identity are leveled and blurred. In her defense, Behn inhabits each of these positions, along with that of writer and plagiarist. In Behn's universe, all centers of authority and authorship are vitiated to such a degree that all we are left with are the leveling effects of commercial forces.

---

[54]   Pacheco, "Rape and the Female Subject," 329.

[55]   See Catherine Gallagher, "Who Was that Masked Woman? The Prostitute and the Playwright in the Comedies of Aphra Behn," *Women's Studies* 15 (1998): 23–42.

Conclusion
The Public Sphere and the Legacy of the Christian Commonwealth

Throughout *Early Modern Catholics, Royalists, and Cosmopolitans*, we have traced a progression from the papal-centered Roman Catholic cosmopolitanism of Campion, Sander, and Persons to the secularized imitations of this model found in fictional works by Munday, Harington, Sidney, and Spenser. In the Stukeley plays and later in the poetry and translations of Fanshawe, we see this secularized version of the Christian commonwealth break down once again in favor of a Christian or European commonwealth based less on the extraordinary power of the Roman curia and more on a horizontal and ecumenical alliance among Christian monarchs. During the English civil war and its aftermath, we see this royalist model of cosmopolitanism give way to a further transformation based on Milton's republican values, which substitute a devout transnational elite for the Episcopal hierarchy of both the Roman and English Churches. Finally, the commercial forces portrayed in Killigrew's and Behn's plays about the buying, selling, and duplication of sexualized bodies constitute a final leveling of the Erastian mythologies surrounding the English monarchy, beginning with the cult of Queen Elizabeth. In the context of Behn's "Language that all nations understand," national and religious identities become interchangeable and duplicable, queens are compared to courtesans, and the exercise of monarchy is compared to prostitution. The trajectory of cosmopolitanism therefore begins with the transnational values inherent in the universalist claims of Roman Catholicism and ends with the anarchic forces of commerce and capitalism. Ultimately, the fictional works explored in these pages show that our current understanding of the early modern English literary tradition as constituting a "writing of the nation" is incomplete, leaving out the way in which English writers also sought to explore political models that incorporated England into various secularized, ecumenical, and commercialized iterations of the Christian commonwealth. Beyond the emergence of the English nation, English writers of fiction sustained a traditional critique of ethnic nationalism that would evolve and continue into the modern age.

There is certainly a temptation to situate this account of a secularizing cosmopolitanism within a Whig interpretation of history, in which the teleological trajectory of historical unfolding inevitably moves towards a secular ideal of humanism, individual rights, and scientific progress. Indeed, most accounts of seventeenth- and eighteenth-century political thought present cosmopolitanism as progressive and arising out of Enlightenment reason or unfettered commerce.[1]

---

[1] Margaret Jacob, *Strangers Nowhere in the World*, 1–12. In contrast to my account, Jacob presents the Roman Catholic Church as impeding the rise of cosmopolitanism (13–40).

Similarly, we might be tempted to situate the Protestant cultural adaptation of certain transnational Catholic forms of hierarchy within the familiar historical account of Protestantism's generation of a secular "spirit of Capitalism," in which medieval Christian values concerning work and Christian duty are internalized and individualized.[2] In general, such accounts are consistent with what Charles Taylor calls the "mainstream secularization theory," whereby a global history of the rise of modernity perceives humanity as abandoning religious faith when humans can control their individual lives and collectively their world and society.[3] But such versions of progressive history constitute a serious error of interpretation. It should be clear by this point that English cosmopolitanism was first and foremost traditional and conservative. A more accurate reading of this book is that it is about the nostalgic, sometimes heroic but ultimately futile attempt to recapitulate some version of the transnational polity by writers that perceived, obliquely in some cases, that the new Erastian sensibility and the establishment of an English national church meant that the old transnational Christian commonwealth was in the process of being splintered by national ideologies and dynastic forces. And in the writings of most of these English writers, we detect a further perception that some transnational authority should step in for what had been lost.

My account of how various English writers used their fictional work to promote secular alternatives to transnational papal authority lends support to Taylor's general historical account of the development of a "secular age" within Western Europe and North America, an age in which (he claims) both belief in religion and unbelief came to be viewed as equally valid options. For Taylor, the early modern Reformation in Northern Europe occurred within an overarching framework of disenchantment, in which the "power of God" was understood not to "operate through various 'sacramentals,' or locations of sacred power which we can draw on" but rather to be present in all human endeavors.[4] Of course, this Protestant tendency towards disenchantment or desacralization occurred with respect to the church hierarchy itself, a process encountered in the fictional writings by Munday, Harington, Sidney, and Spenser in which by means of a process of mimicry and imitation, traditional ecclesiastical hierarchies were reproduced denuded of their spiritual authority. Similarly, Taylor argues that the Reformation had the monumental effect of disembedding the person from the surrounding society such

---

[2] Max Weber, *The Protestant Ethic and the Spirit of Capitalism*, trans. Talcott Parsons, intro. Anthony Giddens (New York, 2001). In turn, Weber's account of the origins of capitalism portrays Benjamin Franklin's secular worldly asceticism as essentially equivalent to the earlier Puritan attitude towards work, in which the "religious basis ... had died away" (123).

[3] Charles Taylor, *A Secular Age* (Cambridge, 2007), 429. Taylor's main interlocutor here is Steve Bruce. See "Pluralism and Religious Vitality," in *Religion and Modernization*, ed. Steve Bruce (New York, 1992), 170–94, Bruce, *Religion in Modern Britain* (New York, 1995).

[4] Taylor, *A Secular Age*, 79.

Conclusion 315

that ultimately we would come to see ourselves as first and foremost free and autonomous individuals.[5] Once again, one reflects on such figures as Munday, Harington, Sidney, and Fanshawe, all of whom fashioned complex authorial identities for themselves by choosing to introduce into the English body politic a conception of transnational authority inherited from a prohibited ideology. Finally, one notes Taylor's theory about how the consciousness of both a public sphere and a sphere of commerce and economic activity replace the old investment in the spiritual realm as the path to peace and orderly governance.[6] These transformations are elements that I explored with respect to Milton and Behn in the second part of this book.

Taylor's history of the seventeenth- and eighteenth-century rise of Enlightenment thought follows Jurgen Habermas's and Michael Warner's account of the rise of an independent public sphere, but what this account omits is how this relates to the corresponding decline of the transnational Christian commonwealth, which the public sphere eventually replaced.[7] Like the Christian commonwealth, Habermas's public sphere extends throughout all of civilized Europe, but as we see in my analysis of Milton's congregational elite, the public sphere was imagined explicitly as replacing the old corrupt ecclesiastical hierarchy, since it served precisely the same function of correcting temporal authorities. Indeed, Milton's conception of an enlightened transnational elite working to guide the nation-states of Europe is largely consistent with Warner's and Habermas's accounts of the public sphere, even if Milton's elite is oriented religiously in ways that do not quite conform to the Enlightenment ideal. To the extent that he is unaware of the important legacy of a transnational ecclesiastical hierarchy for the historical imagination, Taylor's bias here is rooted in the Enlightenment itself, which views the republic of reason as having no historical precedent since its origins were in rational thought rather than the historical process.

Ultimately the bloody history of European civilization beginning in the seventeenth century reveals the inability of a transnational public sphere or republic of letters to compensate for the original ecclesiastical-temporal hierarchy, which itself constituted an unstable edifice. One problem, it seems to me, is that, despite Habermas's and Warner's optimistic account of the international nature of the republic of letters, the emerging nation-states were in reality mostly overseen by separate and distinct religious and secular public spheres, something Taylor acknowledges later in his account.[8] Another problem was the transformation of natural law discourse from a Thomist

---

[5]   Taylor, *A Secular Age*, 146–58.

[6]   Taylor, *A Secular Age*, 176–96.

[7]   Taylor, *A Secular Age*, 186. See Jurgen Habermas, *The Structural Transformation of the Public Sphere*, trans. Thomas Burger (Cambridge, 1989); Michael Warner, *The Letters of the Republic* (Cambridge, 1990).

[8]   Taylor, *A Secular Age*, 377.

account of *ius gentium* into the Hobbesian portrait of a natural state comprising warring individuals and nation-states, an ideological transformation that itself occurred within the emerging republic of letters.[9] Yes, one can point to various eighteenth-century attempts to resurrect the transnational project, such as Kant's cosmopolitan account of perpetual peace. But without the religious convictions that sustained it in the first place, or even the knowledge of its roots in the medieval and early modern religious order, secular cosmopolitanism, it seems to me, lacks any enduring purchase on the collective consciousness. The intellectual, ideological, and cultural transformations that occurred throughout the eighteenth and nineteenth centuries are too complex to explore here, but in the end, such questions inevitably lead to discussion of the relationship between faith and reason both within the modern state and with regard to what has been called the pre-political sphere.

Jurgen Habermas's 2004 debate with Cardinal Joseph Ratzinger (later Pope Benedict XVI) on the place of faith and reason in what Habermas refers to as the contemporary "post-secular society" is instructive of how difficult it remains to discuss the legacy of the transnational sphere.[10] In response to Ernst Wolfgang Bockenforde's question concerning the external foundations of democratic constitutional states, Habermas and Ratzinger are in broad agreement about the importance of the two sides, religion and philosophy, drawing intellectual sustenance from each other.[11] But in the course of their debate, only the theologian, Ratzinger, can entertain the old question of whether there exists a universal law that transcends all national legal systems. After invoking the religious and secular tradition of natural law theory (Vitoria, Hugo Grotius, and Samuel von Pufendorf), Ratzinger acknowledges that the older ordered view of natural law has been capsized by the theory of evolution, even as he calls for an intercultural and interreligious dialogue in order to "grasp anew the relevance of the question of whether there might exist a rationality of nature and, hence, a rational law for man and his existence in the world."[12] In response to the carnage of the twentieth century, the codified system of international law and human rights, drawing from an older tradition of the laws of war, imperfectly overlays

---

[9] See Richard Tuck, *The Rights of War and Peace: Political Thought and the International Order from Grotius to Kant* (New York, 1999), 51–77; 109–39. See also, Tuck, *Natural Rights Theories: The Origin and Development* (New York, 1982); Tuck, *Philosophy and Government, 1572–1651* (New York, 1993).

[10] Joseph Cardinal Ratzinger [Pope Benedict XVI] and Jurgen Habermas, *Dialectics of Secularization: On Reason and Religion*, ed. Florian Schuller, trans. Brian McNeil, C.R.V. (San Francisco, 2006).

[11] Habermas, "Pre-Political Foundations of the Democratic Constitutional State?" in *Dialectics of Secularization*, 21. See E.W. Bockenforde, "Die Entstehung de Staates als Vorgang der Sakularization" (1967), in *Recht, Staat, Freiheit* (Frankfurt am Main, 1991), 112.

[12] Joseph Cardinal Ratzinger, "That Which Holds the World Together: The Pre-political Moral Foundations of a Free State," in *Dialectics of Secularization*, 67–72.

Conclusion 317

a global context that is infinitely more complex than the European one explored in this book, and the extent to which it succeeds in doing so depends more on a convergence of national, ideological, and economic interests than to any appeal to transcendent or temporal authority. In the end, outside of deeply compromised international institutions, there exist on the immediate horizon only imperfect and limited prospects for restraints on acts of invasion and occupation, the excesses of oppressive governments, and extreme nationalistic or religious ideologies.

Works Cited

Manuscript Sources

Archivum Romanum Societatis Iesu, Rome: Anglia Historia VIII, 1579–1624.

Primary Printed Sources

Aldama, Antonio M., S.J. (ed.), *The Formula of the Institute, Notes for a Commentary*, trans. Ignacio Echániz, S.J. (St. Louis: The Institute of Jesuit Sources, 1990).

Alfield, Thomas, *A true reporte of the death & martyrdome of M. Campion Iesuite and prieste, & M. Sherwin, & M. Bryan preistes, at Tiborne the first of December* (London, 1582).

Allen, John (ed.), *The English Hospice in Rome*, vol. 21 (Exeter: Catholic Records Press, 1962).

Allen, Cardinal William [and/or Sixtus V, Pope], *A Declaration of the Sentence and deposition of Elizabeth, the vsurper and pretensed Quene of Englande* (Antwerp, 1588).

Allen, Cardinal William, *A Brief Historie of the Glorious Martyrdom of xii Reverend Priests* (Rheims, 1592), ed. John H. Pollen, S.J. (reprint, London: Burns & Oates, 1908).

———, *Cardinal Allen's defence of Sir William Stanley's surrender of Deventer, January 29, 1586–7*, ed. Thomas Heywood (Manchester: Charles Simms & Co., 1851).

———, *Historia del glorioso martirio di sedici sacerdoti Martirizati in Inghilterra per la confessione, & difesa della fede Catolica, l'anno 1581, 1582, & 1583: con vna prefatione, che dichiara la loro innocenza, composta da quelli, che co[n] essi praticauano mentre erano viui, & si trouorno presenti al lor giuditio, & morte. Tradotta di lingua Inglese in Italiana da vno del Collegio Inglese di Roma. S'è aggiunto il martirio di due altre Sacerdoti, & vno secolare Inglesi, martirizati l'anno 1577 & 1578* (Macerata, 1583).

———, *The Letters and Memorials of William Cardinal Allen (1532–1594)*, ed. Fathers of the Congregation of the London Oratory, intro. Thomas F. Knox (London: David Nutt, 1882).

———, *A true sincere and modest defence of English Catholics that suffer for their faith both at home and abroad: against a false, seditious and slanderous libel entituled; "The execution of iustice in England"* (2 vols, St. Louis: B. Herder, 1914).

Allen, William and Richard Barret, *Letters of William Allen and Richard Barret 1572–1598*, ed. Penelope Renold (London: Catholic Record Society, 1967).

320   *Early Modern Catholics, Royalists, and Cosmopolitans*

Anon., *A Large Examination taken at Lambeth, according to his Maiesties direction, point by point, of M. George Blackwell* (London, 1607).

Anon., *Leicester's Commonwealth: The Copy of a Letter Written by a Master of Art of Cambridge (1584) and Related Documents*, ed. D.C. Peck (Athens: Ohio University Press, 1985).

Anon., *Mr. George Blackwel, (Made by Pope Clement 8. Archpriest of England) his Answeres vpon sundry his Examinations: Together with his Approbation and taking of the Oath of Allegeance: And his Letter written to his Assistants, and brethren, moouing them not onely to take the said Oath, but to aduise all Romish Catholikes so to doe* (London, 1607).

Anon., *A Replication of a Serjeant at the Laws of England*, appended to Christopher St. German, *The Doctor and Student*, ed. William Muchall (Cincinnati: Robert Clark & Co., 1874).

Anon., *The Troublesome Raigne of Iohn King of England* [electronic edition] (Cambridge: Proquest, 1994).

Anon., *Vindiciae, contra tyrannos, or, Concerning the legitimate power of a prince over the people, and of people over a prince*, ed. and trans. George Garnett (New York: Cambridge University Press, 1994).

Anon., *The Wily Jesuits and the Monita Secreta: The Forged Secret Instructions of the Jesuits, Myth and Reality*, ed. Sabina Pavone (St. Louis: Institute of Jesuit Sources, 2005).

Aquinas, Thomas, *Summa Theologiae*, ed. and trans. Thomas Gilby, O.P. (60 vols, New York: McGraw-Hill, 1966).

Ariosto, Lodovico, *Orlando Furioso*, ed. Gioacchino Paparelli (2 vols, Milano: Biblioteca Universale Rizzoli, 1991).

———, *Orlando Furioso, Translated into English Heroical Verse by Sir John Harington (1591)*, ed. Robert McNulty (New York: Oxford University Press, 1972).

Aristotle, *Politics*, ed. and trans. H. Rackham (Cambridge, MA: Harvard University Press, 1990).

Bale, John, *King Johan*, ed. Barry B. Adams (San Marino, CA: Huntington Library, 1969).

Behn, Aphra, *The Works of Aphra Behn*, ed. Janet Todd (7 vols, Columbus: Ohio State University, 1996).

Bellarmine, Robert, *Opera Omnia*, ed. Francesco Romolo and Sisto Riario Sforza (Neapoli: Apud Josephum Giuliano, 1856).

———, *Responsio Matthaei Torti Presbyteri, et theologi papiensis, ad librvm inscriptvm, Triplici nodo triplex cvnevs* (Coloniae Agrippinae, 1608) in J. Fèvre (ed.), *Ven. Cardinalis Roberti Bellarmini Politiani SJ Opera Omnia* (12 vols, Paris, 1870–74).

———, *Tertia Controversia Generalis, De Svmmo Pontifice*, ed. Jacques Amyot and Simon Goulart (Ingolstadii, 1587).

———, *Tractatus de potestate svmmi pontificis in rebvs temporalibvs: aduersus Gvlielmvm Barclaivm* (Coloniae Agrippinae, 1611).

Bilson, Thomas, *The true difference betweene Christian subiection and unchristian rebellion wherein the princes lawfull power to commaund for trueth, and indepriuable right to beare the sword are defended against the Popes censures and the Iesuits sophismes vttered in their apologie and defence of English Catholikes: with a demonstration that the thinges refourmed in the Church of England by the lawes of this realme are truely Catholike, notwithstanding the vaine shew made to the contrary in their late Rhemish Testament* (Oxford, 1585).

Botero, Giovanni, *Delle relationi vniversali* (Roma, 1591).

Bowler, Hugh (ed.), *London Sessions Records, 1605–1685*, vol. 34 (London: Catholic Record Society, 1934).

Bridges, John, *The Supremacie of Christian Princes, ouer all persons throughout their dominions, in all causes so wel Ecclesiastical as temporall, both against the Counterblast of Thomas Stapleton, replying on the Reuerend father in Christe, Robert Bishop of Winchester: and also Against Nicolas Sanders his Uisible Monarchie of the Romaine Church, touching this controuersie of the Princes Supremacie* (London, 1573).

Bristow, Richard, *A briefe Treatise of diuerse plaine and sure wayes to finde out the truthe in this doubtful and dangerous time of Heresie: conteyning sundry worthy Motiues vnto the Catholike faith, or Considerations to moue a man to beleue the Catholikes, and not the Heretikes* (Antwerp, 1574).

Buchanan, George, *George Buchanan: A Memorial 1506–1906*, ed. David Alexander Millar (St. Andrews: W.C. Henderson & Son, 1907).

———, *De jure regni apud Scotos. Or, A dialogue, concerning the due privilege of government, in the kingdom of Scotland: betwixt George Buchanan and Thomas Maitland, by the said George Buchanan. And translated out of the original Latin into English by Philalethes* (Philadelphia, 1766).

Burghley, Lord William Cecil, *Execution of Justice in England, [1583]*, ed. Franklin L. Baumer (New York: Scholars Facsimiles & Reprints, 1938).

———, *The Execution of Justice in England by William Cecil and A True, Sincere, and Modest Defense of English Catholics by William Allen*, ed. Robert McCune Kingdon (Ithaca, NY: Cornell University Press, 1965).

Calvin, Jean, *Two Godly and Learned Sermons*, trans. Robert Horne, ed. Anthony Munday (London, 1584).

Camden, William, *The Historie of the Life and Reigne of the Most Renowned and Victorious Princesse Elizabeth, Late Queene of England* (London, 1630).

Camões, Luís de, *Lusiadas de Luis de Camoens, principe de los poetas de Espana*, ed. and trans. Manuel de Faria i Sousa (Madrid, 1639).

———, *Os Lusíadas*, ed. Frank Pierce (Oxford: Oxford University Press, 1973).

Campion, Edmund, *Ambrosia. A Neo-Latin Drama*, ed. and trans. Joseph Simons (Assen: Van Gorcum & Co., 1970).

———, *Rationes decem quibus fretus B. Edmundus Campianus certamen adversariis obtulit in causa fidei, redditae academicis angliae [Ten Reasons proposed to his adversaries for disputation in the name of the faith and presented to the illustrious members of our universities]*, ed. and trans. John Hungerford Pollen, S.J. (London: The Manresa Press, 1914).

Catholic Record Society, *Miscellanea*, vol. 2 (London: Catholic Record Society, 1906).

322 *Early Modern Catholics, Royalists, and Cosmopolitans*

————, *Miscellanea*, vol. 4 (London: Catholic Record Society, 1907).

————, *Miscellanea*, vol. 7 (London: Catholic Record Society, 1911).

————, *Miscellanea*, vol. 12 (London: Catholic Record Society, 1921).

Celta, Stephano Ivnio Bruto, *Vindiciae, contra tyrannos: sive, De Principis in Populum, Populique in Principem, legitima potestate* (Edimbvrgi, 1579).

Chark, William, *An answere to a seditious pamphlet lately cast abroade by a Iesuite, with a discoverie of that blasphemous sect* (London, 1580).

Charles I, *Eikon Basilike; The portrature of His Sacred Majesty in his Solitudes and Sufferings*, ed. Philip A. Knachel (Ithaca, NY: Cornell University Press, 1966).

Cicero, *De Oratore*, trans. E.W. Sutton, ed. H. Rackham (The Loeb Classical Library, Cambridge, MA: Harvard University Press, 1967).

Circignani, Niccolò, *Ecclesiae Anglicanae Trophaea sive Sanctor. Martyrum, qui pro Christo Catholicaq' fidei Veritate asserenda, antiquo recentioriq' Persecutionum tempore, mortem in Anglia subierunt, Passiones Romae in Collegio Anglico per Nicolaum Circinianum depictae; nuper autem Per Io. Bap. de Cavalleriis aeneis typis repraesentatae. Cum privilegio Gregorii XIII. P.M.* (Rome, 1584).

Coke, Sir Edward, *The Selected Writings of Sir Edward Coke*, ed. Steve Sheppard (3 vols, Indianapolis, IN: Liberty Fund, 2003).

Constable, Henry, *Examen pacifique de la doctrine des Huguenots* (Paris, 1589).

Cowley, Abraham, *The Civil War by Abraham Cowley*, ed. Allan Prichard (Buffalo, NY: University of Toronto Press, 1973).

————, *Poems: Miscellanies, the Mistress, Pindarique Odes, Davideis, Verses Written on Several Occasions*, ed. A.R. Waller (Cambridge: Cambridge University Press, 1905).

————, *Poems: Viz. I. Miscellanies II. The Mistress, or, Love Verses. III. Pindarique Odes. And IV. Davideis, or, A Sacred Poem of the Troubles of David* (London, 1656).

————, *Works of Mr. Abraham Cowley* (London, 1668).

D'Avenant, Sir William, *Sir William Davenant's* Gondibert, ed. David F. Gladish (Oxford: Clarendon Press, 1971).

Davies, Sir John, *Le Reports des cases & matters en Ley, resolves & adjudges en les courts del roy en Ireland [Irish Reports]* (London, 1674).

Dee, John, *The Perfect Arte of Navigation* [London, 1577] (reprint, New York: De Capo Press, 1968).

Donne, John, *Pseudo-Martyr: Wherein out of Certain Propositions and Gradations, This Conclusion is evicted. That those which are of the Romane Religion in this Kingdome, may and ought to take the Oath of Allegeance*, ed. Anthony Raspa (Buffalo, NY: McGill-Queen's University Press, 1993).

Drayton, Michael, "Matilda," in *The Works of Michael Drayton*, ed. William J. Hebel (Oxford: B.H. Blackwell, 1961).

Works Cited

Edelman, Charles (ed.), *The Stukeley Plays: The Battlle of Alcazar by George Peele, The Famous History of the Life and Death of Captain Thomas Stukeley* (New York: Manchester University Press, 2005).

Ellesmere, Lord Chancellor Thomas Egerton, "The Lord Chancellor Egertons Observacions vpon ye Lord Cookes Reportes,"in Louis Knafla (ed.), *Law and Politics in Jacobean England, The Tracts of Lord Chancellor Ellesmere* (New York: Cambridge University Press, 1977), 297–319.

———, "Some Notes, and Remembrances, Concerning Prohibitions, for Staying of Suites in the Ecclesiasticall Courts, and in the Courts of the Admiralty," in Louis Knafla (ed.), *Law and Politics in Jacobean England, The Tracts of Lord Chancellor Ellesmere* (New York: Cambridge University Press, 1977), 282–96.

Fanshawe, Lady Ann, *The Memoirs of Ann Lady Fanshawe*, ed. Herbert Charles Fanshawe (London: John Lane Co., 1907).

Fanshawe, Sir Richard, *La Fida Pastora, Comoedia Pastoralis* [Latin trans. of John Fletcher's *The Faithful Shepherd*] (Londini, 1658).

———, *The Lusiad, or Portugals Historical Poem: Written In the Portingall Language by Luis de Camoens; And Now newly put into English by Richard Fanshaw, Esq* (London, 1655).

———, *Original Letters of his Excellency Sir Richard Fanshaw, During his Embassies in Spain and Portugal* (London, 1701).

———, *Il Pastor Fido: The faithfull Shepheard, With an Addition of divers other Poems Concluding with a short Discourse of the Long Civill Warres of Rome* [English trans. of Battista Guarini's *Il Pastor Fido*] (London, 1648).

———, *The Poems and Translations of Sir Richard Fanshawe*, ed. Peter Davison (2 vols, New York: Oxford University Press, 1997–99).

———, *Querer Por Solo Querer: To Love only for Love Sake: A Dramatick Romance. Represented at Aranjuez Before the King and Queen of Spain, To Celebrate The Birth-Day of that King by the Meninas ... Written in Spanish by Don Antonio de Mendoza, 1623. Paraphrased in English, Anno 1654* (London, 1670).

———, *Selected Parts of Horace, Prince of Lyricks; And Of all the Latin Poets the fullest fraught with Excellent Morality. Concluding With a Piece out of Ausonius and another out of Virgil. Now newly put into English* (London, 1652).

Field, John, *A Caveat for Parsons Howlet, concerning his vntimely flighte, and schriching in the cleare daylighte of the Gospell, necessarie for him, and all the rest of that darke brood, and vncleane cage of papistes, who with their vntimely bookes, seeke the discredite of the trueth, and the disquiet of this Church of England* (London, 1581).

Fletcher, Anthonie, *Certaine very proper, and most profitable similes, wherein sundrie, and very many, most foule vices, and dangerous sinnes, of all sorts, are so plainly laid open, and displaied in their kindes, and so pointed at with the finger of God* (London, 1595).

Foxe, John, *The Acts and Monuments of John Foxe: A New and Complete Edition, with Preliminary Dissertation by Rev. George Townsend*, ed. Stephen Reed Cattley (8 vols, London: Seeley, 1838–41).

324   *Early Modern Catholics, Royalists, and Cosmopolitans*

————, *De Christo gratis iustificante. Contra Osorianam iustitiam, caeterosque eiusdem inhaerentis iustitiae patronos, Stan. Hosium. Andrad. Canisium. Vegam. Tiletanum. Lorichium, contra vniuersam denique Turbam Tridentinam & Iesuiticam. Amica & modesta defensio. Joan. Foxij* (London, 1583).

Friedberg, Emil (ed.), *Corpus Iuris Canonici* (2 vols, Leipzig: Tauchnitz, 1879–81).

Greene, Robert, *Friar Bacon and Friar Bungay*, ed. Daniel Seltzer (Lincoln: University of Nebraska Press, 1963).

Greville, Sir Fulke, "A Dedication to Sir Phillip Sidney," in *The Prose Works of Fulke Greville, Lord Brooke*, ed. John Gouws (New York: Oxford University Press, 1986).

Haddon, Walter, *Gualthieri Haddoni pro Reformatione Anglicana Epistola Apologetica ad Hier. Osorium. Lusitanum* (Paris, 1563).

————, *A sight of the Portugall Pearle, that is, The Answere of D. Haddon Maister of the requests unto our soueraigne Lady Elizabeth by the grace of God quene of England France and Irelande, defendour of the faith, & c. against the epistle of Hieronimus Osorius a Portugall, entitled a Pearle for a Prince. Translated out of lattyn into english by Abraham Hartwell, Student in the kynges college in Cambridge* (London, 1565).

Haddon, Walter and John Foxe, *Against Ierome Osorius Byshopp of Siluane in Portingall and against his slaunderous Inuectiues. An Aunswere Apologeticall: For the necessary defence of the Euangelicall doctrine and veritie* (London, 1581).

————, *Contra Hieron. Osorium, eiusque odiosas insectationes pro Evangelicae veritatis necessaria Defensione, Responsio Apologetica. Per clariss. virum, Gualt. Haddonum inchoata: Deinde suscepta & continuata per Joann. Foxum* (London, 1577).

Hakluyt, Richard, *The Principal Navigations, Voyages, Traffiques, and Discoveries of the English Nation* (12 vols, Glasgow: J. MacLehose and Sons, 1903).

Hanmer, Meredith, *The great bragge and challenge of M. Champion a Iesuite, commonlye called Edmunde Campion, latelye arriued in Englande, contayinge nyne articles here seuerallye laide downe, directed by him to the Lordes of the Counsail, confuted and aunswered by Meredith Hanmer, M. of Art, and student in diuinitie* (London, 1581).

Harington, Sir John, *A Briefe view of the state of the Church of England*, ed. John Chetwynd (London, 1653).

————, *The Englishmans Docter. Or, the Schoole of Salerne* (London, 1607).

————, *The Epigrams of Sir John Harington*, ed. Gerard Kilroy (Burlington, VT: Ashgate, 2009).

————, *The Letters and Epigrams of Sir John Harington together with The Prayse of Private Life*, ed. Norman Egbert McClure (New York: Octagon Books, 1977).

————, *A New Discourse of a Stale Subject, Called the Metamorphosis of Ajax*, ed. Elizabeth Story Donno (New York: Columbia University Press, 1962).

————, *Nugae Antiquae*, ed. Henry Harington (3 vols, London, 1792).

————, *Tract on the Succession*, ed. Clements R. Markham, C.B. (London: Roxburghe Club, 1880).

Heywood, Thomas, *The Fair Maid of the West, Parts I and II*, ed. Robert K. Turner, Jr. (Lincoln: University of Nebraska Press, 1967).

Hinds, Allen B. (ed.), *Calendar of State Papers Relating to English Affairs in the Archives of Venice, 1647–1652* (London: Longman Green, 1927).

Hobbes, Thomas, *Leviathan*, ed. with intro. Richard Tuck (New York: Cambridge University Press, 1991).

Holinshed, Raphael, *The Third volume of Chronicles, beginning at duke William the Norman, commonlie called the Conqueror; and descending by degrees of yeeres to all the kings and queenes of England in their orderlie successions: first compiled by Raphaell Holinshed, and by him extended to the yeare 1577. Now newlie recognized, augmented, and continued (with occurrences and accidents of fresh memorie) to the yeare 1586* (London, 1586).

Hooker, Richard, *The Works of that Learned and Judicious Divine, Mr. Richard Hooker*, ed. John Keble (3 vols, Oxford: Oxford University Press, 1836).

Horne, Robert, *An Answeare Made by Rob. Bishoppe of Wynchester, to a Booke entituled, The Declaration of Suche Scruples, and staies of Conscience, touchinge the Othe of the Supremacy, as M. Iohn Fekenham, by wrytinge did deliuer unto the L. Bishop of Winchester, with his Resolutions made thereunto* (London, 1566).

Humbert, *Libri III Adversus Simoniacos*, in F. Thaner (ed.), *Monumenta Germaniae Historica Libelli de Lite Imperatorum et Pontificum* (3 vols, Hanover, 1891).

James VI and I, *The Political Works of James I*, ed. Charles Howard McIlwain (New York: Russell & Russell, 1965).

————, *Triplici nodo, trplex cuneus* in J.P. Sommerville (ed.), *King James VI and I: Political Writings* (New York: Cambridge University Press, 2006).

————, *Triplici nodo, triplex cuneus: or, an Apologie for the Oath of Allegiance, Against the two Breves of Pope Paulus Quintus, and the late Letter of Cardinal Bellarmine to G. Blackwel the Arch-priest* (London, 1607 [vere 1608]).

Jessop, Augustus, *Letters of Father Henry Walpole, S.J.* (Norwich, 1873).

Jewel, John, *A Defence of the Apologie of the Churche of Englande, Conteininge an Answeare to a certaine Booke lately set foorthe by M. Hardinge, and Entituled, A Confutation* (London, 1567).

————, *Works of John Jewel, Bishop of Salisbury*, ed. Rev. John Ayre (4 vols, Cambridge: Cambridge University Press, 1845–50).

Johnson, Richard, *The Crown Garland of Golden Roses: Consisting of Ballads and Songs*, ed. W. Chappell (London: priv. printing, 1842).

Kant, Immanuel, *Kant: Political Writings* (New York: Cambridge University Press, 1991).

Killigrew, Thomas, *Comedies and Tragedies* (London: Benjamin Blom, 1967).

Knolles, Richard, *The generall historie of the Turkes, from the first beginning of that nation to the rising of the Othoman familie: with all the notable expeditions of the Christian princes against them. Together with the liues and conquests of the Othoman kings and emperours faithfullie collected out of the best histories, both auntient and moderne, and digested into one continuat historie vntill this present yeare 1603* (London, 1603).

Knox, John, *The First Blast of the Trumpet Against the Monstrous Regiment of Women (1558)* in Marvin Arthur Breslow (ed.), *The Political Writings of John Knox* (Washington: The Folger Shakespeare Library, 1985).

Lambarde, William, *Archeion or, a Discourse upon the High Courts of Justice in England*, ed. Charles H. McIlwain et al. (Cambridge: Harvard University Press, 1957).

Languet, Hubert and Sir Philip Sidney, *Huberti Langueti viri clarissimi epistolae politicae et historicae. Scriptae quondam Ad Illustrem, & Generosum Dominum Philippum Sydnaeum, Equitem Anglum, Illustrissimi Pro-Regis Hyberniae filium. Vlissingensem Gubernatorum fortissimum. In quibus variae rerum suo aeuo in Germania, Italia, Gallia, Belgio, Vngaria, Polonia, aliisque Orbis Christiani Prouinciis Pace, Belloque gestarum, narrationes, consilia, & eventûs describuntur. Omnibus Politicarum rerum, & historiarum studiosis, Consiliariis etiam Principum, & ad Reip. Clauum sedentibus, maximè vtiles, ac necessariae. Nunc verò primum publicis typis divulgatae. Francofurti, In Officina Gvlielmi Fitzeri, Librarii Angli. Anno M. DC. XXXIII* (Frankfurt, 1633).

Las Casas, Bartolomé de, *Una brevíssima relación de la destruyción de las Indias* (Sevilla, 1552).

———, *La destruction des Indes*, trans. Jacques de Miggrode, with preface by Alain Milhou (Paris: Chandeigne, 1995).

———, *A Short Account of the Destruction of the Indies*, ed. and trans. Nigel Griffin, intro. Anthony Pagden (London: Penguin, 1992).

———, *The Spanish Colonie, or Briefe chronicle of the acts and gestes of the Spaniardes in the West Indies* (London, 1583).

———, *Tyrannies et cruautés des Espagnols perpétrées ès Indes occidentales qu'on dit le Nouveau Monde, brièvement décrites par l'évêque don frère Barthélemy de Las Casas ou Casaus, de l'ordre de saint Dominique, traduites par Jacques de Migrode pour servir d'exemple et d'avertissement XVII provinces du pays* (Antwerp, 1579).

Laud, William, *A relation of the conference between William Laud, late Lord Arch-Bishop of Canterbury, and Mr Fisher the Jesuite* (London, 1673).

Law, Thomas Graves (ed.), *The Archpriest Controversy: Documents Relating to the Dissensions of the Roman Catholic Clergy 1597–1602* (2 vols, Westminster: Nichols and Sons, 1896–98).

Leake, Richard, *Foure sermons, preached and publikely taught by Richad Leake* (London, 1599).

Lomas, Sophia Crawford (ed.), *The Manuscripts of J.M. Heathcote, Esq., Conington Castle* (Norwich: Norfolk Chronicle, 1899).

Lucan, *Lucan*, trans. J.D. Duff (The Loeb Classical Library, *Cambridge*: Harvard University Press, *1928*).

Lucinge, Rene de, *The beginning, continvance, and decay of estates: VVherein are handled many notable Questions concerning the establishment of Empires and Monarchies*, trans. I.F. (London, 1606).

Lyly, John, *Pap with a Hatchet: Being a Reply to Martin Mar-Prelate* (1589), *Reprinted from the Original Quarto Edition with An Introduction and Notes*, ed. John Petheram (London: J. Petheram, 1844).

Major, John, *In secundum librum sententiarum* (Paris, 1519).

Marprelate, Martin, *Oh read ouer D. Iohn Bridges, for it is worthy worke: Or an epitome of the fyrste Booke, of that right worshipfull volume, written against the Puritanes, in the defense of the noble cleargie, by as worshipfull a prieste, Iohn Bridges, presbyter, priest or elder, doctor of Diuillitie, and Deane of Sarum ... Compiled for the behoofe and overthrow of the vnpreaching Parsons, Fyckers, and Currats, that haue lernt their Catechismes, and are past grace: By the reverend and worthie Martin Marprelate gentleman, and dedicated by a second epistle to the terrible priests* (London, 1588).

May, Thomas, *A continuation of Lucan's historicall poem till the death of Iulius Cæsar by TM* (London, 1630).

———, *Lucan's Pharsalia: or The civill warres of Rome, betweene Pompey the great, and Iulius Cæsar: The whole ten bookes*, Englished by Thomas May (London, 1627).

———, *Supplementum Lvcani librii VII* (Lugduni Batavorum, 1640).

———, *Supplementum Lvcan's Pharsalia: or the Civill Warres of Rome, betweene Pompey the great and Ivlivs Cæsar. The three first Bookes*, trans. into English by Thomas May (London, 1626).

Migne, Jacques-Paul, *Patrologia Latina*, vol. 214 (Paris, 1855).

Milton, John, *The Complete Poems and Major Prose*, ed. Merritt Y. Hughes (New York: Macmillan, 1957).

———, *Complete Prose Works of John Milton*, ed. Don M. Wolfe et al. (8 vols, New Haven, CT: Yale University Press, 1953–82).

Monumenta Ignatiana Sancti Ignatii de Loyola Constitutiones Societatis Jesu (3 vols, Rome: Monumenta Historica Societatis Iesu, 1934–38).

Morney Philippe de, *A Worke concerning the Trewnesse of the Christian Religion: A Facsimile Reproduction with an Introduction by F.J. Sypher*, trans. Arthur Golding and Sir Philip Sidney [London, 1587] (reprint, New York: Scholars Facsimiles and Reprints, 1976).

Morton, Thomas, *A Discharge of Five Imputations of Mis-Allegations, Falsly Charged upon the (now) Bishop of Duresme, by an English Baron* (London, 1633).

Munday, Anthony, *The araignement, and execution, of a wilfull and obstinate traitour, named Eueralde Ducket, alias House* (London, 1581).

———, *A banquet of daintie conceits. Furnished with verie delicate and choyse inventions, to delight their mindes, who take pleasure in musique, and therewithall to sing sweete ditties, either to the lute, bandora, virginalles, or anie other instrument* (London 1588).

328   *Early Modern Catholics, Royalists, and Cosmopolitans*

——, *A breefe and true reporte, of the execution of certaine traytours at Tiborne* (London, 1582).

——, *A breefe answer made unto two seditious pamphlets* (London, 1582).

——, *A breefe discourse of the taking of Edmund Campion, the seditious Iesuit, and diuers other papistes, in Barkeshire: who were brought to the Towre of London, the 22. day of Iuly. 1581. Gathered by A.M.* (London, 1581).

——, *A Briefe Chronicle, of the Successe of times, from the Creation of the World to this instant. Containing, the Originall & liues of our ancient Forefathers, before and after the Floude, As also, of all the Monarchs, Emperours, Kinges, Popes, Kingdomes, Common-weales, Estates, and Gouernments, in most Nations of this Worlde: And how in alteration, or succession, they have continued to this day* (London, 1611).

——, *The Death of Robert, Earl of Huntingdon,* in *The Huntingdon Plays: A Critical Edition,* ed. John Carney Meagher (New York: Garland, 1980).

——, *A discoverie of Edmund Campion, and his confederates* (London 1582).

——, *The Downfall of Robert, Earle of Huntington,* in *Robin Hood and Other Outlaw Tales,* ed. Stephen Knight and Thomas Ohlgren (Kalamazoo: Medieval Institute Publications, 2000).

——, *An Edition of Anthony Munday's* John A Kent and John a Cumber, ed. Arthur E. Pennell (New York: Garland, 1980).

——, *The English Roman Life,* ed. Philip J. Ayres [London, 1582] (reprint, New York: Oxford University Press, 1980).

——, *The Fishmonger's Pageant on Lord Mayor's Day, 1616, Chrysanaleia: The Golden Fishing, Devised by Anthony Munday, Citizen and Draper. Represented in Twelve Plates by Henry Shaw, F.S.A. from Contemporary Drawings in the Possession of the Worshipful Company of Fishmongers, Accompanied with Various Illustrative Documents and an Historical Introduction by John Gough Nichols* (London, 1844).

——, *The Mirrour of Mutabilitie,* ed. Hans Peter Heinrich (New York: P. Lang, 1990).

——, *Pageants and Entertainments of Anthony Munday: A Critical Edition,* ed. David M. Bergeron (New York: Garland, 1985).

——, *Sir John Oldcaste, Part 1,* in *The Oldcastle Controversy:* Sir John Oldcastle, Part 1 *and* The Famous Victories of Henry V, ed. Peter Corbin and Douglas Sedge (New York: Manchester University Press, 1991).

——, *Sir Thomas More: A Play by Anthony Munday and Others,* ed. Vittorio Gabrieli and Georgio Melchiori (New York: Manchester University Press, 1990).

——, *A Watch-vvoord to Englande Englande to beware of traytours and tretcherous practises, which haue beene the ouerthrowe of many famous kingdomes and common weales* (London, 1584).

——, *Zelauto, The Fountain of Fame, 1580,* ed. Jack Stillinger (Carbondale, Southern Illinois University Press, 1963).

Munday, Anthony (trans.), *The first book of Amadis of Gaule* (London, 1589).

——, *The first booke of Primaleon of Greece* (London, 1594).

———, *The [first] seconde [sic] part, of the no lesse rare, historie of Palmerin of England* (London, 1596).

———, *Palmerin D'Oliva.* [Part 1] *The mirrour of nobilitie, mappe of honor, anotamie of rare fortunes, heroycall president of Loue* (London, 1588).

Münster, Sebastian, *Cosmographey oder Beschreibung aller Länder Herrschafften vnd fürnemesten stetten des gantzen Erdbodens sampt ihren Gelegenheiten, Eygenschafften, Religion, Gebreuchen, Geschichten vnnd Handtheirungen ...* (Basil, 1588).

Nadal, Jerónimo, *Epistolae et monumenta. 5, Commentarii de instituto Societatis Jesu*, ed. Michael Nicolau (Rome, 1962).

———, *Epistolae P. Hieronymi Nadal Societatis Jesu ab anno 1546 ad 1577* (4 vols, Madrid: MHSI, 1898–1905).

Nowell, Alexander, *A reproufe, written by Alexander Nowell, of a booke entituled, A proufe of certayne articles in religion denied by M. Iuell, set furth by Thomas Dorman* (London, 1565).

Osório, Jerónimo, *Amplissimi atque Doctissimi Viri D. Hieronymi Osorii, Episcopi Sylvensis, in Gualterum Haddonum Magistrum Libellorum Supplicum apud clarrisimam Principem Helisabetham Angliae, Franciae, & Hiberniae Reginam. libri tres* (Olissipone, 1567).

———, *An Epistle of the Reuerend Father in God Hieronimvs Osorivs Bishop of Arcoburge in Portugale, to the most excellent Princesse Elizabeth by the grace of God Quene of England France, and Ireland. & c. Translated oute of Latten in to Englishe by Richard Shacklock M. of Arte and student of the Ciuill Lawes in Louaine* (Antwerp, 1565).

———, *Epistola reuerendissimi D. Hieronymi Osorij Episcopi Syluensis, ad serenissimam Elisabetam Angliae reginam: cum facultate & approbatione reuerendissimorum patrum supremo Sanctae Inquisitionis consilio praefectorum* (Olysippone, 1575).

———, *A learned and very eloquent Treatie, written in Latin by the famouse man Hieronymus Osorius Bishop of Sylua in Portugal, wherein he confuteth a certayne Aunswere made by M. Walter Haddon against the Epistle of the said Bishoppe unto the Queenes Maiestie*, trans. John Fen (Louvain, 1568).

Parr, Anthony (ed.), *Three Renaissance Travel Plays* (New York: Manchester University Press, 1995).

Peele, George, *A Farewell Entitled to the famous and fortunate generalls of our English forces: Sir Iohn Norris & Syr Frauncis Drake Knights, and all theyr braue and resolute follower* (London, 1589).

———, *The Life and Works of George Peele*, ed. John Yoklavich (New Haven, CT: Yale University Press, 1961).

Persons, Robert, *An Answere to The Fifth Part of Reportes Lately set forth by Syr Edward Cooke, Knight, the Kinges Attorney generall* (St. Omer, 1606).

———, *A Brief Discours contayning certayne reasons why Catholiques refuse to goe to Church* (London, 1580).

———, *The Christian Directory (1582) The First Booke of the Christian Exercise, Appertayning to Resolution*, ed. Victor Houliston (Boston: Brill, 1998).

330   *Early Modern Catholics, Royalists, and Cosmopolitans*

——— [R. Doleman (pseud.)], *A Conference about the next succession to the crowne of Ingland, diuided into two partes. Where-of the first conteyneth the discourse of a ciuill Lawyer, how and in what manner propinquity of blood is to be preferred. And the second the speech of a temporall lawyer, about the particuler titles of all such as do or may pretende within Ingland or without, to the next succession* [1595] (reprint, Amsterdam: Da Capo Press, 1972).

———, *The copie of a double letter ... containing the true aduises of the cause, and maner of the death, of one Richard Atkins, executed by fire, in Rome, the seconde of August 1581* (Rheims, 1581).

———, *A Discussion of the Answere of M. William Barlow, D. of Diuinity, to the Book intituled: The Iudgment of a Catholicke Englishman liuing in banishment for his Religion* (St. Omer, 1612).

———, *Elizabethae Angliae Reginae haeresim Calvinianam propvgnantis, saevissimum in Cathlicos sui regni edictum ... Cum responsione ad singula capita* (Antwerp, 1592).

———, *The Jesuits' Memorial, for the Intended Reformation of England Under their First Popish Prince*, ed. Edward Gee (London, 1690).

———, *The judgment of a catholicke English-man living in banishment for his Religion, Written to his priuate friend in England* [1608] (reprint, New York: De Capo Press, 1972).

———, *Letters and Memorials of Father Robert Persons, S.J.* vol. 1 (to 1588), ed. Leo Hicks, S.J. (London: Catholic Record Society, 1942).

———, *News from Spayne and Holland conteyning. An information of Inglish affayres in Spayne with a conference made theruppon in Amsterdame of Holland* (Antwerp, 1593).

———, *De persecutione Anglicana, epistola. Qua explicantur afflictiones, aerumnae, & calamitates grauissimae, cruciatus etiam & tormenta, & acerbissima martyria, quae Catholici nunc Angli, ob fidem patiuntur* (Rouen, 1581).

———, *De persecvtione Anglicana commentariolvs, a collegio anglicano romano, hoc anno Domini cIɔ. Iɔ xxcii. In Vrbe editus, & iam denuo Ingolstadii escusus: Additis Literis S.D.N.D. Gregoris Papae XIII. Hortatoriis ad subueniendum Anglis, & c.* (Ingolstadt, 1582).

———, *Quaestiones duae De Sacris alienis non aduendis, ad vsum præximque Angliae breuiter explicatae* (St. Omer, 1607).

———, *Relacion de Algunos Martyrios, que de nueuo han hecho los hereges en Inglaterra, y de otras cosas tocantes a nuestra santa y Catolica religion. Traduzida de Ingles en Castellano, por el padre Roberto Personio, etc.* (Madrid, 1590).

———, *A Relation of the King of Spaines Receiving in Valliodolid, and in the Inglish College of the same towne, in August last past of this yere, 1592* (Antwerp, 1592).

——— [Anon.], *Severall speeches delivered at a conference concerning the power of Parliament, to proceed against their King for misgovernment* (London, 1648).

—, "A Storie of Domesticall Difficulties in the English Catholike cause," in John H. Pollen, S.J. (ed.), *Miscellanea II, Publications of the Catholic Record Society* (London: Catholic Record Society, 1906).

—, *A Treatise of Three Conuersions of England from Paganisme to Christian Religion* (3 vols, St. Omer, 1603–4).

Petronius Arbiter, *The Bellum Civile of Petronius*, ed. Florence Theodora Baldwin (New York: Columbia University Press, 1911).

—, *The Satyricon*, ed. and trans. William Arrowsmith (Ann Arbor: University of Michigan Press, 1959).

—, *Satyricon, Seneca, Apocolocyntosis*, ed. E.H. Warmington, trans. W.H.D. Rouse and Michael Heseltine, no. 15 (The Loeb Classical Library, Cambridge, MA: Harvard University Press, 1975).

Polemon, John, *The Second Part of the Booke of Battailes, fought in our age* (London, 1587).

Pollen, John Hungerford, S.J. (ed.), *Unpublished Documents Relating to the English Martyrs, Vol. 1: 1584–1603* (London: Catholic Record Society, 1908).

Pugh, R., *Blacklo's Cabal Discovered in severall of their Letters Clearly expressing Designs Inhvmane against Regulars, Vnivst against the Laity, Scismatical against the Pope, Crvel against Orthodox Clergy men And owning the Nvllity of the chapter, their opposition of Episcopall Authority*, Second Edition (s.l., 1680).

Puttenham, George, *The Art of English Poesy: A Critical Edition*, ed. Frank Whigham and Wayne A. Rebhorn (Ithaca, NY, 2007).

Ralegh, Sir Walter, *The Discovery of Guiana*, NetLibrary eBook (Hoboken, NJ: BiblioBytes, 199-?).

—, *The 21st (and Last) Book of the Ocean to Cynthia*, in *Selected Writings*, ed. Gerald Hammond (Manchester: Manchester University Press, 1984).

Renold, Penelope (ed.), *The Wisbech Stirs, 1595–1598*, vol. 51 (London: Catholic Record Society, 1958).

Richer, Edmond, *A treatise of ecclesiasticall and politike power. Shewing, the Church is a monarchicall gouernment, ordained to a supernaturall and spirituall end, tempered with an aristocraticall order, (which is the best of all and most conformable to nature) by the great Pastor of soules Iesus Christ* (London, 1612).

Roberts, Henry, *The Historie of Pheander, The Mayden Knight* (London, 1617).

—, *A Most Friendly Farewell to Sir Francis Drake* [1585] (reprint, Boston, 1924).

Rogers, Richard, *Seauen treatises containing such direction as is gathered out of the holie Scriptures, leading and guiding to true happines, both in this life, and in the life to come: and may be called the practise of Christianitie. Profitable for all such as heartily desire the same: in the which, more particularly true Christians may learne how to leade a godly and comfortable life euery day* (London, 1603).

Rufinus, *Summa Decretorum*, ed. H. Singer (Paderborn, 1902).

Rushworth, John, *Historical Collections: Abridg'd and Improv'd* (8 vols, London, 1706).

332   *Early Modern Catholics, Royalists, and Cosmopolitans*

Sander, Nicholas, *De visibili monarchia ecclesiae, libri VIII: in quibus diligens instituitur disputatio de certa & perpetua Ecclesiae Dei tum successione tum gubernatione monarchica, ab ipso mundi initio vsque ad finem: deinde etiam ciuitas diaboli persaepè interrupta progressio proponitur, sectaeque omnes & haereses confutantur, quae vnquam contra veram fidem emerserunt: denique de Antichristo ipso & membris eius, deque vera Dei & adulterina diaboli ecclesia, copiosè tractatur ... cum indice rerum & personarum locuplete* (Antuerpiae, 1578).

Seall, Robert, *A comendation of the adue[n]terus viage of the wurthy Captain. M. Thomas Stutely Esquyer and others, towards the land called Terra florida* (London, 1563).

Selden, John, *Table-Talk* (Westminster: A. Constable and Co., 1895).

Sepúlveda, Juan Ginés de, *Demócrates Segundo, o, de las justas causas de la guerra contra los indios*, ed. Ángel Losada (Madrid: Consejo Superior de Investigaciones Científicas, Instituto Francisco de Vitoria, 1984).

Seymour, Edward, *Epistola exhortatoria ad pacem, missa ab illustrissimo Principe, Domino Protectore Angliae, ac caeteris Regiae Maiestatis consiliarijs, ad nobilitatem ac plebem, uniuersumq[ue] populum Regni Scotiae* (Londini, 1548).

Shakespeare, William, *King John*, in *The Riverside Shakespeare*, ed. G. Blakemore Evans (2nd ed., New York: Houghton Mifflin, 1997).

Sidney, Sir Philip, *An Apology for Poetry*, ed. Forrest G. Robinson (Indianapolis, IN: Bobbs-Merrill Educational Publishing, 1970).

———, *The Correspondence of Sir Philip Sidney*, ed. Roger Kuin (2 vols, New York: Oxford University Press, 2012).

———, *The Countess of Pembroke's Arcadia (The New Arcadia)*, ed. Victor Skretkowicz (New York: Oxford University Press, 1987).

———, *A Defense of Poetry*, ed. Jan van Dorsten (New York: Oxford University Press, 1966).

———, *Miscellaneous Prose of Sir Philip Sidney*, ed. Katherine Duncan-Jones and Jan van Dorsten (New York: Oxford University Press, 1973).

———, *The Old Arcadia*, ed. Katherine Duncan-Jones (New York: Oxford University Press, 1999).

Sidney, Sir Philip and Hubert Languet, *The Correspondence of Sir Philip Sidney and Hubert Languet*, ed. Steuart A. Pears (London: W. Pickering, 1845).

Society of Jesus, *Regulae Societatis Iesu. Ad usum nostrorum tantum* (Romae: apud curiam praepositi Generalis, 1935).

———, *Rules of the Society of Jesus: A New Translation from the Latin* (Woodstock, MD: Woodstock College Press, 1956).

Spenser, Edmund, *The Faerie Queene*, ed. A.C. Hamilton (New York: Longman, 1977).

———, *A View of the Present State of Ireland*, vol. 9 in *The Works of Edmund Spenser: A Variorum Edition*, ed. Rudolf Gottfried (Baltimore: Johns Hopkins University Press, 1949).

Sprat, Thomas, "An Account of the Life and Writings of Mr Abraham Cowley," preface to the *Works of Mr. Abraham Cowley* (London, 1668).

St. German, Christopher, *The Doctor and Student Together with Questions and Cases Concerning the Equity Thereof*, ed. T.F.T. Plucknett and J.L. Barton (London: Selden Society, 1975).

Stapleton, Thomas, *A Counterblast to M. Hornes Vayne Blaste Against M. Fekenham. Wherein is set forthe: A ful Reply to M. Horne's Answer, and to euery part thereof made, against the Declaration of my L. Abbat of Westminster, M. Fekenham, touching, The Othe of Supremacy* (Louvain, 1567).

The Statutes at Large From Magna Carta to the Thirteenth Year of King George II in Six Volumes (6 vols, London, 1758).

Stowe, John, *The Annales of England* (London, 1592).

Suárez, Francisco, *Defensio Fidei Catholicae et Apostolicae Adversvs Anglicanae Sectae Errores cum responsione ad Apologiam pro Juramento Fidelitatis, & Praefationem monitoriam Serenissimi Jacobi Magnae Britanniae Regis* (Cologne, 1614).

———, *Selections from Three Works*, ed. James Brown Scott, (2 vols, Oxford: Clarendon Press, 1944).

Swift, Jonathan, *Prose Works*, ed. Herbert Davis et al. (14 vols, Oxford, 1939–68).

Teixeira, José, *A Continvation of the Lamentable and Admirable Adventvres of Dom Sebastian, King of Portugall* (London, 1602).

———, *The Strangest Adventvre That Ever Happened: Either in the ages passed or present. Containing a discourse concerning the successe of the King of Portugall Dom Sebastian*, trans. Anthony Munday (London, 1601).

———, *The Trve Historie of the late and lamentable aduentures of Don Sebastian, King of Portugall* (London 1603).

Travers, Walter, *An Ansvver to a svpplicatorie epistle, of G.T. for the pretended Catholiqves: written to the right honorable Lordes of her Maiesties priuie Counsell* (London, 1583).

Tyler, Margaret, *Margaret Tyler* [reprint of Diego Ortúñez's *The Mirror of Princely Deeds and Knighthood*, trans. M[argaret] T[yler] (London: 1580)], ed. Kathryn Coad (Brookfield, VT: Ashgate, 1996).

[Verstegen, R.], *Praesentis Ecclesiae Anglicanae Typus* (Reims, 1582).

Virgil, *Aeneid*, trans. W.F. Jackson Knight (New York: Penguin, 1956).

Vitkus, Daniel (ed.), *Three Turk Plays from Early Modern England* (New York: Columbia University Press, 2000).

Vitoria, Francisco, *Political Writings*, ed. Anthony Pagden et al. (New York: Cambridge University Press, 1991).

———, *Relecciones teológicas del maestro Fray Francisco de Vitoria*, ed. Luis G. Alonso Getino (3 vols, Madrid: Impr. La Rafa, 1933).

W.W., *A true and iust Recorde, of the Information, Examination and Confession of all the Witches, taken at S. Oses in the countie of Essex; whereof some were executed, and other some entreated according to the determination of lawe. Wherein all men may see what a pestilent people witches are, and how unworthy to lyue in a Christian Commonwealth* (London, 1582).

334   *Early Modern Catholics, Royalists, and Cosmopolitans*

Warner, William, *Syrinx, Or A Sevenfold History*, ed. Wallace A. Bacon (Evanston, IL: Northwestern University Press, 1950).

Webster, John and Thomas Dekker, *The Famous History of Sir Thomas Wyat* [London, 1607] (reprint, New York: AMS Press, 1970).

Wentworth, Peter, *A Treatise Containing M. Wentworths Iudgement Concerning the Person of the Trve and lawfull successor to these Realmes of England and Ireland* (Edinburgh, 1598).

White, Thomas, *The Grounds of Obedience and Government* (London, 1655).

Willet, Andrew, *Synopsis Papismi, that is, A generall view of papistry: wherein the whole mysterie of iniquitie, and summe of Antichristian doctrine is set downe, which is maintained this day by the Synagogue of Rome, against the Church of Christ* (London, 1592).

Yepes, Diego de, *Historia particular de la persecucion de Inglaterra, y de los martirios mas insignes que en ella ha auido, desde el año del Señor. 1570* (Madrid, 1599).

Secondary Sources

Achinstein, Sharon, "John Milton and the Communities of Resistance, 1641–2" in *Writing and Religion in England, 1558–1689: Studies in Community-Making and Cultural Memory,* ed. Roger D. Sell and Anthony W. Johnson (Burlington, VT: Ashgate, 2009), 289–304.

———, *Literature and Dissent in Milton's England* (New York: Cambridge University Press, 2003).

Adams, Simon, "The Outbreak of the Elizabethan Naval War against the Spanish Empire: The Embargo of May 1585 and Sir Francis Drake's West Indies Voyage," in M.J. Rodriguez-Salgado and Simon Adams (eds), *England, Spain and the Gran Armada 1585–1604: Essays from the Anglo-Spanish Conferences, London and Madrid, 1988* (Edinburgh: John Donald, 1991), 45–69.

Adkins, Mary Grace Muse, "Sixteenth-century Religious and Political Implications in *Sir John Oldcastle,*" *University of Texas Studies in English* 22 (1942): 86–104.

Alexander, Gavin, *Writing after Sidney: The Literacy Response to Sir Philip Sidney, 1586–1640* (New York: Oxford University Press, 2006).

Alpers, Paul, *What is Pastoral?* (Chicago: University of Chicago Press, 1996).

Anderson, Benedict, *Imagined Communities: Reflections on the Origin and Spread of Nationalism* (rev. ed., London: Verso, 1991).

Anderson, Judith H., "'Nor Man It Is': The Knight of Justice in Book V of Spenser's *Faerie Queene,*" *PMLA* 85 (1970): 65–77.

Appiah, Kwame Anthony, *Cosmopolitanism: Ethics in a World of Strangers* (New York: Penguin, 2007).

———, "Cosmopolitan Patriots," in Pheng Cheah and Bruce Robbins (eds), *Cosmopolitics: Thinking and Feeling beyond the Nation* (Minneapolis: University of Minnesota Press, 1998), 91–116.

Armitage, David (ed.), *British Political Thought in History, Literature, and Theory, 1500–1800* (New York: Cambridge University Press, 2006).

———, *The Ideological Origins of the British Empire* (New York: Cambridge University Press, 2000).

Armitage, David, Armand Himy, and Quentin Skinner (eds), *Milton and Republicanism* (New York: Cambridge University Press, 1995).

Ashton, John William, "Revision in Munday's *John a Kent and John a Cumber*," *Modern Language Notes* 48 (1993): 531–7.

Astell, Ann W., "Sidney's Didactic Method in the *Old Arcadia*," *Studies in English Literature 1500–1900*, 24.1 (Winter 1984): 39–51.

Auchter, Dorothy, *Dictionary of Literary and Dramatic Censorship in Tudor and Stuart England* (Westport, CT: Greenwood Publishing Group, 2001).

Baker, David J., *Between Nations: Shakespeare, Spenser, Marvell, and the Question of Britain* (Stanford: Stanford University Press, 1997).

Baker, David J. and Willy Maley (eds), *British Identities and English Renaissance Literature* (New York: Cambridge University Press, 2002).

Baker, John H., *Introduction to English Legal History* (London: Butterworths, 1971).

Barbour, Reid, *Literature and Religious Culture in Seventeenth-Century England* (New York: Cambridge University Press, 2002).

Basset, Bernard, S.J., *The English Jesuits: From Campion to Martindale* (New York: Herder and Herder, 1967).

Beach, Adam R., "Carnival Politics, General Satire, and Nationalist Spectacle in Behn's *The Rover*," *Eighteenth-Century Life* 28.3 (2004): 1–19.

Bearden, Elizabeth, "Sidney's 'mongrel tragicomedy' and Anglo-Spanish Exchange in the *New Arcadia*," *Journal for Early Modern Cultural Studies* 10.1 (2010): 29–51.

Bennett, Joan S., *Reviving Liberty: Radical Christian Humanism in Milton's Great Poems* (Cambridge, MA: Harvard University Press, 1989).

Bennett, Josephine W., Oscar Cargill, and Vernon Hall, Jr. (eds), *Studies in the English Renaissance Drama: In Memory of Karl Julius Holzknecht* (New York: New York University Press, 1959).

Bergeron, David, "Anthony Munday: Pageant Poet to the City of London," *Huntington Library Quarterly* 30 (1967): 345–68.

———, *Practicing Renaissance Scholarship: Plays and Pageants, Patrons and Politics* (Pittsburgh: Duquesne University Press, 2000).

Bergvall, Ake, *The "Enabling of Judgement": Sir Philip Sidney and the Education of the Reader* (Stockholm: University of Uppsala, 1989).

Berry, Edward, *The Making of Sir Philip Sidney* (Toronto: University of Toronto Press, 1998).

Bevington, David, *Tudor Drama and Politics. A Critical Approach to Topical Meaning* (Cambridge, MA: Harvard University Press, 1968).

Blayney, Peter, "*The Booke of Sir Thomas Moore* Reexamined," *Studies in Philology* 69 (1972): 167–91.

Bossy, John, *The English Catholic Community, 1570–1850* (New York: Oxford University Press, 1976).

———, *Giordano Bruno and the Embassy Affair* (New Haven, CT: Yale University Press, 1991).

Bowers, Rick, "Sir John Harrington and the Earl of Essex: The Joker as Spy," *Cahiers Élizabéthains* 69 (2006): 13–20.

Bowra, Cecil M., *From Virgil to Milton* (London: Macmillan, 1948).

Bradbook, Muriel C., "The Politics of Pageantry: Social Implications in Jacobean London," in Antony Coleman and Antony Hammond (eds), *Poetry and Drama 1570–1700: Essays in Honour of Harold F. Brooks* (London: Methuen, 1981), 60–75.

Bradley, David, *From Text to Performance in the Elizabethan Theatre: Preparing the Play for the Stage* (New York: Cambridge University Press, 1992).

Bradshaw, Brendan and Peter Roberts (eds), *British Consciousness and Identity: The Making of Britain* (New York: Cambridge University Press, 1998).

Breckenridge, Carol A. and Sheldon Pollock (eds), *Cosmopolitanism* (Durham, NC: Duke University Press, 2002).

Brennan, Gillian, *Patriotism, Power and Print: National Consciousness in Tudor England* (Pittsburgh: Duquesne University Press, 2003).

Brennan, Michael G., *A Sidney Chronology, 1554–1654* (New York: Palgrave Macmillan, 2003).

Brett, Annabel S., *Changes of State: Nature and the Limits of the City in Early Modern Natural Law* (Princeton: Princeton University Press, 2011).

Briggs, William Dinsmore, "Political Ideas in Sidney's *Arcadia*," *Studies in Philology* 28.2 (1931): 137–61.

Brooks, Christopher and Kevin Sharpe, "Debate: History, English Law and the Renaissance," *Past and Present* 72 (1976): 133–42.

Buescu, Ann Isabel, "Um mito das origens da nacionalidade: o milagre de Ourique," in *A memoria da Nação, Colóquio do Gabinete de Estudos de Simbologia, realizada na Fundação Calouste Gulbenkian, 7 a 9 de Outubro de 1987*, ed. Francisco Bethencourt and Diogo Ramada Curto (Lisboa: Livraria Sá *da* Costa Editora, 1991), 49–69.

Burgess, Glen, *The Politics of the Ancient Constitution: An Introduction to English Political Thought, 1603–1642* (University Park, PA: Penn State University Press, 1992).

Callaghan, Dympna, "'And all is semblative a woman's part': Body Politics and *Twelfth Night*," *Textual Practice* 7.3 (1993): 428–52.

Candido, Joseph, "Captain Thomas Stukeley: The Man, the Theatrical Record, and the Origins of Tudor 'Biographical Drama,'" *Anglia-Zeitchrift fur Englische Philologie* 105 (1987): 50–56.

Canny, Nicholas, *Making Ireland British: 1580–1650* (New York: Oxford University Press, 2003).

Carrafiello, Michael, *Robert Parsons and English Catholicism, 1580–1610* (Cranbury, NJ: Associated University Presses, 1998).

Carroll, Clare, "The Construction of Gender and the Cultural and Political Other in *The Faerie Queene* 5 and *A View of the Present State of Ireland*: The Critics, the Context, and the Case of Radigund," *Criticism* 32.2 (1990): 163–92.

Cavanagh, Sheila T., "'The fatal destiny of that land': Elizabethan Views of Ireland," in Brendan Bradshaw, Willy Maley, and Andrew Hadfield (eds), *Representing Ireland: Literature and the Origins of Conflict 1534–1660* (New York: Cambridge University Press, 1993), 116–31.

Cawley, Robert Ralston, *Milton and the Literature of Travel* (New York: Gordian Press, 1970).

Chalifour, Clark L., "Sir Philip Sidney's *Old Arcadia* as Terentian Comedy," *Studies in English Literature* 16.1 (1976): 51–63.

Chrimes, S.B., *English Constitutional History in the Fifteenth Century* (Cambridge: Cambridge University Press, 1936).

Clancy, Thomas, S.J., "English Catholics and the Papal Deposing Power, 1570–1640 [Part I: The Elizabethan Period]," *Recusant History* 6.3 (1962): 114–41.

———, "English Catholics and the Papal Deposing Power, 1570–1640 [Part II: The Jacobean Period]," *Recusant History* 6.5 (1962): 205–28.

———, *Papist Pamphleteers: The Allen-Persons Party and the Political Thought of The Counter-Reformation in England, 1572–1615* (Chicago: Loyola University Press, 1964).

Cleary, J.M., "Dr. Morys Clynnog's Invasion Projects of 1575–76," *Recusant History* 8.5 (1966): 300–322.

Clossey, Luke, *Salvation and Globalization in the Early Jesuit Missions* (New York: Cambridge University Press, 2008).

Cohen, Eileen Z., "Gentle Knight and Pious Servant: A Study of Sidney's Protestantism," Dissertation, University of Maryland, College Park, MD, 1965.

Cohen, Joshua (ed.), *For Love of Country: Debating the Limits of Patriotism* (Boston: Beacon Press, 1996).

Collinson, Patrick, *Godly People: Essays on English Protestantism and Puritanism* (London: Hambledon Press, 1983).

Cooke, Paul J., "The Spanish Romances in Sir Philip Sidney's *Arcadia*," Dissertation, University of Illinois, Urbana-Champaign, 1939.

Copeland, Nancy, "'Once a Whore and Ever'? Whore and Virgin in *The Rover* and its Antecedents," *Restoration: Studies in English Literary Culture 1660–1700* 16.1 (Spring 1992): 20–27.

Cormack, Bradin, *A Power to Do Justice: Jurisdiction, English Literature, and the Rise of the Common Law, 1509–1625* (Chicago: University of Chicago Press, 2008).

Corns, Thomas N., *Uncloistered Virtue: English Political Literature, 1640–1660* (New York: Oxford University Press, 1992).

Corthell, Ronald, "Robert Persons and the Writer's Mission," in Arthur F. Marotti (ed.), *Catholicism and Anti-Catholicism in Early Modern English Texts* (New York: St. Martin's Press, 1999), 35–62.

Coughlan, Patricia, "'Some secret scourge which shall by her come unto England': Ireland and Incivility in Spenser," in Patricia Coughlan (ed.), *Spenser and Ireland: An Interdisciplinary Perspective* (Cork: Cork University Press, 1989), 46–74.

Craft, William, *Labyrinth of Desire: Invention and Culture in the Work of Sir Philip Sidney* (Newark, DE: University of Delaware Press, 1994).

Craig, D.H., *Sir John Harington* (Boston: Twayne Publishers 1985).

Craig, Hugh, "Sir John Harington: Six Letters," in Peter Beal and Jeremey Griffiths (eds), *English Manuscript Studies 1100–1700* (London: The British Library, 1995), 43–63.

Creigh, Geoffrey, "*Zelauto* and Italian Comedy: A Study in Sources," *Modern Language Quarterly* 29 (1968): 161–7.

Cressy, David, "The Protestant Calendar and the Vocabulary of Celebration in Early Modern England," *The Journal of British Studies* 29.1 (1990): 31–52.

Croft, P.J., "Sir John Harington's Manuscript of Sir Philip Sidney's *Arcadia*," in Stephen Parks et al. (eds), *Literary Autographs* (Los Angeles: University of California Press, 1983), 39–75.

Cummins, John, *Francis Drake: The Lives of a Hero* (New York: St. Martin's Press, 1995).

Cummins, Juliet (ed.), *Milton and the Ends of Time* (New York: Cambridge University Press, 2003).

Dahrwadker, Vinay (ed.), *Cosmopolitan Geographies: New Locations in Literary Culture* (New York: Routledge, 2001).

Darbishire, Helen (ed.), *The Early Lives of Milton* (London: Constable, 1932).

Davidson, Clifford, "Nature and Judgement in the *Old Arcadia*," *Papers on Language and Literature* 9 (1970): 34–65.

Davies, Julian, *Caroline Captivity of the Church: Charles I and the Remoulding of Anglicanism, 1625–1641* (New York: Oxford University Press, 1992).

Davis, Alex, *Chivalry and Romance in the English Renaissance* (Rochester, NY: D.S. Brewer, 2003).

Deacon, Richard, *John Dee: Scientist Geographer, Astrologer, and Secret Agent to Elizabeth I* (London: Frederick Muller, 1968).

DeGuzman, Maria, *Spain's Long Shadow: The Black Legend, Off-Whiteness, and Anglo-American Empire* (Minneapolis: University of Minnesota Press, 2005).

Dillon, Anne, *The Construction of Martyrdom in the English Catholic Community, 1535–1603* (Burlington, VT: Ashgate, 2002).

Dipple, Elizabeth, "The Captivity Episode and the *New Arcadia*," *Journal of English and Germanic Philology* 70.3 (1971): 418–31.

———, "Harmony and Pastoral in the *Old Arcadia*," *ELH* 35.3 (1968): 309–28.

———, "'Unjust Justice' in the *Old Arcadia*," *Studies in English Literature 1500–1900* 10 (1970): 83–101.

Dobranski, Stephen B. and John P. Rumrich (eds), *Milton and Heresy* (New York: Cambridge University Press, 1998).

Donnelly, Philip J., *Milton's Scriptural Reasoning: Narrative and Protestant Toleration* (New York: Cambridge University Press, 2009).

Duncan-Jones, Katherine, *Sir Philip Sidney: Courtier Poet* (New Haven, CT: Yale University Press, 1991).

Dunseath, T.K., *Spenser's Allegory of Justice in Book Five of the* Faerie Queene (Princeton: Princeton University Press, 1968).

Edwards, Francis, S.J., *The Jesuits in England: From 1580 to the Present Day* (Tunbridge Wells, Kent: Burns and Oates, 1985).

Eggert, Katherine, *Showing Like a Queen: Female Authority and Literary Experiment in Spenser, Shakespeare, and Milton* (Philadelphia: University of Pennsylvania, 2000).

Engel, William E., "Was Sir John Harington the English Rabelais?," in Barbara C. Bowen (ed.), *Rabelais in Context: Proceedings of the 1991 Vanderbilt Conference* (Birmingham: Summa Publications, 1993), 147–56.

Escobedo, Andrew, *Nationalism and Historical Loss in Renaissance England: Foxe, Dee, Spenser, Milton* (Ithaca, NY: Cornell University Press, 2004).

Eusden, John Dykstra, *Puritans, Lawyers, and Politics in Early Seventeenth-Century England* (2nd ed., New York: Barnes and Noble, 1968).

Fallon, Robert Thomas, *Divided Empire: Milton's Political Imagery* (University Park, PA: Penn State University Press, 1995).

———, *Milton in Government* (University Park, PA: Penn State University Press, 1993).

Fallon, Stephen M., *Milton's Peculiar Grace: Self-Representation and Authority* (Ithaca, NY: Cornell University Press, 2007).

Fichte, Johann G., "Review of Immanuel Kant, *Perpetual Peace: A Philosophical Sketch* (Konigsburg: Nicolovius, 1795)," trans. Daniel Breazeale, *The Philosophical Forum* 32.4 (Winter 2001): 311–21.

Fincham, Kenneth C. and Peter Lake, "The Ecclesiastical Policy of King James I," *Journal of British Studies* 24.2 (1985): 169–207.

Fixler, Michael, *Milton and the Kingdoms of God* (London: Faber and Faber, 1964).

Forker, Charles R., "Two Notes on John Webster and Anthony Munday," *English Language Notes* 6 (1968): 26–34.

Forsyth, V.L., "Polybius's Histories: An Overlooked Source for Sidney's *Arcadia*," *Sidney Journal* 21.2 (2003): 59–65.

———, "The Two Arcadias of Sidney's Two *Arcadias*," *Studies in English Literature 1500–1900* 49.1 (2009): 1–15.

Fortier, Mark, *The Culture of Equity in Early Modern England* (Burlington, VT: Ashgate, 2005).

Fowler, Alistair D.S., *Spenser and the Numbers of Time* (London: Routledge, 1964).

Fowler, Elizabeth, "The Failure of Moral Philosophy in the Work of Edmund Spenser," *Representations* 51 (Summer 1995): 47–76.

340 *Early Modern Catholics, Royalists, and Cosmopolitans*

French, Peter J., *John Dee: The World of an Elizabethan Magus* (London: Routledge, 1972).

Friedrich, Markus, "Communication and Bureaucracy in the Early Modern Society," *Schweizerische Zeitschrift für Religions- und Kulturgeschichte* 101 (2007): 49–75.

Froude, James Anthony, *History of England from the Fall of Wolsey to the Defeat of the Spanish Armada* (12 vols, London: Longmans, Green, and Co., 1893).

Fuchs, Barbara, "An English Picaro in New Spain: Miles Philips and the Framing of National Identity," *The New Centennial Review* 2.1 (Spring 2002): 55–68.

———, *Mimesis and Empire: The New World, Islam, and European Identities* (New York: Cambridge University Press, 2001).

———, "Spanish Lessons: Spenser and the Irish Moriscos," *Studies in English Literature 1500–1900* 42.1 (2002): 43–62.

Gallagher, Catherine, "Embracing the Absolute: The Politics of the Female Subject in Seventeenth-Century England," *Genders* 1 (1988): 24–39.

———, "Who was that Masked Woman? The Prostitute and the Playwright in the Comedies of Aphra Behn," *Women's Studies* 15 (1998): 23–42.

Gibson, Charles, *The Black Legend, Anti-Spanish Attitudes in the Old World and the New* (New York: Knopf, 1971).

Godshalk, William Leigh, "Sidney's Revision of the *Arcadia*, Books III–V," *Philological Quarterly* 43.2 (April 1964): 171–84.

Görtschacher, Wolfgang and Holger Klein (eds), *Narrative Strategies in Early English Fiction* (Lewiston, NY: Edward Mellon Press, 1995).

Greenblatt, Stephen, *Renaissance Self-Fashioning: From More to Shakespeare* (Chicago: University of Chicago Press, 1980).

———, "Sidney's *Arcadia* and the Mixed Mode," *Studies in Philology* 70.3 (1973): 269–78.

Greenfeld, Liah, *Nationalism: Five Roads to Modernity* (Cambridge, MA: Harvard University Press, 1992).

Greenfield, Thelma, *The Eye of Judgment: Reading the* New Arcadia (Toronto: University of Toronto Press, 1982).

Greenlaw, Edwin A., "Sidney's *Arcadia* as an Example of Elizabethan Allegory," in *Anniversary Papers by Colleagues and Pupils of George Lyman Kittredge* (Boston: Ginn and Co., 1913), 327–37.

Griffin, Eric, *Ethno-poetics and Empire: English Renaissance Drama and the Specter of Spain* (Philadelphia: University of Pennsylvania Press, 2009).

Grindal, Edmund, *The Remains of Edmund Grindal*, ed. W. Nicholson (Cambridge: Cambridge University Press, 1843).

Groot, Gerome de, *Royalist Identities* (New York: Palgrave Macmillan, 2004).

Gurr, Andrew, *The Shakespearean Playing Companies* (Oxford: Oxford University Press, 1996).

Guy, John A., *Christopher St German on Chancery and Statute* (London: Selden Society, 1985).

————, "Henry VIII and the Praemunire Maneuvers of 1530–31" *The English Historical Review* 97 (July 1982): 481–503.

————, "Law, Equity, and Conscience in Henrician Juristic Thought" in Alistair Fox and John A. Guy (eds), *Reassessing the Henrician Age: Humanism, Politics and Reform 1500–1550* (New York: Basil Blackwell, 1986), 179–98.

————, *The Public Career of Sir Thomas More* (New Haven, CT: Yale University Press, 1980).

Guy, John A. (ed.), *The Reign of Elizabeth I: Court and Culture in the Last Decade* (Cambridge: Cambridge University Press, 1995).

Haber, Judith, *Pastoral and the Poetics of Self-Contradiction: Theocritus to Marvell* (New York: Cambridge University Press, 1994).

Hadfield, Andrew, *Edmund Spenser: A Life* (New York: Oxford University Press, 2012).

————, *Edmund Spenser's Irish Experience, Wilde Fruit and Salvage Soyl* (New York: Oxford University Press, 1997).

————, *Literature Politics and National Identity: Reformation to Renaissance* (New York: Cambridge University Press, 1994).

Haigh, Christopher, *English Reformations: Religion, Politics, and Society under the Tudors* (New York: Oxford University Press, 1993).

Hall, Kim F., *Things of Darkness: Economies of Race and Gender in Early Modern England* (Ithaca, NY: Cornell University Press, 1995).

Hamilton, A.C., *Sir Philip Sidney: A Study of His Life and Works* (New York: Cambridge University Press, 1977).

Hamilton, A.C. et al. (eds), *The Spenser Encyclopedia* (Buffalo, NY: The University of Toronto Press, 1990).

Hamilton, Donna, *Anthony Munday and the Catholics* (Burlington, VT: Ashgate, 2005).

Hamilton, Gary D., "The History of Britain and its Restoration Audience," in David Loewenstein et al. (eds), *Politics Poetics, and Hermeneutics in Milton's Prose* (New York: Cambridge University Press, 1990), 241-55.

Hammer, Paul, "Essex and Europe: Evidence from Confidential Instructions by the Earl of Essex, 1595–6," *EHR* 111 (1996): 357–81.

————, *The Polarization of Elizabethan Politics: The Political Career of Robert Devereux, 2nd Earl of Essex, 1585–1597* (New York: Cambridge University Press, 1999).

Hampton, Bryan Adams, *Fleshly Tabernacles: Milton and the Incarnational Poetics of Revolutionary England* (Notre Dame, IN: University of Notre Dame Press, 2012).

Harbage, Alfred, *Sir William Davenant, Poet Venturer, 1606–1668* (Philadelphia: University of Pennsylvania Press, 1935).

Hardin, Richard F., *Civil Idolatry: Desacralizing and Monarchy in Spenser, Shakespeare, and Milton* (Newark, DE: University of Delaware Press, 1992).

Harrison, T.P., Jr., "The Relations of Spenser and Sidney," *PMLA* 45.3 (1930): 712–31.

Harvey, David, *Cosmopolitanism and the Geographies of Freedom* (New York: Columbia University Press, 2009).

Heater, Derek Benjamin, *World Citizenship and Government: Cosmopolitan Ideas in the History of Western Political Thought* (New York: St. Martin's Press, 1996).

Hebb, David Delison, *Piracy and the English Government, 1616–1642* (Brookfield, VT: Ashgate, 1994).

Helgerson, Richard, *Forms of Nationhood: The Elizabethan Writing of England* (Chicago: University of Chicago Press, 1992).

Henry, Bruce Ward, "John Dee, Humphrey Llwyd, and the Name 'British Empire,'" *Huntington Library Quarterly* 35 (1971–72): 189–90.

Highley, Christopher, *Catholics Writing the Nation in Early Modern Britain and Ireland* (New York: Oxford University Press, 2008).

Hill, Christopher, *Milton and the English Revolution* (London: Faber and Faber, 1977).

Hill, Tracey, *Anthony Munday and Civic Culture: Theatre, History, and Power in Early Modern London* (New York: Manchester University Press, 2004).

Hobby, Elaine, "No Stolen Object, but Her Own: Aphra Behn's *Rover* and Thomas Killigrew's *Thomaso*," *Women's Writing* 6.1 (1999): 113–27.

Holleran, James V. (ed.), *A Jesuit Challenge: Edmund Campion's Debates at the Tower of London in 1581* (New York: Fordham University Press, 1999).

Holmes, John, "The Guiana Projects: Imperial and Colonial Ideologies in Ralegh and Purchas," *Literature and History* 14.2 (2005): 1–13.

Holmes, Peter, *Resistance and Compromise: The Political Thought of Elizabethan Catholics* (New York: Cambridge University Press, 1982).

Hopkins, Lisa, "Passion and Reason in Sir Philip Sidney's *Arcadia*," in Constance C. Relihan and Goran V. Stanivukovic (eds), *Prose Fiction and Early Modern Sexualities in England, 1570–1640* (New York: Palgrave MacMillan, 2003), 61–76.

Houliston, Victor, *Catholic Resistance in Elizabethan England: Robert Person's Jesuit Polemic, 1580–1610* (Burlington, VT: Ashgate, 2007).

Howard, Jean E., "Gender on the Periphery," in Tom Clayton et al. (eds), *Shakespeare and the Mediterranean* (Newark, DE: University of Delaware Press, 2004), 344–62.

———, *The Stage and Social Struggle in Early Modern England* (New York: Cambridge University Press, 1994).

Hughes, Derek and Janet Todd (eds), *The Cambridge Companion to Aphra Behn* (New York: Cambridge University Press, 2004).

Huillard-Breholles, Jean Louis Alphonse (ed.), *Historia Diplomatica Friderici Secundi* (6 vols, Paris: Plon, 1860).

Huntley, Frank L., "Ben Jonson and Anthony Munday, or, *The Case is Altered* Altered Again," *Philological Quarterly* 41 (1962): 205–14.

Hutner, Heidi (ed.), *Rereading Aphra Behn: History, Theory, and Criticism* (Charlottesville: University of Virginia Press, 1993).

Hutton, Ronald, *The Royalist War Effort 1642–1646* (New York: Longman, 1982).

Isler, Alan, "The Allegory of the Hero and Sidney's Two *Arcadias*," *Studies in Philology* 65.2 (1968): 171–91.

Jacob, Margaret C., *Strangers Nowhere in the World: The Rise of Cosmopolitanism in Early Modern Europe* (Philadelphia: University of Pennsylvania Press, 2006).

Javitch, Daniel, *Proclaiming a Classic: The Canonization of* "Orlando Furioso" (Princeton: Princeton University Press, 1991).

Johnson, Nora, *The Actor as Playwright in Early Modern Drama* (New York: Cambridge University Press, 2003).

Jones, Ann Rosalind and Peter Stallybrass, "The Politics of *Astrophil and Stella*," *Studies in English Literature* 24 (1984): 53–68.

Jones, DeRitter, "The Gypsy, The *Rover*, and The Wanderer: Aphra Behn's Revision of Thomas Killigrew," *Restoration: Studies in English Literary Culture* 10.2 (1986): 82–92.

Jones, W.J., *The Elizabethan Court of Chancery* (Oxford: Clarendon, 1967).

Jordan, Constance, "The Household and the State: Transformations in the Representation of an Analogy," *Modern Language Quarterly* 54.3 (1993): 308–26.

Jowett, John, "Henry Chettle and the Original Text of *Sir Thomas More*," in *Shakespeare and "Sir Thomas More": Essays on the Play and its Shakespearean Interest*, ed. T.H. Howard-Hill (New York: Cambridge University Press, 1989), 131–49.

Jowitt, Claire, "Massinger's *The Renegado* (1624) and the Spanish Marriage," *Cahiers Elizabethains* 65 (2004): 45–54.

_____, *The Culture of Piracy, 1580-1630: English Literature and Seaborne Crime* (Burlington, VT: Ashgate, 2010).

Kalstone, David, "The Transformation of Arcadia: Sannazaro and Sir Philip Sidney," *Comparative Literature* 15.3 (1963): 234–49.

Keen, Maurice H., *Chivalry* (New Haven, CT: Yale University Press, 1984).

———, *The Laws of War in the Late Middle Ages* (Toronto: University of Toronto Press, 1965).

Kelley, Donald R., "History, English Law and the Renaissance," *Past and Present* 65 (1974): 24–51.

Kennedy, Judith M. (ed.), *A Critical Edition of Yong's Translation of George of Montemayor's* Diana *and Gil Polo's* Enamoured Diana (Oxford: Oxford University Press, 1968).

Kenny, Anthony, "Anthony Munday in Rome," *Recusant History* 6 (1962): 158–62.

Kermode, Frank, "The Date of Cowley's *Davideis*," *RES* 25 (1949): 154–8.

Kermode, Lloyd E., *Aliens and Englishness in Elizabethan Drama* (New York: Cambridge University Press, 2009).

Kerrigan, John, *Archipelagic English: Literature, History, and Politics 1603–1707* (New York: Oxford University Press, 2008).

Kilroy, Gerard, "Advertising the Reader: Sir John Harington's 'Directions in the Margent' [with Illustrations]," *English Literary Renaissance* 41.1 (2011): 64–110.

344   *Early Modern Catholics, Royalists, and Cosmopolitans*

————, *Edmund Campion: Memory and Transcription* (Burlington, VT: Ashgate, 2005).

Kinnamon, Noel J., *A Sidney Chronology 1554–1654* (Basingstoke: Palgrave Macmillan, 2003).

Kinney, Arthur, "Text Context, and Authorship of *The Book of Sir Thomas Moore*," in Sigrid King (ed.), *Pilgrimage for Love: Essays in Early Modern Literature in Honor of Josephine A. Roberts* (Tempe, AZ: Arizona Center for Medieval and Renaissance Studies, 1999).

Kouri, E.I., *England and the Attempts to Form a Protestant Alliance* (Helsinki: Suomalainen Tiedeakatemia, 1981).

Knafla, Louis, *Law and Politics in Jacobean England, The Tracts of Lord Chancellor Ellesmere* (New York: Cambridge University Press, 1977).

Knight, Stephen, *Robin Hood, A Complete Study of the English Outlaw* (Cambridge, MA: Blackwell Publishers, 1994).

Knowles, James, "The Spectacle of the Realm: Civic Consciousness, Rhetoric and Ritual in Earl Modern London," in J.R. Mulryne and Margaret Shewring (eds), *Theatre and Government Under the Early Stuarts* (New York: Cambridge University Press, 1993), 157–89.

Kuin, Roger, "Querre-Muhau: Sir Philip Sidney and the New World," *Renaissance Quarterly* 51.2 (Summer 1998): 549–85.

————, "Sir Philip Sidney's Model of the Statesman," *Reformation* 4 (1999): 93–117.

Kumar, Krishan, *The Making of English National Identity* (New York: Cambridge University Press, 2003).

Lake, Peter, *Anglicans and Puritans? Presbyterianism and English Conformist Thought from Whitgift to Hooker* (London: Harper Collins, 1988).

————, *The Boxmaker's Revenge: "Orthodoxy," "Heterodoxy" and the Politics of the Parish in Early Stuart London* (Stanford: Stanford University Press, 2001).

————, "Calvinism and the English Church 1570–1635," *Past and Present* 114 (1987): 32–76.

————, "The Laudian Style: Order, Uniformity, and the Pursuit of Beauty of Holiness in the 1630's" in Kenneth Fincham (ed.), *The Early Stuart Church, 1603–1642* (Stanford: Stanford University Press, 1993), 161–85.

————, *Moderate Puritans and the Elizabethan Church* (Cambridge: Cambridge University Press, 1982).

Lawry, Jon Sherman, *Sidney's Two Arcadias: Pattern and Recording* (Ithaca, NY: Cornell University Press, 1972).

Leinwand, Theodore B., "London Triumphing: The Jacobean Lord Mayor's Show," *Clio* 11.2 (1982): 137–53.

Levack, Brian, *The Civil Lawyers in England 1603–1641* (New York: Clarendon, 1973).

Lim, Walter S.H., *John Milton, Radical Politics, and Biblical Republicans* (Newark: University of Delaware Press, 2006).

Limon, Jerzy, *Dangerous Matter: English Drama and Politics in 1623–24* (Cambridge: Cambridge University Press, 1986).

Lindenbaum, Peter, *Changing Landscapes: Anti-Pastoral Sentiment in the English Renaissance* (Athens, GA: University of Georgia Press, 1986).

Lobanov-Rostovsky, Sergei, "The Triumphes of Gold: Economic Authority in the Jacobean Lord Mayor's Show," *ELH* 60.4 (1993): 879–98.

Lockey, Brian, *Law and Empire in English Renaissance Literature* (New York: Cambridge University Press, 2006).

Loewenstein, David, *Representing Revolution in Milton and his Contemporaries* (New York: Cambridge University Press, 2001).

Loewenstein, David and Paul Steven (eds), *Early Modern Nationalism and Milton's England* (Buffalo, NY: University of Toronto Press, 2008).

Loiseau, Jean, *Abraham Cowley, sa vie, son oeuvre* (Paris: H. Didier, 1931).

Long, A.A., and D.N. Sedley, *The Hellenistic Philosophers* (2 vols, New York: Cambridge University Press, 1987).

Loomie, Albert J., *The Spanish Elizabethans: The English Exiles at the Court of Philip II* (New York: Fordham University Press, 1963).

Loxley, James, *Royalism and Poetry in the English Civil Wars: The Drawn Sword* (New York: Palgrave Macmillan, 1997).

MacCaffrey, Wallace T., *Queen Elizabeth and the Making of Policy, 1572–1588* (Princeton: Princeton University Press, 1981).

Majeske, Andrew, *Equity in English Renaissance Literature: Thomas More and Edmund Spenser* (New York: Routledge, 2006).

Major, Philip, *Thomas Killigrew and the Seventeenth-Century English Stage: New Perspectives* (Burlington, VT: Ashgate, 2013)

Maley, Willy, *Nation, State, and Empire in English Renaissance Literature: Shakespeare to Milton* (New York: Palgrave, 2003).

———, *A Spenser Chronology* (Lanham: Barnes and Noble, 1994).

Maltby, William S., *The Black Legend in England, the Development of Anti-Spanish Sentiment, 1558–1660* (Durham, NC: Duke University Press, 1971).

Marshall, Peter, *The Catholic Priesthood and the English Reformation* (New York: Oxford University Press, 1994).

Martin, Catherine Gimelli, *Milton among the Puritans: The Case for Historical Revisionism* (Burlington, VT: Ashgate, 2010).

Masten, Jeffrey, "More or Less: Editing the Collaborative," *Shakespeare Studies* 29 (2001): 109–31.

Martinez, Miguel, "A Poet of Our Own: The Struggle for *Os Lusíadas* in the Afterlife of Camões," *Journal for Early Modern Cultural Studies* 10.1 (2010): 71–94.

Martz, Louis L., *Milton: Poet of Exile* (New Haven, CT: Yale University Press, 1986).

Matar, Nabil, *Turks, Moors, and Englishmen in the Age of Discovery* (New York: Columbia University Press, 1999).

May, Steven W., *The Elizabethan Courtier Poets: Their Poems and Their Contexts* (Columbia, MO: University of Missouri Press, 1991).

McCabe, Richard, *Spenser's Monstrous Regiment: Elizabethan Ireland and the Poetics of Difference* (New York: Oxford University Press, 2002).

McCabe, William H., S.J., *An Introduction to the Jesuit Theater* (St. Louis: Institute of Jesuit Sources, 1983).

McCoog, Thomas (ed.), *The Reckoned Expense: Edmund Campion and the Early English Jesuits* (Rome: Boydell Press, 2007).

———, *The Society of Jesus in Ireland, Scotland, and England 1541–1588: "Our Way of Proceeding?"* (New York: Brill, 1996).

———, *The Society of Jesus in Ireland, Scotland, and England, 1589–1597* (Burlington, VT: Ashgate, 2012).

McCoy, Richard C., *The Rites of Knighthood: The Literature and Politics of Elizabethan Chivalry* (Berkeley: University of California Press, 1989).

———, *Sir Philip Sidney: A Rebellion in Arcadia* (New Brunswick, NJ: Rutgers University Press, 1979).

McEachern, Clare, *The Poetics of English Nationhood, 1590–1612* (New York: Cambridge University Press, 1996).

McEntegart, Rory, *Henry VIII, the League of Schmalkalden and the English Reformation* (Rochester, NY: Royal Historical Society/Boydell Press, 2002).

McKeon, Michael, "The Pastoral Revolution," in Kevin Sharpe and Steven N. Zwicker (eds), *Refiguring Revolutions: Aesthetics and Politics from the English Revolution to the Romantic Revolution* (Berkeley: University of California Press, 1998), 267–90.

———, *The Secret History of Domesticity: Public, Private, and the Division of Knowledge* (Baltimore: Johns Hopkins University Press, 2005).

McKeown, Adam, *English Mercuries: Soldier Poets in the Age of Shakespeare* (Nashville, TN: Vanderbilt University Press, 2009).

McMillin, Scott, "*The Book of Sir Thomas More*: Dates and Acting Companies," in T.H. Howard-Hill (ed.), *Shakespeare and "Sir Thomas More": Essays on the Play and its Shakespearean Interest* (Cambridge: Cambridge University Press, 1989), 57–76.

———, *The Elizabethan Theatre and* The Book of Sir Thomas More (Ithaca, NY: Cornell University Press 1987).

Mentz, Steven R., "Reason, Faith, and Shipwreck in Sidney's *New Arcadia*," *Studies in English Literature 1500–1900* 44.1 (2004): 1–18.

———, *Romance for Sale in Early Modern England: The Rise of Prose Fiction* (Burlington, VT: Ashgate, 2006).

Meyer, Arnold Oskar, *England and the Catholic Church under Queen Elizabeth*, trans. Rev. J.R. McKee (New York: Routledge and K. Paul, 1967).

Mignolo, Walter, "The Many Faces of Cosmopolis: Border Thinking and Critical Cosmopolitanism," in Carol A. Breckenridge et al. (eds), *Cosmopolitanism* (Durham: Duke University Press, 2002), 157–88.

Works Cited

Mignolo, Walter, Margaret Greer, and Maureen Quilligan (eds), *Rereading the Black Legend: The Discourses of Racism in the Renaissance Empires* (Chicago: University of Chicago Press, 2007).

Mikalachki, Jodi, *The Legacy of Boadicea: Gender and Nation in Early Modern England* (New York: Routledge, 1998).

Milner, Andrew, *John Milton and the English Revolution: A Study in the Sociology of Literature* (Totowa, NJ: Barnes and Noble, 1981).

Milton, Anthony, *Catholic and Reformed: The Roman and Protestant Churches in English Protestant Thought 1600–1640* (New York: Cambridge University Press 1995).

Milward, Peter, *Religious Controversies of the Elizabethan Age: A Survey of Printed Sources*, foreword by G.R. Elton (London: Scolar Press, 1977).

Montrose, Louis Adrian, "*A Midsummer Night's Dream* and the Shaping Fantasies of Elizabethan Culture: Gender, Power, Form," in Margaret Ferguson et al. (eds), *Rewriting the Renaissance* (Chicago: University of Chicago Press, 1986), 65–87.

———, "The Elizabethan Subject and the Spenserian Text," in Patricia Parker and David Quint (eds), *Literary Theory/Renaissance Texts* (Baltimore: Johns Hopkins University Press, 1986), 303–40.

———, "Spenser and the Elizabethan Political Imaginary," *ELH* 69.4 (2002): 907–46.

———, "Spenser's Domestic Domain: Poetry, Property, and the Early Modern Subject," in Margreta de Grazia, Maureen Quilligan, and Peter Stallybrass (eds), *Subject and Object in Renaissance Culture* (Cambridge: Cambridge University Press, 1996), 83–130.

———, "The Work of Gender in the Discourse of Discovery," in Stephen Greenblatt (ed.), *New World Encounters* (Berkeley: University of California Press, 1993), 177–217.

Morey, Adrian, *The Catholic Subjects of Elizabeth I* (Totowa, NJ: Rowman and Littlefield, 1978).

Morina, Claudio, *Chiesa e Stato nella Dottrina di S. Ambrogio* (Roma: Pontificia Università Lateranense, 1963).

Mueller, William A., *Church and State in Luther and Calvin: A Comparative Study* (Nashville: Broadman Press, 1954).

Murray, John Courtney, "St. Robert Bellarmine on the Indirect Power," *Theological Studies* 9 (1948): 491–535.

Nelson, Herbert B., "Amidas v. Bracidas," *Modern Language Quarterly* 1.3 (1940): 393–9.

Nelson, Malcolm Anthony, *The Robin Hood Tradition in the English Renaissance* (Elizabethan and Renaissance Studies, Salzburg Studies in English Literature, Salzburg: Institut für Englische Sprache und Literatur, Univesität Salzburg, 1974).

Nelson, T.G.A., "Death, Dung, the Devil, and Worldly Delights: A Metaphysical Conceit in Harington, Donne, and Herbert," *Studies in Philology* 76 (1979): 272–87.

———, "Sir John Harington and the Renaissance Debate over Allegory," *Studies in Philology* 82 (1985): 359–79.

———, "Sir John Harington as a Critic of Sir Philip Sidney," *Studies in Philology* 67 (1970): 41–56.

Nethercot, Arthur H., *Abraham Cowley: The Muse's Hannibal* (Oxford: Oxford University Press, 1931).

Newcomb, Lori Humphrey, *Reading Popular Romance in Early Modern England* (New York: Columbia University Press, 2002).

Norbrook, David. *Writing the English Republic: Poetry, Rhetoric and Politics, 1627–1660* (New York: Cambridge University Press, 1999).

Oakley-Brown, Liz, "Framing Robin Hood: Temporality and Textuality in Anthony Munday's Huntington Plays," in Helen Philips (ed.), *Robin Hood: Medieval and Post Medieval* (Portland, OR: Four Courts Press, 2005).

O'Connor, John Joseph, *Amadis de Gaule and its Influence on Elizabethan Literature* (New Brunswick, NJ: Rutgers University Press, 1970).

O'Malley, John W., *The First Jesuits* (Cambridge, MA: Harvard University Press, 1993).

———, "To Travel to Any Part of the World: Jeronimo Nadal and the Jesuit Vocation," *Studies in the Spirituality of Jesuits* 16.2 (1984): 1–20.

Osborn, James Marshall, *Young Philip Sidney, 1572–1577* (New Haven, CT: Yale University Press, 1972).

Pacheco, Anita, "Rape and the Female Subject in Aphra Behn's *The Rover*," *ELH* 65.2 (1998): 323–45.

Pagden, Anthony, "Dispossessing the Barbarian: The Language of Spanish Thomism and the Debate over Property Rights of the American Indians," in Anthony Pagden (ed.), *The Languages of Political Theory in Early-Modern Europe* (New York: Cambridge University Press, 1987), 79–98.

———, *The Fall of Natural Man, The American Indian and the Origins of Comparative Ethnology* (Cambridge: Cambridge University Press, 1986).

———, *Lords of All the World: Ideologies of Empire in Spain, Britain and France 1500–1800* (New Haven, CT: Yale University Press, 1995).

———, *Spanish Imperialism and the Political Imagination* (New Haven, CT: Yale University Press, 1990).

Palmer, Daryl W., "Metropolitan Resurrection in Anthony Munday's Lord Mayor's Shows," *Studies in English Literature 1500–1900* 46.2 (2006): 371–87.

Palmer, Patricia, *Language and Conquest in Early Modern Ireland: English Renaissance Literature and Elizabethan Imperial Expansion* (New York: Cambridge University Press, 2001).

Paster, Gail Kern, "The Idea of London in Masque and Pageant," in *Pageantry in the Shakespeare Theater*, ed. David Bergeron (Athens: University of Georgia Press, 1985).

Patterson, Annabel, *Reading Between the Lines* (Madison: University of Wisconsin Press, 1993).

Pattinson, W.B., *King James and the Reunion of Christendom* (New York: Cambridge University Press, 1997).

Payne, Linda R., "The Carnivalesque Regeneration of Corrupt Economics in *The Rover*," *Restoration: Studies in English Literary Culture: 1660–1700* 22.1 (1998): 40–49.

Peck, Harry Thurston, *A History of Classical Philology from the Seventh Century, B.C. to the Twentieth Century A.D.* (New York: Macmillan, 1911).

Perry, Nadra, "Imitatio and Identity: Thomas Rogers, Philip Sidney, and the Protestant Self," *English Literary Renaissance* 35.3 (2005): 365–405.

Phillips, James E., "Renaissance Concepts of Justice and the Structure of *The Faerie Queene*, Book V," *Huntington Library Quarterly* 5 (1941): 211–34.

Phillips, Joshua, "Chronicles of Wasted Time: Anthony Munday, Tudor Romance, and Literary Labor," *ELH* 73.4 (2006): 781–803.

Pincombe, Mike (ed.), *Travels and Translations in the Sixteenth Century, Selected Papers from the Second International Conference of the Tudor Symposium (2000)* (Burlington, VT: Ashgate, 2004).

Plucknett, Theodore F.T., *A Concise History of the Common Law* [1956] (Indianapolis, IN: Liberty Fund, 2010).

Pocock, John G.A., *The Ancient Constitution and the Feudal Law, A Reissue with a Retrospect* (3rd ed., New York: Cambridge University Press, 1990).

———, "British History: A Plea for a New Subject," *Journal of Modern History* 47 (1975): 601–28.

———, *The Machiavellian Moment: Florentine Political Thought and the Atlantic Republican Tradition* (Princeton: Princeton University Press, 1975).

Pollen, John Hungerford, S.J., *The English Catholics in the Reign of Queen Elizabeth: A Study of Their Politics Civil Life and Government* (New York: Burt Franklin, 1971).

Potter, Lois, *Secret Rites and Secret Writing: Royalist Literature, 1641–1660* (New York: Cambridge University Press, 1989).

Pritchard, Arnold, *Catholic Loyalism in Elizabethan England* (Chapel Hill: University of North Carolina Press, 1979).

Pugh, Syrithe, *Herrick, Fanshawe and the Politics of Intertextuality: Classical Literature and Seventeenth-Century Royalism* (Burlington, VT: Ashgate, 2010).

Questier, Michael, *Catholicism and Community in Early Modern England: Politics, Aristocratic Patronage and Religion, c. 1550–1640* (New York: Cambridge University Press, 2006).

Quinn, David Beers, *The Elizabethans and the Irish* (Ithaca, NY: Cornell University Press, 1966).

Quint, David, *Epic and Empire: Politics and Form from Virgil to Milton* (Princeton: Princeton University Press, 1993).

Raber, Karen, "Warrior Women in the Plays of Cavendish and Killigrew," *Studies in English Literature 1500–1900* 40.3 (Summer 2000): 422–4.

Racine, Matthew, "A Pearle for a Prynce: Jeronimo Osorio and Early Elizabethan Catholics," *The Catholic Historical Review* 87.3 (2001): 401–27.

Raitiere, Martin N., *Faire Bitts: Sir Philip Sidney and Renaissance Political Theory* (Pittsburgh: Duquesne University Press, 1984).

Read, Conyers, *Mr. Secretary Walsingham and the Policy of Queen Elizabeth* (3 vols, Oxford: The Clarendon Press, 1925).

Rees, Joan, "Justice, Mercy, and a Shipwreck in *Arcadia*," *Studies in Philology* 87.1 (1990): 75–82.

———, *Sir Philip Sidney and* Arcadia (Cranbury, NJ: Farleigh Dickinson University Press, 1991).

Ribner, Irving, "Machiavelli and Sidney: *The Arcadia* of 1590," *Studies in Philology* 47.2 (1950): 152–72.

———, "Sir Philip Sidney on Civil Insurrection," *Journal of the History of Ideas* 13 (1952): 257–65.

Rodes, Robert E., Jr., *Lay Authority and Reformation in the English Church: Edward I to the Civil War* (Notre Dame, IN: University of Notre Dame Press, 1982).

Rodriguez-Salgado, M.J. and Simon Adams (eds), *England, Spain and the Gran Armada 1585–1604: Essays from the Anglo-Spanish Conferences, London and Madrid, 1988* (Edinburgh: John Donald, 1991).

Rose, K.F.C., *The Date and Author of the Satyricon*, with an introduction by J.P. Sullivan (Leiden: Brill, 1971).

Ross, Charles, *Elizabethan Literature and the Law of Fraudulent Conveyance: Sidney, Spenser, and Shakespeare* (Burlington, VT: Ashgate, 2003).

Rowse, A.L., *Milton the Puritan: Portrait of a Mind* (London: Macmillan, 1977).

Russell, Conrad, *The Causes of the English Civil War: The Ford Lectures Delivered in the University of Oxford, 1987–1988* (New York: Oxford University Press, 1990).

———, *The Fall of the British Monarchies 1637–1642* (New York: Oxford University Press, 1991).

———, *Unrevolutionary England 1603–1642* (Ronceverte: Hambledon Press, 1990).

Ryan, Lawrence V., "The Haddon-Osorio Controversy (1563–1583)," *Church History* 22.2 (1953): 142–54.

Sage, Evan T., *Petronius: Satyricon* (New York: Century, 1929).

Saunders, Ann (ed.), *The Royal Exchange* (London: London Topographical Society, 1997).

Scaglione, Aldo, *Knights at Court: Courtliness, Chivalry, and Courtesy from Ottonian Germany to the Italian Renaissance* (Berkeley: University of California Press, 1991).

Schmidgen, Wolfram, *Exquisite Mixture: The Virtues of Impurity in Early Modern England* (Philadelphia: University of Pennsylvania Press, 2013).

Schmidt, Benjamin, *Innocence Abroad: The Dutch Imagination and the New World, 1570–1670* (New York: Cambridge University Press, 2001).

Schwartz, Regina, *Remembering and Repeating: Biblical Creation in Paradise Lost* (New York: Cambridge University Press, 1988).

Schwyzer, Philip, *Literature, Nationalism, and Memory in Early Modern England and Wales* (New York: Cambridge University Press, 2004).

Scott-Warren, Jason, *Sir John Harington and the Book as Gift* (New York: Oxford University Press, 2001).

Shagan, Ethan H. (ed.), *Catholics and the 'Protestant Nation': Religious Politics and Identity in Early Modern England* (Manchester: Manchester University Press, 2005).

Shapiro, I.A., "Shakespeare and Mundy," *Shakespeare Survey* 14 (1961): 25–33.

Sharpe, Kevin, *Criticism and Compliment: The Politics of Literature in the English of Charles I* (New York: Cambridge University Press, 1987).

———, *The Personal Rule of Charles I* (New Haven, CT: Yale University Press, 1992).

———, *Selling the Tudor Monarchy: Authority and Image in Sixteenth-Century England* (New Haven, CT: Yale University Press, 2009).

Sharpe, Robert Boies, *The Real Wars of the Theatres: Shakespeare's Fellows in Rivalry with the Admiral's Men, 1594–1603* (Boston: D.C. Heath and Company, 1935).

Shawcross, John T., *The Development of Milton's Thought: Law, Government, and Religion* (Pittsburgh: Duquesne University Press, 2008).

Shell, Alison, *Catholicism, Controversy and the English Literary Imagination, 1558–1660* (New York: Cambridge University Press, 1999).

———, *Oral Culture and Catholicism in Early Modern England* (New York: Cambridge University Press, 2007).

Sherman, William, *John Dee: The Politics of Reading and Writing in the English Renaissance* (Amherst: University of Massachusetts Press, 1995).

Sigerist, Henry, "An Elizabethan Poet's Contribution to Public Health: Sir John Harington and the Water Closet," *Bulletin of the History of Medicine* 13 (1943): 229–43.

Simpson, Richard, *Edmund Campion: A Biography* (London: Hodges, 1896).

Sims, James H., "Christened Classicism in *Paradise Lost* and *The Lusiads*," *Comparative Literature* 24 (1972): 338–56.

———, "The Epic Narrator's Mortal Voice in Camoens and Milton," *Revue de Littérature Comparée* 51 (1977): 374–84.

Sinfield, Alan, *Faultlines: Cultural Materialism and the Poetics of Dissident Reading* (Berkeley: University of California Press, 1992).

———, "Sidney and Du Bartas," *Comparative Literature* 27.1 (1975): 8–20.

Singman, Jeffrey L., *Robin Hood: The Shaping of the Legend* (Westport, CT: Praeger, 1998).

352   *Early Modern Catholics, Royalists, and Cosmopolitans*

Skinner, Quentin, *The Foundations of Modern Political Thought* (2 vols, New York: Cambridge University Press, 1978).

Skretkowicz, Victor, "Categorizing Redirection in Sidney's *New Arcadia*," in Wolfgang Görtschacher and Holger Klein (eds), *Narrative Strategies in Early in Early English Fiction* (Lewiston, NY: Edward Mellon Press, 1995), 133–46.

Skura, Merideth, "Anthony Munday's 'Gentrification' of Robin Hood," *English Literary Renaissance* 33.2 (2003): 155–80.

Smith, Alan Gordon Rae, *The Emergence of a Nation State: The Commonwealth of England, 1529–1660* (2nd ed., New York: Longman, 1997).

Smith, Nigel, *Literature and Revolution in England, 1640–1660* (New Haven, CT: Yale University Press, 1994).

———, *Perfection Proclaimed: Language and Literature in English Radical Religion 1640–1660* (New York: Oxford University Press, 1989).

Sochatoff, A. Fred, "The Purpose of Petronius' *Bellum civile*: A Re-examination," *Transactions and Proceedings of the American Philological Association* 93 (1962): 449–58.

Southern, A.C., *Elizabethan Recusant Prose, 1559–1582: A Historical and Critical Account of the Books of the Catholic Refugees* (London: Sands & Co., 1950).

Spelman, Henry, "Of the Union," in Bruce Galloway et al. (eds), *The Jacobean Union, Six Tracts of 1604* (Edinburgh: Clark Constable, 1985), 161–84.

Stanivukovic, Goran V. (ed.), *Remapping the Mediterranean World in Early Modern English Writings* (New York: Palgrave MacMillan, 2007).

Steffen, Lisa, *Defining a British State: Treason and National Identity, 1608–1820* (New York: Palgrave, 2001).

Stevens, Paul, "'Leviticus Thinking' and the Rhetoric of Early Modern Colonialism," *Criticism* 35.3 (1993): 441–61.

———, "Milton's Janus-faced Nationalism: Soliloquy, Subject, and the Modern Nation State," *Journal of English and Germanic Philology* 100.2 (2001): 247–68.

———, "Milton's Nationalism and the Rights of Memory," in *Imagining Death in Spenser and Milton*, ed. E.J. Bellamy et al. (New York: Palgrave Macmillan, 2003), 171–84.

Stewart, Alan, *Philip Sidney: A Double Life* (New York: Thomas Dunne Books, 2001).

Stickler, A.M., "Alanus Anglicus als Verteidiger des monarchischen Papsttums," *Salesianum* 21 (1959): 346–406.

Stickler, A.M. (ed.), "Imperator Vicarius Papae: Die Lehren der französisch-deutschen Dekretistenschule des 12. und beginennden 13. Jahrhunderts über die Beziehungen zwischen Papst und Kaiser," *Mitteilungen des Instituts fur Osterreichische Geschichtsforschung* 62 (1954): 165–212.

Stillman, Robert E., *Philip Sidney and the Poetics of Renaissance Cosmopolitanism* (Burlington, VT: Ashgate, 2008).

———, *Sidney's Poetic Justice: The* Old Arcadia, *its Ecologues, and Renaissance Pastoral Traditions* (Lewisburg, PA: Bucknell University Press, 1986).

—, "The Truths of a Slippery World: Poetry and Tyranny in Sidney's *Defence*," *Renaissance Quarterly* 55.4 (2002): 1287–319.

Stone, Lawrence, *The Causes of the English Revolution 1529–1642* (New York: Harper and Row, 1972).

Sullivan, Margaret M., "Amazons and Aristocrats: The Function of Pyrocles' Amazon Role in Sidney's Revised *Arcadia*," in Jean R. Brink et al. (eds), *Playing with Gender: A Renaissance Pursuit* (Urbana: University of Illinois Press, 1991), 62–81.

Syford, Constance Miriam, "The Direct Source of the Pamela-Cecropia Episode in the *Arcadia*," *PMLA* 49.2 (1934): 472–89.

Tawney, R.H., "The Rise of the Gentry, 1558," *Economic History Review* 11.1 (1941): 1–38.

Tazon, Juan E., *The Life and Times of Thomas Stukeley (c. 1525–78)* (Burlington, VT: Ashgate, 2003).

Taylor, Gary, "The Fortunes of Oldcastle," *Shakespeare Survey* 38 (1985): 85–100.

Thomson, Janice E., *Mercenaries, Pirates, and Sovereigns: State-Building and Extraterritorial Violence in Early Modern Europe* (Princeton: Princeton University Press, 1994).

Tierney, Brian, *The Crisis of Church and State, 1050–1300* (Buffalo, NY: University of Toronto Press, 1988).

Tillyard, Eustace M. W., *The English Epic and its Background* (New York: Oxford University Press, 1954).

Todd, Janet (ed.), *Aphra Behn Studies* (New York: St. Martin's Press, 1996).

Townsend, Freda L., "*Sidney* and *Ariosto*," *PMLA* 61 (1946): 97–108.

Townsend, Rich, *Harington and Ariosto: A Study in Elizabethan Verse Translation* (New Haven, CT: Yale University Press, 1940).

Traub, Valerie, *Desire and Anxiety: Circulation of Sexuality in Shakespearean Drama* (New York: Routledge, 1992).

Trevor-Roper, H.R., "The Elizabethan Aristocracy: An Anatomy Anatomized," *Economic History Review* 3.3 (1951): 279–98.

Trim, David J.B., "Seeking a Protestant Alliance and Liberty of Conscience on the Continent 1558–85," in Susan Doran and Glen Richardson (eds), *Tudor England and its Neighbours* (New York: Palgrave Macmillan, 2005), 139–77.

Trimble, William, *The Catholic Laity in Elizabethan England, 1558–1603* (New York: Belknap Press of Harvard University Press, 1964).

Tubbs, J.W., *The Common Law Mind: Medieval and Early Modern Conceptions* (Baltimore: Johns Hopkins University Press, 2000).

Tuck, Richard, *The Rights of War and Peace: Political Thought and the International Order From Grotius to Kant* (New York: Cambridge University Press, 2001).

Turley, Hans, *Rum, Sodomy, and the Lash: Piracy, Sexuality, and Masculine Identity* (New York: New York University Press, 1999).

Tutino, Stefania, *Empire of Souls: Robert Bellarmine and the Christian Commonwealth* (New York: Oxford University Press, 2010).

———, *Law and Conscience: Catholicism in Early Modern England 1570–1625* (Burlington, VT: Ashgate, 2007).

———, *Thomas White and the Blackloists: Between Politics and Theology during the English Civil War* (Burlington, VT: Ashgate, 2008).

Tyacke, Nicholas, *Anti-Calvinists: The Rise of English Arminianism c. 1590–1640* (New York: Oxford University Press, 1987).

———, "Puritanism, Arminianism, and Counter Revolution," in Conrad Russell (ed.) *The Origins of the English Civil War* (New York: Macmillan, 1973), 119–43.

Ullman, B.L., "Petronius in the Mediavel Florilegia," *Classical Philology* 25 (1930): 11–21.

Ungerer, Gustav, *Anglo-Spanish Relations in Tudor Literature* (Bern, Switzerland: Francke Verlag, 1956).

Van Dorsten, Jan A., *Poets, Patrons, and Professors: Sir Philip Sidney, Daniel Rogers, and the Leiden Humanists* (New York: Oxford University Press, 1962).

Van Dorsten, Jan A., Dominic Baker Smith, and Arthur F. Kinney (eds), *Sir Philip Sidney: 1586 and the Creation of a Legend* (Leiden: Published for the Sir Thomas Browne Institute, E.J. Brill/Leiden University Press, 1986).

Veech, Thomas McNevin, *Dr Nicholas Sanders and the English Reformation 1530–1581* (Louvain: Bureaux Du Recueil, 1935).

Venuti, Lawrence, "The Destruction of Troy: Translation and Royalist Cultural Politics in the Interregnum," *Journal of Medieval and Renaissance Studies* 23.2 (1993): 197–219.

Vitkus, Daniel, "Adventuring Heroes in the Mediterranean: Mapping the Boundaries of Anglo-Islamic Exchange on the Early Modern Stage," *Journal of Medieval and Early Modern Studies* 37.1 (2007): 75–95.

Walker, Roger M., "A Rediscovered Seventeenth Century Literary Friendship: Sir Richard Fanshawe and Dom Francisco Manuel de Melo," *Seventeenth Century* 7.1 (1992): 15–24.

———, "Sir Richard Fanshawe's 'Lusiad' and Manuel de Faria e Sousa's 'Lusíadas Comentadas': New Documentary Evidence," *Portuguese Studies* 10 (1994): 44–64.

Walker, Roger M. and W.H. Liddell, "A Commentary by Sir Richard Fanshawe on the Royal Arms of Portugal," in Helder Macedo (ed.), *Studies in Portuguese Literature and History in Honour of Luis de Sousa Rebelo* (Rochester: Boydell and Brewer, 1992), 155–70.

Weiner, Andrew D., *Sir Philip Sidney and the Poetics of Protestantism: A Study of Contexts* (Minneapolis: University of Minnesota Press, 1978).

Wells, Stanley and Gary Taylor, *William Shakespeare: A Textual Companion* (New York: Oxford University Press, 1987).

Werth, Tiffany, "The Reformation of Romance in Sir Philip Sidney's *The New Arcadia*," *English Literary Renaissance* 40.1 (Winter 2010): 33–55.

Whitney, Lois, "Concerning Nature in *The Countesse of Pembroke's Arcadia*," *Studies in Philology* 23 (1927): 207–22.

Wiles, A.G.D., "Parallel Analyses of the Two Versions of Sidney's *Arcadia*, Including the Major Variations of the Folio of 1593," *Studies in Philology* 39.2 (1942): 167–206.

Williams, J.B. [vere J.G. Muddiman], "Puritan Piracies of Father Persons' 'Conference,'" *The Month* 117 (1911): 270–78.

Williams, Michael E., *The Venerable English College Rome: A History 1579–1979* (London: Gracewing, 1979).

Williams, W. Llewellyn, "Welsh Catholics on the Continent," *Transactions of the Honourable Society of Cymmrodorion* (London, 1903): 46–106.

Willson, David Harris, *King James VI and I* (London: Jonathan Cape Ltd, 1963).

Wilson, Charles, *Profit and Power: A Study of England and the Dutch Wars* (Boston: Longman, 1978).

Wittreich, Joseph, *Interpreting* Samson Agonistes (Princeton: Princeton University Press, 1986).

Womersley, David, "Shakespeare and Anthony Munday," in David Womersley and Richard McCabe (eds), *Literary Milieux: Essays in Text and Context Presented to Howard Erskine-Hill* (Newark: University of Delaware Press, 2008), 72–91.

Woodbridge, Linda, "Palisading the Elizabethan Body Politic," *Texas Studies in Literature and Language* 33.3 (1991): 327–54.

Worden, Blair, *The Sound of Virtue: Philip Sidney's Arcadia and Elizabethan Politics* (New Haven, CT: Yale University Press, 1996).

Woudhuysen, H.R., *Sir Philip Sidney and the Circulation of Manuscripts, 1558–1640* (New York: Routledge, 1996).

Wright, Celeste Turner, "Anthony Mundy and the Bodenham Miscellanies," *Philological Quarterly* 40 (1961): 449–61.

———, *Anthony Mundy: An Elizabethan Man of Letters* (Berkeley: University of California Press, 1928).

———, "Anthony Mundy, 'Edward' Spenser, and E.K.," *PMLA* 76 (1961): 34–9.

———, "Mundy and Chettle in Grub Street," *Boston University Studies in English* 5 (1961): 129–39.

Yates, Francis A., *The Occult Philosophy in the Elizabethan Age* (Boston: Routledge, 1979).

Index

Acts and Monuments, see Foxe, John
Addison, Joseph, ideal of classical
    cosmopolitanism 293
Aeneid, The, see Virgil
Afonso Henriques (king of Portugal) 247,
    249–50, 260–61
Alanus, vision of papal world-monarchy
    23–4
Alfield, Thomas, Munday's response to
    A true report … 104, 105–6
Aljubarrota, Battle of 250, 253
Allen, William (cardinal)
    asked for help with English College
        revolt 62
    on Campion 38
    death 71
    plan to invade England 73
    on power of deposition 55, 179–80
    on *Regnans in Excelsis* 50
Ambrose (Archbishop of Milan)
    in Campion's play *Ambrosia* 93–8
    standing up to Emperor Theodosius
        26–9, 56, 146, 291
Ambrosia, see Campion, Edmund
Amerindians
    Suárez employed Vitoria's natural-law
        reasoning 180
    treatment of conquered peoples 31–2, 177
Amplissimi atque Doctissimi Viri …, see
    Osório de Fonseca, Jerónimo
Anderson, Benedict, account of the rise of
    the modern nation-state 79–80, 81,
    83, 85
Angellica (character)
    Behn's and Killigrew's compared 309–12
    dismantling of image of queen 302,
        304, 307, 309
    focus of collapse of national
        stereotypes 299–300, 310
    portrait central to commercial and
        cosmopolitan sensibility 301, 309–11

anti-popery 214–15
Antonio (Prior of Crato), pretender to
    Portuguese crown 19, 201, 203, 254
Apologia Ecclesiae Anglicanae (Jewel)
    25, 26
appellant/Archpriest controversy 71–2, 216
Arcadia, see Sidney, Philip
Areopagitica, see Milton, John
Ariosto, Lodovico, *Orlando Furioso* 140–48
Aristotle, definition of natural slave 31
arms, royal, of Portugal 255–7
Astrophil and Stella, see Sidney, Philip
Atkins, Richard, English Protestant burned
    at stake 65n98, 78–9, 100–101
Augustus Caesar, and *Supplementum*
    Lucani 229

Baker, David J., on British vs. English
    identity 188–9
Bale, John, *King Johan* 119, 124
Bancroft, Richard (Archbishop of
    Canterbury) 72
banquet of daintie conceits, A (Munday),
    see Munday, Anthony
Barclay, William, on French king's
    authority over church 217
Barrett, Richard, on continuation of
    Welsh-English disputes 64n96
Battle of Alcazar, The (Peele), *see* Peele,
    George
Battle of the Basilicas 26
Behn, Aphra, *The Rover* 9, 293–302, 304,
    308–12
Bellarmine, Robert
    on papal authority 30, 216–19
    Responsio ad librum: Triplici nodo,
        triplex cuneus 129
Bellum Civile (Petronius), *see* Petronius,
    Satiricon
Benedict XVI (pope), *see* Ratzinger,
    Joseph Cardinal (Pope Benedict
    XVI)

Bennet, Henry, on Spanish crown destabilizing its legitimacy 259–60

Bergeron, David, on Munday and the Lord Mayor's Shows 125

Bilson, Thomas, Ambrose incident as exception to proper prince-bishop relations 29

bishops, role of, *see* Church of England; papal supremacy; Roman Catholics/Catholicism; sovereigns/sovereignty; temporal authority

Blackloists, *see* White, Thomas (alias Blackloe)

Blackwell, George
appointed Archpriest 72
on Oath of Allegiance 214–15

Bockeforde, Ernst Wolfgang, question on democratic constitutional states 316

book-licensing, Milton's objections to Catholic origins 269

Book of Sir Thomas More, The (Munday), *see* Munday, Anthony

Bossy, John
on Giordano Bruno 20n72
on Holden and White's plan 220–21

Botero, Giovanni, *Delle relationi universali* 133

"Brag, The", *see* Campion, Edmund

brevíssima relación de la destruyción de las indias, Una (Las Casas) 296–7

Bristow, Richard
Bristow's Motives 48, 55
Campion's denial of possessing his tract questioned by Munday 104

British vs. English perspective 188–89, 194

Brome, Richard, play as basis of *Thomaso* 301

Browne-Montague family, Catholics loyal to Queen 5

Bruno, Giordano, on Sidney 20n72

Buchanan, George
De Jure Regni apud Scotos 20, 158
Genethliacon 227–30

Burghley, 1st Baron of (William Cecil)
Execution of Justice 6, 24–5, 49–50
rivalry with Essex 85

Burke, Helen M., on Behn's English "liberators" 294–5

Calvinists/Calvinism
excluded elector Frederick from alliances in Holy Roman Empire 14
Munday's edition of his Calvin's sermons 110
suggested of Sidney and Spenser 150

Camden, William, on Stukeley 186

Camões, Luís de, *Os Lusíadas*
Fanshawe's translation 240–53, 260–61, 263–5, 270
Milton and 8–9, 263–8, 270, 271, 275–6

Campion, Edmund
Ambrosia 93–8, 122, 145–6, 149
"The Challenge to the Privy Council"/"The Brag" 8, 59–60
cosmopolitan identity predicated upon papal supremacy 7–8, 38
cosmopolitan identity similar to Munday'papal supremacy 102
Harington's interest in his works 132
meeting with Sidney 20
Munday's accounts of treason trials 100, 103–9
Rationes decem 52–5, 93
on *Regnans in Excelsis* 50

Castile, *see* civil war (Castile-Portugal)

Catholicism, *see* Roman Catholics/Catholicism

Catholicism and Community in Early Modern England (Questier), *see* Questier, Michael

Cecil, William, *see* Burghley, 1st Baron of (William Cecil)

censoring of anti-papist works 215

"Challenge to the Privy Council", *see* Campion, Edmund

Charke, William, refutations of Campion's "Challenge" 59

Charlemagne
crowned by Pope Leo III 6, 21, 89, 140, 143–4
in Harington's translation of *Orlando Furioso* 141–2

Charles I (king)
Catholic support for 213–23
in Cowley's *Civil War* 232–3
execution 219, 225, 231, 309
failure to pursue common good and social contract 219–20, 225

Index

Spanish match 215, 306
Charles II (king)
    awarded Fanshawe Chancellor *pro tem*
        of the Order of the Garter 256
    failure of Spain to help him during
        exile 255
    instructions for Fanshawe in Spain
        258–9
    marriage contract with Catherine of
        Braganza 253–4
    parallel with Julius Caesar 245
    public hazard of restoring 220
Charles V (Holy Roman Emperor and King
    of Spain), potential alliance with
    Francis, King of France 13
Childeric (King of the Franks) deposed by
    Pope Zachary 6, 21
chivalry
    in *The Faerie Queene* 175
    in *Orlando Furioso* 141–5
    Stukeley's code 194–5
    universal code enforcing transnational
        justice 141, 142–3, 145, 164
Christian commonwealth; *see also*
    cosmopolitanism; England;
    Munday, Anthony; Persons, Robert
    central to Spenser's imperial
        imagination 184
    differences between Fanshawe and
        Camões 260–61
    English Catholic identity and 76–91
    as equivalent to cosmopolis or city of
        world 58–9
    Jesuit transnational religious order
        37n1, 59–64
    legacy of English Catholic exiles in
        Royalist political theory 222–3
    Osório on 46
    Portugal and Christendom 246–54
    public sphere and legacy of 313–17
    respublica christiana 1, 16–17
    royalist reinvention of 222–3, 225–61
    transnational Christian realm 120
    transnational justice more chivalric
        than Christian 140
    Vindiciae vs. Persons and Sander 154
Christian Directorie Guiding Men to their
    Salvation, A (Persons), *see* Persons,
    Robert

Christian expansionism, Portuguese as
    agents of 266, 268, 270
Christian Turned Turk (Daborne) 199–201,
    206
Chronicle of the First Seven Kings of
    Portugal of 1419 267n9
Chronicles (Holinshed) 1–2
Chrysanaleia: The Golden Fishing: or,
    Honour of Fishmongers (Munday),
    see Munday, Anthony
church and state relations between 5–6,
    8, 21–34, 39–51, 93–8, 132–5,
    213–23, 277–92
Church of England; *see also* conformists/
    conformism
    bishop's role to correct sovereign 25–9,
        57, 291
    blurred boundaries with Roman
        Church 215
    comparisons of Elizabeth to
        Constantine 26–7
    position on supremacy 116
    William Rainold's criticisms 134–5
Cicero, *De republica* 152
citizen of the world 53, 191n25, 293; *see*
    also cosmopolitanism
city of London as cosmopolis in Lord
    Mayor's Show 125–31
civil war (Castile-Portugal) 231, 246–7,
    249, 251–4
Civil War (Cowley), *see* Cowley, Abraham
civil war (English)
    in Fanshawe's translation of *Os*
        Lusíadas 231
    implications of Portuguese war of
        rebellion for 255
    seen as cosmic conflict between God
        and Satan 232
    use of epic as commentary on events of
        225–30, 243–4, 245
civil war (Roman); *see also* Lucan,
    Pharsalia (*De Bello Civi*)
    invoked as historical type 249–50
    moral degeneracy as cause of 241–5
Civitas Dei, *see* Sander, Nicholas
Civitas Diaboli, *see* Sander, Nicholas
Cloots, Anacharsis, *république du genre*
    humain 30

Clynnog, Morys
central to English College revolt 62–4, 66–70, 106
leader of Marian Catholic faction 37, 73–6
Coke, Sir Edward
constructing an English polity through writing 4
equity identified with (foreign) Roman law 180–81, 222
Galfridian view of English history 73, 75n142
Collinson, Patrick, Ambrosian exemplars rarely employed 96
Combes, Thomas, invention of flushable privy ("device") 136
Comendation of the adve[n]terus viage of the worthy Captain M. Thomas Stutely ..., *A* (Seall) 186
commerce/commercialism, *see* cosmopolitanism, commercial
common good and social contract 219–20
common law, *see* law
commonwealth, Christian, *see* Christian commonwealth
Commonwealth of England (1649–1660) 219–20, 259, 264, 269
commonwealth, transnational, Sidney's transnational commonwealth 16, 21, 279
Conference about the next succession ..., *A* (Persons), *see* Persons, Robert
Confession of Augsburg, Henry VIII's refusal to accept 13
conformists/conformism
allegiance to God and king 116–17; *see also* Church of England
allies against both Puritans and Catholic "reformers" 72
Harington's case for James VI as king to 133
jurisdiction of temporal vs. spiritual authority 25
Munday wanted to be seen as conformist 120
questioning purpose of anti-papist works 214–15
Constable, Henry, *Examen pacifique de la doctrine des Huguenots* 133

Constantine
defense of Christians against tyrant Licinius 154–5
parallels with Elizabeth 26–9, 56
Persons on 96
Continuation of Lucan's historicall poem (May), *see* May, Thomas
Copie of a Double Letter, The (Persons), *see* Persons, Robert
Corns, Thomas N., on Milton's *History of Britain* as brimming with anticlericalism 289–90
coronation ceremony as marriage between prince and subject under God 88–9
coronation oath
claim of Charles I to not be bound by 291
Milton on 290–91
Persons on 220
Corpus Juris Canonici, *see* law
Corpus Juris Civilis, *see* law
cosmopolitanism; *see also* Christian commonwealth; citizen of the world; identity, cosmopolitan
Camões's epic and Milton's cosmopolitan republic 263–92
Campion's public persona mirrored by Munday 102, 106
Catholic cosmopolitans and their interlocutors 8, 52–7, 105–6
city within international sphere 125–31
commercial 126–7, 129, 240n37, 293, 295, 300–302, 308–15
ecumenical or transnational 20, 72n127, 90, 126, 133, 240, 260–61
Enlightenment ideal 293
Escurial builders from across Europe 254–5
Kant's cosmopolitan law 30–31, 32
Mignolo's concept of "managerial" 8–9
perspective of English Catholics 31, 58, 65, 136
secular 33, 34, 48, 142, 143, 316
Sidney and 9–16
Society of Jesus as cosmopolitan institution 57–64
transnational justice in *New Arcadia* 159–70

cosmopolitics, *see* Campion, Edmund;
    Dee, John; Harington, Sir John;
    Munday, Anthony; Society of Jesus
Cowley, Abraham
    Civil War 231–5
    Davideis 234–8
    epics about religious history 233–40
Cromwell, Oliver, government justified by
    Charles's failure to pursue common
    good 219–20
Cromwell, Thomas, temporal magistrate as
    head of ecclesiastical affairs 135
cross-dressing, patriarchal ideology and 207
Crowley, Robert
    discussion with Kirby 131
    on sovereign only responsible to
    God 107–8
crucifixion, battle of Ourique as
    re-enactment of events surrounding
    266–8
curia, *see* Roman curia

d'Ablancourt, Frémont, on War of
    Portuguese Restoration 253
Daborne, Robert, *Christian Turned Turk*
    199–201, 206
Davenant, William, *Gondibert: An Heroic
    Poem* 230, 235–40
Davideis (Cowley), *see* Cowley, Abraham
Dawson, Thomas, selling of tract on
    witches 2–3
De Bello Civili, see Petronius, *Satiricon*
De potestate civili [On Civil Power], see
    Vitoria, Francisco de
de Vere, Edward, *see* Oxford, Earl of
    (Edward de Vere)
De visibili monarchia Ecclesiae (Sander),
    see Sander, Nicholas
Death of Robert, Earl of Huntington, The
    (Munday), *see* Munday, Anthony
Decretum, see Gratian
Dee, John
    first uses of "cosmopolitical" and
    "Brytish Impire" 53–4
    secular cosmopolitanism of 8, 59, 105,
    112, 168, 189–90
Defence of English Catholics (Allen), *see*
    Allen, William (cardinal)
Defence of Poetry, see Sidney, Philip

Defensio Fidei Catholicae et Apostolicae
    (Suárez), *see* Suárez, Francisco
Delle relationi universali (Botero), *see*
    Botero, Giovanni
Denham, John, translation of
    The Aeneid 270
deposition of sovereigns, *see* papal
    supremacy; Parliament
Devereux, Robert, *see* Essex, 2nd Earl of
    (Robert Devereux)
Digby, Sir Kenelm, loyalty to the king 219
*Discoverie of Edmund Campion and his
    confederates, A, see* Munday,
    Anthony
Discovery of Guiana, The (Ralegh) 137,
    295–6
*Discussion of the Answer of M. William
    Barlow* (Persons) 217
divine right
    cosmologies developed in wake of
    collapse of 239–40
    Fanshawe's use of epic and 225,
    263–4, 270
    king as earthly representative of God
    232–3
    Portuguese sovereignty and 265–6
Doleman, R., possible derivation of
    name 85
Downfall of Robert, Earl of Huntington, The
    (Munday), *see* Munday, Anthony
Drake, Francis 185–6, 201–2
drapers and international trade 127
Dudley, Robert, *see* Leicester, 1st Earl of
    (Robert Dudley)

ecumenism; *see also* cosmopolitanism,
    ecumenical or transnational
    attempts of Harington to appeal to 133
    ecumenical order envisioned by
    Fanshawe 240, 260–61
    experienced in Europe by Sidney 20
    James I's preference for 129
    in Munday's pageants 126
Edelman, Charles, on *Battle of Alcazar* 198
Eggert, Katherine, on Radigund episode in
    The Faerie Queene 177
Eikon Basilike, posthumous memoir of
    Charles I 290
Eikonoklastes, see Milton, John
Eleutherius (pope) 74–5, 289

Index

Elizabeth I (queen)
  attitudes of English Catholic
    seminarians to 69, 70
  Catholic criticisms of 52–7
  Constantine as example of temporal
    authority and 26–9
  counterpart of Spenser's Britomart 172
  critiques of her defining place in the
    English imagination 294–5
  demand on Archbishop Grindal 25–6
  ecclesiastical sovereignty reaffirmed
    38–48
  equity as justification for her
    usurpation 183–4
  excommunication and attempted
    deposition, *see* Pius V (pope)
  failure to appoint a bishop to Privy
    Council 140, 145, 146
  failure to prevent Philip II's takeover
    of Portugal 254
  foreign policy 11, 14–15, 18–19, 86
  Harington's letter to Traianus instead
    of 138–40
  letter from Sidney against marriage
    with Duke of Alençon 12
  Persons's implicit suggestion of
    deposing 90
  praised for ability to maintain Christian
    commonwealth 3
  Ralegh's presentation of portrait to
    Trinidadians 295–6, 299, 301–4,
    306–7, 309
Elizabethae Angliae Reginae haeresim 82
England; *see also* identity, national
  boundaries dissolved in drama 9,
    298–300, 304–6, 310–12
  as a Christian commonwealth 1–4
  as disseminator of liberty to other
    nations 268–9, 278, 294–300
  Helgerson's account of English
    nationhood incomplete 4, 38,
    140n150
  as part of a Christian commonwealth
    1–34, 37–9, 75–6, 78
  rivalry with Spain 295–300
  Roman Catholicism and English
    nation 71–6
  two conceptions of English nationhood
    4–6, 34, 37–9, 43, 46, 48, 71–2, 76

Englefield, Sir Francis, plan to invade
  England 73
English College at Rome
  1579 student revolt 61–71
  dangers for Munday as student
    104–5, 106
  Stukeley allied with Welsh faction 205
English marriages with Spanish and
  Portuguese 251–2, 253–4
English mission, *see* Society of Jesus
English Romayne Lyfe, see Munday,
  Anthony
epic genre; *see also* Davenant, William;
  Fanshawe, Sir Richard; Lucan,
  Pharsalia; Milton, John; royalists;
  Spenser, Edmund; Virgil
  ancient epics used during civil war
    225–6, 229
  focus on relationship between divine
    and 241–5
  Hakluyt's portrayal of commercial
    voyages as nationalism 209
epieikeia (Greek form of equity) 174
*Epistola ad Elizabethan Angliae Reginam
  de Religione* (Osório), *see* Osório
  de Fonseca, Jerónimo
equity
  legal principle applied in court of
    Chancery and Star Chamber
    112–13, 170–71
  sovereignty and 177–84
Erastian political ideology
  Bellarmine's response to William
    Barclay 217–18
  in *First Part of Sir John Oldcastle*
    116–17
  relationship between English political
    and religious culture 42–3, 313–14
  threat of commerce to 308–9
  threat of precedent set by Ambrose and
    Theodosius 28–9
  trajectory of English Protestant
    politics 2
  Warner's queen as gendered center of
    church and state 302
  White's model of English Catholic
    Church based on 220, 222
Escurial poems (Fanshawe), *see* Fanshawe,
  Sir Richard

Index 363

Essex, 2nd Earl of (Robert Devereux)
    in Harington's writings 134n127,
      138–40, 140, 146–8, 148n163
    Persons's *Conference about the Next*
      Succession dedicated to 85–6
Europe
    chaotic state of affairs reported by
      Sidney 11
    as female body, Portugal as crown 247–8
evolution and natural law theories 316
Examen pacifique de la doctrine des
    Huguenots (Constable) 133
excommunication of Elizabeth I, *see*
    Pius V (pope)
execution; *see also* Charles I (king)
    of Atkins 65n98, 78–9, 100–101
    of Campion and his confederates 49,
      98, 100, 102, 104–7
    of Fisher and More [Catholics] 45–6, 111
    of Kirby 106, 131
    vs. dynastic interests in Sidney's *Old*
      Arcadia 151–2, 152n7
Execution of Justice (Cecil), *see* Burghley,
    1st Baron of (William Cecil)
exiles, English Catholic; *see also* Society
    of Jesus
    aid to Munday and Newell in Rome 102
    appellant party tied to exiles in France
      and Rome 73
    familiarity with Isaiah 49:23 57
    Munday's knowledge of secret world
      of 105
    names 39
    on power of deposition 57
    radicalized by executions of 1580s 50
    republic of letters among 83–5
    Spanish invasion justified by notions of
      equity 178–9
    understanding of relationship between
      temporal and spiritual
      magistrates 93

Faerie Queene, The (Spenser), *see* Spenser,
    Edmund
family/marriage/state analogies 88,
    109–11, 192–3, 247, 249
Famous History of Sir Thomas Wyat, The
    (Webster and Dekker), *see* Webster,
    John, and Thomas Dekker

The Famous History of the Life and Death
    of Captain Thomas Stukeley
    (anonymous) 186–8, 193–9
Fanshawe, Sir Richard
    committed to Church of England 261
    cosmopolitanism in his writings and
      translations 8–9
    diplomatic life 252–61
    Escurial poems 254–5
    Kant's ideal emerging in works of 30
    Maius Lucanizans 228–9
    and Milton on civil wars 286
    Sovereign of the Seas 254–5
    Specimen a Lusitanus 255
    translation of Buchanan's *Genethliacon*
      227–30
    translation of *Os Lusíadas* 240–53,
      260–61, 263–5, 270
    use of epic genre 225–6, 228–31
Farewell Entitled to the famous and
    fortune generals of our English
    forces ..., A (Peele), *see* Peele,
    George
Father Parsons's Greencoat, see
    Leicester's Commonwealth
Feckenham, John, on Constantine giving
    power to bishops 27
fictional works, secularization of
    ecclesiastical figures 98
First Defense of the People of England
    (Milton), *see* Milton, John
First Part of Sir John Oldcastle (Munday),
    see Munday, Anthony
Fisher, John, confrontation with Henry
    VIII 45–6, 146–7
fishmongers, merchants who helped
    European crusaders 127–9, 131
Fitzer, William, publishing of
    Sidney-Languet correspondence
    15–16
Forde, Thomas, testimony at trial 107
foreign policy, *see* Elizabeth I (queen)
Forms of Nationhood (Helgerson), *see*
    Helgerson, Richard
Fornari, Simone, monster in *Orlando*
    Furioso as temporal prince 144
fortune, ebbs and flows 148
Foxe, John
    Acts and Monuments, comparison of
      Constantine with Elizabeth 28–9

Christianity in Britain before papal
authorities 74–5
completed Haddon's second response
to Osório 43, 46
on Constantine as model for Protestant
kings 96
Francis (king of France), potential alliance
with Charles V 13
Frederick II (Holy Roman Emperor) 24
Frederick III (Elector Palatine) 12, 14
Friar Bacon and Friar Bungay (Greene),
see Greene, Robert
Friedrich, Markus
on Jesuits 37n1, 60, 85
on Society of Jesus 60–61
Froude, James Anthony, on English
crown's exploration of joining
Protestant League 13

Gama, Vasco de
portrayal in *Os Lusíadas* 264–6
voyage to India as basis for Milton's
journey by Satan 270n17
gender; *see also* romance genre
in Behn's *Rover* 297–300
patriarchal gender relations in *Faerie
Queene* 172, 176–8, 181–3, 304
patriarchal ideology and 207
prostitutes and royalty in *The
Renegado* 306–9
stereotype reversals 305–6
*General and Rare Memorials pertayning
to the Perfect Arte of Navigation*
(Dee), *see* Dee, John
General Ecumenical Council (1245) 89
Genesis, influence on *Paradise Lost*
regarding slavery 31
Genethliacon (Buchanan) 227–30
Gondibert: An Heroic Poem, see Davenant,
William
Goode, William, Persons's letter on
English vs. Welsh 66–8
governance; *see also* papal supremacy;
secular papal surrogate; sovereigns/
sovereignty; temporal authority
need for discipline in transnational
institutions 282–3
public sphere and commerce replaced
spiritual realm 315

Gratian, *Decretum*, on pope as supreme
judge in temporal and ecclesiastical
affairs 21–3, 25–6
Greenblatt, Stephen, on identity 167–8, 206
Greene, Robert
Friar Bacon and Friar Bungay 109,
304–6
Gregory IX (pope), deposition of
Frederick II 24
Gregory XIII (pope)
clarification of *Regnans in Excelsis* 153
involvement in English College revolt
63, 65, 69–70
provided Stukeley with unseaworthy
ships 205
Greville, Fulke, on Sidney and Protestant
League 15, 21
Grindal, Edmund (archbishop), argument
with Elizabeth 25–6
Grotius, Hugo, ideas of international order
preceded by Vitoria's 31
*Grounds of Obedience and Government,
The* (White), *see* White, Thomas
(alias Blackloe)
Guarini, Giovanni Battista, *Il Pastor
Fido* (Fanshawe's translation) 240,
243, 254
Gunpowder Plot 214, 216
Guzmán, Ramiro Núñez de, *see* Medina
de las Torres, Duke of

Habermas, Jurgen, on place of faith and
reason in "post-secular society" 316
Habermas, Jurgen, and Michael Warner,
on rise of independent public
sphere 315
Haddon, Walter, responses to Osório's
letter to Elizabeth 41–3, 46–8
Hadfield, Andrew, on Spenser 150n2
Hakluyt, Richard 8, 209
Hall, Joseph, and petitioning bishops
excluded from Parliament 288
Hamilton, Donna
on Munday's writings 68n110, 99,
109–10
theory of clandestine Catholic
sympathies 149
Hanmer, Meredith, refutations of
Campion's "Challenge" 59

Harding, Thomas, on prelates seeking favor of secular princes 25, 26

Harington, Sir John
Epigrams presented to James VI and his son Henry 147–8
A New Discourse of a Stale Subject 132, 135–40, 143, 146, 147
Orlando Furioso (translation and commentary) 140–48
and the Privy Council 132–40
on secular version of papal overseer 8
shaped by cosmopolitan perspective of Catholic exiles 149
A Tract on the Succession to the Crown 56–7, 132–7, 139, 145–6

Heimbach, Peter, correspondence with Milton 277–8

Helgerson, Richard, *Forms of Nationhood* 4, 76n144, 140n150, 188, 189, 209

Henry II (king) 1

Henry (Prince of Wales), *Epigrams* presented to 147–8

Henry V (king) in Munday's *Oldcastle* 115–18

Henry VIII (king); *see also* Statute in Restraint of Appeals 1533
appointment of secular overseer of prelates 135
claimed sovereignty over temporal and ecclesiastical realms 38–9
criticism by Harington 57
desired no limits on his sovereignty 13
execution of Catholics 45–6

Henshaw, Henry (Clynnog's replacement) 62

Himatia-Poleos, The Triumphs of olde Draperie, or the rich Cloathing of England (Munday), *see* Munday, Anthony

Historia Particular de la Persecucion de Inglaterra (Yepes) 81

History of Britain, That part especially now called England (Milton), *see* Milton, John

Hobbes, Thomas
Erastian model closer to position of 220
on perpetual war between states 238–9, 238n35

portrait of natural state 315–16
response to Davenant 237–9

Holden, Henry, and White's plan to sever English Catholic Church from pope 220–21

Holinshed, Raphael, *Chronicles* 1–2

Holland, Hugh, convicted through Munday 99

Holliday, Sir Leonard (Lord Mayor) 126

Holy Roman Empire; *see also specific emperors by name*, German Protestant princes and idea of Protestant League 11–15

Hooker, Richard
Ambrose incident as exception to proper prince-bishop relations 29
on Christianity's introduction into England 74
constructing an English polity through writing 4
emperor exempt from ecclesiastical jurisdiction 96

Horne, Robert, on temporal vs. spiritual authority 27

Houliston, Victor
on Persons 77, 220
on Suárez 87–8

Howard, Jean, on adventure play and conversion paradigm 188

Howlet, John (or "I. Howlet"), derivation of name 77–8

Huguenots; *see also Vindiciae, Contra Tyrannos*
Sidney and Spenser identifying with 150

Humbert, on primacy of spiritual over temporal realm 21–2

identity, cosmopolitan; *see also* Dee, John; Stukeley, Thomas
central to Spenser's imperial imagination 184
predicated upon papal supremacy 7–8, 25, 38, 102, 154
transnational identity in *New Arcadia* 167–70
vs. national identity 37–9, 65, 65n99, 185–209

identity, national; *see also* England

adoration of sovereign and 294–5,
302–4, 311
boundaries dissolved in drama 9,
298–300, 304–6, 310–12
interchangeability of religious and 313
Jesuit mission seen as transcending
63, 66
language and emergence of English
nationhood 80–83, 85
Milton's distrust of nationhood 271–9
New Historicist account 167, 169
non-state actors and nationhood 185
Persons's fashioning of English
Catholic 76–91
imperial perspective, preferred to
republican by Fanshawe 245
Innocent III (pope), claims concerning
world governance 23–4
Innocent IV (pope), deposition of Sancho
II 89–90
intemperate violence in *The Faerie
Queene* 174
international order; *see also* chivalry;
cosmopolitanism
Fanshawe's vision 255–6
impetus to construct 33
Kant's ideal of 31–3
Sidney's vision 19–21, 151–9, 161–3
Vindiciae's conception of 154–9
Vitoria's conception of 32–3, 157–9
international trade, *see* cosmopolitanism,
commercial
Ireland
failure of English common law to
reform 178
Irish Catholics supported Charles I 213
Irene (empress, Eastern Roman Empire)
deposed by papal authority in *Orlando
Furioso* 144
deposed by Pope Leo III 89
Isaiah 49:23 54–7, 154–5
Isis and Osyris 175
Israel, role of Christ in, according to
Milton 275–7

James I and VI (king)
Harington presented *Epigrams* to 147–8
Harington's *Tract* in support of James
VI of Scotland 57, 133–4

preference for ecumenism 129–30
*Triplici nodo, triplex cuneus, Or, An
Apologie for the Oath of Allegiance*
(James I) 70, 129, 217
The True Law of Free Monarchies 225
Jesuits, *see* Society of Jesus
Jewel, John
Apologia Ecclesiae Anglicanae 25, 26
defense of Elizabeth 55–6
John a Kent and John a Cumber
(Munday), *see* Munday, Anthony
John I (king), plays portraying 118–25
John II (king of Portugal), design of royal
arms 255
Jones, Ann Rosalind, and Peter Stallybrass,
on Erastian ideology in Sidney's
sonnets 302
*Judgment of a Catholicke English-man,
living in banishment for his
religion ...,* The (Persons) 79, 217
Julius Caesar
and coverage of *Supplementum
Lucani* 229
Fanshawe's parallel with Charles II 245
just-war doctrine 142, 157
justice, fiction of imperial, *see* Sidney,
Philip; Spenser, Edmund

Kahn, Victoria, on *Samson Agonistes* 277
Kant, Immanuel 30–31, 32, 33
Killigrew, Thomas, *Thomaso* 293–4, 301,
309–12
Kilroy, Gerard, on Harington and Campion
132, 136–7, 149
King Johan (Bale) 119, 124
Kirby, Luke 106, 107–8, 131
Knolles, Richard, *General History of the
Turkes* 2
Knox, John, condemned rule of women
based on equity 182
Kouri, E.I., on Elizabethan foreign policy 14

language, emergence of vernacular
print-language 80–83, 85
Languet, Hubert, correspondence with
Sidney 10, 15–18, 162–3, 168–9
Las Casas, Bartolomé de, account of
Spanish atrocities 156–7, 296–7
Laudians, approval of traditional Catholic
doctrines 215

law; *see also* natural law
  common law vs. equity 170–72, 177–8, 180–81
  Corpus Juris Canonici (Roman canon law) 159
  Corpus Juris Civilis (Roman civil law) 90, 159
  cosmopolitan 30–31, 32
  Davenant and Hobbes on 238–9
  gynocentric vs. patriarchal 175
  law of nations (*ius gentium*) 32
  role of parliament in creating 42
  Roman 22, 90, 159
Leicester, 1st Earl of (Robert Dudley) 12, 149–50
Leicester's Commonwealth 5–6, 12, 132, 133
Leo III (pope)
  coronation of Charlemagne 6, 21, 89, 140, 143–4
  deposition of Empress Irene 89, 140
Leo X, capture of monster in *Orlando Furioso* 144
Lesieur, Stephen, preservation of Sidney-Languet letters 16
Life and Death of King John, The (Shakespeare) 118, 123–5
Livery Companies of London 126
London's Love, to the Royal Prince Henrie (Munday's only royal pageant), *see* Munday, Anthony
Lord Mayor's Show, *see* Munday, Anthony
Lucan, *Pharsalia* (*De Bello Civil*)
  analogy in *Os Lusíadas* 250
  Davenant on 235–6
  little attention to moral degeneracy 243
  May's *Supplementum* and translation 226, 228–9
  model for Cowley's *Civil War* 232
  poem of Petronius as response to 242, 244–5
Lucinge, Rene de, *The beginning, continance, and decay of estates* 2
Lucius (king of Britain) 74–5, 289
Lumley, Lord, Harington's marginal notes in *New Discourse* 136–7
Lutheranism, trust of German princes in Emperor Maximilian 14–15
Lyly, John 57n71, 103

McCoog, Thomas, on English Jesuit mission 38
McEachern, Claire, on uniformity through religious texts 80
McEntegart, Rory
  on breakdown of family-state analogy 192–3
  English crown motivated by religion as well as politics 13
McKeon, Michael, on prostitutes 307
Maius Lucanizans (Fanshawe), *see* Fanshawe, Sir Richard
Majeske, Andrew, on Elizabeth's preference for James VI in *The Faerie Queene* 177
Major, John, case for conquering people violating natural law 177
Marlowe, Christopher, *Tamburlaine*, protagonist's refusal to be subject to a king 200–201
Marprelate, Martin (pseudonym), references to England as Christian commonwealth 3
marriage, *see* English marriages; family/marriage/state analogies
masque tradition 125, 236
Massinger, Philip, *The Renegado* 306–8
Matthew, Tobias (archbishop) 57
May, Thomas, translation of and *Supplementum* to *Pharsalia* 226, 228–9
Medina de las Torres, Duke of (Ramiro Núñez de Guzmán) 258, 260
Melanchthon, Philip
  possible influence on Sidney and Spenser 150, 158
  representative of Schmalkaldic states 13
Merchant Taylors, anciently responsible for serving Christian pilgrims in Jerusalem 126
Mercurian, Everard (General, Society of Jesus) 63, 71–2
Mignolo, Walter
  on "managerial" tradition of cosmopolitanism 8, 190–91
Milton, Anthony, on unrest over Spanish match 215
Milton, John; *see also* Camões, Luís de
  comparison between civil and foreign war 285–6

368   *Early Modern Catholics, Royalists, and Cosmopolitans*

correspondence with Peter Heimbach 277–8
idea of transnational elect 264, 277–83, 286–92
perspective on the English nation 264–78
rejection of the episcopal hierarchy 279–80, 286–8, 290–91
replaced by Fanshawe as *Secretarius Pro Lingua Latina* 261
works
    antiprelatical tracts 279–84, 287–90, 291
    Areopagitica 269, 284, 288
    Eikonoklastes 290
    First Defense of the People of England 278
    History of Britain, That part especially now called England 289–90
    Of Reformation 288, 289, 290
    Of True Religion, Heresy, Schism, and Toleration 287
    Paradise Lost 8–9, 232, 264, 268, 269–77, 280–81, 283–4
    Paradise Regained 276–7
    The Readie and Easie Way 286
    The Reason of Church Government 282–3, 288
    Samson Agonistes 276
    A Second Defense of the English People 268–9, 278, 284
    Tenure of Kings and Magistrates 284–5, 287, 291
    Treatise of Civil Power in Ecclesiastical Causes 281–2, 290
Mirrour of Mutabilitie, The (Munday), *see* Munday, Anthony
monarchomach tracts 20–21, 122, 152, 156–7, 161
money, Behn's character Willmore on 295
Moniz, Egas, sacrifice for Afonso Henriques 260–61
Montrose, Louis 77n145, 206, 303–4
moral degeneracy as cause of the Roman and English civil wars 241–5
morality, directed by epic poetry 236–8
More, Sir Thomas
    executed by Henry VIII 45

as portrayed in Munday's play *Book of Sir Thomas More* 111–14
Morone, Giovanni (cardinal), involvement in English College revolt 62–3, 65–8, 70
*Most Friendly Farewell to Sir Francis Drake (*Roberts) 185–6
Munday, Anthony
on English student revolt 62, 64–6, 68–71
Huntington plays compared to Shakespeare's *King John* 123–5
idea of secular version of papal overseer 8, 71, 107–25
membership in Topcliffe's spy network 136
pageants for Lord Mayor's Show 125–31
papal supremacy in his plays 109–25
shaped by cosmopolitan perspective of Catholic exiles 149
works
    A banquet of daintie conceits 99
    The Book of Sir Thomas More 111–14
    Chrysanaleia: The Golden Fishing: or, Honour of Fishmongers (pageant) 127–9, 131
    Death of Robert, Earl of Huntingdon, The 120–23
    The Downfall of Robert, Earl of Huntington 118–20
    English Romayne Lyfe 64–5, 68–71, 100–101, 103, 104, 106, 107, 109
    First Part of Sir John Oldcastle 114–18
    Himatia-Poleos (pageant) 127
    John a Kent and John a Cumber 109–10
    London's Love, to the Royal Prince Henrie (pageant) 130
    The Mirrour of Mutabilitie 102–3
    Palmerin of England, part 1 (translation) 141
    pamphlets/"treason" tracts 103–9
    Primaleon of Greece (translation) 103
    The Strangest Adventvre That Ever Happened (translation) 202–4
    The Triumph of revnited Britania 126
    Zelauto 98–9, 103

Nadal, Jerónimo, on transnational character
of Jesuits 63
nation-state; *see also* identity, national
as a Christian commonwealth 1–4,
17n58, 32
confusion over "country" in Stukeley
plays 197–9
cosmopolitanism predates 207
Fanshawe on 230, 238
interests vs. transnational justice
163–7, 170
legitimacy of sovereignty and 159
and Milton's transnational elite 315
in perpetual state of war 238–9, 238n35
vernacular print-culture and 79–80, 83
national identity, *see* identity, national
nationalism
in Camões and Milton 263–92
English fiction performs critique of
ethnic 313
in Hakluyt 209
natural law; *see also* equity
in *Book of Sir Thomas More* 112–13
consent theory melded with Catholic
theology and 219–20
Kant's cosmopolitan law as secular
expression of 31
no nation more committed to God than
another 277
in Spenser's "Book of Justice" 170–83
Vitoria's concept 31–3, 156–9
vs. chaotic state of nature 238–9,
238n35, 315–16
Neo-Scholasticism 156–7, 172
construction of papal supremacy 172
vs. Protestant monarchomach theory
156–57
New Arcadia, The (Sidney), *see* Sidney,
Philip
*New Discourse of a Stale Subject, Called
the Metamorphosis of Ajax, A*
(Harington) 132–41
New Historicism on identity and
relationship with authority 77n145,
167, 206, 303–4
News from Spayne and Holland
(Persons) 79
Norbrook, David, on use of epic during
English civil war 225–6, 231

Nowell, Alexander, on Ambrose 29
Nowell, Thomas (companion of Munday)
68, 70, 102, 106

Oath of Allegiance of 1606 216–19
*Of True Religion, Heresy, Schism, and
Toleration* (Milton), *see* Milton,
John
Old Arcadia, The (sidney), *see* Sidney,
Philip
Oldcastle (character), *see* Munday,
Anthony, *First Part of Sir John
Oldcastle*
O'Malley, John, on Society of Jesus 61, 63
O'Neill, Shane, condemned by Stukeley 195
*orbis christianus vs. respublica
christiana* 16–17
Order of the Garter 255–7
Os Lusíadas (Camões), *see* Camões, Luís
de; Fanshawe, Sir Richard
Osório de Fonseca, Jerónimo 40–48, 58–9
Osório-Haddon controversy 40–48
Ottoman Empire, threat to Christian
commonwealth 1–2, 16–18
Oxford, Earl of (Edward de Vere), Catholic
patron of Munday 99, 102

Palmerin D'Olivia of Constantinople,
chivalric assistance to "Great
Britain" 141
*Pap with a Hatchet: Being a Reply to
Martin Mar-Prelate* (Lyly) 57n71
papal supremacy; *see also* Sander,
Nicholas; secular papal surrogate;
sovereigns/sovereignty
1579 student revolt and 61–71
Catholic cosmopolitans and their
interlocutors 52–7
Catholicism and the English nation 71–6
clarifications by Bellarmine and
Suárez 217
deposition power over temporal
sovereigns 2, 6–8, 21–5, 49–50,
89–90, 107–8, 144, 172, 287
English Catholic vision of pope's
role 145
Haddon claimed papacy had no
authority over English people 42–3
in Munday's dramatic works 109–25

370 *Early Modern Catholics, Royalists, and Cosmopolitans*

Munday's secularization 109–25
Osório-Haddon controversy and
    responses 40–50
over temporal sovereigns in decline
    after 1570 30–34
resistance from temporal sovereigns
    24–7
Robert Persons's self-fashioning and
    76–91
secularization, *see* secular papal
    surrogate
Sidney's secularization 159–70
spiritual authority only delegated to
    pope 134
transnational aspect of pope's power
    162
parliament; *see also* Milton, John
coronation oath to consult with 290
deposition power to justify removing
    sovereign 90, 221–2
portrayal in Cowley's *Civil War* 232–3
princes invested in 130
Pastor Fido, Il (Guarini) 240, 243, 254
patriotism, Milton's sense of expatriation
    278
Paul V (pope), on Gunpowder Plot and
    Oath of Allegiance 216
Peck, Harry Thurston, on fragment from
    Petronius 241
Peele, George
    The Battle of Alcazar 186–8, 191–3,
        195–9, 201–2, 205, 208
    *A Farewell Entitled to the famous and
        fortune generals of our English
        forces ...* 201–2
Pepys, Samuel, on "bawdy house at
    Whitehall" 307
Persons, Robert
accused by enemies in Archpriest
    controversy 72
clergy as custodians of the people's
    will 220
contractual theory of sovereignty 88, 179
on coronation oath 130, 290
cosmopolitan identity predicated upon
    papal supremacy 7, 25, 154
on demands of James I on his Catholic
    subjects 217
on English student revolt 62, 64–8, 70

"Jurisdiction of Souls" 96
on King John in *Conference* 122
as most influential English Jesuit 38, 58
parliamentarians used *Conference* to
    justify deposition of Charles I 221
on pope and bishops as enlightened
    minority 286
response to Coke on equity 181–2, 222
self-fashioning and the papal monarchy
    76–91
on Sidney's relationship with
    Campion 20
on Stukeley 205
on subjection of women in spiritual
    matters 182
works
    *A Christian Directorie Guiding
        Men to their Salvation* 80, 132
    *A Conference about the next
        succession ...* 85–90, 132–4,
        140, 143–4, 149, 154, 221–2
    The Copie of a Double Letter 78–9
    De persecvtione Anglicana 81
    *Discussion of the Answer of M.
        William Barlow* 89n192, 217
    *Elizabethae Angliae Reginae
        haeresim* (under pseudonym
        Philopater) 82
    *The Judgment of a Catholicke
        English-man, living in
        banishment for his religion ...*
        79, 217
    News from Spayne and Holland 79
    Reasons of Refusal 77–8
    Relacion de Algunos Martyrios 82
    *Relation of the King of Spaines
        Receiving in Valliodolid ...* 79
    "A Storie of Domesticall
        Difficulties in the English
        Catholike cause" 64
    Treatise of the Three Conversions
        74–5, 289
"Petition and Protestation of all the
    Bishops" (1641) 288
Petronius, *Satiricon*, Fanshawe's
    translation 241–5
Pharsalia (Lucan), *see* Lucan, *Pharsalia*
    (*De Bello Civil*)
Pheander, the Maiden Knight (Roberts) 303
Philip II (king of Spain); *see also* Spain

papal authorization to invade England 145

relationship with Stukeley 204–5

Philopater, Andreas (pseudonym for Persons), *Elizabethae Angliae Reginae haeresim* 82

philosophy

poetry comparable to 238

relationship with religious thought 316

Pius V (pope), *Regnans in Excelsis* (Papal Bull of 1570) 6–7, 24–5, 30, 39, 47, 50, 55–6, 68, 135, 153

Plinius Secundus, letter to Emperor Traianus, recounted by Harington 137–9

Pocock, J.G.A., transcultural approach to English history 188–9

poetry

comparable to philosophy 238

defense by Harington 132, 141, 146

poets, as councilors to sovereigns 228–30, 236–8

Pompey

compared to Afonso Henriques of Portugal 249–50

Julius Caesar and 245

portraiture and politics 301–11

Portugal; *see also* Camões, Luís de; Sebastian (king of Portugal)

as English ally against Spain 201–2

Fanshawe's appointment as ambassador to 253

history in *Os Lusíadas* 89–90, 240, 245–54, 264–8

War of Portuguese Restoration as civil or foreign war 253–5

potesta indirecta (indirect power) 217–18

Pounde, Thomas, distributed Campion's "Challenge" 59

praemunire, writs of 114, 181

Primaleon of Greece (translation by Munday), characters from in Munday's *Zelauto* 103

Principal Navigations, see Hakluyt, Richard

Pritchard, Allan, on Cowley's *Civil War* 231–2

property, *see* territory

prostitutes, *see* Angellica (character)

Protestants/Protestantism; *see also* Calvinists/Calvinism; Lutheranism; Puritans/Puritanism

belief in only God over sovereign 116–17

debt to Roman law 159

Osório's warnings 41–3, 47–8

Protestant League 11–15

rejection of correction of temporal sovereigns by ecclesiastics 96

seeing ourselves as free individuals 314–15

spiritual authority only provisionally delegated to pope 134

Psalms, justifying temporal sovereignty 56

public sphere, legacy of Christian commonwealth 315

Pugh, Syrithe, on Fanshawe's views of monarchy 226–30

Puritans/Puritanism

anti-papist zealotry 214

better to fight Catholics than Turks 5

Harington's case for James VI as king to 133

Harington's claim to be "Catholique Puritan" 137

and Jesuit critiques of English church and customs 72

Milton's antiprelatism 277–92

Questier, Michael

on Catholicism and English national identity 4–5

on English Catholic and Protestant communities 99–100

Quint, David, on *Paradise Lost* as repudiation of Catholic ideals of empire 270

Rainolds, John (Puritan) 134

Rainolds, William (Catholic) 134–5, 145

Ralegh, Walter 295–6, 299, 301–4, 306–7, 309

Rationes decem (Campion), *see* Campion, Edmund

Ratzinger, Joseph Cardinal (Pope Benedict XVI), debate with Habermas 316

Readie and Easie Way, The (Milton), *see* Milton, John

Reason of Church Government, The
(Milton), *see* Milton, John
Reasons of Refusal (Persons) 77–8
Reformation, *see* Protestants/Protestantism
Regnans in Excelsis (Papal Bull of 1570),
see Pius V (pope)
Regulae Societatis Iesu ad usum
Nostrorum Tantum 63
Relacion de Algunos Martyrios (Persons) 82
Relation of the King of Spaines Receiving
in Valliodolid ... (Persons) 79
relectiones, see Vitoria, Francisco de
religion; *see also specific religious*
practices by name
Christianity's transnational appeal
236–40
Cowley's epics on religious history
233–6, 238–40
Persons on historical conflicts between
state and 65
poetry and 237
as sustenance for philosophy 316
transcending of territorial loyalties 9, 264
vs. regional solidarity in *Arcadia* 19
Renegado, The (Massinger) 306–8
republic of letters
among English Catholic exiles 83–5
among Jesuits 37n1, 61, 83, 85
republicanism, Milton's investment in 264,
274n25, 286
république du genre humain (Cloots) 30
Responsio ad librum: Triplici nodo,
triplex cuneus (Bellarmine), *see*
Bellarmine, Robert
respublica christiana, see Christian
commonwealth
Richard I (king), portrayal in Munday's
Huntington plays 119–21
Richard II (king), defended by Walworth
during Wat Tyler's Rebellion 131
Richardson, Laurence, testimony at trial 107
Richer, Edmond, on papal deposing
power 2
Roberts, Henry
Most Friendly Farewell to Sir Francis
Drake 185–6
Pheander, the Maiden Knight 303
Robin Hood, portrayal in Munday's
Huntington plays 118–21

Roman Catholics/Catholicism; *see also*
papal supremacy; Society of Jesus
Catholic cosmopolitans and their
interlocutors 52–7
centralized bureaucratic structure 279–80
concerned about pope's deposition
claims 49–50
corrupt clergy in Munday's plays 115–21
cosmopolitan character 136
debt to Roman law 159
distinction between Protestant
approach to tyranny and 50
and the English nation 71–6
and English national identity 4–6, 37–9
as equivalent to loyalty to a foreign
prince 281–2
Harington's case for James VI as king
to 133
Harington's empathy for plight 132
ideals of empire repudiated in *Paradise*
Lost 270
as loyal subjects of English crown 7
Marian faction 37, 73–6
pope blamed for European turmoil 162–3
recusants conforming in increasing
numbers 214–15
as royalists 213–23
secular priests vs. Jesuits 71–2
Sidney's contacts with 19–20
Spanish Dominican use of natural law
172, 177
Roman curia
as head of Christian commonwealth
42, 53, 76, 159
Lord Chancellor as secular analogue
of 114
power of deposition 7–8, 47, 59, 71
and secularization of papal supremacy
131, 313
and Tudor claim of spiritual supremacy
39, 56, 113–16
vs. Roman church, rift in loyalty of
English Catholics 219
romance genre; *see also* Munday, Anthony;
Sidney, Philip
adoration of the sovereign 302–3
cosmopolitan romance 149–84
Orlando Furioso 140–48
portraits in romances 303–9
signature tropes 203–4

Rome, English College at, *see* English College at Rome
Rover, The, see Behn, Aphra
royalists; *see also* divine right
    assumption that European crowns linked by common royalist ideology 259
    Catholic and conformist 222
    conception of Christian kingdom 264
    Cromwell and republicans portrayed as morally depraved 244
    implications of Portuguese War of Restoration for 255
    Milton and ideology of 277, 280, 285–6
    origins of party 213n1
    resonance of Camões's vision with 263–4
    use of epic genre 223, 225–6, 230–41
Rudolf II (Holy Roman Emperor) 9, 12, 15
Rufinus, commentary on Gratian's *Decretum* 23

Samson Agonistes (Milton), *see* Milton, John
Sancho II (king of Portugal), deposed by Pope Innocent IV 89
Sander, Nicholas
    on Church based on monarchy 48–9, 50
    De visibili monarchia Ecclesiae 49–51, 55–6
    pope and bishops as enlightened minority 286
    temporal authority subordinate to ecclesiastical 7, 25, 54–5, 154, 155
Saracen king in *Orlando Furioso* ignores wise councilor 147
Satiricon, see Petronius, *Satiricon*
Schmalkaldic states 13, 279
Scholasticism, Vitoria's cosmology as consistent with 31
Scottish Covenanter rebellion, Irish Catholic support of Charles I 213
Seall, Robert, tribute to Stukeley 186
Sebastian (king of Portugal)
    letter written by Haddon about Osório 46–7
    in *Strangest Adventvre That Ever Happened* … 203–4
    in Stukeley plays 194–7, 208–9

Second Defense of the English People, A (Milton), *see* Milton, John
sectarianism, beneficial in search for truth 283–4
secular papal surrogate; *see also* sovereigns/sovereignty
    as answer to need for secular overseer 70, 91, 140, 146–7, 150
    fiction promoting 314
    in Harington's works 141, 143, 146
    Munday's idea of secular overseer 8, 71, 107–25
    in Sidney's works 21, 155–6, 160, 163
secularization, mainstream secularization theory 314–15
Selden, John, on chancellor's conscience 176
Sepúlveda, Juan Ginés de 31, 177
Severall speeches delivered at a conference concerning the power of Parliament … 221–2
Shakespeare, William, *The Life and Death of King John* 118, 123–5
Shell, Alison, on Ambrose and Theodosius 96
Sherwin, Ralph, complaints about Clynnog 70
Sidney, Philip
    Astrophil and Stella 302
    Defence of Poetry 158
    diplomacy and intelligence gathering 9–13, 15–21
    diplomatic embassy regarding transnational Protestant alliance 279
    The New Arcadia 21, 159–70, 303
    The Old Arcadia 18–20, 151–2, 155–9
    religious leanings 149–50, 150n2, 162
    sympathetic attitude toward Catholicism 20n72
sins, unnatural 30
slavery/enslavement
    concept of natural slave 273–4
    Sepúlveda vs. Vitoria on 31
Smith, Nigel, on use of epic during English civil war 225–6, 231–2
social contract
    basis for deposition of Charles I 219–20, 225
    determined by God Himself 88

Persons vs. Allen 179–80
in *Vindiciae, contra Tyrannos* 225
Society of Jesus; *see also* Campion,
    Edmund; Persons, Robert
    appellant/Archpriest controversy 71–2,
    216
    England as part of a Christian
    commonwealth 7–8, 37
    Jesuits' transnational republic of letters
    37n1, 61, 83, 85
    as transnational religious order 59–64
Sovereign of the Seas (Fanshawe), *see*
    Fanshawe, Sir Richard
sovereigns/sovereignty; *see also* equity;
    papal supremacy; secular papal
    surrogate; social contract; temporal
    authority
    adoration and national identity 294–5,
    302–4, 311
    Fanshawe's idea of network to protect
    and correct 252, 255–6, 260–61, 270
    legitimacy from perspective external to
    nation-state 159
    need to listen to wise councilors 147
    Portuguese 265–6
    right of subjects to resist ruler's 87–90,
    122–3, 153–4, 160–61, 219–20, 287
    Stukeley's sovereignty over self 206
    Stukeley's speech on encounters with
    205–6
    transnational aid to imperiled 161–3,
    165–7
Spain; *see also* civil war (Castile-Portugal)
    Anglo-Spanish rivalry 11, 295–300,
    304–6; *see also* Stukeley, Thomas
    Fanshawe's embassy to 255, 258–60
    natural law and foreign intervention by
    172, 177, 178–9
    Spanish control of Portuguese crown
    202–4, 254
    toleration for English Catholics 86
Spanish match 215, 306
Specimen a Lusitanus (Fanshawe), *see*
    Fanshawe, Sir Richard
Spenser, Edmund
    constructing an English polity through
    writing 4
    The Faerie Queene, Book 5 (justice)
    170–84, 304

religious influences on 149–50, 150n2
A View of the Present State of Ireland
    178, 184
St German, Christopher, on equity 112–13,
    113n77, 170–71, 173, 176–7
Stallybrass, Peter, *see* Jones, Ann Rosalind
Stapleton, Thomas, *A Counterblast to M.*
    Horne's Vayne Blaste against M.
    Fekenham 27–8
Statute in Restraint of Appeals 1533 38–9,
    43, 112–13, 140n150
Steel, Richard, ideal of classical
    cosmopolitanism 293
stereotypes, *see* gender; identity, national
Stevens, Paul, on Milton's "priesthood of
    all believers" 287
Stewart, Alan, on Fulke Greville 15
Stillman, Robert, on Sidney 19, 158
"Storie of Domesticall Difficulties in
    the English Catholike cause, A"
    (Persons), *see* Persons, Robert
Strangest Adventvre That Ever Happened
    …, The (Munday), *see* Munday,
    Anthony
Stukeley, Thomas
    beyond English nation 189–99
    beyond exile and treason 199–202
    death and beyond 205–9
    plays written about him 187–9
    "true" accounts of national character,
    202–5
Suárez, Francisco
    on contractual theory of the state 87–8
    Defensio catholicae fidei contra
    anglicanae sectae errores 129
    on papal authority 30, 180, 217
Summa et est Sciendum 22, 226
Supplementum Lucani (May's
    Continuation of Lucan's historicall
    poem) 226, 228–9
Swift, Jonathan, on "Parsons the Jesuit" 80
Syrinx, Or a Sevenfold History (Warner)
    302

Tamburlaine (Marlowe) 200–201
Taylor, Charles, on mainstream
    secularization theory 314–15
Teixeira, José, recognition of Portuguese
    King Sebastian 203–4

Index

temporal authority; *see also* papal supremacy, secularization; secular papal surrogate; sovereigns/sovereignty
  epic focus on relationship between divine and 240
  need for definitive boundary between jurisdictions of spiritual and 25–6
  right of temporal rulers to depose heretics 155
Tenure of Kings and Magistrates (Milton), *see* Milton, John
territory
  lord's right to property analogous to king's right to govern 265–6
  Milton's desire to separate religion from 9, 271–7
  pope's authority vitiated by interests in 20, 162
Theodosius (Roman Emperor) 26–9, 56, 94–6, 146, 291
Thomaso (Killigrew), *see* Killigrew, Thomas
Thomist perspective on natural law 157, 158–9
Thompson, Sir Edward Maunde, on Munday's *John a Kent* 111
Tilney, Edmund, marginal comments in *John a Kent* 111
toilet, invention of first flushing privy 136
Topcliffe, Richard, anti-Catholic network 71, 98–9, 100, 136
"Towards Perpetual Peace" (Kant) 30
Tract on the Succession to the Crown (Harington), *see* Harington, Sir John
translatio imperii 127
transnational themes; *see also* Christian commonwealth; cosmopolitanism; identity, cosmopolitan; international order; papal supremacy
  Christianity's transnational appeal 236–40
  ecumenical or transnational commonwealth 260–61
  epic genre's transnational appeal 240
  limited institutional restraints on excesses of nationalistic or religious ideologies 316–17

Travers, Walter, response to a papist 3
treason and religious betrayal, Stukeley's plays compared with others 199–202
treason tracts (Munday) 103–9
*Treatise of Civil Power in Ecclesiastical Causes (*Milton), *see* Milton, John
Treatise of the Three Conversions (Persons), *see* Persons, Robert
Triplici nodo, triplex cuneus, Or, An Apologie for the Oath of Allegiance (James I), *see* James I and VI (king)
Triumph of revnited Britania, The (Munday), Munday, Anthony, *see* Munday, Anthony
Troublesome Raigne of Iohn King of England, The (anonymous) 118
Troy legend, use in royalist pamphlets 231
True Law of Free Monarchies, The (James I), *see* James I and VI (king)
truth, search for, and sectarianism 283–4
Tuck, Richard, on Kant's cosmopolitan law 30–31
Turks, *see* Ottoman Empire
Tutino, Stefania, on Digby's loyalty to king 219
21st and Last Book of the Ocean to Cynthia, The (Ralegh) 302–3
tyranny and nationhood as necessary evils 273–5

Unton, Sir Henry, on "stage of Christendome" 86

Van der Noot, Jan, influence on Spenser 150n2
View of a Seditious Bill Sent into England, A (Jewel), *see* Jewel, John
View of the Present State of Ireland, A (Spenser), *see* Spenser, Edmund
Viktus, Daniel
  on *Christian Turned Turk* 200
  on English identity formation 188
Vindiciae, Contra Tyrannos (anonymous Huguenot tract) 122, 130, 152–61, 163, 225
Virgil, *The Aeneid*
  Cowley and 231, 233

influence on Fanshawe 230–31, 240–41, 245–6
Languet's advice to Sidney based on 168–9
prominence during English civil war 225–6
translation by Denham 270
Vitoria, Francisco de 31–3, 156–7, 159, 179

Wales
ancient Catholic identity 73–5
Welsh and English student revolt 61–2, 64, 66–7, 69–70
Walsingham, Francis
correspondence with nephew 10
identified with Huguenots 150
Walworth, William (fishmonger elected Lord Mayor), celebration in *Chrysanaleia* 131
war; *see also* civil war; *specific wars, battles and warring nations by name*
nations in perpetual state of 238–9
War of Portuguese Restoration as civil or foreign war? 253–5
Wardour Castle, Catholic residence 136–7

Warner, Michael, *see* Habermas, Jurgen
Warner, William, *Syrinx, Or a Sevenfold History* 302
Wat Tyler's Rebellion 131
Webster, John, and Thomas Dekker, *The Famous History of Sir Thomas Wyat* 306
Wentworth, Peter, response to Persons's *Conference* 133
White, Thomas (alias Blackloe) 219–21
Whore's Rhetoric, The (anonymous) 307
Wigginton, Giles, on treatment by Munday 99
Williams, W. LLewellyn, on Clynnog faction 73
witches unworthy to live in Christian commonwealth 2–3
women, *see* gender
Worden, Blair, on Sidney's *Arcadia* 18–19
Wycliffe's rejection of papal authority in Munday's *Oldcastle* 115

Yepes, Diego de 81

Zachary (pope), deposition of Childeric 6, 21
Zelauto (Munday), *see* Munday, Anthony

CPSIA information can be obtained
at www.ICGtesting.com
Printed in the USA
BVOW06*1737211216
471404BV00008B/115/P